To. David
with Love
from. Mam.
13.2.94.

CARDIGANSHIRE
COUNTY HISTORY

VOLUME 1

Plate I: Cardiganshire from space. A Landsat 5 Thematic Mapper image derived from visible red, near-infrared and mid-infrared waveband reflectance measurements. Image processing has enhanced the image by contrast stretching and accentuated the differences in land cover. The false colours show clearly areas of upland and lowland and, for example, forestry (dark red), bogs (dark blue), agricultural land (reds, oranges and greens) and settlements (blue). (*Copyright raw data ESM/Eurimage*).

CARDIGANSHIRE COUNTY HISTORY

General Editor : Ieuan Gwynedd Jones

VOLUME 1

From the Earliest Times to the Coming of the Normans

Edited by
J.L.Davies and D.P.Kirby

Published on behalf of the Cardiganshire Antiquarian Society
in association with the
Royal Commission on the Ancient and Historical Monuments of Wales
by the University of Wales Press

CARDIFF

1994

© Cardiganshire Antiquarian Society, 1994

British Library Cataloguing-in-Publication Data

A catalogue record for this book is available from the British Library.

ISBN 0-7083-1170-9

Jacket design by the Royal Commission on the Ancient and Historical Monuments of Wales
Typeset at Alden Multimedia, Northampton
Printed in Wales by Gwasg Gomer, Llandysul

GENERAL EDITOR'S PREFACE

Most county history societies in Wales have aspired to write and to publish histories of their own counties, and some have succeeded magnificently. At the time of their foundation most of them were content to publish lectures, papers, accounts of excavations, editions of documentary sources and so on in printed Transactions, and the historical literature of Wales has been enormously enriched thereby. Invariably, however, in the course of time, with the development of academic history in the University and its colleges, the increasing interest in local history and the need to bring all this work together, the desire grew to replace, where they existed, the old discursive, nineteenth-century county histories with modern, up-to-date, collaborative works.

When the Cardiganshire Antiquarian Society was founded in 1909 it was established mainly to encourage archaeological research, and however amateurish its activities may now appear to have been the Society did succeed in the vitally important task of keeping before the public the importance of historical sites and monuments, such as Ystrad Fflur and Pen Dinas. In the case of Ystrad Fflur, which many would regard as the County's most precious monument, it was this Society which succeeded, after a great deal of pressure and publicity, in persuading its owners to transfer the site to the custody of H. M. Office of Works.

It was not until 1933, however, that serious attention was given to the writing of a County History. In June of that year the then President, the Earl of Lisburne, at a general meeting of the Society at his home in Trawscoed, proposed that a County History should be prepared. Later in that session (1933–4) (Sir) William Llewellyn Davies of the National Library of Wales lectured on the general theme of 'Cardiganshire Local Records and the Compilation of a County History' to meetings of the Society in various parts of the County, and in the same year a County Records Committee was established to encourage the collection of manuscript and other sources for deposit in the National Library where they would be available for scholars. Sir William Llewellyn Davies and David Thomas, HMI, the Honorary Secretary of the Society, were indefatigable in these essential preliminaries, and they fully deserve the honoured place they hold in the annals of the Society. It was in 1934, also, that a young lecturer in the Geography Department of the University College of Wales, Mr Emrys G. Bowen, friend and protégé of Professor Daryl Forde, gave his first lecture to the Society on prehistoric Cardiganshire, thus beginning an association with the Society which was to end only with his death fifty years later.

Preparations of a practical kind were also taken. There were hopeful signs that London 'Cardis', who dominated the capital's milk trade, would support the venture financially, and in August 1939, on the very eve of the war, the Cardiganshire County Council passed a resolution pledging their support and placing all County records at the disposal of the Society. From the beginning, therefore, the County Council, as also the Town Councils of the three boroughs, Aberystwyth, Cardigan and Lampeter, were enthusiastic supporters of the proposal, and it is a matter of great satisfaction to the present Editorial Board that their successor authorities should have continued their generous support. Then came the War, and activities were suspended during the hostilities, and it was not until 1947 that the Society resumed its work.

By 1950 publication of the new Series of Transactions, now entitled *Ceredigion: Journal of the Ceredigion Antiquarian Society*, had been launched, and in 1975 the Society felt that the time had come to proceed with the publication of a County History. The Editorial Board which was then elected determined that the work should be in three volumes, the first on the archaeology and early history of the County to the coming of the Normans, the second on the Middle Ages, and the third on the modern period up to the reorganization of local government in 1974. Because the Editorial Board could count on the ready co-operation of the staff of the Royal Commission on the Ancient and Historical Monuments of Wales, it was decided that Volume 1 should be the first to be written. Professor Emrys Bowen was chosen to plan and to edit this volume.

With the deeply lamented death of Professor Bowen in 1983 (at the age of 82), the Editorial Board invited Dr Jeffrey L. Davies and Dr D. P. Kirby, respectively Senior Lecturer and Reader in the Department of History, to take his place as volume editors, and the shape and structure of the present volume is largely due to them. This has demanded of the Editors, both of whom have themselves contributed substantial chapters to it, not only a most unusual range of scholarship but also much patience and good humour, and I wish to thank them both for their unfailing co-operation. The Society is deeply indebted to them.

A development of major significance was the decision taken in 1988 to publish this volume jointly with the RCAHMW, and the Editorial Committee are happy and proud that this volume should contain the Commission's official record of the prehistory of the County. They are particularly grateful to the Commission's Secretary, Dr Peter Smith and his successor Mr Peter White, to the then Chairman, Emeritus Professor Glanmor Williams, and to the present Chairman, Professor J. Beverley Smith, for their ready advice and co-operation.

County histories are not easily or quickly written and some delay has been inevitable and unavoidable. The original sources for the early history of the County are relatively sparse, almost always obscure and difficult to interpret, while the fundamental archaeological investigations of parts of the County are still incomplete. Above all, most of our contributors are all busy professional persons and obliged to pursue their researches in their spare time. Moreover, ideas of what should constitute a county history have changed very substantially since the 1930s, and contemporary scholarship has likewise moved on.

Ironically perhaps, these delays have worked to the advantage of the History. The volume here presented incorporates the very latest scholarship and includes the most up-to-date archaeological research. It begins where the land of the County began in the unimaginably distant past when it was yet without form, before the graceful curve of its shores had been determined, or the valleys gouged out of the immemorial rocks. It traces the hundreds of thousands of years of changing climates, the successive generations of cold and warm spells, the slow advances and retreats of glaciers and the ageless movements of the seas which shaped our familiar landscape and determined the nature of the soil and the habitats of its flora and fauna. It records how and when the lakes and bogs which now so wonderfully diversify the land were laid down, and what were the succession of grasses, trees and other plants. We dimly discern the coming of Man and study the sparse record which unnumbered generations have left, the relics of their habitations and the artefacts of peace and war, their burial places and the dumb monuments of stone they erected 'Against the Dark and Time's consuming Rage'. It constructs, from evidence much of which has only but recently been uncovered, the extent and location of the long Roman occupation, the routes of their coming and going in pursuit of their military purposes and imperial designs. And finally it traces the slow emergence of the kingdom of Ceredigion out of the confusion of the centuries that followed, a period when historical truth can only with difficulty be distinguished from myth and legend. In doing so it examines forms of economic and social organization and of political structures which are recognizably of our own civilization and which have immeasurably enriched our culture. This volume concludes by tracing the coming of Christianity, the organization of the Church, and the origins of the churches and their dedications which are such an ennobling feature of the landscape today and which have been the most powerful formative influence on the mental and spiritual life of the people.

This Volume has been a number of years in preparation and during that time I have incurred many debts of gratitude which it is now my pleasant duty to acknowledge. Outstanding in his support, especially during the critical initial stages, was the former Honorary Secretary of the Society, Mr Dafydd Morris Jones. It was he who was mainly instrumental in ensuring that the County and District Councils should be closely involved in order to secure a firm financial base for the project. At no stage has our reliance on their generosity been misplaced, and I wish to thank the Dyfed County Council and Ceredigion District Council for the substantial grants they have made towards the costs of publication. The late Mr J. Haulfryn Williams, sometime Honorary Secretary of the Honourable Society of Cymmrodorion, supported the project with a generous gift while it was still at the planning stage. The gift was made 'er cof am Morgan ac Elisabeth Williams, Ynyshir, Morgannwg—gynt o Ystum-tuen' (in memory of Morgan and Elisabeth Williams, Ynyshir, Glamorgan—formerly of Ystum-tuen), and it is a pleasure to record the gift and its dedication here. Miss Martha Phillips of Aberystwyth, a faithful member of the Society, also contributed to the costs of publication. Mr Peter Smith threw his weight behind the project from the beginning, and his successor as Secretary of the RCAHMW, has likewise been very co-operative. I consulted the Commission's Chairmen, Emeritus Professor Glanmor Williams and his successor, Professor J. Beverley Smith, on many occasions when problems of editorial policy arose, and it is a pleasure now to thank them for their wise and steady counsel.

The task of preparing the index was entrusted to Mr William Howells, and I thank him most sincerely for his painstaking work. I am also very grateful to the Editor and the staff of Geiriadur Prifysgol Cymru for advising with the standardization of place-names.

Finally, I wish to thank most sincerely the staff of the University of Wales Press for their efficiency and patience in dealing with what must have been a notably complicated work. Susan Jenkins's calm and expert advice in the early stages was much appreciated and Ceinwen Jones's meticulous editorial work on the volume has been beyond praise.

Ieuan Gwynedd Jones

VOLUME EDITORS' PREFACE

A decade has elapsed since the present editors were invited to take over the task of bringing this first volume of the Cardiganshire County History to completion following the death of the former editor, Professor E. G. Bowen. The project was then at an initial and very incomplete stage, though some chapters had already been submitted. The whole enterprise has since been virtually redesigned. Some of the chapters, which had originally been penned in the late 1970s, have been substantially or wholly rewritten and a large body of new material has been introduced. Inevitably this has been a lengthy and difficult process which has required forbearance and patience from all participants in the enterprise. While every effort has been made to achieve consistency in place-name forms, this has not always been possible and the personal preferences of contributors have on occasion prevailed. We would like to thank all the contributors to this volume for their understanding and co-operation, especially those who agreed to participate in the project at a late stage. We would also like to express our gratitude to Mrs Kate Cooper who undertook the typing of the whole text and its numerous subsequent revisions with cheerful good humour. Mr Geoffrey Ward, senior illustrator at RCAHMW, produced the greater portion of the line-drawings for the Neolithic, Bronze Age, Iron Age and Roman chapters and the Early Christian monuments section, Mrs Jane Durrant drew the Llanbadarn High Cross, and Mr C. R. Musson prepared the aerial photographs for the Iron Age chapter. Dr Neil Chisholm of the Institute of Earth Studies, University of Wales, Aberystwyth, obtained the Landsat image of the County used as the frontispiece. We are most grateful to them all.

This volume in its present form would not have been possible without the generous support and encouragement of Mr Peter Smith, former Secretary of RCAHMW. It is sad to recall that his predecessor, Dr A. H. A. Hogg, enthusiastic contributor to this volume, did not live to see its publication.

CONTENTS

PLATES

FIGURES

THE CONTRIBUTORS

Professor D. Q. Bowen, B.Sc., Ph.D.
Director of the Institute of Earth Studies, University of Wales, Aberystwyth.

C. S. Briggs, BA, Ph.D., FGS, FSA, MIFA
Senior Investigator, RCAHMW.

R. A. Chater, MA
Formerly Head of the Flowering Plant Hiberia, Natural History Museum, London.

William Condry, BA, BA, MA, M.Sc. (*Honoris Causa*)
Author. Nature correspondent for the *Guardian* newspaper.

J. L. Davies, BA, Ph.D. FSA
Senior Lecturer in Archaeology, University of Wales, Aberystwyth.

Professor R. A. Dodgshon, BA, Ph.D.
Institute of Earth Studies, University of Wales, Aberystwyth.

A. P. Fowles, BA, M.Sc.
Invertibrate Ecologist, Countryside Council for Wales.

The late A. H. A. Hogg, CBE, MA, FSA
Formerly Secretary of the RCAHMW.

C. H. Houlder, MA, FSA
Formerly Senior Investigator RCAHMW.

Heather James, BA, FSA
Deputy Director, Dyfed Archaeological Trust.

D. P. Kirby, MA, Ph.D., F.R.Hist.S.
Reader in History, University of Wales, Aberystwyth.

Peter D. Moore, B.Sc., Ph.D.
Reader in Ecology, King's College, London.

Professor P. Ó Riain, MA, Ph.D.
Professor of Early and Medieval Irish, University College, Cork.

C. C. Rudeforth, M.Sc., Ph.D.
Formerly Regional Officer for the Soil Survey of England and Wales.

W. Gwyn Thomas, MA, FSA
Formerly Principal Investigator, RCAHMW.

ABBREVIATIONS

A	*Archaeologia*
Antiq.	*Antiquity*
Ant. J.	*Antiquaries Journal*
Arch.	*Archaeologia*
Arch. Camb.	*Archaeologia Cambrensis*
Arch. J.	*Archaeological Journal*
AW	*Archaeology in Wales*
BAR	*British Archaeological Reports* (Oxford)
BBCS	*Bulletin of the Board of Celtic Studies*
Brit.	*Britannia*
Carms. Antiq.	*The Carmarthenshire Antiquary*
CIIC	R. A. S. Macalister, *Corpus Inscriptionum Insularum Celticarum* I (Dublin, 1945)
ECMW	V. E. Nash-Williams, *Early Christian Monuments of Wales* (Cardiff, 1950)
Econ. Geol.	*Economic Geology*
EHR	*English Historical Review*
EWGT	P. C. Bartrum, *Early Welsh Genealogical Tracts* (Cardiff, 1966)
Gent. Mag.	*Gentleman's Magazine*
JBAA	*Journal of the British Archaeological Association*
JRS	*Journal of Roman Studies*
JRSAI	*Journal of the Royal Society of Antiquaries of Ireland*
Med. Arch.	*Medieval Archaeology*
Mont. Coll.	*Montgomeryshire Collections*
New Phyt.	*New Phytologist*
NLWJ	*National Library of Wales Journal*
PRIA	*Proceedings of the Royal Irish Academy*
PPS	*Proceedings of the Prehistoric Society*
PSAS	*Proceedings of the Society of Antiquaries of Scotland*
TCAS	*Transactions of the Cardiganshire Antiquarian Society*
WHR	*Welsh History Review*

Part I
Land and Environment

CHAPTER 1

THE LAND OF CARDIGANSHIRE*

D. Q. Bowen

IN conventional and elementary terms the topography of Cardiganshire can be described as a series of dissected plateaux. From most vantage points the eye beholds level horizons and gains an impression of a stepped landform, from sea-level to the hilltops of central Wales. Below these 'upland plains' lie the valleys and coastal lowlands of Cardiganshire.

By and large, the valleys are narrow and are deeply incised into the topography. Exceptions do exist and the wide middle reaches of the Teifi are a good example of this. A striking feature of the County is the steep descent to the coastline, followed seawards by an extensive platform submerged daily on its inner landward margin. Features of the coastline are the low-lying area of Cors Fochno and Ynys-las, and the terraces of screes and clays which bury old sea cliffs, for example, at Aberaeron, Llan-non and Morfa Bychan. How did this landscape come into existence; what were the landforming processes; and when did they fashion Cardiganshire scenery? These and other questions are considered in the course of this chapter. First, however, the nature of their foundation, the solid rocks of the County, must be addressed.

When the geological outcrops of Cardiganshire and the immediate offshore are considered it is evident that rocks of three geological systems are present: Palaeozoic, Mesozoic and Cenozoic. Forming Cardiganshire itself, and the inner part of the continental shelf where it abuts on to the coastline, are rocks of the Lower Palaeozoic (Table 1); but seawards of these and lying in troughs, or rifts (graben), are younger Mesozoic rocks. Graben are downfaulted areas which have been subject to long-term subsidence and within which rock sequences have accumulated, whereas

* Acknowledgements: I have been fortunate enough to have discussed aspects of the geology and scenery of Cardiganshire and Wales with those who have made the greatest contributions towards its understanding. The late Professor O. T. Jones, FRS, was kind enough to discuss his work with me at Cambridge in 1963. In May 1964 I was privileged to debate with him his last paper to the Geological Society of London on 'The glacial and post-glacial history of the lower Teifi valley'. To the late Professor T. Neville George, FRS, I owe an incalculable debt for his critical encouragement and friendship between 1966 and 1976. Professor E. H. Brown supervised my postgraduate work at University College London, and continues to debate these matters vigorously with me. I discussed the Cardiganshire landform only briefly with Mr John Challinor when I was Senior Fellow of the University of Wales in 1965–6 at Aberystwyth but still recall and appreciate his pragmatic approach to the topic. In 1966 the late Professor E. G. Bowen invited me to address the Guild of Graduates on the 'Ice Ages', a thoughtful gesture I believe to have been a turning-point in my career, so I am privileged to be a contributor to the County History of which he was a prime instigator. I thank Mr Michael Gelly Jones, Mr Arnold Thawley and Mr Ian Gulley, who drew the illustrations, and Mr David Griffiths who photographed them. I also thank Miss Linda James who assembled the bibliography.

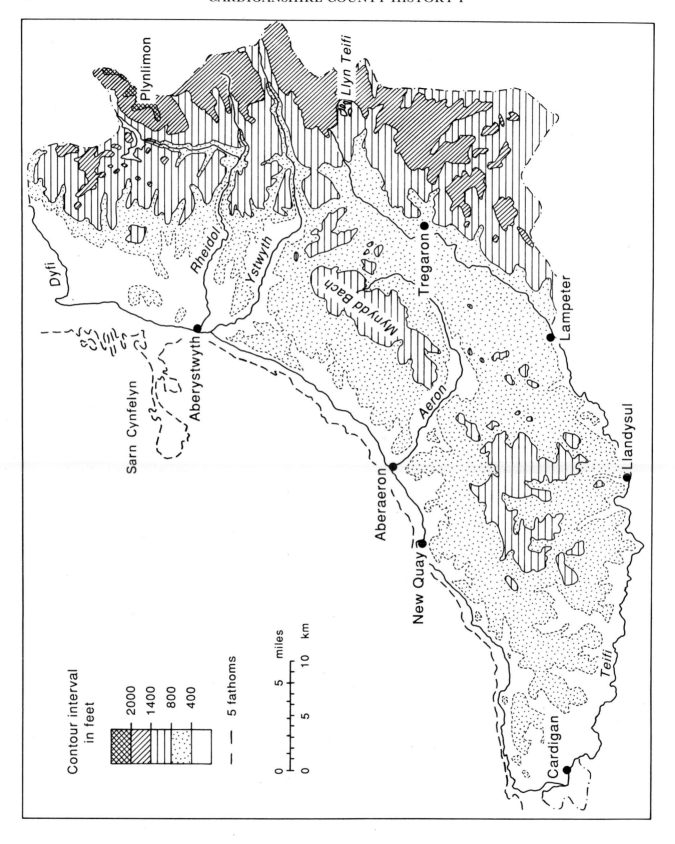

TABLE 1: Stratigraphical Chart of the Rocks of Cardiganshire

Era	System	Series	Stage	Age (Ma)	Rocks in Cardiganshire
C E N O Z O I C	Quaternary	Holocene			Blown sand, beach sand estuarine alluvium river gravels and alluvium colluvium, submerged forest
				0.01	
		Pleistocene	Devensian		Scree, river gravels Glacial sand and gravel Till (boulder clay) Glaciomarine deposits
				0.12	
			Ipswichian		Raised beach (Poppit)
				0.13	
					Unknown in Cardiganshire
				2.40	
	'Tertiary'	Pliocene Miocene Oligocene Eocene Palaeocene			Some rocks in Cardigan Bay
				65.0	
M E S O Z O I C	Cretaceous				
	Jurassic				Rocks in Cardigan Bay
	Triassic				
				250	
P A L A E O Z O I C	Permian Carboniferous Devonian				No rocks in Cardiganshire
				408	
	Silurian	Ludlow Wenlock Llandovery			No rocks in Cardiganshire No rocks in Cardiganshire Sandstones and mudstones
				438	
	Ordovician	Ashgill			Siltstones and mudstones
				505	
	Cambrian				No rocks in Cardiganshire
				590	

The solid rocks of Cardiganshire consist of the Ashgill Series of the Ordovician System and the Llandovery Series of the Silurian System. Between the youngest Llandovery rocks (the Aberystwyth Grits Formation) and the oldest deposits of the Quaternary System, is a time interval of well over 400 million years. No rocks from this interval of time are known in Cardiganshire. Offshore, however, on the floor of Cardigan Bay some Mesozoic and Cenozoic rocks are known. It was towards the end of this 'lost' interval of time in Cardiganshire that its landforms were fashioned. (Subdivisions and ages from the 1989 Global Stratigraphic Chart of the International Union of Geological Sciences). Ma: millions of years.

that part of the Welsh massif of which Cardiganshire forms a part, has been a positive (horst-like) area of net uplift through time. Indeed, throughout western Europe there exists a similar pattern of alternating horst and graben, which has influenced the accumulating rock sequences. The pattern of horst and graben was initiated when sea-floor spreading (plate-tectonic movements) started in the early Mesozoic, and was strongly accentuated during the early

Fig. 1: The relief and drainage of Cardiganshire. The contour interval has been chosen to emphasize the plateau-like quality of the topography.

Cenozoic when the North Atlantic as we know it today began to open. Thus the broad controls on the landform started to take shape at least 290 million years ago.

The solid rocks of Cardiganshire are older and they accumulated in a marine basin, many hundreds of metres deep, from Cambrian to Devonian times. The *Welsh Basin* extended between the present-day Welsh borderland to the south and east, and the north Wales coast to the north and west. Its geological history and the age of the sediments which accumulated in it were debated by Sedgwick and Murchison during the heroic age of geology.[1] But major advances had to await O. T. Jones and his students after 1902.[2] In recent years the *Aberystwyth Sheet* of the British Geological Survey (1984), and the sheet memoir (1986), have given detailed accounts of the rocks of north Cardiganshire.[3] South Cardiganshire remains largely unsurveyed by modern methods.

Most of the rocks are turbidites, although two rare, very thin, volcanic layers are known from north Cardiganshire. Turbidites are rocks which were deposited from turbidity currents of suspended sediments flowing down a submarine slope.[4] In Cardiganshire they consist of muds and sands. An account of their deposition in north Cardiganshire was given in the celebrated work of Wood and Smith on the Aberystwyth Grits.[5]

These Lower Palaeozoic rocks were deformed into folds by faulting and by cleavage. Traditionally it has been assumed that this occurred during an end-Silurian event, the Caledonian earth movements. But the work of Cave and Haines[6] has suggested that some of the deformation took place more or less continuously as the sediments accumulated. This may have occurred when the sediments were still wet and before they became completely lithified. Much of this would have occurred by downslope slumping and related processes (Fig. 2). During the Silurian the rocks were deformed along ENE–WSW lines, the trend that is so dominant in rock outcrops and the 'grain' of Cardiganshire notably exemplified by the trend of its coastline, and also the line of the middle Teifi Valley between Ystrad Meurig and Llanllwni. The geological structure of Cardiganshire has been integrated into the plate-tectonic development of the British Isles by Dewey.[7] Its main structures are: the Central Wales Syncline, the Teifi Anticline and the

[1] J. Challinor, 'Geological research in Cardiganshire: 1842–1949', *Ceredigion*, 1 (1951), 144–76; idem, 'A review of geological research in Cardiganshire: 1842–1967', *The Welsh Geological Quarterly*, 4 (1969), 3–40.

[2] O. T. Jones, 'The Hartfell-Valentian succession in the district around Plynlimon and Pont Erwyd (north Cardiganshire)', *Quarterly J. of Geological Soc. of London*, 64 (1909), 463–537; idem, 'The geological structure of Central Wales and the adjoining regions', op. cit., 68 (1912), 328-44; idem, 'On the evolution of a geosyncline', op. cit., 94 (1938), lx–cx; idem, 'The geological evolution of Wales and the adjacent regions', op. cit., 111 (1956), 323–51. See also O. T. Jones and W. J. Pugh, 'The geology of the district around Machynlleth and the Llyfnant valley', op. cit., 71 (1916), 343–85, and idem, 'The geology of the districts around Machynlleth and Aberystwyth', *Proc. of the Geologists' Association* (1935a), 247–300.

[3] R. Cave and B. A. Haines, 'Geology of the country between Aberystwyth and Machynlleth', *Memoir, British Geological Survey*, 1986.

[4] D. Wilson, 'Rapid mapping in Central Wales', *Natural Environment Research Council News*, July 1989 (1989), 27–9.

[5] A. Wood and A. J. Smith, 'The sedimentation and sedimentary history of the Aberystwyth Grits (Upper Llandoverian)', *Quarterly J. of Geological Soc. of London*, 114 (1958), 163–95.

[6] See above n.3.

[7] J. F. Dewey, 'Plate tectonics and the evolution of the British Isles', *Quarterly J. of Geological Soc. of London*, 139 (1982), 371–412.

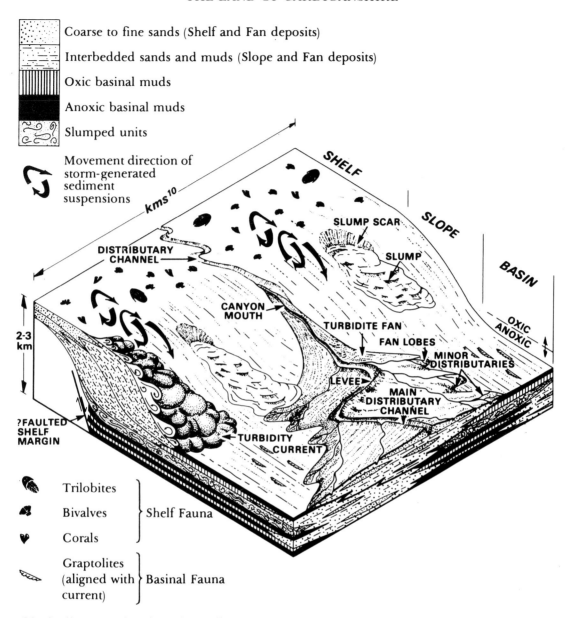

Coarse to fine sands (Shelf and Fan deposits)

Interbedded sands and muds (Slope and Fan deposits)

Oxic basinal muds

Anoxic basinal muds

Slumped units

Movement direction of storm-generated sediment suspensions

Trilobites

Bivalves   } Shelf Fauna

Corals

Graptolites (aligned with current)   } Basinal Fauna

Fig. 2: Block diagram showing the sedimentary environments in which the rocks of Cardiganshire accumulated (from Wilson). The Welsh Basin lay between the Welsh borderland to the south and east and the coast of north Wales to the north and west.

Ystwyth Fault (Fig. 3), but in detail innumerable smaller folds and faults occur. The mineralized rocks of north Cardiganshire are described in a masterly synthesis by O. T. Jones, while more recently W. J. Phillips discussed the mineralization process.[8]

[8] O. T. Jones, 'Lead and zinc. The mining district of north Cardiganshire and west Montgomeryshire', *Special Report Mineral Resources, Geological Survey, Great Britain*, 20 (1922), and W. J. Phillips, 'Hydraulic fracturing and mineralization', *Quarterly J. of Geological Soc. of London*, 128 (1972), 337–59.

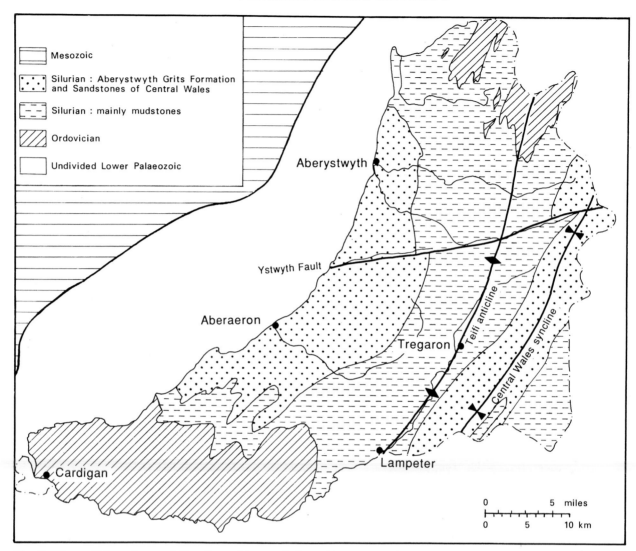

Fig. 3: The solid geology of Cardiganshire and the adjacent sea floor, adapted from maps of the British Geological Survey, Aberystwyth Sheet 163 (1984), Institute of Geological Sciences (British Geological Survey) Cardigan Bay Sheet (1982), and Institute of Geological Sciences, Central Wales Mining Field Map (1974). The boundary of the Mesozoic rocks on the floor of Cardigan Bay is from M. R. Dobson and R. J. Whittington, 'The Geology of Cardigan Bay', *Proc. Geologists' Assoc.*, 98 (1987), 331–53.

The fossils in the Lower Palaeozoic rocks are almost entirely graptolites, marine animals of planktonic lifestyle, which have been used to subdivide the succession into Biostratigraphical Zones. The Twenty-seventh International Geological Congress (Moscow 1985) used them to redefine the international base of the Silurian System.

How was the scenery of Cardiganshire fashioned?

The solid rocks of Cardiganshire are of Lower Palaeozoic age. Younger Mesozoic rocks are preserved in downfaulted areas offshore but it is controversial if they formerly extended east to cover the County. Immediately overlying the Silurian rocks are Pleistocene clays, gravels and sands, and Holocene ('postglacial') marine deposits, valley alluvium and hillslope colluvium, which provide the parent materials for soils.[9] Thus, between the Silurian (400 million years ago) and the oldest Pleistocene sediments (c.130,000 years ago) is a great 'lost' interval for which no known evidence survives. Sometime during this period the main elements of the scenery of Cardiganshire were fashioned.

Because this was so long ago, and because no evidence of the landforming processes survives in the form of sediments, the origin of the scenery continues to be controversial and inferences about origin have to be drawn from the shape of the landforms themselves. This is unsatisfactory because different landforming processes can produce similar landforms. Three major themes have dominated debate: first, the origin of the drainage system; secondly, the origin of the plateaux; and thirdly, the history of the Pleistocene ice ages.

i) The origin of the drainage system

Perhaps the greatest single influence on ideas about the Welsh drainage system has been the notion that it came into existence on a great dome of chalk, which covered Wales and was tilted south-eastwards from Snowdonia. It has always been difficult to reconcile the directions of Cardiganshire rivers with this, but reconstructions have shown an original master river flowing southwards from Trawsfynydd to join the line of the upper Rheidol, which flowed into the upper Teifi, which then became a tributary to an early Tywi stream. Thus drainage evolution in Cardiganshire fell into the radial pattern advanced for Wales.

This singularly failed, however, to account for the westward flowing Dyfi, Llyfnant, Rheidol, Ystwyth, Wyre, Aeron and lower Teifi streams. In the case of the Rheidol and Ystwyth the idea was advanced that they developed by cutting backwards from the coastline, eventually to intersect the Rheidol–Teifi stream respectively at Devil's Bridge and Ysbyty Ystwyth, thus effecting 'river capture'. Most river captures, on the other hand, involve streams cutting headwards along the grain (strike) of soft rocks or lines of weakness formed, for example, by a fault. The Rheidol and Ystwyth did neither. In fact it was the supposed original Rheidol–Teifi stream which followed the grain of the rocks! It is far more likely that the westward-flowing streams of the County are original features. They all flowed towards the graben of Cardigan Bay, which had been a 'negative' area for millions of years. Instances of river capture so as to break up this original drainage system occurred in the case of the later development of the middle Teifi and also the middle and upper reaches of the Aeron, both of which developed along the grain of the geology (Fig. 4: inset). The supposed river captures at Devil's Bridge and Ysbyty Ystwyth are no more than tributary valley development in a NE to SW direction along the grain of the rocks. The valleys south of Devil's Bridge and south of Ysbyty Ystwyth are topographic depressions because they coincide with belts of weaker rock.

[9] C. C. Rudeforth, 'Soils of north Cardiganshire', *Memoir, Soil Survey of Great Britain* (Harpenden, 1970); R. I. Bradley, *Soils in Dyfed* V: Sheet SN 24 (Llechryd), *Memoir, Soil Survey Record of Great Britain*, No.63 (Harpenden, 1980).

Having established the primary drainage pattern of Cardiganshire, which is consistent with the views of T. N. George on the plateaux[10], the question remains as to how they originated. The geological evidence from around Wales, notably from the Tremadoc Bay basin, shows that a possible starting-point was during the Oligocene Epoch (Table 1), when Wales as a whole was reduced to a low-lying area. During the subsequent Oligocene–Miocene earth movements this low-lying landscape was uplifted and on its slopes the drainage system initiated, including the westward-flowing rivers of Cardiganshire. Considerable uplift occurred at this time, as, for example, some 1,350 m along the Llanbedr Fault near Harlech.

ii) The origin of the Cardiganshire 'plateau'

Many have been impressed by the overall plateau-like quality of Cardiganshire: take the views looking north and north-east from the top of the hill overlooking Aberaeron, or the view north from the highest point on the Llanrhystud–Lampeter road, or the view inland from the golf course at Aberystwyth. It is difficult to deny the impression of the senses, that is of a vast upland plain or a series of plains at different elevations (Figs. 4 and 6).

Debate on these themes has continued ever since 1846 when Ramsay[11] described the uplands of central Wales as a plain of marine erosion. O. T. Jones, however, believed that the High Plateau (his 'tableland' of 1951) (Figs. 4 and 6) was a landsurface originally fashioned in Permo-Triassic times, then buried by Mesozoic rocks, and subsequently exposed by erosion consequent upon uplift in Cenozoic times.[12] T. N. George linked plateaux and drainage by arguing that the plateaux were marine in origin, and that the streams had extended their courses seawards across such emergent wave-cut platforms as the sea-level fell, or as the land rose (or both), during late Tertiary time. E. H. Brown was the first to map the plateaux systematically throughout Wales, thus extending his early work in north Cardiganshire (Figs. 4 and 6). Below 600 ft. he believed that the plateaux were marine platforms, but above that height he argued they were the remnants of *peneplains*, former landsurfaces which were the outcome of long surface weathering and erosion.[13]

[10] T. N. George, 'The development of the Towy and upper Usk drainage pattern', *Quarterly J. of Geological Soc. of London*, 98 (1942), 89–137 (see also O. T. Jones, 'The Upper Towy drainage-system', op. cit., 80 (1924), 568–609); T. N. George, 'The Welsh landscape', *Science Progress*, 49 (1961), 242–64; idem, 'The Cenozoic evolution of Wales', *The Upper Palaeozoic and Post Palaeozoic Rocks of Wales*, ed. T. R. Owen (Cardiff, 1974), 341–71; idem, 'Prologue to a geomorphology of Britain', *Special Publication No.7, Institute of British Geographers* (1974), 113–25.

[11] A. C. Ramsay, 'On the denudation of South Wales and the adjacent counties of England', *Memoir, Geological Survey. Great Britain*, 1 (1846), 297–335.

[12] O. T. Jones, 'Some episodes in the geological history of the Bristol Channel region', *Report of the British Association* (Bristol, 1930), 57–82; see also idem, 'The drainage system of Wales and the adjacent regions', *Quarterly J. of Geological Soc. of London*, 107 (1952), 201–25.

[13] E. H. Brown, 'Erosion surfaces in north Cardiganshire', *Trans. Inst. British Geog.*, 16 (1950), 49–66; idem, 'The river Ystwyth, Cardiganshire: a geomorphological analysis', *Proc. of the Geologists' Association of London*, 63 (1952), 244–69; idem, 'The physique of Wales', *Geographical Journal*, 123 (1957), 208–30; idem, *The Relief and Drainage of Wales: A Study in Geomorphological Development* (Cardiff, 1960).

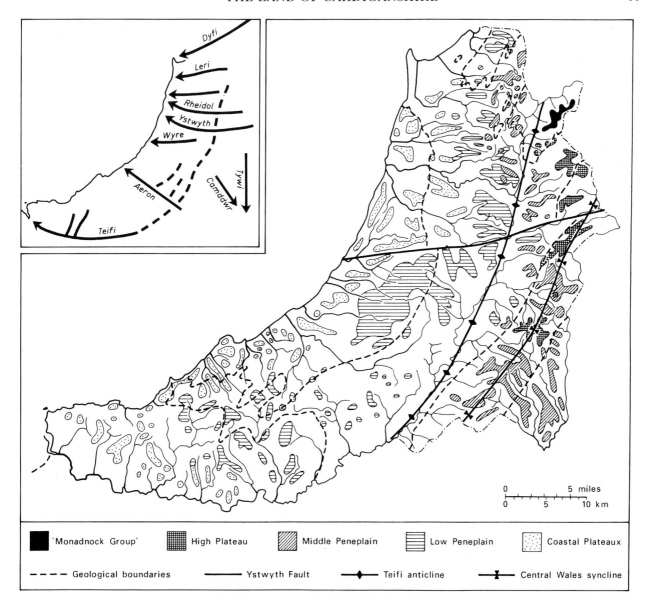

Fig. 4: Plateaux remnants ('upland plains'/planation surfaces/erosion surfaces) of Cardiganshire as mapped by E. H. Brown. Brown's classification is used, but no inference about the origin of the plateaux is intended, and it is used simply to illustrate the broad altitudinal groupings of the plateaux remnants. Note that the plateaux are indifferent to the principal geological boundaries (but see Challinor). Brown's classification, applicable to all of Wales, recognized: coastal plateau up to 600 ft; the Low Peneplain between 700 and 1100 ft; the Middle Peneplain between 1200 and 1600 ft; the High Plateau between 1700 and 2000 ft; and the Summit Plain above 2100 ft, in this instance Plynlimon (2468 ft).

Inset map shows the reconstructed original drainage pattern of Cardiganshire (from D. Q. Bowen). The broken lines indicate later development along less resistant rock outcrops: for example, the upper Aeron, upper Teifi and upper Rheidol.

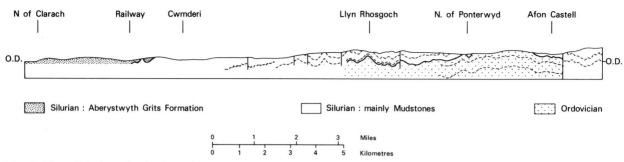

Fig. 5: Simplified geological section across north Cardiganshire from between Clarach and Wallog to the Castell Valley near Dyffryn Castell (adapted from the British Geological Survey, Aberystwyth Sheet 163). The base of the Silurian and the base of the Aberystwyth Grits Formation is shown as a heavy line. The broken lines show the geological structure of the rocks.

More recently the evidence has been reviewed and reinterpreted by D. Q. Bowen[14] to show that all pre-existing theories are applicable to some extent in space and time, but that new discoveries have invalidated some arguments. It is an integral part of his hypothesis that the origin of the centrifugal drainage pattern he deduced for Wales, and Cardiganshire, was genetically related to present-day summit areas (shown by the development of river captures just below existing summits). The starting-point for development of both the drainage and plateaux would have been the uplift of an end-Oligocene (*c*.30 million years ago) landsurface, but the exact nature of its subsequent history is indeterminate without further evidence. Given the considerable fluctuations of global sea-level, which are known to have occurred in late Cenozoic times, and probable uplift of the earth's crust in Wales, formation of plateaux by marine and subaerial ('peneplain') development cannot be excluded. In a radical challenge to all such theories, however, John Challinor suggested that the plateaux were illusory and only existed in 'the eye of the indoctrinated beholder'.[15] Challinor believed that the 'hill-top surface' of Cardiganshire is a logical outcome of long-continued weathering and erosion, and that all watershed areas may be incorporated into a smooth curve from Plynlimon to sea-level (Fig. 5). This would appear to be corroborated by the study of the detailed form of the ground and a comparison of it with variations in the geology, especially the distribution of resistant and soft rocks. The more resistant rocks should generally conform to positive or upstanding elements in the scenery, and the softer or less resistant rocks should correspond with the negative elements or depressions.[16]

[14] D. Q. Bowen, 'The land of Wales', *Wales: A New Study*, ed. D. Thomas (Newton Abbot, 1977), 11–35; idem, *The Llanelli Landscape: The Geology and Geomorphology of the Country around Llanelli* (Llanelli, 1980); idem, in *National Atlas of Wales*, ed. H. Carter (Cardiff, 1982); idem, 'The Welsh landform', *Settlement and Society in Wales*, ed. D. Huw Owen (Cardiff, 1989), 27–44.

[15] J. Challinor, 'The hill-top surface of north Cardiganshire', *Geography*, 15 (1930), 651–6. Note that, despite his objection to the recognition of plateaux, Challinor agreed that a hill-top surface may have a 'plateau quality'. He also seems to have had doubts about the proposed river capture at Devil's Bridge. He wrote: 'The Rheidol above Devil's Bridge is a tributary of the Mynach–Lower Rheidol, which has developed along the softer rocks of the anticlinal axis and has worked back northwards into the high ground of Plynlimon, so as to outgrow its "parent"' (J. Challinor, 'The physiography of the two localities Ponterwyd and Devil's Bridge', *Report of the Centenary Meeting, Arch.Camb.*, 99 (1947), 139–40. See also D. Q. Bowen, *The Llanelli Landscape*, 14.

[16] See also D. Q. Bowen, 'Y Tirffurf Cymreig', *Y Gwyddonydd*, 5 (1967), 14–22, who explored similar ideas to those of Challinor in the Talerddig region of Montgomeryshire.

This is certainly the case in detail, and it appears to hold good to some extent even if broader tracts of land are considered. For example, the belt of high ground adjacent to the coastline and its hinterland between Borth and Llangrannog consists of the Aberystwyth Grits Formation with its comparatively thick turbidite sandstones. Landwards the Silurian rocks consist mostly of mudstones, and they form a broad strath of ground between the high coastal belt and the upland of Plynlimon, which owes its elevation to late Cenozoic uplift. Such scenic contrasts, as well as the 'resistant rock upland' of Cader Idris, may be readily appreciated from excellent roadside vantage points on the northern flank of Mynydd Bach. Although the Plynlimon upland consists largely of silty mudstones with subordinate sandstones and siltstones, these are distributed throughout the Ordovician succession and probably determine its steep slope angles.

These relationships between rock hardness and landform, both in detail and at large, appear to lend support to Challinor's view that no plateaux exist in Cardiganshire. On the other hand, those who recognize the existence of plateaux remnants would maintain that the correlation between rock resistance and topography is predictable because of weathering and erosion of formerly more extensive plateaux. Indeed plateaux remnants will be preferentially preserved on more resistant rocks.

iii) The Ice Ages

A general cooling of the northern hemisphere commenced about 3 million years ago and by 2.4 million years ago evidence for mid-latitude glaciation appears, but it was not until about 800,000 years ago that Britain experienced severe and extensive glaciation.[17] Between 2.4 million and 800,000 years ago the frequency of glaciations followed a 41,000-year cycle, when it is likely that glaciers occurred on the high ground throughout Wales; but after 800,000 years ago they followed a 100,000-year cycle, and the extent of glaciation underwent a dramatic increase in extent so as to cover Wales completely on occasion.

From evidence beyond Cardiganshire it is possible to show that the County was completely covered by some of the earlier glaciations.[18] At these times glacial erosion occurred in both overdeepening valley floors and oversteepening valley side slopes, as, for example, in the Rheidol

---

[17] N. J. Shackleton, R. G. West and D. Q. Bowen (eds.), *The Past Three Million Years: Evolution of Climatic Variability in the North Atlantic Region* (The Royal Society, London, 1988); see also D. Q. Bowen, 'The last 130,000 years', *The University of Wales Science and Technology Review*, 5 (1989), 39–46.

[18] D. Q. Bowen, 'The Pleistocene history of Wales and the Borderland', *Geological Journal*, 8 (1973), 207–24; idem, 'The Pleistocene succession of the Irish Sea', *Proc. Geologists' Association*, 84 (1973), 249–72; idem, 'The Quaternary of Wales', *The Upper Palaeozoic and Post Palaeozoic Rocks of Wales*, ed. T. R. Owen (Cardiff, 1974), 373–426; idem, 'An introduction to the Quaternary', *Geological Conservation Review: Quaternary of Wales*, ed. S. Campbell and D. Q. Bowen (Nature Conservancy Council, Peterborough, 1989), 7–19; idem, 'The Quaternary rocks and landforms of Wales', ibid., 15–20.

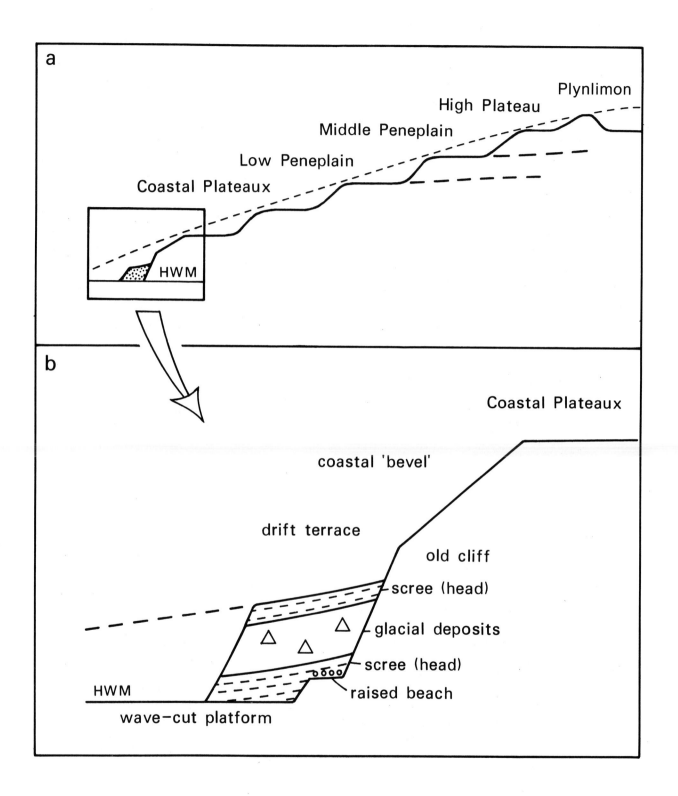

and Ystwyth valleys. The deep, glaciated rock basins at the mouth of the Dyfi[19] and Teifi[20] were probably overdeepened by Welsh ice during such early glaciations.

In Cardiganshire the only evidence for the last Ice Age (120,000 to 10,000 years ago) is represented by sedimentary deposits, but because some of these deposits immediately overlie an old cliff-line along the coast it is possible to say something about the last major interglaciation (125,000 years ago). At Poppit, near St Dogmaels, a raised beach lies on a shore-platform. Both the platform and its sea cliff are buried by a terrace consisting of scree and glacial deposits. The same shore-platform occurs across the estuary of the Teifi near Gwbert, and similar platforms and cliffs are buried by a terrace of 'drift' deposits at different places along the coastline (Fig. 6). The terrace, consisting of glacial and periglacial deposits is spectacularly displayed between New Quay and Cei Bach, between Aberaeron and Aber-arth, between Morfa and Llanrhystud and along the coast at Morfa Bychan south of Aberystwyth. Traces of the rock platform which the terrace buried are seen from place to place: in the stream bottom at Aber-arth and at Morfa Bychan where at one point the sea has removed the terrace deposits to exhume the old cliff. Elsewhere the old cliff-line is a prominent feature of the landscape between Llanrhystud and Morfa, between Aber-arth and Aberaeron, and around New Quay. Indeed present-day rock cliffs are relics of this and earlier events.[21]

Glaciers developed in northern Britain and the uplands of Wales during the Early Devensian glaciation (Table 1)[22] but at this time Cardiganshire was ice-free (except possibly for Plynlimon)

[19] D. J. Blundell, D. H. Griffiths and R. F. King, 'Geophysical investigations of buried river valleys around Cardigan Bay', *Geological Journal*, 6 (1969), 161–80.

[20] D. L. Lear, 'The Quaternary deposits of the Lower Teifi Valley' (unpublished Univ. of Wales Ph.D. thesis, Aberystwyth, 1986); D. Q. Bowen and D. L. Lear, 'The Quaternary geology of the Lower Teifi Valley', *Geological Excursions in Dyfed, South-west Wales*, ed. M. G. Bassett (Cardiff, 1982), 297–302.

[21] D. Q. Bowen, 'Time and place on the British coast', *Geography*, 58 (3) (1973), 207–16; idem, 'The coast of Wales', *Geological Journal*, Special Issue, No.7 (1977), 223–56.

[22] D. Q. Bowen and G. A. Sykes, 'Correlation of the marine events and glaciations on the North-east Atlantic Margin', *Philosophical Transactions of the Royal Society of London*, Series B, 318 (1988), 619–35; D. Q. Bowen, 'Time and space in the glacial sediment systems of the British Isles', *Glacial Deposits of Great Britain and Ireland*, eds. J. Ehlers, P. L. Gibbard and J. Rose (Balkema, Rotterdam, 1991), 1–13; idem, 'The last Interglacial-Glacial Cycle in the British Isles', *Quaternary International*, 3/4 (1989), 41–7.

Fig. 6: (a) Diagrammatic profile across the Cardiganshire plateaux using the classification and terminology of E. H. Brown (see caption for Fig. 2). The broken line represents J. Challinor's view of the 'hill-top surface of North Cardiganshire' as one unitary surface that has been 'continuously lowered by subaerial erosion'; in other words, he disbelieved the existence of plateaux. But, using a statistical analysis of summit elevations throughout Wales, O. T. Jones showed that different topographic levels (plateaux) did exist. Similarly, trend surface analysis of the topography of north Cardiganshire by J. Rodda confirmed the existence of the plateaux subdivision proposed by Brown. (b) Diagrammatic illustration of coastal topography along parts of the Cardiganshire coastline. Where the drift terrace has been removed by marine erosion, the ancient cliffs and marine platforms are subject to wave action today. The sequence of coastal events may be summarized thus: (a) formation of the cliffed coast, (b) burial by the deposits of the drift terrace, consequent upon a fall (ice age) in sea-level, (c) recovery of sea-level (postglacial) and erosion of the drift terrace.

and cold, periglacial conditions prevailed. Frost shattering of bedrock occurred and scree (head) materials accumulated. These may be seen at the base of the coastal terrace at New Quay, Aber-arth and Morfa Bychan. At this time and previously during cycles of cold, the upper cliff slopes were eroded to produce the scree. This resulted in lessening the angle of the slope, so that a 'cliff-bevel'[23] was formed (Fig. 6). Examples of bevelled cliffs may be seen in profile along the entire Cardiganshire coast, but the most spectacular examples are around Llangrannog, and between Aber-arth and Morfa, where the Aberystwyth–Aberaeron road runs along the crest of the bevel.

The Late Devensian glaciation was complex because Cardiganshire was affected by mid-Wales ice, and by ice from the Irish Sea which had its origins to the north. Evidence for glaciation by mid-Wales ice is provided by glacial deposits which occur principally along valley sides and on valley floors.[24] Although most of these do not form glacial depositional landforms, important exceptions occur throughout the Teifi Valley,[25] where kames, kame terraces and kettle holes occur. Rock surfaces scratched during the passage of ice have been identified in the north of the County,[26] while classical erosional forms, similar to *roches moutonnées* occur in the Teifi Pools area.[27] The pattern of glaciation may be inferred from the distribution of the deposits of mid-Wales ice. Ice from the Plynlimon area flowed east to west along the valleys of northern Cardiganshire to extend over the floor of Cardigan Bay where the extent of different ice lobes is marked by the *sarnau*, which are end-moraines (that is, ridges composed of glacial deposits). In the north of the County the ice carried felsite erratics from Mynydd Aran, a glacier which terminated at Sarn Cynfelyn. The floor of Cardigan Bay is covered by Welsh glacial deposits for up to 12 km offshore from the present coastline.[28] Farther south ice moved along the Teifi Valley, at least as far as Pentre-cwrt, but the extent to which it overrode Mynydd Bach is unknown.

Ice from the Irish Sea met the Welsh ice offshore in a zone which trends south-eastwards, and which meets the coastline at Llanrhystud. South of Llanrhystud the entire coastline appears to have been glaciated by Irish Sea ice.[29] The main evidence used to show this is a stiff blue-black calcareous clay which contains far-travelled rocks and marine shell fragments. This deposit is, or has been, exposed at Llanrhystud, Aber-arth, Aberaeron, Gilfachyrhalen, New Quay, Traeth y Mwnt, Gwbert, and upstream as far as Cenarth in the lower Teifi Valley. Boulders of Irish Sea rocks have been identified at Llandysul.[30] Similar clay deposits in the left-bank tributary valleys

[23] A. Wood, 'The erosional history of the cliffs around Aberystwyth', *Liverpool and Manchester Geological Journal*, 2 (1959), 271–87; idem, 'Coastal cliffs of Cardigan Bay', *Coastal Cliffs: Report of a Symposium, Geographical Journal* (1962), 303–20.

[24] See above, n.3.

[25] A. Price, 'The Quaternary deposits of the Middle Teifi Valley between Llanllwni and Pentrecwrt' (unpublished Univ. of Wales M. Sc. thesis, Aberystwyth, 1976); see also D. Q. Bowen and D. L. Lear, 'The Quaternary geology of the Lower Teifi Valley' (see above, n.20).

[26] O. T. Jones and W. J. Pugh, 'The geology of the district around Machynlleth and the Llyfnant valley' (see above, n.2).

[27] D. Q. Bowen in *National Atlas of Wales* (see above, n.14).

[28] R. A. Garrard and M. R. Dobson, 'The nature and maximum extent of glacial sediments off the west coast of Wales', *Marine Geology*, 16 (1974), 31–44.

[29] K. E. Williams, 'The glacial drift of western Cardiganshire', *Geological Magazine*, 64 (1927), 205–27.

[30] O. T. Jones, 'The glacial and post-glacial history of the lower Teifi valley', *Quarterly J. of Geological Soc. of London*, 121 (1965), 247–81.

of the Teifi have been described by the Soil Survey of England and Wales.[31] Infilling the old valley of the Teifi south of Cilgerran is a vast thickness of glacial deposits. Geophysical investigations have indicated that much of this glacial deposit may consist of Irish Sea clays.[32] It is possible that the similar old valley of the Teifi at Cenarth is also infilled with the same material.[33]

The origin of the blue-black calcareous clay has become controversial. Traditionally it has been interpreted as a deposit laid down beneath an ice-sheet, but it is now believed by many that it was deposited in the sea as a glacio-marine mud at a time when the Irish Sea ice-sheet was 'retreating' northwards.[34] The folded and contorted deposits at Traeth y Mwnt[35] show deformation of some of these deposits by submarine slumping. But was the lower Teifi Valley ever an arm of a glacial sea? There is abundant evidence for waterlain clays, sometimes beautifully laminated, as far upstream as Pentre-cwrt,[36] and for deltas at Bancywarren near Cardigan, and in the middle Teifi, for example, at Llanybydder and Lampeter.[37] These have been used to show the existence of an ice-dammed proglacial 'Lake Teifi' much as envisaged by Charlesworth[38] and O. T. Jones[39]. It seems reasonable to assume that 'Lake Teifi' consisted of meltwater, especially in its upper reaches around Lampeter and Llanybydder. In the north of the County scattered laminated clays show the former existence of small, probably ephemeral, glacial lakes. In the lower Teifi, Lear has shown that the Irish Sea clays predate the development of 'Lake Teifi' as well as the deposition of the delta gravels at Bancywarren.[40] The source of meltwater for the Bancywarren gravels was from ice immediately to the north of that locality,[41] so that the presence of an Irish Sea ice mass appears confirmed. Certainly, at one point, it covered the entire high ground to the south of the Teifi estuary to a height of well over 182 m (600 ft.) OD.[42] The date of the glaciation is shown by age determinations from the protein content of the marine shells collected from Irish Sea deposits (amino-acid dating). This evidence which has been confirmed by radiocarbon dating, shows that the glaciation occurred about 20,000 to 17,000 years ago.[43]

A feature of the Cardiganshire landscape is the short, deep, narrow and often 'dry' (that is, streamless) valley. Some of them cut across present-day watersheds and are thus unrelated to the

[31] R. I. Bradley, *Soils in Dyfed* V (see above, n.9).

[32] K. R. Nunn and M. Boztas, 'Shallow seismic reflection profiling on land using a controlled source', *Geoexploration*, 15 (1977), 87–97.

[33] See above, n.30, and D. Q. Bowen and D. L. Lear, 'The Quaternary geology of the Lower Teifi Valley' (see above, n.20).

[34] N. J. Eyles and A. M. McCabe, 'The Late Devensian (22,000 YBP) Irish Sea sheet margin', *Quaternary Science Review*, 8 (4) (1989), 307–52.

[35] D. Q. Bowen, 'The last 130,000 years' (see above, n.17).

[36] See above, n.30; D. Q. Bowen and D. L. Lear, 'The Quaternary geology of the Lower Teifi valley (see above, n.20).

[37] D. Q. Bowen in *National Atlas of Wales* (see above, n.14).

[38] J. K. Charlesworth, 'The South Wales end-moraine', *Quarterly J. of Geological Soc. of London*, 85 (1929), 335–58.

[39] See above, n.30.

[40] D. L. Lear, 'The Quaternary Deposits of the Lower Teifi Valley' (see above, n.20).

[41] J. R. L. Allen, 'Late Pleistocene (Devensian) glaciofluvial outwash at Banc-y-Warren, near Cardigan (west Wales)', *Geological Journal*, 17 (1982), 31–47.

[42] D. Q. Bowen, 'Pleistocene deposits and fluvioglacial landforms of north Preseli', *Geological Excursions in Dyfed, South-west Wales*, ed. M. G. Bassett, 289–95.

[43] D. Q. Bowen, 'An introduction to the Quaternary' and 'The Quaternary rocks and landforms of Wales' (see above, n.18).

present drainage system. Such valleys are attributed to erosion by meltwater streams towards the close of glaciation when the ice was melting rapidly. Some of them may have drained temporary lakes but the majority either formed along an ice-margin or were cut beneath the ice by subglacial streams. Excellent examples occur at Tal-y-bont[44] and across the watersheds between the valleys north of Aberystwyth. Farther south the gorges occupied by the River Teifi today were also fashioned by meltwater erosion. Running parallel to each of them at Cilgerran, Cenarth, Henllan, Alltcavan, Llandysul and Llanllwni, are abandoned, wide and glacial drift-infilled (or plugged) valleys which were formerly occupied by the Teifi. The sequence of events which led to the formation of the gorges appears to have been as follows: a pre-glaciation Teifi occupied the wide, but now abandoned, valleys; then glaciation and submergence of the valley by ice; and finally during deglaciation, meltwater streams, either within (englacial) or upon (supraglacial) the ice, cut downwards into bedrock where they fashioned the gorges.[45] After the ice had disappeared, the 'postglacial' Teifi followed the route of the gorges because its former courses were blocked by thick infills of glacial deposits. Examples of this, but on a greatly reduced scale, occur in some of the smaller valleys, for example, at Llechryd and Aber-arth, and just downstream from Ponterwyd.[46]

During and after the disappearance of the ice, between about 17,000 and 10,000 years ago, the landscape was subjected to harsh periglacial conditions with sub-zero temperatures for much of the year. During this time some of the glacial deposits on slopes were moved downslope by solifluction and many were mixed with scree deposits formed by severe frost action on bedrock. On the softer mudstones, stratified screes were formed.[47] In Cwm Ystwyth the huge amphitheatre-like hollows of Cwm Tinwen and Cwm Du were still filled with snow and possibly some ice, and erosion produced thick platforms of sediments. Watson called these nivation (predominant frost action) cirques.[48] Ubiquitous, though almost certainly discontinuous, permafrost (ground permanently frozen, although its top layer would melt during the short summer season), was present in Cardiganshire; its principal legacies were ice-wedge pseudomorphs into superficial materials,[49] and the remains of open-system pingos.[50] These consist of circular depressions surrounded by ramparts and mark the former position of ice-cored mounds or hillocks. They were supplied with water, which then froze, by a sub-permafrost artesian flow of water from higher ground. Locally

[44] O. T. Jones and W. J. Pugh, 'The geology of the district around Machynlleth' (see above, n.2).

[45] D. Q. Bowen, 'On the supposed ice-dammed lakes of South Wales', *Trans. Cardiff Naturalist Society*, 93 (1967), 4–17.

[46] J. Challinor, 'The "incised meanders" near Pont-erwyd, Cardiganshire', *Geological Magazine*, 70 (1933), 90–2; see also T. D. Adams, 'Buried valleys of the upper Rheidol (Cardiganshire)', *Geological Magazine*, 98 (1961), 406–8.

[47] E. Watson, 'Grèzes litées ou éboulis ordonnées tardi-glaciaires dans la région d'Aberystwyth au centre du Pays de Galles', *Bull. de l'Assoc. de Géographes Français*, 338–9 (1965), 16–25.

[48] E. Watson, 'Two nivation cirques near Aberystwyth, Wales', *Biuletyn Peryglacjalny*, 15 (1966), 79–101.

[49] E. Watson, 'Periglacial structures in the Aberystwyth region of Central Wales', *Proc. of the Geologists' Association*, 76(4) (1965), 443–62.

[50] E. Watson and S. Watson, 'Remains of pingos in Wales and the Isle of Man', *Geological Journal*, 7 (1971), 381–92; E. Watson, 'Two nivation cirques near Aberystwyth' (see above, n.48); idem, 'Field excursions in the Aberystwyth region, 1–10 July, 1975', *Biuletyn Peryglacjalny*, 26 (1976), 79-112; and E. Watson and S. Watson, 'Remains of pingos in the Cletwr Basin, south-west Wales', *Geografisca Annaler*, 56, Series A (1974), 3–4.

spectacular concentrations of such pingo scars occur at Talgarreg, Cwrtnewydd, and throughout Cardiganshire.[51] The evidence indicates that they formed between 11,000 and 10,000 years ago, long after the ice had disappeared. Indeed, this short period of 1,000 years or less (corresponding to the Loch Lomond Glaciation in Scotland, and a dramatic southward shift of the Gulf Stream to the latitude of northern Portugal), witnessed spectacular periglacial erosion (frost action), downslope movement of deposits (solifluction),[52] and the accumulation of alluvial fans, notably those near Llan-non, where they were deposited by the Peris and Clydan streams,[53] and at Tre'r-ddôl, by the River Cletwr. Along some streams river terraces were also formed by aggradation of gravels and subsequent stream downcutting.[54] In the Teifi Valley the Dôl-haidd and Cilgwyn terraces were described by O. T. Jones,[55] while Cave and Hains have described smaller ones in the valleys of the Myherin, Castell, Rheidol (notably near Capel Bangor[56]), Melindwr and Leri. Some spectacular river incision (downcutting) also took place at this time when, for example, the bedrock channels of present-day streams were fashioned, as well as other spectacular features such as the Mynach falls at Devil's Bridge. The intensity of erosion and landscape sculpturing during this short time can be paralleled elsewhere in the British Isles. As such, it probably holds a key to earlier episodes of erosion when the British landscape was modified by periglacial (frost-dominated) action. The history of global Quaternary Ice Ages is dominated by many such cycles of episodic erosion which probably hold the key to interpreting many mid-latitude landscapes, not least that of Cardiganshire. The evidence for such repetitive cycles in our County may have been destroyed, but the evidence of the latest may be used as a 'key to the past'.

The most recent and ongoing event of the Quaternary Ice Ages is the present interglaciation (the Holocene Epoch), which commenced with the great climatic improvement some 10,000 years or so ago. From that time onwards Mesolithic, Neolithic, Bronze Age and Iron Age peoples successively colonized and modified the landscape, particularly its vegetation. But what of the environments they inhabited? J. A. Taylor has synthesized the immediate climatic, vegetational, landform and prehistoric antecedents of the present-day Cardiganshire landscape.[57] During these successive cultural episodes the hillsides, floodplains and coastline of the County were modified anew.

Perhaps the most spectacular changes occurred along the coastline. At the maximum of the Late Devensian (last) Glaciation, world sea-level was about 130m below present, a figure which represents the abstraction of sea-water locked into the world's ice-sheets. When ice-sheets all over

[51] E. Watson, 'Pingos of Cardiganshire and the latest ice limit', *Nature*, 236 (1972), 343–4. Investigations by A. S. Handa and P. D. Moore, 'Studies in the vegetational history of mid-Wales IV. Pollen analysis of some pingo basins', *New Phyt.*, 77 (1976), 205–25, show that the age of the pingos is probably Late-glacial, between 11,000 and 10,000 years ago. This invalidates their use as an artefact to delimit the extent of the last (Late Devensian) glaciation.

[52] E. Watson and S. Watson, 'The periglacial origin of the drifts at Morfa Bychan near Aberystwyth', *Geological Journal*, 5 (1967), 419–40.

[53] E. Watson, 'Field excursions in the Aberystwyth region' (see above, n.50).

[54] M. G. Macklin and J. Lewin, 'Terraced fills of Pleistocene and Holocene age in the Rheidol Valley, Wales', *J. Quaternary Science*, 1(1) (1986), 21–34.

[55] O. T. Jones, 'The glacial and post-glacial history of the lower Teifi valley' (see above, n.30).

[56] R. Cave and B. A. Haines, 'Geology of the country between Aberystwyth and Machynlleth' (see above, n.3).

[57] J. A. Taylor (ed.), *Culture and Environment in Prehistoric Wales* (BAR 76, 1980).

the world started to disappear the global sea-level rose. Initially the rise was rapid but it slowed appreciably after about 5,000 years ago. Cardigan Bay became progressively submerged, and therein lies the substance for a lost province (Cantre'r Gwaelod) beneath the waters of the bay. Records of the events of these times are preserved below the present-day surface in Cors Fochno (Borth Bog)[58] and at Clarach.[59] On the foreshore at Ynys-las may be seen the remains of a submerged forest (mainly pine) which has been radiocarbon-dated to 6,000 years ago.[60] Other patches of submerged forest have been seen at Clarach. Marine and estuarine deposits are extensive on the south side of the Dyfi estuary.

Along the contemporary shoreline of Cardigan Bay is found a variety of marine deposits. These include storm beach gravels, sands, silts and muds. Extensive sand beaches occur in the Dyfi estuary, between Ynys-las and Borth, and at New Quay. Storm beaches, consisting of gravels heaped into ridges and beach berms (small platforms on the gravels), occur between Aberaeron and Aber-arth, between Morfa and Llanrhystud, at Tan-y-bwlch and along the Aberystwyth foreshore, at Clarach and between Borth and Ynys-las. The development of the Aberystwyth storm beaches is no longer supplied naturally, which has led to problems of erosion.[61] Tracts of blown sand occur at Ynys-las and towards Borth and at Gwbert.

Inland the present interglacial saw the development of deep soil profiles and widespread peat[62] which contain the fossil pollen record showing the development of the Cardiganshire vegetation (and by inference the climate) and its progressive modification by Man. During the Holocene, three raised bogs developed behind the end-moraine at Tregaron. The stratigraphical and pollen analytical investigation of these bogs was an early classic in the field.[63] Hillslope colluvium was transferred by soil creep and slope-wash downslope. On flood plains evidence from sequences of alluvium shows that the Ystwyth formerly entered the sea at Tan-y-bwlch, before it was diverted into Aberystwyth harbour in the late eighteenth century.[64] The development of the meanders of the Rheidol and Ystwyth streams have been studied by John Lewin.[65]

[58] R. H. Yapp, D. Johns and O. T. Jones, 'The salt marshes of the Dovey estuary. Part 1', *J. Ecology*, 4 and 5 (1916–17), 27–42 and 65–103; J. Haynes and M. R. Dobson, 'Physiography, foraminifera and sedimentation in the Dyfi estuary, Wales', *Geological Journal*, 6 (1969), 217–56; P. J. Wilkes, 'Mid-Holocene sea-level and sedimentation interactions in the Dyfi estuary area, Wales', *Palaeogeography, Palaeoclimatology, Palaeoecology*, 26 (1979), 17–36; H. Godwin, 'Coastal peat beds of the British Isles and North Sea', *J. Ecology*, 31 (1943), 199–247; J. A. Taylor, 'Chronometers and chronicles', *Progress in Geography*, 5 (1973), 250–334.

[59] A. Heyworth, C. Kidson and P. J. Wilkes, 'Late-glacial and Holocene sediments at Clarach Bay, near Aberystwyth', *J. Ecology*, 73(2) (1985), 459–80.

[60] J. A. Taylor, 'Chronometers and chronicles' (see above, n.58).

[61] A. Wood, 'Coast erosion at Aberystwyth: the geological and human factors involved', *Geological Journal*, 13 (1978), 61–72; idem, 'Prevention of beach erosion at Aberystwyth: a success story', *Geological Journal*, 15 (1980), 135–6.

[62] J. A. Taylor (ed.), *Culture and Environment* (see above, n.57).

[63] H. Godwin and G. F. Mitchell, 'Stratigraphy and development of two raised bogs near Tregaron, Cardiganshire', *New Phyt.*, 37 (1938), 425–54.

[64] See above, n.61.

[65] J. Lewin, 'Meander development and floodplain sedimentation: a case study from mid-Wales', *Geological Journal*, 13 (1978), 25–36.

CHAPTER 2

SOILS AND LAND USE

C. C. Rudeforth

Cardiganshire's varied soils have developed mainly since the Ice Age from rocks and drift materials under the influence of slope shapes, past climates, vegetation, animals and Man. The resulting contrasts in soil thickness, composition and drainage, together with current climate and topography, have greatly affected how Man has been able to use the land. A brief description of the soils and how they have formed provides a useful background for understanding the County's history.

About 12,000 years ago when Cardiganshire was emerging from the glacial epoch, rocks were exposed and shattered by heavy frosts, and torrents from melting glaciers deposited thick gravels along the valley floors. Compact tills blanketed lower hill slopes and plateaux. Permafrost was widespread.[1] Wedges and lenses of ice accumulated in the drifts; gravels were heaved and convoluted by frost action. Fed by downslope seepage, ice lenses in some valley-side drifts became thick enough to burst through the surface as pingos,[2] later to melt and leave a characteristic uneven topography of curved ramparts and rounded hollows. The generally warmer and moister climates that followed favoured chemical weathering which dissolved and further comminuted components in the rocks and drifts. These finer materials were washed into streams and often accumulated over the earlier, coarser deposits.

The picture which thus emerges is of weathered soil materials thinned by erosion from convex slopes contrasting with those in concave sites where deposits are often thick. Water is also shed from convex slopes and accumulates in hollows. Contrasts in soil formation, therefore, developed in the rolling landscape leaving thin, stony, coarse-textured, well aerated and often dry brown soils on the upper slopes, and deep, finer-textured, poorly aerated, grey-coloured gleyed soils on the wetter concave slopes. At the same time different plants and animals colonized the contrasting sites and contributed to the development of different ecosystems.

Under a cover of vegetation, plant remains are added to the soil where they are more or less decomposed and incorporated with the mineral material. Part of the organic matter decays, releasing nutrients for plant growth, but part is transformed into dark-coloured humus which decomposes more slowly. In relatively base-rich, well aerated soils, rapid decomposition and faunal activity, particularly that of earthworms, achieve intimate mixing of mineral and organic

---

[1] V. I. Stewart, *A Perma-frost Horizon in the Soils of Cardiganshire*, Welsh Soils Discussion Group Report 2 (Aberystwyth, 1961), 19–22.
[2] E. Watson, 'Remains of pingos in Wales and the Isle of Man', *Geological Journal*, 7 (1971), 381–92.

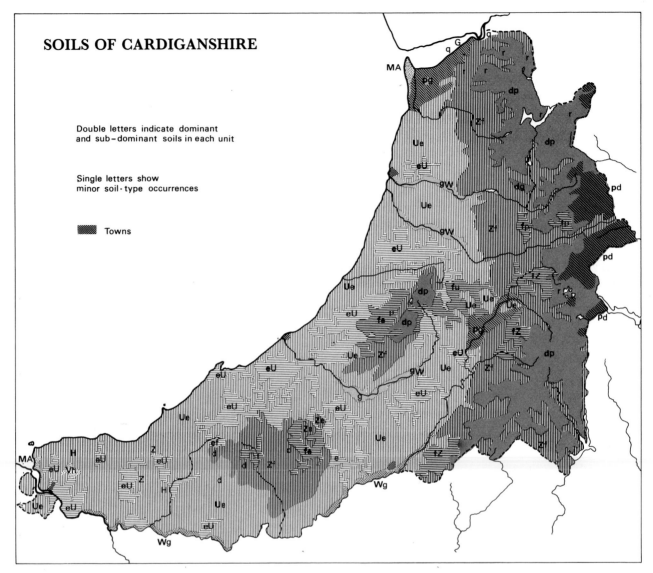

SOILS OF CARDIGANSHIRE

Double letters indicate dominant
and sub-dominant soils in each unit

Single letters show
minor soil-type occurrences

▓▓ Towns

Fig. 7:

components. In strongly acid soils where there is little mixing by fauna, breakdown is retarded
so that partly decomposed plant litter accumulates on the mineral soil surface. Where waterlog-
ging or low summer temperature severely inhibits decomposition, thick accumulations of organic
matter or peat develop at the surface. With low temperatures and high rainfall, acid peats have
accumulated on the Cambrian Mountains even where subsoils drain freely. The relevant soil
profiles display striking horizon contrasts characteristic of stagnopodzols. The black surface peat
overlies a bleached, seasonally waterlogged, greyish loamy horizon from which most iron oxides
have been removed and this in turn passes to a bright orange-coloured, iron-rich, well aerated
and permeable subsoil.

Soil formation, erosion and redeposition have operated with varying intensity since the glaciers
retreated and these processes have often been modified by Man's activities. Charcoal fragments

Symbol	Soil Group	Brief Description of Soil
	Terrestrial raw soils	
A	Raw sands	Unstable coastal dune sand
	Raw gley soils	
G	Unripened gley soils	Soft permanently wet estuarine muds
	Lithomorphic soils	
H	Rankers	Shallow non-calcareous loamy or peaty soils on rock or rock debris
M	Sand-parendzinas	Calcareous sandy soils in stabilized coastal sands
	Brown soils	
U	Brown earths	Well drained loamy non-calcareous soils with brownish subsurface horizon
V	Brown sands	Well drained sandy non-calcareous soils, locally gravelly, with brownish subsurface horizon
W	Brown alluvial soils	Well drained loamy non-calcareous alluvial soils with brownish subsurface horizon, often over gravelly substratum; liable to flood
	Podzolic soils	
Z	Brown podzolic soils	Well drained loamy acid soils with ochreous subsurface horizon
d	Stagnopodzols	Loamy acid soils with periodically wet peaty surface and bleached subsurface horizon over a permeable ochreous horizon with or without a thin ironpan
	Surface-water gley soils	
e	Stagnogley soils	Poorly drained slowly permeable loamy or clayey non-calcareous soils with greyish or mottled subsoils
f	Stagnohumic gley soils	Poorly drained slowly permeable loamy or clayey acid soils with humose or peaty surface
	Ground-water gley soils	
g	Alluvial gley soils	Poorly drained loamy or clayey alluvial soils with greyish or mottled subsurface horizons; liable to flood
h	Sandy gley soils	Poorly drained permeable sandy soils with greyish or mottled subsurface horizons affected by high groundwater
	Peat soils	
p	Raw peat soils	Poorly drained hill and raised bog peats with soft or fibrous topsoils
q	Earthy peat soils	Poorly drained lowland peats with earthy (crumbly) topsoil
r	**Rock**	Rock outcrops with scree and raw skeletal soils

Key to Fig 7: Soils of Cardiganshire

in subsoils suggest that erosion sometimes followed forest fires, caused perhaps by Man or lightning. Since forest clearance, land enclosure and cultivation, soil has also washed periodically downslope leaving subsoil exposed below field boundaries and thick topsoil accumulations above them. Contamination of valley floors by toxic particles carried from lead-mine spoil heaps in floodwaters during the last hundred years[3] and the recently increased acidity of afforested catchments demonstrate that Man's influence continues to this day.

Fig. 7 identifies the main soils found in Cardiganshire. The soils form distinctive patterns which have influenced Man's activities since he first colonized the County. His footpaths and trackways

---

[3]B. E. Davies and J. Lewin, 'Chronosequences in alluvial soils with special reference to historic lead pollution in Cardiganshire, Wales', *Environmental Pollution*, 6 (1) (1974), 49–58.

followed the drier land wherever possible. Early settlements were built on hilltops for defence, taking advantage of the well-drained soils usually found at such sites. Many farmsteads have since been built on sheltered, well-drained, lower slopes but close to wetter land where there is a good water supply but no risk of flooding. Stock could then be grazed conveniently on the drier land in wet seasons and the wetter land when drought stopped growth on the dry banks.

The map (Fig. 7)[4] has pairs of symbols. The first symbol of each pair represents the dominant soil and the second the main ancillary soil. Unripened gley soils (G) are restricted to the tidal salt marshes of the Dyfi estuary. They are partly grazed by sheep, but also valued as wildlife habitats and for recreation. Sandy soils (M and A) include the nearby Ynys-las sand dunes accumulated on a shingle bar running northwards from Borth. These soils support recreational activity (for example, golfing and camping). A similar tract lies between Cardigan and Gwbert where sand has been blown from the Teifi estuary over solid rocks.

Cardiganshire's most extensive soils are the Brown earths (U). These well-drained loamy soils, although thin in places, support some of the best land for livestock farming. The land is firm for much of the grazing season, and most of it supplies adequate moisture for grass growth except in very dry years. Most farmers also have some wetter land represented by the Stagnogley soils (e). Shallow, drought-prone Ranker soils (H), however, are more common in parts of the south-west, where cereals, particularly barley for stock feed, are also grown. Woodland, much of it deciduous, covers many of the steep valley sides. Two other units of Brown soils are the Brown sands (V), near Cardigan, prized as the best source of sands and gravels in the County, and the deep, silty Brown alluvial soils (W) along the lower Teifi Valley. Flooding precludes a wide cropping range but these soils can produce excellent grass and other crops where the risk is acceptable.

On higher land, Brown podzolic soils (Z) are similar to the Brown earths, but are more acid and have an iron-enriched subsoil likely to inhibit phosphate uptake by crops. Lower temperatures on the hills also inhibit growth. However, on hard rocks in the north (r), these soils extend almost to sea level and their use here is limited more by steep slopes and rock outcrops. Brown podzolic soils are used extensively for forestry and are suited to a range of species such as Sitka spruce, Douglas fir, Japanese and European larches, Noble and Grand firs and Western hemlock, with sessile oak and beech in sheltered sites. Stagnopodzols (d) on the Cambrian Mountains are even more acid and the surface peat which has accumulated supports *Molinia*, *Nardus* and heather moorland or forest.

The wetter lands are represented by gley soils. The surface-water gley soils (e,f) have slowly permeable horizons that impede water flow and render them waterlogged for part or all of the year. Most are unsuitable for cultivation except in the driest areas, and even here repeated cultivation would cause damage and prove costly unless done in very dry periods. The land is often soft and wet near the surface, especially where peaty (f), so that the grazing period is limited; yet with careful management—including artificial drainage—grass yields can be excellent in the warmer districts. Gley soils on valley floors (g) are affected by groundwater. They

---

[4]The map is derived from C. C. Rudeforth: (Soils. Sheet 1.5a) *National Atlas of Wales*, ed. H. Carter (Cardiff, 1983).

provide excellent grazings but wetness and liability to flood make most of the fields unsuited to regular cultivation.

Thicker peats (p,q) range from the open heather and *Molinia* moorlands of the mountain tops where they are associated with stagnopodzols (d) to deeper valley bogs with alluvial gley soils (g). Near the Dyfi estuary, earthy peats (q) have been formed under cultivation and are partly used for arable crops as well as for grazing. The peat soils of the hills have particular additional value in holding large amounts of water which is released steadily, thereby maintaining base stream flow during dry periods. The peats, extensively cut for fuel in the past, are now a potential source for the horticultural industry, although also highly valued by conservationists.[5]

[5]For a full account of the soils of north Cardiganshire, see C. C. Rudeforth, 'Soils of north Cardiganshire', *Memoir, Soil Survey of Great Britain* (Harpenden, 1970), and of the south-west, see R. I. Bradley, *Soils in Dyfed* V: Sheet SN 24 (Llechryd), *Soil Survey Record*, No.63 (Harpenden, 1980). Further information about the soils of the whole county and their use can be found in C. C. Rudeforth, R. Hartnup, J. W. Lea, T. R. E. Thompson and P. S. Wright, *Soils and their Use in Wales*, Bulletin No.11, Soil Survey of England and Wales (1984).

CHAPTER 3

THE HISTORY OF VEGETATION IN CARDIGANSHIRE

P. D. Moore

THE history of Man in Cardiganshire is intricately interwoven with the history of the County's vegetation. The changing vegetation represents more than a backcloth to the unfolding story of Man's emergence and cultural development; coupled with climate and soils, it has exerted a profound influence upon his settlement patterns and has often been a determining factor in the development of agricultural practices. It has offered a source of food and shelter though presenting at times a formidable obstacle to the improvement of agricultural productivity. This being so, it is not surprising that Man in his turn has profoundly modified the vegetation of Cardiganshire. There remains no part of the landscape, even the open peatlands of Borth and Tregaron, the upland valley woodlands and the montane grasslands, which has escaped human-induced pressures of one sort or another. Thus Man and vegetation have a long established relationship, though whether this approximates to the relationship of predator and prey, parasite and host, or one of mutual symbiosis is open to debate.

The investigation of vegetational history is dependent upon the survival of fragments of plants in a recognizable form and in sufficient numbers to provide a reasonable statistical basis for the reconstruction of plant communities. Cardiganshire has proved particularly fortunate in its possession of deposits of peat and lake sediments scattered over a large portion of its surface area, both in the uplands and the lowlands. These deposits are rich in plant fossils, both macroscopic (for example seeds, fruits, leaves, wood, etc.) and microscopic (pollen grains and spores). Macrofossils are particularly valuable because they can often be identified to a specific level, but owing to their size they tend largely to comprise fragments of local, often wetland plant species. Microfossils, being small, may travel considerable distances and in suitable deposits are present in very high concentrations, but cannot always be identified with the precision of macrofossils. For example, different sedge species can be identified on the basis of their fruits, or even by the cells in their epidermal layers, but their pollen grains are indistinguishable from one another. Thus sedge pollen is recorded simply under the family, Cyperaceae.

Apart from the identification problems, pollen grain records are not always easy to interpret in terms of the vegetation which has given rise to them. Pollen grains differ in size, weight and aerodynamic properties, so that some travel further than others. Plants differ in the number of pollen grains which they produce and the height at which their pollen grains are released from the anthers. They also differ in the technique employed in the transfer of pollen from anther to stigma. A wind-pollinated species, such as grass, produces more pollen than an insect-pollinated one, such as clover; hence there is a better chance of finding fossil evidence for the former than

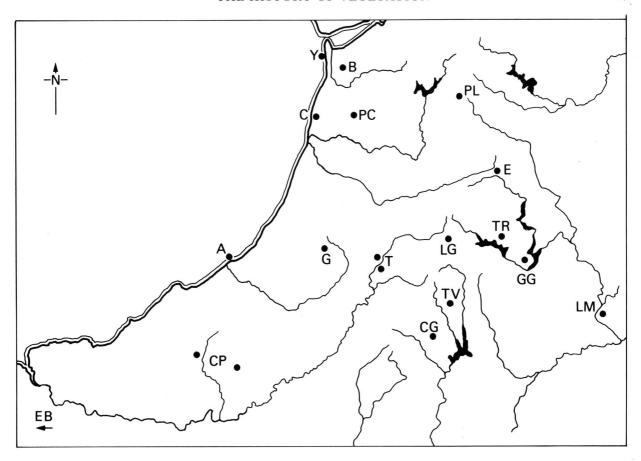

Fig. 8: Map of Central Wales showing sites at which pollen profiles have been described, most of which are referred to in the text. Key to sites:

Y	Ynys-las submerged forest	A	Aberaeron	EB	Esgyrn Bottom
B	Borth bog	G	Gwarllyn	CP	Cledlyn and Cletwr pingos
PL	Plynlimon	T	Tregaron	CG	Cefn Gwernffrwd
C	Clarach	LG	Llyn Gynon	TV	Tywi Valley
PC	Penrhyn-coch	TR	Trumau	LM	Llyn Mire
E	Elan Valley (Gors Llwyd)	GG	Gors Goch		

the latter. Many other factors are also important, such as whether the plant in question flowers in the deep shelter of a forest or out on an exposed hillside and, of course, how far away it is located from the site at which the pollen has come to rest.[1] It is necessary, therefore, to be aware that many pitfalls exist in the interpretation of pollen data.

[1]See K. Faegri and J. Iversen, *Textbook of Pollen Analysis* (3rd edn., Oxford, 1975), P. D. Moore, J. A. Webb and M. E. Collinson, *Pollen Analysis* (Oxford, 1991), and H. J. B. and H. H. Birks, *Quaternary Palaeoecology* (London, 1980), for more detailed critiques of methods of pollen analysis.

Work on the vegetational history of Cardiganshire began with the analyses of Godwin and Mitchell on Cors Tregaron,[2] Godwin and Newton at Ynys-las,[3] Davies at Figyn Blaen Brefi,[4] and Godwin at Cors Fochno,[5] but it was not until the mid-1960s that the results of pollen analyses from other parts of Cardiganshire were published. The locations of published (and some unpublished) pollen sites in Cardiganshire and adjacent areas are shown in Fig. 8.

The history of vegetation in Cardiganshire may be subdivided into the following periods:

Interglacial

Although no interglacial site containing good pollen material has been found in Cardiganshire, information from south Wales can reasonably be applied to the County, though even here only one detailed set of information is available, from West Angle (Pembs.).[6] There is some doubt concerning which interglacial it represents; it could belong to the penultimate Hoxnian or to one of the two phases of the final, Ipswichian interglacial.[7] The sediments involved at this site are from an estuarine stream channel and record a sequence of vegetation from birch (*Betula*) forest, through alder (*Alnus*)/oak (*Quercus*) woodland to a mixed forest of alder, spruce (*Picea*) and fir (*Abies*). It is only in the final stages of this sequence that hazel (*Corylus*) is prominent, and this, together with the presence of fir, is indicative of the earlier of the interglacials, namely the Hoxnian.

It is unwise to speculate too far on the vegetation of Cardiganshire during this interglacial on the basis of one site, but it is reasonable to suppose that a progression from sub-alpine birch woodland, through deciduous into mixed forest with coniferous, boreal elements took place. Within the pollen record, there is also evidence for some major disturbance, marked particularly by a peak in ash (*Fraxinus*) pollen, but it cannot be determined whether this is a natural feature, perhaps resulting from a local flood, or whether it resulted from human impact.

There is little botanical material from the last, Devensian glaciation in Cardiganshire, and most is confined to the final stages. In south Wales there are records of wood of willow (*Salix*) or aspen (*Populus*) found at Broughton Bay, Gower, by Campbell and Shakesby.[8] This material probably comes from an interstadial, warmer break in the cold, glacial climate, and it has been

[2]H. Godwin and G. F. Mitchell, 'Stratigraphy and development of two raised bogs near Tregaron, Cards.', *New Phyt.*, 37 (1938), 425–54.

[3]H. Godwin and C. Newton, 'The submerged forest at Borth and Ynyslas, Cardiganshire; data for the study of post-glacial history, I', *New Phyt.*, 37 (1938), 333–44.

[4]E. G. Davies, 'Figyn Blaen Brefi; a Welsh upland bog', *J. Ecology*, 32 (1944), 147–66.

[5]H. Godwin, 'Coastal peat beds of the British Isles and North Sea', *J. Ecology*, 31 (1943), 199–247; idem, *History of the British Flora* (Cambridge, 1956) (and cf. 2nd edn., 1975).

[6]A. C. Stevenson and P. D. Moore, 'Pollen analysis of an interglacial deposit at West Angle, Dyfed, Wales', *New Phyt.*, 90 (1982), 327–37.

[7]P. D. Moore, 'Hydrological changes in mires', *Handbook of Holocene Palaeoecology and Palaeohydrology*, ed. B. E. Berglund (Chichester, 1986), 91–107.

[8]S. Campbell and R. A. Shakesby, 'Wood fragments of possible Chelford Interstadial age from till at Broughton Bay, Gower, South Wales', *Quaternary Newsletter*, 47 (1985), 33–6.

proposed that it was growing at the same time that spruce woodland was found in Cheshire at the site of Chelford, which has given its name to this important early Devensian interstadial.[9] Such forested interludes, however, were probably exceptional and the landscape of Cardiganshire, when not actually covered with ice, must have been of a tundra nature for most of the Devensian glacial period.

Late-glacial (late-Devensian)

The earliest Quaternary sediments which have been subjected to pollen analysis in Cardiganshire belong to the closing phases of the last (Devensian) glaciation. The upland site at which this work was carried out is a small infilled lake, now bog-covered, at the watershed between the Ystwyth and the Elan, directly on the County boundary.[10] The position of the site is shown in Fig. 8 and a simplified diagram of a selection of the results is shown in Fig. 9. A second site with late-Devensian sediments from a cliff section near Aberaeron has also been described.[11]

Although there are no radiocarbon dates available from these sites, their distinctive system of layering and the vegetation sequence recorded within permit an estimate of their age to be made. They probably formed some time between 13,000 to about 10,000 years ago. It is likely that there are many such locations in the County, especially in the lakes of the highland region, but these have yet to be discovered and described.

Three features are most prominent in the pollen record from the Elan Valley site. The first is the overall lack of tree pollen and the dominance of herbaceous pollen in the sediments, the second is the very high diversity of pollen types found at the site, and the third is the instability of the vegetation which gave rise to the pollen, as evidenced by the changing proportions of the pollen types with depth. The general conclusion which is reached from these three features is that the contemporary vegetation was of a tundra type with a high proportion of montane and alpine species, the fortunes of which varied considerably over these three thousand years as the climate underwent extreme fluctuations.

As has been observed in the late-Devensian sites in many parts of the British Isles, it is possible to discern from the sediment and pollen sequence a pattern of climatic change in which cold conditions give way to warmer ones, only to be replaced by a cold event once again. The beginning of our present interglacial was interrupted by a return to extremely cold conditions, which are thought to have lasted from about 11,000 to about 10,000 years ago (normally expressed in radiocarbon years bp, i.e. 'before present', 1950).

Among the pollen types in the Elan Valley, birch, juniper (*Juniperus*) and grasses (*Gramineae*) provide the clearest indication of the fluctuating climate. In the basal sediments grasses pre-

[9]I. M. Simpson and R. G. West, 'The stratigraphical palaeo-botany of the late Pleistocene deposit at Chelford, Cheshire', *New Phyt.*, 57 (1958), 239–50.

[10]P. D. Moore, 'Studies in the vegetational history of mid-Wales II: the late-glacial period in Cardiganshire', *New Phyt.*, 69 (1970), 363–75.

[11]R. T. Smith and J. A. Taylor, 'The post-glacial development of vegetation and soils in northern Cardiganshire', *Trans. Inst. British Geog.*, 48 (1969), 75–96, and J. A. Taylor, 'Chronometers and chronicles: a study of palaeo-environments in west central Wales', *Progress in Geography*, 5 (1973), 247–334.

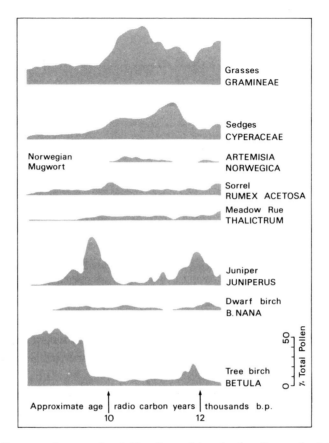

Fig. 9: Simplified pollen diagram from upland Cardiganshire during Late-glacial times. Based upon data from Elan Valley.

dominate, although juniper is commencing its rise, presumably in response to the warming of the climate. Some detailed radiocarbon dates on similar deposits in north Wales place the juniper rise at about 13,000 bp.[12] Tree birches are low in abundance and the dwarf birch, a low-growing tundra shrub, is present in similar proportions. One must envisage the landscape as open grassland, with soils disturbed by frosty conditions. Sorrels (*Rumex* and *Oxyria*) and mugworts (*Artemisia*) would have been particularly prevalent on the wind-blasted ridges where the winter snow did not accumulate to produce an insulating blanket. In the sheltered, north-facing hollows, where snow survived late into the summer, the dwarf willow (*Salix herbacea*) was best developed. The valleys may have contained small copses of tree birches, perhaps even here contorted by the stunting effect of the wind. Junipers may also have formed local scrub in these valleys, but over the hilltops in the more exposed areas they would take on a more prostrate form, hugging the surface of the ground.

The response to warmer conditions is seen first among the tree birches and the juniper, which probably expanded their cover within the valley to form a dense scrub. This open woodland may even have overflowed the valley sides onto the surrounding plateaux, for the grass component

[12]S. Lowe, 'Radiocarbon dating and stratigraphic resolution in Welsh glacial chronology', *Nature*, 293 (1981), 210–12.

of the pollen diagram decreases very considerably with woodland expansion. This means that birch woodland was probably found up to 400 m altitude during this warm stage. Soils became more stable, so some of the plants characteristic of disturbed locations, such as the mugworts, decreased in abundance. Many of the arctic and alpine types of plant found in the basal sediments became less frequent in the warm interval, perhaps as a consequence of the higher summer temperatures which were inappropriate for the growth of many such plants.[13] The presence of birch woodland suggests that summer temperatures attained at least 12°C July mean.[14] In fact, the evidence of beetle fauna from north Wales at this time indicates that temperatures were considerably greater than this, perhaps even higher in summer than at present day, but possibly with colder winters.[15]

It is possible that the high altitude site at Elan Valley from which our late glacial picture is derived does not adequately reflect the state of affairs in lowland Cardiganshire, and since there are currently no lowland sites available which provide information on this point we must look elsewhere for evidence. A comparative study has been carried out by Dominguez on the vegetation sequence in the upper Elan Valley and at Llyn Mire in the Wye Valley during the late-Devensian.[16] The main difference between these sites was that birch was a much more important and juniper a much less important component of the late-glacial vegetation in the lowland. Whereas birch values in the Elan site rose only to about 20 per cent of the total pollen input during the warm interstadial, values exceeding 40 per cent were recorded at the lowland Llyn Mire site: in contrast, juniper values in the lowland were only about half those found in the uplands. The lowland site also showed a much richer aquatic and wetland flora, with marsh species like meadowsweet (*Filipendula*) and submerged aquatics like water milfoil (*Myriophyllum*) reaching higher proportions. On the other hand, and perhaps predictably, the arctic/alpine element in the flora was poorer. In particular, the values for the sorrels (including the mountain sorrel, *Oxyria digyna*), were far lower at Llyn Mire. A similar contrast between upland and lowland vegetation in late-glacial times has been demonstrated in Snowdonia and the Llŷn peninsula. The arctic/alpine species associated with Nant Ffrancon[17] are not found in the sediments on the Llŷn peninsula at Glanllynau.[18]

It is entirely likely that the coastal lowlands of Cardiganshire shared these features with the Wye Valley and bore extensive, if open, birch woodland during the interstadial. The only data

[13]E. Dahl, 'On the relation between summer temperature and the distribution of alpine vascular plants in the lowlands of Fennoscandia', *Oikos*, 3 (1951), 22–52; and A. P. Conolly and E. Dahl, 'Maximum summer temperatures in the modern and Quaternary distribution of certain arctic-montane species in the British Isles', *Studies in the Vegetational History of the British Isles*, ed. D. Walker and R. G. West (Cambridge, 1970), 159–223.

[14]J. Iversen, 'The late-glacial flora of Denmark in relation to climate and soil', *Danmarks Geologiske Undersoegelse* (IIR), 80 (1954), 87–119.

[15]G. R. Coope and J. A. Brophy, 'Late glacial environmental changes indicated by a coleopteran succession in North Wales', *Boreas*, 1 (1972), 97–142.

[16]L. S. de Dominguez, 'A study of altitudinal variation in the late-Devensian flora of mid-Wales' (unpublished Univ. of London M. Phil. dissertation, 1982).

[17]B. Seddon, 'Late-glacial deposits at Llyn Dwythwch and Nant Ffrancon, Caernarvonshire', *Phil. Trans. Royal Society of London*, B244 (1962), 459–81, and C. J. Burrows, 'Plant macrofossils from late-Devensian deposits at Nant Ffrancon, Caernarvonshire', *New Phyt.*, 73 (1974), 1003–33.

[18]K. Simpkins, 'The late-glacial deposits at Glanllynau, Caernarvonshire', *New Phyt.*, 73 (1974), 605–18.

from the Cardiganshire lowlands at this time derive from the Aberaeron section but here the stratigraphic sequence is difficult to interpret, so the evidence should be treated with a degree of caution.[19] Some organic material from the section has been radiocarbon dated to 11,260 $\pm$ 160 bp,[20] which confirms its late Devensian affinities. As in the other sites, grasses, sedges and herbaceous plants dominate the pollen spectrum, suggesting that open tundra conditions extended through the lowlands at this late stage in the interstadial.

The return to colder conditions, which is marked at both the lowland Wye Valley and the upland Elan Valley sites by a change in sediment type, from organic mud to silty clay, resulted in a considerable decline in the pollen of both birch and juniper, and a return to the open grassland tundra landscape. In north Wales this cooling has been dated to around 11,000 bp[21] but at neither site is it likely that birch or juniper became extinct. They simply became reduced in the vigour of their growth and flowering, and survived until the return of warmer conditions permitted their expansion once more at about 10,000 bp.

It is important to remember that at this time the sea levels to the west of Cardiganshire were considerably lower than at present. A land bridge existed during late-glacial times extending from the Llŷn Peninsula to the Wicklow Mountains in Ireland, so the coastal plain of Cardiganshire was an extensive, gently sloping region which became important to many species of plants and animals as a migration route to Ireland. Evidently many animals, like snakes and the common shrew, and some plants, like herb paris (*Paris quadrifolia*) had not arrived in west Wales before the land bridge was severed, probably during the interstadial of about 12,000 years ago.[22] A more southerly land bridge, linking Cornwall and Brittany to Ireland, may have remained intact for a longer period.

Some sediments dating from the end of the cold period are found in the lowermost parts of the pingo basins in west Cardiganshire.[23] Tree pollen is scarce and open, disturbed habitat species are frequent. So the cold, stadial episode must have reduced the cover of woodland and juniper scrub over the Cardiganshire lowland, or at least reduced its rate of flowering.

Early Post-Glacial (Holocene)

The recommencement of the warming process has been dated from various parts of Wales, including Llyn Peris and Cwm Cywion in Snowdonia,[24] the Brecon Beacons[25] and the small basins in the Cledlyn and Cletwr valleys in west Cardiganshire.[26] All are agreed on a date close to

[19]See above, n. 11.
[20]See Taylor, art. cit., above, n. 11.
[21]See above, n. 12 and C. J. Burrows, 'Radiocarbon dates from late-Devensian deposits at Nant Ffrancon, Caernarvonshire', *New Phyt.*, 75 (1975), 167–71.
[22]F. M. Synge, 'Coastal evolution', *The Quaternary History of Ireland*, ed. K. J. Edwards and W. P. Warren (London, 1985), 115–31.
[23]S. Handa and P. D. Moore, 'Studies in the vegetational history of mid-Wales, IV; Pollen analysis of some pingo basins', *New Phyt.*, 77 (1976), 205–25.
[24]See above, n. 12 and J. Ince, 'Two post-glacial pollen profiles from the uplands of Snowdonia, Gwynedd, North Wales', *New Phyt.*, 95 (1983), 159–72.
[25]M. J. C. Walker, 'Late-glacial history of the Brecon Beacons, South Wales', *Nature*, 287 (1980), 133–5.
[26]See above, n. 23.

10,000 bp for that expansion of juniper and birch pollen which is indicative of the climatic warming. This is also taken as marking the beginning of the Holocene, or the current Flandrian interglacial. The very rapid response of these two plants confirms that they had not become extinct in the area.

Juniper does not appear to have retained its position of importance for very long as it soon gave way to birch, which proved a more competitive species. Perhaps it continued as an understorey in the birch woodland, from where its pollen would not be as readily dispersed as in the open conditions that formerly prevailed.

Unfortunately it is impossible, on the basis of pollen grains, to separate the two species of birch trees, silver (*Betula pendula*) and hairy (*B. pubescens*). They differ markedly in their ecology, the latter preferring the damp soils in low-lying basins and lake margins, whilst the former tolerates dry, well-drained soils. It is likely that both species were expanding their populations at this time but, since *B. pubescens* grew around the lakes and damp sites which have been used for analyses, the picture is distorted by its greater representation as a macrofossil. The apparently rapid birch expansion and domination may simply reflect immediate local changes and juniper scrub may have persisted longer and in greater density away from deposition sites.

Another scrub species which expanded rapidly in the west of the County was hazel (*Corylus avellana*), and the biogeographical implications of this pattern of invasion are considerable. It means that the hazel migration into Britain was not entirely from the continental east, but also took place along the low-lying areas to the west. It is possible that this migration route reflects the glacial survival of hazel in areas of land now submerged to the west of Britain.[27] The early arrival of the hazel in Cardiganshire is recorded best at a site on the Mynydd Bach called Gwarllyn.[28] There hazel begins to expand while juniper and birch are still rising. In the uplands, on the other hand, hazel is not recorded in any profusion until after the fall of the early post-glacial juniper peak, when birch is the dominant pollen type.

The radiocarbon date for the commencement of hazel expansion at Tregaron Bog, near the Mynydd Bach, is given by Hibbert and Switsur as 9725 ± 220 bp[29] which is early when compared with other parts of Britain,[30] so confirming the migration pattern of this shrub up the western side of Britain at this time. The pattern is not entirely simple, however, and not all sites fit in well. Further south in Cardiganshire at the Cledlyn pingos the hazel rise does not appear to have been quite so early,[31] and at a site in north Pembrokeshire, Esgyrn Bottom, the juniper levels are low, so that it is not possible to discern the sequence of vegetation change.[32]

There has been some speculation about the relationship of Mesolithic communities to hazel. Some time ago Rawitscher proposed that a casual management of forest could have been

[27]P. D. Moore, 'Studies in the vegetational history of mid-Wales, III; Early Flandrian pollen data from west Cardiganshire', *New Phyt.*, 71 (1972), 947–59; and J. Deacon, 'The location of refugia of *Corylus avellana* L. during the Weichselian glaciation', *New Phyt.*, 73 (1974), 1055–63.

[28]See Moore, art. cit., above, n. 27.

[29]F. A. Hibbert and V. R. Switsur, 'Radiocarbon dating of Flandrian pollen zones in Wales and northern England', *New Phyt.*, 77 (1976), 739–807.

[30]See Deacon, art. cit., above, n. 27.

[31]See above, n. 23.

[32]F. M. Slater and E. J. Seymour, 'Esgyrn Bottom—the most westerly raised bog in Wales', *Proc. Birmingham Nat. Hist. Soc.*, 32(3) (1977), 193–205.

TABLE 2: Maximum hazel (*Corylus avellana*) pollen levels achieved in the early Flandrian (prior to the rise in *Alnus* at about 7,000 bp). Data is expressed as percentage of arboreal pollen

Site	Footnote	Position	%AP
Esgyrn Bottom	32	Coastal	656
Gwarllyn	27	Mynydd Bach	270
Cledlyn Pingo W	23	Teifi Valley	152
Tregaron	2	Teifi Valley	140
Tregaron	29	Teifi Valley	100
Llyn Gynon	36	Uplands	350
Elan Valley	36	Uplands	330

conducted by Mesolithic people using fire.[33] This, he claims, would have favoured hazel which is able to regenerate from the basal stems. There is no direct evidence for this from the Cardiganshire data, although it is interesting to examine the maximum levels of hazel at different sites in relation to geographical position. Table 2 shows these maxima, which are indicative of the comparative proportion of hazel pollen between these sites in the early Flandrian. The low values from the Teifi Valley system are particularly noticeable, as are the high values from the uplands and what is now the coastal area and Mynydd Bach. Work on the distribution of Mesolithic artefacts in Dyfed shows a high concentration in Pembrokeshire, extending northwards up what is now the coastline of Cardiganshire. These are the areas in which hazel reached very high levels, but a direct, causal relationship between hazel abundance and Mesolithic activity cannot as yet be proved.

Hazel does not flower well under a closed canopy, and the changing values for hazel pollen in different geographical areas of Cardiganshire may simply be a reflection of how dense was the high canopy of forest trees. It is reasonable to expect that during this time of forest expansion, the uplands would still possess an open canopy woodland as a result of climatic constraints upon tree growth. In the lowlands, however, it is surprising to find high levels such as those at Gwarllyn and even more so at Esgyrn Bottom. The open canopy in these areas could well have resulted from a measure of disturbance, possibly as a result of Mesolithic forest fires. Other changes occur in Slater and Seymour's Esgyrn Bottom diagram at the same depths as the peak hazel pollen,[34] which may be considered to support this hypothesis. Grass pollen, fern spores and pollen of *Ericaceae*, *Succisa* and *Helianthemum*, which has been found in association with human disturbance in southern England,[35] also have inflated values at the hazel peak. The case for an open canopy is, therefore, a strong one, though a human role cannot be conclusively demonstrated. Fire resulting from lightning strikes is an alternative possibility, but the overall pattern of hazel distribution shown in Table 2 is difficult to explain in these terms.

[33]S. Rawitscher, 'The hazel period in the post-glacial development of forests', *Nature*, 156 (1945), 302–3.
[34]See above, n. 32.
[35]P. D. Moore and A. Willmot, 'Prehistoric forest clearance and the development of peatlands in the uplands and lowlands of Britain', *Proc. Fifth Int. Peat Congress: Poznan, Poland* (1976), 1–15.

The open birch/hazel woods of coastal Cardiganshire also soon became dominant on the uplands of the Cambrian Mountains, and extended from the upper Ystwyth[36] right down to the Tywi Valley above Llandovery.[37] Hazel arrived in force at this latter site soon after 9,000 bp and with birch dominated the pollen rain there for almost 2,000 years. This is quite typical of the upland areas where hazel remained an important canopy-forming shrub over a very long period of time, perhaps right up to 5,000 years ago in places like Plynlimon.[38]

On the eastern flank of the Cambrian range, in Radnorshire and Breconshire, hazel was still an important forest component, though oak (*Quercus* sp.) and pine (*Pinus sylvestris*) were more strongly represented than in the uplands. In the Wye valley it is oak which is the major tree species,[39] whereas pine is more important further east still, as at Rhos-goch Common.[40]

The early post-glacial on this eastern fringe of the Cambrian Mountains may have had a more continental type of climate than the western side. There are some unusual plants currently growing in isolated patches in these eastern localities, many of which have their main areas of distribution in mainland Europe, especially in central Poland. Some of these species were present in Wales in late-glacial and early post-glacial times, such as the perennial knawel (*Scleranthus perennis*), and these may have been able to survive in the more continental, early post-glacial climate east of the mountain massif.[41]

The general sequence of tree pollen types in the Flandrian post-glacial of Cardiganshire is shown in Fig. 10. The data here is based largely upon the pollen diagrams published from Tregaron,[42] Elan Valley[43] and Plynlimon.[44] The series of radiocarbon dates given by Hibbert and Switsur permit the construction of a summary pollen diagram in which time (rather than depth of sediment) can be used as a horizontal axis.[45] This should facilitate cross-correlations between pollen rain and prehistoric or historic periods. It should be noted that the recent part of the diagram is based largely upon the data from the upland site of Plynlimon, at which no radiocarbon dates were available. The correlations with cultural phases must therefore be regarded as tentative, although cross-dating from archaeological artefacts in the peats of Cardiganshire does support the interpretation placed upon the data.[46]

The pollen sequence shown in Fig. 10 differs little from those found in other parts of western Britain. Elm appears to expand before oak, but then the latter becomes the more abundant of

[36]P. D. Moore and E. H. Chater, 'Studies in the vegetational history of Mid-Wales, I; the post-glacial period in Cardiganshire', *New Phyt.*, 68 (1969), 183–96.
[37]F. M. Chambers, 'Date of blanket peat initiation in upland South Wales', *Quaternary Newsletter*, 35 (1981), 24–9.
[38]P. D. Moore, 'Human influence upon vegetational history in North Cardiganshire', *Nature*, 217 (1968), 1006–9.
[39]P. D. Moore, 'Studies in the Welsh Quaternary: vegetational history', *Cambria*, 4(1977), 73–83, and 'Studies in the vegetational history of mid-Wales, V; Stratigraphy and pollen analysis of Llyn Mire in the Wye Valley', *New Phyt.*, 80 (1978), 281–302.
[40]D. D. Bartley, 'Rhosgoch Common: stratigraphy and pollen analysis', *New Phyt.*, 59 (1960), 238–62.
[41]P. D. Moore, 'A new British flower', *Nature*, 295 (1982), 189.
[42]See above, n. 29.
[43]See above, n. 36.
[44]P. D. Moore and E. H. Chater, 'The changing vegetation of west-central Wales in the light of human history', *J. Ecology*, 57 (1969), 361–79.
[45]See above, n. 29.
[46]See above, n. 44.

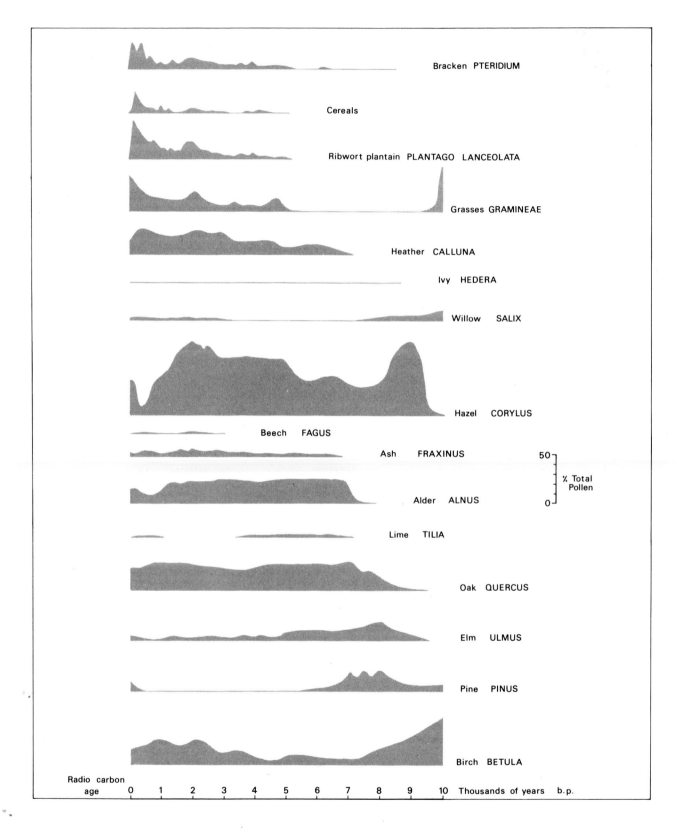

Bracken PTERIDIUM

Cereals

Ribwort plantain PLANTAGO LANCEOLATA

Grasses GRAMINEAE

Heather CALLUNA

Ivy HEDERA

Willow SALIX

Hazel CORYLUS

Beech FAGUS

Ash FRAXINUS

50

% Total Pollen

0

Alder ALNUS

Lime TILIA

Oak QUERCUS

Elm ULMUS

Pine PINUS

Birch BETULA

Radio carbon age   0   1   2   3   4   5   6   7   8   9   10   Thousands of years   b.p.

the two. Pine is a major contributor to the pollen rain as birch dies away, but its behaviour is erratic and varies from one site to another. In the Teifi Valley sites the situation is made more complex by the persistence of birch in quite high quantities throughout the early Flandrian. The erratic behaviour of pine at other sites (for example, Elan Valley, Tregaron and Esgyrn Bottom) suggests that local factors played an important part. The most even course for the pine curve is observed at Gwarllyn, where a level of about 15 per cent arboreal pollen is established soon after the hazel rise and is maintained until the expansion of alder. The pine rise is dated at Tregaron at about 8,200 bp.[47] Tregaron has higher values for pine than the neighbouring Gwarllyn, reaching 40 per cent arboreal pollen at times, and Elan Valley has higher levels still, with three peaks exceeding 50 per cent. The possibility that these represent periods when pine grew very locally, possibly even upon the contemporaneous mire surface, cannot be excluded. Caution must be applied, therefore, before one concludes that pine was more abundant in the uplands, which is what an initial inspection of the Cardiganshire data suggests. In all sites pine reaches its maximum extent shortly before the alder rise. Pine may have been less abundant in south Cardiganshire, since its representation at Cefn Gwernffrwd[48] and at Llan-llwch in Carmarthenshire[49] is very low, but sedimentation occurred on both of these sites only when the alder rise had already begun.

The rise in alder (*Alnus glutinosa*) in the mid-Flandrian is accompanied by a fall in pine to very low levels. At Tregaron this major vegetation change has been dated to about 7,000 bp, which corresponds well with dates for many parts of England.[50] At Llangorse Lake, Chambers has recorded a very early expansion of alder, dated at about 7,900 bp,[51] and speculates that alder, like hazel, may have entered Wales from the west.[52] There are scattered records for alder right through the post-glacial, and Godwin regards such evidence as indicative of small populations living in sub-optimal conditions,[53] but its expansion at the beginning of 'Atlantic' times is extremely marked. Work by Chambers and Price in north Wales[54] and also by Smith in Ireland,[55] suggests that Mesolithic cultures may have played a part in the process. Clearance of woodland and the consequent hydrological change may have provided alder with certain advantages in the competition for space in the forest.

[47]See above, n. 29.
[48]F. M. Chambers, 'Two radiocarbon dated pollen diagrams from high altitude blanket peats in South Wales', *J. Ecology*, 70 (1983), 445–59.
[49]K. W. Thomas, 'The stratigraphy and pollen analysis of a raised peat bog at Llanllwch, near Carmarthen', *New Phyt.*, 64 (1965), 101–17.
[50]A. G. Smith and J. R. Pilcher, 'Radiocarbon data and the vegetational history of the British Isles', *New Phyt.*, 72 (1973), 903–14.
[51]F. M. Chambers, 'Flandrian environmental history of the Llynfi catchment, South Wales', *Ecologia Mediterranea*, 11 (1985), 73–80.
[52]See above, n. 48.
[53]H. Godwin, *History of British Flora*, cited note 5.
[54]F. M. Chambers and S. M. Price, 'Palaeoecology of *Alnus* (alder): early post-glacial rise in a valley mire, north-west Wales', *New Phyt.*, 101 (1985), 333–4.
[55]A. G. Smith, 'Newferry and the Boreal Atlantic transition', *New Phyt.*, 98 (1984), 35–55.

Fig. 10: Simplified pollen diagram from Cardiganshire showing the development of vegetation during post-glacial times. The main sources of information are Elan Valley, Tregaron and Plynlimon. Data is expressed as percentage of tree pollen.

Alder very rapidly assumes a pollen representation exceeding that of oak, but this does not necessarily imply a greater abundance in population terms. Alder produces larger quantities of pollen than oak; its pollen has more efficient dispersal and it is also a frequent member of the communities in and around mires and lakes where pollen is being preserved. Hence it tends to be over-represented in the pollen record.

Evidence for the dominance of alder in some low-lying areas of Cardiganshire is provided by the submerged forests of Cardigan Bay. The Ynys-las/Borth forest contains a preponderance of alder, with pine, oak, birch and hazel.[56] Godwin and Willis have obtained radiocarbon dates of about 6,000 bp for this submerged forest,[57] and Taylor has published a similar date for a pine root from submerged peats at Clarach, north of Aberystwyth.[58] There is, therefore, direct evidence for the survival of pine into 'Atlantic' times. Indeed at Borth there is evidence to suggest that it succeeded alder in the local mire succession.[59] In the uplands pine is also likely to have survived locally, as is suggested by the pine pollen in the soil underlying blanket peat at Plynlimon.[60] Alder was also demonstrably present in the form of wood remains at Llyn Gynon. Lime (probably *Tilia cordata*) may have been present locally in Cardiganshire at this time, but is unlikely to have been common, judging from the very low pollen values throughout the County. In their soil pollen studies, however, Smith and Taylor describe one site at Penrhyn-coch which exhibits fairly high lime values and which may well reflect the local presence of a lime-rich woodland.[61]

Although it is safe to assume that the bulk of the County was clothed with dense forest at this time (7,000–5,000 years ago), the higher peaks along the ridge of the Cambrian Mountain chain may have been open or only very lightly wooded. P. E. J. Wiltshire's unpublished diagrams from the Claerwen Valley area are of considerable interest in this respect. Her diagram from Trumau has a large proportion of hazel, together with grasses at the base and also has features suggestive of woodland disturbance antedating the Neolithic elm decline (see below, p. 39). It is possible that these areas were exploited by late Mesolithic people. The radiocarbon-dated pollen diagram of Hibbert and Switsur from Tregaron has indications of Mesolithic activity between 6,000 and 5,000 bp.[62] Similar signs of Mesolithic activity have been described from the Lake District where it has been suggested that some form of agriculture was being practised.[63] It is not easy to provide conclusive evidence concerning the impact made by Mesolithic people upon the vegetation of Cardiganshire, but it seems probable that it was locally very considerable and that it has been underestimated in the past.

[56]See above, n. 3.
[57]H. Godwin and E. H. Willis, 'Cambridge University natural radiocarbon measurements, II', *Radiocarbon*, 3 (1961), 60–76.
[58]See Taylor, art. cit., above, n. 11.
[59]See above, nn. 3 and 38.
[60]See above, n. 44.
[61]See Smith and Taylor, art. cit., above, n. 11.
[62]See above, n. 29.
[63]K. J. Edwards and K. R. Hirons, 'Cereal pollen grains in pre-elm decline deposits; implications for the earliest agriculture in Britain and Ireland', *J. Archaeol. Science*, 11 (1984), 71–80.

The Neolithic Elm decline

The fall in elm pollen is extremely well marked in most diagrams from Cardiganshire, such as that of Hibbert and Switsur from Tregaron. Here the elm declines at 5,000 bp which agrees very precisely with dates from elsewhere in Britain, adding support to Smith and Pilcher's contention that the elm decline in Britain was a remarkably synchronous event across the country.[64] It is almost invariably accompanied by pollen types such as *Plantago lanceolata*, *P. major* and *Artemisia*, which are normally regarded as indicative of a human presence and involvement in forest disturbance. In some sites from the uplands there is clear evidence of the use of fire for forest clearance, as at Pwll-nant-ddu and Esgair Nantybeddau.[65]

There are no sites in Cardiganshire where pollen evidence can be used to indicate Neolithic arable agriculture at the time of the elm decline. There is, however, a site at Llyn Mire in the Wye Valley at which cereal-type pollen grains have been found in association with the elm decline.[66] There the occupation period following the collapse in elm pollen appears to have lasted about a century and some close sampling of sediments has produced pollen data that is suggestive of a rotational farming system in which arable land lay fallow and was subsequently invaded by bracken, only to be cleared again after a period of perhaps 10–12 years. There is no reason to suppose that such communities were geographically restricted and this could well prove to be the pattern of early Neolithic land use all over the County. The inhabitants of small settlements in the valleys are likely to have cleared parts of the upland areas for the grazing of stock and cultivated the valley floors where the stock may also have been housed in winter. Whether the decline in elm was itself caused by the gathering of elm branches for winter feeding or whether it resulted from disease, perhaps assisted in its movement by man, is still in contention.[67] The finding of the *Scolytus* beetle, vector of the disease, in sediments of approximately elm decline age[68] has given new impetus to the disease hypothesis, but it still does not account for the associated declines in certain other palatable tree species such as lime. Although lime is present in too small a quantity to be observed falling at this stage in the Cardiganshire diagrams, it can clearly be seen to decline in some valleys of the Black Mountains in Breconshire.[69]

It is noticeable that the Neolithic elm decline is found at or near the base of many of the upland blanket peat sites in Cardiganshire, such as Plynlimon,[70] the Tywi Valley[71] and the Claerwen

---

[64]See above, n. 50.

[65]P. E. J. Wiltshire and P. D. Moore, 'Palaeovegetation and palaeohydrology in upland Britain', *Background to Palaeohydrology*, ed. K. J. Gregory (Chichester, 1983), 433–51.

[66]See above, n. 39 and P. D. Moore, 'The resolution limits of pollen analysis as applied to archaeology', *MASCA Journal* (University of Pennsylvania), I (4) (1980), 118–20, and 'Neolithic land use in mid-Wales', *Proc. Fourth Int. Palynological Congress: Lucknow*, 3 (1981), 279–90.

[67]P. D. Moore, 'The death of the elm', *New Scientist*, 107 (1985), 30–4.

[68]M. A. Girling and J. Greig, 'A first fossil record for *Scolytus scolytus* (F.) (elm bark beetle): its occurrence in elm decline deposits and the implications for Neolithic elm disease', *J. Archaeol. Science*, 5 (1985), 347–51.

[69]M. D. R. Price and P. D. Moore, 'Pollen dispersion in the hills of Wales: a pollen shed hypothesis', *Pollen Spores*, 26 (1984), 127–36.

[70]See above, n. 44.

[71]P. D. Moore, 'The influence of prehistoric cultures upon the initiation and spread of blanket bog in upland Wales', *Nature*, 241 (1973), 350–3.

Valley,[72] as at Cefn Brwynog, Gors Goch and Trumau. The same is true at sites further north, as in the western Rhinogau.[73] It has been postulated elsewhere that the influence of Neolithic clearance, burning and grazing on the lightly wooded summits and higher ridges of mid Wales could have resulted in increased soil moisture and the initiation of blanket peat accumulation.[74] Such a process would have continued, especially on lower altitudes and more steeply sloping sites, into the Bronze Age.[75] The precise involvement of climatic deterioration and soil maturation at this time is difficult to discern but, whatever the complex causes of the process,[76] the development of extensive blanket peats in upland mid-Wales undoubtedly commenced in Mesolithic/ Neolithic times on the high ridges and plateaux and extended at the expense of forest through late Neolithic into Bronze and Iron Age times.

The Bronze and Iron Ages

Bronze Age clearances and settlement episodes are known from the pollen diagrams of Cardiganshire, the most detailed account of which is given by Turner of an episode at Tregaron which she considers to have lasted only about fifty years.[77] The clearance of woodland is followed by rising bracken, then grasses and sorrel (*Rumex acetosa*). Similar episodes can be seen in the upland diagrams from Plynlimon, where ash (*Fraxinus excelsior*) can be seen to increase in consequence of the opening of the woodland canopy,[78] and at Pwll-nant-ddu where bracken benefits.[79]

The Iron Age/Roman period in Cardiganshire is marked by extensive evidence of clearance from Tregaron,[80] Plynlimon and the lowlands at Borth Bog[81] and from Blaen yr Esgair.[82] At these sites, it is salutary to note that the ratio of tree to non-tree pollen fell to levels resembling those of present day. The implication is that Cardiganshire may well have been largely deforested by the end of the Roman occupation. The evidence suggests that the deforestation of the Bronze Age continued into the Iron Age with perhaps an increased degree of clearance in the lowlands.[83] The process was then further accelerated during the Roman period. Although the Iron Age/Roman phase is pronounced in the upland diagrams from Plynlimon, it is not conspicuous at the Elan Valley site.[84] This may be because the location of a fort at Cae Gaer may have resulted in local

[72]See above, n. 65.

[73]M. F. Walker and J. A. Taylor, 'Post Neolithic vegetation changes in the western Rhinogau, Gwynedd, north-west Wales', *Trans. Inst. British Geog.*, NS1 (1976), 323–45.

[74]P. D. Moore, 'The initiation of peat formation and the development of peat deposits in mid-Wales', *Proc. Fourth Int. Peat Congress: Helsinki*, I (1972), 89–100.

[75]See Smith and Taylor, art. cit., above, nn. 11 and 48.

[76]P. D. Moore, D. C. Merryfield and M. D. R. Price, 'The vegetation and development of blanket mires', *European Mires*, ed. P. D. Moore (London, 1984), 203–35, and note 7.

[77]J. Turner, 'The anthropogenic factor in vegetational history, I: Tregaron and Whixall Moss', *New Phyt.*, 63 (1964), 73–90, and 'A contribution to the history of forest clearance', *Proc. Royal Society of London*, B161, (1965), 343–53.

[78]See above, n. 44.

[79]See above, n. 65.

[80]See above, n. 77.

[81]See above, n. 38.

[82]See above, n. 44.

[83]See Turner, 'A contribution to the history of forest clearance', above, n. 77.

[84]See above, n. 36.

deforestation whereas the Ystwyth and Elan Valleys remained undisturbed. By contrast, sites in the Claerwen Valley generally show a marked Iron Age impact,[85] and the same is true of the upper Tywi catchment as shown at Cefn Gwernffrwd, where there is direct stratigraphic evidence of forest removal shortly after 2,580 bp, that is, in the Iron Age.[86] At the same site, but in the analysis of blanket peat deposits, Chambers shows two very clear periods of deforestation, one in the Bronze Age at about 3,450 bp, when oak and hazel are most strongly affected, and another in the Roman/Iron Age at about 1,900 bp when hazel is again reduced but this time concurrently with all the other trees.[87] It is reasonable to conclude that the impact of the Bronze Age peoples on the uplands was very considerable and that the subsequent complete deforestation was effected during the Roman/Iron Age.

Evident also in the Claerwen area are the hydrological changes which took place at this time. It is widely accepted that the Iron Age climate became appreciably cooler and wetter—the upland peats show a tendency towards more rapid growth and poorer humification. Some of the upland valley mires undoubtedly became much wetter and grew more rapidly as a result. But one cannot attribute all these effects simply to a changing climate. The intensive deforestation and resulting soil erosion of Iron Age times is recorded as layers of silt and charcoal in the peats, as at Esgair Nantybeddau where valley birch woods growing on the surface of the mires were destroyed and replaced by *Sphagnum* bogs.[88] The destruction of woodland on surrounding slopes would also have led to increased flooding in the valleys and faster valley bog growth and spread.

These observations are supported by the work of Chambers at Cefn Graeanog in north Wales.[89] He was able to demonstrate a statistically significant negative relationship between weed pollen in a peat deposit and the degree of humification of that peat. In other words, poorly humified, fast-growing peats were rich in weed pollen, thus supporting the hypothesis that forest clearance is associated with the changes in the hydrological regime.

The massive vegetation changes which took place in the Roman/Iron Age period become even more apparent to the south and east of the county of Cardiganshire, as at Llangorse Lake (Breconshire), where the entire course of sedimentation in the basin probably changed as a result of alterations in land use.[90]

The historic period

The decline in pollen types such as grasses, plantain (*Plantago lanceolata*) and bracken at the close of the Roman period is most marked and abrupt in the lowland diagrams, such as the Tregaron example published by Turner.[91] This is associated with a regeneration of forest during the post-Roman period.

[85]See above, n. 65.
[86]F. M. Chambers, 'Environmental history of Cefn Gwernffrwd, near Rhandirmwyn, mid Wales', *New Phyt.*, 92 (1982), 607–15.
[87]See above, n. 48.
[88]See above, n. 65.
[89]See above, n. 48.
[90]R. Jones, K. Benson-Evans and F. M. Chambers, 'Human influence upon sedimentation in Llangorse Lake, Wales', *Earth Processes and Landforms*, 10 (1985), 227–35.
[91]See Turner, 'The anthropogenic factor', above, n. 77.

The indicators of disturbance rise again at Tregaron at a point which Turner has radiocarbon-dated (non-calibrated) to 1182 AD, which corresponds well (allowing for the inherent errors in radiocarbon dating) with the foundation of Strata Florida Abbey. A rise in plantain pollen is also found at the upland site of Plynlimon, but there the rise in Rosaceae pollen (largely *Potentilla* type) is even more marked. This is likely to be due to a local abundance of the tormentil (*Potentilla erecta*) which is a trailing species that thrives under conditions of intensive grazing. The Cistercian use of the uplands as pasture is thus amply confirmed by the pollen record.

There is a very sudden fall in tree and shrub pollen at a slightly higher level in the peat at Plynlimon, accompanied by a rapid expansion of the disturbance indicators. Circumstantial evidence suggests that this could be linked with the demands made by Edward I in the closing years of the thirteenth century, that a programme of forest clearance should be embarked upon to assist in the control of local rebels who indulged in 'robberies, homicides and other enormities against the King's peace',[92] but in the absence of radiocarbon dates, such an interpretation must remain speculative.

The general pattern of woodland decline and rising levels of those pollen types usually indicative of disturbance continues with but a single interruption, the apparent setback to agricultural expansion in the later Middle Ages which could reflect the combined effects of the Black Death and the repercussions of Owain Glyndŵr's rebellion. The eventual peak in agriculture, evidenced by high cereal pollen and arable weeds at the Plynlimon site can be fairly conclusively identified with the cultivation of the marginal uplands during the Napoleonic Wars (1793–1815). This forms quite the most distinctive horizon in many of the Cardiganshire pollen diagrams from both the uplands and the lowlands.

Finally, the Cardiganshire pollen diagrams record the decreased agricultural activity of the nineteenth and twentieth centuries. One can observe the increased tree pollen associated with the arrival of forestry interests, both those of private individuals such as Thomas Johnes of Hafod in the early nineteenth century and those of the Forestry Commission in the twentieth.

Despite the importance of vegetation to Man and his settlement and agricultural interests, the naturalists, travellers and historians of the past have left us rather little documentary evidence concerning its nature in Cardiganshire. Even those remarkable figures Giraldus Cambrensis and John Leland make only passing reference to the landscape and its flora. The accumulating evidence gleaned from the microscopic analysis of peat deposits, however, is gradually filling in this gap in our knowledge. As this continues, it becomes evident that the Man/vegetation interaction has been a complex one. Occasionally the vegetation has exerted strong pressure upon Man, perhaps limiting the distribution patterns of Mesolithic cultures, or causing shifts in populations from the uplands to the lowlands in the Bronze Age and Iron Age as extensive bogs began to form. At other times the vegetation itself has undergone considerable modification at the hands of Man, as during the Roman occupation, for example, or during the Napoleonic Wars. Pollen studies, in that they are a guide to past vegetation, provide us with more than a backcloth against which the drama of human history has taken place; they represent a sensitive instrument with which one can measure the changing fortunes of mankind.

[92]See above, note 44, and S. W. Williams, *The Cistercian Abbey of Strata Florida* (London, 1889).

CHAPTER 4

THE HIGHER PLANTS AND VEGETATION OF CARDIGANSHIRE*

A. O. Chater

Historical introduction

THE earliest botanical records of the flora of Cardiganshire that have come down to us were made in the second half of the seventeenth century by John Ray (1627–1705) and Edward Lhuyd (Llwyd) (1660–1709). Both independently climbed Plynlimon, and found it disappointing botanically in comparison with the mountains of north Wales. Lhuyd, whose mother came from Glanfred near Tal-y-bont, and who had an uncle at Tyno-hir just across the County boundary in Montgomeryshire, also left notes of plants he saw along the Dyfi estuary and at Borth and Aberystwyth.[1] Eighteenth-century travellers, notably the Revd Littleton Brown (1699–1749), reported a few interesting species that they found in the County. The numbers recorded increased rapidly after 1800.[2] James Edward Smith (1759–1828), founder of the Linnean Society of London and the most eminent British botanist of his day, visited Thomas Johnes's family at Hafod in the Ystwyth Valley several times from 1795,[3] and he and Johnes's daughter Mariamne recorded several interesting species. The first attempt at a complete list of plants for any part of the County was by Thomas Owen Morgan (1799–1878), a barrister and printer at Aberystwyth. His list of plants from within a 16-mile radius of Aberystwyth was published as *Flora Cereticae superioris* in 1849 and included 455 species of vascular plants. He had published a shorter version in his *New Guide to Aberystwith* in the previous year, and in five later editions he gave variously modified versions of it.[4] Most of the records are localized and of considerable interest in giving a picture of the flora at this period, but two dozen or so are clearly erroneous and his work needs to be treated with caution. The second edition of Watson's

---

* This chapter was written in 1984 and updated in 1986 and thus predates the general availability of the National Vegetation Classification (A.O.C., April 1992).

[1] A. O. Chater, 'Nodlyfr llysieuol anghyhoeddedig Edward Llwyd', *Y Naturiaethwr*, 10 (1983), 2–13, and 'An unpublished botanical notebook of Edward Llwyd', *Botanical Soc. British Isles: Welsh Bulletin*, 40 (1984), 4–15.

[2] P. W. Carter, 'Botanical exploration in Cardiganshire', *Ceredigion*, 1 (1950), 77–96, an extensive but in several respects incomplete account.

[3] E. Inglis-Jones, *Peacocks in Paradise* (London, 1950), and J. E. Smith, *A Tour to Hafod in Cardiganshire* (London, 1810).

[4] T. O. Morgan, *New Guide to Aberystwith and its Environs* (Aberystwyth, 1848: 2nd edn., 1851: 3rd edn., 1858: 4th edn., 1864: 5th edn., 1869), and *Morgan's New Guide to Aberystwyth and Neighbourhood* (Aberystwyth, 1874).

Topographical Botany in 1883 listed 491 vascular plants from Cardiganshire, all culled from earlier authors. Towards the end of the century, however, much detailed recording was done by such eminent visiting botanists as the Revd Augustin Ley, J. H. Burkill and J. C. Willis, E. S. Marshall and the Revd W. H. Painter.[5]

The founding of the University College of Wales at Aberystwyth in 1872, and in particular the appointment of J. H. Salter as assistant lecturer in Botany in 1891 and later professor in 1899, provided an immense stimulus to the study of the flora. Salter's unpublished natural history diaries[6] are an incomparable source of information about the flora and vegetation of the County from 1891 until his death in 1942. His researches on altitudinal ranges of plants in mid Wales were chiefly carried out in Cardiganshire.[7] His *Flowering Plants and Ferns of Cardiganshire* and its *Supplement* is the only Flora of the whole County.[8] Salter's successor as Professor of Botany, R. H. Yapp, began the tradition of ecological study of the vegetation of the County with a classic series of papers on the salt marshes of the Dyfi estuary,[9] and Professor L. Newton later published a useful survey of the plant communities of the County in 1933.[10] This tradition is still very much alive at the University College, with special emphasis on the raised mires of Cors Fochno and Cors Caron — the first true raised mire in Britain to be described in detail[11] — on blanket and valley mires elsewhere in the County, and on the Ynys-las sand dunes as well as on the Dyfi salt marshes. The foundation of the Welsh Plant Breeding Station in 1919 augmented work done on the grasslands of the County, in particular on the upland sheep-walks, by Sir R. G. Stapledon.[12] The opening of a regional office of the Nature Conservancy Council in Wales at Plas Gogerddan has led to a great deal of largely unpublished ecological survey work in the County. Its statutory obligations have led to the designating of three National Nature Reserves and sixty-four Sites of Special Scientific Interest (SSSI), most of them primarily on botanical grounds, and a high proportion of the sites mentioned in this chapter fall into this category. The West Wales Naturalists' Trust has twenty reserves in the County, forming a parallel and often overlapping series with the SSSIs.

The sites of real botanical interest in the County form only a small proportion of the land of the County which has largely been reseeded, afforested or otherwise, from a botanical point of view, adversely developed. Such sites are dwindling rapidly. The protection afforded for sites which are Nature Reserves, and the more precarious protection provided for the SSSIs, together with the informed interest of many landowners, however, should mean that something of the richness and variety described here will be preserved.

[5] See above, n. 2.

[6] J. H. Salter, 'Natural History Diaries' 1891–1942, National Library of Wales MSS 14432B-14451B. I am indebted to A. P. Fowles for making available to me extracts from these diaries.

[7] J. H. Salter, 'The altitudinal range of Flowering Plants and Ferns in mid Wales', *North Western Naturalist*, 3 (1928), 131–5, 170–4.

[8] J. H. Salter, *The Flowering Plants and Ferns of Cardiganshire* (Cardiff, 1935), and A. E. Wade, *A Supplement to Dr J. H. Salter's The Flowering Plants and Ferns of Cardiganshire* (Cardiff, 1952).

[9] R. H. Yapp, D. Johns, O. T. Jones, 'The salt marshes of the Dovey Estuary, I, Introductory', *J. Ecology*, 4 (1916), 27–42, and R. H. Yapp, 'The Dovey salt marshes in 1921', *J. Ecology*, 10 (1922), 18–23.

[10] L. Newton, *Plant Distribution in the Aberystwyth District* (Aberystwyth, n.d. [1933]).

[11] H. Godwin and V. M. Conway, 'The ecology of a raised bog near Tregaron, Cardiganshire', *J. Ecology*, 27 (1939), 313–63.

[12] R. G. Stapledon, *The Sheep Walks of Mid Wales* (Aberystwyth, 1914).

Much of the more floristic, rather than ecological, work in the County in recent decades has been carried out in connection with the recording and mapping schemes of the Botanical Society of the British Isles,[13] most recently in connection with R. G. Ellis's work on the *Flowering Plants of Wales*.[14] This work, listing 1,070 species for the County, provides an up-to-date account of the state of the flora of Cardiganshire and places it in context with the rest of Wales. The nomenclature, both English and Latin, of this work is followed in the present chapter. The ferns are similarly well covered in the latest edition of H. A. Hyde and A. E. Wade's *Welsh Ferns*,[15] and the nomenclature of this work is here followed. Much of the classification of vegetation in this chapter follows the pattern established by D. A. Ratcliffe, who as well as providing a general description of vegetation types in Britain, identified and described a series of key sites in Britain, of which five are in Cardiganshire.[16]

Salter quotes E. S. Marshall as saying that Cardiganshire is 'botanically remarkable rather from the absence of many species common elsewhere than from the presence of many interesting or rare ones'.[17] Even Edward Lhuyd noticed this and it remains to some extent true, in spite of many interesting discoveries made in recent decades. Although the species may be unexciting in comparison with several other Welsh counties, it is now clear that certain habitats and plant communities are as well or better displayed in Cardiganshire than anywhere else in the British Isles, and it is on these communities rather than on the constituent species that this inevitably highly selective account will concentrate.[18]

Maritime communities

Most of the Cardiganshire coast consists of rocky shoreline or boulder beaches beneath rock or drift cliffs and lacks any permanent communities of higher plants except on the cliffs themselves. At the northern and southern extremities of the County, however, the Dyfi and Teifi estuaries are protected by well-developed sand dune and shingle spit systems and contain areas of salt marsh. Small areas of salt marsh occur in between, as at Aberystwyth and Aberaeron, and as minute isolated patches on the cliffs. Small areas of sand dune and sandy foreshore occur in such places as Clarach, Tan-y-bwlch, Penbryn and Mwnt. Shingle beaches with significant plant communities are the most interesting coastal features away from the two estuaries, and are best seen at Tan-y-bwlch and just north of Aberaeron. Many of the coastal sites, partly because of the restorative effects of tides and storms, are among the least disturbed by Man in the County.

[13]F. H. Perring and S. M. Walters (eds.), *Atlas of the British Flora* (London, 1962), and F. H. Perring and P. D. Sell (eds.), *Critical Supplement to the Atlas of the British Flora* (London, 1968).

[14]R. G. Ellis, *Flowering Plants of Wales* (Cardiff, 1983).

[15]H. A. Hyde and A. E. Wade, *Welsh Ferns*, ed. S. G. Harrison (6th edn., Cardiff, 1978); A. C. Jermy *et al.*, *Atlas of Ferns of the British Isles* (London, 1978).

[16]D. A. Ratcliffe (ed.), *A Nature Conservation Review* (Cambridge, 1977). A further two or three sites of comparable national significance for conservation have been identified since.

[17]J. H. Salter, *The Flowering Plants and Ferns of Cardiganshire* (Cardiff, 1935), vi.

[18]Much of what I know of the flora of Cardiganshire has come from discussion and excursions with D. Glyn Jones of the Nature Conservancy, as well as with my late father, E. H. Chater, and with W. M. Condry. I also wish to acknowledge much detailed information from P. M. Benoit, R. G. Ellis, A. P. Fowles, N. T. H. Holmes, J. P. Savidge, and D. A. Wells among many others.

i) Shingle beaches

Ephemeral communities of Oraches (*Atriplex* spp.), Curled Dock (*Rumex crispus*), Cleavers (*Galium aparine*) and sometimes Yellow-horned Poppy (*Glaucium flavum*) occur on many of the storm beaches, as at South Marine Terrace, Aberystwyth (SN 580 812), and at Wallog (SN 590 857), but storm action never allows the natural succession of communities to get beyond this phase of primary colonization. Purple Spurge (*Euphorbia peplis*) and Oysterplant (*Mertensia maritima*), plants of otherwise uncolonized shingle, grew on the beaches of Aberystwyth and Borth respectively in the nineteenth century but are now extinct in mid Wales.[19] Similarly, Ray's Knot-grass (*Polygonum oxyspermum* subsp. *raii*) occurs on Tan-y-bwlch and Ynys-las beaches and was known at Clarach from 1894 to 1918.

The effects of successful colonization can best be seen on Tan-y-bwlch shingle spit (SN 580 802), the unstable crest of which, depending on storm action, has varying numbers of primary colonizers. Down the landward slope, mats of Sea Campion (*Silene vulgaris* subsp. *maritima*), along with scattered plants of Sea Herb-Robert (*Geranium robertianum* subsp. *maritimum*), are the first permanent vegetation. Next follow Wild Thyme (*Thymus drucei*) and Biting Stonecrop (*Sedum acre*), after which Red Fescue (*Festuca rubra*) appears and becomes dominant, binding and stabilizing the shingle so that this part of the beach is normally undisturbed by storms, although every few years it is buried by fresh shingle and the plants either grow up through this or, if the new shingle is too deep, the process of colonization begins anew. In this Fescue-dominated vegetation many other characteristically coastal species occur, including Sea Mouse-ear (*Cerastium diffusum*), Little Mouse-ear (*C. semidecandrum*), Sea Fern-grass (*Desmazeria marina*), Rough Clover (*Trifolium scabrum*), Knotted Clover (*T. striatum*), Kidney Vetch (*Anthyllis vulneraria*) and Crested Hair-grass (*Koeleria cristata*). Such a community and succession is characteristic of shingle beaches and the one running east from Aberaeron (SN 461 635) has a similar but less rich flora. In Cardiganshire the last two species are good examples of plants which are more or less restricted to the coast where salt and shell debris provide the necessary calcareous conditions.

On the landward side of Tan-y-bwlch beach, mats of prostrate Blackthorn (*Prunus spinosa*), photographed in 1910 and described by Salter in 1935 as 'probably of great age',[20] either genetically a prostrate form or the upper tips of largely submerged bushes, can be seen on the shingle — certainly one of the botanical curiosities of the County.

ii) Sandy foreshores and dunes

On sandy foreshores the early stages of colonization are as precarious as those on the shingle beaches, and can be seen at Ynys-las, Clarach, Tan-y-bwlch beach, Traeth Penbryn (SN 293 526) and Penyrergyd (SN 162 488). The most characteristic species are as follows: Sand Couch (*Elymus farctus* subsp. *boreali-atlanticus*), Sea Rocket (*Cakile maritima*), Prickly Saltwort (*Salsola kali*), Sea Sandwort (*Honkenya peploides*) and Sea Holly (*Eryngium maritimum*), with Sea Spurge (*Euphorbia paralias*) at the larger sites. Embryonic dunes are formed by blown sand collecting around these plants, or around driftwood and other bulky debris, which becomes colonized by

[19]C. E. Salmon, '*Euphorbia peplis* in Britain', *J. Botany*, 45 (1907), 158–60.
[20]J. Ballinger (ed.), *Aberystwyth and District* (Aberystwyth, 1911), 78; J. H. Salter, *The Flowering Plants and Ferns of Cardiganshire*, 41.

Marram (*Ammophila arenaria*). At Mwnt (SN 194 519) the sand blown up the cliff above Traeth y Mwnt forms a well developed stabilized Marram dune 30 m above the beach. Lyme-grass (*Leymus arenarius*), an associated colonizer, does not now occur in Cardiganshire.

The dune system at Ynys-las (SN 605 940), now part of the Dyfi National Nature Reserve, has been studied and described in considerable detail.[21] All stages of dune formation from the strand line colonists, described above, through mobile and fixed dunes to dune scrub occur, as well as a complex of dune slacks. The total area is some 60 ha, but the dunes, which are probably mostly less than 300 or 400 years old, are constantly changing, blow-outs are frequent, and much protection work is carried out by the Nature Conservancy Council to prevent too great changes taking place. The highly calcareous mobile dunes, mostly along the seaward side of the sand spit which juts northwards across the mouth of the Dyfi estuary, are dominated by, and largely formed as a result of the growth of, Marram. On the landward side other colonizers such as Sand Sedge (*Carex arenaria*), Sea Spurge, Ragwort (*Senecio jacobaea*), Hairy Hawkbit (*Leontodon taraxacoides*) and Red Fescue occur.

Inland of these mobile dunes, which are the highest of all, are slightly lower and less calcareous, semi-consolidated dunes which support much Restharrow (*Ononis repens*), Creeping Buttercup (*Ranunculus repens*), Hare's-foot Clover (*Trifolium arvense*) and Portland Spurge (*Euphorbia portlandica*), but especially conspicuous and characteristic are the numerous ephemeral annual species, including the Common Whitlow-grass (*Erophila verna*), Rue-leaved Saxifrage (*Saxifraga tridactylites*), Hairy Bitter-cress (*Cardamine hirsuta*), Common Cornsalad (*Valerianella locusta*), Early Forget-me-not (*Myosotis ramosissima*), Slender Sandwort (*Arenaria serpyllifolia* subsp. *leptoclados*) and Thyme-leaved Sandwort (subsp. *serpyllifolia*). Rabbits, now abundant again after their decline caused by myxomatosis, have done much to shape the vegetation of these dunes, making here their maximum effect. Still further inland lie mature, neutral or slightly acidic, completely vegetated dunes. The extremely rich flora of these inland dunes contains many species, confined in Cardiganshire to Ynys-las or Penyrergyd, including Bee Orchid (*Ophrys apifera*), Blue Fleabane (*Erigeron acer*), Ploughman's Spikenard (*Inula conyza*), Yellow-wort (*Blackstonia perfoliata*), Lesser Chickweed (*Stellaria pallida*) and Spring Vetch (*Vicia lathyroides*).

The dune-slacks at Ynys-las are hollows in which the vegetation is partially submerged in fresh water each winter. They contain Variegated Horsetail (*Equisetum variegatum*), Creeping Bent (*Agrostis stolonifera*), Glaucous Sedge (*Carex flacca*), Small-fruited Yellow-sedge (*C. serotina*), Water Mint (*Mentha aquatica*), Silverweed (*Potentilla anserina*), Bog Pimpernel (*Anagallis tenella*), Strawberry Clover (*Trifolium fragiferum*), Lesser Spearwort (*Ranunculus flammula*), Common Marsh Bedstraw (*Galium palustre*), Common Reed (*Phragmites australis*), Sea Rush (*Juncus maritimus*) and Black Bog-rush (*Schoenus nigricans*). Orchids are often extremely abundant in the slacks: Marsh Helleborine (*Epipactis palustris*), Early Marsh Orchid (*Dactylorhiza incarnata* subsp. *incarnata*), Welsh Marsh Orchid (*D. majalis* subsp. *cambrensis*), Southern Marsh Orchid (subsp. *praetermissa*) and Northern Marsh Orchid (subsp. *purpurella*), as well as hybrids.

At Penyrergyd, the only other substantial sand-dune system in the County, is a sand and shingle spit on boulder clay containing a strikingly rich and different flora, the present absence of dune-slacks explaining the absence of many Ynys-las species. The Penyrergyd dunes contain

[21]E. E. Watkin (ed.), *A Handbook for Ynyslas* (Aberystwyth, 1976), 37–66, 143–6.

patches of Ash (*Fraxinus excelsior*) and Oak (*Quercus* sp.) scrub with such species as Broom (*Cytisus scoparius*), Herb-Robert and False Brome (*Brachypodium sylvaticum*), which do not occur at Ynys-las. Parts are more acidic than anything at Ynys-las and approximate to dune heath, with Sheep's Sorrel (*Rumex acetosella*), Heath Milkwort (*Polygala serpyllifolia*) and Downy Oat Grass (*Helictotrichon pubescens*). Other parts, where the boulder clay is near the surface, have species characteristic of this formation, and thus largely confined to the south-west of the County, such as Great Horsetail (*Equisetum telmateia*), Common Fleabane (*Pulicaria dysenterica*) and Greater Knapweed (*Centaurea scabiosa*). Parts of the mature dunes at Ynys-las, when the Wild Thyme, Restharrow and Bird's-foot Trefoil (*Lotus corniculatus*) flower, and the semi-consolidated dunes at Penyrergyd, with their Pyramidal Orchid (*Anacamptis pyramidalis*) and Sea Bindweed (*Calystegia soldanella*), are as colourful a spectacle as anything on the Cardiganshire coast.

iii) Salt marshes

The extensive salt marshes of the Dyfi estuary show the characteristic zonation of species common to most salt marshes. Glassworts (*Salicornia* spp.) colonize the mud-flats at the lowest level, then Common Salt-marsh Grass (*Puccinellia maritima*) forms a close sward which, as it collects sediment brought down by the river and its tributary streams, is replaced by Thrift (*Armeria maritima*) and then Red Fescue (*Festuca rubra*). Much of the marsh contains small permanent pools in the sward, and most of it has been heavily sheep-grazed. Many characteristic salt-marsh species such as Sea Arrowgrass (*Triglochin maritimum*), Long-bracted Sedge (*Carex extensa*), Annual Sea-blite (*Suaeda maritima*), Sea Plantain (*Plantago maritima*), and Sea Aster (*Aster tripolium*) occur, but the marsh is comparatively poor in species and floristically is most remarkable for the absence of such expected species as Sea-purslane (*Halimione portulacoides*) and Common Sea-lavender (*Limonium vulgare*). Common Cord-grass (*Spartina anglica*), imported in 1920, has colonized the lowest levels of the marsh, replacing to a considerable extent the earlier colonizers (Glassworts and Common Salt-marsh Grass), and drastically altering the vegetational character of the estuary. The tradition of ecological work on the site has continued with important studies on the behaviour of this *Spartina*.[22]

Apart from the salt marshes of the Teifi estuary, the features of which mostly resemble those of the Dyfi but on a much smaller scale, small areas of salt marsh occur elsewhere, notably in Aberystwyth and Aberaeron harbours, in the latter supporting Reflexed Salt-marsh Grass (*Puccinella distans*) and Greater Sea-spurrey (*Spergularia media*). In several places along the coast in the south-west of the County isolated patches on the hard Ordovician cliffs can have a quite rich flora, including Brooklime (*Samolus valerandi*) and Salt-marsh Rush (*Juncus gerardii*).

[22]Papers dealing with the ecology of the *Spartina* and of the Dyfi estuary include: R. H. Yapp, 'The salt marshes of the Dovey Estuary, I, Introductory', *J. Ecology*, 4 (1916), 27–42, and 'The salt marshes of the Dovey Estuary, II, The salt marshes', *J. Ecology*, 5 (1917), 65–103; 'The Dovey Salt Marshes in 1921', *J. Ecology*, 10 (1922), 18–23; J. H. Salter, '*Spartina* ...in western Wales', *North Western Naturalist*, 6 (1931), 229–30; R. H. Yapp, '*Spartina townsendii* on the Dovey salt marshes: a correction', *J. Ecology*, 11 (1923), 102; E. H. Chater, 'New forms of *Spartina townsendii* (Groves)', *Nature*, 168 (1951), 126; E. H. Chater and H. Jones, 'Some observations on *Spartina townsendii* H. and J. Groves in the Dovey Estuary', *J. Ecology*, 45 (1957), 157–67; and E. H. Chater, 'Ecological aspects of the Dwarf Brown form of *Spartina* in the Dovey Estuary', *J. Ecology*, 53 (1965), 178–97.

iv) Sea cliffs and screes

The lower zones of cliffs and scree slopes, where the influence of salt spray is very strong, have a sparse but very characteristic assemblage of higher plants. Sea Spleenwort (*Asplenium marinum*) is usually the lowest species on the cliffs, although there is also a large colony of it, sometimes severely reduced after hard winters, on the north tower of the Aberystwyth Castle ruins. Sea Campion, Thrift, Scentless Mayweed (*Tripeurospermum inodorum*), Rock Sea-spurrey (*Spergularia rupicola*), White Stonecrop (*Sedum anglicum*) and Sea Plantain are common, and Ivy Broomrape (*Orobanche hederae*), parasitic on Ivy, Wood Spurge (*Euphorbia amygaloides*), normally a woodland species, and Wild Madder (*Rubia peregrina*) occur in a few sites. Rock Samphire (*Crithmum maritimum*) is still abundant in a few places, but is no longer common near Aberystwyth as it was in the last century when it was sold as a vegetable in the market.

The lowest levels of scree slopes which are especially well developed at such sites as Allt-wen (SN 575 794) have much White Stonecrop and Ivy, and at the richer and damper sites such as Cribach Bay there are extensive colonies of Wood Vetch (*Vicia sylvatica*) and Narrow-leaved Everlasting Pea (*Lathyrus sylvestris*). On the more exposed and level cliff tops, as around Gwbert and Llangrannog Head, an often somewhat open, very low-growing community has developed characterized by Spring Squill (*Scilla verna*) and Heath Pearlwort (*Sagina subulata*), with much Red Fescue, Sea Plantain, Buck's-horn Plantain and Thrift. The most spectacular displays of Spring Squill, however, are on the site of long-abandoned arable fields along the cliff tops east of Mwnt.

Native woodlands

Almost all the older woods in the County and many of those that have developed naturally in the last century or two show extensive signs of former management, mostly in the form of coppicing. Many, if not most, of the woods have lost whatever floristic richness and ecological variety they may once have had because of lapsed management. A large number of woods are no longer fenced off and grazing, especially by sheep, has drastically reduced ground flora as well as regeneration from coppice stools or seed of many of the potentially most interesting woodlands.[23]

Woods of Sessile Oak (*Quercus petraea*) are the most familiar and extensive over most of the County, clothing the steep, freely drained sides of the valleys from almost sea-level up to 350m. Most of these woods appear on the earliest Ordnance Survey maps (*c.*1825–35), and almost all appear to have been coppiced within the last 150 years, the majority most recently in one or other of the two World Wars. On many of these steep slopes the woods are entirely of Sessile Oak mixed with Downy Birch (*Betula pubescens*), containing no shrub layer or only occasional Rowan (*Sorbus aucuparia*), and a very poor ground flora dominated by Wavy Hair-grass (*Deschampsia flexuosa*),

[23]The history and former management of woods in Wales is described by W. Linnard, *Welsh Woods and Forests* (Cardiff, 1982), and L. J. Mincher, 'Broadleaved woodland in Ceredigion—history, present state and future role' (unpublished M. Sc. thesis, University of Salford, 1986). The present account generally follows the classification of woodlands proposed in G. F. Peterken, *Woodland Conservation and Management* (London and New York, 1981).

Sweet Vernal-grass (*Anthoxanthum odoratum*) and Bilberry (*Vaccinium myrtillus*), with the abundant and conspicuous mosses *Leucobryum glaucum* and *Dicranum majus*. Coed Troed Rhiw Seiri (SN 670 850) and Allt Hoffnant (SN 325 521) are good examples. Where the soil is slightly heavier and deeper on less steep slopes, the Oak and Birch have an under-storey of Hazel (*Corylus avellana*). Rowan is often more frequent and there is usually some Hawthorn (*Crataegus monogyna*), Holly (*Ilex aquifolium*), Honeysuckle (*Lonicera periclymenum*) and Bramble (*Rubus fruticosus* agg.) present. The ground flora is dominated by such species as Creeping Soft-grass (*Holcus mollis*), Great Wood-rush (*Luzula sylvatica*), Bluebell (*Hyacinthoides non-scriptus*) and Broad Buckler-fern (*Dryopteris austriaca*). This type of woodland was familiar to Dafydd ap Gwilym, and many of the woods in Cwm Llyfnant, Cwm Cletwr, the Leri Valley, the Marchnant and Gwenffrwd Valleys and at innumerable other sites in the County are still of this kind.

On well-drained slopes where stands of Ash form quite narrow strips marking the presence of flushes, Ash (*Fraxinum excelsior*) is present with Sessile Oak, Hazel is dominant in the shrub layer (unless it has been grazed out), and there is a richer ground flora with Sanicle (*Sanicula europaea*), Dog's Mercury (*Mercurialis perennis*), Yellow Pimpernel (*Lysimachia nemorum*), Wood Speedwell (*Veronica montana*), Wood Anemone (*Anemone nemorosa*), Hart's-tongue (*Phyllitis scolopendrium*) and Enchanter's Nightshade (*Circaea lutetiana*). Within Sessile Oak woods, outcrops of rock in a variety of strata can have an even richer vegetation. These include most notably outcrops of the Bryn-glas and Drosgol Formations of the upper part of the Ordovician in Cwm Llyfnant and Cwm Einion, outcrops of the Devil's Bridge Formation of the Silurian by the River Melindwr, south of Cymerau, and in the Cwm Rheidol National Nature Reserve, outcrops of the Cwmsym-log Formation of the Silurian at another site by the River Melindwr, and outcrops of the Derwen-las Formation of the Silurian in Cwm Cletwr. Further south in the County similar rich woodland vegetation occurs in such sites as the Gwenffrwd (SN 596 598) and Marchnant (SN 607 579) valleys. These rocks contain very little calcareous material, but locally they presumably contain just enough to affect the vegetation, especially where flushing occurs. The dominant trees of these outcrops are Wych Elm (*Ulmus glabra*), subject now to Elm Disease, and Ash, usually with some Sessile Oak. The ground flora of these much richer sites includes such locally uncommon species as Wood Stitchwort (*Stellaria nemorum* subsp. *glochidisperma*), Yellow Archangel (*Lamiastrum galeobdolon*), Upland Enchanter's Nightshade (*Circaea x intermedia*), Oak Fern (*Gymnocarpium dryopteris*), Hay-scented Buckler-fern (*Dryopteris aemula*), Wood Fescue (*Festuca altissima*), abundant Ramsons (*Allium ursinum*) and, in very sheltered, damp sites, Tunbridge Filmy Fern (*Hymenophyllum tunbrigense*). In many of these same valleys a further type of woodland, with Small-leaved Lime (*Tilia cordata*) amongst the Sessile Oak and with a Hazel shrub layer is found, but only as very small stands.

The few areas of uncoppiced old Sessile Oak Woodland include Coed Mynachlog-fawr (SN 745 654) and the Teifi gorge woods at Coedmor (SN 194 445). Coed Mynachlog-fawr approximates most closely of all the woods in the County to wood pasture, and supports Pedunculate Oak (*Quercus robur*) as well as Sessile Oak, together with a rich shrub community of Hazel, Rowan, Hawthorn, Sallow (*Salix cinerea*) and Guelder Rose (*Viburnum opulus*). Clearings contain either Bracken (*Pteridium aquilinum*), Purple Moor-grass (*Molina caerulea*) or small mires. This type of woodland is probably of considerable age, although it is doubtless secondary, judging from the absence of very old trees and from evidence that the woods in this area were destroyed and not just coppiced in the Middle Ages.[24] The Coedmor woods are extremely rich in woody and herbaceous species, and contain besides Sessile and Pedunculate Oaks and their hybrids, much Ash, Wych Elm and ancient trees of Small-leaved Lime as well as the Wild Service-tree (*Sorbus torminalis*). A few other coastal valleys, notably that of the Afon Arth (SN 495 625 etc.), have very similar woodland but show signs of coppicing.

On the steep slopes along the coast, notably at the Penderi Reserve (SN 552 735) and between Cribach Bay and Craig y Filain are windblown woods of Sessile and Pedunculate Oaks and their hybrids, probably of great age, parts of which may well be quite unmodified by Man. They often have a shrub layer of Hazel, Hawthorn, Wild Privet (*Ligustrum vulgare*) and Spindle (*Euonymus europaeus*), and sometimes a distinctly calcicole ground flora, and occasionally Small-leaved Lime. Pedunculate Oak is a large component of these woods but nowhere is it dominant. Where the hybrid is dominant, as in the plateau woods just north of Coedmor Mansion, it is probably planted.

Alder woodland occurs on a small scale both as acidic woodland on flushed slopes, for example in Cwm Llyfnant, and as wet woodland or Alder carr on valley floors, for example at Highmead on the Teifi. At Rosehill Marsh (SN189 454) is a rare example of estuarine Alder carr, inundated at high spring tides and with a ground flora dominated by Common Reed (*Phragmites australis*) with tussocks of Dotted Sedge (*Carex punctata*).

Ancient woodland, that is woodland that has existed continuously since at least the Middle Ages, can be identified not only by documentary means but also by the presence of indicator species of plants (and animals). Although such indicators have not been specifically worked out for Cardiganshire, recent work in Pembrokeshire describes a very comparable series of woodlands and discusses the problems of indicators.[25] How much of the woodland in Cardiganshire is secondary, in the sense that it has developed on previously treeless land, is uncertain, and over-grazing has destroyed much of the evidence. Most of the estate plans, which might have provided further evidence, are less than 200 years old, and the earliest Ordnance Survey maps are only about 150. Tree-trunks are often sawn and susceptible to dating, but not so the coppiced stools which in most of our woods must be of great age. The total number of broadleaved woods in Cardiganshire (including those with less than 50 per cent admixture of conifers) is almost as great as 150 years ago, and the aggregate area which they now cover is about 75 per cent of the area they covered then.[26] This estimate includes ancient and planted as well as secondary broadleaved woods. Broadleaved woodland of all sorts, including plantations, now covers some 4,100 ha, or 2.3 per cent of the County.

The speed with which secondary woodland can develop is surprising and may be observed south-east of Tyddyn-du (SN 272 426). An area of ten hectares or so which has become dense

[24]P. D. Moore and E. H. Chater, 'The changing vegetation of west-central Wales in the light of human history', *J. Ecology*, 57 (1969), 361–79, and L. J. Mincher, 'Broadleaved woodland in Ceredigion', 15, 22–3.

[25]J. Buchanan and M. Fuller, *Pembrokeshire Ancient Woodlands Survey*, Nature Conservancy Council, Aberystwyth and West Wales Naturalists' Trust (Haverfordwest, 1980).

[26]This estimate is my own calculation of the area shown as broadleaved woodland based on the first edition of the Ordnance Survey maps (1825–35) and the latest tables produced by the Forestry Commission Surveys of 1978–82. Both these measurements, 4,840 ha and 3,742 ha, may be very misleading for a variety of reasons, but the visual impression from the relevant OS maps suggests that the estimate of about 75 per cent is not far wrong.

woodland, colonized first by Downy Birch, then by Sessile Oak and Ash, with a well-developed shrub layer of Hazel and Holly, was rough pasture less than a century ago. Secondary as well as planted woodland, however, never acquires so rich a flora as ancient woodland,[27] and sites such as Coed Rheidol and the Gwenffrwd and Coedmor woods will, if they survive, always remain unsurpassed for woodland diversity in the County.

Pastures and hay meadows

Most of the County consists of grassland variously managed for grazing by sheep, cattle and horses and, increasingly, for silage. Hay meadows are few and decreasing. The amount of grassland recently ploughed and reseeded vastly exceeds that which has retained a rich variety of species under traditional management, and mostly consists of virtual monocultural leys of forms of Perennial Ryegrass (*Lolium perenne*), sometimes mixed with sown or naturally spreading species such as Crested Dog's-tail (*Cynosurus cristatus*), Cock's-foot (*Dactylis glomerata*) and Bents (*Agrostis* spp.), Red and White Clover (*Trifolium pratense* and *T. repens*) and Buttercups (*Ranunculus* spp.).

The unimproved sheepwalks still covering much of the drier parts of the uplands, probably derived from heathland by grazing and burning, are dominated by Sheep's-fescue (*Festuca ovina*) and Common Bent (*Agrostis capillaris*), with Heath Bedstraw (*Galium saxatile*) and Tormentil (*Potentilla erecta*) as the commonest associates. Mat-grass (*Nardus stricta*) is locally the dominant on damper sites; Heath Rush (*Juncus squarrosus*) becomes abundant on still wetter sites. Areas of tussocky Purple Moor-grass (*Molinia caerulea*), grading into wet heath, are common. These communities have few species, and it is only where they are flushed or merge into heath that more than half a dozen can be found. Mountain Pansy (*Viola lutea*), abundant fifty years ago, is no longer a common spectacle on the sheepwalks.

Below 300 m only a few remaining sites show the richness that was common earlier this century. Near Elerch a slope dominated by Sheep's-fescue, Heath-grass (*Danthonia decumbens*) and Sweet Vernal-grass (*Anthoxanthum odoratum*), has abundant Spring-sedge (*Carex caryophyllea*), Common Dog-violet (*Viola riviniana*), Harebell (*Campanula rotundiflora*), Tormentil, Mountain Pansy, Common Bird's-foot-trefoil (*Lotus corniculatus*), Bluebell (*Hyacinthoides non-scripta*), the locally very rare and decreasing fern Moonwort (*Botrychium lunaria*) and many other species. A similar site near Strata Florida is one of the few remaining pasture sites for the Wood Bitter-vetch (*Vicia orobus*), formerly so abundant that Salter[28] described it as 'a great ornament to the hill pastures'. Much of the middle altitude grassland in the southern half of the County, especially where periglacial pingo remains occur, is of a type recently recognized as especially characteristic of, and largely confined to, Cardiganshire and adjacent parts of Carmarthenshire and

---

[27]G. F. Peterken and M. Game, 'Historical factors affecting number and distribution of vascular plant species in the woodlands of central Lincolnshire', *J. Ecology*, 72 (1984), 155–82.
[28]J. H. Salter, *Flowering Plants and Ferns*, 39.

Pembrokeshire. Named for convenience *rhos*, as such grassland is usually called *rhos* locally,[29] it is essentially a Purple Moor-grass pasture, grazing having prevented the formation of the characteristic tussocks of this species. It consists of a series or mosaic of communities, usually containing small areas of heath with Heather (*Calluna vulgaris*), as well as small areas of mire with Sedges (*Carex* spp.) and Bog Mosses (*Sphagnum* spp.), and flushes with Sharp-flowered Rush (*Juncus acutiflorus*). The water-table is always high in places, and there are often areas of standing water. Devil's-bit Scabious (*Succisa pratensis*), Tormentil, Mat-grass, and Heath Spotted-orchid (*Dactylorhiza maculata*) are very characteristic and almost constant species of *rhos*. Creeping Willow (*Salix repens*) and Meadow Thistle (*Cirsium dissectum*) appear locally but rarely. Whorled Caraway (*Carum verticillatum*) is characteristic especially of horse-grazed and perhaps shallow-ploughed *rhos*. Pingo groups with their series of dry banks and wet, often mire-filled hollows, provide ideal topography for *rhos*, with extensive areas remaining at the Llawr-cwrt National Nature Reserve, on the upper Cledlyn, and at Glwydwern and Glynyrhelyg near Gors-goch. Ridge-and-furrow pasture, rare in Cardiganshire, can also provide an ideal site for *rhos*, as exemplified on a small area at Comins Capel Betws.

At lower altitudes, most of the remaining unimproved dry pastures are acidic and dominated by Common Bent, Sweet Vernal-grass, Red Fescue and Heath-grass, and the characteristic herbs include Knapweed (*Centaurea nigra*), Common Bird's-foot-trefoil, Ribwort Plantain (*Plantago lanceolata*) and Yarrow (*Achillea millefolium*). Slightly more base-rich sites, such as the neutral grasslands on the east slope of Pendinas (SN 586 806), horse-grazed like so many of the best grassland sites in Cardiganshire, are very rich in species with no clear dominants. The same species are all on Pendinas, together with Rough Hawkbit (*Leontodon hispidus*), Bulbous Buttercup (*Ranunculus bulbosus*), Burnet-saxifrage (*Pimpinella saxifraga*), Common Restharrow (*Ononis repens*), Fairy Flax (*Linum catharticum*), Pignut (*Conopodium majus*) and many others. Quaking-grass (*Briza media*), now largely confined to a few relic grassland sites, half of them in churchyards, occurred here until about 1960. Another calcicole, Yellow Oat-grass (*Trisetum flavescens*), is similarly and significantly rare in the County. Apart from churchyards and a few coastal sites near lime-kilns, where it may have been introduced with limestone, it was found in only one pasture, near Caerwedros, where it was dominant until the site was reseeded in 1985. In sloping pastures near Llangybi, Greater Butterfly-orchid (*Platanthera chlorantha*) occurs in some quantity, Tall Fescue (*Festuca arundinacea*) is abundant and, until recently, Bladder Campion (*Silene vulgaris*) occurred in one of its only two grassland sites in the County.

The few hay meadows that remain in the lowlands, damp and herb-rich, as in the Aeron valley between Tal-sarn and Llangeitho, and the similarly managed communities in many church-yards, are usually dominated by Yorkshire-fog (*Holcus lanatus*), Sweet Vernal-grass, Crested Dog's-tail, Lesser Soft-brome (*Bromus thominii*) and Rough Meadow-grass (*Poa trivialis*), with Common Sorrel (*Rumex acetosa*), Greater Bird's-foot-trefoil (*Lotus uliginosus*), Greater Burnet (*Sanguisorba officinalis*) and many other species. Upland hay meadows above 300 m survive only near Ystumtuen and in the Camddwr valley below Soar-y-mynydd. At this latter site the

[29]E. Price Evans, 'Cader Idris: a study of certain plant communities in south-west Merionethshire', *J. Ecology*, 20 (1932), 1–52, used the word in a wider sense, but it has been little used in his sense in the ecological literature. It is proposed here as the term for this type of grassland in the narrow sense.

management, unchanged in essentials for many decades, has established and preserved an extremely rich association of species with Red Fescue, Soft-brome (*Bromus mollis*), Crested Dog's-tail, Sweet Vernal-grass, and Rough Meadow-grass as the dominants. The abundance of Wood Bitter-vetch, Saw-wort (*Serratula tinctoria*), Pignut and Yellow Rattle (*Rhinanthus minor*) with many other species makes these meadows a rare survival of the sort of richness that characterized the Cardiganshire uplands half a century and more ago.

Peatlands

Peatland, or mire, communities form when vegetation builds up over its own undecayed remains in waterlogged contexts. In acidic conditions this vegetation consists largely of Bog Mosses (*Sphagnum* spp.) overlying moss peat, whereas in alkaline or eutrophic conditions the vegetation is usually a fen community of sedges, grasses and other herbs overlying sedge peat. Mires are classified according to their topography and the way in which they acquire water. The high rainfall of western Britain allows extensive development of raised and blanket mires which are conspicuous in Cardiganshire.

Raised mires, developed on the alluvial plains of rivers and estuaries, consisting of large, perceptibly convex areas dominated by Bog Mosses and deriving their water from rainfall on their surface, are undoubtedly the most widely known and extensively studied habitats in the County. Cors Fochno or Borth Bog, encompassing some 550 ha contains the largest area of comparatively unspoilt raised mire in Britain, and its development has been intensively studied.[30] It has a very high water table, and a characteristic mosaic of wet hollows with White Beak-sedge (*Rhynchospora alba*), Hare's-tail Cottongrass (*Eriophorum vaginatum*), Bog Asphodel (*Narthecium ossifragum*), all three Sundews (*Drosera* spp.), Cross-leaved Heath (*Erica tetralix*), Deergrass (*Scirpus cespitosus*) and Bog-rosemary (*Andromeda polifolia*), and drier hummocks with Heather (*Calluna vulgaris*), Bog Myrtle (*Myrica gale*) and lichens cover much of the central part. Near the margins, where water draining from the surrounding land provides some enrichment, there are Grey Willow (*Salix cinerea*), thickets and huge plants of Greater Tussock-sedge (*Carex paniculata*) and Royal Fern (*Osmunda regalis*), which in recent decades has become abundant again after near-extermination. Other marginal areas are dominated by an intermediate community of Purple Moor-grass (*Molinia caerulea*) and Bog Myrtle. Sites transitional to the salt marsh along the River Leri contain such species as Black Bog-rush (*Schoenus nigricans*) and Sea Rush (*Juncus maritimus*), but Saltmarsh Flat-sedge (*Blysmus rufus*) has not been seen here (one of its most southerly sites in Britain) in recent years.

---

[30]See for example W. M. Condry, 'A peat bog worth preserving', *Country Life* (August, 1962), 472–3; F. M. Slater, 'Contributions to the ecology of Borth Bog, Wales: general considerations', *Proc. of the Fourth Int. Peat Congress, Helsinki* (1972), I, 277–88; F. M. Slater, 'The vegetation of Cors Fochno and other Welsh peatlands' (unpublished Univ. of Wales Ph.D. thesis, Aberystwyth, 1974); A. D. Fox, 'Aspects of the hydrology of Cors Fochno National Nature Reserve' (unpublished Univ. of Wales Ph.D. thesis, Aberystwyth, 1984); and F. M. Slater, 'The *Schoenus nigricans* area of Cors Fochno (Borth Bog)', *Nature in Wales*, 16 (1978), 16–19.

Cors Caron or Tregaron Bog, a complex of several separate raised mires covering some 800 ha at an altitude of 160 m, has a lower water table than Cors Fochno.[31] Stratigraphical studies show that the mires developed over a late-glacial lake, through Sedge-dominated flood-plain mire, such as can still be seen a little lower down the Teifi between Ystradcaron and the river, and by the confluence with the Nant Bryn-maen, to raised mire no longer relying on water from below but entirely dependent on rainfall. Bog Myrtle is absent, but Crowberry (*Empetrum nigrum*), absent from Cors Fochno, Deergrass and Purple Moor-grass are abundant. The site is very varied, the marginal enriched areas containing Bog-sedge (*Carex limosa*) and the river terraces Reed Canary-grass (*Phalaris arundinacea*) and Water Sedge (*Carex aquatilis*). Both here and at Cors Fochno peat-cutting for fuel, attempts at draining, and burning have modified parts of the site and added to the variation. The scientific importance of these sites is such that both are National Nature Reserves.

Blanket mires, covering large areas of upland chiefly on gentle slopes above 300 m, on relatively impermeable rock, and deriving their water supply from rainfall, consist of poor communities dominated by Purple Moor-grass, Deergrass, Hare's-tail Cottongrass, Common Cottongrass (*Eriophorum angustifolium*) and Bog Mosses. Extensive blanket mires with Heather, and in places Bog-rosemary, are found especially at 400–500 m on the plateau between the Llyfnant and Einion, and between the Ystwyth and Claerwen, though south-west of Tyn-y-graig (SN 683 686) are the substantial remains of an unusually low-altitude blanket mire. Watershed mires, where blanket mires often become eroded by the headwaters of streams so that peat hags are formed, occur in a few places. Those at Figyn Blaen Brefi[32] (SN 717 547) and Gors Lwyd [33] (SN 857 754) have been extensively studied, the latter being of special floristic interest with a large colony of Slender Sedge (*Carex lasiocarpa*).

The four other main types of mire derive their water from ground-water supply—flood-plain, basin, valley and soligenous.

Flood-plain mires, previously mentioned, are well developed beside the Dyfi near Ynys-fach. Here one of the most eutrophic mires in Cardiganshire has Blunt-flowered Rush (*Juncus subnodulosus*) in its only site, amongst Common Reed (*Phragmites australis*) and Bog Myrtle.

Basin mires, formed in waterlogged hollows, have a vegetation usually akin to that of raised mires, good examples being in the pingo depressions on the Nant Cledlyn (SN 475 481) and at the south end of Gors-goch valley mire (SN 483 499) where a raised mire community with abundant Round-leaved Sundew (*Drosera rotundifolia*) and Cranberry (*Vaccinium oxycoccus*) grows on dominant Bog Mosses, though examples of basin mires with vegetation akin to blanket mires can be seen on the western slopes of Plynlimon (SN 779 880) and on the Mynydd Bach.

Valley mires develop in comparatively small valleys where there is movement of water into and along the mire. In Cardiganshire they occur mainly in the gently sloping valleys of the coastal plateau, and the communities in them vary from very poor, acidic, raised mire to mesotrophic poor fen, these extremes sometimes only being a few metres apart. Conspicuous examples occur

[31] H. Godwin and V. M. Conway, 'The ecology of a raised Bog near Tregaron, Cardiganshire', *J. Ecology*, 27 (1939), 313–63, and R. T. Johnston, 'Ecological studies on the West Bog, Tregaron, and on Borth Bog' (unpublished Univ. of Wales M.Sc. thesis, Aberystwyth, 1970).

[32] E. G. Davies, 'Figyn Blaen Brefi: a Welsh upland bog', *J. Ecology*, 32 (1945), 147–66.

[33] F. M. Slater, 'Gors Lwyd—a peat bog under threat', *Nature in Wales*, 15 (1976), 60–72.

to the west of Gors-goch village and along the east side of the old railway south of Tyn-y-graig. The great variety of habitats within such valley mires gives them a natural history interest comparable to that of the *rhosydd*, and many are closely associated with areas of *rhos*. At Gors-goch the surviving undrained valley mire covers some 25 ha. Where drainage begins on the slight slope and water drains down from the adjacent *rhos*, rather oligotrophic poor fen has developed with Bottle Sedge (*Carex rostrata*), White Sedge (*C. curta*), Water Horsetail (*Equisetum fluviatile*) and Common Marsh-bedstraw (*Galium palustre*). Soft Rush (*Juncus effusus*), Marsh Pennywort (*Hydrocotyle vulgaris*) and Common Spotted-orchid (*Dactylorhiza fuchsii*) are found on drier areas. At a lower altitude, extensive wet stretches are dominated by Bog Mosses and contain Bogbean (*Menyanthes trifoliata*), Purple Moor-grass, White Sedge, Common and Hare's-tail Cottongrass, Wavy Hair-grass (*Deschampsia flexuosa*) and Cranberry, while drier areas have Tussock-moss (*Polytrichum commune*) and Heather. Narrow Buckler-fern (*Dryopteris carthusiana*) is a very characteristic plant of these valley mires, along with the less common Royal Fern. In the middle of this mire, where there is a water-channel, more mesotrophic poor fen has developed and Soft Rush, Sharp-flowered Rush (*Juncus acutiflorus*), Marsh Bedstraw and Common Valerian (*Valeriana officinalis*) are the dominants, with Marsh Cinquefoil (*Potentilla palustris*), Ragged Robin (*Lychnis flos-cuculi*) and Lesser Butterfly-orchid (*Platanthera bifolia*). Grey Willow forms dense carr in places, and *rhos* continues along its west margin. By the outflow at the north-western end Greater Tussock-sedge occurs. A valley mire complex near Ciliau Aeron has even more eutrophic areas which contain both Great Fen-sedge (*Cladium mariscus*) and Cyperus Sedge (*Carex pseodocyperus*).

Small soligenous mires, where peat has formed on slopes with water coming predominantly from springs or flushes, are common in the uplands where they frequently interrupt blanket mires on otherwise dry slopes. They are also a regular constituent of *rhos*. In the most oligotrophic and acidic examples Star Sedge (*Carex echinata*), Long-stalked Yellow-sedge (*C. demissa*) and Bulbous Rush are found amongst the Bog Mosses, but in the more mesotrophic ones, where the seepage is more mineral-rich, Tawny Sedge (*Carex hostiana*), Carnation Sedge (*C. panicea*), Flea Sedge (*C. pulicaris*), Sharp-flowered Rush and a great range of other plants appear. The Bog Orchid (*Hammarbya paludosa*) is confined to a few such flush mires in the north of the County, and Lesser Clubmoss (*Selaginella selaginoides*) reaches its southernmost site in Britain in such a flush in the Tywi valley. The most eutrophic and calcareous soligenous mires in the County occur along the banks of the Afon Mwldan north-east of Cardigan, attaining an area of 2 ha or more and dominated in places by Lesser Pond-sedge (*Carex acutiformis*) and Greater Tussock-sedge (*C. paniculata*) with abundant Long-stalked Yellow-sedge (*C. lepidocarpa*), Dioecious Sedge (*C. dioica*), Few-flowered Spike-rush (*Eleocharis quinqueflora*), Broad-leaved Cotton-grass (*Eriophorum latifolium*), Quaking-grass (*Briza media*), Marsh Heleborine (*Epipactis palustris*) and Fragrant Orchid (*Gymnadenia conopsea*). In one place an extensive, very wet eutrophic fen with Common Reed, Lesser Pond-sedge, Long-stalked Yellow-sedge and Fragrant Orchid has developed.

Heaths

Extensive tracts over 300 m, which are neither covered by wet peat nor improved to become grasslands or conifer plantations, are heath, dominated by Heather (*Calluna vulgaris*), Bell

Heather (*Erica cinerea*) and Bilberry (*Vaccinium myrtillus*). This heath is mostly comparatively dry and the species amongst these dwarf shrubs are those characteristic of the grassland of the sheepwalks, together with Lemon-scented Fern (*Oreopteris limbosperma*) and Hard Fern (*Blechnum spicant*). In a few areas, for example near the summit of Plynlimon and on Disgwylfa Fawr (SN 737 847), other dwarf shrubs such as Crowberry (*Empetrum nigrum*) and Cowberry (*Vaccinium vitis-idaea*), and the Alpine Clubmoss (*Diphasiastrum alpinum*) and Stag's-horn Clubmoss (*Lycopodium clavatum*) occur. Dwarf Willow (*Salix herbacea*) occurs only at one site, at 700 m on Plynlimon. Heaths are especially sensitive to changes in management, and rapid changes caused by the exclusion of grazing animals can be seen wherever an area of heath has been enclosed for afforestation. For a few years the Heather and Western Gorse (*Ulex gallii*) will grow up, often to 1 or 2 m, and flower prolifically before being shaded out. In the extreme north of Cardiganshire, along the often very steep slopes of Cwm Llyfnant and on Pencarreg-gopa, the combination of high rainfall and light grazing has led to the development of very tall heath, similar to that developing briefly in afforested areas, but with deep Bog Mosses (*Sphagnum* spp.) under the Heather, abundant Crowberry, herbs such as Common Cow-wheat (*Melampyrum pratense*) and Tormentil (*Potentilla erecta*), and the rare orchid Lesser Twayblade (*Listera cordata*).

At lower and middle altitudes heaths are often dominated by Western Gorse. The acidic heaths of the middle altitudes are mostly overgrazed, and most have been lost to ploughing or afforestation in recent years, one of their characteristic species, Mountain Everlasting (*Antennaria dioica*), having been lost from most of its sites. Dry heath occurs down to less than 100 m, for example on the slopes east of Cors Fochno. Lowland wet acidic heath has mostly been destroyed, but small areas remain as at Comins Capel Betws (SN 616 574). Here Western Gorse, Cross-leaved Heath (*Erica tetralix*) and Purple Moor-grass (*Molinia caerulea*) are dominant, together with locally abundant Bog Mosses, Deergrass (*Scirpus cespitosus*), Carnation Sedge (*Carex panicea*), Lousewort (*Pedicularis sylvatica*), Heath Spotted-orchid (*Dactylorhiza maculata*), Heather and Petty Whin (*Genista anglica*). Areas of heath nearer the coast are usually less acidic and often contain great abundance of Creeping Willow (*Salix repens*) as well as Heath Milkwort (*Polygala serpyllifolia*) and Bog Pimpernel (*Anagallis tenella*). They are similar in their ecology to some of the more oceanic heaths of Pembrokeshire, and this particular heath element is a very characteristic constituent of *rhos*.

Within a few hundred metres of the coast submaritime heath has developed. Never extensive, it is often confined to comparatively inaccessible and thus uncultivated sea-cliff slopes, and can be seen at Allt-wen (SN 575 795), New Quay Head (SN 384 604), Penmoelciliau (SN 342 563), Craig y Filain (SN 234 521) and Pen Peles (SN 218 524). Heather and Bell Heather are constantly present, and usually such species as the early-autumn-flowering Western Gorse and the late-autumn and spring-flowering Gorse (*Ulex europaeus*), with Slender St John's-wort (*Hypericum pulchrum*), Heath Milkwort, Tormentil, Red Fescue (*Festuca rubra*), Heath Bedstraw (*Galium saxatile*), Sea Plantain (*Plantago maritima*), Saw-wort (*Serratula tinctoria*) and a coastal ecotype of Heath Grass (*Danthonia decumbens*). This submaritime heath is usually very windblown, like the cliff oakwoods with which it is sometimes associated, and is probably a truly natural community uninfluenced by Man. The inland heaths, by contrast, are probably all, except for the very highest, the result of Man's management and would probably revert to scrub or forest if left untouched for long.

Coastal gorse heath usually develops on abandoned cultivated land, but on Tywyn Warren, Gwbert (SN 165 487), it occurs on a slope which has probably never been cultivated, but it may be that this site is best regarded as dune heath.

Mountain rocks

On rock outcrops above 300 m, especially where these are base-rich, species with a restricted, often arctic-alpine, distribution can be found, but Cardiganshire has few such sites.[34] Most of the Ordovician outcrops of Plynlimon and around Foel Goch and Pencarreg-gopa are very acidic and have few species, and only on the wet rocks above Llyn Llygad Rheidol do any species occur which are not more abundant in other habitats nearby. Here, Starry Saxifrage (*Saxifraga stellaris*) is abundant, one of only seven arctic-alpines in the County. It also occurs in the Rheidol gorge as far down as Devil's Bridge where it has been presumably washed down from its higher sites. One large cushion of Mossy Saxifrage (*S. hypnoides*) has been known on Plynlimon since 1903,[35] another on Lluest Graig having long since disappeared. This species is usually a calcicole but it is here unassociated with any other calcicolous plants, Vivaparous Fescue (*Festuca vivipara*) and Water Avens (*Geum rivale*) being almost the only other species of interest on these cliffs.

Certain outcrops of the Silurian have species or assemblages thereof that are distinctly calcicole. These outcrops occur notably on Craig y Pistyll in the north and Craig Ddu in the south-east where they are part of the Derwen-las formation, and at Hirgoed-ddu near Eisteddfa Gurig and on Craig Clyngwyn in the south-east where they are part of the Devil's Bridge formation.[36] The general calcareous content of these rocks is very low, but they presumably contain just sufficient to affect the vegetation, while springs and seepage may help to make this material more available. Stone Bramble (*Rubus saxatilis*), Wood Spurge (*Euphorbia amygdaloides*), Marjoram (*Origanum vulgare*), Rock Stonecrop (*Sedum forsteranum*) and certain Hawkweeds (notably *Hieracium lasiophyllum*) are largely or entirely confined to these outcrops.[37] Outcrops of other Silurian strata when flushed occasionally have a characteristic assemblage of species which, while less calcicolous, in the context of the Cardiganshire uplands may indicate very slightly base-rich conditions. Lady's Mantle (*Alchemilla glabra*), Pale Sedge (*Carex pallescens*), Ash (*Fraxinus excelsior*), Woodruff (*Galium odoratum*), Water Avens, Primrose (*Primula vulgaris*), Sanicle (*Sanicula europaea*), Common Valerian (*Valeriana officinalis*), and Globeflower (*Trollius europaeus*) are among such indicators.

[34] W. M. Condry, *The Natural History of Wales* (London, 1981), 27–8.
[35] J. H. Salter, *Natural History Diaries* (entry for 26 September 1903).
[36] *British Geological Survey of England and Wales*. Sheet 163 (Southampton, 1984). I am grateful to Dr B. A. Hains of the British Geological Survey, Aberystwyth, for details of these outcrops and of those mentioned in the section on woodlands.
[37] See R. H. Roberts, 'A note on the Cardiganshire localities of *Sedum forsteranum* Sm.', *Nature in Wales*, 9 (1964), 19–21, and resulting correspondence, ibid., 96.

Rivers

Cardiganshire possesses four main rivers, but the Dyfi, being entirely tidal within the County, need not concern us.

The Teifi is a river of exceptional botanical interest, and recent work[38] has shown it to be of outstanding importance in Britain for the variety of communities it contains and the unusual arrangement of these communities, and for the presence of several nationally rare species. The headwaters of the Teifi, which rises at 540 m, flow through high-altitude acidic moorland, with a very oligotrophic community, dominated by mosses and liverworts with such higher plants as Bog Pondweed (*Potamogeton polygonifolius*) and Intermediate Water-starwort (*Callitriche intermedia*). When it has fallen to 175 m, it meanders slowly through the extensive raised mire complex of Cors Caron, and the combination of peaty, nutrient-poor, slow-flowing water and the much richer, more mesotrophic bed of silts and clays, produces communities with Floating Water-plantain (*Luronium natans*), Broad-leaved Pondweed (*Potamogeton natans*), Stream Water-crowfoot (*Ranunculus penicillatus* subsp. *penicillatus*), Lesser Marshwort (*Apium inundatum*) and Yellow Water-lily (*Nuphar lutea*), with stands of Common Club-rush (*Scirpus lacustris*), Water Sedge (*Carex aquatilis*) and Slender Tufted-sedge (*C. acuta*) at the river's edge. Mosses and liverworts are few. For much of the rest of its length the Teifi is comparatively fast-flowing, rocky and only slightly mesotrophic, but because it has its slow-flowing and most mesotrophic section high up at Cors Caron, and not nearest its mouth as is normally the case, the influence of this section, particularly in the dispersal of various species by seed or flood-washed fragments, is felt along the whole course of the lower part of the river. The Teifi is also unusual in having no large tributaries, and this results in the Cors Caron stretch having an unexpectedly dominating influence. Common Club-rush is abundant opposite Tregaron and occurs as far downstream as Newcastle Emlyn, Water Sedge is scattered all down the river, and Water Dock (*Rumex hydrolapathum*) occurs from Lampeter to Llanybydder. These are plants characteristic of enriched, static or slow-moving lowland waters, but here they occur alongside species such as Intermediate Water-starwort and Alternate Water-milfoil (*Myriophyllum alterniflorum*), which are characteristic of nutrient-poor, upland waters. Among the more interesting plants of the Teifi is a hybrid Pondweed (*Potamogeton* x *olivaceus*, *P. alpinus* x *P. crispus*), abundant between Llanybydder and Cenarth, otherwise unknown south of Cumbria. Neither parent occurs in the Teifi watershed.

The tributaries of the Teifi are extremely varied in geology and vegetation. The Egnant, Mwyro and Groes, like the Teifi's own headwaters, are acidic and dominated by bryophytes, whilst the Dulas is slower-flowing, with much Broad-leaved Pondweed and Stream Water-crowfoot. The Grannell and Cletwr make a particularly interesting comparison. The headwaters of the former, with a substrate of boulders and large stones, are dominated by bryophytes, but further downstream the substrate changes to shingle and fine gravel, with fewer bryophytes and increasingly dominant higher plants such as Stream Water-crowfoot. This is the typical sequence. The Cletwr, however, rather like the Teifi itself, reverses this sequence. The upper

---

[38]N. T. H. Holmes, *Typing British Rivers according to their Flora* (Focus on Conservation, 4: Nature Conservancy Council, 1983). The writer is indebted to Dr Holmes who kindly supplied much additional information and many ideas.

reaches have a fine substrate of clays and silt with few bryophytes and abundant Stream Water-crowfoot and Alternate Water-milfoil, while the lower reaches have a substrate of boulders and shingle with dominant bryophytes.

The Rheidol, rising at 650 m, is very fast-flowing on rocky substrates, largely through deep gorges, for the upper half of its length. The conditions are very oligotrophic, with many bryophytes and few higher plants. Damming of the river and diversion of much of its flow for hydroelectric purposes have completely altered the ecology between Nant-y-moch and Aber-ffrwd, below which there is shingle and silt substrate along the alluvial plain. In these lower reaches there is a moderately rich flora with such species as Alternate Water-milfoil, Intermediate Water-starwort, Broad-leaved Pondweed and Pond Water-crowfoot (*Ranunculus peltatus*). Pond Water-crowfoot, which tolerates very unstable substrates and can even behave as an annual when winter floods destroy the colonies, is in marked contrast to the Stream Water-crowfoot of the Teifi and Ystwyth which also grows in fast water but requires a more stable substrate.

The Rheidol and the Ystwyth have both suffered from heavy metal pollution from lead-mines in their upper reaches, and much work has been done, especially on the Rheidol, to discover the nature of the pollution and to chart and hasten the river's recovery.[39] The Rheidol, rising at such an altitude in an area of high rainfall, was one of the fastest-flowing rivers in Britain and this in itself will have restricted the flora, but the combination of flow-regulation and pollution has now obscured the true picture. The Ystwyth has suffered worse pollution than the Rheidol and is recovering more slowly. Until recently there were few if any higher plants in the main river. Bryophytes dominate the upper reaches, and for much of its length, especially for several. kilometres above Llanafan Bridge and similarly above Llanilar, the river flows over unstable alluvial shingle. Higher plants are significant only in the lower reaches where Stream Water-crowfoot is rapidly spreading as the pollution decreases.

Standing waters

There are two natural, upland lakes on the Mynydd Bach, Llyn Eiddwen and Llyn Fanod, and a score further inland stretching from the pool on Moel y Llyn to Llyn Berwyn. The great majority of lakes and pools in the County, though, are reservoirs constructed in connection with lead-mining, and most have developed a flora virtually indistinguishable from that of most of the natural lakes. Several, however, contain sufficient quantities of toxic metals to prevent any aquatic vegetation developing, for example Bwlch Gwyn Reservoir (SN 741 790) at Ystumtuen. The very large recent reservoirs, Llyn Brianne and Nant-y-moch Reservoir, have yet to acquire a distinctive flora.[40]

[39]L. Newton, 'Pollution of the rivers of West Wales by lead and zinc mine effluent', *Annals of Applied Biology*, 31 (1944), 1–11; idem, 'Pollution problems of the River Rheidol, Cardiganshire', *Trans. Botanical Soc. of Edinburgh*, 38 (1959),141–50; and H. Jones and W. R. Howells, 'Recovery of the River Rheidol', *Effluent and Water Treatment J.*, 9 (1969), 695–710.

[40]B. Seddon, 'Aquatic plants of Welsh Lakes', *Nature in Wales*, 9 (1964), 3–8; idem, '"Operation Wellington": some results of a lake flora survey of Wales', *Botanical Soc. British Isles: Welsh Region Bulletin*, I (1964), 3–6; and idem, 'Aquatic macrophytes as limnological indicators', *Freshwater Biology*, 2 (1972), 107–30.

The most nutrient-poor and dystrophic of the unpolluted water bodies are the numerous very acid peaty pools of the upland mires, containing Bog Mosses (*Sphagnum* spp.), Bog Pondweed (*Potamogeton polygonifolius*), Common Cottongrass (*Eriophorum angustifolium*), Bulbous Rush (*Juncus bulbosus*), Bogbean (*Menyanthes trifoliata*) and little else. Lesser Bladderwort (*Utricularia minor*) occurs in a few of these pools but has decreased in recent decades for unknown reasons.

The majority of the larger water bodies in the uplands are oligotrophic, slightly more nutrient-rich and less acidic. Natural deep but artificially enlarged lakes such as Llyn Llygad Rheidol (SN 792 877) or Llyn Penrhaiadr (SN 752 932) have Shoreweed (*Littorella uniflora*), Floating Bur-reed (*Sparganium angustifolium*) and Quillwort (*Isoetes lacustris*), but few other species. Spring Quillwort (*I. echinospora*) often replaces Quillwort, especially in shallower lakes and in reservoirs such as Llyn Plas-y-mynydd (SN 748 928) and Llyn Pendam (SN 708 838). In the latter, at low water, extensive lawns of Shoreweed and Spring Quillwort can be seen on the mud. Water Lobelia (*Lobelia dortmanna*) occurs in many of these lakes. The entirely natural Llyn Eiddwen (SN 605 670) has an exceptionally rich flora and is one of the most interesting oligotrophic or slightly mesotrophic lakes. Besides Quillwort, Water Lobelia, Bog and Broad-leaved Pondweed (*Potamogeton natans*), Floating Bur-reed, Shoreweed and others, there are such rarities as Floating Water-plantain (*Luronium natans*) and Awlwort (*Subularia aquatica*.) Llyn Gynon (SN 797 647), another natural lake, has the same species, but Quillwort is replaced by Spring Quillwort, there is Yellow Water-lily (*Nuphar lutea*), and a sterile, deep-water form of Pillwort (*Pilularia globulifera*) in its only extant site in Cardiganshire. Llyn Fanod (SN 603 643) has much the same species but, being slightly more mesotrophic, Spring Quillwort replaces Quillwort, and Yellow and White Water-lily (*Nymphaea alba*) both occur as well as Six-stamened Waterwort (*Elatine hexandra*).

There is only one natural lowland lake in Cardiganshire, Maes-llyn Pool (SN 693 628), a 2 ha kettle-hole lake on the margin of Cors Caron. Species with a wide tolerance such as Shoreweed, Yellow Water-lily and Small Pondweed (*Potamogeton berchtoldii*) occur here, and it is the only site in the County for Rigid Hornwort (*Ceratophyllum demersum*) which requires distinctly base-rich conditions, and the lake is the most mesotrophic natural one in the County. The richest of the artificial lowland lakes is the 3 ha Falcondale Pond (SN 570 500), fringed by the only colony in the County of Reed Sweet-grass (*Glyceria maxima*) and containing the equally restricted Blunt-leaved Pondweed (*Potamogeton obtusifolius*), as well as Broad-leaved Pondweed and Spiked Water-milfoil (*Myriophyllum spicatum*).

Although small, some of the ox-bows and backwaters of the Teifi from Tregaron downwards are among the most eutrophic of the permanent natural water bodies in the County, some even containing Water Dock (*Rumex hydrolapathum*). The ox-bows of the Rheidol at Lovesgrove are much more oligotrophic.[41]

Plantations and conifers

Much present woodland in Cardiganshire is plantation, and several estates, for example Gogerddan, had plantations by the mid-eighteenth century. Some 13,000 ha are currently under

[41]H. Jones, 'Studies on the ecology of the River Rheidol, II: an ox-bow of the lower Rheidol', *J. Ecology*, 44 (1956), 12–27.

conifer, as against 4,100 under broadleaved woodlands (almost 7.2 per cent of the County as opposed to just under 2.3 per cent). The earliest well-documented planting operation is that carried out by Thomas Johnes of some five million trees on the Hafod estate between 1782 and 1816,[42] over half being European Larch (*Larix decidua*) and the rest chiefly Oaks (*Quercus* sp.) and Beech (*Fagus sylvatica*), although Norway Spruce (*Picea abies*) and half a dozen more broadleaved species were used in smaller numbers. An estate nursery provided most of the stock. Virtually all that remains are scattered groups of Beeches, notably south-west of Dologau (SN 773 730) and by The Arch (SN 765 756). Although Beech has been planted extensively in other parts of the County, it is presumably nowhere native.[43] By the Teifi at Henllan (SN 360 404) there is a pure, mature Beech wood with characteristically poor ground flora of little but Great Wood-rush (*Luzula sylvatica*). Other mature Beech plantations on more open sites, as on the Nanteos estate, have been overgrazed and have a very poor community of grasses. Many broadleaved woods in the County were planted or replanted in the nineteenth century as mixed woodland, for example Cwm Woods (SN 600 834), Penglais Woods (SN 592 822) and Gwachal Dwmlo (SN 258 430). These woods can be quite rich in ground flora species, and Cwm Woods, for example, has been known for Bird's-nest Orchid (*Neottia nidus-avis*) since 1921. After Beech, the most frequent non-native broadleaved tree is Sycamore (*Acer pseudoplatanus*); it has often been planted, but in innumerable cases it has invaded natural or semi-natural woodland. English Elm (*Ulmus procera*) and Hornbeam (*Carpinus betulus*), neither of them native, are occasionally abundant where they do occur.

Groups and single trees of various conifers have been planted for decoration, chiefly on estates and around the larger country houses and farms. Species of Fir (*Abies* spp.) are the most conspicuous and frequently regenerate from seed. The largest, with trunks *c*.400 cm in girth, perhaps 150–250 years old, are at Nanteos (SN 610 786). There are fine specimens of Douglas Fir (*Pseudotsuga menziesii*) and Norway Spruce on many estates. The older Wellingtonias (*Sequoiadendron giganteum*) and Monkey Puzzles (*Araucaria araucana*) were probably planted about a century ago. Monterey Cypress (*Cupressus macrocarpa*) and Monterey Pine (*Pinus radiata*) occur mostly near the coast, whilst the ubiquitous Scots Pine (*Pinus sylvestris*) and Austrian and Corsican Pine (subspecies of *P. nigra*) have been widely used for decoration as well as timber.

Until the First World War, conifer plantations for timber were mostly of European Larch, Scots and Austrian Pine and Norway Spruce. With the start of operations by the Forestry Commission in 1919, and more recently with the development of private forestry, Japanese Larch (*Larix kaempferi*) has largely replaced European Larch (which is more susceptible to canker and die-back) and has been extensively planted on well-drained soils. With its abundant hybrid (*L.* x *henryana*), it now covers some 1,200 ha while European Larch covers only about 250.[44] Scots Pine (220 ha) and Corsican Pine (170 ha) have been scarcely planted since 1970, but, especially

[42]W. Linnard, 'Thomas Johnes (1748–1816)—pioneer of upland afforestation in Wales', *Forestry*, 44 (1971),135–43; idem, *Ceredigion*, 6 (1970), 309–19; and idem, *Welsh Woods and Forests* (Cardiff, 1982).

[43]W. Linnard, 'Historical distribution of Beech in Wales', *Nature in Wales*, 16 (1979), 154–9.

[44]See H. A. Hyde, *Welsh Timber Trees*, ed. S. G. Harrison (4th edn., Cardiff, 1977) and *Dyfed: Census of Woodlands and Trees, 1978–82* (Forestry Commission, Edinburgh, 1985). I am grateful to Mr A. H. A. Scott, Forestry Commission, Aberystwyth, who kindly made these statistics available to me.

on the exposed high altitude moorlands, Lodge-pole Pine (*Pinus contorta*) now covers 680 ha, virtually all planted since 1950. Norway Spruce (900 ha) is now seldom planted except on the wetter lowland soils, but Sitka Spruce (*Picea sitchensis*) (8,250 ha) is by far the most abundant conifer, and perhaps tree, in the County. It grows well on wet, acid, peaty soils, is very resistant to wind, and has been widely planted on the Cardiganshire uplands since the 1920s. Douglas Fir (620 ha), requiring well-drained soils and susceptible to frosts and wind, is mostly found in more sheltered valleys. Western Hemlock (*Tsuga heterophylla*) is often used for underplanting broad-leaved woodland, as it withstands shade well; it regenerates more abundantly than any other of the planted conifers. Noble Fir (*Abies procera*), Giant Fir (*A. grandis*), Japanese Cedar (*Cryptomeria japonica*) and Lawson Cypress (*Chamaecyparis lawsoniana*) are among the other conifers planted on a smaller scale for timber.

Apart from the first few years when grazing animals are excluded and the light is not yet drastically reduced, the ground flora of these mostly monocultural plantations is monotonous and extremely poor in species, even when compared with Sessile Oak woods on similarly poor soils. Broad Buckler-fern (*Dryopteris austriaca*), however, is often spectacularly abundant. On some damp upland slopes, where light penetrates more effectively as at Hirgoed-ddu (SN 805 835), deep Heather (*Calluna vulgaris*) and Bog Mosses (*Sphagnum* spp.) are dominant, and on drier slopes, where the trees grow poorly or are well-spaced, Bell Heather (*Erica cinerea*), Hard Fern (*Blechnum spicant*) and Wavy Hair-grass (*Deschampsia flexuosa*) may persist.

Conifer plantations, although in themselves poor in species, do sometimes have a long-lasting protective or even enriching effect on natural communities. In steep-sided stream gulleys too difficult to plant, the native woodland has sometimes been left with its ground vegetation intact, often as strips no more than 10–30 m wide. The extreme shelter and dampness of the micro-climate is enhanced by the proximity of the conifer stands and this, together with the absence of grazing, allows many species that have been lost from larger and grazed areas of native woodlands to survive and spread. Outstanding examples are the narrow, rocky stream gorges on the west side of Llyn Brianne, which contain under their original Oak and Birch trees a wealth of locally rare species such as Globeflower (*Trollius europaeus*), Stone Bramble (*Rubus saxatilis*), Oak fern (*Gymnocarpium dryopteris*) and Wilson's Filmy Fern (*Hymenophyllum wilsonii*).

Trees

Some trees are worthy of mention because of their size or historic associations. Many churchyards have Yews (*Taxus baccata*), and the Yew in Strata Florida churchyard, under which Dafydd ap Gwilym is reputed to have been buried in about 1370,[45] is or was the largest in girth. Although only about two-thirds of the trunk remains,[46] when complete the trunk must have been at the very least 750 cm in girth, indicating that it may well have been a sizeable tree in the fourteenth century. The following churchyards also have old Yews or stumps of Yews: Llanfair Clydogau (with a girth of 693 cm), Llangeitho (with girths of 599, 570, 439 and 427 cm), Llanafan, St

---

[45]H. I. Bell and D. Bell, *Dafydd ap Gwilym: Fifty Poems* (London, 1942), 306–9.

[46]Measurements of girth of trees in this section are all taken at 1. 5 m above ground level, or lower down if at any point below 1. 5 m the trunk is narrower.

Peter's at Lampeter (with girths of 500 and 434 cm), Eglwys Newydd (Hafod), Llanfihangel Genau'r-glyn, and Gartheli. While it is impossible accurately to estimate the age of these various trees, a Yew with a girth of 700 cm may be approximately 750 years old. The rate of growth of younger trees is faster. The three largest Yews in Eglwys Newydd (Hafod) churchyard, two of them fused together at the base, are 413, 412 and 410 cm in girth; they must all be the same age and presumably date from the founding of the church here in c. 1620. Certain groups of Yews, such as those on the mound just north-east of Llanfihangel Genau'r-glyn church, may be the fragments of single trees of great age.[47] The recently felled Yew at Gartheli churchyard is only 333 cm in girth, yet must have been already a substantial tree in the late eighteenth century when marriages were celebrated beneath it[48] (if indeed this tree is the same one). The largest Yew outside a churchyard is at Pantybeudy, Llanbadarn Odwyn, with a trunk no less than 549 cm in girth, the field adjoining being called Cae'r Ywen on eighteenth-century estate maps.

The deciduous tree with the largest trunk in Cardiganshire is a now largely dead Sweet Chestnut (*Castanea sativa*), 690 cm in girth, near Dolgwibedyn, Llanafan. No Oak approaches this size, although many large trees remain on the Trawscoed estate. A magnificent Sessile Oak (*Quercus petraea*) on the north bank of the Ystwyth at Trawscoed is 610 cm in girth and another near Dolfor (SN 668 717) attains 500 cm. Many Pedunculate Oaks (*Q. robur*) on this estate are 500–600 cm in girth. As recently as 1946 there was said to be an Oak 966 cm in girth at Trawscoed,[49] which would probably have been at least 350 years old and may well have been there before the first Vaughan arrived about 1200 AD.[50] The oldest of the remaining Trawscoed oaks must be between 200 and 400 years old. The variation in rate of growth from tree to tree is indicated by the fact that, judging from the annual rings of recently felled trees between 100 and 200 years old, Oaks in the County put on, on average, anything from 0.9 to 3 cm of girth annually throughout their lives. Among other notable Oaks in the County, one of the largest is a pollarded Pedunculate Oak, 594 cm in girth, in Llanfair-fawr farmyard, Llanfair Clydogau.

Two of the best remaining preaching Oaks are Sessiles, one at Tanyralltuchaf near Tregaron, 432 cm in girth, under which William Williams of Pantycelyn preached in about 1744,[51] and the other at Llwynrhydowen (SN 444 450), 495 cm in girth, under which David Davis of Castell Hywel is said to have been ordained in 1733.[52]

The oldest Ash (*Fraxinus excelsior*) trees in the County are undoubtedly the enormous coppiced stools, most easily seen on hedgebanks, some of which are over 500 cm in girth and probably several centuries old. One of the largest uncoppiced trees is a relic on the streambank in the plantation by the River Peithyll (SN 623 834), 474 cm in girth, probably some 200 years old and thus nearing the age limit for a maiden Ash.

[47] E. Lees, 'An old Yew Tree', *Gardeners' Chronicle*, 9 (1878), 44.

[48] G. E. Evans, *Cardiganshire* (Aberystwyth, 1903), 231.

[49] H. A. Hyde, *Welsh Timber Trees*, 122.

[50] For discussion of the relation between size and age of Oaks, see M. G. Morris and F. H. Perring (eds.), *The British Oak* (Faringdon, 1974), 355–6, and O. Rackham, *Trees and Woodland in the British Landscape* (London, 1976), 26–9.

[51] D. C. Rees, *Tregaron* (Llandysul, 1936), 46; T. H. Parry-Williams (ed.), *Caniadau Isgarn* (Aberystwyth, 1949), 30; and S. Jones, H. Jones and C. Davies, *Yr Hen Dderwen* (Llandysul, 1976), 12 (and plate facing p. 17).

[52] A. J. Martin, *Hanes Llwynrhydowen* (Llandysul, 1977), 33 (and cf. postcard in National Library of Wales, Acc. No. P. 6998. L. N. Card 389a, c. 1911).

Hedges

Hedges are one of the most conspicuous features of the vegetation of the County and are of considerable botanical and historical interest. Much of Cardiganshire was probably well hedged in the Middle Ages, although the earliest evidence in most cases for the amount of hedging (as distinct from enclosure by simple embankment) is the estate maps of the late eighteenth century. These show that 200 years ago lowland Cardiganshire had something like two-thirds of its present hedging.

Almost all, with the exception of some of the most recent hedges, are found on banks which vary from massive ancient parish or other boundaries to low, narrow, baulk-like banks seemingly caused largely by ploughing. Almost all the older hedges and some of the younger show signs of having been laid or pleached, and on many farms this is still carried out.[53] Hawthorn (*Crataegus monogyna*) is the dominant and still widely used hedge-forming shrub. Hawthorn hedges in the County planted from non-indigenous stock can often readily be noticed in spring when they leaf and flower several weeks earlier than the local bushes. There were probably no local nurseries providing quick-sets for hedges until after 1800, and until recent decades hedges were mostly planted from locally collected saplings or cuttings. Mixed hedges, without any clearly dominant species, are common. In today's lowlands, the commonest dominants and co-dominants in the hedges are very much the same as they were nearly two centuries ago:[54] Hawthorn, Blackthorn (*Prunus spinosa*), Grey Willow (*Salix cinerea*), Hawthorn and Blackthorn, Hawthorn and Hazel (*Corylus avellana*), Hawthorn and Sessile Oak (*Quercus petraea*), and Hazel and Sessile Oak. Many hedges in the coastal belt are of Gorse (*Ulex europaeus*). In the uplands, and perhaps most conspicuously between the Mynydd Bach and Tregaron and between Lampeter and Tregaron, hedges of mixed Hawthorn and Beech (*Fagus sylvatica*) are common, the former making the stockproof barrier and the latter providing a greater degree of shelter.[55]

In some parts of Britain the age of a hedge appears to be deducible by counting the number of shrub species in a given length, and interpreting the result with reference to the composition of hedges of known age in the same area.[56] In general such a hedge appears to acquire additional shrub species, by natural colonization, at a rate of about one a century, so that a Hawthorn hedge planted *c.* 1680 will be found to contain on average an extra two species in a 30 m length by 1980. The equation that seems widely applicable in southern England is: age in years = (number of species × 110) − 30. In Cardiganshire, however, the number of species as often as not appears to bear no relation to the age of the hedge. For example, accumulating the fairly comparable results from a survey of a total of 272 hedges in three areas near Llangeitho, the 170 hedges shown on 1791 estate maps (and thus probably at least 200 years old) average 7.4 shrub species per standard 30 m length, while the 102 not shown on the 1791 maps (and thus definitely less than

[53]E. Scourfield, 'Regional variation of hedging styles in Wales', *Folk Life*, 15 (1977), 106–15.
[54]W. Davies, *General View of the Agriculture and Domestic Economy of South Wales* (London, 1815), I, 224–72.
[55]For a description of the planting of such a hedge at Llain in Llanbadarn Odwyn parish, 'tair draenen wen a ffawydden', by Kitchener Davies, see M. I. Davies (ed.), *Gwaith James Kitchener Davies* (Llandysul, 1980), 13–26, and cf. A. O. Chater, 'Perthi'r Llain', *Y Naturiaethwr*, 14 (1985), 2–15.
[56]See E. Pollard, M. D. Hooper and N. W. Moore, *Hedges* (London, 1974).

200 years old) average 7.7 shrub species. The younger hedges are the richer, and furthermore are three or four times as rich as might have been expected if hedge-dating in the conventional way were valid for Cardiganshire. One explanation may be that the later hedges were planted with more species than the earlier ones, or that older hedges were allowed to become overgrown, thereby losing many of their more easily shaded-out species.

Many hedges in Cardiganshire average nine or more species in a standard length. Many of those on ancient boundaries are very rich, though whether this is due to their age or to the width of the banks marking these boundaries is uncertain. In one of the richest in the County, on a massive curved bank bounding former glebe-land near Llanbadarn Odwyn church, is a remarkable total of 21 tree and shrub species in a 120 m length, so mixed that two bushes of the same species are scarcely ever in contact. The average is 13.5 per 30 m length, which might suggest that it is 1,350 years old, but on historical grounds it is unlikely to be more than 600 to 700 years old and may, of course, be much younger.

The practice of leaving standard trees in hedges is widespread, and some of the most attractive are the Beeches south of Bronnant and the Oaks in Dyffryn Aeron. Hedges are the main habitat in the County for seven of the Rose species and most of the thirty-five Bramble species, and their herbaceous vegetation is often very rich. Bluebell (*Hyacinthoides non-scriptus*), Dog's Mercury (*Mercurialis perennis*) and other woodland species are widespread even in hedges less than two centuries old. In late May, the Laburnum (*Laburnum anagyroides*) hedges, most prevalent in the south-west of the county, are a spectacular feature, mostly on high banks and regularly coppiced.[57]

Banks

Field and roadside banks are even more abundant than hedges and many are probably older. They vary from low baulks to elaborate structures 2 m or more in height, built up of stones, turves and earth in the manner of Pembrokeshire banks, and are important plant habitats. For many species such as Black Spleenwort (*Asplenium adiantum-nigrum*), Sheep's-bit (*Jasione montana*) and Pennywort (*Umbilicus rupestris*), whose natural habitat is dry, often rocky coastal slopes or screes and outcrops, banks are an acceptable substitute and provide their most abundant habitats in the County. The high, well-vegetated and not particularly dry banks of the coastal tract from New Quay to Gwbert are the chief habitat in the County for a rather different group of plants, including Early-purple Orchid (*Orchis mascula*) and Field Scabious (*Knautia arvensis*), in other counties characteristic of somewhat calcareous pastures. In many places, banks are a refuge for species that have been lost from the adjacent fields by agricultural improvement. On Gernos Mountain (SN 355 465) the banks have a heathy vegetation with Bilberry (*Vaccinium myrtillus*), Bell Heather (*Erica cinerea*), Heath Bedstraw (*Galium saxatile*), Wavy Hair-grass (*Deschampsia flexuosa*) and many others, the only indication of the extensive heath that once covered the

---

[57]W. M. Condry, *The Natural History of Wales*, 167. The reasons for the abundance of these laburnum hedges and the dates when most of them were planted are unknown.

mountain. Banks may thus act as reservoirs from which native species may colonize surrounding ground when fields are abandoned.

Banks contribute greatly to the diversity of species even in semi-natural sites, particularly in wet areas where a dry bank can add a whole range of extra habitats and species. The two sides of a bank can be ecologically very different, not only because of variations of sun and shade, but because on road margins one side may be regularly cut and the other allowed to grow unchecked. The change from manual to mechanical cutting in recent years has had a striking effect on their flora. Frequent close shaving often results in bare patches, and this opens up the bank for colonization by such species as Cat's Ear (*Hypochaeris radicata*), Sheep's-bit and English Stonecrop (*Sedum anglicum*). Perhaps for similar reasons, Shining Crane's-bill (*Geranium lucidum*), a rare plant in Cardiganshire fifty years ago,[58] has spread rapidly in recent decades along roadside banks and is now very abundant.

As elsewhere in Britain the increasing frequency of road salting is probably the cause of the spread of coastal Common Scurvygrass (*Cochlearia officinalis*) along inland roadside banks.[59] It began to appear there in Cardiganshire a decade or more ago and is now very conspicuous when in flower in April between Blaen-porth and Blaenannerch along the A487.

Arable weeds

Predominantly poor, acidic soils, modern farming practices and the comparatively small area devoted to arable all mean that the arable weed flora is generally rather uniform and poor throughout the County. The main weed association, reduced to just a few of its constituent species in most parts of Cardiganshire, is seen at its best in the coastal Barley fields between Aber-porth and Gwbert, where the following are found: Black-bindweed (*Polygonum convolvulus*), Redshank (*P. persicaria*), Knotgrass (*P. aviculare*), Field Woundwort (*Stachys arvensis*), Sun Spurge (*Euphorbia helioscopia*), Petty Spurge (*E. peplus*), Scarlet Pimpernel (*Anagallis arvensis*), Fat Hen (*Chenopodium album*), Chickweed (*Stellaria media*), Corn Marigold (*Chrysanthemum segetum*), Field Pansy (*Viola arvensis*), Changing Forget-me-not (*Myosotis discolor*), Field Forget-me-not (*M. arvensis*), Pineappleweed (*Matricaria matricarioides*), Prickly Sow-thistle (*Sonchus asper*), Perennial Sow-thistle (*S. arvensis*), Lesser Snapdragon (*Misopates orontium*), Sharp-leaved Fluellen (*Kickxia elatine*), Red Dead-nettle (*Lamium purpureum*), Corn Spurrey (*Spergula arvensis*), Shepherd's Purse (*Capsella bursa-pastoris*), Tall Ramping-fumitory (*Fumaria bastardii*), Common Ramping-fumitory (*F. muralis* subsp. *boraei*) and Common Fumitory (*F. officinalis*). Fifty and more years ago many other weed species were common here, and in 1979–80 the excavation of a trench at Aber-porth[60] brought up dormant seeds on the site of a field last ploughed in 1936 and since under pasture. Twenty-one species germinated and flowered as follows: Black-bindweed, Redshank, Knotgrass,

[58] J. H. Salter, *Flowering Plants and Ferns*, 29.

[59] N. E. Scott and A. W. Davison, 'De-icing salt and the invasion of road verges by maritime plants', *Watsonia*, 14 (1982), 41–52.

[60] A. O. Chater, 'Floristic archaeology at RAE Aberporth', *Sanctuary: Conservation Bulletin MOD*, 9 (1982), 11–13, and G. Ellis, 'Decreasing and endangered agricultural Weeds in Wales', *Aus Liebe der Natur*, 3 (1983), 55–60.

Sun Spurge, Scarlet Pimpernel, Fat Hen, Chickweed, Corn Marigold, Corn Spurrey, Tall Ramping-fumitory, Parsley-piert (*Aphanes arvensis*), Wood Bitter-cress (*Cardamine flexuosa*), Toad Rush (*Juncus bufonius*), Long-headed Poppy (*Papaver dubium*), Pale Persicaria (*Polygonum lapathifolium*), Groundsel (*Senecio vulgaris*), Wood Groundsel (*S. sylvaticus*), Wild Radish (*Raphanus raphanistrum*), Dwarf Spurge (*Euphorbia exigua*), Annual Knawel (*Scleranthus annuus*), and Field Madder (*Sherardia arvensis*). The last three are now virtually extinct as arable weeds in Cardiganshire and even such species as Long-headed Poppy and Wild Radish are fast disappearing. Ninety years ago additional weed species were present in these same fields at Aber-porth, including Small-flowered Buttercup (*Ranunculus parviflorus*), Field Pepperwort (*Lepidium campestre*) and Prickly Poppy (*Papaver argemone*). All three are now probably extinct in the County. The resurrection of arable weeds from disused fields can also be seen around the edges of the Pen-parc sand quarries, where species such as Annual Knawel and Wild Radish appear in abundance when the topsoil is removed. Corn Marigold, which in the nineteenth and earlier twentieth century grew profusely in Cardiganshire,[61] is still an occasionally abundant arable weed and may be increasing.

Lead-mines

Mining activity has simultaneously impoverished and enriched the flora.[62] Heavy metal residues can be so toxic in high concentrations as to prevent any higher plants growing on the spoil heaps. This lack of vegetation cover allows the fine-particled heaps to become more eroded by wind and rain, and to combat the resulting pollution of the surroundings a number of heaps have been reclaimed by flattening and covering them with topsoil and seeding, as at the west end of Cwmsymlog mine (SN 697 837). Slightly less toxic waste is frequently colonized by resistant races of Common Bent (*Agrostis capillaris*)[63] and a very few other species, notably resistant races of Sea Campion (*Silene vulgaris* subsp. *maritima*), which can even be seen in many church and chapel graveyards, such as at Ysbyty Cynfyn church (SN 752 791), Trisant chapel (SN 716 757), and Jezreel chapel, Goginan (SN 690 813), where spoil from Sea Campion-colonized mines has been used to cover graves. Alpine Penny-cress (*Thlaspi alpestre*) and Spring Sandwort (*Minuartia verna*),

[61] J. A. Webb, 'Plant records', *Proc. Swansea Scientific and Field Naturalists' Soc.*, 2 (1941), 128–30, and W. H. Purchas, 'Plants noticed in the immediate neighbourhood of Aberystwith: Septr. and October 1848' (Royal Botanic Gardens, Kew, MS).

[62] D. A. Ratcliffe, 'Ecological effects of mineral exploitation in the United Kingdom and their significance to nature conservation', *Proc. Royal Society of London*, 339A (1974), 355–72; M. S. Johnson, 'Land reclamation and the botanical significance of some former mining and manufacturing sites in Britain', *Environmental Conservation*, 5 (1978), 223–8, and M. S. Johnson, P. D. Putwain and R. J. Holliday, 'Wildlife conservation value of derelict metalliferous mine workings in Wales', *Biological Conservation*, 14 (1978), 131–48. Some of the Cardiganshire records in this last paper require confirmation.

[63] A. D. Bradshaw, 'Populations of *Agrostis tenuis* resistant to lead and zinc poisoning', *Nature*, 169 (1952), 1098; A. J. M. Baker, 'Ecophysiological aspects of zinc tolerance in *Silene maritima* With.', *New Phyt.*, 80 (1978), 635–42; and A. J. M. Baker and D. H. Dalby, 'Morphological variation between isolated populations of *Silene maritima* With. in the British Isles with particular reference to inland populations on metalliferous soils', *New Phyt.*, 84 (1980), 123–38.

two other resistant species, occasionally appear on mine waste. Neither occurs in unpolluted sites in the County but Alpine Penny-cress has grown in several places on the banks of the Ystwyth where the soil is so heavily contaminated that few other species are able to compete. It has recently disappeared from the lower reaches as the pollution has decreased, but it is still abundant in places between Llanilar and Llanafan Bridge.

Mining also often brings minerals to the surface which are beneficial to plants, as at Cwmsymlog where colonies of Fairy Flax (*Linum catharticum*) and Moonwort (*Botrychium lunaria*), the latter known only in four other sites in the County, are found. Forked Spleenwort (*Asplenium septentrionale*) is almost exclusively confined in Cardiganshire to lead-mines where it occurs both on worked rock surfaces and on walls and buildings.

Graveyards

The three hundred or so graveyards in the County have a disproportionately rich flora for their size.[64] Unaffected by modern agricultural practices, often enclosed from permanent pasture in the last century and managed only by traditional methods of cutting, in many parishes they are unique relics of the former vegetation. Examples are Gwenlli (SN 392 535), Gartheli (SN 586 567), Cribyn (SN 521 514) and Capel Rhiwbwys, Llanrhystud (SN 546 693), where parts of the nineteenth-century pasture are as yet undisturbed even by burials. These graveyards, enclosed wholly or in part comparatively recently, are usually the most interesting, the older ones having been disturbed repeatedly by burials so that although often rich in species, their grassland structure is much disturbed. Graveyards often contain a large number of species, St Peter's at Lampeter having the most with 151, and even one so small as the half acre at Henllan (SN 354 402) having 124. It may be that the enrichment of the soil by burials is one reason why certain calcicoles such as Hedge-bedstraw (*Galium mollugo*), Yellow Oat-grass (*Trisetum flavescens*) and Quaking Grass (*Briza media*) have the majority of their Cardiganshire sites in graveyards, but since such species often occur where burials have not yet taken place, it may equally be that they are relics of permanent pasture and were formerly more widespread throughout Cardiganshire.

Of the 1,500 or so plants of the somewhat calcicolous Green-winged Orchid (*Orchis morio*) that flower in Cardiganshire in a good year, over 90 per cent are shared between the chapel cemetery at Aber-porth (SN 266 506) and Llangeitho churchyard (SN 621 601). The only extant sites for Common Calamint (*Calamintha sylvatica* subsp. *ascendens*) and Tor-grass (*Brachypodium pinnatum*) are Llangoedmor (SN 199 458) where it has been known since 1907,[65] and Lampeter churchyards respectively. Both species are calcicoles.

Several naturalized species, nowhere native in Cardiganshire, are restricted to churchyards, notably Broad-leaved Meadow-grass (*Poa chaixii*), abundant at Maestir (SN 554 493) and Llanfihangel Ystrad (SN 524 562), White Wood-rush (*Luzula luzuloides*) at Maestir, and Summer

[64]A. O. Chater, 'Life in the graveyard', *Nat.World*, 6 (1982), 17–19; idem, 'God's acre: the conservation of consecrated vegetation', *Churchscape: Annual Review of the Council for the Care of Churches*, 3 (1984), 21–7; and idem, 'The flora of Ceredigion churchyards', *Botanical Soc. British Isles: Welsh Bulletin*, 43 (1986), 24–31.

[65]J. H. Salter, *Natural History Diaries* (entry for 15 August 1907).

Snowflake (*Leucojum aestivum*), known at Llanychaearn (SN 585 786) since 1906.[66] Virtually all the many sites where Dropwort (*Filipendula vulgaris*) and Star-of-Bethlehem (*Ornithogalum umbellatum*) are naturalized occur in graveyards. Few Cardiganshire graveyards have been destroyed —like St Michael's, Aberystwyth, and the old part of Llanbadarn Fawr churchyard—by clearance schemes, and they remain among the most botanically rewarding sites in the County.

Aliens

Among the numerous aliens established in the County are some which reflect patterns of particular interest. The development of the lime industry in the early nineteenth century led both to the building of limekilns along the coast and the spreading of lime on fields throughout the County.[67] Imported limestone came mostly from Pembrokeshire and the Gower, and several species probably never native to Cardiganshire, including Bristly Oxtongue (*Picris echioides*) and Teasel (*Dipsacus fullonum*), still confined to the neighbourhood of limekilns, presumably arrived in this way. Other species such as Hedge-bedstraw (*Galium mollugo*) and Yellow Oat-grass (*Trisetum flavescens*) also occur in their vicinity but whether native or alien is uncertain. The effect of deliberate liming on the semi-natural grassland vegetation of the County has been scarcely studied.

The coming of the railways in the 1860s opened up linear corridors of open habitat along which species could spread. The well-known railway alien, Oxford Ragwort (*Senecio squalidus*), was first seen at Cardigan in 1917, twenty-one years after the arrival of the railway there,[68] and in the north of the County at Capel Bangor station in 1925.[69] It is still confined to the immediate vicinity of the former and present railway system. Spear-leaved Willowherb (*Epilobium lanceolatum*) and Narrow-leaved Meadow-grass (*Poa angustifolia*) entered Cardiganshire along the railway via Glandyfi twenty-five or thirty years ago,[70] and Rat's-tail Fescue (*Vulpia myuros*) first appeared, at Aberystwyth, in 1956 before spreading via Lampeter along the line to Aberaeron prior to its closure in 1965.

Sawmills are another frequent source of introductions and American Willowherb (*Epilobium ciliatum*), now common all over the County, was first recorded in 1962 at the Llanilar woodyard. Along forest and farm tracks, as well as along roadsides, Slender Rush (*Juncus tenuis*), another native of North America, first found in Wales near Portmadoc in 1890,[71] and formerly one of the most abundant aliens, has decreased markedly for unknown reasons in recent years. New Zealand Willowherb (*Epilobium brunnescens*), first found in Wales in Snowdonia in 1930,[72] seems to have reached Cwm Llyfnant in Cardiganshire by 1955 by spreading south through Merioneth. Favouring damp, open, shaly habitats, it spreads on newly constructed roads, especially in the uplands where it can be seen in great abundance around the Nant-y-moch and Llyn Brianne

[66] J. H. Salter, *Natural History Diaries* (entry for 26 Feb. 1906).
[67] R. Lewis, 'Lime kilns of Ceredigion', *Rural Wales*, 50 (1984) 31–2.
[68] D. H. Kent, '*Senecio squalidus* L. in the British Isles—7 Wales', *Nature in Wales*, 8 (1963), 175–8.
[69] J. H. Salter, *Flowering Plants and Ferns*, 82.
[70] P. M. Benoit, 'Field notes', *Nature in Wales*, 6 (1960), 91–2 and 8 (1962), 72.
[71] J. H. Salter, *Flowering Plants and Ferns*, 145.
[72] S. G. Harrison, 'A New Zealand Willow-herb in Wales', *Nature in Wales*, 11 (1968), 74–8.

dams, and occurs also by undisturbed rocky streams where flood debris and natural erosion keep the ground open.

Decorative planting has often led to various species becoming extensively naturalized. Rhododendron (*Rhododendron ponticum*) is now so widespread in woodland that it has often completely shaded out the native ground flora. Of two Iberian species, Spanish Gorse (*Genista hispanica* subsp. *occidentalis*), perhaps originally planted in the 1890s, is abundant on the south-west slope of Constitution Hill, Aberystwyth, and Hairy-podded Broom (*Cytisus striatus*), planted in about 1970, is now abundant on the slope above the A487 between Aberystwyth and Penparcau.[73] Tree lupin (*Lupinus arboreus*), a native of North America, was planted at some unknown date on Tywyn Warren, Gwbert, and is now abundant there.

Relationships of the Cardiganshire flora

Cardiganshire has approximately 812 native species and subspecies of vascular plants and 265 naturalized aliens, as well as perhaps 50 occasionally occurring casuals, not counting the 120 or so microspecies or apomicts in Hawkweeds (*Hieracium* spp.), Brambles (*Rubus* spp.) and Dandelions (*Taraxacum* spp.), and ranks eighth in richness among the thirteen former counties of Wales.[74] Absence of variety as regards soil and geological formation[75] and of naturally occurring strongly calcareous soils are certainly factors which explain the absence of many species including some calcicoles, although a surprising number of these are found in small quantities on the coast and on certain rock outcrops and in churchyards. Climate and geographical factors must also account for the absence of many other species.

Several attempts have been made to assign species in the British and Irish flora to geographical elements characterized by their world distributions. R. G. Ellis, following J. R. Matthews, classified the Welsh flowering plants on this basis and, although Matthews's system is necessarily crude and many of its details misleading, some useful general observations can be made by applying it.[76] Table 3 shows the Cardiganshire flora analysed according to this system, with the figures for ferns added.

Three widespread, general elements need not detain us here, their importance for Cardiganshire being undifferentiated from the rest of the British Isles—the General Northern Element with species common to temperate Europe, Asia and North America, including cosmopolitan species; the Eurasian Element with species widespread in Europe and at least in west or south-west Asia; and the General European Element with species widespread in Europe and sometimes also in North America but not in Asia. The Endemic Elements are similarly not differentiated in any particular way in Cardiganshire, and the North American Element with species occurring in western Britain, Ireland and North America, is not represented at all.

[73] A. O. Chater, 'Genista hispanica and Cytisus striatus naturalised in Ceredigion', *Nature in Wales*, 16 (1978), 56–7.

[74] R. G. Ellis, *Flowering Plants of Wales*, 9.

[75] J. H. Salter, *Flowering Plants and Ferns*, vi.

[76] R. G. Ellis, *Flowering Plants of Wales*, 18–32, 294–5; J. R. Matthews, *Origin and Distribution of the British Flora* (London, 1955); and D. A. Webb, 'The Flora of Ireland in its European context', *J. Life Sciences: Royal Dublin Society*, 4 (1983), 143–60.

TABLE 3: Native species and subspecies of vascular plants, excluding *Rubus*, *Taraxacum* and *Hieracium*.

Element	Britain & Ireland	Wales	Wales as % of Britain & Ireland	Cardiganshire	Cardiganshire as % of Wales	Cardiganshire as % of Britain & Ireland
Alpine	21	11	52	2	18	10
Arctic–Alpine	84	29	35	7	24	8
Arctic–Subarctic	33	6	18	1	16	3
Continental	71	57	80	23	40	32
Continental Northern	92	88	96	41	47	45
Continental Southern	116	98	84	41	42	35
Eurasian	460	403	88	295	73	64
Endemic (Britain & Ireland)	27	12	44	4	33	15
Endemic (Wales)	18	6	33	2	33	11
General European	211	171	81	130	76	62
General Northern or Wide	199	173	87	127	73	64
Mediterranean	36	21	58	6	29	17
North American	6	1	17	0	–	–
Northern Montane	27	17	63	8	47	30
Oceanic Northern	34	31	91	27	87	79
Oceanic Southern	77	63	82	40	63	52
Oceanic West European	104	100	96	58	58	56
Total	1616	1287	80	812	63	50
Alpine + Arctic–Alpine + Arctic–Subarctic	138	46	33	10	22	7
Continental + Continental-Northern + Continental-Southern	297	243	82	105	43	35
Oceanic Northern + Oceanic Southern + Oceanic West European	215	194	90	125	64	58

Of those elements which are worthy of consideration in a Cardiganshire context, the Arctic and Alpine Elements are the most poorly represented, largely due to the absence of high mountains with base-rich rocks. The Alpine Element consists of species occurring in the mountains of west, central or south-eastern Europe, but which are absent from northern Europe; the only species in Cardiganshire is Mossy Saxifrage (*Saxifraga hypnoides*), apart from the anomalous occurrence of Alpine Penny-cress (*Thlaspi alpestre*) on heavily polluted soils. This is only 18 per cent of the Welsh or 10 per cent of the British and Irish Alpine species. The Arctic-Alpine Element consists of species chiefly of the arctic or subarctic which reappear further south, mostly only at relatively high altitude in the mountains of Europe and sometimes Asia and America, and has seven representatives in Cardiganshire, 24 per cent of the Welsh or 8 per cent of the British and Irish Arctic-Alpine species. Dwarf Willow (*Salix herbacea*), Starry Saxifrage (*Saxifraga stellaris*), Cowberry (*Vaccinium vitis-idaea*), Parsley Fern (*Cryptogramma crispa*) and Alpine Clubmoss (*Diphasiastrum alpinum*) are generally confined to high ground over 300 m but Crowberry (*Empetrum nigrum*) occurs on Cors Caron at only 160 m and reaches its westernmost point in Wales on the Llawr-cwrt National Nature Reserve at 200 m. The occurrence of the seventh species, Spring Sandwort (*Minuartia verna*) on polluted mine soils is, like that of Alpine Penny-cress, somewhat anomalous in Cardiganshire. The Arctic-Subarctic Element, species exclusively northern in Europe, is represented in Cardiganshire only by Water Sedge (*Carex aquatilis*), which reaches its absolute southern limit just south of Cardiganshire at the Talley lakes in Carmarthenshire.

The Northern Montane Element is a less extreme form of the Arctic-Alpine Element and consists of species of northern Europe, which reappear in the mountains of central and southern Europe but which are usually absent from the intervening low-lying tracts. It is better represented in Cardiganshire, with eight species, including Lesser Twayblade (*Listera cordata*), Stone Bramble (*Rubus saxatilis*) and Globe-flower (*Trollius europaeus*), amounting to 47 per cent of the Welsh and 30 per cent of the British and Irish totals for this element.

The three Continental Elements are somewhat better represented but their showing is still poor in relation to the British Isles as a whole. The Continental Element consists of species characteristic of central Europe, frequently extending eastwards into Asia, but which thin out westwards as they favour cold winters, hot summers and a relatively high moisture deficit. In Wales it is only in the east that such conditions occur, but some of its species which reach Cardiganshire, such as Marsh Helleborine (*Epipactis palustris*) and Chaffweed (*Anagallis minima*), grow in wet, more or less coastal habitats, or, like Burnet Rose (*Rosa pimpinellifolia*) and Ploughman's Spikenard (*Inula conyza*), are characteristic of dry, sandy, often open habitats. This element also includes the all-important Oaks and other woodland species such as Yellow Archangel (*Lamiastrum galeobdolon*) and Wood Speedwell (*Veronica montana*). The twenty-three Cardiganshire species comprise 40 per cent of the Welsh and 32 per cent of the British and Irish total. Of the Continental Northern Element, consisting of species whose main distribution in Europe is central and northern but which die out or occur only in the mountains in southern Europe, Cardiganshire's forty-one species comprise 47 per cent of the Welsh and 45 per cent of the British and Irish totals and include many mire and aquatic species such as all three Cottongrasses (*Eriophorum* spp.) and Shoreweed (*Littorella uniflora*). Cardiganshire's forty-one species of the Continental Southern Element, which consists of species chiefly of central and southern Europe, thinning out northwards and often extending into north Africa and south-west Asia, include such familiar plants as Honeysuckle (*Lonicera periclymenum*), Alexanders (*Smyrnium olusatrum*) and Yellow-horned Poppy (*Glaucium flavum*), and comprise 42 per cent of the Welsh and 35 per cent of the British and Irish totals.

The Mediterranean Element, consisting of species whose chief centre of distribution is in the Mediterranean region, often extending up through western France, is proportionately much less well represented in Cardiganshire than in Wales as a whole, with only six species, 29 per cent of the Welsh and 17 per cent of the British and Irish species. All are coastal, such as the Tree Mallow (*Lavatera arborea*), which reaches its northern limit at the northern tip of Ireland and on the west coast of southern Scotland.

The Oceanic Elements are the best represented in Cardiganshire, reflecting the general oceanity of the climate's mild winters and cool summers, high rainfall and low moisture deficit. The total percentages in Cardiganshire of the Oceanic, the Continental and the Arctic and Alpine Elements are 64 per cent, 43 per cent and 22 per cent of the Welsh, and 58 per cent, 35 per cent and 7 per cent of the British and Irish species respectively, showing clearly the relative significance of the Oceanic in the County. The Oceanic Northern Element consists of species characteristic of north-west Europe, sometimes also occurring in eastern North America, and Cardiganshire's twenty-seven species comprise 87 per cent of the Welsh and 79 per cent of the British and Irish, the highest percentages of any element. It includes coastal species such as Sea Purslane (*Honkenya peploides*), and species characteristic of the north-west European mires such as Bog Asphodel (*Narthecium ossifragum*) and Bog Myrtle (*Myrica gale*). The Oceanic Southern Element consisting of species characteristic of south-western Europe is represented by forty species in Cardiganshire, which comprise 63 per cent of the Welsh and 52 per cent of the British and Irish. Most, such as Wild Madder (*Rubia peregrina*) and Ivy Broomrape (*Orobanche hederae*), are predominantly coastal in Cardiganshire, but the few inland species include such abundant plants as Pennywort (*Umbilicus rupestris*), Bog Pimpernel (*Anagallis tenella*) and Holly (*Ilex aquifolium*). The Oceanic West European Element, its species confined to western Europe, neither particularly northern nor southern nor mediterranean, is the element most favoured by an oceanic climate. It is proportionately less well represented than the Oceanic Northern Element, but has a much greater number of species. The fifty-eight in Cardiganshire comprise 58 per cent of the Welsh and 56 per cent of the British and Irish. Some of these, such as Wavy St John's-wort (*Hypericum undulatum*), Ivy-leaved Bellflower (*Wahlenbergia hederacea*), Wood Bitter-vetch (*Vicia orobus*), Whorled Caraway (*Carum verticillatum*) and Spring Squill (*Scilla verna*) are probably as well represented in Cardiganshire as anywhere in Britain.

Two species reach their southern limit in Britain and Ireland in Cardiganshire, Lesser Clubmoss (*Selaginella selaginoides*) by Llyn Brianne, a constituent of the General Northern Element, and Awlwort (*Subularia aquatica*) at Llyn Fanod, a constituent of the Northern Montane Element. The Arctic Alpine Starry Saxifrage (*Saxifraga stellaris*) has its southernmost British sites on Plynlimon and in the Rheidol gorge. It is unclear why these species do not occur in the mountains of south Wales since both are widespread in the mountains of continental Europe much further south. If the early nineteenth-century record of Oysterplant (*Mertensia maritima*) near Borth is correct,[77] this Arctic-Subarctic species once reached its southern limit in the County. Another

[77]T. O. Morgan, *New Guide to Aberystwith*, 149.

plant of the shingle beaches, Purple Spurge (*Euphorbia peplis*), a member of the Mediterranean Element, once reached its northern limit in the County and was described as growing 'in great plenty on ye shore at Aberystwyth' in 1731, but it was last recorded about 1804.[78] Bastard Balm (*Melittis melissophyllum*), a member of the Continental Southern Element not seen in Cardiganshire for thirty years, once had its northern limit in Allt Hoffnant near Llangrannog. Cornish Moneywort (*Sibthorpia europaea*), an Oceanic West European species, attains its northernmost site in Britain at Bangor Teifi.

Two well-known species have been described as new to science from Cardiganshire, both belonging to the Oceanic West European Element. Rock Stonecrop (*Sedum forsteranum*) was described by Smith in 1808 from material collected by Forster in 1805 'on a rock not far from the fall of the Rhydol near the Devil's bridge'[79] where it still grows. Northern Marsh-orchid (*Dactylorhiza majalis* subsp. *purpurella*) was described under the name *Orchis purpurella* by the Stephensons in 1920 from specimens collected on the Cwm estate near Llangorwen.[80] It is a characteristic species of the *rhosydd* and of certain flushes on the boulder clay cliff slopes of the coast. Two Dandelions, *Taraxacum cambricum* and *T. celticum*, were described as recently as 1984, from specimens collected near Llanafan Bridge and in Aber-porth churchyard respectively;[81] the former is believed to be confined to but is fairly widespread in Britain, whilst the latter is apparently confined to central and northern Wales.

There is still a great deal to be learnt about the Cardiganshire flora. That it is worth conserving so that it can be further investigated is clear, whether for species new to science or for distributional patterns which illuminate phytogeographical problems. The County's habitats and plant communities contain examples that have proved worthy of selection as among the best representatives of their kind in Britain, and they contain many features that illustrate the continual interaction between Man and Nature.

[78]G. C. Druce and S. H. Vines, *The Dillenian Herbaria* (Oxford, 1907), lxxv; J. Evans, *Letters Written during a Tour through South Wales* (London, 1804), 338.

[79]E. Forster, 'Botanical notes', British Museum (Natural History), London, MS (notes for July and August 1905); J. E. Smith, *English Botany*, vol.26, t.1802 (1808), which erroneously gives the date as 1806.

[80]T. and T. A. Stephenson, 'A new Marsh Orchis', *J. Botany*, 58 (1920), 164–70.

[81]A. J. Richards and C. C. Haworth, 'Further new species of *Taraxacum* from the British Isles', *Watsonia*, 15 (1984), 85–94.

CHAPTER 5

THE VERTEBRATE ANIMALS OF CARDIGANSHIRE*

William Condry

Mammals

REMOTE from any outcrops of Carboniferous Limestone, Cardiganshire has no caves where the bones of prehistoric animals might have been preserved, so that the only sources of ancient bones are deep peat-beds such as occur near Borth, Tregaron and, on a smaller scale, elsewhere. As this peat is a post-glacial formation, however, it cannot take our enquiry into a remote era of prehistory.

One ancient mammal whose bones have been found in peat is the urus or aurochs (*Bos primigenius*), the remains of which were exposed in 1968 on the shore near Borth from peat-beds which had been subject to marine transgression about 5,000 years ago. A similar discovery reported by Edward Lhuyd in Camden's *Britannia* (1695) was that of a huge aurochs' horn dug out of moorland peat, probably not far from Llanddewi Brefi and kept in the church there. What little is left of it is now in the Welsh Folk Museum at St Fagans. There is much uncertainty about when the aurochs became extinct in Britain but it probably did not survive into the historic period.

Brown bears are believed to have survived in parts of Britain until about the tenth century and, if they were ever widespread in Wales, then the formerly tree-covered Cardiganshire uplands may well have been included in their range; but we have no evidence for this and certainly any references to bears and bearskins in medieval literature should be treated with caution since in the early Middle Ages bearskins were an object of trade. It is known that bears used in medieval bear-baiting in Britain were imported from the Continent. We should likewise be wary of reading too much into the place-name element *arth*, Welsh for 'bear', which could be a corruption or the product of folklore.

A mammal whose history is particularly enigmatic is the beaver. Travelling up the coast to Cardigan in 1188 Giraldus Cambrensis enlivened his *Itinerary through Wales* with a detailed essay

* In gathering information about the County's fauna I am happy to acknowledge the help of the County Archivist, Cardigan Record Office (deer-parks); David Austin, St David's University College, Lampeter (pillow mounds); Dr John Cule (history of the black rat); Revd Canon J. Cunnane (deer-parks); Tony Fox, formerly of UCW Aberystwyth (history of the aurochs); David Gardner, Welsh Water (freshwater fish); Tom McOwat (bats); the late Col. Morrey Salmon (heronries); C. J. Spurgeon, RCAM (pillow mounds); Hywel Roderick (sea birds); and Peter Walters Davies (lake fish). Arthur Chater and Peter Davis read an early draft of the script and made valuable comments.

on the natural history of beavers, a digression which he justified on the grounds that the Teifi was the only river in England and Wales where beavers then survived, but Giraldus nowhere says that he personally saw a beaver. While the survival of a colony of beavers at this date is not impossible, it is conceivable that the Teifi's beavers had vanished long before and that what Giraldus, who admits that part of his information derived from Cicero, learnt at Cardigan was folklore which he adapted to provide a detailed account of the life of the beaver. We remain on uncertain ground with the Laws of Hywel Dda which certainly testify to the value of beaver-skins —120 pence each compared with a mere 8 pence for wolf, fox and other skins—but do not reveal whether the reference is to native beaver skins or to continental imports. Along the upper reaches of the Cledlyn and Grannell in more recent times there was a cottage industry producing beaver fur hats, but they were made from imported fur.[1]

How long the wolf and the wild boar survived in Cardiganshire is not recorded. Both are reckoned to have persisted in densely wooded parts of Britain until as late as the sixteenth century, but Cardiganshire had probably lost much of its remaining tree cover long before, partly through the creation of the great Cistercian sheepwalks and partly as a consequence of early lead-smelting. Similarly, the date of the extinction of the wild cat is impossible to determine because of a possibility of confusing them with feral domestic cats.[2] Loss of continuous woodland cover brought about the demise of the only two species of native deer, the red and the roe, which were probably as abundant here as in other parts of Wales where they are known to have survived into the seventeenth century. The story of domesticated deer in the County is little known. There is a record of a deer-park in the sixteenth century at Plas Ciliau Aeron, presumably what is now called Parc Neuadd which is still partly walled and dotted with ancient oaks, and in 1637 Thomas Bushell, in the terms of his lease of Lodge Park, Tre'r-ddôl, from the Pryses of Gogerddan, had to agree that the Pryses would continue to keep and hunt deer at Lodge Park.[3] Maps also show a deer-park at Llanfair Clydogau in the eighteenth century. Fallow deer is the species most likely to have been kept in these parks.

There were no wild goats in post-glacial Britain, but domesticated goats have often run wild and small herds long persisted on the Welsh uplands and on steep slopes above the sea. None now survive in Cardiganshire but a herd is said to have lived on Plynlimon[4] and according to local report a small group frequented the cliff slopes south of Cwmtudu in the first half of this century. While domesticated sheep practically all belong to modern breeds, there is one semi-wild flock —the small, dark brown Soay or Viking sheep established on Cardigan Island by the West Wales Field Society in 1944 as an exercise in rare breeds conservation. These particular animals derived from Woburn Park, Bedfordshire, and Walcot Hall, Shropshire,[5] but the parent stock had kept its genetic purity through isolation on the Scottish island of Soay since Viking times.

Cardiganshire's common wild mammals are largely those familiar in much of Britain. Four insectivores—hedgehog, mole, common shrew and pygmy shrew—are widespread and

---

[1] C. Matheson, 'Notes on the mammals of Cardiganshire', *Ceredigion*, 4 (1962), 231–43.

[2] J. H. Salter, *Natural History Diaries*, (entry for 12 Oct. 1895) reveals how confusion could arise over the identity of a dead cat which he mistakenly thought to be a wild specimen. MS in NLW.

[3] T. I. Davies, 'The Vale of Aeron in the making', *Ceredigion*, 3 (1958), 194–206; for Lodge Park, see *NLWJ*, 8 (1953–4), 355.

[4] G. K. Whitehead, *The Wild Goats of Great Britain and Ireland* (Newton Abbot, 1972).

[5] C. Lever, *The Naturalised Animals of the British Isles* (London, 1977), 222.

abundant. The hedgehog belongs to woodlands, hedgerows and gardens, chiefly in the lowlands, and is now a frequent road victim. Moles are found in all types of soil containing plenty of earthworms and are therefore usually absent from very peaty ground such as the blanket bogs which cover much of the moorlands. Common and pygmy shrews are found in a wide range of habitats from the coast to high moorland. A third species, the little-known water shrew, is much more local but it may be less restricted to aquatic habitats than its name suggests. It is probably distributed, though very thinly, from near sea-level to well up into the hill country. The water shrew is easily known by its black upper parts, the other two species being brown-backed.

For reasons of conservation the bats of Britain are now better studied than in the past. Eight species have been recorded in Cardiganshire: pipistrelle, whiskered, common longeared, Natterer's, Daubenton's, Brandt's, greater horseshoe and noctule; and there may well be others, such as the lesser horseshoe, serotine, barbastelle and Leisler's.

J. H. Salter, who frequently refers to specimens in the possession of local taxidermists, provides valuable insight into the status of some of the rarer mammals in the late nineteenth and early twentieth centuries. He shows, for example, that the pine marten was certainly present but very rare. In 1893 one or two were received from the Tregaron district, and in 1916 one was sent from Crosswood. So here was an animal which, well known in much of Britain until far into the nineteenth century, had now been brought to the edge of extinction. During this century, with the reduction in the hunting of such predators, the marten should have recovered in Cardiganshire but has not, and there are still only occasional reports of it, mainly from the north of the County. Its most likely haunts are the margins of upland forestry plantations from where it can emerge to hunt for voles and other prey on the open moorlands. Cliffs, gorges, block screes and caves are also likely refuges.

The marten's failure to increase its numbers contrasts markedly with the fortunes of its cousin, the polecat. This is the mammal for which Cardiganshire is most distinguished because, when it had become rare or extinct nearly everywhere else in Britain earlier this century, it survived in quite good numbers here, though why, given that they were even sometimes hunted by 'polecat-hounds' (presumably foxhounds), is still unexplained. The First World War brought an upturn in the numbers of several rare predatory mammals and birds by diverting gamekeepers to other duties, and in the western half of Wales gamekeeping was never resumed on its pre-war scale, in many places dying out completely. The polecat was thereby able to spread from Cardiganshire, recolonizing most of rural Wales and eventually spilling over into the English border counties, and it still remains widespread in Cardiganshire, occupying many habitats. Earlier this century the north Cardiganshire polecat population which, as elsewhere, is normally black-furred, began to produce unique red or yellow forms which eventually spread to south Merioneth.[6] Since the 1950s, however, less has been heard of these varieties.

Four other carnivores—stoat, weasel, badger and fox—seem to be under no immediate threat. Stoats and weasels are now possibly outnumbered by polecats but both are still widespread from the coast to the hills, with stoats apparently more common than weasels. Very occasionally white or partially white stoats are seen in winter. Though very little is known about stoat and weasel numbers, the badger population is easier to measure. It thrives in many lowland woods and also

[6] C. Matheson, 'Notes on the mammals of Cardiganshire', 240.

has large ancestral sets along the slopes above the sea cliffs, especially where there is cover from brambles or bracken. So far, neither the criminal activity of badger-digging nor the official destruction of badgers to prevent bovine tuberculosis has seriously affected the badger population of Cardiganshire. The fox, despite unending persecution from farmers, continues to flourish, though whether it can withstand such a rate of destruction indefinitely is debatable.

The otter could once be seen playing with its young in Aberystwyth harbour and until mid-century seems to have been a resident on streams throughout Cardiganshire, but there must be some concern about its future because in many parts of Britain its numbers have declined drastically in recent years through a combination of hunting, habitat-destruction and water-pollution. Today there are probably fewer otters in Cardiganshire than before 1950. Even so they are surviving better here than in many other districts and are reported as not uncommon on the Teifi, the Ystwyth and the Rheidol. The Teifi is also known, since 1960, as the haunt of another fish-eating predator, the American mink, an escapee from fur farms which has been spreading along many British rivers.[7]

Cardiganshire's marine mammals belong to two quite distinct orders. The seals are members of the *Pinnipedia*, while whales, dolphins and porpoises form the *Cetacea*. Seals often come to land and have a distinctive place among the County's fauna, but the cetaceans are entirely aquatic and are only relevant here because some of them are frequently seen from the shore and occasionally become stranded. The now protected grey seal is not uncommon along the Cardiganshire coast. It breeds locally in small numbers and there are records of up to eighty adults lying together on rocks at low tide. The other British species, the common seal, has never been satisfactorily recorded in Cardiganshire but it might be an overlooked sporadic visitor since it breeds in fair numbers on the east coast of Ireland. The cetacean most likely to be seen from the shore is the bottle-nosed dolphin with its blackish back and a prominent, backward-pointing dorsal fin. The seven cetacean species recorded as stranded on the Cardiganshire coast in the twentieth century are: bottle-nosed dolphin, common dolphin, Risso's dolphin, common porpoise, lesser rorqual, pilot whale and bottle-nosed whale.[8] These days there are growing fears that industrial pollution of the Irish Sea could be adversely affecting dolphins and other animals in Cardigan Bay.

Ever since their introduction, probably very soon after the Norman Conquest, rabbits have been a source of meat and fur in many parts of Britain. Throughout the Middle Ages rabbits were the perquisite of kings, bishops, abbots and lords and were kept in enclosures carefully guarded by warreners, the few rabbits that escaped into the countryside being quickly seized by a hungry peasantry or by predatory animals. It may seem incredible to present-day farmers, accustomed to the rabbit as a major pest, that until well into the nineteenth century it was a carefully husbanded animal which in the wild was rather uncommon.

Several factors explain the increase in feral rabbits which took place during the nineteenth century. Firstly, they could more easily survive on the improved farmlands with their winter vegetable crops and better grasslands; secondly, predatory mammals and birds had been destroyed on a huge scale by gamekeepers, so allowing rabbits to multiply unchecked; thirdly,

---

[7] C. Lever, *The Naturalised Animals of the British Isles*, 137.
[8] C. Matheson, 'Notes on the mammals of Cardiganshire', 242.

the earth banks raised to mark the bounds of newly enclosed fields provided perfect breeding quarters; fourthly, with other sources of meat and fur becoming more generally available, many of the old keepered warrens were neglected, allowing the rabbits to escape; and fifthly, and perhaps most importantly, many farmers introduced rabbits into their fields with the idea of cropping them.

Rabbits have not only entered into rural history but have also an archaeological legacy. As long ago as the Middle Ages the practice was adopted of building mounds, usually in clusters, in which rabbits could burrow more easily and so breed more prolifically than in hard, level ground. Such mounds were still being built well into the nineteenth century though scarcely recorded in literature, and when they finally went out of use their purpose was quickly forgotten. Inevitably, since they so resembled prehistoric burial mounds, they attracted the interest of archaeologists who, ignorant of their true purpose, called them 'pillow mounds', a term still in use and marked on some older maps. Eventually when their true character was revealed most archaeologists lost interest in them. Pillow mounds were widespread in Wales and are best known in the old counties of Montgomery, Radnor, Brecon and Glamorgan. [9] In Cardiganshire they are recorded from only four localities: near Llangrannog (SN 314553), Pen y Bannau hillfort (SN 742669), Cellan (SN 627499), and Llanfair Clydogau (SN 652518). From the last-named site a possible medieval dating has been obtained for one of the mounds. [10]

Very little is known of the pre-twentieth-century history of the rabbit in Cardiganshire but much might be gleaned from estate papers, game books and maps showing sites of warrens—in Welsh, *cwnigaer*, a name clearly connected with 'coney', as the rabbit was first called in English. In the records of the Royal Commission on Ancient and Historic Monuments (Wales) there exists a particularly interesting reference to a warren at Aberystwyth Castle in 1593, which consisted of 'one acre of pasture called the Conygre lying on the north side of the castle of Aberustwith', and in 1748 the site, known today as Castle Point, was named on Lewis Morris's famous map of the Welsh coast as Pen Gwningen. In this connection we may note that Kidwelly Castle, Carmarthenshire, had a field called the *cwnigaer* on its north side. [11] It seems likely that most of the larger estates had warrens though perhaps not as extensive as those at Crosswood. In its report of 1894/5 the Royal Commission on Land in Wales and Monmouthshire quotes Richard Theophilus Evans of Llanfihangel-y-Creuddyn, from whom we learn that the Earl of Lisburne kept over 300 acres 'in this parish' and about '1,000 acres between the parishes of Llanafan and Gwnnws' almost entirely for rabbits. Evans was a neighbouring farmer complaining about the damage rabbits were causing. This large-scale exercise in rabbit farming, which produced up to 15,000 rabbits a year, is reported to have been discontinued *c.*1899. [12] A 1791 map of the Nanteos estate shows an enclosed rabbit warren forming part of intended improvements though the work was never carried out. The rabbits long established in the dunes at Ynys-las could represent descendants from a warren of the Gogerddan estate. Similarly the warren in the dunes at Gwbert was presumably once a guarded possession of some local estate, such as Coedmor or maybe the castle at Cardigan.

[9] C. J. Spurgeon, *RCAM Inventory of the Ancient Monuments in Glamorgan* III, Pt.II (Cardiff, 1982), 312–22.

[10] D. Austin, pers. comm.

[11] A. Price, *Nature in Wales*, 5 (1959), 845.

[12] C. Matheson, 'Notes on the mammals of Cardiganshire', 236.

In the twentieth century the rabbit got completely out of hand and spread widely over woodlands and farmlands, with the exception of the high moors. By mid-century Cardiganshire, along with parts of Carmarthenshire and Pembrokeshire, was one of the worst affected areas of Britain. Some of the coastal farms could almost be described as rabbit farms for there was a large-scale trapping industry, and a comment of the time is particularly revealing: 'When we were concerned with the first attempted large-scale clearance schemes in west Wales from 1946 onwards, we found that many small farmers had received the equivalent of their rent, or more, from the granting of trapping rights. Many of them needed a great deal of convincing that the benefits they would gain from the increased production of rabbit-free land would more than compensate them for their loss of income.'[13] The scene changed abruptly after 1954 with the introduction of myxomatosis which achieved an over 90 per cent kill, and there followed five or six virtually rabbit-free years, after which a slow recovery became evident. Since then local increases have often been kept in check by the illegal reintroduction of myxomatosis. In future, however, the disease is likely to have far less impact because rabbits are beginning to develop a natural resistance and a new population explosion now seems a real possibility.

The history of the common or brown hare has been wholly different. As a native species more at home on open ground than in woodland, though always scarce on high moorland, the hare presumably increased steadily during the long centuries which saw the replacement of tree cover by grassland. If so it was probably a familiar inhabitant of lowland farms by the end of the Middle Ages. At present its numbers seem to have reached a low point and certainly cannot be compared with those of the 1890s on the Crosswood estate where there were occasional annual bags of over 200, as in 1898, when 229 were shot.[14] Such figures, however, indicate the artificially swollen populations of a preserved animal and give no indication of what numbers were like in the wild. Another species, the blue or mountain hare, was introduced into Wales from Scotland in the nineteenth century in the hope of improving sport on the uplands. They were released on several north Welsh moorlands, and a similar but failed experiment took place on Plynlimon.[15]

The triumph of the American grey squirrel over the red squirrel represents a rare event—the apparently complete ousting of a native by an alien species, and several theories have been put forward to explain it, though none so far is universally accepted. This process had its origins between the 1870s and the 1920s when grey squirrels were released at many different sites in England and Wales. They spread out steadily and there was a corresponding sharp fall in red squirrel numbers. In Cardiganshire the native squirrel was abundant until the 1950s when the greys began to invade, but by the 1970s the greys were widespread and common whereas the reds had become hard to find, being only known at Devil's Bridge and a few other places. The total absence of any small animal is impossible to demonstrate but at present it seems doubtful whether there are any red squirrels in the County.

Cardiganshire has nine other rodents, besides squirrels, seven of which are native. Field vole, bank vole and wood mouse are extremely common and are important in the diet of both furred and feathered predators. Field voles are especially significant in this respect because in some years they are very abundant on high moorlands. A species only locally frequent is the water vole,

[13]H. V. Thompson and A. N. Worden, *The Rabbit* (London, 1956), 4.
[14]The Earl of Lisburne, pers. comm.
[15]C. Matheson, 'Notes on the mammals of Cardiganshire', 237.

being restricted to stream-sides and ditches mainly in the lowlands. In some sheltered woods of oak and hazel there are dormice but very little is known about their numbers and distribution. The yellow-necked mouse, so curiously local in Britain, is probably very rare in Cardiganshire for the sole record is of one at Rhydyfelin near Aberystwyth in 1913.[16] Only in the last few years has the harvest mouse been found here—not in cornfields but in wild, grassy places like the margins of Cors Fochno, especially in tussocks of purple moor-grass where it hides its spherical nests. How long it has existed here is a matter for speculation.

Two alien rodents, apart from grey squirrel, are the house mouse and the common or brown rat. The arrival of the mouse in Britain takes us back at least as far as the Iron Age.[17] The Asiatic brown rat, still so resistant to efforts to destroy it, spread through Britain in the eighteenth century,[18] quickly replacing the black or ship rat which had been in Britain since at least Roman times,[19] usually living in the warmth and security of human habitations. It is a reasonable assumption that the black rat, now absent, was long established in Cardiganshire, and certainly the Black Death, with which this rat was intimately linked, made serious ravages here in the mid-fourteenth century, especially in the commote of Cardigan.[20]

Birds

Bird reporting in Cardiganshire begins with a mystery. Edward Lhuyd in a letter of September 1696 writes: 'There came this last May into Cardiganshire two strange birds (as I guess by the description given them) of the aquatic fissiped tribe. They say they were almost two yards tall and of a whitish colour, with the tips of their wings dark. I took 'em to be some sort of Exotic Crane.'[21] What these birds were is quite uncertain.

Until Salter listed 209 Cardiganshire species in 1895 in *The Zoologist*, only news of occasional rare birds (almost invariably killed) had reached the ornithological world from the County. Among such rarities were a cape pigeon (a species of petrel), shot on the Dyfi estuary in 1879, a cream-coloured courser, shot at Ynys-las in 1886, and a collared petrel, shot near Aberystwyth in 1889. It was 1966 before a second list of Cardiganshire birds was produced, this time by the West Wales Naturalists' Trust.[22] In this list 235 species were included and their status briefly summarized. Since then 30 others, mostly rare visitors, have been added. About 104 species nest regularly or fairly frequently in Cardiganshire and a further 23 have bred here in the past eighty years.

Because of its western aspect Cardiganshire has a number of breeding birds which are less common or even quite absent at a comparable English latitude. Noteworthy examples are raven,

---

[16]F. S. Wright, *The Zoologist*, 20 (1916), 329.
[17]G. B. Corbet and H. N. Southern, *The Handbook of British Mammals* (Oxford, 1977), 229.
[18]Ibid., 243.
[19]J. Rackham, '*Rattus rattus*: the introduction of the black rat into Britain', *Antiq.*, 53 (1979), 112–20.
[20]W. Rees, 'The Black Death in Wales', *TRHS*, 3 (1920), 115–35.
[21]R. W. T. Gunther, *Life and Letters of Edward Lhwyd* (Oxford, 1945), 309.
[22]G. C. S. Ingram, H. M. Salmon and W. M. Condry, *The Birds of Cardiganshire* (Haverfordwest, 1966).

buzzard, peregrine and red kite, all of which were savagely dealt with by the nineteenth-century gamekeepers in England but were able to survive better in west Wales because the country here was wilder and in many places less intensively keepered. Recent studies of a large area of upland Cardiganshire have shown that both raven and buzzard are more numerous than in any area of comparable size in Britain, an important factor in their survival being the year-round availability of carrion sheep.[23]

Of these once persecuted predators the red kite, though it has declined greatly since the early nineteenth century, is still fairly well represented in parts of Cardiganshire. Formerly widespread in Britain and common even in London, where it was protected in the Middle Ages as a street scavenger, the kite has been throughout this century virtually restricted as a British breeding species to west mid Wales, and even here it escaped extinction only by a hair's breadth. Kites were very easy to poison or shoot, while buzzards, harriers and owls could be destroyed without difficulty because of their habit of using poles as observation posts. All a gamekeeper needed to do was set traps on the tops of the poles. J. H. Salter in 1902 wrote that he 'pulled down two pole traps on a walk up the Ystwyth to Llanilar'.[24] Though the pole trap was made illegal as early as 1904, it continued to be used illicitly for many decades. As well as taking such direct action Salter also became a pioneer of organized conservation in 1903 when he gathered together a group of well-wishers dedicated to ensuring the survival of the kite, an enterprise that has since continued.[25] Thus protected, the Welsh kite population has slowly increased from about twelve at the beginning of the century to about 370 in 1992. More than half of the breeding pairs are in Cardiganshire, many of them nesting in steep valley-side oakwoods. In recent years the kite has been closely studied and much new light has been shed on its natural history and ecology.[26]

Another species confined to western Britain is the chough, 'a very tender bird and unable to bear very severe weather', as Thomas Pennant described it in the eighteenth century.[27] A striking bird with red beak and legs contrasting with glossy black plumage, there are usually about 15–20 breeding pairs in Cardiganshire, most of them in coastal habitats, nesting in caves or holes in cliffs and feeding on ants, beetles and other small life. The stonechat, another delicate bird which is familiar along the coast, declines not only in hard weather but whenever gorse, its chief habitat, is destroyed.

Cardiganshire suffers from a shortage or total absence of a number of breeding species such as the great crested grebe, shoveler, tufted duck, pochard, mute swan, red-legged partridge, common partridge, turtle dove, lesser whitethroat, yellow wagtail, hawfinch and tree sparrow. Certain passage birds are likewise scarce here, for while there are regular movements of seabirds

[23] I. Newton, P. E. Davies and J. E. Davis, 'Ravens and buzzards in relation to sheep farming and forestry in Wales', *J. Applied Ecology*, 19 (1982), 681–706.

[24] J. H. Salter, *Natural History Diaries* (entry for 28 Feb. 1902).

[25] H. M. Salmon, 'The Red Kites of Wales: the story of their preservation', *Welsh Wildlife in Trust*, ed. W. S. Lacey (Bangor, 1970), 68.

[26] See for example, P. W. Davies and P. E. Davis, 'The ecology and conservation of the red kite in Wales', *British Birds*, 66 (1973), 183–224, 241–70, and idem, 'The food of the red kite in Wales', *Bird Study*, 28 (1981), 33–40; P. E. Davis and I. Newton, 'Population and breeding of red kites in Wales over a 30-year period', *J. Animal Ecology*, 50 (1981), 759–72; and I. Newton, P. E. Davis and D. Moss, 'Distribution and breeding of red kites in relation to land use in Wales', *J. Applied Ecology*, 18 (1981), 173–86.

[27] T. Pennant, *British Zoology*, I (London, 1776), 229.

and waders along the Cardiganshire coast, the passage of many small land birds is slight compared with that on the east coast of England which has the advantage of being closer to the Continent and its migrant multitudes.

It is an enormous loss that Edward Lhuyd never wrote his projected natural history of Wales, for he lived at a time when sizeable fragments of the late medieval landscape were still intact but were soon to be swept away by the agrarian revolution and the enclosures, and since Cors Fochno was well known to him his account of it would have complemented what George Owen relates of swamps that were the breeding haunts of spoonbill and bittern in Pembrokeshire.[28] It is probable that Cors Fochno, Cors Caron and other Cardiganshire wetlands also had these and other water birds now known here only as rare casuals. Even as late as the 1820s, when Cors Fochno was visited by the first ordnance surveyors, there were ten areas of open water. These pools have long since disappeared as has much of Cors Fochno itself, being now confined to the area usually referred to as Borth Bog, whereas it formerly extended along the Dyfi estuary to the Llyfnant. Now only a rare migrant, the marsh harrier or 'moor buzzard' as it used to be known, was doubtless a familiar breeding species in the former wetlands of Cardiganshire as elsewhere in Britain, and may have lingered late into the nineteenth century on Borth Bog.

In these former fens and meres when fish and frogs were common, we can assume that grey herons too were more abundant. That such a large and conspicuous bird has managed to survive as a breeding species is probably because it was one of the earliest wild birds to be protected. In the Middle Ages the gentry carefully conserved herons as a quarry for falconry, encouraging them to make their heronries in tall trees close to their dwellings. Young herons were also valued as a source of food. The superstition that a family line would die out if ever the heronry ceased to be occupied served as a powerful reason to guard the nesting birds from disturbance. Several of the Cardiganshire heronries are still on private estates close to what are or were country houses. The heronries—about nine in number—some of them quite old, vary in size from year to year, the largest usually not greater than about twenty pairs, the total number being on average about ninety to a hundred. Among the present-day heronries are those at Ynys-hir (Glandyfi), Llidiardau (Llanilar), Llanllŷr (Tal-sarn), Cockshead (Olmarch), Llanerch-aeron (Ciliau Aeron), Highmead (Llanwenog), Llanfair (Llandysul), Henllan and Llechryd. Now only a rare visitor, the heron's cousin, the bittern, was evidently better known by sound than by sight for it was familiar to country folk throughout Wales as *aderyn y bwn*, the booming bird; and even in this century, when it has long since ceased to breed here, its impressive springtime voice has been heard, though rarely, at Cors Fochno and Cors Caron. While the draining of wetlands was the major reason for the decline of the bittern, there can be little doubt that it was eventually hunted out of existence, for its flesh, along with that of the crane and heron, was much sought after. Two other species have also disappeared within this century from Cors Caron. A colony of lesser black-backed gulls bred here until they were exterminated by gamekeepers in the early 1930s, and up to 600 white-fronted geese used to winter regularly but ceased to return after the 1960s. In recompense the whooper swan now winters on the bog in much better numbers than in the first half of the century.

In the few thousand years which have seen the replacement of wild-wood by farmlands a whole world of sylvan birds and other fauna has largely vanished, its remnants surviving as relict

[28]G. Owen, *The Description of Penbrokshire* (London, 1892).

populations in the remaining fragments of broad-leaved woodland. Even surviving ribbons of sessile oak, birch and a few other trees strung out along steep valley sides, may be doomed to disappear either by clear felling or through neglect. Many are unfenced and have become sheep and cattle pastures with no hope of tree generation. Such woods are important as the breeding places of kite, buzzard, raven, tawny owl, nuthatch, tree creeper, three kinds of woodpecker, various tits, warblers, thrushes and other species. Especially characteristic are three small spring migrants from Africa—redstart, wood warbler and pied flycatcher—for they are much commoner here than in most woodlands further east. That well-known hole nester, the starling, has recently fluctuated as a breeding species. Historically it was known as a winter visitor, as indicated by one of its old names, *aderyn du yr eira* ('blackbird of the snow').[29] A survey of 1948 revealed it as a thinly distributed breeding bird in Cardiganshire, nesting in buildings in villages and towns, very rarely in trees.[30] Then came a change: by the 1970s it was nesting widely in woodlands. But the increase was not maintained and by the early 1990s it had again become scarce as a woodland breeder.

A very celebrated English woodland bird, but almost unknown throughout Wales, is the nightingale. Its absence from Wales was recognized as long ago as the twelfth century when two writers, Alexander Neckham[31] and Giraldus Cambrensis,[32] both pointed it out. This did nothing to prevent the poets from rhapsodizing about Welsh nightingales but these were clearly birds of poetic licence, imported as an integral part of the English and classical poetic tradition. In Welsh the nightingale is *eos* but the existence of place-names like Nanteos cannot be taken as indicating the former presence of nightingales because long ago *eos* may well have meant some other singing bird. Many place-names, after all, have come to us out of the shadows of early history.

Although the destruction of the primal forest by Man resulted in the disappearance of much of their habitat, many forest species proved to be so adaptable that they readily accepted a farmland existence. Some of the birds, for instance, learned to make the best of both worlds by using relict pockets of woodland for nesting and roosting and the farmlands for foraging. It may well be that chaffinches, greenfinches, thrushes, magpies, rooks, jackdaws, carrion crows, wood-pigeons, kites, buzzards and sparrowhawks have become more abundant in the post-medieval countryside than they ever were formerly. Concurrently the farmlands have become a welcome habitat for newcomers such as lapwings, curlews, gulls, larks, pipits and starlings which spread out as woodland diminished. In north Cardiganshire the rook, that much persecuted, though on balance beneficial, bird of farmland, has been carefully counted by A. O. Chater who has reported an increase in the number of nests from 1,410 in 1974 to 2,466 in 1992, and in the number of rookeries from 42 to 59, despite the fact that at this time rooks seem to be decreasing in much of Britain.

In the twentieth century we have seen the decline of several well-known farmland birds. Anyone old enough to recall the countryside of the 1930s will remember how all the hayfields were loud with the rasping of corncrakes until fast-moving machinery replaced old cutting methods. This change meant that hay could be cut earlier, when the birds were on their eggs.

[29]T. Davies, *Nature in Wales*, 2 (1956), 274.
[30]J. L. Davies, 'The breeding status of the Starling in west Wales,' *British Birds*, 42 (1949), 373.
[31]T. Wright (ed.), *Alexandri Neckham De Naturis Rerum* (Rolls series: London, 1863), 102.
[32]J. F. Dimock (ed.), *Giraldi Cambrensis Opera*, vi (Rolls series: London, 1868), 125.

The result was that the nests were destroyed nearly everywhere and the corncrake quickly became very rare, and so it still is. The decline in the partridge was also extremely severe though very much slower: the bird changed from being common last century to scarce today, the victim, gamebird experts have said, of colder late spring weather and perhaps agricultural changes too.

Two other birds, meadow pipit and skylark, are also now much less common in enclosed farmland than formerly, and one attractive little bird of hedgerows and scattered thorn bushes, the red-backed shrike, formerly common, is now quite absent as a breeding species from Cardiganshire as it is from nearly all of Britain. The disappearance of another farmland bird earlier in the twentieth century, the corn bunting, which was an abundant all-year-round resident in arable districts, was presumably due in part at least to the decline in cereal cultivation. The woodlark, a bird mainly of fields and hillsides, frequently misreported as a nightingale because it often sings at night, was devastated by the prolonged and intense frosts of the winter of 1962–3 which rendered it extremely rare throughout Wales. Why it has not recovered, as bird numbers usually do in a few years after severe winters, is a mystery.

A predator of the farming scene is the little owl. Introduced to south-east England in the late nineteenth century, it reached Cardiganshire about 1918 and by mid-century was widespread and fairly common when its numbers inexplicably slumped, remaining low ever since though with some slight recovery since the mid-1970s. Another alien, the collared dove, reached Cardiganshire in about 1961 as part of a general colonization of Britain and is now familiar.

Pairs and small groups of breeding seabirds are thinly scattered along the Cardiganshire coast. There is a large colony of cormorants six miles south of Aberystwyth; and a major site on Birds Rock, south-west of New Quay Head, supports sizeable populations of kittiwakes, herring gulls, guillemots, razorbills, shags and fulmars. Two are recent colonists: the fulmar began breeding in Cardiganshire in 1947 and the kittiwake, which first nested at New Quay in 1962, has recently established a second colony at Lochdyn.

The Dyfi and Teifi estuaries are the main wintering grounds for waders, geese and ducks and the chief summer haunts of shelducks. The red-breasted merganser, first recorded breeding in this area at Aberdyfi in 1957, has continued to increase and spread while its cousin, the goosander, has been colonizing rivers such as the Ystwyth since the mid-1970s.

A few oystercatchers and ringed plovers have long nested along Cardiganshire's sandy or stony beaches but today they do so with ever more difficulty because of increasing human disturbance. Most of our oystercatchers now nest on the cliffs; and ringed plovers, which used to breed along Tan-y-bwlch beach, are now confined to the National Nature Reserve at Ynys-las. Small numbers of little terns used to nest just above the high-water mark at the mouth of the Dyfi until the site became a rocket range during the Second World War. They have never returned.

Gannets from Grassholm are often to be seen off the Cardiganshire coast as are foraging flocks of Manx shearwaters from their large nesting colonies on Bardsey, Skomer and Skokholm. The shearwater has never been known to breed in Cardiganshire but there is currently an attempt to introduce it on Cardigan Island. An 1899 *Guide to Cardigan* mentions 'Welsh parrots', that is puffins, on Cardigan Island, but the only reliable report of puffins was that of Bertram Lloyd who found 25–30 pairs breeding there in 1924—the only site ever recorded in Cardiganshire. The decline and disappearance of the puffins is undocumented but it is a reasonable assumption that they were driven away by rats which came ashore probably following the wreck of the *Hereford* in 1934. The puffins had gone by 1944. In recent years the Dyfed Wildlife Trust (the rats having been exterminated in 1969) has attempted to attract puffins back to the island by a display of cut-out models and three-dimensional models of the birds, but so far without success.

Few species breed on Cardiganshire's treeless uplands but they include some which are highly localized nesting birds in southern Britain. Red grouse and merlin live chiefly among the heather; snipe, golden plover, dunlin and curlew nest on the peat bogs; teal and black-headed gulls on the lakes; skylark and meadow pipit are widespread on the grasslands; common sandpiper, dipper and grey wagtail belong to the watersides; the wheatear prefers the screes; and the ring ouzel hides its nest among heathery rocks. The rarest of these moorlanders are merlin, dunlin, golden plover and ring ouzel. Largely deserted in winter except for occasional ravens, crows, buzzards and kites looking for carrion sheep, the uplands are summer foraging grounds for a number of lowland birds. Most obvious are the rooks and jackdaws which gather in noisy flocks after the breeding season in search of grassland insects. Other birds such as woodpigeons, mistle thrushes and various finches go on similar daily excursions as part of the dispersal from their breeding quarters. In both spring and autumn many diurnal migrants regularly pass over the high ground, among them starlings, redwings, fieldfares, swallows, martins and lesser black-backed gulls. Swifts may occur on any summer's day, sometimes in large flocks, moving with frontal weather systems. One rare wader's migration is unique: the dotterel crosses Wales from peak to peak northwards in spring and back again in autumn and has occasionally been seen on Plynlimon, but there is no record of it breeding anywhere in Cardiganshire.

When the moors are planted with conifers, as they have been increasingly since the end of the First World War, the birds which breed or feed on open ground are displaced, but behind the forest fences that keep out the sheep, there soon develops a jungle of grasses, heather, bilberry, crowberry and other plants, which, with the young trees, creates a habitat attractive to birds which enjoy this deep cover. During a forest's first few years there may be whinchats, warblers, finches, robins, song thrushes, blackbirds, yellowhammers and other birds breeding where there were none before. Black grouse also seek this type of cover, and kestrels, buzzards and short-eared owls may be attracted by the voles that often swarm where grass grows tall. Soon, however, the conifers grow into each other, suppressing the ground vegetation by their shade, and the original bird colonists decline through loss of habitat, most of them disappearing altogether. The nearly mature forests may have many goldcrests, coal tits and locally siskins, and Cardiganshire's first breeding records of crossbills were in tall spruces in Myherin Forest, Devil's Bridge, and in Ystwyth Forest, Llanafan, in 1977. Sparrowhawks particularly benefit from the maturing forests and some buzzards also breed in them. The rare but increasing goshawk is a likely future colonizer of the conifers for it has already begun to breed in the County.

Amphibians and reptiles

Three amphibians are known in Cardiganshire: common frog, common toad and palmate newt. All are widespread in aquatic habitats in the breeding season, after which they may be found far from water. While frogs and palmate newts breed in lowlands and uplands alike, the toad seems to be absent from high ground. It is just possible that another species, the smooth newt, may occur for it is known not only in Ireland but also in eastern Wales.

Cardiganshire has four reptiles: slow worm, common lizard, grass snake and adder, but none seems to be abundant except very locally and temporarily. The slow worm may well be the commonest for it seems to be well known throughout the lowlands. The lizard is widely but thinly distributed from the coast to the uplands and although perhaps most typical of dry banks can also be found in really damp conditions, even sphagnum bogs. The grass snake, its distribution poorly known, frequents lowland watersides where it finds its chief prey, the frog, but it seems scarce at present. The adder is equally local and is best known on or near the peat bogs of Cors Fochno and Cors Caron and on cliff slopes in the south of the County.

Fish

The lakes and streams of Cardiganshire, isolated by the Cambrian Mountains from the rivers of eastern Wales, are very poor in fish species compared with the middle and lower reaches of the Severn and the Wye. What is distinctive about the fresh waters of west Wales, including Cardiganshire, is the predominance of game fish: salmon, and brown and sea trout.

Doubtless men were taking salmon from the Dyfi and Teifi estuaries in seine nets in the remote past just as today; and salmon-fishing from coracles, which is still practised on the lower Teifi, is of similar antiquity. So are the *goredi* (fish traps) made from semicircles of boulders still visible on the shore at Aber-arth and Llan-non and which no doubt caught salmon along with mullet and bass. Although salmon enter the mouths of all but the smallest rivers, they are particularly prevalent in the Teifi, Aeron, Ystwyth, Rheidol and Dyfi. They spawn from December to March, not only in the lower reaches of these rivers but also as far as the headwaters except where there are insuperable natural barriers. To the impoverished hill people of long ago the arrival of these large and easily captured fish must have seemed a divine intervention, especially as it happened just when other food was in shortest supply. The majority of young Cardiganshire salmon descend to the sea as smolts in the spring at two years of age. One of the biggest salmon ever caught was a cock fish of 53 lb taken at Llandysul in the 1930s. The future of the salmon is considered by some to be in the balance now that their feeding grounds off Greenland and the Faroes are known and subjected to over-exploitation.

One of the most widespread fish in Cardiganshire is the brown trout, found in nearly every stream and the majority of lakes. In a few of the lakes, however, especially those surrounded by conifers, a recent increase in acidity has rendered the water uninhabitable by even this hardy fish. It remains to be seen what effects alien brown trout, introduced from fish farms, may have on the genetic make-up of the native population. The sea trout (known in Wales as *sewin*) used to be regarded as a distinct species but is now thought to be a migratory form of brown trout. It is an increasing species, perhaps because of the salmon decline, and many more sewin than salmon are now caught in the Teifi. The sea trout's life cycle is very different from that of the salmon, for whereas the majority of salmon make only one spawning migration to the river of their birth, sea trout return for eight or nine successive years. Sea trout will enter even very small streams such as the Clydan and Peris at Llan-non and the Arth at Aber-arth, and they spawn even higher up shallow tributaries than the salmon.

At a time when many mines were being worked, lead and zinc were a major cause of water pollution. As one writer complained in 1913, the Ystwyth and Rheidol formerly held salmon and sea trout in some numbers but 'the pollutions from various mines have quite wiped them out'. This calamity had only come about because the rivers were 'used almost solely for the lawless and selfish benefit of industries which could well afford to take proper means to effectually prevent the poisoning of the waters'.[33] In 1919 a report confirmed that the Rheidol was quite devoid of fish, but the gradual improvement of the quality of the water has resulted in a successful restocking with salmon and trout. Precautionary measures during the completion of the Rheidol hydro-electric works in the early 1960s 'have resulted in stabilization of the river bed and in the establishment of rooted vegetation such as water crowfoot and water starwort. This must be of considerable benefit to the salmon parr population in the main river.'[34] Nevertheless pollution problems from the lead-zinc mines can still occur, especially after floods.

Both bullhead and stone loach are widespread in gravelly or pebbly streams while minnow and three-spined stickleback, though sparsely scattered in lakes and pools, belong chiefly to the middle reaches of the larger rivers. All four seem scarce or absent in many of the streams in north Cardiganshire, although brackish ditches alongside the Dyfi estuary have the ten-spined stickleback and even more salty pools on the estuary marshes have the three-spined species.

The common eel is perhaps even more widespread and numerous than the brown trout. It spawns at sea and the elvers running up the rivers in their thousands in spring show astonishing determination to struggle up almost vertical rocks, as at Cenarth Falls on the Teifi, eventually finding their way to almost every ditch, pond, stream and lake, irrespective of altitude, provided the water is not too polluted. Indigenous to Cardiganshire rivers are all three British species of lamprey. The brook lamprey, widespread and relatively common, spends its whole life in fresh water, whereas river and sea lamprey spend most of their adult lives at sea but return to spawn in the rivers. Both seem to be restricted to the major rivers like the Teifi, Aeron, Ystwyth and Rheidol.

A few other British fish species have been introduced into Cardiganshire. Among them is the grayling of which there is a small, very localized population in the Teifi near Llanybydder. Also restricted are the pike further upstream near Tregaron where efforts are being made to get rid of them. The lake at Falcondale has many rudd and also perch which have occasionally found their way into the Teifi and which are also in Maes-llyn, Tregaron.

There are at present three truly exotic fish in Cardiganshire: the North American rainbow trout, the North American brook char and the Far Eastern grass carp. Rainbow trout have been introduced with varying degrees of success to some of the upland lakes but their future looks uncertain at a time of increasing water acidity. Rainbows do much better in fertile lowland fish farms. The brook char, commonly called the 'brook trout', is appreciably more tolerant of acidity than either the rainbow or the brown trout and has in recent years been introduced into Llyn Berwyn, the Teifi Pools and other waters. The grass carp, a native of the Far East, has been

---

[33]A. Grimble, *The Salmon Rivers of England and Wales* (London, 1913), 162.
[34]A. N. Jones and W. R. Howells, 'Recovery of the River Rheidol', *Effluent and Water Treatment J.* (Nov. 1969).

introduced at a small number of privately owned pools where heavy weed growth has been a problem. Its appetite for weed is prodigious and it can be of great help in keeping ponds and ditches clear. It is not known to breed naturally in Britain for it needs water temperatures above 22° C to induce spawning.

In recent years, because of the growing concern about acidification and the decline in fish, experiments have been made to improve certain lakes by adding lime to the water, and so far the results have been promising. Clearly the problem is a complicated one which will remain of concern well into the future and involve many other life-forms besides fish.

CHAPTER 6

THE LEPIDOPTERA OF CARDIGANSHIRE

Adrian Fowles

Cardiganshire seems to be a neglected county entomologically, which is a pity since it is quite obvious that it has a most interesting and varied fauna.[1]

D R Birkett was one of many visiting naturalists who have been delighted by the riches of the County's Lepidoptera and surprised by the discoveries they have made. Over twenty years later, and despite an accelerated interest in the region's invertebrate fauna, Cardiganshire is still largely underworked and new species are continually being added to the County list. The excitement generated by the finding of Rosy Marsh Moths on Cors Fochno has focused much attention on the Lepidoptera of the Dyfi Valley in recent years, but elsewhere in the County there are a great many fine sites that remain completely unsurveyed. For many English counties, and a few Welsh ones, a comparison is possible between the status of the populations of butterflies and moths over the last 150 years or so. Nationwide the picture is not an encouraging one and a high proportion of the British fauna has declined significantly. Unfortunately such a review is not applicable in Cardiganshire as the region has received scant attention until recent years but it is possible to draw some conclusions from the available records.

Since 1970 thirty-five butterfly species have been confirmed as resident in the district, with a further seven or eight occurring as migrants. There has been little change in composition of species this century, with the County list remaining remarkably similar. This is a commendable situation as most county reports lament the loss of one or other species, but we are now at the point where Cardiganshire may also have its casualties. The presumed extinction of the High Brown Fritillary and the Brimstone as resident species suggests that it is high time our butterflies received more attention from conservationists. Without sympathetic management, and possibly acquisition, of prime sites, the next few years could see the disappearance of Pearl-bordered Fritillaries, White-letter Hairstreaks and Grizzled Skippers. On a more optimistic note, both Purple Hairstreaks and Commas have become far more common recently and the same may also be true of Small Skippers. Many other species continue to be abundant in suitable habitats and it is particularly pleasing that Marsh Fritillaries and Graylings have so many strong colonies since both are declining in other parts of Britain. In terms of the number of individual butterflies to be seen on the wing, there are still many sites where the delights of former days can be enjoyed.

---

[1]N. L. Birkett, 'Further records of Cardiganshire Lepidoptera, 1965', *Entomologist's Record and Journal of Variation*, 78 (1966), 11–13.

Dr Salter, the County's foremost naturalist, wrote of a visit to Cwm Clettwr in 1895, 'Above the woods I came to a warm corner in which Green Hairstreaks fairly swarmed. With a net I could have caught twenty without moving a dozen yards. Nothing in butterflies has pleased me more.'[2] In good years they can still be disturbed from the upland Bilberry moors in astonishing numbers and this was also the case with Marsh Fritillaries on southern pastures in 1983.

Of the larger moths 552 species have been reported from Cardiganshire but with the level of recording that has taken place over the years it is difficult to assess the changing fortunes of most of these, particularly as the different methods of detection that have been employed attract different species. H. Ll. Roberts suggested a novel way to collect moths: 'An effective method of catching moths at Borth is as follows: open the bedroom window, place a candle on the windowsill facing the bog, close the window in half-an-hour, or much sooner, and move out of the room until dawn. Then armed with daylight courage, a soft brush and ten large biscuit tins, advance to the attack and go for fresh tins after the first ten are filled.'[3]

Salter employed various methods to amass his collection—including beating for larvae, digging for pupae, and inspecting Ivy-bloom at dusk—but he chiefly relied on the appeal of 'sugar'. He relates that he applied this tempting mixture to a tree-trunk in his garden more or less nightly for ten years.[4] P. M. Miles has also favoured 'sugaring', and designed a trap which could be left in position overnight and inspected the following morning.[5] His four-year survey on Ynys-las Dunes NNR used 44 kg of malt extract, cider, and demerara sugar.[6] Artificial light has always been popular, though technological advances in trap-design have made life easier for the present-day lepidopterist. In 1956 J. R. Langmaid had to prevail upon 'Owen the Post' to plug in his mercury-vapour lamp at the village shop[7] but nowadays actinic lamps can be operated even in the most remote districts.

Taking into account the inherent problems of interpreting data gathered in so many different ways, it is possible tentatively to interpret the changes in status of some of the County's moths. In a sense it is perhaps premature to make such generalizations when species are still regularly being added to the County list (eighteen since 1980). However, for some of our moths a pattern is already discernible. Notable declines have taken place amongst ten species, some of them mirrored elsewhere in Britain; others are currently inexplicable. The Goat Moth, Narrow-bordered Bee Hawk, Vapourer, Wood Tiger, and Sword-grass have all become much scarcer in Cardiganshire since the mid-1950s and some of these may have become extinct. These species have all been reported less commonly from other parts of their British range over the same period. Blomer's Rivulet, Clouded Magpie, and perhaps the Brick, have suffered as Dutch Elm Disease has swept through Cardiganshire, although significantly White-letter Hairstreaks had a good year nationally in 1984 and hopefully the moths will also stage a come-back. The remaining species that have been reported less frequently of late—Round-winged Muslin and Beautiful

[2] J. H. Salter, *Natural History Diaries*, (entry for 8 May 1895).
[3] H. Ll. Roberts, *Borth Guide Book* (undated), 15.
[4] J. H. Salter, 'Scarcity of Lepidoptera', *North Western Naturalist*, 12 (1937), 400–1.
[5] P. M. Miles, 'Successful sugar-trapping', *Bull. Amateur Entomologist's Soc.*, 14 (1955), 57–8.
[6] P. M. Miles, 'Heterocera of Dyfi National Nature Reserve—Ynyslas Dunes, Cards., Wales, 1974–1978', *Entomologist's Monthly Mag.*, 116 (1981), 246–52.
[7] J. R. Langmaid, 'Three days in Wales, 1956', *Entomologist's Gazette*, 8 (1957), 37–8.

Yellow Underwing—are moorland and peat-bog inhabitants. As with the Wood Tiger (another peatland species), it is curious that they should have been so rarely encountered at a time when there has been the greatest interest in the ecology of their preferred habitat. There are a further twenty-one species on the County list which have not been seen since at least 1960. Some of these are rare migrants and a handful are possibly mistaken identifications, but for the remainder there are too few records to judge their past status.

On the positive side, there are six species which are sufficiently conspicuous to suppose that they would not have been overlooked had they always been present in the County. They were all reported for the first time in the last twenty years and are now frequently recorded. The most likely explanation is that they have extended their range, but it is too early to say how permanent the colonization will be. The Peacock, Sharp-angled Peacock, White-pinion Spotted, White Satin and Blackneck have presumably spread northwards in recent years. The Barred Umber has possibly always been resident at low density but it is strange that it was unnoticed until 1969. In the late 1930s it looked as though the Golden Plusia was ready to colonize the County but after a few sightings between 1937 and 1939 it disappeared again. Blair's Shoulder-knot may be on the verge of colonizing west Wales as Cardiganshire has just had its first record[8] and it appears to be well established now in many parts of England and Wales. In future years we may possibly anticipate the arrival of Cypress Pug and Varied Coronet as they continue to advance northwards from southern England.

Unfortunately our knowledge of the microlepidoptera of Cardiganshire is extremely limited. The Salter Collection, held in the National Museum of Wales, contains seventy-seven species of Alucitidae, Pyralidae, and Pterophoridae but there are also nine boxes of unsorted micros, undoubtedly the most comprehensive assemblage made of this group in the County. Recently Dr A. N. B. Simpson has sampled many sites in southern Cardiganshire and there is every indication that further work will reveal many exciting finds.

Collecting, recording and conservation

Our knowledge of the past status of Cardiganshire moths is rather limited in comparison with most of England and south Wales. Although the first published record goes back to 1839, when John Curtis described the Welsh Wave as a species new to science from a specimen collected at Hafod, very few lepidopterists worked within the County until the present century. H. Jenner-Fust[9] and Neville Chamberlain[10] recorded a handful of species but it was not until Salter returned to the County in 1923 that any extensive work was carried out. His unpublished *Natural History Diaries* from 1891 to 1908 include several observations of diurnal moths but his interest in entomology only really developed during his residence in Tenerife and southern France from 1908 to 1916. By the time he returned to Llanbadarn Fawr he had already formed a substantial

[8]P. R. Holmes, 'Blair's Shoulder-knot *Lithophane leautieri* in west Wales', *British Journal of Entomology and Natural History*, 1 (1988), 127.
[9]H. Jenner-Fust, 'Lepidoptera in north Wales', *Entomologist's Monthly Mag.*, 10 (1874), 179–80.
[10]W. Bowater, 'Neville Chamberlain's entomological diary', *Entomologist's Record and Journal of Variation*, 71 (1959), 236–8.

collection of British Lepidoptera which he continued to add to with Welsh specimens. His collection contains 306 species of macrolepidoptera acquired in Cardiganshire—four of which have not been recorded since.

The first County list of the larger moths was published by S. G. Smith[11] as part of his valuable series on the butterflies and moths of north Wales. The bulk of the 296 species reported were observed by J. P. Robson at Aberystwyth between 1937 and 1942 and E. C. Pelham-Clinton in the Glandyfi–Borth area from 1948 to 1950. Later supplements[12] and additional records collated by H. N. Michaelis[13] brought the published records up to a total of 330 species. These publications undoubtedly generated a great deal of interest in the County's moths and prompted a spate of short articles by visiting lepidopterists.[14] In the meantime, P. M. Miles embarked upon his major contribution to our knowledge of the County fauna, initially through annual reports of immigrant Lepidoptera,[15] and his thorough local surveys at Trawscoed, Ynys-las Dunes NNR and Cnwch-coch have provided much valuable information on the distribution of the County's moths.[16]

After the discovery of Rosy Marsh Moths in 1967 put Cardiganshire firmly on the lepidopterist's map, the late 1960s saw many famous entomologists active in the County. Regrettably, few of them ventured away from the immediate vicinity of Cors Fochno and the bulk of modern records has come from locally-based naturalists. Foremost in this respect has been the wealth of information provided by the permanent traps of the Rothamsted Insect Survey, which have been in operation at various sites since 1966. We are fortunate that they have sampled representative habitats in both halves of the County from sea-level to 274 m. A complete review of the larger

[11]S. G. Smith, 'The Butterflies and Moths found in the County of Cardiganshire', *Cheshire, North and Mid-Wales Nat. Hist.*, IV (1951), 5–46.

[12]S. G. Smith, 'The Butterflies and Moths found in the County of Radnorshire', *Cheshire, North and Mid-Wales Nat. Hist.*, V (1954), 5–51; idem, 'Records of Butterflies and Moths found in the County of Lancashire', *Annual Report of the Proc. of Lancs. and Cheshire Entomologist's Soc.*, 77/8 (1956), 39–54.

[13]H. N. Michaelis, 'New and additional records of Lepidoptera', *Annual Report of the Proc. of Lancs. and Cheshire Entomologist's Soc.*, 85/7 (1966), 78–81; idem, 'Records of Lepidoptera from Lancashire, Cheshire and Wales', ibid., 107–11.

[14]N. L. Birkett, 'Some Cardiganshire Lepidoptera records', *Entomologist's Record and Journal of Variation*, 66 (1954), 244–5; idem, 'Further records of Cardiganshire Lepidoptera', ibid., 78 (1966), 11–13; G. G. E. Scudder, 'Insects recorded from Tregaron Bog Nature Reserve, Cards.', *Entomologist's Monthly Mag.*, 92 (1956), 221–5; J. O. T. Howard, 'Collecting on the Welsh coast', *Entomologist's Record and Journal of Variation*, 67 (1955), 299–300; J. R. Langmaid, 'Three days in Wales, 1956', *Entomologist's Gazette*, 8 (1957), 37–8; idem, 'Three days in Wales, 1956', ibid., 9 (1958), 18–20; and J. R. G. Turner, 'Notes on Lepidoptera at Tregaron', *Annual Report of the Proc. of Lancs. and Cheshire Entomologist's Soc.*, 85/7 (1966), 111–15.

[15]P. M. Miles, 'Some Welsh records of *Colias croceus* and other migrant lepidoptera', *Entomologist's Monthly Mag.*, 84 (1948), 57; idem, 'Some Welsh records of Lepidoptera including migrants', ibid., 87 (1951), 18; idem, 'Immigrant Lepidoptera observed in Wales during 1952', ibid., 89 (1953), 271–2; idem, 'Immigrant Lepidoptera observed in Wales during 1953', ibid., 90 (1954), 248–50; idem, 'Immigrant Lepidoptera observed in Wales during 1954 and 1955', ibid., 93 (1957), 184–7.

[16]P. M. Miles, 'Records of moths trapped at Trawscoed, near Aberystwyth, Cards., Wales', *Entomologist's Monthly Mag.*, 92 (1956), 289–95; idem, 'Heterocera of Dyfi National Nature Reserve—Ynyslas Dunes, Cards., Wales, 1974–1978', *Entomologist's Monthly Mag.*, 116 (1981), 246–52; idem, 'Moths (Heterocera) of north Cardiganshire, 1981–1983', *Nature in Wales* (New Series), 5 (1987), 48–53.

moths occurring in Cardiganshire, including all records received up to the end of 1984, has recently appeared[17] and annual updates are produced by the Dyfed Invertebrate Group.[18]

Whilst in southern England butterfly collectors are still very active, in contrast, I have never seen a butterfly collector in Cardiganshire and the County Museum has no knowledge of any local collections. Visiting lepidopterists must undoubtedly take specimens, and the Large Heath is their most likely quarry, but it would seem that the species to be found in Cardiganshire are not of sufficient national interest to attract collectors from afar. The Marsh Fritillary, however, could become an attractive quarry in the future as populations decline in England.

As most of the early lepidopterists were collectors, it follows that historical records of the region's butterflies are limited. The first published record appears to be of Green-veined Whites at Aberystwyth by Jenner-Fust in 1873[19] and the earliest local list was printed as an appendix to a parish history in 1896.[20] Salter seems to have been the first naturalist to take an interest in the recording of the County's Lepidoptera and his valuable records span the period 1891–1942. His annotated list of butterflies found in the Aberystwyth district[21] was followed by several short notes in the *North Western Naturalist* but little further information appeared until 1942 when J. A. Whellan contributed his observations of butterflies in southern Cardiganshire.[22] This was followed in 1951 by the first County list with the publication of the Cardiganshire section of S. Gordon Smith's summaries of the distribution of Lepidoptera in north Wales,[23] supplemented four years later.[24] More recently, there have been studies of Large Heaths[25] and Marsh Fritillaries[26] in the County and a number of site lists for established reserves have appeared—for example, Cors Caron National Nature Reserve (NNR)[27], Royal Society for the Protection of Birds (RSPB) Ynys-hir[28], and Ynys-las Dunes NNR.[29] Information derived from the growing interest in butter-

[17]A. P. Fowles, 'The Moths of Ceredigion', *Research and Survey in Nature Conservation*, 8 (1988).

[18]A. P. Fowles, 'Butterflies and Moths in Ceredigion in 1986', *Newsletter Dyfed Invertebrate Group*, 4 (1986), 2–4; idem, 'Lepidoptera records from Ceredigion in 1987', ibid., 9 (1988), 5–7; idem, 'Lepidoptera records from Ceredigion in 1988', ibid., 12 (1989), 5–7; idem, 'Records of butterflies and moths in Ceredigion (VC 46), with particular reference to 1984 and 1985', ibid., 13 (1989), 1–5.

[19]See above, n.9.

[20]W. J. Davies, 'Gieir Bach yr Haf neu Loynod Byw (Butterflies)', *Hanes Plwyf Llandysul* (1896), 331–2.

[21]J. H. Salter, 'The mammals, birds and butterflies of Cardiganshire', *Aberystwyth and District National Union of Teachers Guide* (1911), 95–6.

[22]J. A. Whellan, 'Notes on Rhopalocera and Odonata observed in south-west Wales', *North Western Naturalist*, 17 (1942), 108–9.

[23]See above, n.11.

[24]See above, n.12.

[25]J. R. G. Turner, 'A quantitative study of a Welsh colony of the Large Heath butterfly *Coenonympha tullia*', *Proc. Royal Entomological Soc. of London (A)*, 38 (1963), 101–12.

[26]A. P. Fowles, 'The Marsh Fritillary in Ceredigion', *British Butterfly Conservation Soc. News*, 35 (1985), 36–9.

[27]G. G. E. Scudder, 'Insects recorded from Tregaron Bog', *Entomologist's Monthly Mag.*, 92 (1956), 221–5.

[28]R. Squires, 'A checklist of Butterflies recorded at Ynyshir', *Ynyshir Report* (RSPB, 1979), 17–18.

[29]S. Pester, 'Butterflies of Ynyslas Dunes', *Ynyslas Nature Reserve Handbook* 3B (Edition 5) (1988), 111–24.

flies by local naturalists has recently resulted in a comprehensive account of the County fauna[30] and annual reviews now appear in the Newsletter of the Dyfed Invertebrate Group.[31]

The conservation of butterflies in Cardiganshire has, thus far, largely been achieved as an indirect result of the need to safeguard general habitat-types. Most nature reserves contain locally important populations and the majority of the best butterfly sites are designated Sites of Special Scientific Interest (SSSIs). This is a step in the right direction but the legislation allows little scope for positive management and the colonies of some scarcer species could suffer from neglect. A representative selection of habitats is protected within the County through the purchase of reserves by the Countryside Council for Wales, Dyfed Wildlife Trust, National Trust and Woodland Trust and of all the resident butterflies only the Brown Hairstreak lacks a formally conserved breeding locality. However, the only 'butterfly reserve' is at Coed Allt-fedw, a young conifer plantation which is managed by Forest Enterprise under the guidance of the Dyfed Wildlife Trust. In 1973 this site held an abundance of interesting species[32] but the diversity has since dwindled, despite the encouragement of larval foodplants. The existence of an exceptionally large colony of Marsh Fritillaries was a significant factor in the acquisition of the National Nature Reserve at Rhos Llawr-cwrt and management is directed towards maintaining the strength of this population. The purchase, however, would not have been agreed solely because of the importance of this butterfly and the reserve largely owes its protection to the quality of its flora. The truth is that conservation bodies do not have the resources available to concern themselves with single-species protection and must aim to conserve representative pockets of vegetation in the hope that wildlife in general will benefit. It is likely that the future of many colonies of our scarcer species will depend upon sympathetic management by private landowners and the conservation effort of butterfly enthusiasts in Cardiganshire. With the growing interest in the study of moths locally, it is to be hoped that their most important localities can also be identified and conserved.

Habitat

The status of butterflies and moths in a region is dependent primarily upon the broad-scale environmental factors of geology and climate which shape the landscape. In Cardiganshire our natural heritage has derived from the habitats which have formed on essentially poor soils under the influence of a mild, wet climate. The County is predominantly rural with few major towns and no heavy industries. Agriculture occupies almost nine-tenths of the total area (mainly sheep and dairy farming with a little arable in the south) and the general character of the land reflects the balance that has been struck between wildlife and farming traditions. Whilst there has always been a process of agricultural improvement at work in the County, the rate of change has been leisurely and wildlife has had time to adapt or move on. Unfortunately this is now no longer the case and financial incentives have brought about an acceleration in the loss of many fine sites.

[30]A. P. Fowles, 'The Butterflies of Ceredigion', *Nature in Wales* (New Series), 3 (1986), 25–43.

[31]See above, n.18.

[32]P. M. Miles, 'A changing environment', *Nature in Wales*, 14 (1975), 241–2.

Butterflies can, of course, be found in almost every type of habitat—from urban gardens to mountain tops. Some species, such as the ubiquitous Green-veined White, can be seen in nearly all of them while others are restricted to specific localities where their specialized ecological requirements are fulfilled. Moths have adapted to live in all of the major habitats of Cardiganshire and can be found from the salt-spattered rocks of the shoreline to the wind-swept summit of Plynlimon. The oceanic climate that prevails in west Wales, coupled with the relatively high ground, favours the creation of damp habitats and it is largely for the species of our wet woodlands and peatlands that Cardiganshire is important. The cooler summers and absence of calcareous rock formations restrict the fauna in comparison with many southern counties but we are fortunate in being at the margin of the range of several species. For example, a number of Oakwood inhabitants approach their northern limit in the County—such as the Lobster, Black Arches and Double-line—whilst our moorlands support several moths approaching their southern limit, including Haworth's Minor, Light Knot Grass and Large Ear. The healthy condition of our lichen flora, the unspoilt variety of the coastline, the unique character of the raised bogs, the richness of the southern valleys, and the wealth of the unimproved pastures all add to the diversity of the County fauna.

i) Coastal habitats

Few species are capable of withstanding the environmental rigours of saltmarshes and in Cardiganshire only three moth species are clearly associated with this habitat. The Rosy Wave, Dog's Tooth and Saltern Ear are all present in the Dyfi estuary but the Teifi marshes are less well worked and only the Rosy Wave is known there at present. The dune systems at Gwbert and Ynys-las are home to thousands of Common Blues, Meadow Browns, Dark Green Fritillaries and other butterflies whilst a number of moths occur there which are found nowhere else in the County. This is mainly due to the range of larval foodplants that are restricted to sandy areas but other factors, such as the ease of pupation in deep sand, are also significant. In comparison with many other localities in the County sand dunes have a rather poor diversity, only 169 species, for example, of the larger moths having been recorded from Ynys-las.[33] However, because of the localized distribution of their inhabitants they have received far more attention than most other habitats and several interesting species have been discovered. Many moths are common to both Ynys-las dunes and Pen-yr-ergyd dunes at Gwbert—such as the Cinnabar, Six-spot Burnet and Archer's Dart—whilst Ynys-las alone (on current knowledge) supports Sand Dart, Portland Moth, Thyme Pug, Shore Wainscot and White Colon. Each of these could be expected to occur at Gwbert and further fieldwork will no doubt reveal some of them.

There are approximately 60 km of cliffs of varying height along the coastline of Cardiganshire and yet this is the least studied of the lowland habitats. Here a narrow band of coastal heath, sandwiched between improved pasture and the sea, supports large numbers of butterflies and is particularly important for the widespread colonies of Graylings and Dark Green Fritillaries. Small Blues have been found in a few sheltered, south-facing coves where their larvae feed on the

[33]A. P. Fowles, 'The Moths of Ynyslas Dunes', *Ynyslas Nature Reserve Handbook* 3B (Edition 5) (1988), 125–7.

profusion of Kidney Vetch. A number of scarce and extremely interesting moths also breed along the coast, several of which are very local in Britain. Amongst the jumble of rocks at the foot of the cliffs two rare species feed on lichens as caterpillars—Dew Moth and Hoary Footman—whilst Thrift Clearwings inhabit the spindly plants of Thrift that cling precariously to cracks in the rock within the reach of the salt-spray. A little higher up the slope the Black-banded, Barret's Marbled Coronet and Northern Rustic will be found, whereas the Crescent Dart and Annulet occupy more stable soils as scree gives way to heath. Where cliff-top gulleys have Umbellifer stands the Brindled Ochre—only recently identified in the County—may occur. Most of these species have only been seen on a few occasions though this probably reflects a lack of observation rather than their own scarcity.

ii) Unimproved pastures

Little grassland in the coastal belt has escaped improvement but further inland, between 100 and 200 m, less of the land has been ploughed. Many of the finest sites here are *rhos* pastures, an almost unique mosaic of grassland communities that are largely confined to Cardiganshire and which support a colourful mixture of Orange Tips, Green Hairstreaks, Marsh Fritillaries, Ringlets etc. However, financial incentives for the reclamation of marginal land have persuaded many farmers to re-seed their *rhos* and the character of the landscape has changed accordingly. In 1977 the Nature Conservancy Council, recognizing that drainage had increased on farmland throughout west Wales, organized a survey of wet meadows. This brought to light many fine sites which have now received SSSI designation, but even so vast areas of pasture have been drained and ploughed, and, at the present rate of decline, the Marsh Fritillaries of England and Wales could be restricted to local strongholds in south-west England, Anglesey and Dyfed. As Cardiganshire holds about a quarter of all Welsh colonies identified to date it is important that an effort is made to conserve as many of these sites as possible.

The botanical diversity of these pastures also supports many species of moths which are more characteristic of other habitats, such as marshes, moorland and woodland clearings. A striking feature of *rhos* is the large number of day-flying moths present. At various times throughout the summer, the Forester, Five-spot Burnet, Chimney Sweeper, Scarlet Tiger, Small Yellow Underwing, Burnet Companion and Small Purple-barred can be found on the wing. This habitat is also significant for several species which are declining in Britain as a result of wetland drainage—the Silver Hook, Scarlet Tiger and Forester, for example. The Devon Carpet, Anomalous and Marbled White-spot are also interesting inhabitants closely associated with *rhos*.

iii) Peat-bogs

The two internationally important raised mires of Cors Fochno and Cors Caron are protected as NNRs and, with the control of peripheral drainage, there appears to be no foreseeable threat to their existence. Cors Caron is largely intact but Cors Fochno has shrunk considerably to its present extent as the bog has been steadily reclaimed over the past 150 years or so. The central domes of each bog are inhabited only by Large and Small Heaths, with other butterflies occurring as casual visitors from the fringes. Small Pearl-Bordered Fritillaries are another characteristic butterfly of Cardiganshire's peatlands, breeding here on Marsh Violets rather than the Dog Violets they favour in the open woodlands of southern England.

The mires and bogs of the County have relatively few species of larger moths, most of which are also found in damp grassland sites or on the upland moors. The Rosy Marsh Moth is the most famous inhabitant of our peat-bogs but several other scarce species also occur. The Silver Hook and Devon Carpet are found on bogs as well as *rhos* pastures, whilst the Ling Pug and Purple-bordered Gold have only been found on Cors Caron and Cors Fochno respectively. Cors Caron has strong colonies of Haworth's Minor, Heath Rustic and Light Knot Grass whilst the Grey Scalloped Bar is probably also common. Day-fliers are less frequent than in other open habitats —only the Common Heath is abundant, though males of the Fox Moth, Northern Eggar and Emperor dash past at high speed in search of females. The Beautiful Yellow Underwing is now scarce in the County and the Orange Underwing is very local.

iv) Woodlands

Of the blanket of Sessile Oakwood that once covered the region only a fragment now remains, and apart from the steep sides of gorges, as in Coed Rheidol NNR where ancient Oaks still cling to inaccessible ledges, most of the woods now remaining in the County are even-aged stands of Sessile Oak with varying amounts of Alder, Ash, Beech, Birch, Rowan, Small-leaved Lime and Wych Elm. Regrettably few of these are fenced off from livestock and a healthy understorey is a rare sight—grazing has drastically affected the ground flora and hence the distribution of woodland Lepidoptera. Purple Hairstreaks, feeding on Oak itself, are widespread but Silver-washed Fritillaries and Commas are restricted to the larger, protected woods, as at Ynys-hir RSPB. Another crucial factor limiting the abundance of butterflies in Cardiganshire's woods is the virtual absence of broad rides and clearings. These sunny, sheltered areas are the favoured haunts of many species. Another preferred habitat is the tangled thicket that forms the woodland edge but far too many of our woods end abruptly where sheep pasture begins. This has certainly contributed to the scarcity of Brown Hairstreaks in the area.

An astonishing number of moth species feed as larvae on our native trees, and woodlands are the richest habitat for the lepidopterist to study. Weekly trapping at Coed Penrhynmawr, Ynys-hir RSPB, in 1982 yielded 218 species of larger moths[34] whilst in a single night 108 species were captured on the Coedmor estate at Llechryd. In Britain the Oak is the most important tree, being host to about 130 species of the larger moths. Birch, too, is important as some 120 species will feast upon its foliage. Beech supports about 50 species, Alder 50 and Ash 30. The Sessile Oakwoods contain such interesting species as Small Brindled Beauty, Spring Usher, Black Arches, Blossom Underwing and Merveille-du-jour and the Cloaked Carpet and Double-line are ground-layer inhabitants commonly found in the better oakwoods. The wealth of lichens on the older trunks and branches are fed upon by the larvae of the Brussels Lace and Dotted Carpet, species which shun the pollution of urban areas and thrive in the clean air of west Wales. Birch scrub in the northern woods is the home of the Satin Lutestring, here at its southernmost limit in Wales. It is strange that the species typical of Wych Elm are all scarce in the County. This tree is widespread and not uncommon, particularly in the valley woods, but Blomer's Rivulet,

[34] A. P. Fowles, 'The Moths of Ynyshir', *Ynyshir 1982 Report* (RSPB, 1983), 24–5.

Clouded Magpie, Dusky-lemon Sallow and Lesser-spotted Pinion are all localized or rare. Only the Brick is at all frequent, and it is also known to feed on Ash as an alternative foodplant. The White-letter Hairstreak is also scarce and Dutch Elm Disease may eventually cause the extinction of all these host-specific Lepidoptera.

Conifers have been planted extensively in Cardiganshire and now cover some 13,000 hectares. Although there are no native conifers, a small number of moth species have spread with the plantations and there are a dozen moths which feed on one or other of the Spruces and Pines. The commonest members of the group are the Pine Carpet, Grey Pine Carpet, Spruce Carpet, Bordered White, Barred Red and Tawny-barred Angle. The Cloaked Pug, Ochreous Pug, Larch Pug, Dwarf Pug, Pine Beauty and Satin Beauty are rarely observed at present, though the Pugs are under-recorded and probably widespread. Another species occasionally found in coniferous woods is the Red-necked Footman—this species feeds on woodland lichens and is also encountered in broad-leaved woods but seems to prefer conifers in Cardiganshire.

v) Uplands

In an attempt to restore forests to the denuded landscape the Forestry Commission began planting conifers on agriculturally unproductive soil as early as 1920 and the afforestation programme gained considerable momentum in the 1950s. The majority of these plantations are at altitudes above the normal range of many of our scarcer butterflies and as such even the younger stages do not harbour the diversity of species encountered in similar woods in other parts of Britain. However, the Green Hairstreak, once abundant on the open moors, but now seriously reduced by the grazing of its foodplants, has probably benefited by the exclusion of livestock from plantations—allowing Bilberry to flourish along the edge of the forest tracks.

The upland sheep-walk has probably always been a poor habitat for butterflies and Small Heaths are the only species the naturalist is likely to encounter on the open high ground. Where sheltered valleys intrude into this bleak countryside Meadow Browns, Small Coppers, Peacocks etc. add to the fauna. Local lepidopterists have always suspected that Large Heaths probably inhabit some of the remote blanket bogs but, although many of these areas are infrequently visited, it seems unlikely that any colonies await discovery. Further north, Large Heaths feed on Purple Moor-grass and Cotton-grass but at this latitude they may be restricted to White-beaked Sedge which is itself recorded from less than a dozen sites.

The open habitats of the uplands consist mainly of moorland pasture, blanket mires and heaths composed of relatively few plant species. The moth fauna is similarly limited and light-traps generally attract many individuals of a few species. A high proportion of the moths in these habitats are diurnal, or at least easily flushed from the vegetation during the day. The sheep-walks are the poorest habitat with only a handful of resident moths—typical inhabitants are Marbled Minor, Small Dotted Buff, Small Wainscot and Antler. Heaths and mires are noticeably richer—Ling and Bilberry serving as foodplants for a number of species. Common Heaths and male Northern Eggars and Fox Moths are on the wing during the day, whilst True-lover's Knot, Northern Spinach, Striped Twin-spot Carpet and Narrow-winged Pug are common nocturnal residents. Scarcer species of the uplands include Glaucous Shears, Smoky Wave, Haworth's Minor and Grey Mountain Carpet, whilst the Scarce Silver Y is possibly a rare inhabitant of the higher moors. The few lepidopterists that have worked at the highest altitudes in the County have failed to find the diversity that graces Snowdonia but a couple of species are of interest. F. C. Best reported the Ashworth's Rustic as scarce in one site,[35] whilst Salter captured the Red Carpet and Beech Green Carpet at the northern extremity of the County but they have not been seen in Cardiganshire for many years.

vi) Artificial habitats

The moth fauna of the County's towns and villages has received little study but the indications are that several species which are common elsewhere in England and Wales are rather scarce. The Currant-feeders—the Spinach, V-moth, Currant Pug and Currant Clearwing—are all infrequently recorded and the garden pests, Cabbage Moth and Dot, are also relatively uncommon. The Privet Hawk is regrettably local but the Nettle-bed inhabitants, the Snout and Burnished Brass, for example, are well established. The Golden Plusia appeared to be colonizing gardens in Aberystwyth during the 1930s but has since vanished. Many nectar-bearing flowers which attract Red Admirals and Small Tortoiseshells during the day are also visited by moths during the night and the Large Yellow Underwing is one of the commonest moths to be seen feeding on Buddleia, whilst Hummingbird Hawks in the daytime and Convolvulus Hawks at dusk feed from many garden flowers.

Wherever local highways departments can be persuaded to treat road verges sympathetically they can provide a haven for wildlife. Away from the main trunk roads in Cardiganshire, the network of narrow lanes criss-crossing the County are bordered by grassy verges that are infrequently mown. Tall grasses are interspersed with many herbs and in some places, particularly in the south, orchids such as the Lesser Butterfly, Heath Spotted and Early Purple flourish. Thistles, Knapweeds and Bramble provide a nectar source for butterflies from adjacent habitats whilst the presence of larval foodplants allow Large and Small Skippers, Orange Tips and Ringlets to breed in abundance. Along the coastal lanes of the south-west the profusion of Dog Violets in the hedgebanks supports colonies of Pearl-bordered Fritillaries and is of great significance to the future of this species in the County.

Our hedgerows, too, are generally in a similarly healthy position. There appears to be an increasing number of farmers who are laying their hedges, although machine-flailing is also widespread. Most farms are comparatively small and are content to retain manageable-sized fields—a situation which relates to livestock farming as opposed to the arable 'wastelands' of East Anglia. 'Grubbing out' is a rare occurrence and the chess-board pattern of well-maintained hedges is a noticeable component of panoramas from the higher hills. The spraying of herbicides to control undergrowth is almost unknown (nor is it practised on verges) and this also contributes to the diversity of the hedgerow. Whilst some adult butterflies obtain nectar from Hawthorn blossom there are few species which breed on the hedge itself. Holly Blues are scarce but have

[35]F. C. Best, 'Agrotis ashworthii in mid-Wales', Entomologist, 70 (1937), 312.

been reported from hedgerow Hollies and White-letter Hairstreaks make use of the widely planted Elms, although most of these have succumbed to Dutch Elm Disease.

The natural history value of churchyards is well known and in some urbanized counties they serve the function of nature reserves. In a county such as Cardiganshire, where the soils are predominantly acid, the enrichment resulting from the recurrent digging of graves in the older churchyards allows many plants to thrive that have a restricted distribution. Calciphiles, such as Hedge Bedstraw and Quaking Grass, have over half of their sites in churchyards (cf., above p. 69) but their butterfly counterparts have yet to follow suit. The stability of the habitat and the shelter provided by the churchyard walls allow several butterflies to extend their altitudinal range—Ringlets, Orange Tips and Small Skippers are all commonly found in churchyards at altitudes where they are otherwise scarce. The Small Pearl-bordered Fritillary is another interesting inhabitant, with at least five churchyards in the southern part of the County containing moderate colonies, often accompanied by the Chimney Sweeper.

The mining of lead was a boom industry in the north of the County in the nineteenth century and spawned many prosperous upland villages, but by the 1920s most mines had closed. Their abandoned spoil heaps have dominated the immediate landscape ever since, and the high toxicity of the lead and zinc in the spoil inhibits plant colonization. However, the high rainfall has gradually leached out the poisons and a scrubby heath, principally of Ling, has formed on several sites. This has now become an important habitat for invertebrates—for instance, all four species of grasshopper in Cardiganshire are found here in incredible abundance. Butterflies also thrive and the largest Grayling colonies in the County occur on mine spoil. Small Coppers and Small Heaths are also common inhabitants and the wetter hollows around the mounds support Small Skippers and Small Pearl-bordered Fritillaries.

Several commentators on the natural history and geology of Cardiganshire have referred to the remarkable absence of calcareous rocks in the County. The Carboniferous Limestone which brings Silver-studded Blues to north Wales and Marbled Whites to the south does not penetrate the County and calcium carbonate is only naturally present on the sand-dunes at the mouths of the Dyfi and Teifi. This has inevitably restricted the distribution of those butterflies which favour such formations, and hence the railways have played a significant role in extending their range. The permanent ways upon which the tracks were laid are largely constructed from imported iron-slag which has a high lime content and this has enabled plants and animals characteristic of calcareous soils to spread along them. Dr Beeching could justly be called 'the butterflies' friend' for it was his closure of the Aberystwyth–Lampeter and Cardigan–Newcastle Emlyn lines in 1965 that opened up this artificial habitat as an unofficial nature reserve. The importance of the old railway lines in this respect is now widely recognized and, indeed, the Dyfed Wildlife Trust has managed the disused cutting at Allt-fedw as a reserve since 1981. It is not only the minerals present in the permanent way that have attracted butterflies but also the free-draining nature of its construction and the warmth and shelter provided by the numerous cuttings—conditions which appeal to Wall Browns, Common Blues and many other species. Dingy Skippers have almost certainly spread along the railway lines from coastal localities as sheets of Bird's-foot Trefoil have colonized the track. The larval foodplant of the Brown Argus in west Wales is still not known but its recent occurrence in the County must surely be attributable to the closure of the Cardigan line and the subsequent establishment of lime-loving plants.

Migrants

Whilst it is possible to encounter immigrant lepidoptera anywhere in the County, there are greater chances of finding them in coastal districts. It has been suggested that most immigrants recorded in Cardiganshire will have originated in north Africa (*pers. comm.* R. F. Bretherton). Twenty species of immigrant moths have been recorded, two of which—Stephen's Gem and Oak Yellow Underwing—were the first of their kind to be captured in Britain. More or less annual visitors in varying abundance are Vestal, Gem, Hummingbird Hawk, Dark Swordgrass, Pearly Underwing and Silver Y, each of which probably manage to breed after their arrival in the County. Occasional specimens of Convolvulus Hawk, Death's Head Hawk and Small Mottled Willow also occur whilst the Bedstraw Hawk, Striped Hawk, Great Brocade, Delicate, Cosmopolitan, Scarce Bordered Straw, Bordered Straw, Ni Moth and Clifden Nonpareil are very rarely recorded. In addition, there are several species which, although resident in some parts of Britain, are also believed to migrate here from the Continent. In Cardiganshire the commonest of this group is the Angle Shades, whilst the Four-spotted Footman and Angle-striped Sallow have probably only occurred as immigrants. The status of many species on the County list suggests that they may also belong to this category, although small colonies could be established locally—the Scarce Silver Y, Golden-rod Brindle and White Satin being examples. A third type of migrant may be recognized, namely those species which are resident elsewhere in Britain but occasionally undertake short-range, dispersive journeys to areas away from their breeding colonies. There could be anything up to thirty species which could have visited Cardiganshire in this manner. Species whose occurrence at present suggests that they may have wandered from other parts of Britain include Dotted Rustic, Stout Dart, Pale Shining Brown and Scarce Tissue.

Three butterfly species are regular immigrants to Cardiganshire and a further four or five are rare visitors. Red Admirals and Painted Ladies appear most years, usually commonly, and manage to rear a second brood which brightens the autumn countryside. They generally arrive in early summer from the Mediterranean and perhaps try to return there as winter draws on. Hibernation in Britain is suspected for the Red Admiral but apart from the occasional appearance of individuals early in the year this has yet to be confirmed in Cardiganshire. The Clouded Yellow has been increasingly less frequent over the last couple of decades but occasionally they reach west Wales in abundance, as in 1983. The Camberwell Beauty, a Scandinavian immigrant, has only been recorded once, in the autumn of 1976, whereas the Milkweed (or Monarch) has been found on four occasions. There have been a handful of records of Marbled Whites, a species which breeds no closer than south-east Carmarthenshire but is known to disperse long distances during hot summers. Large Tortoiseshells have been recorded twice in recent years although we are as yet unaware of their place of origin. The Pale Clouded Yellow has been reported three times but confirmation is required due to the similarities with the pale form *helice* of the Clouded Yellow. Evidence of return migrations of species which have managed to breed in Britain is more difficult to detect although Miles reported an eastward flight of Silver Y's at Ynys-las in September 1958.[36] The moths were accompanying Red Admirals and Small Tortoiseshells coming in off the sea and continuing inland over the dunes.

[36]P. M. Miles, 'Field notes: Moths', *Nature in Wales*, 5 (1958), 743.

Local populations of Large Whites and Small Whites are reinforced annually by migrations from the Continent and the latter species is probably quite rare as a resident in Cardiganshire. Other species, such as Dark Green Fritillaries and Small Tortoiseshells, are often seen flying purposefully across high ground which is unsuitable for breeding and, whilst some of our butterflies are extremely sedentary, others are clearly highly mobile. The importance of these movements in maintaining populations or establishing new colonies, for both butterflies and moths, is relatively unknown. It is just one of a series of unresolved questions that have been thrown up by the history of Lepidoptera studies in Cardiganshire—questions that ensure the future still holds an endless fascination and enjoyment in these delightful insects for the generations of local naturalists to come.

Part II
Archaeology and History

CHAPTER 1

THE STONE AGE

C. H. Houlder

WHILE it is in general true that the extant structures of any period of prehistory on their own can only provide a skeletal, lifeless picture of the human scene, for the Stone Age in Cardiganshire there is no picture at all from this source. There is not even one remaining example of the substantial stone burial chambers which typify the neolithic occupation of other parts of the Welsh countryside, though the former existence of a handful of such sites can be detected. The presence of Man in the County before the Bronze Age can be reviewed best, therefore, in broadly geographical terms and on a scale that treats Cardiganshire as only the centre part of a dissected coastal landscape rising to the Cambrian Mountains from Cardigan Bay on the west. Earlier chapters have defined the potential environment of this larger region through successive climatic and topographical changes, and provide a basis for interpretation of the archaeological evidence for each stage of human progress.

The yield of structural evidence from excavation is equally poor, even on recognizable settlement sites, usually leaving only small artefacts and waste products for study, but in a few instances there are features that may be assigned to the Stone Age at sites where the main phase of activity was later. For chance finds of artefacts the distribution map has to serve as the medium for relating the record to the environment. The character of artefacts, however, not only provides the essential link with the time-scale for the local study but sometimes allows their significance for British prehistory as a whole to be recognized.[1]

The Earlier Stone Age—Palaeolithic and Mesolithic periods

The palaeolithic period falls within the Pleistocene geological era and in terms of prehistoric human cultures consists of a succession of occupations of the land surface during the warm phases that alternated with glacial. Each advance of the ice tended to obliterate Man's imprint on the land with the result that any surviving relics of his former existence behind a later ice-margin consists only of much weathered artefacts in secondary deposits, though in rare cases primary deposits may be sealed in the protected conditions of caves or in the lower levels of an open site

[1] Additional details of sites and finds discussed in this chapter may be found in Appendix I: Stone Age Settlement Sites and Finds, Appendix II: Neolithic Burial Monuments, and Appendix III: Neolithic Stone Implements.

fortuitously untouched by erosion. Cardiganshire, however, has neither the limestone formations which have yielded such early relics in north and south Wales, nor has chance produced any stray objects from those glacial or riverine deposits that have been scientifically examined or exploited for commercial purposes.

It is possible, nevertheless, to regard one find of a flint specimen from Dôl-y-bont (Appendix [App.] I,1 and Fig. 12.2) as probably having preceded the geologically defined end of the Pleistocene. Typologically it is a core from which flakes have been detached all round, but its size is such as to distinguish it from the smaller cores which typify the microlithic industries of the ensuing Mesolithic period. Comparison with well-documented settlement sites of the final Upper Palaeolithic period in Europe provides almost exact parallels[2] as by-products of industries based on larger flake-tools such as may be equated chronologically with the Creswellian culture of British caves but belonging rather to open, summer hunting stations. To add Dôl-y-bont to the handful of cognate sites known in Britain, notably Hengistbury Head, Portland Bill and two sites in East Anglia[3], would be to extend the range of this early penetration of the emerging hunting terrain, not to an unacceptable degree but to the extent of requiring confirmation from discoveries of artefacts or collateral dating evidence within the Leri Valley deposits. Its dating is particularly crucial since a possible post-glacial alternative might lie in the recognition of a later, truly Mesolithic, flake-tool tradition on the coast of Wales similar in aspect to that recently defined as developing in the north of Ireland between about 6000 and 3000 BC.[4]

It is well to remember that during the transition around 8000 BC from a glacial to a post-glacial climatic regime, the sea-level, though intermittently rising with the release of previously ice-bound water, would have allowed a considerable area of Cardigan Bay to remain as dry land for several centuries. The fauna would have become increasingly diverse as the vegetation cover developed, improving from the limited number of species that could survive in late-glacial tundra conditions to a greater range of species reliant on cover. Food-bearing trees such as hazel appeared, as well as a corresponding diversity of fresh-water and marine food. Though it is inevitable that any evidence of Man's presence on the now submerged coastal plain before about 4000 BC must be as tenuous as it is fortuitous, a recently discovered antler object from Ynys-las (App.I,2 and Plate II) may be placed in a Mesolithic cultural context with some confidence. As part of a composite axe or adze, it compares closely with tools belonging to the generalized Maglemosian cultural tradition that extended across southern Britain into the western mainland of Europe before final severance of the land bridge at about 6000 BC.[5] Its find-spot on a foreshore that contains the stumps of forest trees, a natural component of the environment favoured by species such as the deer that bore the antler, invokes a scene which contrasts with that suggested by finds of Mesolithic character from the land mass rising to the east.

Apart from the settlement site at Aberystwyth discussed below, the only Mesolithic finds in Cardiganshire admitted to a 1977 national list are those from Llangrannog (App.I,3), all

[2] J. G. D. Clark, *The Mesolithic Settlement of Northern Europe* (Cambridge, 1936), 56 and fig.16.
[3] P. A. Mellars, 'The palaeolithic and mesolithic', *British Prehistory*, ed.A. C. Renfrew (London, 1974), 41–99 (p. 76).
[4] P. C. Woodman, 'Recent excavations at Newferry, Co. Antrim', *PPS*, 43 (1977), 155–99.
[5] E.g. J. G. D. Clark, *The Mesolithic Settlement of Northern Europe*, 110–12; idem, *Excavations at Star Carr* (Cambridge, 1954), 157–9.

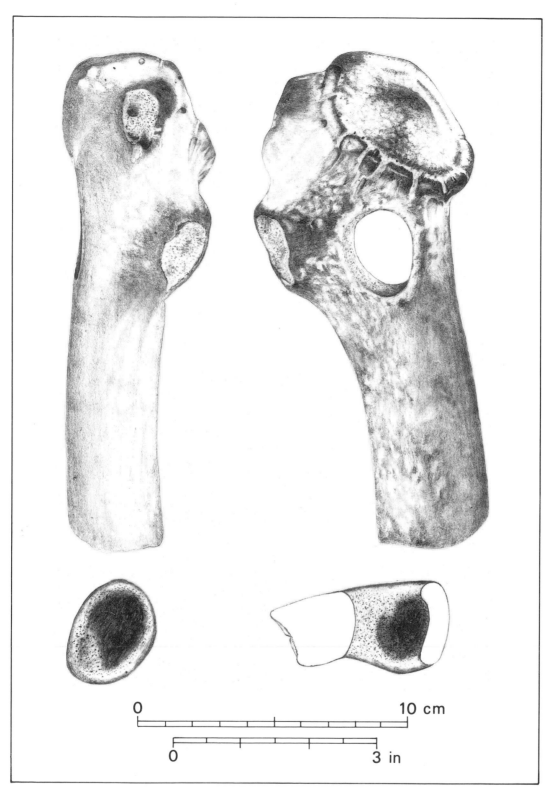

0

10 cm

0

3 in

Plate II: Mesolithic antler object from Ynys-las (drawing).

Plate III: Gogerddan: cropmark of circular enclosure. (*Copyright Cambridge University Collection of Air Photographs*).

Plate IV: Hillforts: (a) Pen Dinas, Aberystwyth. (*Crown copyright RCAHM (Wales)*). (b) Castell Moeddyn. (*Crown copyright RCAHM (Wales)*). (c) Cnwc y Bugail and Castell Disgwylfa. (*Crown copyright RCAHM (Wales)*).

Plate V: Hillforts: (a) Pen y Bannau (*Crown copyright RCAHM (Wales)*). (b) Castell, Cilcennin (Castell Perthi Mawr). (*Copyright Dyfed Archaeological Trust*). (c) Castell Nadolig. (*Crown copyright RCAHM (Wales)*).

Plate VI: Farmstead enclosures: (a) Waunlle, sub-circular enclosure with tangential circular enclosure, SN 225 491 (a new discovery). (*Crown copyright RCAHM (Wales)*). (b) Oval enclosure, Llwyn y Brain. (*Copyright Cambridge University Collection of Air Photographs*). (c) Rectilinear enclosure NE of Capel Tygwydd, SN 276 439 (a new discovery). (*Crown copyright RCAHM (Wales)*). (d) Adjacent rectilinear enclosures, Bailey A and B, SN 252 439 (a new discovery). (*Crown copyright RCAHM (Wales)*).

Plate VII: Trawscoed Roman fort and *vicus*, vertical view (July 1975), K 17 A1 178. (*Copyright Cambridge University Collection of Air Photographs*).

Plate VIII: Llanio Roman fort and *vicus*, from the north (July 1975), CBH 49. (*Copyright Cambridge University Collection of Air Photographs*).

Plate IX: Penllwyn Roman fort, from the north-west (July 1976), BZX 61. (*Copyright Cambridge University Collection of Air Photographs*).

Plate X: Erglodd Roman fortlet, from the south-west (July 1976), CBH 49. (*Copyright Cambridge University Collection of Air Photographs*).

suggestive of an economy dependent on the sea and its food supply at the end of the period of submergence. The inland mountain areas have yielded no traces of settlement to compare with recent discoveries in south-east Wales.[6] Even the fairly prolific finds in the Glaslyn and Bugeilyn region of western Montgomeryshire must be attributed to a hunting tradition more properly belonging to the ensuing Neolithic and Bronze Age periods.

The archaeological status of the Aberystwyth site (App.I,4) can only be defined from a very limited range of observed facts. In the absence of any kind of structure, the only witnesses of domestic activity (apart from the flint industry itself and the limpet hammers) were charcoal, fragmentary bone and burnt flint; but if the working of flint obtained from nearby beaches, providing amongst other things tips and barbs of composite game-hunting weapons, was the principal use of this low headland, this must be seen as only one aspect of a more extensive settlement.

Recent studies equate the Aberystwyth flint industry variously with those from Nab Head and Daylight Rock, Caldey (Pembs.), Prestatyn (Flints.) and Burry Holm (Glam.), observing the relative abundance of individual microlithic forms. Clark included Aberystwyth in a longer list of British sites with continental, Sauveterrian affinities,[7] but Wainwright conservatively puts it among 'sites with coastal economies' without reference to external influence on tool forms.[8] Both, however, exclude the term Tardenoisian, used in the 1925 excavation report and by Grimes,[9] which they would reserve for industries exhibiting a far greater tendency to strictly geometric forms.

The stratigraphic position of the flint industry was originally taken to indicate a comparatively early date in post-glacial times, but certainty is not possible because it was assumed that the overlying darker loam is a rainwash deposit formed in the warm, wetter Atlantic climate which set in soon after 6000 BC (pollen zone VIIa), and this might not be the case. But when it is remembered that the present coastline was not established until about 4000 BC, the supposed partial dependence of the inhabitants of the Aberystwyth site on a marine food supply forces the conclusion that occupation here should be dated shortly before the coastal inundation was complete, and thus somewhat after the time of the maker of the Borth antler axe.

The Later Stone Age—the Neolithic period

i) Settlement sites

Recognition of the Neolithic period as a cultural phase is of very long standing. It is typified by settled occupation of the land coupled with controlled exploitation of preferred food and material resources. In the British artefact record the signals of its inception are conventionally taken to

[6] E.g. J. J. Wymer (ed.), *Gazetteer of Mesolithic Sites in England and Wales* (CBA Research Report 20: London, 1977), 18, 98–9.

[7] J. G. D. Clark, 'A microlithic industry from the Cambridgeshire fenland and other industries of Sauveterrian affinities from Britain', *PPS*, 21 (1955), 3–20 (p. 15).

[8] G. J. Wainwright, 'A reinterpretation of the microlithic industries of Wales', *PPS*, 29 (1963), 99–132.

[9] W. F. Grimes, *The Prehistory of Wales* (Cardiff, 1951), 12.

be the making of pottery, the polishing of stone implements and the building of homesteads of some permanence. The use of the term 'colonization' to describe the arrival of these traditions in Britain as a westward spread from the Continent has tended to suggest a deliberate folk movement, rather than the gradual process of land-winning that is now recognized.

By about 4000 BC the high average temperatures and rainfall of the Atlantic climatic period had created in western Britain a generally forested terrain, but one offering adequate return for pioneers of simple agriculture. Such evidence as is available suggests that stock-raising was dominant over crop husbandry, with some support from hunting and food-collection in the manner of the indigenous Mesolithic population who maintained a separate existence alongside the newcomers.

In assessing Cardiganshire's position in this period of culture-contact it is noteworthy that the Irish Sea formed an integral part of a western channel belonging to the European seaboard as a whole.[10] Radiocarbon dating places the first known Neolithic pottery in northern Ireland well before 3000 BC,[11] and out of the handful of settlements that can be dated within the bracket 3500 to 3000 BC around the Irish Sea two are significantly located in the western promontories of Wales, at Coygan, Carms.,[12] and Llandegai, Caerns.[13] These two are sited on limestone and gravel respectively, where land clearance would have been a less onerous process and the soil immediately suitable for primitive cultivation. The hinterland of Cardigan Bay would have been less attractive, and until recently the absence there of known settlement sites suggested that any isolated finds of Neolithic character probably belonged to later phases of expansion from the areas of primary landfall. There is now evidence of settlement of early Neolithic character from two sites near Aberystwyth, in both cases preceding phases of Bronze Age settlement, and from a third beneath an Iron Age enclosure. At Plas Gogerddan (App.I,5; also Fig. 42) a single pit, radiocarbon-dated to about 3500 BC, contained charred plant remains that included not only grains of wheat (both spelt and emmer) and barley, but fragments of apple and hazel-nut. This mixture is directly comparable with that found on Neolithic sites elsewhere in Britain and reflects a continuing dependence on the collection of woodland wild plants alongside the cultivation of cereals. At Llanilar (App.I,6) pottery fragments in a hill-wash deposit represent a vessel of Early-Middle Neolithic type, potentially datable even earlier than the Plas Gogerddan site. An assortment of Late Neolithic pottery indicates reoccupation after a long hiatus, followed in turn by Early Bronze Age features, but the character of the Neolithic settlement remains obscure. At Bryn Maen Caerau (App.1,7) the evidence, though slight, confirms that of the stone axe finds (see below) that occupation of riverine as well as coastal lowland was a normal feature of the settlement pattern from an early date. Studies of peat deposits may eventually give independent evidence on the role of cultivation through changes registered in the overall pollen record, but

[10] E. G. Bowen, 'Britain and the British Seas', *The Irish Sea Province in Archaeology and History*, ed. D. Moore (Cambrian Archaeol. Assoc., 1970), 13–28.

[11] P. C. Woodman, 'The Irish mesolithic/neolithic transition', *Dissertationes Archaeologicae Gandenses*, 16 (1975), 296–307.

[12] G. J. Wainwright, *Coygan Camp: A Prehistoric, Romano-British and Dark Age Settlement in Carmarthenshire* (Cambrian Archaeol. Assoc., 1967), 14–20.

[13] C. H. Houlder, 'The henge monuments at Llandegai', *Antiquity*, 42 (1968), 216–21 (p. 219) and *AW*, 9 (1969), 8 (radiocarbon date).

the effect of Man on the landscape in Cardiganshire may not have been as positive as has been shown to be the case elsewhere.[14] At least it can be noted that the decline in elm pollen at about 3000 BC, usually attributed to human interference, has been recorded in Borth Bog and in mountain locations, but with a less prominent rise in weed pollen than is to be expected as a result of land clearance for tillage.[15]

It remains then to note the location of recognizably Neolithic monuments and finds and to comment on their typological, and hence cultural, significance in geographical terms. Neolithic house structures are rare in Britain and are usually found by chance or by intensive excavation of sites yielding relevant finds. Cardiganshire has not yet contributed in this way, but in addition to the potential of the sites noted above it may be assumed that settlements of some permanence would have existed fairly close to the communal megalithic tombs of the period which are likely to have been sited near the margin of the particular tract of land favoured by a primitive agricultural group.[16]

ii) Megalithic tombs

In reviewing all possible cases for inclusion in a list of acceptable tombs, all known references have been considered alongside the results of twentieth-century field study. In the two descriptive compilations available to date, A. R. Sansbury treated the pre-Celtic monuments of Cardiganshire in some detail, combining antiquarian sources with observation and local enquiry,[17] while G. E. Daniel in his listing for all counties of England and Wales detailed only those sites which he could accept as surviving prehistoric chambered tombs, but added notes on 'doubtful, disputed and certain vanished sites'.[18] W. F. Grimes's list of Welsh megalithic sites contained no entries for Cardiganshire, since his purpose was to synthesize the diagnostic features of tombs, including their cairn structure.[19]

Poverty of detail renders such a review particularly tentative in Cardiganshire. The inventory of sites now given in Appendix II (entries numbered as in this chapter), though more rigorous in its criteria than Sansbury's list, is based on fuller and more recent information than Daniel's, with recourse to the records of Ordnance Survey and Royal Commission field investigations.[20] Eight of Daniel's thirteen contenders are acceptably prehistoric but only four invite interpretation as Neolithic tombs and one of those admittedly on the sole evidence of a surviving field name; the other four are lacking in detail and could be of Bronze Age date. A further four sites are rejected as fortuitous boulder formations, and the thirteenth dismissed as an error of siting.

[14] I. F. Smith, 'The neolithic', *British Prehistory*, ed. A. C. Renfrew, 100–36 (p. 101) and 281,.n.8.

[15] P. D. Moore, 'Human influence upon vegetational history in north Cardiganshire', *Nature*, 217 (1968), 1006–9, and see this volume, above, pp. 39–40.

[16] RCAHM *Glamorgan*, Vol.I, 1 (1976), 26–7.

[17] A. R. Sansbury, 'The Megalithic Monuments of Cardiganshire' (unpublished University of Wales BA thesis, Dept. of Geography, Aberystwyth, 1932).

[18] G. E. Daniel, *The Prehistoric Chambered Tombs of England and Wales* (Cambridge, 1950), 215–16.

[19] W. F. Grimes, 'The megalithic monuments of Wales', *PPS*, 2 (1936), 106–39.

[20] The Ordnance Survey's archaeological record cards and maps, now known as the National Archaeological Record, are housed and maintained by the Royal Commission on Ancient and Historical Monuments as part of its own National Monuments Record. The Commission's Inventory for Cardiganshire has not yet been compiled.

Of the four sites now accepted as Neolithic tombs, that at Wileirog Uchaf (App.II, 4) has vanished without even an antiquarian description, yet its former existence is preserved in the name 'Cerrig cromlach' in the nineteenth-century tithe survey, applied to a pair of fields at the eastern edge of a cultivable coastal ridge. The other three are known from early descriptions and can all be seen to have stood near well-drained land suitable for clearance for light tillage. Llech y Gawres (App.II, 2) and Garreg Fawr (App.II, 3) occupied positions raised above major valley deposits of gravel and alluvium, while Llech yr Ast (App.II, 1) is at the eastern margin of gravel left on the coast by the final glaciation.[21] Such detail as is recorded of three of these tombs allows little comment on their comparative morphology. All were formed by the raising of a massive slab or boulder onto uprights, at Llech yr Ast to a height of at least three feet (c.1 m) but at Llech y Gawres to five or six feet (c.1.5–2 m). The height of Garreg Fawr is not recorded. The interior of the Llech yr Ast chamber could have measured six feet by three (c.2 x 1m), and Garreg Fawr could have been of similar size. The 'less and lower' monument referred to by Edward Lhuyd (see App.II, 1) at Llech yr Ast is the only possible example of subsidiary structure, perhaps a secondary chamber of the same monument, but the further mention of 'five beds' and a circle indicates the nearby presence of a complex of structures covering a potentially wide time-span.

There is no mention of the mounds that might be expected to have covered these bare remains, but the 'small bank or rising' (see App.II, 2) on which Llech y Gawres stood might have been a denuded artificial mound rather than a natural elevation chosen for effective siting. In the absence of any clue as to the refinements of the stone structures and the shape of the mounds it would be unwise to speculate on the wider significance of any of these tombs, either their relationship to other, better preserved examples in west Wales or the origins of their builders. It is nevertheless notable that the most southerly sites, Llech yr Ast and Llech y Gawres, are close to the major concentration of megalithic sites recorded for northern Pembrokeshire and were only omitted by Grimes from his survey of megalithic monuments for lack of recorded detail.[22] The two sites at the centre of the Cardigan Bay coast, Wileirog and Garreg Fawr, stand in isolation between the Pembrokeshire and Merioneth concentration of tombs, the nearest sites northward being beyond the Mawddach estuary.

iii) Sites not acceptable as Neolithic tombs

Though megalithic in the literal sense of the word, and acceptably the work of prehistoric man, four sites (App.II, 5–8) which have been proposed as Neolithic tombs under the terms *cromlech* or *dolmen* must now be omitted from the list. The two boulders on Banc Rhosgoch Fach (App.II, 5), once accompanied by a third, smaller stone, are uninformative in themselves, lying in a bleak tract of poor land with no suggestion of the former presence of a mound. Llech Gybi (App.II, 6) as a name alone need signify no more than a single stone of any shape or disposition, and the placing of the sick 'under the llech' does not necessarily imply that the stone was raised on supports. The stones at Meini (App.II, 7) were never reported as consisting of more than two in an upright position, which at about twelve feet high (c.4m) are more likely to have been

[21] R. A. Garrard and M. R. Dobson, 'The nature and maximum extent of glacial sediments off the west coast of Wales', *Marine Geology*, 16 (1974), 31–44.
[22] W. F. Grimes, 'The megalithic monuments of Wales', *PPS*, 2 (1936), 106–39.

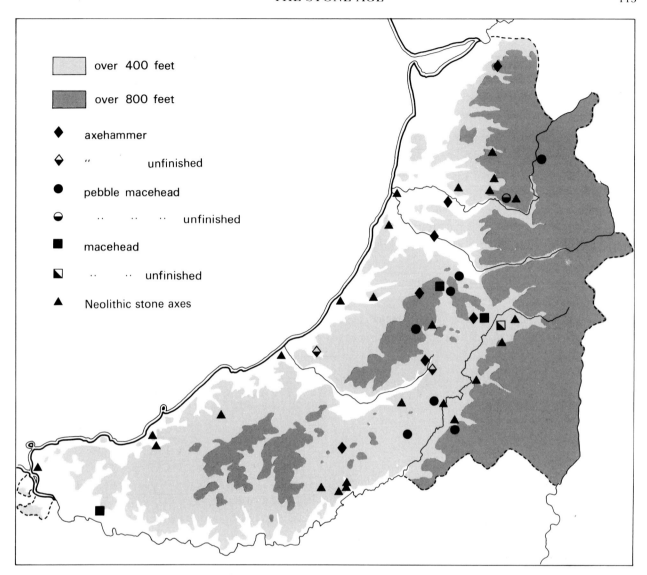

Fig. 11: Distribution of Neolithic and Bronze Age stone implements.

individual standing stones than members of a chambered tomb. Lhuyd's description of Meini Kyvrivol (App.II, 8) lacks the informative detail of size and plan that would place the site in any particular phase of prehistory. The huge stone known as Carreg y Bwci (App.II, 9) must now be recognized as one of a scatter of natural boulders, though it was included, and arguably by design, in the circuit of what appears to be a Roman watchtower. Finally, four sites (App.II, 10–13) must now be removed from any list of prehistoric interest, for reasons given under their entries in the Appendix.

Apart from the few tombs already listed, the County contains no proven examples of monumental construction prior to those accepted for description in later chapters. In particular there is no reliable evidence that the standing stones now incorporated in the churchyard wall at Ysbyty Cynfyn (see p. 199) ever stood on the perimeter of a prehistoric enclosure. W. F. Grimes, in a review of stone circles in Wales, admits that only the largest, most northerly stone can reasonably be regarded as retaining its original prehistoric siting, but seems prepared to accept the bank as prehistoric also and worth comparing with the embanked circles of supposed late Neolithic date in south-west Wales.[23] A curvilinear bank was certainly used here as the earliest limit of the churchyard, faced with stone in a later stage and finally partly levelled on the north when the cemetery was enlarged, but critical survey shows the original enclosure to have been far from circular and without any features suggestive of a prehistoric origin. The stones may be considered as of Bronze Age origin, if indeed they are not themselves the product of an early nineteenth-century attempt to add interest to a poorly endowed churchyard (see p. 136).[24]

iv) Casual finds of Neolithic artefacts

Of the few flint artefacts recorded from Cardiganshire some have already been noted as possibly of Mesolithic date. Certainly there are no items, such as flint leaf-shaped arrowheads, which would be typically Neolithic. On the other hand, there are examples of stone axes of simple, unperforated type, usually ground smooth and polished at least at the cutting edge, to serve as the most characteristic indicators of Neolithic activity in the countryside. Though not providing precise location of settlement sites, axe finds do at least show the extent of penetration of the terrain through the whole of this period, presumably having been lost or discarded during agricultural clearance or the procurement of timber for construction work, but their use for field tillage is improbable for sharp-edged tools.

Out of twenty-two axes from known locations, all but one were found below the 200 m (656 ft) contour, nine of them (App.III, 1–9) within 4 km of the coast; ten more (App.III, 10–18, 22) were within 5 km of the Teifi in its middle reaches, four of them (App.III, 10–13) grouped closely north of Llanybydder. The significance of the distribution is unlikely to lie in simple criteria such as accessibility by sea or river valley but rather in a whole range of environmental factors which must have presented the Neolithic population with strongly contrasting mountain and lowland regimes. Two axes (App.III, 19–20) from the Melindwr valley indicate choice of a sheltered enclave in the foothills east of Aberystwyth.

Evidence is now accumulating from botanical and soil studies, in the interpretation of which it is now possible to discern the influence of man on his environment through such processes as forest clearance and animal husbandry, though the initial choice of terrain for settlement would have been dependent on soil type, vegetation and other factors of ecology.[25]

[23] W. F. Grimes, 'The stone circles and related monuments of Wales', *Culture and Environment*, ed. I. Ll.Foster and L. Alcock (London, 1963), 93–152 (pp. 127–8).

[24] C. S. Briggs, 'Ysbyty Cynfyn churchyard wall', *Arch.Camb.*, 128 (1979), 138–46.

[25] J. G. Evans, *The Environment of Early Man in the British Isles* (London, 1975), chs. 5, 6; *The Effects of Man on the Landscape: The Highland Zone*, ed. J. G. Evans, S. Limbrey and H. Cleere (CBA Research Report, 11, 1975); P. D. Moore, 'Human influence upon vegetational history in north Cardiganshire', *Nature*, 217 (1968), 1006–9.

APPENDIX I: STONE AGE SETTLEMENT SITES AND FINDS

The information at the head of each entry includes the site name, parish and national grid reference.

1. Dôl-y-bont   Genau'r-glyn   SN 626 882

A flint core (Fig. 12.2) was found in 1974 on the driveway of a caravan site at Mill House, Dôl-y-bont. Gravel from the River Leri had been brought there from time to time but from a number of different locations so that the exact stratigraphic source of this object is uncertain. A search of the river banks yielded no further specimens nor clearly observable stratigraphy. The specimen is in Ceredigion Museum.

2. Ynys-las   Borth   SN 60 92

An object made of red deer antler (Plate II), found on the foreshore between Borth and Ynys-las *c.* 1980, appears to be the main body of a composite tool. The base of a shed antler has been perforated close to the burr for insertion of a handle. The distal end of the shaft is abraded, so that it is uncertain whether it was originally cut obliquely to provide a sharp axe or adze blade or whether it served as a sleeve to hold a flint blade or pick. The precise findspot cannot now be determined. The object remains in private possession.

3. Llangrannog   Llangrannog   SN 310 540

A total of nine specimens of flint or chert, consisting of one core and eight unworked blades or flakes, were found at five locations at Llangrannog, either on or close to the beach. There are undoubtedly other finds of similar undiagnostic character from similar locations elsewhere on the Cardiganshire coastline that have escaped record as lacking in interest.

J. J. Wymer (ed.), *Gazetteer of Mesolithic Sites*, 31.

4. Penyranchor   Aberystwyth   SN 579 807

Situated at the north-western foot of Pen Dinas, the site, often characterized as a 'flint factory', was found in 1911 during geological survey.[1] Spoil from a building site yielded finds ranging from distinctive microlithic tools and flint waste to coarse pottery and clay pipes. Only in 1922 was it possible to examine what remained of the relevant deposits.[2] It was estimated that less than one-fifth of the Mesolithic site was still undisturbed, consist-ing of two raised areas to north and south of the road to Tan-y-bwlch beach, called the Harbour Bluff and Hospital Bluff respectively. The rock and its overlying deposits had been deeply breached for this road, as well as for an earlier tramway and for the emergence of the Ystwyth into the harbour.

The flint industry recovered amounts to several thousand pieces (including chert in a proportion of about 1 in 30), the majority being waste flakes and spalls, though some show signs of casual use. Some of the 200 cores indicate, by their reduction to less than 2 cm in length, the smallness of blades acceptable for final shaping; larger flakes, up to 8 cm long, were also used as coarse knives. The characteristic end-product was a microlithic point, reduced from a longer piece by notching or oblique trimming with steep secondary flaking. The so-called micro-burin, the waste portion detached at a notch, was present though not recorded in the original report. Also among the stone tools was a number of 'limpet-scoops', apparently natural pebbles up to 13 cm long with ends abraded by supposed use in hammering limpets from rocks.

The stratigraphy of the site in general terms consists, at the base, of contorted strata of grit and shale, on which is superimposed glacial drift of variable depth followed by a sequence of loams. The drift is barely perceptible towards the eastern end of the Harbour Bluff, but attains a considerable depth towards the sea; the loams also increase westwards from about 30 to 75 cm in depth, a trend which is even more marked on the Harbour Bluff, where the flint industry is contained in a distinctly lighter and more friable soil up to 25 cm thick at the base.

[1] R. Thomas, *Arch. Camb.*, 67 (1912), 211–16.
[2] R. Thomas and E.R. Dudlyke, 'A flint chipping floor at Aberystwyth', *J. Royal Anthrop. Inst.*, 25 (1925), 73–89. The original collection of Thomas and Dudlyke is in the National Museum of Wales, as listed by Grimes, *Prehist. of Wales*, 137–8 (nos. 13, 14). Other small collections are in private hands.

5. Plas   Trefeurig   SN 626 835
Gogerddan

Excavations around a standing stone in 1986

revealed remains of several periods, of which the Neolithic is known to be represented by only one pit, the contents of which may be dated to 3530 BC on the basis of a radiocarbon date of 4700 ± 70 bp (CAR-994). Other features could be contemporary but cannot be so assigned in the absence of corroborative dating or artefactual evidence. The favourable location of this site on deposits of well-drained glacial origin, rare in this part of west Wales, accounts for its continued use throughout ensuing centuries of agricultural use.

K. Murphy, *AW*, 26 (1986), 29–31; 27 (1987), 36.

6. Llanilar   Llanilar   SN 625 751

The chance discovery in 1980 during house-building of five cremation burials, two of them accompanied by Bronze Age urns, led to a more extensive examination by the Dyfed Archaeological Trust in 1983 and 1984 of the ground that remained undisturbed. Several hearths and pits disposed in three groups were probably all roughly contemporary components of an early Bronze Age settlement along with the cremations, which were found to lie within a small ditched enclosure. A range of Neolithic pottery[1] was also present, contained in soil deposits that had entered some of the pits, though only as secondary filling derived from an earlier phase of settlement activity that cannot be fully defined. A single open, round-bottomed bowl of early- to middle-Neolithic character compares closely with forms dated elsewhere in Wales to about 4000 BC. In addition to and distinct from this early specimen were vessels of late Neolithic Peterborough ware, similar to the Mortlake sub-style that occurred in southern England at least 1,500 years later. Probably of the same date were sherds of a Welsh variant of the Grooved Ware tradition.

[1] Opinion on the Neolithic pottery by Dr T. Darvill has been kindly supplied in advance of publication of the full report on the 1983–4 excavation by the Dyfed Archaeological Trust.

D. G. Benson *et al.*, *Ceredigion*, 9 (1982), 281–92.

7. Bryn Maen   Cellan   SN 597 483
Caerau

Excavation by the Dyfed Archaeological Trust in 1987 within an Iron Age defended enclosure revealed a pit sealed beneath a pre-enclosure soil. A date centred on 3655 BC may be deduced from a radiocarbon determination of 4820 ± 70 bp (CAR-1071) from charcoal in the filling. No artefacts were present.

G. Williams, *AW*, 27 (1987), 32–3.

APPENDIX II: NEOLITHIC BURIAL MONUMENTS

The information at the head of each entry includes alternative names, parish, and national grid reference. The final references at the end of each entry are to the numbering in inventories by:
A. R. Sansbury, 'The Megalithic Monuments of Cardiganshire' (unpublished University of Wales BA thesis, Dept. of Geography, Aberystwyth, 1932).
G. E. Daniel, *The Prehistoric Chamber Tombs of England and Wales* (Cambridge, 1950), 215–16.
The National Archaeological Record (hitherto OS) number completes the entry.

A. Sites acceptable as megalithic structures

1. Llech yr   Llangoedmor   SN 222 483
Ast or
Penllech yr
Ast

It is now impossible to establish the precise location of this chamber tomb, but it probably lay near the northern edge of a field named Parkyrast on the 1838 Tithe Survey map. This agrees with Fenton's siting, in 1860, 'a little beyond the third milestone' from Cardigan.[1] An 1859 excursion report refers to it as 'near the road',[2] and Lhuyd's placing of it 'in the parish of Lhan Goedmor'[3] indicates the south side of the road.

Though the site had been mentioned by George Owen in 1603[4] the first and fullest description was by Lhuyd who stated that 'Lhech yr Ast . . . is a vast rude stone of about eight or nine yards in circumference, and at least half a yard thick. It is plac'd inclining, the one side of it on the ground, the other supported by a pillar of about three foot high.' He described several other features in the vicinity, most of which are likely to have been of

Bronze Age date, but the one noted as 'such another monument, but much less and lower' could have been a second chamber of the Neolithic tomb. It seems unlikely that Meyrick, whose description[5] is a slight variant of Lhuyd's, had ever seen the structure. Fenton's recorded observations, made 'during a pedestrian ramble in 1838', stated that 'the large incumbent stone has been long since removed or destroyed, but there are some of its supporters yet in existence'. The 1859 excursion report noted that 'some of the stones have been converted into gateposts', but there was still 'one solitary stone remaining'.

There is thus evidence that a stone measuring (say) 3.0 m by 1.5 m and 0.5 m thick had served as the capstone of a megalithic chamber here, though there is no unequivocal report of more than one upright support in position.

[1] Fenton, *Arch. Camb.*, 15 (1860), 58–9.
[2] *Arch. Camb.*, 14 (1859), 329.
[3] E. Lhuyd, in Gibson (ed.), Camden's *Britannia* (London, 1695), cols. 646–7.
[4] H. Owen, *The Description of Pembrokeshire by George Owen of Henllys, Lord of Kemes* (Cymmrodorion Record Series, no. 1 London, 1892), 251–2.
[5] S. R. Meyrick, *Hist.and Antiquities of the County of Cardigan* (London, 1808), 119.
Sansbury, *Meg.Mons.*, no. 52; Daniel, *Prehistoric Chamber Tombs*, no. 1.
OS SN 24 NW 3

2. Llech y Gawres   Llangoedmor   SN 200 449

In a small field named 'Parc domen' on the tithe map of 1838 there is a broad and ill-defined mound about 1.5 m high. This is the only position so far suggested as fitting Lhuyd's description. After describing other antiquities 'near Neuodd' (*sic* for Neuadd-Wilym) he continues:

> Lhech y Gowres (a monument well known also in this neighbourhood) seems much more worth our observation; being an exceeding vast stone, placed on four other very large pillars or supporters, about the height of five or six foot. Besides which four, there are two others pitch'd on end under the top-stone, but much lower, so that they bear no part of the weight. There are also three stones (two large ones, and behind those a lesser) lying on the ground at each end of this monument: and at some distance, another

rude stone, which has probably some reference to it. This Lhech y Gowres stands on such a small bank or rising, in a plain open field, as the five stones near the circular monument call'd Rolrich stones in Oxfordshire.[1]

Meyrick recorded that all traces of the monument had disappeared.[2]

Though the size of the capstone is not stated, there seems to have been a tomb of truly megalithic proportions here, with at least six stones of the chamber remaining in Lhuyd's time. The other stones mentioned could have belonged to further chambers, though their distance from the main chamber is in doubt. The apparent mound today has an east to west elongation to about 30 m, reaching but not continuing beyond the hedge to the east, and spread to a maximum width of 15 m.

[1] Lhuyd, in Gibson (ed.), Camden's *Britannia*, col. 647.
[2] Meyrick, *Hist.and Antiq.*, 119.
Sansbury, *Meg.Mons.*, no. 53; Daniel, *Prehistoric Chamber Tombs*, no. 2.
OS SN 24 NW (*sic*) 12

3. Garreg Fawr   Llanbadarn Fawr   SN 6000 8093

Samuel Meyrick seems to have been the first to allude to this large slab, set on a masonry plinth in the square of Llanbadarn village, but without attaching particular antiquarian significance to it. He records that 'an immense stone still remains in the centre of the village, but this has of late been broken by some wicked boys making a bonfire on it'.[1] This information is enhanced by the depiction on an unpublished map of 1810 by William Couling of a large stone on supporting uprights.[2] It was noted in successive editions of T. O. Morgan's guidebook to Aberystwyth, of which the first in 1848 states that 'in the centre of the open space are the two fragments of a large slab of stone, whence the crier used to proclaim all matters of public interest. It formerly stood upon pillars of the same material, but being fractured by the kindling of a bonfire upon it some years ago, it was afterwards placed upon a foundation of masonry'.[3] George Eyre Evans referred to Garreg Fawr as 'the huge top stone of the Cromlech which, within memory in 1899, used to stand on its four legs'.[4]

The stone measures 3.3 m long by 1.05 m at its widest, the west and east ends being respectively 0.75 and 0.95 m wide. It has a regular thickness of 0.2 m above the masonry, with well-weathered and level upper and vertical surfaces. The stone has been reassembled by adding the four smallest fragments, about two-fifths of the whole, to the eastern end of the largest. The SE and NW corners have been slightly damaged, and the lower arris has been trimmed on the south side and part of the north side where it overlapped the masonry. The map depiction and the two later mentions of supporting pillars create a strong case for regarding this slab as the former capstone of a chambered tomb. Admittedly no human memory could have extended from 1899 to before 1808, and at that date, soon after the breaking of the stone, Meyrick had recorded no such function. Nevertheless this is clearly what it was considered to have been at the beginning of the nineteenth century, in spite of what may now seem to be rather narrow proportions for a capstone. Only one other large stone is to be seen in the vicinity, lying in a corner of the square 20 m to the east. Though its longest dimension of 1.1 m is barely adequate for its interpretation as a support, it is apparently the remnant of a larger original.

[1] Meyrick, *Hist.and Antiq.*, 376.
[2] E. G. Bowen, *A History of Llanbadarn Fawr* (Llandysul, 1979), 4–5 (and end-paper).
[3] T. O. Morgan, *New Guide to Aberystwith* (Aberystwyth, 1848), 46.
[4] *Arch. Camb.*, 72 (1917), 407–24.
Sansbury, *Meg.Mons.*, no. 38; Daniel, *Prehistoric Chamber Tombs*, no. 3.
OS SN 68 SW 8

4. Wileirog   Genau'r-glyn   SN 616 860
Uchaf
Two adjacent fields on the tithe map are named 'Cerrig Cromlach'. They occupy the eastern shoulder of a rounded ridge, where the land has long been intensively farmed. The ground shows no marked changes of surface level, apart from a broad rise at the SW corner of the fields, and the only large stones are three used as gateposts between the fields, of which the largest is 1.2 m long and 0.5 m wide, of triangular section.

This site deserves to be noted as the probable location of a vanished structure on the evidence of the name alone, which is sufficiently definitive to allow its inclusion in a list of possible megalithic tombs.
Sansbury, *Meg. Mons.*, no. 24; Daniel, *Prehistoric Chamber Tombs*, no. 8.
OS SN 68 NW.

B. Sites acceptably prehistoric, but not of Neolithic character

5. Banc   Llannarth   SN 4362 5409
Rhosgoch
Fach
The two rough grit boulders, first noted as a 'supposed ruined cromlech',[1] are unlikely to have been part of a large structure, nor is a third stone, removed c.1935.[2]
[1] R. E. Bevan, *TCAS*, 4 (1926), 60–70.
[2] OS field report, 1972.
Sansbury, *Meg.Mons.*, no. 41; Daniel, *Prehistoric Chamber Tombs*, no. 6.
OS SN 45 SW 5

6. Llech Gybi   Llangybi   SN 60 52
There is no precise location to suggest for this vanished stone. Lhuyd's remark that it was 'supported by other stones'[1] cannot in itself be taken to indicate that this was a tomb chamber, since he would surely have made that suggestion also, but the opposite view was taken by Canon Fisher on the grounds that 'the earlier term for cromlech was undoubtedly *llech*'.[2] The site is included in the Bronze Age chapter of this volume (App. III, no. 51).
[1] R. H. Morris (ed.), *The Parochialia of Edward Lhuyd* (Cambrian Arch. Assoc., Supplement, 1911), III, 88.
[2] *Arch.Camb.*, 74 (1919), 540–1.
Sansbury, *Meg. Mons.*, no. 55; Daniel, *Prehistoric Chamber Tombs*, no. 10.
OS SN 65 SW 3

7. Meini   Llanychaearn   SN 560 735
The various large stones here, some of them formerly standing, and now removed from the positions in which they were observed in 1797, 1800 and 1804 by Wyndham, Malkin and Evans respectively,[1] can hardly be thought of as components of a megalithic chamber on the available evidence. A reference is included in the Bronze Age chapter of this volume (App. III, no. 60).
[1] *Arch.Camb.*, 13 (1858), 319.
Sansbury, *Meg.Mons.*, no. 56; Daniel, *Prehistoric Chamber Tombs*, no. 4.
OS SN 57 SE 4

8. Meini   Llangoedmor   SN 20 44
Kyvrivol
(Cyfrifol)

The nineteen stones first noted here by Lhuyd,[1] of which no trace or siting is now recoverable, do not seem to have represented the remains of a megalithic chamber. A reference is included in the Bronze Age chapter of this volume (App. II, no. 5).

[1] Lhuyd, in Gibson (ed.), Camden's *Britannia*, col. 647.
Sansbury, *Meg. Mons.*, no. 54; Daniel, *Prehistoric Chamber Tombs*, no. 11.
OS SN 24 SW

C. Sites rejected as fortuitous boulder formations, or not located

9. Carreg y   Cellan   SN 6457 4790
Bwci or Llech
Cynon or
Maen y
Prenfol

First noted and described by Lhuyd,[1] this massive boulder has been repeatedly the subject of folklore and conjecture. It is now recognized as a naturally deposited boulder incorporated, arguably by design, in the bank of an earthwork, for which an interpretation as a watchtower of Roman date[2] is noted on pp. 307–8 of this volume.

[1] Lhuyd, in Gibson (ed.), Camden's *Britannia*, col.647; idem, *Parochialia*, III, 86.
[2] J. L. Davies, *Arch.Camb.*, 135 (1986), 147–53, and *infra*, II, ch. 4.
Sansbury, *Meg.Mons.*, no. 5; Daniel, *Prehistoric Chamber Tombs*, no. 9.
OS SN 64 NW 1

10. Cerrig y   Genau'r-glyn   SN 5937 8678
Gath

Prior to Sansbury's elevation of this site to the status of 'dolmen (partly destroyed)', or 'remains of a cromlech, or a cist', there seems to have been no tradition of a chambered structure nor can the three irregular stones that bear this name be inter-preted as anything other than fortuitous in arrangement, resulting perhaps from field clearance.

[1] Sansbury, *TCAS*, 5 (1927), 108–9.
Sansbury, *Meg. Mons.*, no. 25; Daniel, *Prehistoric Chamber Tombs*, no. 7.
OS SN 58 NE 1

11. Bwlch   Ysgubor-y-   SN 730 945
Gorog   coed

First noted by Fleure as 'what may be a rude dolmen',[1] this was more fully described by Sansbury: 'A monument of problematic form, presumably a dolmen, is situated on the south-western flank of Bwlch Gorog. It consists of a number of large blocks of stone placed one upon the other and has the appearance of a dolmen with a capstone formed of a number instead of a single slab. The structure is approximately 6 ft in height, 9 ft in length and 6 ft in breadth.' Without verification of such an unusual structure in so remote a situation, which has not been possible on the basis of the scanty locational evidence provided, the site has not been accepted.

[1] H. J. Fleure, *Arch. Camb.*, 70 (1915), 405–20.
Sansbury, *Meg.Mons.*, no. 79; Daniel, *Prehistoric Chamber Tombs*, no. 12b.
OS SN 79 SW 6

12. Bwlch-   Trefeurig   SN 73 86
ystyllen

'The remains of a dolmen at Bwlch Ystyllen' were recorded by Fleure[1] but not described by Sansbury. The site has not been rediscovered.

[1] H. J. Fleure, *Arch. Camb.*, 70 (1915), 405–20.
Daniel, *Prehistoric Chamber Tombs*, no. 12a.
OS SN 78 NW 3

13. Llan-
ddeiniol

Daniel's listing of a supposed site in Llanddeiniol parish resulted from an early mislocation of Meini (No. 7 of this inventory).

Daniel, *Prehistoric Chamber Tombs*, no. 5.

APPENDIX III: NEOLITHIC STONE IMPLEMENTS

Full petrological descriptions, under the given reference numbers of the Council for British Archaeology, are available from the National Monuments Record for Wales, Aberystwyth.

1. Tywyn   Y Ferwig   SN 162 489
Warren
(Fig. 12.4)
Axe (half), pecked/ground. Polished only at narrow cutting edge. Oval section. Length (?)200 mm, width 61 mm, thickness 39 mm. Petrology CA37 Greywacke. Found at edge of eroding sea cliff. In private possession.

2. Troed-y-   Penbryn   SN 299 524
rhiw
Axe, ground/polished. Rounded cutting edge, pointed butt. Pointed oval section. Length 142 mm, width 63 mm, thickness 28 mm. Petrology CA14 Welded tuff. Surface find in field. Nat. Museum of Wales Acc. no. 53.378.
H. N. Savory, *BBCS*, 15 (1953), 225.

3. Cefngranod   Penbryn   SN 303 518
Adze, flaked/ground. Rounded cutting edge, pointed butt. Asymmetric pointed oval section. Length 189 mm, width 69 mm, thickness 35 mm. Petrology CA19 Group VIII (SW Wales). Surface find in field. Nat. Museum of Wales Acc. no. 72.18H.
H. N. Savory, *BBCS*, 26 (1975), 241–2 and fig.

4. Llain-wen   Llan-   SN 387 550
(Fig. 12.1)   llwchaearn
Axe, flaked/ground. Crescentic cutting edge, narrow butt. Quasi-triangular section. Length 141 mm, width 55 mm, thickness 23 mm. Petrology CA41 Group VIII (SW Wales). In private possession.

5. Nr. Aberaeron   SN 45 62
Axe, flaked/ground. Polished at crescentic cutting edge. Pointed oval section. Length 101 mm, width 42 mm, thickness 23 mm. Petrology CA20 Flint, not sectioned. Nat. Museum of Wales Acc. no. 33.279.
Grimes, *Prehist. of Wales*, 145, no. 95 and fig.

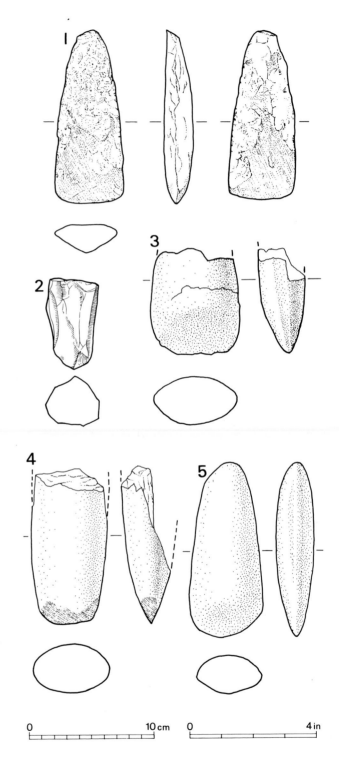

Fig. 12: Stone implements I.

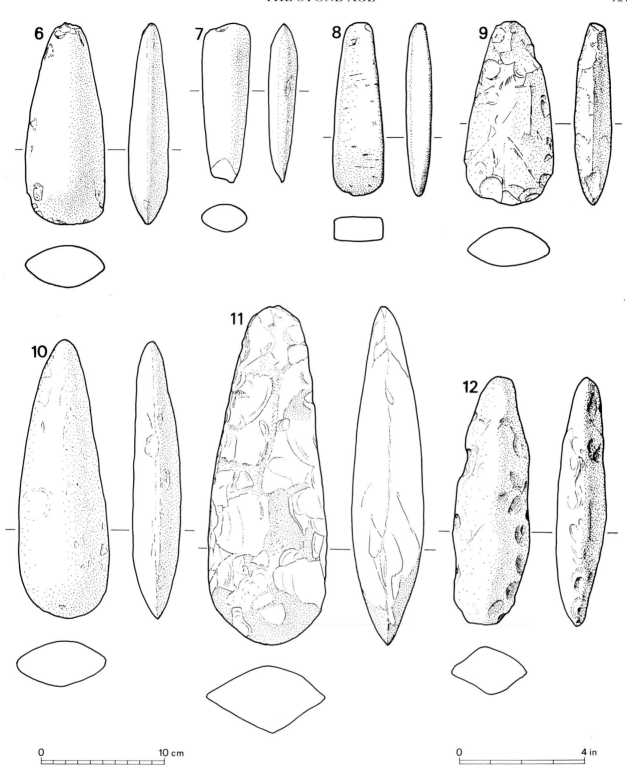

Fig. 13: Stone implements II.

6. Allt-lwyd   Llansanffraid   SN 514 682
beach
(Fig 13.12)
Axe, flaked/ground. Much abraded. Rounded cutting edge. Pointed oval section. Length 197 mm, width 63 mm, thickness 39 mm. Petrology CA36 Group VIII (SW Wales). Found on beach below eroding cliff. In private possession.

7. Tynrhelyg   Llanrhystud   SN 555 682
(Fig. 13.11)   Anhuniog
Axe, flaked/ground. Polished only at rounded cutting edge. Pointed oval section. Length 273 mm, width 96 mm, thickness 57 mm. Petrology CA34 near Group VIII. Found in lane, probably from ditch. In private possession.

8. Ffosrhyd-   Llanychaearn   SN 578 765
galed
(Fig. 13.7)
Axe (part), flaked/ground. Slender form. Pointed oval section, truncated at sides. Length (?)128 mm, width 39 mm, thickness 22 mm. Petrology CA4 Rhyolite. Nat. Museum of Wales Acc. no. 47.164/98.
Grimes, *Prehist. of Wales*, 148, no. 128.

9. Pen Dinas   Aberystwyth   SN 583 802
Axe, small, reflaked from flaked/ground axe with some polish. Pointed oval section. Length 60 mm, width 31 mm, thickness 17 mm. Petrology CA2 Group XXI (Mynydd Rhiw). Surface find on hillside. Nat. Museum of Wales Acc. no. 47. 164/94.
Grimes, *Prehist. of Wales*, 148, no. 126; Houlder, *PPS*, 27 (1961), 142 and fig.

10. Rhiw-siôn   Llanwenog   SN 500 468
Isaf
Axe, flaked/ground. Polished only at crescentic cutting end. Pointed oval section. Length 109 mm, width 40 mm, thickness 20 mm. Petrology CA38 Flint, not sectioned. Nat. Museum of Wales Acc. no. 37.702.
Grimes, *Prehist. of Wales*, 146, no. 105 and fig.

11. Ffinnant   Llanwenog   SN 524 462
Ganol
(Fig. 13.10)
Axe, flaked/ground. Rounded cutting edge, pointed butt. Pointed oval section. Length

221 mm, width 73 mm, thickness 38 mm. Petrology CA35 Tuff. In University of Wales, Aberystwyth, collection.

12. Castell-du   Llanwnnen   SN 531 468
(Fig. 13.6)
Axe, flaked/ground/polished. Rounded cutting edge, pointed butt. Pointed oval section. Length 159 mm, width 64 mm, thickness 33 mm. Petrology CA39 Group VIII (SW Wales). Found in garden topsoil. In private possession.

13. Castell-du   Llanwnnen   SN 531 468
(Fig. 13.8)
Axe. Rounded cutting edge on natural stone. Narrow straight sides. Squared section. Length 136 mm, width 40 mm, thickness 20 mm. Petrology CA40 Group VIII (SW Wales). Found in farmyard, possibly imported. In private possession.

14. Llwyn-y-   Gartheli   SN 594 565
groes
Axe, fragment of butt. Petrology CA17 Rhyolitic ash. In Tregaron Comprehensive School Collection.
H. N. Savory, *BBCS*, 24 (1970), 97–8.

15. Llanio   Llanddewi-   SN 644 563
                brefi
Axe, flaked/ground/polished. Concave sides, square butt. Pointed oval section. Length 206 mm, width 65 mm, thickness 20 mm. Petrology CA16 Rhyolitic ash. Found in plough soil. In private possession.
H. N. Savory, *BBCS*, 24 (1970), 97 and fig.

16. Nant-   Caron-is-   SN 68 59
llwyd   clawdd(?)
Axe, pecked/ground. Pointed butt, rounded cutting edge. Oval section. Length 175 mm, width 68 mm, thickness 45 mm. Petrology CA13 Group I (SW England). Nat. Museum of Wales Acc. no. 52.299/1.
H. N. Savory, *BBCS*, 15 (1953), 68.

17. Bwlchy-   Caron-uwch-   SN 710 633
ddwyallt   clawdd
Axe, pecked/ground. Parallel-sided, pointed butt. Expands to cutting edge. Oval section. Length 157 mm, width 44 mm, thickness 34 mm. Petrol-

ogy CA7 Group XXIIIb (SW Wales). Nat. Museum of Wales Acc. no. 47. 164/101.
Grimes, *Prehist. of Wales*, 144, no. 78 and fig.

18. Pontrhyd-   Caron-uwch-   SN 73 66
fendigaid   clawdd
Axe, pecked/ground/partly polished. Crescentic edge, pointed butt. Oval section. Length 218 mm, width 70 mm, thickness 50 mm. Petrology CA6 Greywacke. Nat. Museum of Wales Acc. no. 47. 464/100.
Grimes, *Prehist. of Wales*, 148, no. 130.

19. Pen-   Parsel Canol   SN 667 810
lanoleu
(Fig. 12.3)
Axe (half), ground/polished. Rounded cutting edge. Flat oval section. Length (?)180 mm, width 72 mm, thickness 37 mm. Petrology CA32 Altered dolerite. Surface find in field. In private possession.

20. Pencraig-   Melindwr   SN 703 816
ddu Mine
Axe, flaked/ground. Rounded cutting edge, thin broad butt. Thick pointed oval section. Length

(?)202 mm, width 74 mm, thickness 44 mm. Petrology CA1 Group VII (Graig Lwyd). Found on road surface. Nat. Museum of Wales Acc. no. 25. 203/2.
Grimes, *Prehist. of Wales*, 144, no. 80 and fig.

21. Banc y   Trefeurig   SN 707 843
Garn (Fig.
12.5)
Axe, ground. Rounded cutting edge and butt. Flattened oval section. Length 137 mm, width 58 mm, thickness 31 mm. Petrology CA33 Altered lava. Surface find. In Carmarthen Museum, Acc. no. 26/1631.
Trans. Carms. Antiq. Soc., 19 (1926), xv.

22. Esgair-   Blaenpennal   SN 636 654
gors-fach
(Fig. 13.9)
Axe, flaked/ground. Rounded cutting edge, narrow rounded butt. Pointed oval section. Length 144 mm, width 73 mm, thickness 29 mm. Petrology CA43 Group VIII (SW Wales). Surface find. In Ceredigion Museum, Acc. no. 2329.

CHAPTER 2

THE BRONZE AGE*

C. S. Briggs

Introduction

THE Bronze Age is a term arbitrarily employed by prehistorians to encompass the period *c.* 2500–600 BC.[1] Despite the metal-using technology of the period, however, the use of non-ferrous metallurgy need not imply that metal-working was central to the existence or economy of what were essentially static farming communities. Rather, metal-working should be seen as an incidental activity but one which has left some of the few known artefacts of the period. Differences in the mode of burial or pottery styles are just as important as metal in establishing a chronological distinction between the Neolithic and Bronze Ages. During the centuries *c.* 2500–2000 BC, large communal chambered graves were giving way to circular burial monuments, containing single or multiple cremations or inhumations, often accompanied by funerary vessels and sometimes by items of worked copper or bronze, gold or fragments of worked minerals such as lignite or amber which were probably personal ornaments during the lives of the deceased. Funerary pottery and ornaments therefore serve as important indicators of burial practices. Little is known of settlement sites and domestic pottery or the crafts of daily life. The later part of the Bronze Age is characterized by the absence of recognizable burial and funerary pottery at least in the west of Britain. Greater reliance, therefore, has to be placed on metalwork

* This study was undertaken as a project of the National Monuments Record (Wales) (1976–81) and appears through the courtesy of the Commissioners on Ancient Monuments and Mr P. Smith, (Secretary). It was carried out originally under the supervision of Mr C. H. Houlder.

    While the study of the monuments owes much to Mr A. R. Sansbury and the late Mr D. Sansbury, the artefactual studies have drawn heavily upon information collected by Mr W. E. Griffiths. Details of implement petrology were provided by Mr C. H. Houlder. Numerous scholars have assisted in answering queries; these include Mr D. G. Benson, Mr G. C. Boon, Mr W. J. Britnell, Mr C. B. Burgess, Dr J. L. Davies, Mr M. Freeman, Dr H. S. Green, Miss F. M. Lynch, Dr P. Manning, Mr D. M. Metcalfe, Dr S. P. Needham, Mr E. R. D. Prosser, Dr J. D. Owen, Dr H. N. Savory and Mrs G. Varndell. Landowners and farmers too numerous to mention treated the writer with courtesy, even when he strayed upon their land under the most inauspicious of circumstances. Mr G. A. Ward illustrated the artefacts from the writer's sketches and drawings, while Mr D. K. Leighton put the results of his own fieldwork at the writer's disposal and drew the site plans from surveys in which he originally assisted. The staff of RCAHM (Wales) are to be thanked for help in various ways. The writer alone is responsible for the views expressed.
[1]C. B. Burgess, 'The Bronze Age in Wales', *Culture and Environment in Prehistoric Wales*, ed. J. A. Taylor (BAR 76: Oxford, 1980), 243–86, and idem, *The Age of Stonehenge* (London, 1980).

studies for an understanding of the period even though these provide an inadequate alternative to a fuller knowledge of settlement sites and domestic economy. In some respects in Wales the period might be better divided into two and renamed the 'Round Grave Burial Period' (c. 2500–1400 BC) and the 'Bronze-Using Dark Age'(c. 1400–600 BC), since virtually all known funerary monuments fall into the earlier part of our period and the majority of the known metalwork into the later.[2] In the use of these two main types of evidence—the monumental and the artefactual—it is necessary to stress that the known monuments are those which have been recorded and the artefacts those which have found their way into museums or are noticed in the literature. Many other sites and finds may exist but await recognition, description and publication. Present knowledge, therefore, gives but a tiny glimpse of the whole. In this quest environmental sciences also have a valuable contribution to make in the study of these early communities and on occasion provide a tantalizingly different story from that which emerges from a study of the monumental and artefactual evidence alone.

Monuments

i) A history of site discovery

Bronze Age monuments and artefacts have figured in the topographical literature for about three centuries.[3] In his travels and through parochial questionnaires Edward Lhuyd in the 1690s recorded a variety of sites to the south and east of the County, among them a notable group in Cellan parish.[4] Incidental evidence from the surveys of mining speculators, notably by Lewis Morris and William Waller, appeared soon after. Other contemporary eighteenth-century surveys, particularly of the Gogerddan and Nanteos estates, early roadbooks and the earliest Ordnance Survey maps also adventitiously include useful archaeological information.

Although numerous eighteenth-century tourists passed through the County it is to Samuel Rush Meyrick, the County historian, that we are most indebted.[5] He not only described cairns and putative stone circles but also excavations (which produced only urns) undertaken upon burial mounds at his express command. Later nineteenth-century discoveries are recorded in the accounts of the meetings of the Cambrian Archaeological Association at Aberystwyth in 1846, Cardigan in 1859, Machynlleth in 1866, and Lampeter in 1878.[6] The founding of the Cardiganshire Antiquarian Society in 1909 ensured that a more local base was given to prehistoric

[2]Cf. the contributions of Burgess on chronology, op.cit., n.1 above, and F. M. Lynch, 'Bronze Age monuments in Wales', *Culture and Environment in Prehistoric Wales*, ed. J. A. Taylor, 233–41.
[3]For a fuller critical account of antiquarian sources see C. S. Briggs, 'Notes on the study of Megalithic and Bronze Age sites and finds from Ceredigion', *Ceredigion*, 9 (1982), 264–80.
[4]E. Gibson (ed.), *Camden's Britannia* (1st edn., London, 1695), cols. 645–7; (2nd edn., 1722), cols. 771–6. See also the new edition of 1722 publ. as *Camden's Wales*, introd. by G. Walters (Carmarthen, 1984), 61–3.
[5]S. R. Meyrick, *The History and Antiquities of Cardiganshire* (London, 1808 and 1810). Original manuscripts relative to the compilation of this have not been located.
[6]Aberystwyth Meeting, *Arch. Camb.*, 2 (1847), 351–72; Cardigan Meeting, ibid., 12 (1859), 349–52; Machynlleth Meeting, ibid., 22 (1866), 544–9; Lampeter Meeting, ibid., 33 (1878), 65–8.

studies, although the earliest diggings under its auspices left a great deal to be desired. Daryll Forde, H. J. Fleure and latterly E. G. Bowen all contributed in some measure to the investigation of local sites, but it was one of their students, Arthur Sansbury, who made the greatest contribution in his assiduous publication of Bronze Age sites and finds. Regrettably, his most important work, a thesis surveying local cairns and standing stones, was never published, although it has proved a sound introduction to further investigation.[7] Random discoveries brought about by farming, forestry and industrial activity, together with planned excavation notably by C. H. Houlder, A. H. A. Hogg and K. Murphy, whilst not appreciably altering site distribution patterns, have vastly expanded our knowledge and expectation of the cultural range and artefactual types to be recognized in west Wales. The full effects of the application of environmental and scientific archaeology have yet to be felt in Cardiganshire, although R. T. Smith, J. A. Taylor and P. D. Moore have laid the foundations.

During the period of investigation for this chapter (1976–85) the known distribution of upland cairns has been dramatically altered by field discoveries by the writer and D. K. Leighton. A number of ploughed-out lowland monuments have also been recognized through aerial photography, most notably by officers of the Ordnance Survey, while results from the recently excavated barrows at Gogerddan have yet to be assessed.

ii) Monument recognition and discovery

Our knowledge of burial and settlement sites is limited by factors of recognition and discovery. As barrows are easily ploughed out and cairns offer suitable quarrystone or hardcore, those which are known and recorded probably represent only a small fraction of the original total. Unless burials happen to be protected by stone slabs which offer resistance to the plough, unprotected urns and their contents are easily lost without trace. Urnless burial pits, distinguished only by soil discoloration, are likely to pass quite unnoticed. Similarly, only the more permanently fixed parts of stone-built cairns tend to survive the attentions of the stone-picker, leaving structures which only confuse the archaeologist.[8]

Until recently it was commonly believed that prehistoric man lived almost exclusively in the hills. This view is particularly easy to uphold if strong emphasis is placed upon the visually spectacular hilltop settings of some cairns.[9] But barrow sites also litter the lowlands and there is now no evidence to demonstrate preference for upland or lowland situations for early settlement and agriculture. Aerial photography illustrates valley bottoms covered in cropmarks of prehistoric sites, even though centuries of ploughing and erosion have pared down surface features beyond recognition. Damaged or near-obliterated sites are only likely to be recognized where the ground is disturbed, and in this respect early recognition of archaeological features (for example,

[7]A. R. Sansbury, 'The Megalithic Monuments of Cardiganshire' (unpublished Univ. of Wales BA thesis, Aberystwyth, 1932). The earliest excavations of the Antiquarian Society appear in *TCAS*, 2 (1909), 99–100.

[8]J. B. Stevenson, 'Survival and discovery', *The Effect of Man on the Landscape: The Highland Zone*, ed. J. G. Evans and S. Limbrey (CBA Research Report No.11; London, 1976), 104–8.

[9]P. Crew, 'The excavation of a group of mountain-top cairns on Drosgl, Llanllechid, Gwynedd', *BBCS*, 33 (1985), 290–325.

discoloured soil, scattered potsherds or a damaged cist) is crucial. Everyone with an interest in local history should be encouraged to observe and report this type of information. The point is well illustrated with reference to the discovery of several Bronze Age burials in 1980 at Llanilar, only drawn to the attention of archaeologists through the watchfulness and goodwill of a trio of workmen digging a trench which disturbed one of the burials.[10]

iii) Settlement sites

a) Enclosures: Whereas there is a great deal of information available about burial in the earlier part of the Bronze Age, our knowledge of contemporary settlement sites is relatively poor. It is likely that some of the cropmarks plotted from aerial photographs have their origins in this period. One such potential site is the circular feature on land of the Plant Breeding Station at Plas Gogerddan, Bow Street (Plate III). Excavations there might reveal traces of timber buildings and drainage gulleys with related field boundaries. Despite the apparent absence of entrances it remains possible that the site could have been a henge monument (see p. 142) or may belong to a later period. If finds elsewhere in Britain are taken as a guide, early palisaded enclosures, both defensive and agricultural, originating in the Later Bronze Age after *c.* 1200 BC may in future be recognized beneath many local hill forts, like, for example, at Pilcornswell (Pembs.).[11] Another habitation site of *c.* 1300 BC, comprising a hut loosely associated with enclosures, has been excavated at Stackpole Warren (Pembs.) and there is every reason to believe that the nearby site at Longstone Field, St Ishmael, which yielded a comparable date, also formed part of an agriculturally orientated community.[12] Sites such as these, represented only by postholes and burnt stone with occasional fragments of burnt flint and potsherds, must also exist in Cardiganshire, though they await recognition.

b) Burnt mounds: Further evidence of settlement is beginning to emerge in the form of 'boiling mounds', or 'burnt mounds' in several parts of the County and beyond.[13] These mounds comprise a heap of red and black burned stone and charcoal and sometimes peat or other vegetable matter. They are common in the neighbourhood of Cors Fochno and more generally on the poorly drained soils of the upper Teifi Valley, though examples are constantly being recognized elsewhere. The excavation of such a mound at Fullbrook Mill, Tregaron, has yielded a radio-carbon date of 1925 ± 70 bc (CAR 469) which places it firmly in the Early Bronze Age. It now seems likely that the base of a tanged and barbed flint arrowhead of Bronze Age type, found among burned debris in another deposit near the mill, might also be taken as a rough indication

[10]D. G. Benson, C. S. Briggs, J. L. Davies and G. H. Williams, 'A Bronze Age cemetery at Llanilar, Cardiganshire', *Ceredigion*, 9 (1982), 281–92.

[11][G. H. Williams], 'Fighting and farming in Iron Age Pembrokeshire', *Current Archaeology*, 82 (1982), 332–5.

[12][G. H. Williams], 'Standing stones', *Current Archaeology*, 82 (1982), 337–9; G. H. Williams, *The Standing Stones of Wales and South West England* (BAR 197: Oxford, 1988).

[13]T. C. Cantrill, 'Prehistoric cooking-places in south Wales', *Arch. Camb.*, 66 (1911), 253–86; idem, 'Some chemical characters of ancient charcoals', *Arch. Camb.*, 74 (1919), 365–92; T. C. Cantrill and O. T. Jones, 'The discovery of prehistoric hearths in south Wales', *Arch. Camb.*, 61 (1906), 17–34.

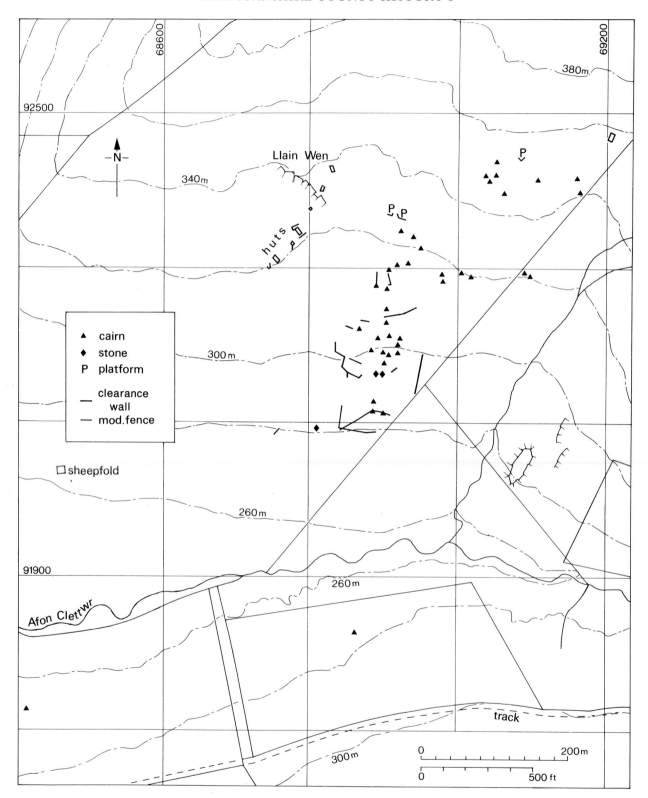

Fig. 14: Upper Cletwr valley early landscape and cairns.

of contemporary use.[14] A slightly later date was obtained from a similar site at Troedrhiwgwinau in 1986.[15] However, lest it be thought that all such mounds are of the Bronze Age, it should be pointed out that some have yielded Dark Age or even medieval radiocarbon dates.[16] The radiocarbon method provides only the date of the timber, not necessarily the date it was burnt: the burning of fossil fuel in the form of bogwood could provide an unrealistically early date for a much later event.

c) Other types of settlement: It is now generally believed that much of upland Britain was farmed during the earlier part of the Bronze Age.[17] In many upland areas of Wales evidence is emerging for field clearance and even field systems, mostly of unknown date, though many are thought to date from the Bronze Age.[18] Not only are widespread clearances known in Snowdonia and on the Brecon Beacons, but they are also preserved upon lower-lying heathlands like Dyffryn Ardudwy, Mynydd Presely and Skomer Island.[19] Some sites have associated huts, and in some areas Bronze Age burial cairns are interdigitated among these settlements.[20]

Clearance and enclosure features are currently known from only a handful of areas in Cardiganshire. Clearances with huts were noted in the 1870s on the stony ridge between Cellan and Cynwil Gaeo,[21] but these have since been swept away. During the 1960s a group of low stone mounds were noted on the south-facing slope of Hafod Ithel, Trefenter, by Mr Eric Whatmore (Fig. 15).[22] These presumed agricultural clearances may be contemporary with the Bronze Age cairns capping Garn Wen (Garn Wen 1 and 2) about 1 km to the north. Similar cairn groups were planned at Nant Groes Fawr by D. M. Metcalfe in 1976 (Fig. 16). More extensive fieldstone clearances clutter the northern, south-facing valley side of the Upper Cletwr (Fig. 14). Lying below the outcropping rock north of Llain Wen are 30–40 cairns, a handful of which were almost certainly Bronze Age burial sites (Llain Wen nos. 240–1; Fig. 20.2). These clearance features comprise odd formless stone heaps along with low dispersed and fugitive fieldwalls, up to 50–60 m in length. Some cairns may originally have punctuated lines of less durable fencing, but without excavation it is difficult to distinguish any particular pattern. Nearby, to the west are the remains

[14]G. H. Williams *et al.*, 'A burnt mound at Felin Fullbrook, Tregaron, Ceredigion', *BBCS*, 34 (1987), 228–43.

[15]A. E. Caseldine and K. Murphy, 'A Bronze Age burnt mound on Troedrhiwgwinau Farm, near Aberystwyth, Dyfed', *AW*, 29 (1989), 1–5.

[16]G. H. Williams, 'A group of burnt mounds at Morfa Mawr, Aberaeron', *Ceredigion*, 10 (1985), 181–8.

[17]For useful discussion see R. Mercer (ed.), *Farming Practice in British Prehistory* (Edinburgh, 1981).

[18]For Britain generally, see C. B. Burgess and D. A. Spratt (eds.), *Upland Settlement in Britain: The Second Millennium BC and After* (BAR 143: Oxford, 1985). For a general survey of Wales, see C. S. Briggs, 'Problems of the early agricultural landscape in Upland Wales, as illustrated by an example from the Brecon Beacons', in loc. cit., 285–315.

[19]R. S. Kelly, 'The Ardudwy Survey: fieldwork in western Merioneth 1979–81', *J. Merioneth Hist. and Record Soc.*, 9 (2) (1982), 121–62; P. Drewett, 'An archaeological survey of Mynydd Preseli, Dyfed', *AW*, 27 (1987), 14–17; J. G. Evans, *Prehistoric Farmers of Skomer Island* (West Wales Trust for Nature Conservation: Haverfordwest, 1986).

[20]C. S. Briggs, n. 18 above, 298–302; A. H. Ward, 'Cairns and cairn fields: evidence for early agriculture on Cefn Bryn, West Glamorgan', *Landscape History*, 8 (1986), 5–14.

[21]D. R. Thomas, 'Prehistoric and other remains in Cynwil Gaio', *Arch. Camb.*, 34 (1879), 345–56.

[22]C. S. Briggs, 'Hafod Ithel', *AW*, 14 (1974), 9–10; C. Stenger, 'Lloft Lloyd; Y Bryn; Nant Groes Fawr', *AW*, 23 (1983), 6–7.

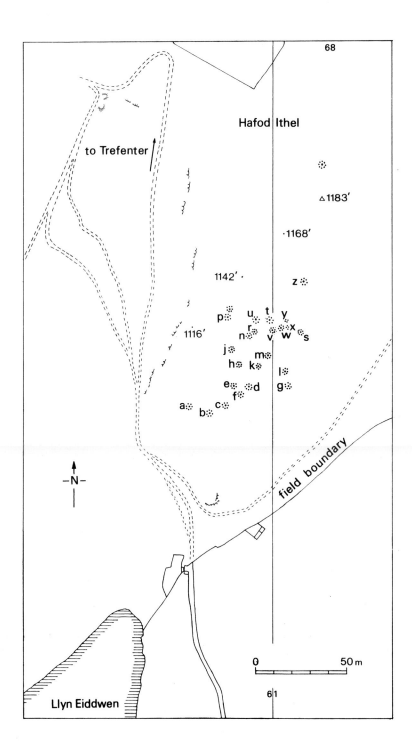

Fig. 15: Hafod Ithel early landscape and clearance cairns.

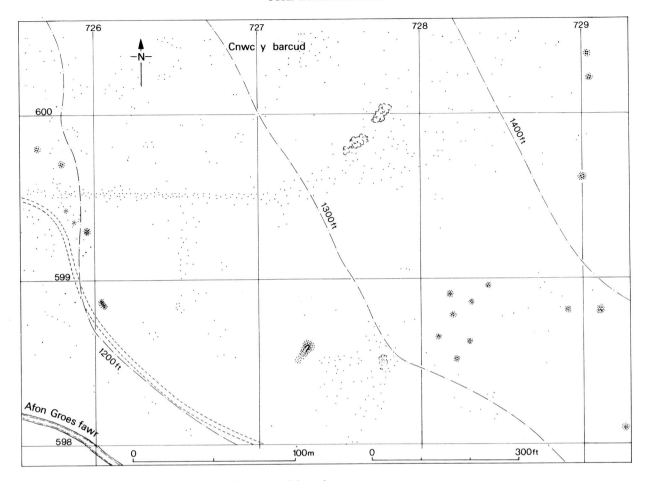

Fig. 16: Nant Groes Fawr, early landscape with cairn groups

of seven huts, most probably medieval or later in date. Presumably their occupants modified the later prehistoric landscape. During the 1984 drought prehistoric settlement enclosures, a land boundary, field clearance cairns and early ploughsoils were exposed from beneath areas of peat erosion within the confines of Nant-y-moch reservoir.[23]

As already hinted, lowland settlement is very difficult to recognize, owing to erosional factors. At Llanilar in 1983 Early Bronze Age pottery fragments, possibly of domestic origin, were excavated from pits within an enigmatic Neolithic–Early Bronze Age burial complex (see Appendix 1, no. 233, Fig. 26). Radiocarbon samples from the excavation of a similar site at Gogerddan in 1985 also hint at a local presence there during the later part of the Early Bronze Age.

Another early settlement site may have been the so-called 'crannog' close to the source of the Tywi, described by Peate in 1927.[24] According to Peate's informant there were ten pointed

[23]C. S. Briggs and K. Murphy, 'Nant-y-Moch Reservoir', *AW*, 24 (1984), 28–33.
[24]I. C. Peate, 'A reputed Lake Dwelling site near Tregaron', *BBCS*, 4 (1927), 283–4; idem, *Antiq.*, 2 (1928), 473.

wooden piles about 2 ft high, set into a subsoil of whitish clay (in which were fragments of charcoal) in a straight line about 12 ft apart. It seems probable that these were vestiges of an early wooden field boundary of a type well known and often preserved in Ireland. A similar example has been described from Trallong (Brecs.) not far to the east of the Tywi site.[25] Savory was inclined to regard them as possibly connected with stock-raising during the Middle Bronze Age.[26] Although at this stage dating can only be conjectural, these structures do appear to have been erected before the growth of peat by communities practising plant or animal husbandry, which demanded clearance of the ground and its division, as part of their social or agricultural organization. Such features may be easily overlooked when encountered in modern drainage or afforestation schemes.

d) Farming and the Bronze Age landscape: From the limited evidence it is difficult to judge just what sort of farming was being undertaken. Some palaeoecologists have recently explained forest clearances simply in terms of slash-and-burn agriculture.[27] One pollen analysis of peat from Tregaron Bog suggested the total duration of a clearance episode might have been about fifty years, including a deforestation episode of ten years followed by some fifteen years' occupation.[28] These estimates provide an indication of the processes involved in land-taking, though they might not be representative of non-boggy soils which were probably long-used once colonized. Until recently it was possible to conjecture a shift from arable to pastoralism at the end of the Neolithic[29] but emerging evidence for widespread land division and clearance cairns from field surveys must indicate continuing common practices of crop-husbandry. Certainly, in lowland Britain such arable farming was complemented by animal husbandry, though the bones which could demonstrate this diversity have been dissolved by acid upland soils.

What effect had these early farming practices upon landscape and soils? Forest or woodland clearances are discernible in pollen diagrams documenting the vegetational history already described by Dr Moore (see above, I. ch. 3). It is more difficult to establish how far landforms may have been altered by agriculture, for, although valley sediment studies in north Cardiganshire probably indicate increases in arable farming during historic times, there is at present only a hint of comparable accelerating sedimentation during the prehistoric period.[30] Evidence is also beginning to emerge which suggests considerable degradation of soils during later prehistoric times. Some thirty years ago Dr Victor Stewart noticed 'that a discontinuous charcoal

[25] H. N. Jerman, 'Oak piles from the Peat in North Breconshire', *Ant. J.*, 15 (1935), 68–9; W. F. Grimes, *The Prehistory of Wales* (Cardiff, 1951), 232.

[26] H. N. Savory, 'Prehistoric Brecknock', *Brycheiniog*, 1 (1955), 79–126 (p. 114).

[27] J. R. Pilcher and A. G. Smith, 'Palaeoecological investigations at Ballynagilly, a Neolithic and Bronze Age settlement in Co. Tyrone, Northern Ireland', *Philosophical Transactions of the Royal Society of London*, 286(B) (1979), 345–69. The association between apparently limited vegetational clearance with slash-and-burn agriculture was first made locally by P. D. Moore, 'Human influence upon vegetational history in North Cardiganshire', *Nature*, 217 (1968), 1006–9.

[28] J. Turner, 'The anthropogenic factor in vegetation history', *New Phyt.*, 63 (1964), 73–89; idem, 'A contribution to the history of forest clearance', *Proc. Royal Society of London*, 161(B) (1965), 343–54.

[29] R. Bradley, *The Prehistoric Settlement of Britain* (London, 1978).

[30] M. G. Macklin and J. Lewin, 'Terraced fills of Pleistocene and Holocene age in the Rheidol Valley, Wales', *J. Quaternary Science*, 1 (1986), 21–34.

horizon may exist at about 3–4 ft (about 1 m) in places within the mantle of erosion debris' in a soil transect running through the University farm, Penglais, Aberystwyth. This suggested that 'erosion on a massive scale must at one time have followed removal of the surface vegetation by fire'.[31] Discussing further aspects of local soil development in 1961, in which evidence was based upon transects at Trawscoed, in the Dyfi Forest and from a cliff section at Aberaeron, Dr Stewart concluded that in the wake of conditions which enabled a 'climate suitable for full forest cover', soil development had been dramatically affected by 'fire, followed by massive but localised erosion'.[32] The recent recognition by Mr M. Nixon of an as yet uninvestigated but extensive deeply buried charcoal-rich soil profile situated within a silted valley bottom near Borth also suggests early forest clearance and subsequent agricultural activity. Interestingly, the Nant-y-moch Bronze Age burial monuments and presumed field clearances were actually discovered beneath peat surrounded by a grey, charcoal-rich soil. This begs a further question: as charcoal-rich soils are often indicators of later prehistoric farming activity, did this accelerating peat growth on exhausted agricultural soils have a more far-reaching effect upon climate?

During the earlier part of the Bronze Age, the climate of north-west Europe is generally considered to have deteriorated significantly from drier and warmer before *c.* 2000 BC to cooler and far more humid by 1200 BC.[33] Recent speculation suggests this change specifically resulted from the cooling effects of atmospheric ash from an eruption of the volcano Santorini in the eastern Mediterranean in 1626 BC. Transported volcanic dust has been recognized during peat profile investigation in the British Isles.[34] However, although a single short-term catastrophic factor like this might be invoked to explain climatic deterioration, it seems equally possible that this eruption exacerbated an already delicate environmental balance—the cumulative, long-term effect of man-made vegetational changes. Further documentation of these changes, and evidence of the dust itself must now be sought beneath the peat covering unafforested areas of upland Wales.

iv) Burial and ritual monuments

a) Cairns: i. Cairn classification. The plethora of terms propounded for Bronze Age cairn typology in recent years has become too cumbersome for practical field use, and something approaching the simplicity of W. E. Griffiths's definition is preferred here.[35] A full discussion is

[31] V. I. Stewart, 'A morphological study of the inter-relationships of selected soils in Mid-Wales', *Welsh Soil Discussion Group Report*, No.1 (1959–60), 11–16.

[32] V. I. Stewart, 'A perma-frost horizon in the soils of Cardiganshire', *Glaciation in Wales as related to Soil Profile Development* (Welsh Soils Discussion Group; Aberystwyth, 1961), 19–22. Wider aspects of prehistoric soil development are usefully discussed by R. T. Smith and J. A. Taylor, 'The post-glacial development of vegetation and soils in northern Cardiganshire', *Trans. Inst. Brit. Geog.*, 48 (1969), 75–95.

[33] A. F. Harding, *Climatic Change in Later Prehistory* (Edinburgh, 1985). For much important local information about vegetation and climate see J. A. Taylor, 'Chronometers and chronicles: a study of palaeoenvironments in west-central Wales', *Progress in Geography*, 5 (1973), 247–334, and idem, *Timescales of Environmental Change* (Inaugural lecture, Aberystwyth, 1987).

[34] M. G. L. Baillie, 'Irish Oaks record volcanic dust veils drama', *Arch. in Ireland*, 2. 2 (1988), 71–4; idem, 'Irish tree rings, Santorini and volcanic dust veils', *Nature*, 332 (1988), 344–6; idem, *Current Archaeology*, 117 (1989), 310–13.

[35] W. E. Griffiths, 'Burial and ritual structures, Bronze Age', in RCAHM, *Glamorgan*, I, i, *The Stone and Bronze Ages* (HMSO, London, 1976), 42–9.

to be found in the introduction to Appendix I. The term *Kerb Cairn* is adopted to describe any burial monument demonstrably encompassed by larger perimeter stones, whether flat or ortho-static flags or amorphous boulders. A *Ring Cairn* is taken to be an annular bank of small stones encompassing an area free of cairn mass with or without inner or outer revetment. *Barrow* is used to define a site in which no stabilizing perimeter may be seen upon field inspection, but in which either stone or timber may originally have acted as such. Finally, *Cairn* is used to convey that insufficient evidence of structure is detectable for further typological refinement to be possible without excavation. It is hoped that this simplification will eliminate any future confusion created by the tendency to overcategorize burial sites.

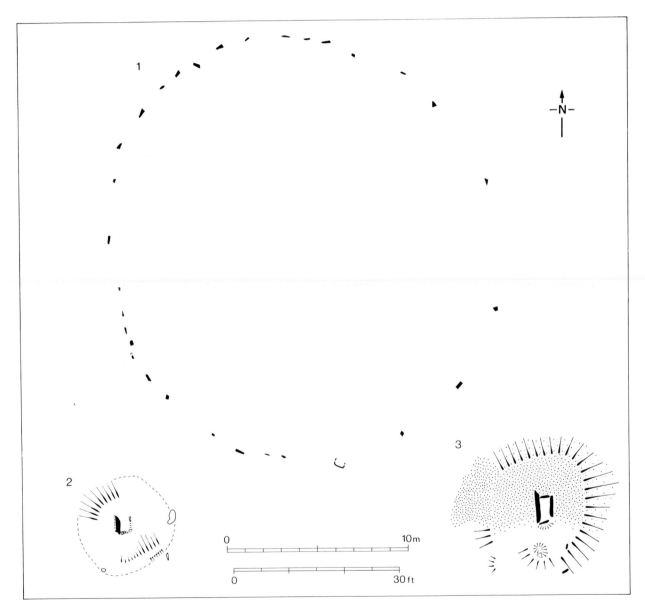

Fig. 17: 1. Moel y Llyn stone circle, 2–3. Cae'r Arglwyddes cairns 1 and 2.

ii. Morphology, building materials and location. Cairns in Cardiganshire are conventionally circular, although in some cases recent destruction has brought about shapelessness. Where the site was an earthen barrow, or of earth and stone, the diameter may vary from about 10 m to over 20 m, with some as high as 3 m, for example at Mynydd Trichrug. Few stone cairns survive to this height though many must have been higher than at present.

The materials employed in building upland cairns without doubt derive from the localities in which the monuments stand, and a small number of cairns utilizing different types of stone may be observed within quite a close compass of ground. The point is well illustrated with reference to the Cletwr Valley (Fig. 14). At the top, eastern end of the valley survives a stone circle, Moel y Llyn (Appendix II, no. 6, Fig. 17.1), which comprises a peristalith of flat orthostatic slabs, stones of similar material appearing in the subsoil where recent drainage ditches have trenched it.[36] Two or three other cairns litter its immediate vicinity, one having been robbed of all but its central cist, the others retaining more boulder-like cairn masses; here the cairn material is of a type which may have been picked up in nearby field clearance.

On the northern slope of the valley are two small encised cairns at the east end of Llain Wen (Fig. 20.2). In these the stones have rounded faces; whilst the large quartz boulders which revet the cairn could only be derived from one of the quartz veins which outcrop visibly nearby and to the north. Stones of a similar size are present in scree between 10 and 20 m from the cairns. Llain Wen Cairn, some 200 m to the west, comprises larger boulders, but again there is none larger than the stones which literally clothe the slopes behind and to its north. About 80 m to the north-west stands another burial cairn upon a slight eminence, its massive slab cist-cover dragged away to the south. To the west and south of these burial cairns there is an area covered in vestigial walls, probably of field enclosures, together with innumerable field clearance cairns. Their age is at present unclear. Across the valley near the farm of Cae'r Arglwyddes, the matrix of the most easterly cairn (App. II, no. 99, Fig. 17.3) comprises rounded fieldstones and some pebbles and boulders deriving from an hitherto unrecognized glacial deposit which forms a slight ridge along the southern side of the Cletwr, and which is deeply incised, exposing gravels and clay, not far from the cairn.

About 500 m to the west another cairn (App. II, no. 98, Fig. 17.2) lies on the slope below a craggy outcrop. The sharpness of the stones which form its cist and kerb contrasts with the roundness of its neighbour's boulders, and it seems reasonable to assume that here the material derives directly from the rock exposure above it. Further west Bedd Taliesin (Fig. 37.4) occupies a rocky shelf, and incorporates slabs comparable to exposures in its immediate vicinity.[37] Some observers, most notably Burl, have suggested that white quartz boulders were added to prehistoric cairns in order to enhance their general appearance.[38] However, in south Wales quartz

[36] P. Manning 'Circles of the druids: monuments in the Upper Clettwr Valley', *Country Quest*, 26 (1985), 59–60.

[37] It seems worth noting that both name and preservation of this site are probably owed to the cairn's use as a marker on the old coach road which passed by here until the late eighteenth century. Today the southern side of the Cletwr Valley is under cultivation, and recent heaps of fieldstone litter the fields like scatters of the earlier stone-heaps on the opposite, northern side of the valley (Llain Wen 3).

[38] It is hard to deny that such cosmetic treatment was deliberate at sites like Newgrange, Co.Meath; see H. A. W. Burl, 'Stone circles and ring cairns', *Scottish Arch. Forum*, 4 (1972), 31–47.

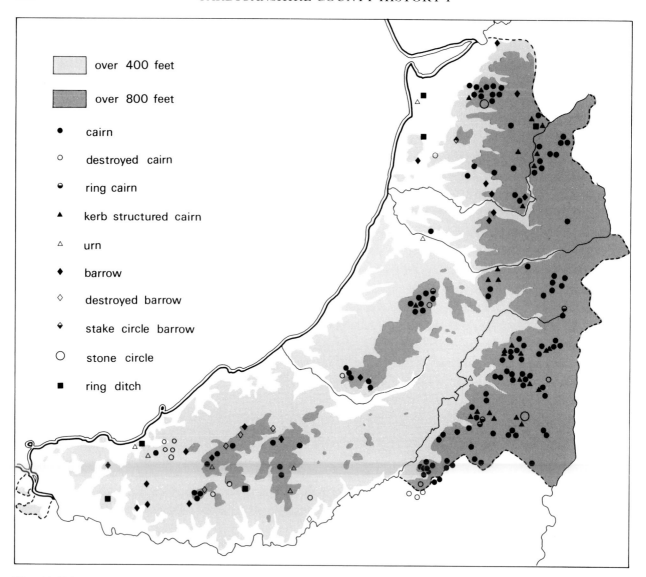

Fig. 18: Distribution of Bronze Age burial monuments.

is a common component of cairns.[39] Locally there was apparent unconcern for such ostentation. For example the builders of Carn Owen ignored a massive quartz vein about 100 m away.

Besides the Cletwr Valley grouping of Bronze Age sites there are several others of interest in the County. Between Ponterwyd and Nant-y-moch is a particularly fine group, at least in terms of surviving stone structures, and other notable groupings survive on Plynlimon, in the reservoir of Nant-y-moch, and at Blaen Glas Ffrwd, Bryngwyn Bach, Bryn y Gorlan, Carn Fflur, Castell Rhyfel, Esgair Gerwyn, Tair and Mynydd Trichrug. These occupy a variety of topographical situations, a few on hilltops, some on flat or even sloping platforms on valley sites whilst Bryn y

[39] Quartz is a common component of cairns in south Wales. During the early nineteenth century its natural abundance was commented upon by Walter Davies in his *General View of the Agriculture and Domestic Economy of South Wales*, 1 (London, 1809), 569, who observed that 'in the uplands . . . it [quartz] was . . . much impeding the progress of agriculture'.

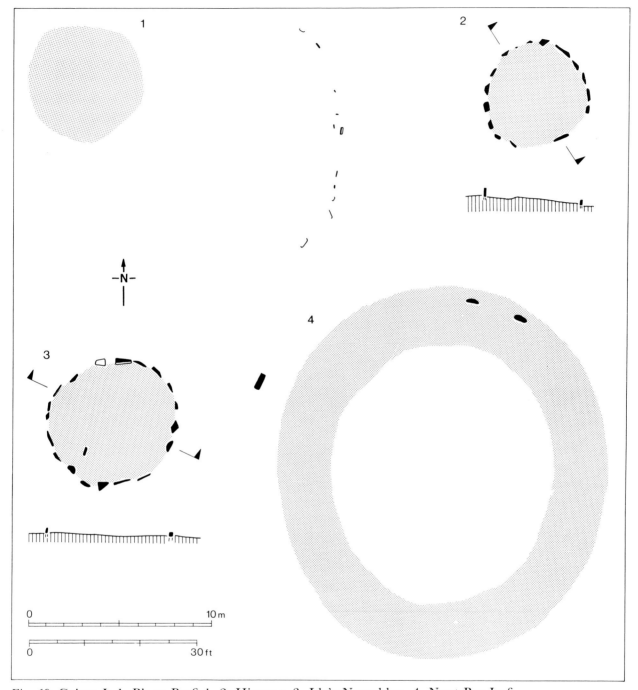

Fig. 19: Cairns I: 1. Blaen Brefi 1, 2. Hirnant, 3. Lle'r Neuaddau, 4. Nant Bry Isaf.

Gorlan occupies a plateau at about 400 m above OD. These cairns, often with structural features now exposed, are widespread over much of the upland of eastern Cardiganshire. Cairns and barrows are also quite common in the lowland western area, where structural features are rarely in evidence.

The materials employed in the construction of local burial sites in this County seem largely to reflect those which were available. In general, the siting of the monuments appears to have been

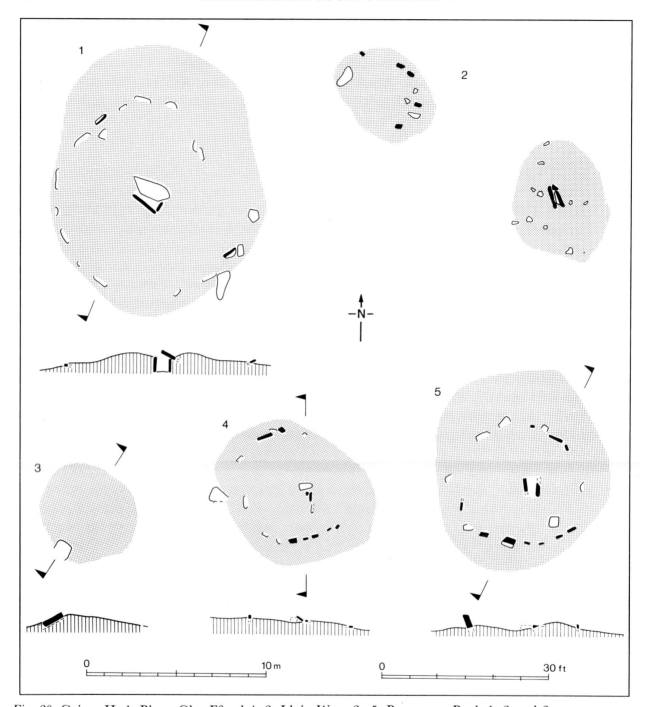

Fig. 20: Cairns II: 1. Blaen Glas Ffrwd 4, 2. Llain Wen, 3.–5. Bryngwyn Bach 1, 2 and 3.

of little importance to the builders; whereas some were built in exposed situations, remote at the present day, many destroyed sites are currently being recognized upon good farmland.[40]

[40] D. K. Leighton discusses cairn distribution in greater detail, particularly in relation to forestry and agricultural improvement: 'Structured round cairns in west central Wales', *PPS*, 50 (1984), 319–50 (pp. 328–30).

It has been demonstrated that too few monuments have so far been examined in detail to justify any complex classification of the structured sites at present, and it is felt that classification along the lines advocated here may highlight rather than obscure the problems, many of which we are only just beginning to recognize.

b) Barrows: Regrettably, few unploughed barrows now remain in the well-drained, fertile lowland of Cardiganshire. Many lowland burial monuments appear to have been built almost entirely of earth and stone, and examples of barrows once stabilized by concentric wooden posts rather than stone revetments include Banc Troed Rhiw Seiri (App. I, no. 12), Pen-y-glogau (App. I, no. 306) and possibly the large barrow at Gogerddan. Such structural features are well matched elsewhere in Wales, in Britain and on the Continent.[41] Excavation and field clearance, however, suggest that in common with upland cairns many barrows incorporated considerable amounts of fieldstone. Some barrows mask rows of concentrically set boulders, though unfortunately barrow excavation or destruction has not always provided clear details. At Crug Du, for example, whereas the cists appear to have been of flat flagstones, the cairn revetment was a more mundane stone construction and Maes yr Haf may well have been built similarly. It is difficult to believe that Pen-y-glogau did not also possess some structural form which went unrecognized by the roadmen who carried it away. Some of the reports of what were thought to be stone circles (for example, Meini Kyvrivol) and indeed, even some of the apparent surviving examples, could have formed the revetments or internal structural features of denuded barrows or cairns.[42]

All these burial sites, irrespective of composition and structural elements, fall within the same tradition of monument building.

c) Stone circles: When investigations for this chapter began in 1976, stone circles were believed to survive at Ysbyty Cynfyn and Hirnant.[43] A further site was claimed to have existed at Stepaside Farm, just outside Cardigan. According to Professor O. T. Jones, the Presellite stones utilized as gateposts here and elsewhere had probably once formed a model for Stonehenge, having been carried there from Garn Meini.[44] Their reuse as gateposts provided a rough guide to the extent of the original stone circle. The authenticity of the orthostats incorporated into the churchyard wall at Ysbyty Cynfyn, however, must now be called into question,[45] and, similarly, re-examination by the writer of the Stepaside stones shows them to be natural, glacially transported boulders of varied petrographic composition. The undulating configuration of the local topography makes it unlikely that a prehistoric circle of such large dimensions could ever have been built there. It has also been established that the circle at Hirnant (Fig. 19.2) was originally part of a cairn revetment and never intended to be free-standing (see Appendix 1, no. 235). In common with other small free-standing circles—for example, Lle'r Neuaddau (Fig. 19.3)—Hirnant has been

---

[41] W. Glasbergen, *Barrow Excavations in the Eight Beatitudes* (Groningen, 1954).

[42] C. S. Briggs, 'Druids' circles in Wales', *Landscape History*, 8 (1986), 5–12.

[43] H. A. W. Burl, *The Stone Circles of the British Isles* (London, 1976).

[44] O. T. Jones, 'The Blue-stones of the Cardigan District', *Antiq.*, 30 (1955), 34–6; *Cardigan and Tivy-side Advertiser*, 26 Aug. 1955 and 2 Sept. 1955.

[45] C. S. Briggs, 'Ysbyty Cynfyn churchyard wall', *Arch. Camb.*, 128 (1979), 138–46.

robbed of its cairn, most likely within the last hundred years. The problem of defining the original intention of free-standing stone circles of greater diameter is thus emphasized.

Excavations outside the County—for example, at Y Drosgl (Caerns.)[46]—show that very large hilltop cairns, which appear amorphous externally, may be revetted internally and externally by large hidden boulders or orthostatic slabs. In such cases the removal of the cairn mass would leave a perimeter feature indistinguishable from many stone circles. However, it is often very difficult to establish that such cairn mass existed originally. It is fairly easy to explain why the surrounding stones would not have been removed along with the rest of the cairn. First, many of the kerbstones might have been too heavy; secondly, the growing awareness of druidical tradition from the seventeenth to the nineteenth century probably did more for the protection of cairn-kerbs and free-standing stone circles than the Ancient Monuments Acts do at the present day.[47]

Despite these reservations, there are two authentic examples of stone circles in Cardiganshire. One on Bryn y Gorlan has been described by D. K. Leighton.[48] This half-circle forms part of a complex which comprises a massive fallen monolith as well as vestigial or putative cairn sites. The other, originally well known to mid-nineteenth-century antiquaries has been relocated by Dr P. Manning. Lying midway between Moel y Llyn and Moel y Garn, the site preserves at least 33 orthostats forming a circle of 26 m diameter, its stones not rising more than about 0.4 m above the ground (Fig. 17.1). A further circle was said to have existed nearby. This was also relocated by Dr Manning but seems more likely to be the remains of a hut group.[49]

Since Grimes's review of Welsh stone circles in 1963[50] a number of additional discoveries have been made. One is a recently located example at Pen y Rhaglen Wynt, just south of the Cardiganshire border with Carmarthenshire where the presence of stone alignments prompted comparison with supposed astronomically significant sites. Rigorous examination of its potential as a solar indicator failed to confirm this, unless constructed c. 8500 BC, well before the accepted date-range.[51] There is now a growing body of opinion which suggests that free-standing circles and their associated menhirs may never have had any astronomical significance beyond that of recording solstices. In any case, at many sites there were probably too many trees to allow successful sightings in the Bronze Age.[52] What then was their function? Those having wide diameters or tall orthostatic perimeters must embrace rituals of indeterminate nature, together with the simple recording of sunrise and sunset, perhaps in connection with the agricultural year,

[46] P. Crew, 'The excavation of a group of mountain-top cairns', *BBCS*, 33 (1985), 290–325.

[47] See n. 42 above. An awareness of the druidical tradition began in Wales with Edward Lhuyd during the 1690s. It was championed by Henry Rowlands in *Mona Antiqua Restaurata* (Dublin, 1723) and William Stukeley, particularly in *Stonehenge. A Temple Restor'd to the British Druids* (London, 1740), and became a fundamental feature of Welsh tradition through the works of Iolo Morganwg and Taliesin Williams during the early nineteenth century.

[48] D. K. Leighton, 'A stone circle and associated structures on Bryn y Gorlan, Cardiganshire', *Arch. Camb.*, 129 (1980), 154–7.

[49] See n. 36 above.

[50] W. F. Grimes, 'The stone circles and related monuments of Wales', *Culture and Environment: Essays in Honour of Sir Cyril Fox*, ed. I. Ll. Foster and L. Alcock (London, 1963), 93–152.

[51] C. S. Briggs, 'A prehistoric complex on Cefn Gwernffrwd, Carmarthenshire', *Arch. Camb.*, 124 (1974), 111–13; J. G. Morgan and C. N. L. Ruggles, 'Indications at the Cefn Gwernffrwd site', *Arch. Camb.*, 125 (1976), 162–5.

[52] R. Norris, 'Megalithic observatories in England, real or imagined?', *Records in Stone: Papers in Memory of Alexander Thom*, ed. C. N. L. Ruggles (Cambridge, 1988), 262–76.

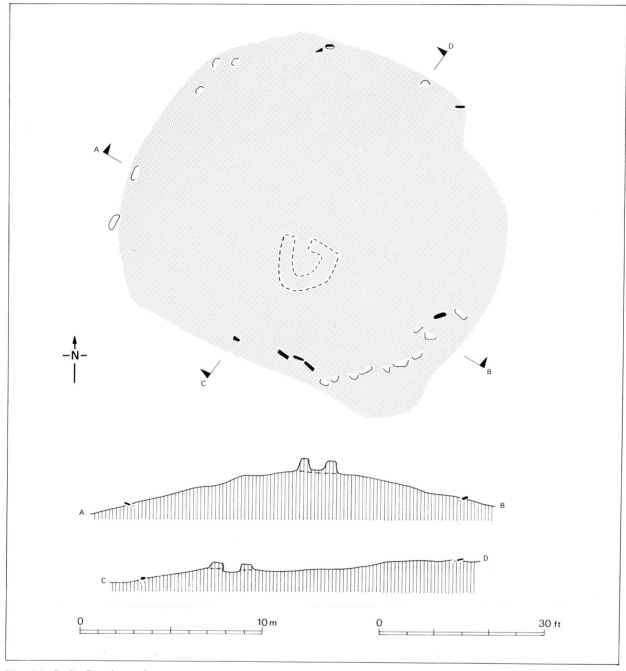

Fig. 21: Cefn Cerrig, cairn.

but even these sightings may have been inhibited by trees. It must, however, be emphasized that most excavated stone circles have also yielded some evidence for burial, which illustrates their close relationship to structured cairns and round barrows.

d) Henge monuments: Not all prehistoric ritual monuments incorporate visible stone. One class of Neolithic–Bronze Age monument, the henge, comprised circular enclosures up to and greater than 100 m in diameter, usually delimited by a bank and ditch.[53] The chronology of the type is dependent upon the number of entrances, Neolithic sites having one, Bronze Age two, opposed entrances. No monuments of henge type are certainly known from the County, but during the dry summers of 1976 and 1984 a circular feature was photographed from the air between Bow Street and Gogerddan (Pl. III),[54] which if not a settlement enclosure (see p. 127) might be a henge. Others have recently been recognized elsewhere in south-west Wales.[55]

e) Standing stones: Standing stones are the most difficult monuments to interpret and date. After the Ice Age numerous large boulders strewed the landscape, some even in upstanding positions. Indubitably, it was the clearance of these for agricultural purposes which led to their incorporation into tombs, cairns and stone circles, although it remains probable that communal ritual activities were undertaken around single large stones with or without a readjustment of posture. In Cardiganshire a number of these sites, some of which may have originally comprised vestiges of composite stone monuments, are recorded in the antiquarian literature. Others were remarked upon either because they served as mute signposts along post-medieval roads or had been preserved as boundary markers in unwritten legal agreements.

In compiling a catalogue we are faced with problems of inclusion and rejection. Boulders are constantly being swept from the drift-ridden landscape in a continuous process going back to the origins of agriculture. Many large boulders now incorporated into hedge-banks, field walls or even buildings, are archaeologically unremarkable; others of similar size or smaller, sited upon uncultivated ground or moorland or close to known cairns could on occasion be of greater significance. Size might appear a diagnostic factor, though after the excavation of quite small upstanding stones deliberately placed over pits at Aber Camddwr almost any size or shape of stone may repay investigation in the right circumstances. Fieldstones abound which might once have served as prehistoric standing stones (*meinihirion*). Some caution is necessary, however, before many of the stones listed in the pioneering work of A. J. Bird,[56] some of which are no higher than 1.5 m and often sitting upon rather than in the ground along hedge-banks, can be regarded as archaeologically significant. Some stones are marked up on the Ordnance Survey 6-inch and 25-inch maps, but local enquiry rarely demonstrates them to be of any great age. Some are clearly unmoved erratics whilst others are of recent erection.

Of those stones named on old maps or described by travellers, some stood up to 2 m in height, though several have since fallen or are now lost. These include Byrfaen (Cellan),[57] probably though not certainly prehistoric, and Llech Mihangel (Lledrod), a lost roadside monument. The

[53] A. F. Harding and G. E. Lee, *Henge Monuments and Related Sites of Great Britain* (BAR 175: Oxford, 1988).

[54] CUAP BYA 35, and also aerial photographs taken by T. James and C. S. Briggs in NMR (Wales).

[55] G. H. Williams, 'A Henge monument at Ffynnon Newydd, Nantgaredig', *BBCS*, 31 (1984), 177–90.

[56] A. J. Bird, 'The Menhir in Cardiganshire: a re-assessment', *Ceredigion*, 11 (1972), 40–5.

[57] First published by E. L. Barnwell, 'On Pillar Stones in Wales', *Arch. Camb.*, 28 (1875), 299–306. The illustration (p. 306) by Henry Longueville Jones is entitled simply 'Maen Hir near Lampeter'. In an earlier discussion Briggs, 'Notes on the study of Megalithic and Bronze Age sites' (see above n. 3), p.267, mistakenly transposes nearby Byrfaen, which is upstanding, for Hirfaen which is not.

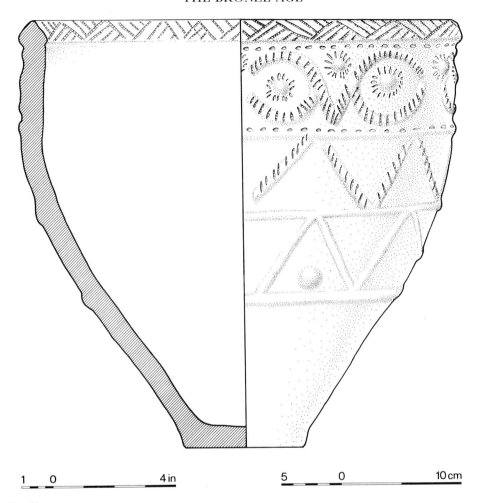

Fig. 22: The Penllwyn urn.

former stone later served to mark the parish boundary and stands to an imposing height of 4 m. The tantalizing late seventeenth-century account of a stone at Cardigan 'of considerable height above the ground and about 3 yards deep', which 'of a sudden fell flat to the admiration of many spectators that came on purpose to see it',[58] leaves its origin and nature unclear, but it may have been the stone which stood near Olmarch House (App. III, no. 65).

Until the kerb cairn at Aber Camddwr was excavated there was no certain example of a standing stone incorporated into a Bronze Age burial or ritual site in Cardiganshire,[59] although the massive example at Bryn y Gorlan, now fallen, may have been one.[60] The nature of the two stones, Cerrig Llwydion (local memory suggests there was a third), apparently associated with a round barrow near Plas Gogerddan, is uncertain because excavation has shown that the stone

[58] R. H. Morris (ed.), *The Parochialia of Edward Lhwyd, Cambrian Arch. Assoc.*, Supplement III (1911), 4; Bodleian Lib. Ashmole MS 1829, fo. 104.
[59] E. C. Marshall and K. Murphy, 'The excavation of two Bronze Age cairns with associated standing stones in Dyfed: Parc maen and Aber Camddwr II', *Arch. Camb.*, 140 (1991), 28–76.
[60] See above, n. 48.

nearest the barrow was erected or re-erected when the area was used as a racecourse in the eighteenth or nineteenth centuries. In any case the stones are not marked on the First Edition O.S. 25-inch map.

Stones impressive in their size or position are to be seen at Llech Gron, Nebo, Carreg Samson, Llanddewibrefi and Nant-y-maen, Caron-is-clawdd. The massive stone in the churchyard wall at Ysbyty Cynfyn (see above pp. 114, 139) remains a mystery since there is no mention of it until the close of the nineteenth century.[61]

In his study of Cardiganshire standing stones Bird listed twenty-seven examples and suggested that their valleyward distribution indicated the lines of early trackways, or that the more upland groupings constituted the boundaries of agricultural land.[62] The standing stones and burial monuments used to postulate trackways in Cardiganshire and Merioneth are more likely only parts of an original distribution pattern rather than deliberate markers set up along early routes.[63]

Although no certain prehistoric standing stone has been excavated in this County, great interest attaches to the excavations undertaken elsewhere in Dyfed. At Rhosyclegyrn (Pembs.) J. M. Lewis found huts, possibly of Neolithic or Bronze Age date, associated with two standing stones,[64] whilst excavations by the Dyfed Archaeological Trust around standing stones at Stackpole and St Ishmael (Pembs.) have brought to light indications of more circular huts.[65]

v) Burial in the Bronze Age

Towards the end of the third millennium BC there was a change in the mode of burial practices during which oblong or trapezoidal-shaped barrows and megalithic tombs began to be slowly replaced by circular barrows and cairns. It is difficult to pinpoint a precise origin for the new burial form, but the roots of individual, rather than of collective, burial were to be found on the Continent. Part of the fashion for round monuments probably came from the circularity of passage graves which had evolved in the western Mediterranean during the early fourth millennium BC and then spread slowly north along the Atlantic coast, to be adopted in British-Irish contexts by about 2500 BC. Circular burial monuments were current for almost a thousand years after about 2000 BC. Thereafter the burial record is scarcely known or understood until later Iron Age times, about 200 BC, when burials accompanied by blue glass beads and bronze or iron safety-pin (*fibula*) brooches began to appear in Britain and Ireland.

The characteristic mode of early Bronze Age round barrow and cairn burial is in a central pit or stone-lined cist. Grave goods are common. There may be one or more urns. If the body was

[61] See above, n. 45.

[62] See above, n. 56.

[63] *Pace* E. G. Bowen and C. A. Gresham, *The History of Merioneth*, I (Dolgellau, 1967), 56–63. For later development of the idea, see also C. B. Crampton and D. Webley, 'How the West was won: prehistoric land-use in the Southern Marches', *Welsh Antiquity*, ed. G. C. Boon and J. M. Lewis (Cardiff, 1976), 19–36. For further useful work on standing stones see J. C. Wilson, 'The standing stones of Anglesey: a discussion', *BBCS*, 30 (1983), 363–89 and H. E. Roese, 'Some aspects of topographical locations of Neolithic and Bronze Age monuments in Wales: 1 Menhirs', *BBCS*, 28 (1980), 645–55.

[64] J. M. Lewis, 'Excavations at Rhos-y-clegyrn Prehistoric Site, St Nicholas, Pembrokeshire', *Arch. Camb.*, 123 (1974), 13–42.

[65] G. H. Williams, *The Standing Stones of Wales and South-West England* (BAR 197: Oxford, 1988). D. G. Benson *et al.*, 'Excavations at Stackpole Warren, Dyfed', *PPS*, 56 (1990), 179–245.

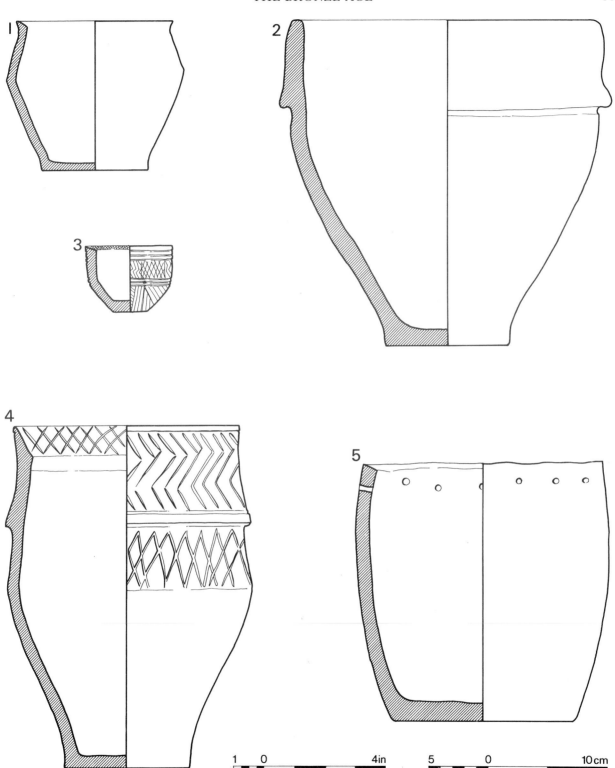

Fig. 23: Early Bronze Age pottery I. 1. Crug Du, 2.–4. Maes yr Haf, 5. Crug Cou (from a barrow near).

cremated, the ashes would invariably be contained in this vessel. Occasionally in upland Wales a fragmentary bronze awl, razor or knife survives the adverse soil conditions. Flint arrowheads or a flint dagger might be among other expected grave-goods.

Before the introduction of radiocarbon dating relative chronologies for burials were ascertained through comparison of the accompanying pottery. The term *urn* merely describes any one of several types of pottery vessel current throughout this period. *Beakers*, current from *c.* 2500–1500 BC, were the earliest among these pottery traditions. Comprising a number of sub-types, regional and chronological, their forms evolved in Britain under both continental and local influences. *Food vessels* developed from Beakers. A miniature version of these urns was the *Pygmy Cup*. From Food Vessels evolved a series of *Urns* of different forms, many of which are encompassed by the *Collared Urn Series*. As currently understood, these ceramic traditions probably culminated *c.* 1200 BC. There is considerable overlap in the currency of pottery types, and it is likely that the future discovery of greater numbers will result in a clearer understanding of both chronological and regional relationships.

a) Discovery of burials: Around forty instances of burial are known from the County, nine or ten from cairns and a dozen or so from barrows, with possibly as many as twenty more deriving from unmarked or unknown sites, probably representing instances of discovery where a covering mound had been entirely eroded away. In percentage terms these figures are comparable to totals known from other Welsh counties and, when the pattern of farming and the history of discovery is taken into consideration, the recorded figure for Cardiganshire reflects a considerable level of archaeological awareness. Only about 5–10 per cent of Cardiganshire's burial monuments, however, have produced any real evidence of burial. Many cairns have obviously been robbed. Few have been investigated in recent years. Furthermore, certain of the antiquarian finds must derive from sites now completely destroyed without record. Sadly, the total of recorded burials producing artefacts through recent scientific excavation probably comprises less than 1 per cent of the known total. The present conclusions are therefore necessarily tentative and a systematic campaign of excavation upon selected sites would dramatically alter them.

b) Mode of burial: Where it has been possible to ascertain the mode of interment, eight sites have yielded burials of over sixteen individuals from pit-graves. The same number yielded a further twenty-six interred in cists, sixteen of which derived from one site, namely Pen-y-glogau. Observations at the Llanilar site in 1980 make it clear that vast numbers of unassociated urnless cremation pits might easily go unrecognized unless the ground is deliberately examined, and such examination is normally unlikely without the prior discovery of urns or other recognizable artefacts.[66] Recent excavation at Gogerddan has brought to light a group of circular ditched burial enclosures, with central platforms some 3 to 5 m in diameter, but completely lacking any

---

[66] See above, n. 10. Though not mentioned in the excavation report a green-blue copper-coloured deposit between 3 and 5 cm long among the cremated bone fell from the urn at the time of discovery but appears not to have survived. A list of Welsh burials incorporating small copper or bronze ornaments is in preparation by the writer, following a similar discovery at Fan y Big, Brecs. in 1981 (see C. S. Briggs, W. J. Britnell and A. M. Gibson 'Two Cordoned Urns from Fan y Big, Brecon Beacons, Powys', *PPS*, 56 (1990), 173–8).

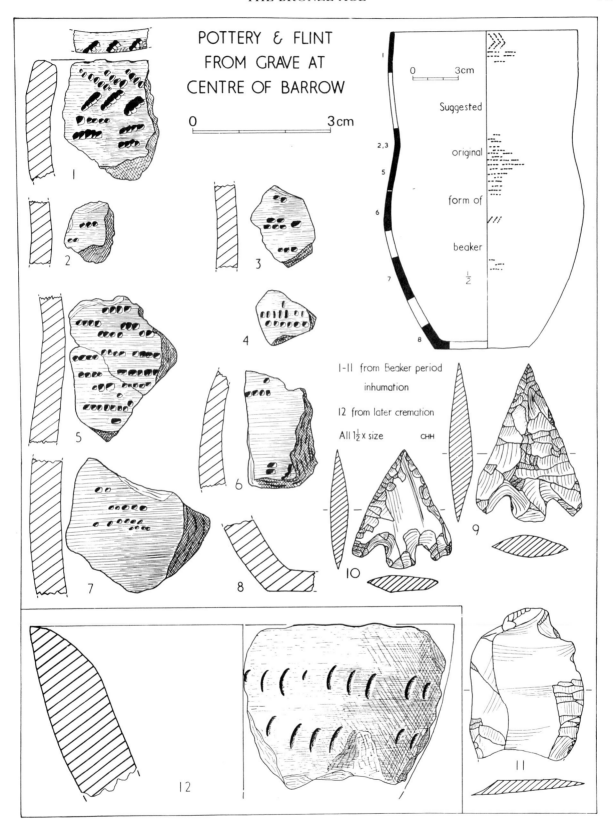

POTTERY & FLINT
FROM GRAVE AT
CENTRE OF BARROW

0   3cm

Suggested

original

form of

beaker

$\frac{1}{2}$

1-11 from Beaker period
inhumation

12 from later cremation

All 1½ × size   CHH

Fig. 24: Grave group from Banc Troed Rhiw Seiri (reproduced from *Ceredigion*, 3(1957), with permission).

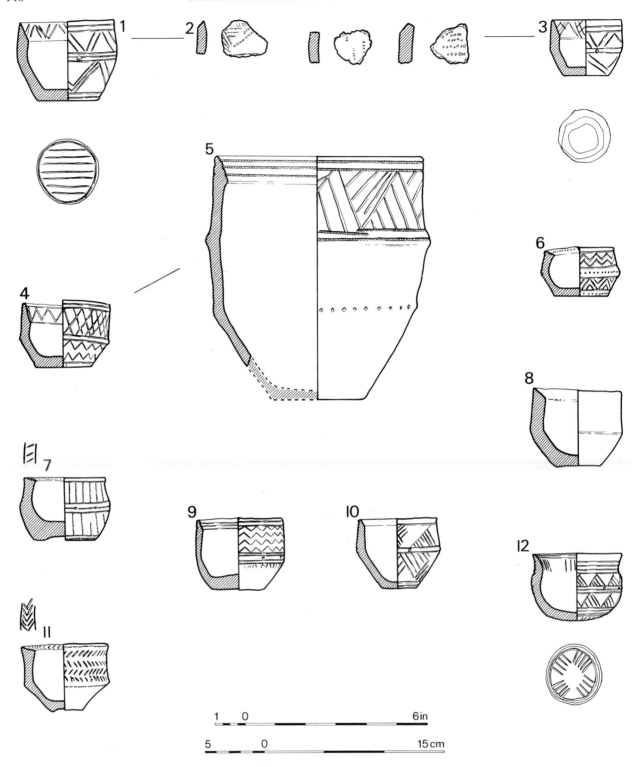

Fig. 25: Early Bronze Age pottery II. 1.–3. Crug Du, 4.–5. Pyllau Isaf (Gloucester Hall), 6. Crug Cou (from a barrow near), 7. Pantglas, 8. Neuadd Fawr, 9. Fan, 10. unlocalized, 11. Pen-y-glogau, 12. Neuadd Fawr.

artefacts ascribable to the Bronze Age. Their absence is due either to grave-robbing during the Later Iron Age or in the Romano-British period when the ditches were reused for burials (with artefacts), or to dissolution of both artefacts and inhumations through highly acidic soil conditions.[67] It can therefore be said with some confidence that traditions of both cist and pit burial in west Wales are incompletely known at the time of writing.

c) The tradition of single-grave burial: Single-grave burial was a pan-European tradition. As already noted, burials in this tradition are conventionally treated in two separate categories —those in pits and those encisted in stone. As cremation and inhumation traditions coexisted within the Early Bronze Age in Britain and Ireland, considerable importance now attaches to differentiating between the long pits or cists presumed to have been for extended or crouched inhumation on the one hand, and the small receptacles intended only for cremation on the other. These distinctions tend to overshadow both the source of available stone suited to the task of cist-building and the sufficiency of fuel for the pyre. Single burial, though often the focus in cairns and barrows, was often accompanied by other single burials in the same vicinity. Careful excavation of the monuments and their environs usually shows that individuals continued to be inserted into pits in or around the monument over a considerable period. Although cremation became an important component of this new burial fashion, burning was not absolutely necessary to its practitioners. The nature of the resting place of the deceased, of the ritual which preceded burial, or the factors attracting further burials to the same spot were variables strongly dependent upon environmental factors. The isolation by scholars of one factor from another without reference to these many local variables can, therefore, create quite a biased impression of overall burial practice. The recognition of commonly recurring features over wide areas need not indicate, therefore, that there was direct contact or conscious copying between distant culture groups.

No full survey or analysis of burial tradition exists for Wales as a whole, so it is difficult to reach conclusions about the genesis of specific integral traits. Although it has been suggested that culture contact may have brought extended inhumation burial from Ireland to south Wales,[68] equally it is possible that local inhumation traditions relate to eastern, English counterparts. By the same token, it is likely that multiple Beaker burials and associated copper artefacts, which characterize the earliest Bronze Age outside mid Wales,[69] did exist there also but have not yet been recognized.

The burials at Crug Coe, Crug Du, Crug Mawr, Maes yr Haf, Pyllau Isaf and Tyll Coed between them yielded over 30 pots, as well as bone of uncertain nature. Overall, the County has yielded in excess of 67 pottery vessels. Of these, only 27 survive in museum or private collections. Lost grave-goods must have included sherds of Beakers and of other later Urn-forms.

---

[67] K. Murphy, 'Excavations at Gogerddan', *Arch. J.* (forthcoming); idem, 'Plas Gogerddan', *AW*, 26 (1987), 29–31.

[68] H. N. Savory, 'Copper-Age cists and cist-cairns in Wales, with special reference to Newton, Swansea and other 'multiple-cist' cairns', *Prehistoric Man in Wales and the West*, ed. F. M. Lynch and C. B. Burgess (London, 1972), 117–39 (p. 118, fig. 1).

[69] Ibid., 123, fig. 2.

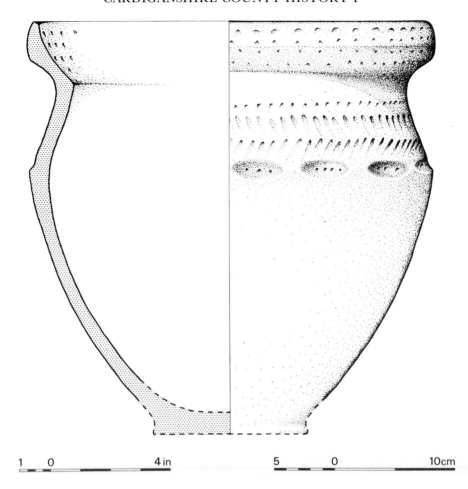

Fig. 26: The Llanilar Urn.

d) Burial practices: Burnt bone is known from at least half the urn burials in the County. At first sight this might suggest that cremation was the more dominant practice, but the skeletal contents of long pits scarcely survive acidic soils, so inhumation is unlikely to be recognized without scientific excavation. Calcined, cremated bone, being less vulnerable to adverse soil conditions, survives better, helping to create a preservation bias in favour of cremation burials. Despite soil conditions which should have mitigated against its survival, an unusual human frontal bone was found at Strata Florida in 1896. This has been put forward as a medieval discovery, possibly having been found by the monks 'amongst, or in, the local rocks, perhaps in a cist vaen'.[70] Of course, this might have been the remnant of a reinterred bog body, but that seems unlikely.[71]

[70] W. G. Smith, 'Human frontal bone from Strata Florida', *Arch. Camb.*, 51 (1896), 94–7 (p. 97).
[71] Only one bog-body, of unknown date, is known from the County. It was disinterred from Dolfawr Fair bog (SN 711 670) in 1811 and reburied in Ystrad Meurig churchyard. Noted from NLW MS 1755B, fols. 14, *bis*–15, in C. S. Briggs and R. C. Turner, 'A gazetteer of bog burials from Britain and Ireland', *Lindow Man: The Body in the Bog*, ed. I. M. Stead, J. B. Bourke and D. Brothwell (London, 1986), 181–95 (p. 187). There are otherwise unsubstantiated stories of persons lost crossing Borth Bog late in the nineteenth century or in the early twentieth.

The relative number of individuals originally buried unaccompanied by, as opposed to those interred with, grave-goods is difficult to assess. At Llanilar the discovery of urnless burial pits suggests that a greater proportion of the prehistoric community might have been buried without grave-goods.

e) The pottery: All known surviving funerary pottery has been drawn (Figs. 23–27). Owing to its fragmented condition, ascription to precise pottery traditions can sometimes be difficult. Nonetheless, basic lists within the broadly defined categories of Beaker Food Vessels and Cinerary Urns have been compiled.[72]

Although Beaker-users, metallurgy, and single grave burial were at one time thought to have arrived in north-west Europe through a series of invasions, a rather more slow development of events is now envisaged, in which these elements are seen to have developed separately under both local and intrusive influences.[73] Although the detail of these introductions into west Wales has yet to be properly documented, a local adoption of Beaker-use by the early second millennium BC is shown by the handful of classic Beaker sherds from Crug Du, Wstrws and Banc Troed Rhiw Seiri. A few other equally diagnostic cultural indicators of Beaker presence have survived. The best is the flint dagger from Bryn'reithin (Fig. 32),[74] although scattered tanged and barbed arrow-heads are also important.[75]

A variety of common ornamental and morphological features are recognizable among Beakers and their lineal descendants, Food Vessels. Only three Food Vessels have survived in their entirety; at Disgwylfa Fawr (Fig. 27.5), Garn Wen (Fig. 27.1) and Llanilar (Fig. 26). Although the Disgwylfa vessel is of a form known as the Irish-Scottish Vase, a type numerically best known from Irish burials, it probably owes more to English rather than to Irish influence. That it might have been locally manufactured by Irish women, as was once suggested,[76] now seems extremely unlikely.

Interestingly, traits of most Food Vessel traditions are represented in these local vessels, and Collared Urn elements are also recognizable.[77] In common with the Disgwylfa find, the Garn Wen 'Urn' seems to be characteristic of the Enlarged Food Vessel group,[78] and, though having a different shape, the Llanilar 'Urn' seems to be of a similar tradition, exhibiting ornament which would not have been out of place on a European Pot Beaker.[79]

[72] H. N. Savory, 'A corpus of Welsh Bronze Age pottery, I', *BBCS*, 16 (1955), 215–38; 'A corpus of Welsh Bronze Age pottery, II', 17 (1957), 89–118; and 'A corpus of Welsh Bronze Age pottery, III', 18 (1958), 196–233 (cf. R. H. Kavanagh, 'Pygmy Cups in Ireland', *J. Royal Soc. Antiq. Ireland*, 107 (1977), 61–95); H. N. Savory, 'The Late Bronze Age in Wales: some new discoveries and interpretations', *Arch. Camb.*, 107 (1958), 3–63 and I. H. Longworth, *A Corpus of Collared Urns* (Cambridge, 1984).

[73] J. D. G. Clark, 'The invasion hypothesis in British archaeology', *Antiq.*, 40 (1966), 172–89.

[74] H. S. Green, C. H. Houlder and L. H. Keeley, 'A flint dagger from Ffair Rhos, Ceredigion, Dyfed', *PPS*, 48 (1982), 492–501.

[75] H. N. Savory, 'A corpus of Welsh Bronze Age pottery, III', *BBCS*, 18 (1958), 199.

[76] L. F. Chitty, 'Notes on the Irish affinities of the Bronze Age food vessels of type 1a found in Wales', *BBCS*, 9 (1938), 275–83.

[77] I. H. Longworth, *A Corpus of Collared Urns* (see above, n. 72).

[78] T. G. Cowie, *Bronze Age Food Vessel Urns* (BAR 55: Oxford, 1978).

[79] J. Brennan, A. M. Ap Simon and C. S. Briggs, 'The Giant Beaker from Cluntyganny', *Ulster J. Arch.*, 41 (1978), 33–6.

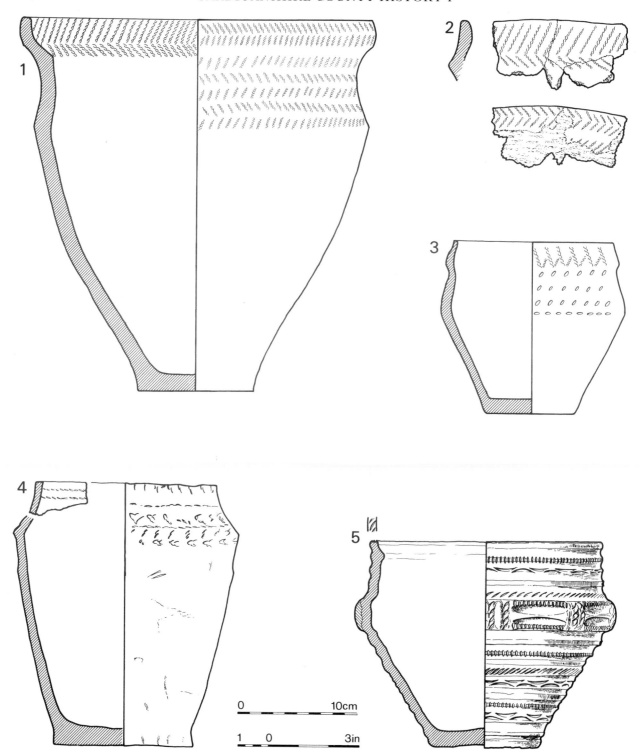

Fig. 27: Early Bronze Age pottery III. 1. Garn Wen, 2. Possibly Garn Wen, 3. Aber Camddwr, 4. Tresaith, 5. Disgwylfa Fawr.

Distinctive prehistoric pottery traditions were at one time thought to be products of massive invasion rather than peaceful long-term acculturation. Some still believe that Pygmy Cups (Fig. 25.1, 3, 4, 6–12 and Fig. 23.3), Encrusted Urns (Fig. 22) and other single-grave pottery were transported by population movement from one area to another.[80]

West Wales has the greatest concentration of Pygmy Cups in Britain and Ireland.[81] These small vessels, locally biconical in form in west Wales, bear incised decoration, and resemble miniature Food Vessels. Their decorative motifs are reminiscent of Beaker, Food Vessel or Collared Urn traditions. Where findspots are known, they often accompanied cremations, and were placed there as accessories to larger cremation Urns, a practice common elsewhere in the British Isles. Cremation may have been practised at Maes yr Haf, Pen-y-glogau and Pyllau Isaf, though regrettably their documentation is insufficiently clear to be certain of direct association. Elsewhere, for example at Banc Troed Rhiw Seiri, a Pygmy Cup appears to have belonged to a secondary burial within a barrow of Beaker origin. In the main, however, Pygmy Cups from west Wales do not come from associated contexts. They occurred singly at Crug Cou, Nantglas, Tyll Coed (were there really twelve?) (see App. I, no. 332) and Ty'n-y-rhos.

Records survive of over forty urns besides those already enumerated. These fall into the categories of Encrusted, Collared, Overhanging Rim Urns and those of anomalous form.

One of the most spectacular urns from Wales is that found at Penllwyn Chapel in 1926 (Fig. 22). It is a good example of the cosmopolitan pottery tradition of that time in west Wales, and while thought by some to have been an element of Irish influence there is no need to invoke widespread population movement to account for its presence here.[82] Only one example of a Collared Urn is recorded; that from Maes yr Haf (Fig. 23.4). It is associated with an Overhanging Rim Urn (Fig. 23.2) and a Pygmy Cup (Fig. 23.3). The Garn Wen Food Vessel displays certain Collared Urn features, and although difficult to judge from early drawings, the cordon-decorated pieces from Gilfach-wen-isaf (Fig. 40) appear to have been of the Collared tradition, the decoration having something in common with the Pyllau Isaf or Gloucester Hall Urn (Fig. 25.4–5). Of those vessels best described as anomalous, the slightly waisted Tresaith Urn appears to be a hybrid Food Vessel with a Collared Urn, though its rough cord impression may be more a local trade mark. Similarly the urn from Aber Camddwr, while assuming the shape of a Food Vessel, is cord-decorated more in the manner of a Beaker or Urn.

The interest of these local grave-groups lies in the association of several pottery traditions within one burial monument. Good examples are Banc Troed Rhiw Seiri, Crug Du, Maes yr Haf, and also possibly Llanilar, Pen-y-glogau and Pyllau Isaf. These grave-groups suggest the continued sanctity of one site for several hundred years. Although such continuity shows early farming communities were fairly static, the presence of successive pottery traditions suggests receptiveness to influences current elsewhere within the British Isles. The ceramic traditions must

[80] For example R. M. Kavanagh, 'The Encrusted Urn in Ireland', *PRIA*, 73C (1973), 507–617, and 'Collared and Cordoned Cinerary Urns in Ireland', 76C (1976), 293–403; cf. J. Waddell, 'The invasion hypothesis in Irish prehistory', *Antiq.*, 52 (1978), 121–8.

[81] H. N. Savory, 'A corpus of Welsh Bronze Age pottery, I', *BBCS*, 16 (1955), 101, fig. 3.

[82] A. L. Brindley, 'The cinerary urn in Ireland—an alternative interpretation', *PRIA*, 80C (1980), 197–206; J. Waddell, 'The invasion hypothesis in Irish prehistory', op cit.

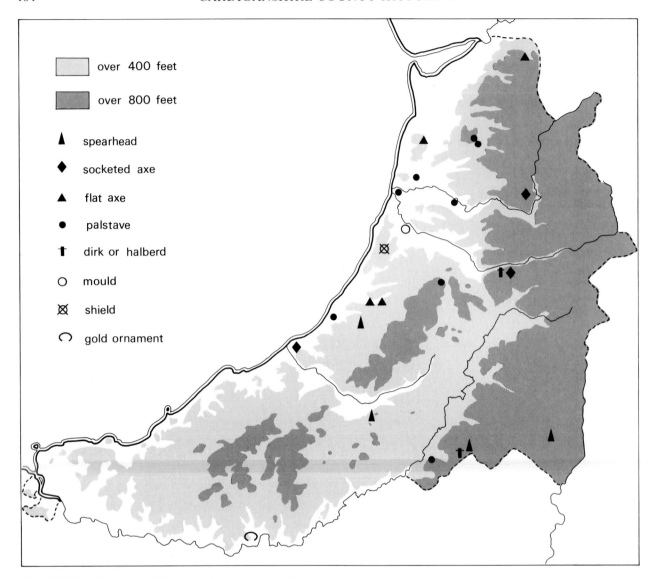

Fig. 28: Distribution of Bronze Age metalwork.

have changed more through slow absorption of ideas, intermarriage, barter and minor tribal wars, rather than through the wholesale movement of population groups.

Although grave-goods other than the ceramic are rare, the surviving pottery and its burial contexts helps paint a backcloth in ritual and burial to a stage otherwise virtually empty of Bronze Age life.

Artefacts

i) Prehistoric metallurgy

a) Implements of bronze: Because some specimens have been inadequately described in the antiquarian literature or remain in private possession, it is difficult to say precisely how many

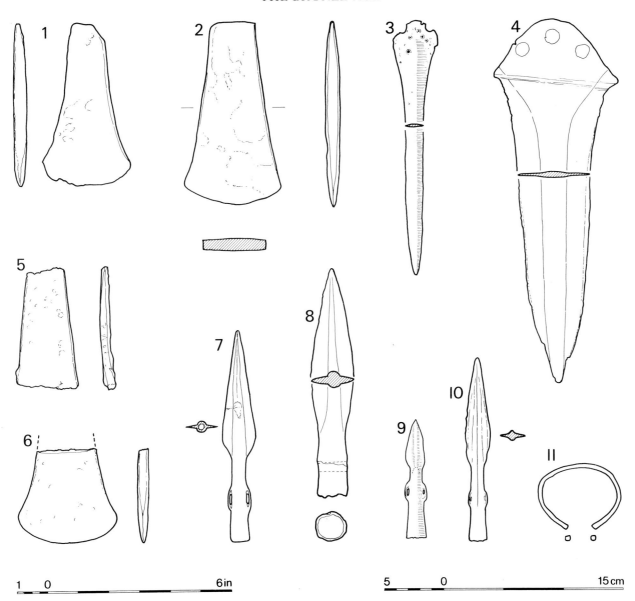

Fig. 29: Bronze Age metalwork I. 1. Cefn Coch Sheepwalk, 2. Rhyd-y-pennau, 3. Nant Clywedog Ganol, 4. Pont-rhyd-y-groes, 5.–6. Rhyd-y-torth, 7. Near Abermeurig, 8. Carn Saith Wraig, 9. Tregaron, 10. Nant Clywedog Ganol, 11. Llandysul.

pieces of Bronze Age metalwork now survive from the County. Over thirty are listed here, of which five are of the Early Bronze Age, thirteen from the Middle and eleven from the Late, though some examples cannot be confidently ascribed to any particular phase (App. V, nos.16, 19, 28).

The Early Bronze Age metalwork comprises four flat axes from Rhyd-y-torth, Llan-non (App. V, no. 21, i, ii; Fig. 29.5 and 6), Cefn Coch Sheepwalk (no. 7, Fig. 29.1), and Rhyd-y-pennau (no. 22, Fig. 29.2), together with one halberd, found 'near a copper mine' at

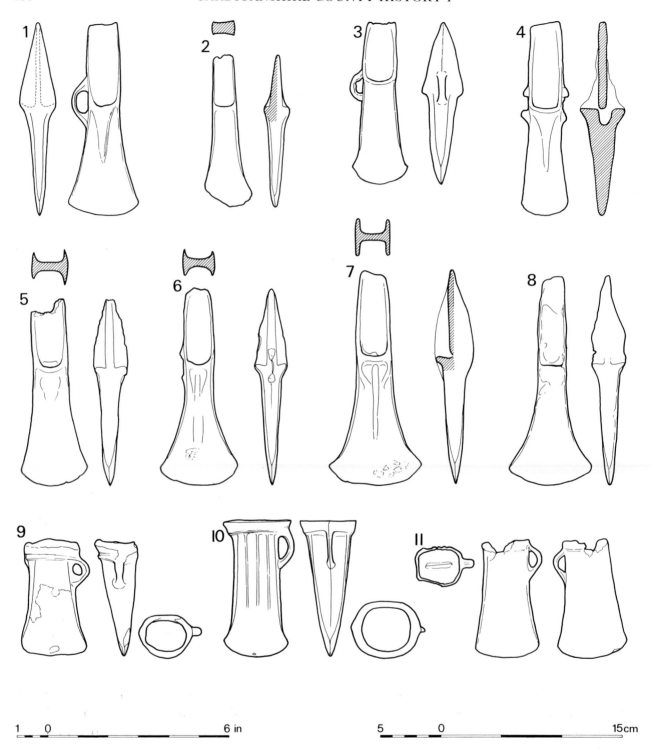

Fig. 30: Bronze Age metalwork II. 1. Ysbyty Cynfyn, 2. 'Pen Dinas', Aberystwyth, 3. Tan-y-bwlch, 4. Aberystwyth, 5. Ash Grange, 6. Llan-non, 7. Tŷ-gwyn, Cwmere, 8. Glanrheidol, 9. Tan-y-bwlch, Cellan, 10. Aberaeron, 11. Cae Maen Arthur.

Pont-rhyd-y-groes (no. 17, Fig. 29.4). According to metal-analytical evidence, the latter was of 'International' type[83] although the fact that it is of copper and was discovered near a post-medieval copper mine at Pont-rhyd-y-groes may suggest that it was more likely of local work-manship and metal. Similarly, the Rhyd-y-pennau flat axe, thought to be of Irish metal,[84] might more convincingly have been derived from a local metal source. This handful of Early Bronze Age implements are of types which had a wide currency in the British Isles between *c.* 2200 and 1450 BC. They are of unalloyed copper in which trace-elements might easily have derived from a variety of copper ore types. These tools would have been cast in open sand or clay moulds, and cleaning up or 'fettling' would have been effected using stone burnishers. Whereas the halberd might have had a ceremonial use, the axes could have served to strip or fell trees or even have been used as hoes for tilling lighter soils.

The Middle Bronze Age metalwork of *c.* 1450–900 BC comprises nine palstaves, a dirk, a spearhead and a gold bar-torc. The immediate precursor of the palstave was the haft-flanged axe, one of which was known from Rhydlwyd (Lledrod) (no. 20). Palstaves form the most important element of the Middle Bronze Age implement repertory in Wales. They are classified according to decoration. An undecorated example was found at Tan-y-bwlch (Tirymynach) (no. 24, Fig. 30.3). Those from Ash Grange (no.4, Fig. 30.5) and Glanrheidol (no. 9, Fig. 30.8) have hollows beneath the stopridge. Three from Llan-non (no. 13, Fig. 30.6), Pen Dinas (no. 14, Fig. 30.2) and Ty-gwyn (no. 26, Fig. 30.7) are 'shield-pattern' palstaves. The example from Ysbyty Cynfyn (no. 27, Fig. 30.1) exhibits a well-developed midrib, whilst a similar example of this 'south-western' type is alleged to have been found at Cae Mawr Farm.[85] It has much in common with those from Tan-y-bwlch (Tirymynach) and Ysbyty Cynfyn, and is possibly a lost find from the former place.[86] Mystery still surrounds the original findspot of the ribbed and double-looped palstave (Fig. 30.4), rescued from a cellar in Aberystwyth, purporting to have been discovered with a gold multi-flanged torc found 'somewhere in mid Wales'. Despite the fact that gold deposits are known from recent workings in the counties north and south of Cardiganshire, there is little evidence that gold was being recognized and collected locally in mid Wales in any quantity for the fashioning of ornaments during the Bronze Age.[87] Apart from the multi-flanged torc from Aberystwyth, there is only a small gold bar-torc of square section, reputed to have come from Llandysul (no. 12, Fig. 29.11), but even its provenance is questionable since its collector, Canon William Greenwell, acquired his artefacts with little concern for the integrity of their provenances.

The dirk from Nant Clywedog Ganol (no. 10, Fig. 29.3) has been analysed and its composition found to be similar to other artefacts of the 'Acton Park' phase of the Middle Bronze Age.[88] It is

---

[83] H. N. Savory, *Guide Catalogue of the Bronze Age Collections* (Cardiff, 1980), 43.

[84] Ibid., 100.

[85] Y. C. Stanton, 'A palstave from Ciliau-Aeron, Dyfed', *BBCS*, 30 (1983), 399–400.

[86] C. S. Briggs in *AW*, 26 (1986), 31–2.

[87] R. Hunt, *A Historical Sketch of British Mining* (London, 1887; repr. Wakefield, 1978), 42–3. His discussion about finding gold in Cardiganshire (p. 20) is based entirely upon uncorroborated literary references cited by Meyrick. T. A. Morrison, *Goldmining in Western Merioneth* (Llandysul, 1975), and A. E. Annels and B. C. Burnham, *The Dolaucothi Gold Mines* (National Trust Guide, *c.* 1985), provide more up-to-date accounts.

[88] J. P. Northover, 'The analysis of Welsh Bronze Age metalwork', in Savory, *Guide Catalogue*, 229–43.

one of only a handful of similar weapons at present known from Wales, and, although it might appear that the type had a limited local currency,[89] few thin bronzes have survived Welsh upland acidic soils. From the same findspot, though unassociated with the dirk so far as is known, came a socket-looped spearhead (no. 11), which, to judge from the sharp state of its casting seams, may have seen little use.

There are no certain associations of implements which could be described as hoards from the County, though the remaining two socket-looped spearheads were each at one time thought to have belonged to group finds. One (no. 25, Fig. 29.9) from 'a peat-bog near Tregaron', described along with two palstaves, was probably brought together with them for the purpose of an exhibition, and thereby comprised an amalgam from two or three different provenances.[90] The second was thought to have been found with a Pygmy Cup in a burial at Abermeurig (no. 3, Fig. 29.7). This spear is, however, almost certainly from near Tregaron.

Of the Late Bronze Age metalwork, four examples are socketed axes, one a pegged spearhead, and there is a shield and the stone matrix for casting a socketed chisel. The main form of axe in use during the Late Bronze Age was socketed and comprised two basic types; decorated three-ribbed axes in the west known as south Welsh or Bulford-Helsbury axes,[91] and plain, bag-shaped axes with an angularity in the form of their faceting. The former type is characteristically square-cast with a rather coarse socket and three-ribbed decoration on the outer face, examples of which come from Aberaeron (no. 1, Fig. 30.10) and Ffynnoncadno Quarry (no. 8). The faceted axe without decoration from Cellan (no. 23, Fig. 30.9) and the plain bag-shaped variety from Ysbyty Ystwyth (no. 6, Fig. 30.11) are probably local variants of more widely distributed implement types.

The only pegged socketed spear is that from Carn Saith Wraig (no. 5, Fig. 29.8). Spearheads have a limited distribution in west Wales, but it is impossible to know whether this reflects restricted currency in antiquity or again is due to poor survival rates once discarded. The Aber-mad socketed chisel mould, one of a handful of casting matrices known from Wales, is of considerable interest in that no known implements appear to have been cast from it, or even from similar moulds. Its discovery serves again to emphasize not only the low survival rates of any implement type from such a remote period, but also how little is known of the destructive casting process, which presumably consumed the majority of sand or clay moulds.

Technically and aesthetically, and as a potential indicator of social and political conditions, the most exciting piece of metalwork is the shield from Rhos Rydd, Aberllolwyn (no. 19; Fig. 35). The dating and function of this class of metalwork in Britain and Europe has attracted considerable attention.[92] Such shields tend to be found in or close to water or waterlogged ground, and, whereas this association is often taken to indicate ritual deposition in rivers or bogs, the fact that these fragile beaten bronzes would have stood little chance of survival outside such conditions

[89] H. N. Savory, *Guide Catalogue*, 54 and 112.

[90] 'Catalogue of the Museum formed for the Dolgellau Meeting of the Cambrian Archaeological Association', *Arch.Camb.*, 5 (1850), 331–4.

[91] The discussion and catalogue by S. P. Needham, *The Bulford-Helsbury Manufacturing Tradition: The Production of Stogursey Socketed Axes during the later Bronze Age in Southern Britain* (London, 1981), supersedes that of C. N. Moore, 'The South Welsh Axe: its origins and distribution', *Arch. J.*, 135 . (1978), 57–66.

[92] J. M. Coles, 'European Bronze Age shields', *PPS*, 28 (1962), 156–90 and S. P. Needham, 'Two recent British shield finds and their Continental parallels', *PPS*, 45 (1979), 111–34.

tends to be overlooked. Certainly, in Wales the four known shields are from bogs rather than lakes or rivers. As may be seen from the illustration, like its counterparts elsewhere, the Aber-llolwyn shield is well equipped with a handle and a small tab for the attachment of a carrying strap. It is generally agreed that these shields served more of a ritual or symbolic, rather than a bellicose function, though one English example has been penetrated by a spear. Nevertheless they could hardly have survived the onslaught of more than a single encounter as defensive pieces, and it seems more likely that they were made for mock combat, perhaps as part of warrior initiation. Shields of hide and possibly wood were certainly stronger as repellents of sharp spears than their metallic counterparts. Their date of currency is difficult to ascertain, since they tend to be found unassociated with contemporary artefacts, and the chronology used to date Late Bronze Age finds hinges on a system evolved in Middle Europe for which there are few carbon-14 dates. However, their use between the twelfth and eighth centuries BC appears probable.

The society which made such shields was probably one in which chieftains exercised some control and highly skilled smiths played an important role. Sadly, little is yet known of the nature of settlement, domestic economy and burial during this period in Wales. Elsewhere, in north Wales and in parts of England, contemporary settlement sites are now being recognized and excavated. Results from them should help to shed light on events further afield and may lead to the discovery of local settlement sites.

b) Metal production: Considerable interest attaches to the localities where metal in its various mineral forms may be recognized, since it is generally believed that they were known to prehistoric man and exploited by him. This belief has led to considerable detailed investigation and speculation about the age of the metal mines of mid Wales. During the 1930s Oliver Davies excavated shallow trench-mines at Copa Hill, Cwmystwyth. The site produced stone hammers and crushing or grinding querns, believed to date from Roman or prehistoric times. Among the finds Davies distinguished between what he believed to be an older, saddle-quern type of ore-crushing stone associated with stone hammers, and younger stones bearing deeper, ovoid, hollow faces. These hollows were thought to have resulted from percussion with iron hammers (Fig. 31.4). They might have continued in use 'until the end of the eighteenth century', because 'stone would be cheaper and easier to procure than other material, so long as ore was crushed by hand'. Interestingly, tradition survived into the 1930s to suggest that girls had pounded the ore on the dumps by hand.[93] Although he suggested that the sites may have been Roman, no Roman artefacts were found. His pioneering investigation was inconclusive and failed to establish a reliable chronology for the site.

The site was reinvestigated in 1986, 1989 and 1990 with a view to establishing whether or not these primitive mining techniques could have survived from Bronze Age times.[94] It is currently claimed by some that grooved stone 'mauls' were ore-excavating tools;[95] others, however, still see

---

[93] O. Davies, 'Cwm Ystwyth Mines', *Arch. Camb.*, 99 (1946), 57–63.

[94] S. Timberlake, 'An archaeological investigation of early mineworkings on Copa Hill, Cwmyst-wyth', *AW*, 27 (1987), 18–20; S. Timberlake, 'Bronze Age mining at Cwmystwyth: the radio-carbon dates', *AW*, 28 (1988), 50.

[95] P. Craddock and D. Gale, 'Evidence for early mining and extractive metallurgy in the British Isles: problems and potentials', *Science and Archaeology: Glasgow 1987*, ed. E. O. Slater and J. O. Tate (BAR 196: Oxford, 1988), 167–91.

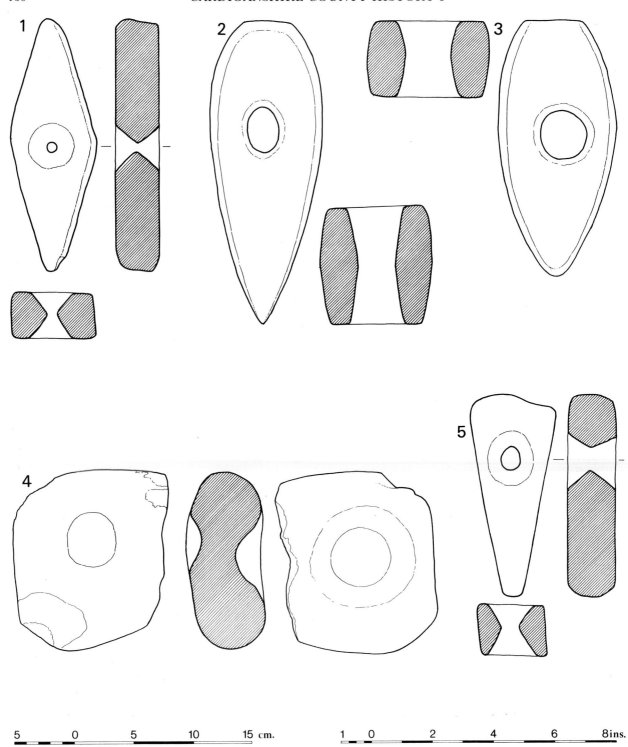

Fig. 31: Perforated stone implements I. 1. Llanfeiliog, 2. Cwrt Mawr, 3. Llyn Eiddwen (N of), 4. Copa Hill (Cwmystwyth), 5. Llwyn-rhys.

them only as ore grinders.[96] In Sweden, similar artefacts are dated to recent historic mining.[97] Despite thorough excavation, Copa Hill has still produced no diagnostic Bronze Age artefacts. However, alderwood and oak charcoal excavated from debris within a mine opencast has produced uncalibrated radiocarbon dates ranging from 3500 ± 50 bp (BM-2732) to 2990 ± 190 bp (Q-3077), which when calibrated cover the spectrum 1964–1733 to 1680–800 BC, that is, entirely within the Bronze Age.[98] Interestingly, this hillside was exploited early in the eighteenth century.[99] A large peat-cutting lying east and north-east of the trenches can still be approached along tracks through the 'ancient' workings. The peatbog base forms several hollows which could have been post-Glacial alder carr. Extracting timber from peat for domestic and industrial use was a commonplace in the recent past.[100] Some nineteenth-century mines even possessed peat storage sheds,[101] clear indication of contemporary industrial peat exploitation. So in the continued absence of either a Bronze Age stratigraphy or artefacts it seems reasonable to consider the likelihood that Bronze Age charcoal could be that of timber won from the nearby bog and burned in fire setting or in other processes upon a medieval or post-medieval exploitation. Dates of a comparable age have been obtained from reconnaissance at several other mines in Wales, sites excavated because preliminary investigation had yielded stone mauls. These include the Great Orme, Parys Mountain and Nant yr Eira (on the east side of Plynlimon). Because diagnostic Bronze Age artefacts have still not been found stratified in these workings, or at similar Irish mines, and because contemporary associated settlement and burial sites also elude recognition, archaeologists remain divided as to their precise date of exploitation.[102]

Unfortunately, metallic minerals tend to be mapped by geologists concerned with an economic viability at the present day, so that only larger deposits are drawn to the attention of pre-historians. The outcome is that the plethora of localities in which both primary and recycled metallic minerals could have been recognized and used by prehistoric man remain overlooked. Similarly the economic values which accompanied the demand for metals in the Roman and

[96]C. S. Briggs, 'Copper mining at Mount Gabriel: Bronze Age bonanza or post-famine fiasco?', *PPS*, 49 (1983), 17–35; idem, 'The discovery and description of Trench Mines at Derricarhoon Td., Co. Cork, in 1846', *J. Irish Arch.*, 2 (1984), 33–40; G. Warrington, 'The Copper Mines of Alderley Edge and Mottram St Andrew, Cheshire', *J. Chester Arch. Soc.*, 64 (1981), 47–73.

[97] L. Stentik, 'Steinkoller med Skaftfure', *Festskrift til Anders Hagen, Arkeoligiske Skriften Historisk Museum Univ. i Bergen*, 4 (1988), 292–300.

[98] S. Timberlake and R. Switsur, 'An archaeological investigation of early mineworkings on Copa Hill, Cwm Ystwyth: new evidence for prehistoric mining', *PPS*, 54 (1988), 329–33; S. Timberlake, 'Excavations at an early mining site on Copa Hill, Cwmystwyth, Dyfed, 1989 and 1990', *AW*, 30 (1990), 7–13; Timberlake, loc. cit., n. 94.

[99] S. R. Meyrick, *Hist. and Antiq. of Cardiganshire*, 561, 563.

[100]T. M. Owen, 'Historical aspects of peat-cutting in Wales', *Studies in Folk Life*, ed. G. Jenkins (London, 1969), 123–56.

[101]M. Palmer, *The Richest in All Wales* [*Esgair-hir*] (Northern Mines Res. Group, Sheffield, 1983), Fig. 5, 26.

[102]J. Ambers, 'Radiocarbon, calibration and early mining: some British Museum radiocarbon dates for Welsh copper mines', *Early Mining in the British Isles*, ed. P. Crew and S. Crew (Maentwrog, 1990), 59–63; D. James, 'Prehistoric copper mining on the Great Orme Head, Llandudno, Gwynedd', *Acta of British School at Athens Centenary Conference on Ancient Mining and Metallurgy*, ed. J. Ellis-Jones (U.C.N.W., Bangor, 1988), 115–21; P. Crew and S. Crew, op. cit., *passim*. For the alternative view see C. S. Briggs, 'Early mines in Wales: the date of Copa Hill', *AW*, 31 (1991), 5–7.

medieval periods are easily transposed upon earlier periods when technology and society were at very different stages of development. Archaeologists assume that those regions which today or in the recent past have produced tin, gold, copper and lead were actually well known in antiquity. This assumption is strengthened by the longevity of mining and processing techniques. However, it is now becoming clear that there exists no proven connection between the whereabouts of the mined metals and the provenances of the known artefacts. For example, there are no Bronze Age tin artefacts from Cornwall, no prehistoric gold ornaments from the Dolau Cothi or Dolgellau areas, and pre-Roman copper finds from Parys Mountain, Anglesey, and the Dolfrwynog Turf Copper Mine area of Merioneth are unremarkable. In short, there is no 'fall-off' in distribution from the presumed 'production zones' to the artefact findspots, such as is known for Roman pig lead or for medieval pottery.[103]

Recent estimates suggest that only about $\frac{2}{3}$ tonne of metal may have been smelted during the whole of the Irish Early Bronze Age.[104] Such a low figure suggests that small amounts of ore, perhaps of mixed minerals, might have been collected during agricultural work over a relatively long period and then worked up into an artefact or group of artefacts by a specialist craftsman within a particular community. This seems a practical alternative to the idea of independent prospectors who travelled long distances to locate ore bodies, such as are known from medieval and later times.

In Cardiganshire there was certainly sufficient copper ore to be had for making small artefacts without recourse to much travel. Post-medieval copper-working is known from over twenty mines, including Esgair Fraith (SN 742 911), Esgair Hir (SN 733 913), South Darren (SN 684 831), Cwmystwyth (Copa Hill SN 815 755), and from a handful of mines in which production was otherwise limited to lead.[105] Besides larger commercially exploitable copper lodes there are many smaller. Their general occurrence has been mapped through the stream sediment analyses of J. S. Webb's geochemical survey,[106] which graphically show that copper minerals are common throughout Wales.[107] Similarly, other important associated trace elements, commonly recognized by analysis in early artefacts, have been noted in the surveys. Tin is also known in very small quantities in Wales, though its relative insolubility in water probably inhibits current geochemical detection, exaggerating its scarcity. Specimens of ore have not, so far, been systematically collected for trace element analysis, but preliminary study suggests that it may in future be possible to localize ores through some of their more obscure trace elements.[108]

[103]C. S. Briggs, 'The location and recognition of metal ores in pre-Roman and Roman Britain and their contemporary exploitation', *Acta*, ed. J. Ellis-Jones (1988), 106–14.

[104]L. N. W. Flanagan, 'Industrial resources, production and distribution in earlier Bronze Age Ireland', *The Beginnings of Metallurgy in Atlantic Europe*, ed. M. Ryan (Dublin, 1980), 145–63.

[105]O. T. Jones, *Lead and Zinc: The Mining District of North Cardiganshire and West Montgomeryshire*, Mems. Geol. Survey Spec. Reports on Mineral Resources, G. B. Vol XX, HMSO (London, 1922), 188–91; Palmer, *The Richest in All Wales [Esgair-hir]*, 45.

[106]J. S. Webb, *The Wolfson Geochemical Atlas* (Oxford, 1976).

[107]C. S. Briggs, 'Notes on the distribution of some raw materials in later prehistoric Britain', *Settlement and Economy in the Third and Second Millennia BC*, ed. C. B. Burgess and R. Miket (BAR 33: Oxford, 1976), 267–82 (Fig. 15.4).

[108]D. A. Jenkins, 'Trace element analysis in the study of ancient metallurgy', in J. Ellis-Jones (ed.), *Acta* (1988), 95–105. Those trace elements found to be diagnostic for ore provenancing are generally not ones which have been looked for in the artefacts, so no correlation between the two sets of data seems possible at the moment.

Although copper may be recognized in a variety of ways—for example, by plant type or through eccentric (usually stunted) plant growth, and through water discoloration, it is unlikely that such sophisticated diagnosis was necessary in prehistoric times.[109] Apart from ore collection from areas of primary mineralization, mineral ore would have been recognized in superficial drift deposits, river and stream beds, or even in maritime locations.[110] A brief period of experimentation with the quartz pebbles tinged various shades of green and probably containing several copper and iron minerals might have provided the smith with the necessary experience to distinguish one ore-bearing pebble from another and thereby select examples suitable for smelting.

After ore is extracted from parent rock its fragmentation is necessary. If this work had been undertaken upon any scale, theoretically cobbing floors should be recognizable since the smelting hearth need have been no more than a metre or so in diameter, so its chance of survival is poor and few certain examples are known. Because flue construction might well have been undertaken into steep stream or river banks or into natural bluffs, neither type of site would remain long in the archaeological record since stream erosion or soil creep easily destroys or covers them. Nevertheless, smelting or working-hearths have been recognized in Anglesey,[111] so that their discovery elsewhere is not impossible. An enormous amount of fuel and extremely strong draught are both required to reduce ore to a malleable or liquid state.

In Wales some of the so-called 'boiling mounds' may have been connected with this early industrial activity, though there are no recorded instances of clinker from them to add weight to the suggestion. It is disappointing to note that the socketed chisel mould from Aber-mad was accompanied by neither hearth nor clinker, though its discovery under different circumstances might have brought to light more evidence.

In recent years numerous technical analyses of prehistoric metal artefacts have been under-taken in order to help determine their composition, likely origin and mode of manufacture, involving the quantification of major and minor constituents in the alloy. According to an as yet unpublished analysis of bronze implements, during the Bronze Age mid Wales was an area in which the current metal carried arsenic and nickel as its principal impurities. In common with

---

[109]The notion that prehistoric man may have located minerals through geobotanical observation was advanced in 1976; C. S. Briggs, 'Notes on the distribution of some raw materials in later prehistoric Britain', op. cit., 267–82, citing H. L. Cannon's article on recent techniques, 'Botanical prospecting for ore deposits', *Science*, 132, no. 3427 (1960), 591–8. The earliest documentation for this practice in Britain is from the early 1800s at Turf Bog Mine, Llanfachreth (Gwynedd), and it seems unlikely that locally geobotany was appreciated much earlier than this (unpublished research by the author). According to Meyrick (who obviously thought copper ore abundant in the County), *Hist. and Antiq. of Cardiganshire*, ccvii–ccviii, 'Mines, especially those of copper, may . . . be discovered by the harsh and disagreeable taste of the waters which issue from them. . . . A candle, or a piece of tallow, put into water of this kind, will, in a short time, be tinged of a green colour.' It has yet to be shown, however, that 'The Ancient Britons wrought the mines of Cardiganshire' (ibid., ccxli).

[110]C. T. Morley, 'Mines and where you find them', *Technology Ireland*, 3:7 (1971), 14–17; P. E. Nawrocki and D. M. Romer, 'A buried anomaly associated with a float train in central Ireland', *Prospecting in Glaciated Terrain, 1979* (Institute of Mining and Metallurgy; London, 1979), 40–4; E. Grip, 'Tracing of glacial boulders as an aid to ore prospecting in Sweden', *Econ. Geol.*, 48 (1953), 715–25; V.-P. Salonen, 'Length of boulder transport in Finland', *Prospecting in Glaciated Terrain, 1986* (Institute of Mining and Metallurgy; London, 1986), 211–15.

[111]R. B. White, 'Rhosgoch to Stanlow Shell Oil Pipeline', *BBCS*, 27 (1976–7), 463–90 (pp. 470–6).

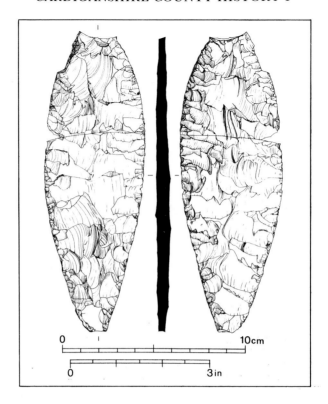

Fig. 32: Flint dagger, Bryn'reithin.

much of the rest of Wales during the Middle Bronze Age (the Acton Park Phase) casting metal was characterized by nickel, arsenic, cobalt and possibly a trace of antimony. Later Bronze Age artefacts are characterized by higher or lower levels of lead,[112] and the inclusion of antimony. The apparent absence of antimony from the geological record in Wales suggested to the investigators that much of the metal was being imported.[113] Evaluation of the data is hampered, however, by the absence of similarly detailed geochemical knowledge of Welsh ores since hardly any have so far been collected for analysis.[114] A further problem highlighted by this analytical research programme is the growth of a belief that later Bronze Age smiths increasingly relied upon scrap almost to the exclusion of newly-won metal.[115] It would be odd if the knowledge of ore collection by scavenging or by prospecting and trading (if either of the latter were necessary) should have been lost or ignored. Clearly the collection and analysis of ores can help provide clues about early metallurgy which are often as important as those which derive from artefact analysis.

[112]J. P. Northover in Savory, *Guide Catalogue*, 242–3.
[113]J. P. Northover, op. cit., and 'Bronze in the British Bronze Age', *Aspects of Early Metallurgy*, ed. W. A. Oddy (London, 1977), 63–70.
[114]D. A. Jenkins, *loc. cit.* (n. 108), 123.
[115]J. P. Northover in Savory, *Guide Catalogue*, 234.

ii) Stone industries

a) Early Bronze Age flintwork: Most implements in everyday use in later prehistoric times were of flint, chert or similar suitably worked stone. Although neither flint nor chert occurs in the bedrock of mid Wales,[116] flint is a minor component of the Irish Sea Drift and is commonly found in beach exposures and more rarely in pebble form inland.

During the Late Neolithic, standards of flint craftsmanship attained a very high order to the extent that it became possible to knap notches into fine pressure-flaked artefacts, from which evolved the tanged-and-barbed arrowheads current during Beaker and Early Bronze Age times. One such example was found on the crest of the south-east rampart of Pen Dinas in the early 1930s,[117] a group of about a dozen on Pen Plynlimon Arwystli in 1967, two of which are now in the National Museum of Wales,[118] and upwards of forty on the Bugeilyn Moorland.[119] More archaeological value attaches to specimens found in excavated contexts. Two arrowheads accompanying a comb-decorated beaker and a cremation burial, together with a retouched flint flake, were excavated at Banc Troed Rhiw Seiri, the assemblage comprising a classic Beaker grave (Fig. 24).[120] Another, found in unrecorded circumstances and now lost, came from the cist of the cairn Cae'r Arglwyddes 1.[121]

It seems likely that the finest piece of flintwork from the County, a Beaker dagger, now in the National Museum of Wales, originally accompanied a burial (Fig. 32). It was discovered in 1976 in a garden at Bryn'reithin (SN 7455 9779). Although broken, the implement was originally about 17.5 cm long, 5.5 cm wide and 0.7 cm thick, and made of brownish-grey flint. A plano-convex flint blade was found nearby. It is presumed that the nearby house may occupy the former site of a cairn, the destruction of which resulted in the general scattering of grave-goods within a fairly close compass of ground.[122] Only five similar specimens are known from Wales,[123] and it has been suggested that these derived from East Anglia, the Cotswolds, Devon or even Yorkshire as part of a flint trade.[124] This, however, would seem unlikely on present evidence, since sizeable pieces of locally occurring flint are occasionally to be found in the Irish Sea Drift and it has yet to be scientifically demonstrated that the Welsh daggers and other flint artefacts are not made from these.[125]

[116]C. S. Briggs, 'Transported flint in Ireland: a charter of investigation for prehistory and geology', *Proc. Fourth Int. Congress on Flint, Brighton 1983*, ed. M. Hart and G. de G. Sieveking (Cambridge, 1985), 185–90.
[117]H. N. Savory, *Guide Catalogue*, 97; NMW 33, 409,1.
[118]H. N. Savory, 'Deposit of Bronze Age flint arrow-heads on the Plynlimon moorland', *BBCS*, 23 (1969) 291–4; *Guide Catalogue*, 99, Fig. 49.
[119]I. C. Peate, 'Arrowheads from Bugeilyn', *Arch. Camb.*, 80 (1925), 196–202.
[120]C. H. Houlder, 'The excavation of a Barrow in Cardiganshire', *Ceredigion*, 3 (1957), 11–23 (pp. 15–16, Fig. 3), 118–23.
[121]A. R. Sansbury, *Meg. Mons.*, 10.
[122]See above, n. 74.
[123]W. F. Grimes, 'The early Bronze Age Flint Dagger in England and Wales', *Proc. Prehist. Soc. E. Anglia*, 6 (1932), 340–55.
[124]See above, n. 74.
[125]See above, n. 116.

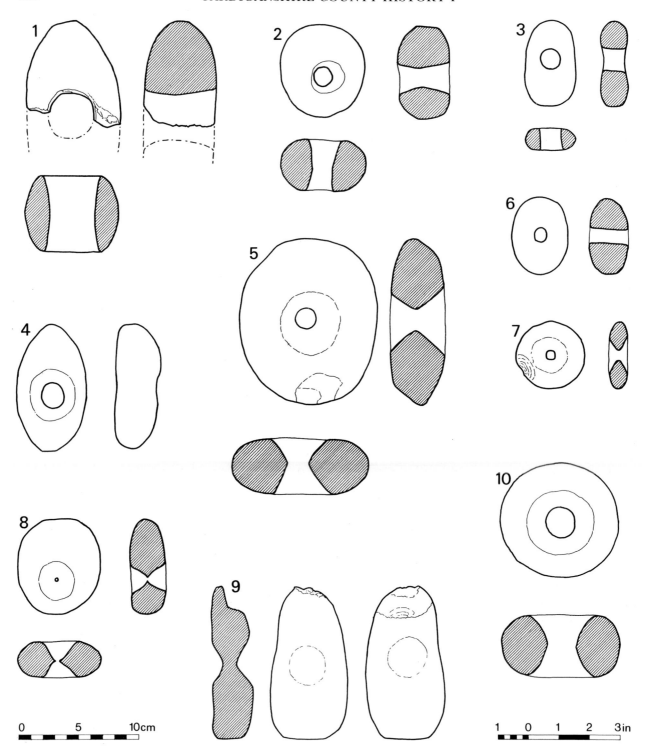

Fig. 33: Perforated stone implements II. 1. Penlan, Swyddffynnon, 2. Rhiwgoch Farm, Ponterwyd, 3. Cwmllechwedd-isaf, 4. unlocalized, 5. Ffosgwy, 6. Llanddewibrefi, 7. Tŷ Neuadd, Pen-uwch, 8. Ffynnon Wen, 9. Wern Felen, 10. Llwyndyrys, Llechryd.

b) Perforated stone implements: Perforated stone implements have a generally widespread distribution throughout west Wales.[126] Of twenty-three from the County, ten are certainly of the axe-hammer class (App. IV, nos. 4, 7, 12, 13, 14, 15, 16, 17, 19 and 20). Those from Llanfeiliog (no. 9) and Penlan (no. 15) are of related forms, whilst those from Llwyn-rhys (no. 12) and Wern Felen (no. 23) may also have been intended to serve as axe-hammers but are either unfinished or do not quite attain the shape normally associated with this type. Into the category of maceheads fall the implements unlocalized from Cardiganshire (no. 1), Cae-y-Maes Mawr (no. 2), Cwmllechwedd-isaf (no. 3) and Ffynnon Wen, Cwmrheidol (no. 6). Those from Ty Neuadd (no. 22) and Llanddewibrefi (no. 8) are so small as to be termed miniatures and may not be of any great antiquity. It is difficult to classify the examples from Ffosgwy (no. 5), Llangybi (no. 10), Llechryd (no. 11) and Rhiwgoch Farm (no. 18).

A wide range of lithic raw materials has been employed in their manufacture. Some (nos. 5 and 23, for example) are of local rock, which in general is more fissile or more soft than some of the others. The major groups of igneous rock type represented include fine-grained crystalline and possibly more compact volcanic rocks probably from the Preseli–St David's area (nos. 3, 15, 18 and 20 and perhaps nos. 4, 13 and 17). From Cwm Mawr near Corndon Hill on the Welsh border comes a distinctive picrite (nos. 7, 14, 16 and 19). Although their material is petrographically defined, the sources of several remain unlocated, including nos. 1 (grit), 6 (conglomerate), 8 and 9 (sandstone), 21 (volcanic grit) and 22 (volcanic ash or greywacke). Seven of the implements are drilled pebbles (nos. 3, 5, 11, 18, 21, 22 and 23). These artefacts comprise two already noted to be of local stone (nos. 5 and 23) and two possibly from the Preseli–St David's area (nos. 3, 18) and perhaps another (no. 22). The source of rock for nos. 11 and 21 is yet to be localized.

These axe-hammers might have been put to several uses. Smaller examples may have been intended as symbols for the kind of ritual deposition that was practised in the Wessex Bronze Age. But there are few parallels from southern England for the massive axe-hammers of Pembrokeshire or Border rocks which form an important proportion of the totals in Wales, the Midlands and beyond. Their use might have included a percussive industrial role such as service in sinking fence posts, beating hide to soften it, or log-splitting for fuel or planks.

c) Lithic resources: Was there a trade in stone implements? Most archaeologists now believe that stone or the implements themselves were transported by Man over long distances from their source. Before initiation of an implement survey by the Council for British Archaeology during the 1930s, however, there was a widespread belief that prehistoric implement-making material derived from superficial deposits rather than from trade.

Unfortunately the imprecise petrographic information available about superficial deposits which currently satisfies the demands of Quaternary geology is quite inadequate for archaeological purposes. Nevertheless, an amazing variety of far-travelled rock-types is known from local pebble-beaches. Only three detailed studies of glacial erratics have been undertaken in Cardiganshire.

---

[126]This growing distribution is underlined by recent discoveries of a fragmentary macehead and battle axe close to hand in eastern Powys at Caeadda, Llanwrin; J. Barfoot, 'Inventory of prehistoric shaft-hole implements from Caeadda, Llanwrin', *Mont. Coll.*, 75 (1987), 96–9.

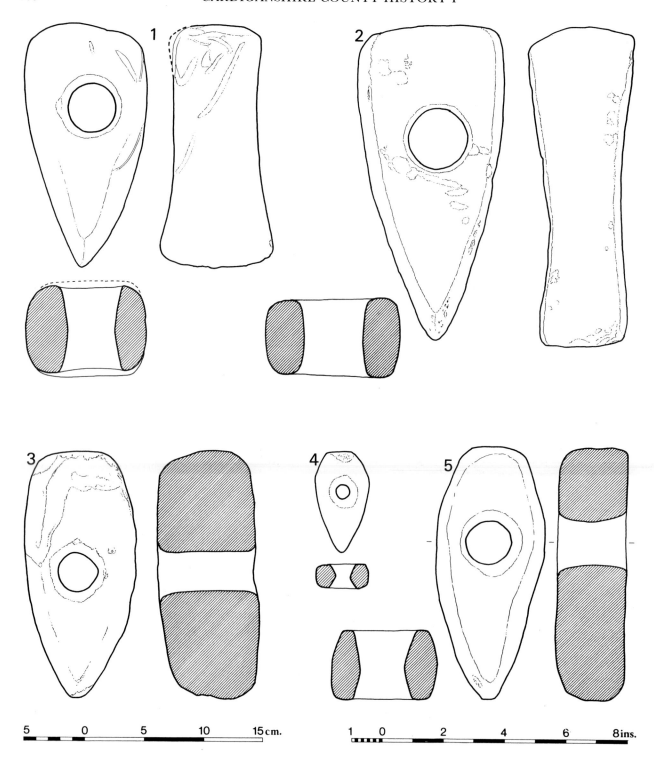

Fig. 34: Perforated stone implements III. 1. Tafarn Crug Isaf, 2. Glan Ystwyth, 3–4. 'Teifiside', 5. Penlan, Swyddffynnon.

The most important, by J. C. Griffiths,[127] remains unpublished. The other two studies by H. E. Hope-Macdonald and K. E. Williams[128] demonstrate the presence of rock-types from Llŷn, including material from the vicinity of Mynydd Rhiw (the site of the axe-making factory, the floors of which have a Bronze Age radiocarbon date),[129] and erratics from Merioneth, Cumbria and Scotland, which were also carried as far south as the Vale of Glamorgan. The conclusions drawn from these studies are largely superseded by recent advances in petrology, and fresh investigations are therefore now required.[130] Natural processes have also at some time carried Preseli rocks north into the Teifi estuary, which accords with the theory that ice-dispersal from areas of high ground tended to be radial and multi-directional. An examination of boulders around Cardigan suggests that many have derived from the Preseli–St David's area.[131] Given the generally unsystematic nature of geological studies and the random activities of collectors, little or no attempt has been made to relate artefacts to the occurrence of glacial erratics. In contrast prehistoric Man must have examined and selected stones disturbed by agricultural practices, fashioning implements out of the heaviest and hardest. Several of the perforated implements from Cardiganshire were certainly made from pebbles which were presumably acquired locally. Some, weighing two or three kg, are unlikely to have been transported far by human agency. While so much remains uncertain about the sources of raw materials, it seems reasonable to regard those implements described above as having been basically the products of local production.

Discussion

i) Bronze Age communities in west Wales

The Bronze Age is the earliest period in the prehistory of west Wales for which both artefacts and sites have been recorded in some numbers. The ubiquity of Bronze Age burial monuments, from river valley to mountain top, is suggestive of a colonization of enormous tracts of land between about 2200 and 1400 BC. Pollen analytical studies indicate that climatic change to warmer conditions obtained during the earlier part of this period. Indeed, it is often suggested that these conditions made the uplands more hospitable to farming, but there are unknown factors to be taken into the reckoning, such as how far Man's alteration of vegetation cover affected the

[127]J. C. Griffiths, 'The glacial deposits west of the Taf' (unpublished University of London Ph.D. thesis, 1940). Griffiths's thesis has been extensively drawn upon in publications by many students of the Welsh Quaternary.

[128]H. A. Hope Macdonald, 'Some erratics from the Teifi Estuary, Western Cardiganshire', *Geological Magazine*, 98 (1961), 81–4; K. E Williams, 'The glacial drift of western Cardiganshire', idem, 64 (1927), 205–27, based upon an unpublished M.Sc. thesis (UCW Aberystwyth, 1927).

[129]C. H. Houlder, 'The excavation of a Neolithic stone implement site on Mynydd Rhiw, in Caernarvonshire', *PPS*, 27 (1961), 108–43.

[130]More general problems besetting prehistoric studies arising from an absence of information about petrology of erratics are raised by C. S. Briggs, 'Axe-making traditions in Cumbrian Stone', *Arch. J.*, 146 (1989), 1–43.

[131]This radial movement is suggested *inter alia* by an unpublished petrographic section from near Gwbert in the British Geological Survey, London, of ophitic dolerite from Garn Meini or its locality. M. Baines and C. S. Briggs have also demonstrated the widespread occurrence of crystalline igneous rocks used as gate posts in the Cardigan area in unpublished fieldwork.

climate, and it remains probable that a combination of anthropogenic, vegetational and climatic factors interacted to force an eventual near-abandonment of upland farms and fields towards the approach of the Later Bronze Age.

Nevertheless, much has been learned from an examination of both monuments and artefacts. We can now see prehistoric communities erecting cairns and barrows for the burial of their dead while at the same time clearing away stones from their small fields as a preliminary to primitive agricultural practice. Although it has not been certainly demonstrated that any early boundaries discovered in peat or elsewhere were directly related to this agriculture, or that settlement sites were situated close to the known burial sites, nevertheless a variety of putative domestic sites have been described and there is every indication that sites like those at Stackpole (Pembs.) will eventually be recognized and excavated locally.

A wide range of pottery types and metal implements are represented from the County, the origins of which lie in contemporary Bronze Age traditions within the British Isles. Some bronze implement types should be seen more as regional variants and there is a strong suspicion that further discoveries will show both pottery and metalwork to have well-developed local traits. When the typology of the perforated stone implements is considered, it is clear that their size owes much to the ready availability of suitably large pebbles. And whilst flint implements are not very plentiful, the possibility remains that in this locality fissile volcanic rocks or quartz industries may have been substitutes for flint, and that these are not easily recognizable. It is now a common-place among prehistorians to assume that all like artefacts had a common origin and must be products of trade or exchange. This is potentially misleading. It has been demonstrated that there is no general shortage of flint or of hard stone or of the numerous requisites for copper-bronze alloys, and that these are more likely to have constituted the materials from which prehistoric artefacts were fashioned locally rather than imported stone or metal.

The prevailing belief in a great mobility of population and artefacts manifest by ancient trackways and trade routes and distribution patterns is one which requires substantial modification. Distribution maps are the fickle records of survival, not accurate guides to human activity in prehistoric times. We can, however, be certain from our examination of sites and of artefacts that ideas and technologies spread through the contact of one population group with another, and that this process, though slow by present standards, carried contemporary knowledge to all corners of the land.

ii) The Bronze-Iron transition

Our picture of Bronze Age society and the processes which brought about the transformation from the presumably smaller communities which erected burial mounds to the greater tribal populations which constructed hillforts is obscure. Few answers are to be found in the artefacts and, though it may be possible to see a coincidence between the distribution of certain Middle Bronze Age and Later Bronze Age metal types and the later, Iron Age, tribal areas, [132] complex metallurgical and geological factors still need to be explored in relation to these distributions. Unfortunately, topographical and morphological studies of Iron Age settlements cannot be assessed alongside those as yet undiscovered Bronze Age settlement sites.

[132]See above, n. 1.

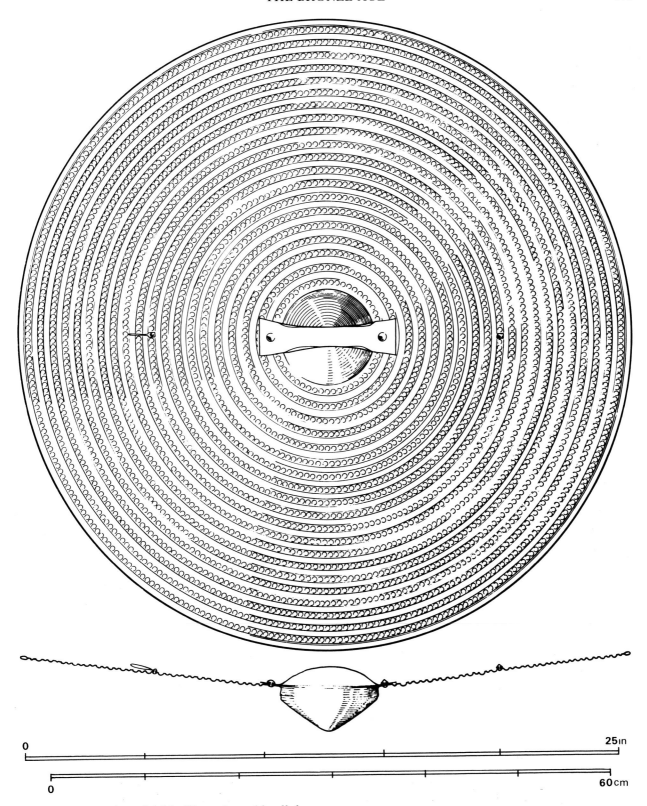

Fig. 35: Bronze Age shield, Glan-rhos, Aberllolwyn.

Although the Bronze Age begins with the certain introduction of copper-bronze or of gold metallurgy, its termination is far less easy to define. For, whereas the widespread use of iron is barely demonstrable archaeologically until the final centuries BC, evidence is mounting to suggest that small quantities of the metal were used alongside bronze perhaps as early as the tenth to eighth centuries BC.[133] Whether or not it was the abandonment of bronze and the adoption of an iron technology in warfare which had a profound effect upon the need to construct hillforts, at the same time welding together smaller communities into larger for purposes of self-defence, or whether such a process was brought about by as yet ill-defined environmental factors, will remain a matter of conjecture without further evidence. Whatever the causes, the end of the Bronze Age between *c.* 800 and 500 BC is likely to have witnessed great social and economic changes. As will be seen from the chapter which follows, the evidence from west Wales indicates that these changes were no less profound here than elsewhere in the British Isles.

APPENDIX I: CAIRNS, BARROWS AND BURIALS

Key

The sites are arranged alphabetically under placename and numbered consecutively, each feature having its own number.

Abbreviations

(i) site condition

c.   cairn
d.   destroyed
dil. dilapidated
mutil. mutilated

(ii) authorities

AW: Archaeology in Wales (The Annual Newsletter of the Council for British Archaeology, Group 2 (Wales)).

CAS: Ceredigion Archaeological Survey (1986–9). Unpublished reports by Manpower Services Commission project administered from St David's University College, Lampeter.

Hist. and Antiq.: S. R. Meyrick, *The History and Antiquities of the County of Cardigan* (London, 1808).

Handlist: A Handlist of the Field Monuments of Wales (1) Cardiganshire RCAHM, 1970 (HMSO).

Muckle: MS Unpubl. typescript on 'Field Survey in Blaencaron, Caron is Clawdd, Dyfed' (Cardiff, 1989).

---

[133]C. S. Briggs, 'Buckets and cauldrons in the Late Bronze Age of North-west Europe: a review' (with an appendix on buckets by M. Holland), *Les Relations entre le Continent et les Iles Britanniques à L'Age du Bronze: Actes du colloque de Lille dans le cadre du 22ième Congrès Préhistorique de France, 2–7 Septembre, 1984,* supplément de la Revue Archéologique de Picardie, Société Préhistorique Français, ed. J. C. Blanchet *et al.* (Amiens, 1987), 161–86.

NAS: National Archaeological Survey Card (formerly Ordnance Survey Antiquity Card). Records held at RCAHM(Wales), Aberystwyth.

NLW MS: National Library of Wales Manuscript.

NMW Rec.: Annotated Record Map at National Museum of Wales.

OS 1818–20: Ordnance Survey two-inch MS Survey in British Library (Photocopy in Dept. of Maps and Prints, NLW).

OS 1830–6: First Edition printed Ordnance Survey Maps.

OS SN refers to OS/NAS Card (see above).

SAM: Scheduled Ancient Monument.

Sansbury *Meg. Mons.*: A. R. Sansbury, 'The Megalithic Monuments of Cardiganshire' (unpublished BA thesis, Dept. of Geography, UCW, Aberystwyth, 1932).

Where known, the initials of the first observer are noted. Where none is given, information has been taken from the National Monuments Record Index.

A bracketed date following the entry indicates the time at which the most recent known observation was made upon the the site. Some dates indicate the first time a site was known to be damaged or destroyed. Where no date is provided the last known reference comes from the cited publication.

C.S.B. (C. S. Briggs); A.O.C. (A. O. Chater); A.H.A.H. (A. H. A. Hogg); C.H.H. (C. H. Houlder); C.R.K. (C. R. Kerkham); D.K.L. (D. K. Leighton); D.M.M. (D. M. Metcalfe); A.J.P. (A. J. Parkinson); E.W. (E. Whatmore). For further references see footnotes.

Introduction: Cairn Classification

Since a good part of this appendix is given over to burial monuments an explanation of the terminology may be found useful.

Wales has been the focus of a strong interest in Bronze Age cairns in recent years. This interest is owed to Sir Cyril Fox,[134] W. F. Grimes,[135] and, more directly bearing on this discussion, to the industry of Frances Lynch.[136] This interest formed the theme for discussion at the Fourth Scottish Archaeological Research Forum in 1972 and resulted in the advancing of a rather complex system of cairn classification for Wales.[137] Drawing together terms current in south-west England and Wales, two main cairn types were defined;[138] on the one hand those monuments having an area completely free of stone, though encompassed by some sort of overall stone enclosure, and on the other hand those comprising amorphous heaps of stone in which the outer structure was recognizable. Of the former group *Stone Ring, Ring Cairn* and *Embanked*

[134]C. Fox, *Life and Death in the Bronze Age* (London, 1959).
[135]W. F. Grimes, *The Prehistory of Wales* (Cardiff, 1951); idem, 'The stone circles and related monuments of Wales', *Culture and Environment*, ed. I. L. Foster and L. Alcock (London, 1963), 93–152.
[136]F. M. Lynch, 'Ring-cairns and related monuments in Wales', *Scottish Arch. Forum*, 4 (1972), 61–80; idem, 'The impact of the landscape on prehistoric man', *The Effect of Man on the Landscape: The Highland Zone*, ed. J. G. Evans, S. Limbrey and H. Cleere (CBA Res. Rep. no. 7; London, 1975), 124–7; idem, 'Ring Cairns in Britain and Ireland: their design and purpose', *Ulster J. Arch.*, 42 (1979), 1–19; idem, 'Bronze Age monuments in Wales', *Culture and Environment in Prehistoric Wales*, ed. J. A. Taylor (BAR 76; Oxford, 1980), 233–41.
[137]It is noteworthy that in the same year (1972), having examined the Caernarfonshire and Glamorgan cairns, W. E. Griffiths felt it 'too early to be dogmatic about typology . . .', *AW*, 12 (1972), 9.
[138]What follows is a condensed version of a discussion which has now appeared in a slightly different form; see D. K. Leighton, 'Structured round cairns in West Central Wales', *PPS*, 50 (1984), 319–50.

Stone Circle were the main sub-types. A *Stone Ring* was seen merely as a shallow, circular heap of stones without larger structural features; a *Ring Cairn*, also a ring of stones, but with concentric revetments of larger stones on both the outside and inside. *Embanked Stone Circles* lacked the outer revetment and the central hollow which had been approached through an 'entrance' in the stone ring.

Of the amorphous cairn structures, *Cairn Circles* and *Kerb Circles* formed the main types. The classification was later extended to include *Kerb Cairns* which were thought to have been much smaller than *Kerb Circles*. A *Cairn Circle* was felt to be an amorphous cairn with spaced uprights 'often leaning outwards . . . important points [being] the obvious filling of the centre and the spacing of the uprights'. This structure differed from the *Kerb Circle* in that the latter had 'a contiguous or a very close-set ring of stones surrounding a level area . . . which will . . . normally appear empty, but may in fact be filled with a shallow spread of stones. There may also be a slight bank outside the ring.' Besides being smaller, *Kerb Cairns* were often revetted by boulders, and rose prominently from the ground surface, resembling a 'charlotte rousse'.[139]

In his description of the cairns of Glamorgan, W. E. Griffiths adopted a simpler approach, using the general terms *mound, ring* and *platform cairns*.[140]

Bearing in mind these different approaches, care was exercised when categorizing the sites and when applying existing classifications. Since existing classifications seemed not to take into consideration either rates of destruction or the lithology and availability of cairn material, in this survey types and sizes of stone, the extent of arable farming in the neighbourhood and any other factors felt to have a direct bearing upon the morphology, survival, denudation or destruction of the cairn, were recorded. However, difficulties were encountered from the outset in accepting the more complex classification. Included among the *Simple* or more *Complex Ring Cairns* were the sites at Banc Troed Rhiw Seiri, Crug Du and three of the Upper Rheidol-Hirnant Group (as adduced from the distribution map,[141] Fig. 18). Of these, only the excavated site at Aber Camddwr[142] actually fitted the proposed definition of a *Ring Cairn*. On the face of it the Hirnant and Lle'r Neuaddau sites are good examples of free-standing stone circles so it is difficult to appreciate why they too, should have been included in the same category. The existence of a peristalith at these sites suggests the intention of a kerb to protect or revet cairn mass. Although an abundance of cairn material is not now in evidence at these sites, buried stone can easily be detected by probe, confirming records of its presence made by Hemp, Sansbury and Griffiths.[143] These monuments appear to have been invisible until the early years of the present century, when, in common with many other similar sites they were exposed by cultivation from beneath peat. At that time much cairn mass was incorporated into fences and tracks in the immediate vicinity. The use of current aesthetic or architectural terms suggesting that such monuments had been deliberately 'designed', whether or not as *Ring Cairns* or as *Stone Circles*, imposes certain value-judgements upon both builder and environment which it is difficult to demonstrate were present in prehistoric times. Certainly, it is often impossible to show that sites like this were ever intended to be free-standing without a central rubble filling. As noted elsewhere, some peristalithic circles and ring-cairns are merely the disembodied cadavers of their intended structures.[144]

The net effect of the spirit of this discussion upon fieldwork undertaken mainly by the writer from 1976–80, and subsequently by Mr D. K. Leighton, has been to increase the number of recorded *Kerb Cairns* in west-central mid Wales to

[139]F. M. Lynch and J. N. G. Ritchie, 'Kerb Cairns', in J. N. G. Ritchie *et al.*, 'Small cairns in Argyll: some recent work', *PSAS*, 106 (1975), 15–38.

[140] RCAHM, *Glamorgan* I, Part I, 42–9 (HMSO, 1976).

[141]F. M. Lynch, 'Ring-cairns and related monuments in Wales', *Scottish Arch. Forum*, 4 (1972), Figs. 3 and 4.

[142]A. H. A. Hogg, 'Two cairns at Aber Camddwr, near Ponterwyd, Cardiganshire', *Arch. Camb.*, 126 (1977), 24–37.

[143]MSS fieldnotes in NMR Wales.

[144]C. S. Briggs, 'Druids' circles in Wales', *Landscape History*, 8 (1986), 5–12.

around thirty, to reduce the number of *Ring Cairns* mapped in 1972, and to question the existence of *Stone Circles* as a separate class of monument. Besides the *Ring Cairn* at Aber Camddwr, similar sites have since been recognized at Bryn y Crofftau, Caron-uwch-clawdd, Carn Fflur (site 1), Pen y Craig Ddu and at Carnau, Cellan. The number of *Kerb Cairns* listed by Leighton has not changed significantly. From the foregoing it will be appreciated that the plethora of terms propounded for cairn typology was found too cumbersome for practical use in the field, and something approaching the simplicity of Griffiths's definition is therefore advocated as an alternative.

Aber Camddwr
1. ring cairn   Cwmrheidol   SN 7540 8670
2. kerb cairn   Trefeurig   SN 7510 8690
In the Nant-y-moch valley at a height of 330 m above OD, two cairns, noted from aerial photographs, were excavated by A. H. A. Hogg in 1955 and 1962,[1] prior to the flooding of the valley. Further survey and excavation was undertaken during drought and reservoir engineering operations, from 1984 to 1986.[2]

1. Ring cairn, about 10 m in diameter, surrounded by a band of small stones about 2 m wide and 0.5 m high, had a neat, central, rock-cut pit containing a small Collared Urn. Around this were six shallow hollows in a ring about 2.75 m in diameter, outside which was a depression with the headless dismembered remains of a child, burnt *in situ* and covered with flat slabs. Occupying the central space were thirty irregularly placed stake holes. Several other pits were noted, some containing charcoal; an unstratified fire-damaged flint scraper 3.5 cm × 0.9 cm, steeply trimmed at the non-bulbar end of the flake, was also found.

The urn (Fig. 27.3), now in the National Museum of Wales (Acc. No. 64.59.2), is of brown ware, 14 cm high, 13.6 cm in diameter at the mouth, 15 cm high at the shoulder and with a flat base 7.5 cm in diameter. Its interior was blackened and the exterior surface decorated with parallel sloping cord impressions, between which a fainter series sloped in the opposite direction. The shallow neck was ornamented with three equidistant horizontal rows of small oval pits, each placed diagonally: the shoulder bore a row of similar pits end to end.[3]

A tiny fragment of a polished stone axe was also discovered here in 1986 by James Barfoot.

2. Kerb cairn, some 3.3 × 3.75 m in diameter and 0.3 m high, produced no finds when first excavated. Within the interior was an empty hollow area 2 × 0.75 m and 0.4 m deep. This may have housed a burial which had not survived the acid soil conditions.

When the water level was lowered in 1984 and 1986 a denuded square annexe was revealed to the SE of the cairn. Excavation by K. Murphy for the Dyfed Archaeological Trust revealed evidence of *in situ* burning beneath this feature. Several pits, two of them charcoal-filled, probably held large upright stones. Two of them contained indications of stakes. Overall, there was a large number of stakeholes, but these formed no obvious pattern, except for an alignment on the south side of the cairn. Some appeared to have been markers predating the upright stones. A small Bronze Age sherd was discovered in a stakehole beneath one of the main kerbstones, and the only other artefact, a perforated spindle-whorl, was a stray find.[4] Charcoal from beneath the annexe yielded C14 dates calibrated to around 1550 BC, and from pits around the cairn to 1200–1100 BC. The cairn was moved *en masse* during 1986 as part of an MSC–NACRO Conservation Scheme, and it now overlooks the reservoir from a site some 100 m to the SSW of its original site.

[1] Hogg, *Arch. Camb.*, 126 (1977), 23–37; Leighton, *PPS*, 50 (1984), 332–3.
[2] Murphy, *AW*, 26 (1986), 26, 31 and *Arch. Camb.*, 140 (1991), 28–76.
[3] Griffiths, *Arch. Camb.*, 126 (1977), 33–5; Savory, *Guide Catalogue* (1980), 152 (no. 456); I. H. Longworth, *A Corpus of Collared Urns* (Cambridge, 1984), 320 (no. 2069).
[4] By Miss E. O'Tuomey, who kindly donated it to the Ceredigion Museum.
OS SN 78 NE 2. (1986)
OS SN 78 NE 7. (1986)

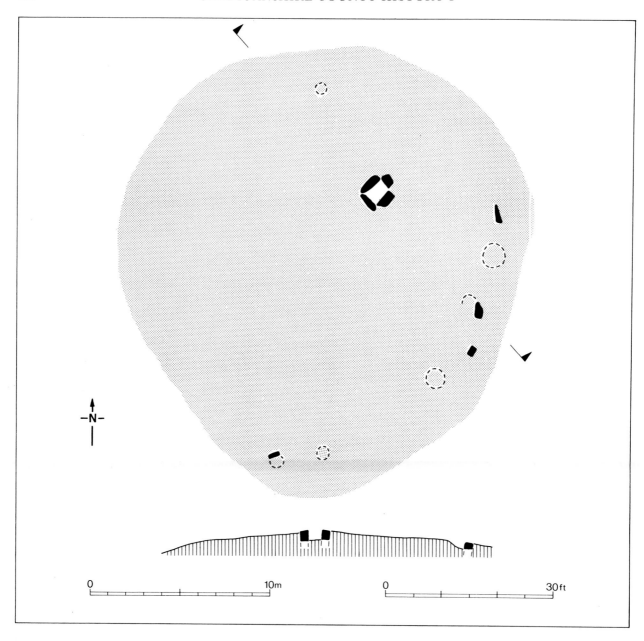

Fig. 36: Garn Wen, cairn.

Aberpeithnant
3. barrow   Melindwr   SN 7518 8400
Briggs & Murphy, *AW*, 24 (1984), 24. (1986)

Afon Tywi   Caron-uwch-   SN 80 62
(W of)   clawdd
4. cairn
Peate, *BBCS*, 4 (1927–9), 284; OS SN 86 SW 2.

Allt Pencraig
5. barrow   Llandygwydd   SN 2487 4537
Handlist; OS SN 24 NW 14. (1975)
6. barrow   Llandygwydd   SN 2493 4547
Handlist; OS SN 24 NW 14. (1975)

Banc   Llangoedmor   SN 2496 4898
7. barrow
Fenton, *Arch. Camb.*, 7 (1861), 316; OS SN 24 NW 9.
(1975)

Banc Blaeneg-   Caron-uwch-   SN 7885 6642
nant   clawdd
8. cairn
D.K.L. (1983)

Banc Dolau-Couon, Pont-rhyd-y-groes
9. kerb cairn   Upper Llanfi-   SN 7318 7428
                   hangel-y-
                   Creuddyn
Thorburn, *Arch. Camb.* (forthcoming). (1989)

Banc Geufron (Fig. 37.3)
10. kerb cairn   Gwnnws Isaf   SN 7163 7033
This kerb cairn stands on a low eminence within
an open hollow 305 m above OD about 70 m W of
B. M. 987 and close to the forestry and farm track.
The diameter of the mound exceeds 10 m, with the
ground falling away steeply particularly on the W
and S. There are currently eleven kerbstones
visible, though the inner faces of five are still
obscured by the mound. Two internal orthostats,
each over a metre long, and a flat stone half that
length could have formed parts of a cist or cists,
now robbed out. One of the largest kerbstones is
well over a metre high, but has fallen. A further
upright formerly stood without the cairn mass to
the SW but has now disappeared. This could be
the flat stone now lying partly buried to the W of
the cairn. Although slightly damaged by the farm

track, the cairn is still in fairly good condition,
largely grass- and bracken-covered.
C.S.B.; SAM 139; Sansbury, *Meg. Mons.*, no. 32;
Leighton, *PPS*, 50 (1984), fig. 4.2; OS SN 77 SW 3. (1990)

Banciau Duon: Y Garn
11. barrow   Llanddewi-   SN 6917 5297
                   brefi

Banc Troed Rhiw Seiri (Fig. 24)
12. barrow   Tirymynach   SN 6677 8560
A double-banked barrow with a single ditch,
excavated by C. H. Houlder in 1955. In 1956 the
monument was described as follows: 'The ground
it occupied had first been cleared of vegetation by
burning. Sharpened stakes had been driven in at
intervals of about 18 ins (0.5 m), delimiting a
burial circle about 35 ft (11 m) in diameter. A
bank was then built on the line of the stakes from
a ditch on the outside. Surplus material appears to
have formed the second discontinuous bank. The
barrow was probably re-fashioned at the time of
the secondary burial.'[1]
   From a central burial pit came fragments of
burnt bone, two barbed and tanged flint arrow
heads (Fig. 24), and beaker sherds representing a
vessel about 20 cm high, decorated with horizontal lines of impressions placed end to end or with
narrow bands of chevrons and oblique lines. Felt
by Griffiths[2] to belong to the 'A' Beaker Tradition,
this vessel was more recently cast in his 'Northern'
Tradition by Clarke.[3] A further cremation had
probably occupied the same pit but was represented only by fragments of a coarse vessel,
possibly a Pygmy Cup (Fig. 24). The only other
discovery was a flint flake (Fig. 24).
[1] Houlder, *Ceredigion* 3 (1957), 11–23, 118–23.
[2] Griffiths, *PPS*, 23 (1957), 59, 75, 78.
[3] D. L. Clarke, *Beaker Pottery of Great Britain* (Cambridge,
1970), II, C19, 524.
C.H.H.; SAM 67; OS SN 68 NE 1. (1981)

Banc-y-   Llanddewi-   SN 6823 5602
gwyngoed   brefi
13. cairn

Bedd Taliesin (Fig. 37.4)
14. kerb cairn   Ceulan-a-   SN 6714 9120
                  Maesmor

This well-known site is situated on a level shelf

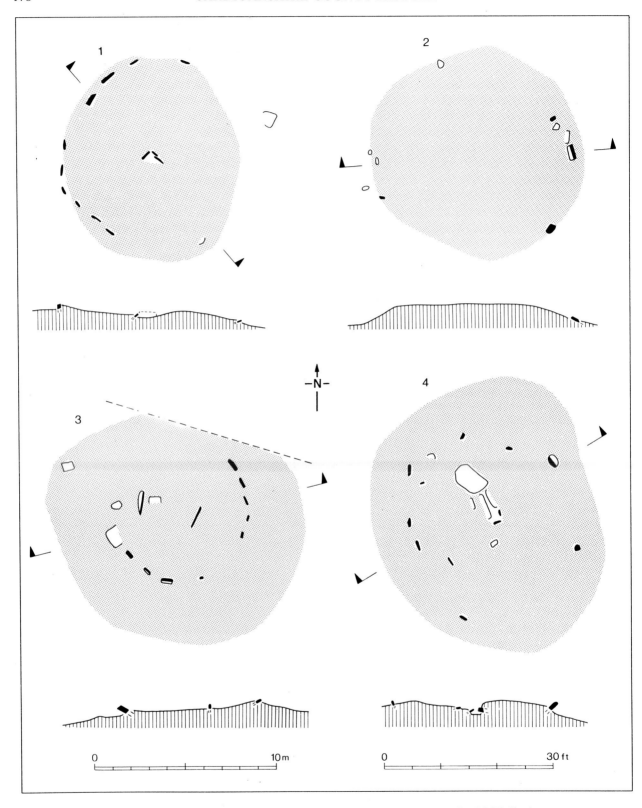

Fig. 37: Cairns: 1. Moelau, 2. Nant Maesnant Fach, 3. Banc Geufron, 4. Bedd Taliesin.

immediately above the track and below a craggy hill about 230 m above OD. The surviving cairn mass is slightly asymmetrical, measuring 12 m (NNE–SSW) by 13 m (NNW–SSE) and standing about 1m high. It appears to have been revetted by a kerb, also rather asymmetrical, about 6 m in diameter, of which ten stones are now visible, two having become overgrown since Sansbury's day.[1] In the centre of the cairn is a cist, collapsed inwards, about 2 m long, 0.5 m wide and deep. A massive capstone, 1.75 m long × 1.1 m wide and up to 0.4 m thick, lies to the north of the cist, supported on smaller stones.

The cairn has a well-documented history and is believed to have been dug into before Meyrick's time, producing a large skull. There now seems little evidence to support T. Rees's contention that it was formerly surrounded by two concentric circles.[2] Although Lhuyd rejected the idea that Taliesin ever lay in it, more romantic topographers have seen bards or druids as its incumbents.[3]

[1] Sansbury, *Meg. Mons.* no. 14; Leighton, *PPS*, 50 (1984), no. 3, 334, fig. 5.3.
[2] T. Rees, *A Topographical and Historical Description of South Wales* (2nd edn., London, 1815), 454; A. Nicholson, *The Cambrian Travellers' Guide* (London, 1813), 42–3.
[3] R. J. Thomas, *Bedd Taliesin* (Aberystwyth, 1968); Wood, *Ceredigion*, 8 (1979), 414–18.
Handlist; SAM; OS SN 69 SW 1. (1990)

Bedd y Forwyn (alternatively Virwyn)
15. cairn (d.)   Cellan   SN 6203 4727

16. barrow   SN 6246 4767
OS 1-inch 1834; Morris, *Lhuyd's Parochialia* III, (1911), 86; Sansbury, *Meg. Mons.* no. 6; S. Lewis, *Topog. Dict.* (1833); OS SN 64 NW 11. (1990)

Black Lion (nr.), Tal-y-bont
17. robbed   Ceulan-a-   SN 6560 8925
cist (d.)   Maesmor
Murphy, *AW*, 26 (1986), 32.

Blaenaugwenog
18. barrow   Llanwenog   SN 478 514
burial
There appear to have been two cairns or urn cemeteries, one in a field called Cae Rhyd Las, in which four urns were adventitiously discovered. Of these, one had been found around 1850, the other three about 1909. The second cemetery, in

an adjacent field known as Cae Hyttir, was excavated by workmen during the winter of 1910. It seems that the two fields covered a single deposit about 100 m in length. In Cae Hyttir a patch 20 yds (18 m) in diameter was excavated and from beneath a capstone 14 ins (0.33 m) × 10 ins (0.25 m) × 3 ins (0.07 m) thick, were four circular deposits, presumably individual burials. These comprised dark earth incorporating calcined bones and charred wood. Bones from the fourth deposit were recognizable as parts of a left femur, tibia, ribs and skull. Other features containing charcoal which were noted at that time could have been pre-barrow domestic pits or postholes (cf., Pen y Glogau). With the exception of two small fragments of plain pottery and the flints, no identifiable artefacts appear to have been recovered from this exploration.

Both flints appear to have been undistinguished flakes. The potsherds were of 'coarse fabric mixed ... with quartz stones between the size of a pin's head and a pea and having the usual outer coating of lighter-coloured and finer paste over the dark, coarse clay within'. Quartz was noticeably absent from the fabric of the other urns.

Three pottery vessels can be recognized from the original report: (a) An urn of undecorated, light-coloured friable fabric of unknown height, 7.6 cm in diameter at the mouth and 4 cm at the base. It contained dark earth and charred wood with small stones. A flint was found nearby. The base is among surviving sherds. (b) An undecorated urn, better baked with an internal bevel 1.5 ins (3.8 cm) below the rim. It was 7 ins (17.8 cm) high and about the same in diameter at the mouth. This is no longer identifiable. (c) A Collared Urn, found inverted upon a flat, oval stone, some 15.25 ins (38.5 cm) × 9 ins (22.9 cm). It stood 10.5 ins (26.7 cm) high with a rim circumference of 23.75 ins (29 cm), and basal circumference of 12.5 ins (31 cm) with a collar 2.5 ins (6.4 cm) wide. The rim was decorated with a vertical zigzag ornamentation and below this was a criss-cross twisted cord pattern for a further 1.5 ins (3.8 cm) of the vessel. Surviving fragments include the base and some rim sherds.

Further urns were discovered in 1910 and 1911, but only one survived and its form and fate are not known.
Thomas, *Arch. Camb.*, 65 (1910), 373–9; 67 (1912), 345–56.

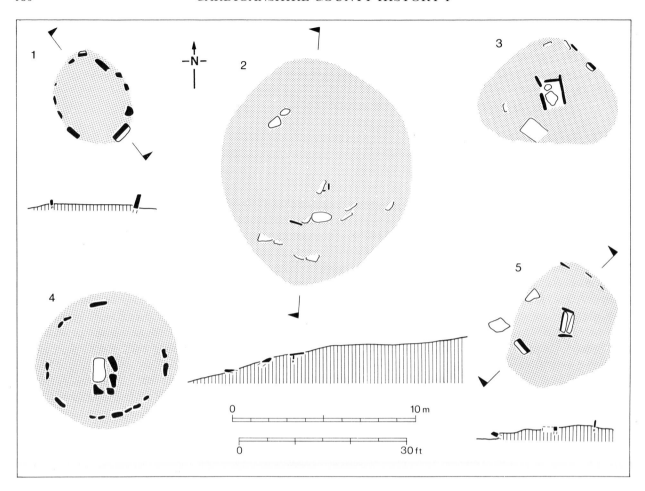

Fig. 38: Cairns: 1. Dolgamfa, 2. Blaen Brefi 2, 3. Blaen Glas Ffrwd 3, 4. Coed Craig yr Ogof, 5. Blaen Camddwr.

Blaen Brefi

19. cairn with cist (Fig. 38.2)	Llanddewi-brefi	SN 7082 5560

Lying at about 375 m above OD on the hillslope is a cairn measuring 12.2 m (N–S) × 10.5 m, revetted on the lower side by several orthostats possibly arranged in concentric arcs. There is a central cist. The site has probably been denuded by robbing for nearby buildings. (1990)

20. ?kerb cairn (Fig. 19.1)		SN 7110 5535

Situated on level ground on a sheltered knoll at 415 m above OD is a single arc of stones comprising some ten upright or leaning, barely exposed slabs providing an irregular kerb to a now largely stoneless cairn putatively 12 m in diameter.
Leighton, *PPS*, 50 (1984), nos. 4–5, 334–5, figs. 5 and 6.
CAS *Carnau* (1988), 12.

Blaen Bwch Isaf (cropmarks)

21. barrow (d.)	Llangynllo	SN 3658 4659
22. barrow (d.)		SN 3712 4698

OS SN 34 NE 12. (1975)

Blaen Camddwr (Esgair Ffrwd) (Fig. 38.5)

23. kerb cairn	Caron-is-clawdd	SN 7516 5890

A small cairn about 6 m in diameter, of which very little now remains, lying at about 427 m above OD. The kerb consists of four orthostats and two fallen stones by the side of the track. The limits of cairn material lie immediately outside the NE orthostats and the remainder were probably incorporated into the nearby track. Two other larger slabs lie close to the site and appear to derive from a collapsed and robbed cist 1.5 m × 0.7 m aligned NNE–SSW.

C.S.B.; Leighton, *PPS*, 50 (1984), no. 6, 334 and 336, fig. 6; OS SN 75 NE 1. (1990)

Blaen Dyffryn Isaf
24. 'mound'   Melindwr   SN 700 812

BlaenDyffryn
25–27. barrow   Orllwyn Teifi   SN 393 417
burials

Three mounds formerly existed in the locality in a field called Cae Cnwc, one devoid of finds, located about 100 yards (91.4 m) from the other two. Upon attempting to remove these two while 'improving the field by carting the mounds away to get it more level, seeing that it was good soil', bones and urns were found in one, and bones in the other.[1] The two urns were from the larger mound, which had a 'trench with rough stones placed on edge ... about 15 ins (37.6 cm) deep, 18 ins (54.2 cm) wide and 6 to 8 feet (1.83–2.44 m) long' (probably a cist). It was full of human bones and charcoal, including one complete lower jaw. The smaller mound appears to have been uncisted. The urns were found at ground level after most of the covering material had gone, and both contained 'the remains of a human being'.[2] Interestingly, one was also 'covered with a rough grey stone, about 15 to 18 ins (37.6–45.2 cm) square'.

The urns were 9.5 ins (24 cm) high, about 5–5.5 ins (13–14 cms) in diameter, both at mouth and base, of a 'dark umber brown', the necks about 1.5 ins (3.8 cm) above the bodies and were ornamented with diagonal incised lines about 0.25 ins (0.6 cm) apart. Both disintegrated soon after discovery.

A contemporary pen and ink sketch was made of one urn, but this has not been located.

[1] G. E. Evans, *Trans. Carms. Antiq. Soc.*, 18 (1924–5), 76.
[2] Anon., *Red Dragon* (1885), ii, 89; *Cardigan and Tivyside Advertiser* 18 May 1885.

Blaen Glas Ffrwd   Caron-uwch-clawdd
A group of cairns and cists situated on a NE to SW ridge at about 395 m above OD. The cists, formed of large slabs set on edge, have all been opened and the capstones displaced.

28. cairn   SN 7697 6310
A low bank of stones about 1.25 m wide formed of fairly large boulders embedded in turf, encircling a central area about 2 m in diameter. (1990)

29. cist   SN 7698 6316
A cist measuring 2 × 1 m, aligned N–S without covering cairn. (1990)

30. cairn with   SN 7708 6309
cist (Fig. 20.1)
A cairn composed of medium to large stones, about 12 m in diameter and 0.8 m high. A kerb may be traced on the W and a further concentric circle may also be present. In the centre is a cist measuring 2 × 1 m and 0.8 m deep on a NW–SE axis. (1990)

31. cairn with   SN 7714 6315
cist (Fig. 38.3)
A cairn of medium-sized boulders, 5 m in diameter with a good kerb of upright slabs, protruding only a few centimetres above the turf. (1990)

32. cairn with   SN 7732 6332
cist
Traces of a cairn measuring about 3 × 2.5 m, now almost invisible, with a cist aligned WNW × ESE at the centre. (1990)

33. cairn   SN 771 628
A kerb cairn about 5 m in diameter and 0.4 m high with remnants of an orthostatic kerb on N, S and W.

A.H.A.H. (nos. 28–32); D.K.L.; SAM 138; Leighton, *PPS*, 50 (1984), nos. 7–8, 334, 336–7, figs. 6, 7. (1990)

Blaenglowon Fawr
34. barrow   Llandysilio-   SN 3990 5142
gogo
SAM 88; *Handlist*; Davies, *Arch. Camb.*, 59 (1905), 62; OS SN 35 SE 7. (1988)

Blaenhirbant-uchaf
35. ?barrow   Llanwenog   SN 4685 4632
with cist
A circular cropmark about 25 m in diameter. OS SN 44 NE 7. (1975)

Blaenhoffnant Uchaf
36. cairn (d.)   Penbryn   SN 3321 5183
Described by Meyrick as having been 'close to two

others', but no cairn traced by OS in 1973.
Meyrick, *Hist. and Antiq.*, 433; OS SN 35 SW 5. (1973)

Blaen Llwernog
37. ?barrow   Melindwr   SN 7305 8195
and stone pair
OS SN 78 SW 19. (1978)

Blaen Marchnant
38. cairn   Ysbyty   SN 7783 7040
                   Ystwyth
OS SN 77 SE 1. (1978)
39. cairn with   SN 7791 7031
cist (mutil.)
OS SN 77 SE 3. (1978)

Blaen Nant-y-rhiw
40. cairn   Llanddewi-   SN 7712 5291
                   brefi
D.K.L. (1980)
41. ?barrow,   SN 7660 5333
hut or ring
cairn
D.M.M. (1980)
42. barrow   SN 7676 5347
(1980)

Blaen-porth
43. burials   Aber-porth   SN 26 49
'In the adjacent fields, funeral urns, probably
British, have been lately found, containing
fragments of burnt bones, which find was understood not to have been the only one on or near the
same spot.' The finds appear to have been lost.
'Cardigan Meeting', *Arch. Camb.*, 14 (1859), 329; Anwyl,
Arch. Camb., 61 (1906), 110.

Blaenyffynnon
44. barrow   Bron-gwyn   SN 2998 4433
(d.)
NMW Rec. from O. T. Jones; OS SN 24 SE 3. (1972)

(Y) Bryn
45. ring cairn   Caron-is-   SN 7249 6168
                        clawdd
D.M.M.; Stenger, *AW*, 23 (1983), 6.

Bryn Beddau
46. ring cairn   Caron-is-   SN 7678 8766
                        clawdd
C.S.B. (1984)

Bryn Bras
47. barrows   Cwmrheidol   SN 7465 8014
OS SN 77 NW 10. (not loc. 1978)

Bryn Cosyn
48. cairn   Caron-is-   SN 7444 5952
                   clawdd
A badly damaged cairn spread of 9 m diameter,
lying on the moorland track, out of which a
modern beacon has been built. It is just possible to
distinguish several orthostats, perhaps of a structural concentric circle of about 5 m in diameter, of
which only two survive. (1984)
49. cairn   SN 7448 5945
A low structureless cairn which appears to have
been robbed. A small heap of stones now lying to
its SW may be the result of such robbing. A large
flat stone at least 35cm thick lies on the peat some
20 m W and could have been the capstone to a
cist. (1984)
50. cairn   SN 7422 5959
A robbed cairn about 11 m NW–SE. Some
massive stones have been used to build a wall, on
the N end of which stands an orthostat about
0.5 m square and 1 m high. At least two further
orthostats can be recognized on either side of the
one already described. It seems likely that all once
formed part of the cairn. (1984)
51. cairn   SN 7430 5758
OS SN 75 NW 5, 10.

Bryn Cysegrfan
52. ?ring   Llanfair   SN 64 52
barrow   Clydogau
T. Lewis, *TCAS*, 5 (1927), 92. It is possible that this
'monument' was in fact part of a rabbit-warren (D.
Austin, 'Excavation and survey at Bryn Cysegrfan,
Llanfair Clydogau, Dyfed, 1979', *Medieval Archaeology*, 32
(1988), 130–65).

Brynehedydd
53. cairn (d.)   Penbryn   SN 3310 5119
OS SN 35 SW 6. (1973)

Bryn Goleu (NNW of)
54. cairn   Cellan   SN 6243 4712
(mutil.)
OS SN 64 NW 19. (1975)

Bryn Granod
55. urn burial   Llanwenog   SN 472 490
According to E. Lorimer Thomas, 'One urn,
found years ago on the farm of Bryn Granod, and
left on a hedge to crumble away, has disappeared,
but the exact spot in a ploughed field whence it
was unearthed is known, and charcoal, white
stones and dark earth may still be seen there on
the surface.'[1] This appears to be the find referred
to by G. E. Evans who asserted that, 'some time
ago one of those (tumps) was ploughed through',
having seen the rim of an urn and noted the
accompanying white stones in a field at Llanwenog.[2]

[1] E. L. Thomas, *Arch. Camb.*, 65 (1910), 373.
[2] *Minutes of Evidence* : Report from the Joint Select Committee of the Consolidation and Amendment (H.L.) and
the Ancient Monuments Protection (N.2) Bill (H.L.),
together with the Proceedings of the Committee and
Minutes of Evidence (HMSO, 1912), 10 (paras 282–4).
OS SN 44 NE 4.

Bryngwrog
56. barrow   Bron-gwyn   SN 2828 4423
(d.)
NMW Rec. inf. from O. T. Jones; OS SN 24 SE 4. (1972)

Bryn Gwyddel (nr.)
57. cairn   Llanddewi-   SN 733 527
                  brefi
D.K.L. (1980)

Bryngwyn Bach cairn cemetery (Fig. 20.3–5)
58. kerb cairn   Caron-uwch-   SN 7284 6282
with cist   clawdd
Kerb cairn about 9.5 m in diameter and about
0.6 m high with an orthostatic circle about 6.5 m
in diameter set within the circumference of the
cairn. A robbed and shattered cist lies in a hollow
on the south.
59. kerb cairn   SN 7282 6282
with cist
Kerb cairn measuring about 9 × 8 m and about
0.5 m high with an orthostatic circle about 6.5 m
in diameter set within the circumference of the

cairn. A robbed and shattered cist lies in a roughly
central position.
60. cairn with   SN 7281 6284
cist
Cairn about 6.5 m in diameter and about 0.4 m
high. A robbed cist lies roughly centrally.
61. cairn   SN 7283 6287
Cairn about 4.5 m × 4 m and 0.3 m high.
62. cairn   SN 7285 6290
Cairn about 6.5 m × 5 m and about 0.5 m high.
There is a depression on the east.
63. cairn   SN 7282 6291
Cairn about 6.5 m × 5 m and about 0.5 m high.
There is a central depression.
Sites 61–3 lie some 30 m north of 58–60.
A.O.C.; Leighton, *AW*, 17 (1977), 16; *PPS*, 50 (1984),
nos. 9–11, 334, 337, fig. 7, 338; OS SN 76 SW 11. (1984)

64. cairn   (E of   SN 7302 6293
cemetery   Bryngwyn
                  Bach)
D.K.L.

Bryn Herlwn
65. barrow   Penbryn   SN 3454 5049

Bryn Hirfaen
66. cairn (d.)   Cellan   SN 6220 4660
OS SN 64 NW 13.
67. cairn (d.)   SN 6208 4633
OS SN 64 NW 14.
68. cairn (d.)   SN 6180 4625
NMW Rec.; OS SN 64 NW 15. (1975)

Bryn Llwyd
69. cairn   Llanwenog   SN 4562 4805
When first noted by W. F. Grimes in 1939 this
cairn was 55 ft (16–17 m) in diameter and stood
about 1 ft (0.3 m) high with the centre dug out.
Aerial photographs taken in 1946 indicate a
cropmark feature 16 m in diameter.
NMW Record; OS SN 44 NE 2. (1975)

Brynmeniog
70. barrow   Llanddewi-   SN 6504 5285
                  brefi
71. barrow   SN 6516 8285
D.K.L. (1980)

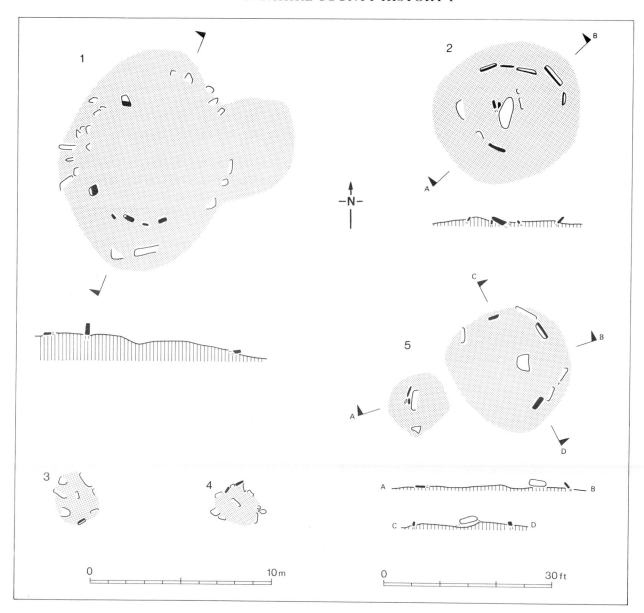

Fig. 39: Cairns: 1. Carn Fflur, 2. Bryn Rhudd, 3.–4. Bryn y Gorlan, 5. Bryn Poeth.

Bryn Poeth (Fig. 39.5)

72. cairn	Llanddewi-	SN 6840 5510
(?kerb cairn)	brefi	

This site was possibly the focus of attention in digging and survey by the Cardiganshire Antiquarian Association and a group from Tregaron School in 1915 and 1927.

D.K.L.; SAM 137; *TCAS*, 2 (1) (1915), 98–100; T. Lewis, *TCAS*, 5 (1927), 83–99. The suggestion is made by K. Ray, CAS *Carnau* (1988), 4–9. (1988)

Bryn Rhosau

73. cairn   Cwmrheidol   SN 7334 7999

A turf-covered cairn measuring 13.5 m N–S × 12.5 E–W and 1.3 m high, surrounded by a ditch 2 m wide and 0.5 m deep. The northern half of the mound is revetted by massive stone slabs, and the centre is mutilated.

74. cairn   SN 7332 7997

8 m NS × 7.5 m EW and 0.8 m high with a ditch

on its western side. This also has a mutilated centre and NW quadrant.

C.S.B.; SAM 137; OS SN 77 NW 6. (1988)

Bryn Rhudd (Fig. 39.2)

75. ring cairn (site II)	Llanddewi-brefi	SN 6994 5540
76. ring cairn (site III)		SN 6921 5549
77. ring cairn (site IV)		SN 6917 5537

For 76–7 see OS SN 65 NE 31. (1988)

| 78. ring cairn (site V) | | SN 6897 5510 |

(1981)

| 79–81. three small cairns | | SN 6888 5530 |

D.K.L.; SAM 137; OS SN 65 NE 30. (1981)

| 82. cairn | | SN 6923 5545 |

CAS *Carnau* (1988), 16–20. (1987)

| 83. cairn | | SN 6919 5598 |

D.K.L.; CAS *Carnau* (1988), 14. (1987)

Bryn y Crofftau

| 84. ring cairns | Caron-uwch-clawdd | SN 7423 6344 |

S.R.H. and A.J.P.; OS SN 76 SW 10. (1978)

Bryn y Gorlan prehistoric monument complex (Fig. 39.3–4) (see *Standing Stones* no. 6 and *Circles* no. 1).

circle (mutil.)	Llanddewi-brefi	SN 750 546
standing stone (fallen)		SN 7494 5473
standing stone ?setting		SN 7498 5476
85. cairn		SN 7434 5464
86. cairn		SN 7488 5463

This monument complex is situated on moorland plateau at between 400–40 m OD and comprises the following: a stone circle with ten surviving standing stones, representing an original circle of approximately 18 m diameter. One monolith is fallen and three stones protrude to heights of up to 0.9 m, and six are only stumps. The circle is one of currently only two authenticated examples in the County and is probably connected with a fallen standing stone 1.8 m in height some 90 m to the SE. Three further sites are located nearby. The first was probably the setting for a further monolith, the other two are cairns, possibly of the kerb variety.

Leighton, *Arch. Camb.*, 129 (1980), 154–7; *PPS*, 50 (1984), nos. 14–15, 338–9, fig. 8. (1990)

Bryn yr Afr (E of)

87. cairn	Trefeurig	SN 7486 8725
88. cairn		SN 7463 8764
89. cairn		SN 7491 8752

Briggs and Murphy, *AW*, 24 (1984), 32. (1986)

Bwlch Blaen Carnau

| 90. cairn | Llanddewi-brefi | SN 7005 5630 |
| 91. cairn | | SN 7008 5633 |

D.K.L.; CAS *Carnau* (1988). (1987)

Bwlch Corog (nr. Ffynnon Drewi)

| 92. barrow | Lledrod Isaf | SN 6190 6741 |

OS SN 66 NW 9. (1990)

Bwlch Graig Goch (nr.)

| 93. ?kerb/ clearance cairn | Trefeurig | SN 7655 8701 |

Briggs and Murphy, *AW*, 24 (1984), 31. (1984)

Bwlch Mawr: Crud yr Udon

| 94. barrow (d.) | Llanwenog | SN 4885 3452 |

According to Meyrick, here there was 'a barrow . . . which on being opened, was found to contain a coffin of glazed earth, in which were human bones placed in an upright position.' Slight indications of a platform some 20 m in diameter.

Meyrick, *Hist. and Antiq.*, 188; CAS *Capel Dewi* (1988), no. 4843/5.

Bwlch y Crwys

| 95. barrow | Upper Llanfi-hangel-y-Creuddyn | SN 7102 7760 |

OS SN 77 NW 3. (1978)

Bwlch y Groes (see Maes yr Haf)

Bwlch y Maen

| 96. ?ring barrow | Ceulan-a-Maesmor | SN 6989 8595 |

APs RAF 541/515/3644–6. (1978)

Bwlch yr   Tirymynach   SN 7198 8685
Adwy
97. cairn
D.K.L. (1984)

Cae'r Arglwyddes (Fig. 17.2–3)
98. cairn with   Ceulan-a-   SN 6840 9168
cist   Maesmor

Lying at 270 m above OD this badly damaged mound, of largely water-worn pebbles, has altered little in the past fifty years, although used as a dump for field stones. It displays no traces of a kerb and contains the vestiges of a cist, comprising one side slab over 1 m long and still providing a depth of 0.25 m. A further large, loose stone, lying on the edge of the mound, was probably its capstone.
OS SN 69 SE 13.

99. cairn with   SN 6886 9179
cist

This cairn is situated at about 260 m above OD immediately north of an intermittent rocky outcrop, hidden away from view except from the N and E. It is about 7.9 m in diameter, stands over 0.5 m high and contains a fine, upstanding cist measuring 1.75 by just under 1 m wide and 0.45 m deep. The cist is slightly damaged, the largest stone being split down the middle, its opposite leaning inwards. Both endstones are still practically vertical. According to Sansbury this cist produced two flint arrowheads, one barbed and tanged, the other triangular and tanged, both now lost. The cairn matrix is of fairly angular rock, probably derived from the rock exposed in its vicinity. There is one upstanding stone 2.5 m to the south of the cist which may have formed a part of a kerb. The mound is somewhat mutilated, with slight robbing to the south of the cist and in a small hollow about a metre from it. To the west further stone has accumulated in recent years due to field clearance.
SAM 140; Sansbury, *Meg. Mons.*, no. 16; OS SN 69 SE 14. (1990)

Carnau, E of,
100. ring   Llanddewi-   SN 691 552
cairn   brefi
101. ring   SN 691 552
cairn
D.K.L. (1981)

Carnau (Graig Twrch) (see also Craig Twrch)
102. Find   Cellan   SN 688 482
(? in cairn)

Here E. L. Thomas recorded the discovery of a fragment of an urn (?in a cairn). There are several cairns on Craig Twrch, and it is not clear to which this alludes.
Thomas, *Arch. Camb.*, 67 (1912), 345–56.

Carn Dôl-gau
103. cairn   Trefeurig   SN 7079 8266
SAM 65; OS SN 78 SW 4. (1986)

Carneddau (Y Drosgl)
104. cairn   Trefeurig   SN 7595 8786
(dilap.)
105. cairn   SN 7595 8785
(dilap.)
106. cairn   SN 7598 8847
(?clearance)
107. cairns   SN 7514 8735
and clearance
108. clearance   SN 755 879
cairns
Briggs, *AW*, 24 (1984), 33. (1984)

Carn fach Bugeilyn
109. cairn   Trefeurig/   SN 8264 9037
              Trefeglwys
RCAHM (Montgomeryshire Inventory), 1911, 171, no. 872; OS SN 89 SW 1. (1977)

Carn Fflur (Fig. 39.1)
110. ?ring   Caron-uwch-   SN 7397 6235
cairn with cist clawdd

A probable ring cairn about 16 m in diameter and 0.75 m high, set eccentrically within a possible later turf-covered stone ring approximately 36 m in diameter. Two huts or sheep shelters have been built on the N of this outer ring. The cairn encloses a robbed cist of massive size.
C.S.B.; S.R.H.; D.K.L.; A.J.P.; *AW*, 17 (1977), 16; OS SN 76 SW 13. (1978)

111. kerb cairn   SN 7420 6245

Lying to the E of no. 110 amongst a number of clearance cairns, a kerb cairn 10 m in diameter and about 0.5 m high. Remnants of an orthostatic ring survive on the S and W (Fig. 27.5).
Leighton, *PPS*, 50 (1984), 338–9, fig. 8; OS SN 76 SW 15.

112. cairn   SN 7427 6229
with cist

A rocky knoll is capped by a large and apparently featureless cairn in which are some large boulders which may have formed part of a collapsed cist.
OS SN 76 SW 5. (1978)

113. cairn   SN 7423 6235
Carn Fflur is capped by a large, apparently structureless heap about 20 m in diameter.
(Ref. as 110 above).

Carn Nant y Llys
114. cairn   Upper Llanfi-   SN 7984 7708
(?d.)   hangel-y-
                    Creuddyn
OS 1820.

Carn Owen
115. cairn   Ceulan-a-   SN 7324 8819
                    Maesmor
This is an amorphous cairn about 12 m in diameter on top of Carn Owen, with small satellites to the NE.
SAM 45; OS SN 78 NW 1. (1988)

Carn Pen Moelfryn
116. cairn   Melindwr   SN 6855 8235
CAS *Melindwr and Trefeirig* (1988), no. 6882/1. (1987)

Carn Pen y Foel Goch
117. ?barrow   Ysgubor-y-   SN 6951 9285
(d.)   coed
NLW Mapbook 37, fol. 9.

Carn Philip Gwyddel
118. cairn (d.)   Llanwenog   SN 4891 4609
This mound was destroyed about 1806 but was originally said to have taken the form of a human body, and need not have been a prehistoric cairn. Although Meyrick's description accords with that of a Neolithic court-cairn, it may even have been a pillow mound. No traces now remain.
Meyrick, *Hist. and Antiq.*, 188; *Handlist*; OS SN 44 NE 3. (1976)

Carn
Rhyrddod   Ysbyty   SN 7905 7041
119. cairn   Ystwyth
OS SN 77 SE 1. (1978)

Carn Saith Wraig
120. cairn (N)   Llanddewi-   SN 7710 5297
                    brefi
121. cairn (S)   SN 7718 5288
A socketed bronze spearhead reputedly came from one of these cairns (see *Metalwork* no. 5 p. 215).

Carn Wen
122. cairn   Troed-yr-aur   SN 3730 4938
This cairn of no more than 10 m in diameter is largely reduced to a grass-covered spread of stone and soil and was noted by John Fenton. The OS Trig point is probably centrally positioned upon the monument.
Fenton, *Arch. Camb.*, 15 (1860), 61; OS SN 34 NE 3.

Carn Wyn
123. barrow   Llandysul   SN 4560 4628
A place-name where there is no trace of the feature in an arable field, although there is an indistinct cropmark about 19 m in diameter on an aerial photograph.
OS SN 44 NE 6. (1975)

Carreg Fihangel
124. cairns   Llanfihangel-
(3d.)   y-Creuddyn
This parish was formerly of greater extent than the present one and it is possible that one or more of these cairns do survive.
Lewis, *Topog. Dict.* (1833), s.v. Llanfihangel-y-Creuddyn.

Carreg Tryr Croes (see also *Standing Stones* no. 79)
125. cairn   Cellan   SN 6082 4623
with cist (d.)
Morris, *Lhuyd's Parochialia* III (1911), 87; Meyrick, *Hist. and Antiq.*, 216–17; Sansbury, *Meg. Mons.* no. 5.
Carreg y Bwci (see *Neolithic burial monuments*; also II ch. 4, Appendix I (d)).

Castell Nadolig
126. ?urn   Penbryn   SN 298 504
burials (d.)
The site was visited during the Cambrians' 1859 meeting. Within the area adjoining the main hillfort had been 'lately found, under a large stone now lying on the spot, three urns containing ashes'.
Cardigan Meeting, *Arch. Camb.*, 14 (1859), 328. OS SN 25 SE 4. (1973)

Castell Rhyfel (nr.) (see Nant Groes Fawr)

Castell Rhyfel
127. cairn   Caron-is-   SN 7273 5987
                    clawdd
A cairn 6 m in diameter with a robbed cist about
1.5 × 1 m wide, situated on the slope to the south
of Castell Rhyfel. It is apparently attached to
another cairn measuring about 10 × 6 m.
OS SN 75 NW 4. (1989)
128. cairns   SN 729 600
(group)
A group of seven clearance cairns spaced
approximately equidistant from one another.
(1989)
129. cairns   SN 728 598
(group)
Six small cairns lie to the E side of the track. This
hillside appears to have been cleared of stone for
agricultural purposes.
D.M.M.; Stenger, *AW*, 23 (1983), 67; Muckle MS.
(1989)

Cefn Cerrig (Fig. 21)
130. kerb   Caron-uwch-   SN 7646 5801
cairn   clawdd
A collection of loose rocks at 442 m above OD
which takes advantage of the steeply dipping
rock exposure. It stands about 2 m high and is
roughly 21 m (NW–SE) × 18 m. Its matrix is
mainly of angular stone. Projecting from the
cairn, and close to its perimeter, is a discontinuous
ring of upright and leaning slabs, protruding but
slightly above the level of the cairn. These slabs
appear largest on the S where a number lie con-
tiguously. A shooting box occupies the centre of
the cairn.
Leighton, *PPS*, 50 (1984), no. 17, 338 fig. 9; OS SN 75 NE
4. (1990)
131. cairn   SN 7672 5833
OS SN 75 NE 2.

Cefn Lletre
132. cist with   Penbryn   SN 2890 5137
urn
Meyrick records the discovery of a cinerary urn in
a destroyed cairn.
133. barrow   SN ?29/30 49
Meyrick, *Hist. and Antiq.*, 178 (1907 reprint, 209).

Cefn y Cnwc
134. cairn (d.)   Caron-is-   SN 775 589
                   clawdd
A much denuded cairn with a central depression
measuring 6.5 m N–S by 5.5 m E–W and 0.25 m
high.
D.K.L. (1981)

Cerrig-Blaen-Clettwr-Fach
135. cairn   Llangynfelyn   SN 7077 9256
OS SN 79 SW 1. (1978)

Cerrig Llwydion prehistoric complex (see Gogerddan).

Cerrig Maes y Carnau
136. cairn   Caron-uwch-   SN 258 463
                   clawdd
A low heap of stones about 18 m in diameter,
much disturbed by a sheep shelter which lies to
the south.

Cil Garn
137. cairn (d.)   Caron-uwch-   SN 7366 6414
                   clawdd
OS SN 76 SW 9. (1978)

Cil y Bryn
138. cist   Caron-uwch-   SN 732 629
(unlocated)   clawdd
S.R.H.; A.J.P.; OS SN 76 SW 12. (1978)

Cnwch Eithiniog prehistoric complex (see also
Standing Stones nos. 28–9).
139. cairn (E)   Llanddewi-   SN 7577 4965
                   brefi
140. cairn (W)   SN 7575 4966
(?)standing   SN 7573 4965
stone (Maen
Bach)
A complex comprising two cairns and possibly a
standing stone. A square monolith (Maen Bach)
of local grit about 1 m high and about 1.6 m in
girth stands on a low cairn about 12 m in
diameter.
OS MS 2-inch 1820 marked 'Carns and Erect Stone';
Sansbury, *Meg. Mons.*, no. 27, 16; OS SN 74 NE 5.

Cnwc Mawr

141. kerb	Llanddewi-	SN 6830 5358
cairn	brefi	

D.K.L. (1980)

142. cairn		SN 685 538

Morgan, *AW*, 27 (1987), 33. (1986)

Coed Craig yr Ogof (Fig. 38.4)

143. kerb	Gwnnws Isaf	SN 7127 7131
cairn with cist		

A badly denuded cairn, described in 1932 as about 7 m in diameter and about 1m high and then comprising fourteen visible kerbstones, although the cairn was sufficiently high to mask other orthostats which may have existed in the S quadrant. The stones protruded only slightly above the surface and two had been uprooted. Sansbury noted that the cairn was constructed of local stone with a considerable amount of white quartz. Within lay a cist, 1.8 m long × 1.4 m wide, consisting of five stones, though one, possibly the lid of the cist, then covered part of the walls and made difficult its true identification. The site is now badly disturbed.

Sansbury, *Meg. Mons.*, no. 3; Leighton, *PPS*, 50 (1984), no. 18, 338, 341, fig. 10; OS SN 77 SW 5. (1990)

Craig Twrch

144–5. cairns	Cellan	SN 660 490
(2)		(approx.)

D.K.L. (1981)

Craig yr Eglwys

146. cairn	Trefeurig	SN 8074 8968

This is probably a boundary marker cairn of no great antiquity.

OS SN 88 NW 3. (1978)

Craig y Foelallt

147. ?barrow	Llanddewi-	SN 67 55
cemetery	brefi	

Craig Ystradmeurig

148. cairn	Gwnnws Isaf	SN 7058 6865

'A cairn 10 m in diameter with maximum height of 1.8 m, situated on a natural outcropping rock.'

SAM; *Handlist*; OS SN 76 NW 10. (1970)

Creigiau Duon

149. barrow	Ceulan-a-	SN 7026 0110
	Maesmor	

Crug

150. cairn	Llanddewi-	SN 6685 5312
	brefi	

OS 65 SE 3. (1978)

Crug Bach

151. barrow	Penbryn	SN 3755 4996

A grass-covered bowl barrow 19 m in diameter and *c.* 2 m high with some superficial disturbance.

OS 1975; SAM; *Handlist*; OS SN 34 NE 2. (1988)

Crug Bychan

152. barrow	Y Ferwig	SN 1785 5111
(largely d.)		

SAM 105; *Handlist*; OS SN 15 SE 1. (1988)

Crug Coe (Sarnau)

153. cairn	Penbryn	SN 3077 5057

Marked on OS 1-inch map; condition not ascertained. According to D. Prys Williams, 'this burial place was first discovered *circa* 1790, by a man of the name of Dafydd Siencyn Siors, while searching for some building stones. Some time after this another urn was found near the same spot by some labourers; and a third discovery was brought about in a curious way by some people while digging after a fox, about the year 1833. They came across a cist of stone, and within the fox with several young ones, and a large urn with some ashes. This urn was . . . destroyed, having been exposed in a hedge near Sarnau and pelted to pieces with stones.'

SAM 63; Williams, *Arch. Camb.*, 60 (1905), 159; *Handlist*; OS SN 35 SW 2. (1976)

Crug Cou

154. barrow	Llannarth	SN 4097 5284

An earthen barrow 31 m in diameter, 1.2 m high; under active cultivation and suffering from plough damage.

C.S.B. (1988)

Crug Cou (finds in a barrow, near)

155. barrow	Llannarth	SN 4102 5289

Undirected digging by a local farmer in two places on a barrow 66 yds to the north-east of Crug Cou produced three, possibly four, pottery vessels.[1] Little appears to be known of the barrow site and enquiry failed to locate it in 1976. The pottery vessels comprise:

(a) (Fig. 25.6). A Pygmy Cup 'of biconical form, of good brown ware, with internally bevelled rim. Decoration consists of a double chevron in the upper part and alternating triangles in the lower, enclosed by horizontal lines and all incised with a row of fine stabbed dots around the angle and just above the base, and on the internal bevel of the rim. There is an incised circle on the base.' It is 6.4 cm in diameter (at angle) and 3.95 cm high.[2]

(b) (Fig. 23.5). A second pottery vessel, not certainly associated with the first. This is of 'coarse ware, with poorly-finished surface of slightly barrel shape, with internally bevelled rim. Undecorated, with a row of small holes in the wall below the lip. (There are 19 holes in the restored vessel and these are presumably largely conjectural.) Also (still accompanied by) the small slab with which the the mouth was covered.' This vessel is 20.9 cm high and 19.5 cm in diameter at the mouth.[3]

(c) The cast of a further urn is thus described: 'Fragmentary overhanging rim cinerary urn (cast) of coarse brown ware. The collar and flange are missing; decoration on the remaining portion consists of incised lattice pattern on the neck. Found . . . with burnt bones.' It is 17.6 cm high and 19.35 cm in diameter.[4]

[1] Grimes, *BBCS*, 8 (1936), 271–2.

[2] Grimes, *Prehist. of Wales* (1951), 217, no. 669; Savory, *Guide Catalogue*, 149, no. 476; NMW Acc. No. 39.563.4.

[3] Grimes, *Prehist. of Wales*, 211, no. 645; Savory, *Guide Catalogue*, 153, no. 462.

[4] Grimes, *Prehist. of Wales*, 211, no. 643; Savory, *Guide Catalogue*, 149, no. 431; I. H. Longworth, *Corpus of Collared Urns* (1984), 318, no. 2047, describes it as 'Unclassified Series [of Collared Urn], North Western Style Form— [unspec.].' The cast of this vessel was not available for study in 1977 and there are no published illustrations of it. For further discussion: see Grimes, *Arch. Camb.*, 92 (1937), 296, no. 2; *Prehist. of Wales*, 217, no. 669. fig. 31.5; Savory, *Arch. Camb.*, 107 (1958), 45, 49, fig. 4, 14; Savory, *Guide Catalogue* (1980), 155, no. 475 (where a grid ref. of 411 529 is given); NMW Acc. No. 37.62. (1976)

Crug Du (Fig. 25.1–3 and Fig. 23.1 [pottery])

| 156. | kerb cairn with cists | Llandysilio-gogo | SN 3807 5039 |

According to J. Davies (Ioan Dafydd) the site was accidentally discovered while stones were being dug out for road-mending by a contractor to the County Council in 1904.[1] A circle of stones about 19 m in diameter, up to 1 m high and about 2 m wide, surrounded an elevated saucer of rough ground, within which were the remains of three stone cists, each of six large flagstones; the one from which pot (a) derived being 12 in. (0.3 m) wide × 14 in. (0.35 m) long. Another cist was about 1.3 m long × 0.3 m wide, and contained ashes and half-burned and calcined bones. A second urn (b) containing ashes and portions of calcined bones was associated with a well-preserved cist and was accompanied by an incense cup (c). A further Pygmy Cup (d) was also encisted, and sherds of Beaker fabric (e) were also picked up casually on the site.

(a) (Fig. 23.1) the cast of an urn in Carmarthen Museum has been described as an 'overhanging rim cinerary urn of devolved, biconical form, with flattened, everted rim and shoulder ridge marking the base of the collar; undecorated H.12.2; diam. (mouth) 12.9 cm'.[2]

(b) Fragments representing an overhanging rim urn[3] about 12 in. (0.3 m) high and about 12 to 15 in. (0.3–0.38 m) in diameter, with incised diagonal lines forming a band 4 in. (0.1 m) wide below the rim which swells out to form a ridge around its body, before tapering towards the base. It was believed to have been about the same size as vessel (a). The fabric is of a uniform colour throughout and is the same thickness as the first vessel.

(c) (Fig. 25.1) A Pygmy Cup with two perforations accompanied (b), the base decorated with seven parallel incised strokes within an incised circle. The tapered rim is decorated internally with double V-shaped incisions. External decoration is in two horizontal panels, divided by three incised horizontal lines both above and below. The panels contain single double zigzag incisions.[4]

(d) (Fig. 25.3) A Pygmy Cup, the base decorated with three concentric incisions; otherwise its form and decoration are similar to vessel (c) except for fewer horizontal incisions separating the decorated panels, whilst the interior of the rim is criss-crossed with incisions.

(e) (Fig. 25.2) Three Beaker sherds also derive from the site. These are comb-decorated and of a sandy buff fabric. Clearly, none is of Barbed Wire Beaker type as suggested by Clarke.[5]

[1] Davies, *Arch. Camb.*, 60 (1905), 62–9.

[2] Grimes, *Prehist. of Wales* (1951), 213, no. 653; I. H. Longworth, *Corpus of Collared Urns* (1984), 318, no. 2056.
[3] Davies, *Arch. Camb.*, 60 (1905), 65, fig. 3B. It is not possible to discover whether or not this urn was ever properly restored (see Anon., *Trans. Carms. Antiq. Soc.*, 28 (1938), ix).
[4] Davies, loc.cit., figs. 4A, 5A.
[5] D. L. Clarke, *Beaker Pottery* (1970), II, 524 (nos. 1847, 1–2).
See also Anwyl, *Arch. Camb.*, 61 (1906), 93–110; Griffiths, *PPS*, 23 (1957), 57; I. H. Longworth, *Corpus of Collared Urns* (1984), 38–9; Savory, *Carms. Antiq.*, 3 (1960), 53–5; *BBCS*, 20 (1963), 325; Thomas, *Arch. Camb.*, 67 (1912), 345–56.
OS SN 35 SE 2. (1981)

Crug Ffa
157. barrow   Cardigan/   SN 202 478
(d.)   Y Ferwig
Fenton, *Arch. Camb.*, 15 (1860), 58; OS SN 24 NW 1. (1975)

Crug Las
158. barrow   Cardigan/   SN 3880 5154
                Y Ferwig
OS 1834; OS SN 35 SE 1. (1973)

Crug Mawr
159. barrow   Betws Ifan   SN 2983 4661
'A tumulus in this parish, called Crug Mawr, was opened in the year 1829, under the direction of the Rev. Thomas Bowen, upon whose estate it is situated; and was found to contain two earthen vases, and two lachrymatories . . . One of the vases, soon after its exposure, crumbled to pieces; the other, together with the lachrymatories, was presented to the Museum at Oxford.'

No record exists of such a presentation to either the Ashmolean Museum, Oxford, or to the British Museum. It can only be assumed that this was hearsay.
Lewis, *Topog. Dict.* (1833), *s.v.* Troed-yr-aur; *Handlist*.

Crug Moel
160. barrow   Llannarth   SN 4569 5200
Handlist; OS SN 45 SE 2. (1972)

Crug y Balog
161. barrows   Troed-yr-aur   SN 3418 4528
Meyrick, *Hist. and Antiq.*, 346; *Handlist*; OS SN 34 NW 1. (1975)

Crug yr Udon *see* Bwlch Mawr.

Cwm yr Olchfa
162. cairns   Caron-is-   SN 7237 6009
(?burial or   clawdd
clearance)
C.S.B.; D.M.M.; D.K.L.; Muckle MS. (1989)

Devil's Bridge (nr.)
163. cairn   Upper Llanfi-   SN 7362 7713
                hangel-y-
                Creuddyn

Dinas
164. ?barrow   Cwmrheidol   SN 7491 8360
(N)
165. ?barrow   SN 7487 8324
(Central)
166. ?barrow   SN 7489 8319
(S)
OS SN 78 SW 22. (1978)

Disgwylfa Fawr
167. kerb   Melindwr   SN 7373 8473
cairn
Lying in an exposed position at 506 m above OD, this cairn is now grass-grown. It is some 20 m in diameter and about 3 m high.[1] It was examined in 1937 by trenching across the site. No first-hand excavation report survives and no proper plans appear to have been drawn up. Within the mound was found 'a large ring of rock slabs set up in an outward facing position. Within this ring lay a dug-out trunk some 8 or 9 feet (2.4–2.7 m) long, of which the greater part at one end has been preserved. Above this lay a second smaller dug-out 3 ft 6 ins (1.08 m) long. The larger trunk is said to have lain at a depth about 5 ft (1.5 m) below the present summit of the barrow and the smaller approximately 1 ft higher.' Within the hollow of the smaller trunk were cremated human bones, a small flint blade (now lost), and a Food Vessel standing on its base. Animal skin, which, it was claimed, had covered these finds, was not preserved, but some reddish animal hair, subsequently determined as fox or stoat, was.[2] The coffins, which then still had bark adhering, were of *Quercus robur*.[3] The larger yielded a C14 date of 1910 ± 70 bc (HAR-2187), the smaller, of 1350 ± 80 bc (HAR-2677).[4]

The Food Vessel (Fig. 27.5) is described as 'of coarse, well-fired ware with a dark brown surface, with single vertical rim and several unperforated lugs spanning a double shoulder-groove. The decoration consists of seventeen broad horizontal furrows (including the shoulder furrows) at regular intervals from the rim to the base, the intervening ridges and the flat rim being decorated with vertical or slanting incisions, or a false-relief pattern executed with the finger nail, and transverse incisions on the raised vertical edges of the lugs.'[5] It is 17 cm high and 20.03 cm in diameter at the shoulder.

[1] Leighton, *PPS*, 50 (1984), no. 19, 342.
[2] Forde, *TCAS*, 13 (1938), 72–3: *BBCS*, 9 (1939), 188–9; Chitty, *BBCS*, 8 (1938), 275–83; V. E. Nash-Williams, *A Hundred Years of Welsh Archaeology* (Cardiff, 1946), 53 (Pl.11a).
[3] Coles *et al.*, *PPS*, 44 (1978), 22 (fig. 12).
[4] Green, *Arch. Camb.*, 136 (1987), 43–50.
[5] Grimes, *Prehist. of Wales*, 205 (no. 617).
SAM 30; OS SN 78 SW 5. (1988)

Dolgamfa (Fig. 38.1)
168. kerb   Cwmrheidol   SN 7457 7916
cairn
Lying at 300 m above OD this is a fine example of a denuded kerb cairn, originally comprising twelve orthostats (of which only eleven are now visible), mostly leaning out from the centre. Three stones are over 1 m high and others stand up to about 0.75 m. Those on the N side are almost overgrown and a smaller amount of the original cairn material is still embanked against them on the interior. The stones, set in an oval, appear to be of local origin and measure 5 m (NW–SE) × 4 m. There is a slight hollow in the centre which may have been the site of a cist.
C.S.B.; C.R.K.; Sansbury, *Meg. Mons.* no. 21; Leighton, *PPS*, 50 (1984), no. 20, 341, fig. 10, 342; OS SN 77 NW 5. (1990)

Y Drosgl (see Carneddau)

(Y) Drum
169. cairn   Caron-is-   SN 7170 5941
                    clawdd
170. cairn   SN 7166 5941
Leighton, *AW*, 17 (1977), 16. (1976)

Dyffryn Castell (see Dolgamfa)
Alleged kerb   Cwmrheidol   SN 77 81
cairn or stone
circle (?d.)

Dyffryn Saith
171. urn   Penbryn   SN 2859 5135
burial (Fig. 27.4)
An urn and cremated bones were found at a depth of 1 m in digging a pipe-trench by the Welsh Water Authority in 1975. A spread of burnt material was also noted nearby. The vessel, which was shattered on removal, is of a type related to the Cordoned Urn, 21 cm high and about 15 cm in diameter with cord-impressed decoration on shoulder, neck and rim.
Dyfed Archaeological Trust Report 1975–6, 20–1; Barnie, *AW*, 15 (1975), 30; OS SN 25 SE 8.

Dyll Faen (Y Garn)
172. ?kerb   Melindwr   SN 7756 8531
cairn
A roughly circular cairn at 660 m above OD with a diameter of about 20 m and about 1.3 m high. It is cut by a drystone wall and has been mutilated by climbers.
W.E.G.; C.S.B.; D.K.L.; D.M.M.; SAM 34; OS SN 78 NE 1. (1989)

Esgair Fraith
173. barrow   Llangynfelyn/   SN 7426 9154
                 Uwchygarreg
This site, marked as 'Tump' on the OS 6-inch sheet (1964), might be an ancient cairn, but as it is sited upon the parish boundary could be a more recent feature, having been connected with nearby mines.
(1990)

Esgair Ffrwd (see Blaen Camddwr)

Esgair Garn
174. cairn   Llanddewi-   SN 6499 5278
with cist   brefi
175. cairn   SN 6507 5288
with cist
Although considered by the OS to be 'modern stone heaps', it is possible that the nuclei to these cairns were among those tackled by the Cardiganshire Antiquarian Society during the first decade of this century.

Sansbury, *Meg. Mons.*, no. 28; Lewis, *TCAS*, 5 (1928), 93; D.K.L.; OS SN 65 SE 9.

Esgair Gerwyn

| cairn cemetery | Caron-uwch-clawdd | SN 8027 5737 |

176. robbed cist about 1.75 m with one missing side slab.
177. grass-covered cairn about 5 m in diameter and about 0.3 m high with a central hollow.
178. grass-covered cairn about 6.5 m in diameter and about 3 m high with a hollow and possible orthostats indicating the site of a former cist.
179. cairn.
SAM 135; Leighton and Metcalfe, *Ceredigion*, 8 (1978), 360–2. (1989)

Esgair Perfedd

| 180. cairn | Caron-uwch-clawdd | SN 7476 5929 |

A low cairn, situated immediately east of a rocky knoll clothed in large boulders. The cairn is about 5 m in diameter and about 0.4 m high, of angular rock fragments. It is now moss and grass-covered. C.S.B.; D.K.L.; D.M.M.; *AW*, 17 (1977), 17; OS SN 75 NW 17. (1989)

Esgair y Garn

| 181. burial or ?clearance cairn (E) | Gwnnws Uchaf | SN 7599 6770 |
| 182. burial or ?clearance cairn (W) | | SN 7581 6769 |

Fan (see Ty'n-y-rhos)

| 183. cairn | Nancwnlle | SN 565 587 |

According to the earliest account of this site, a pottery vessel was 'found in a field near Talsarn'.[1] G. E. Evans offered more positive information: 'It is within my knowledge that there was a little tumulus there which had been excavated some years before, and a very fine little food vessel had been found in it.'[2] Wheeler illustrated the vessel and associated with it a spearhead with which it was supposed to have been found.[3] Edward Anwyl provided no further information.[4] In the absence of conclusive evidence it seems better to regard these finds as unassociated.

The Pygmy Cup (Fig. 25.9) is described by Grimes as 'of good buff ware, biconical, with internal bevel to lip, and two small holes about 1 inch apart on shoulder. Decoration (incised throughout) consists of three parallel lines on bevel, quadruple series of zigzags between horizontal lines on upper part, and traces of what may be a series of hanging triangles around the somewhat poorly-modelled lower part.'[5] Its height is 5.8 cm and diameter 7.2 cm.

[1] Lampeter Meeting, *Arch. Camb.*, 33 (1878), 65; Barnwell, *Arch. Camb.*, 34 (1879), 223.
[2] *Mins. of Evidence* (1912), 16 (para. 420).
[3] R. E. M. Wheeler, *Prehist. and Roman Wales* (Oxford, 1925), fig. 78.2.
[4] Anwyl, *Arch. Camb.*, 61 (1906), 111, 113.
[5] Grimes, *Prehist. of Wales*, 198 (no. 585) (and fig. 31.4); Savory, *Guide Catalogue*, 132. (1988)

Fedw Lwyd (nr.)

| 184. cairn | Caron-uwch-clawdd | SN 764 628 |

D.K.L. (1981)

Ffynnon Drewi (nr.)

| 185. cairn | Lledrod Isaf | SN 6216 6733 |

A peat-covered mound of miscellaneous stone about 8 m in diameter and about 1 m high, either a burial monument or the result of field clearance. It was badly damaged by the removal of hardcore for the repair of a nearby track in Spring 1976. (1989)

Ffynnon Drewi

| 186. cairn (dil.) | Blaenpennal | SN 6190 6741 |

C.S.B.; OS SN 66 NW 9. (1989)

Ffynnon Tysul (approx. area)

| 187. barrows 4(d.) | Llandysul | SN 42 41 |

According to Meyrick, there were originally four 'carneddau' here, from one of which three encisted urns containing ashes were excavated. Meyrick, *Hist. and Antiq.*, 146; (1907), 192; *Arch. Camb.*, 67 (1912), 351.

Fron Ddu

| 188. barrow | Upper Llanfihangel-y-Creuddyn | SN 7022 7698 |

SAM 124; OS SN 77 NW 7. (1988)

Fron Felen Uchaf
189. cairn   Penbryn   SN 3230 5123
OS SN 35 SW 14. (1973)

Fuwch Wen a Llo (see Garn Fawr)

(Y) Garn
190. cairn   Llandysul   SN 4548 4916
NMW Rec., *Handlist*; OS SN 44 NE 1. (1975)

(Y) Garnedd
cairns   Melindwr
In 1965 J. Evans noted the following cairns:
191.   SN 7491 8360
Circular, 7.5 m in diameter and 1 m high,
apparently undisturbed, with a few stones
scattered on the surface.
OS SN 78 SW 26.
192.   SN 7539 8400
Circular, about 8 m in diameter and 0.6 m high.
193.   SN 7535 8404
Stones, embedded in the ground, over 3 m
diameter. No elevation.
194.   SN 7540 8410
A slight change of altitude over a diameter of 6 m.
195.   SN 7533 8413
196.   SN 7529 8390
197.   SN 7518 8400
C.S.B.; D.K.L.; A.J.P.; SAM 41; OS SN 75 NW 12.
During visits in 1971, 1977 and 1978 it was not possible to
confirm the existence of 196 and 197.
J. Evans, *Arch. Camb.*, 126 (1977), 36–7. (1988)

Garn Fawr
198. cairn   Caron-is-   SN 7079 5713
                    clawdd
OS SN 75 NW 1. (1975)

Garn Fawr (Fuwch Wen a Llo) (see *Standing Stones*
no. 9)
199. cairn   Trefeurig   SN 7218 8332

Garn Felen
200. cairn   Caron-is-   SN 7010 5696
                    clawdd and
                    Llanddewi-
                    brefi
OS SN 75 NW 2. (1975)

Garn Gron
201. cairn (W)   Caron-is-   SN 7297 6115
                       clawdd
202. cairn   SN 7397 6106
(middle)
203. cairn (E)   SN 7400 6108

Garn Lwyd
204. cairn   Cwmrheidol   SN 7525 8335
The spread of stones in this area appears to derive
from a natural outcrop.
W.E.G.; Hogg, *Arch. Camb.*, 111 (1977), 24–37; Briggs and
Leighton, *Arch. Camb.*, 111 (1977), 37; OS SN 78 SE 2.
(1979)

Garn Lwyd
205. cairn (d.)   Blaenpennal   SN 6317 6749
OS 1834 (sheet 12); OS SN 66 NW 6. (1974)

Garn Nant y   Upper Llanfi-   SN 7984 7708
Llys   hangel-y-
                     Creuddyn
206. cairn
OS SN 77 NE 3. (1978)

Garn Wen
207. cairn (d.)   Llandysul   SN 3960 4707

Garn Wen
208. cairn (d.)   Penbryn   SN 35 51
                                          (approx.)
N.L.W. Mapbook 39, fols. 14 and 20.

Garn Wen
209. cairn   Trefeurig   SN 6851 8421
CAS *Capel Bangor Trefeirig Report* (1988), no. 6884/2; OS
SN 68 SE 6. (1988)

Garn Wen (Mynydd Bach) (Fig. 36) There are
two cairns sited on the N–S ridge.
210. cairn (N)   Lledrod Isaf   SN 6176 6775
Situated about 340 m above OD the more
northerly cairn may formerly have been 16–20 m
in diameter with a 0.4 m deep hollow almost in the
centre, possibly the remains of a robbed cist, of
which only one stone remains upright on the west.
There is no trace of an outer revetment. Its
destruction is probably largely due to the building
of a platform house on the lee of the hill to the
ENE, and only 35 m from the perimeter. Much
cairn material is also scattered down the slope to

the W, and the cairn is still suffering from human and animal interference.
OS SN 66 NW 2.
211. kerb cairn
This cairn was first described by Daryll Forde in 1939, shortly after its massive cist had yielded a fine Food Vessel.[1] Plans to excavate the cairn at the time did not come to fruition. Since then the site has been shamefully damaged by the displacement and removal of stones, and it is now almost impossible to ascertain its precise original diameter. If the cist was off-centre, however, and the surviving kerb-stones represent the original line of the kerb, then it was about 20 m.[2] The two larger surviving kerb-stones are each over 1 m long. The interior of the cist measures about 1.25 by 1 m, and 0.6 m deep. The side slabs are all at least half a metre in thickness and the base of the eastern slab is wedged with smaller stones. The mound is covered by boulders of up to 1 m in diameter and the cairn is being actively eroded by humans and animals.

The vessel (Fig. 27.1) was a 'Cinerary Urn of "enlarged food-vessel type", of good brown ware, with well marked neck, and short rim with internal hollow bevel. Decoration consists of herring-bone pattern of corded lines on the internal bevel and seven lines of oblique stabbed impressions also forming a herring bone pattern on the rim, neck and shoulder.'[3] Height is 30.8 cm and diameter at mouth 29 cm.

Rim fragments of a similar vessel are deposited both at Tregaron County School and in the Visual Arts Department, UCW Aberystwyth (Fig. 27.2), but the provenance of these sherds is not above suspicion.
(1991)
[1] Forde, *BBCS*, 8 (1936), 271; Bowen, *TCAS* (1936), 14–15.
[2] Leighton, *PPS*, 30 (1984), no. 21, 342, 343 (fig. 11).
[3] Grimes, *Prehist. of Wales*, 210 (no. 641); Savory, *BBCS*, 20 (1963), 317; *Guide Catalogue*, 149.

Garreg Wen (or Pant Camddwr)
212. cairn   Lledrod Isaf   SN 6350 6836
Although described by the OS as a ring cairn, this is an upstanding mound of earth and stone, 18 × 15 m in diameter and about 0.7 m high, lying to the E of the farmhouse of that name.
C.S.B.; SAM 131; OS SN 66 NW 8. (1991)

Gelli (nr.)
213. barrow   Cwmrheidol   SN 7053 8003
A barrow, close to the junction of three walls, about 1.25 m high and apparently undisturbed.
A.H.A.H.; OS SN 78 SW 1. (1972)

Gilfach-wen-isaf (see *Standing Stones*, no. 47)
214. cist   Llandysul   SN 405 407
burial with
standing stone
An account written for *The Cambrian* in April 1805 records the recent discovery on the farm of the Revd John Llwyd of Gilfach, Cardiganshire, of 'a number of human bones mixed with ashes, and also two urns, placed under a prodigious large stone, which measured about 16 ft (4.9 m) in length, 4 ft (1.2 m) in breadth and 8 ft (2.5 m) in height. This mass of rock took the workmen near a fortnight to remove by powder and other means. It was encircled round the edge with small stones, which were placed to receive the weight of the large one and to keep it from pressing upon the centre and which covered a space of near six feet (1.8 m) square. It evidently was not the burial place of one person, but probably of a whole family. The rudeness of this structure carried with it the appearance of very remote times.'[1] Although the account is anonymous, it seems to have been from the pen of Richard Fenton. In his diary for Saturday 6 September 1806, he wrote '. . . to Gilfach Wen the seat of the Revd Mr Lloyd, a very gentlemanly, well informed man—he showed us fragments of two Urns with Charcoal and Bones he dug from under an immense Clegyr stone which induced us to think that an adit must have been made under this immense stone to introduce the urns which were deposited in a circular cell lined with coarse stones just under the great stone. The stone was blasted for the purpose of building and in the process the urns were discovered. We rode up to see the place.'[2]

In the back of the same notebook are crude sketches of urn fragments which probably came from the site (Fig. 40). The upper drawing is of a vessel upon a base about 4.5 in. (13 cm) in diameter with whip-cord decoration around the exterior of a wide, collared-type rim, 1.5 in. (3.8 cm) high, everted above a channel about 0.5 in. wide. The lower of the sketches is certainly in the Collared tradition with a rim 2 in. high and with a basal diameter of 3.75 in. (about 9.5 cm).[3]

[1] *The Cambrian* 1805, quoted by G. E. Evans, *Trans. Carms. Antiq. Soc.*, 20 (1926–7), 70.
[2] Cardiff Public Library MS 2.65, fols 17–18.
[3] Cardiff Public Library MS 2.65, fol. 136. The writer is indebted to Miss P. Ward for drawing this to his attention.

Gilvin Park (W of)
215. cairn   Cellan   SN 6298 4896
(mutil.)
A mutilated cairn 11 m in diameter and 0.4 m high with no trace of structures.
NMW Record; OS SN 64 NW 16. (1975)

Gistfaen Farm
216. ?cist (d.)   Ysbyty   SN 7435 7155
                    Ystwyth
Sansbury, *Meg. Mons.*, no. 81.

Gloucester Hall (see Penyberth)
217. cairn (d.)   Trefeurig   SN 638 839

Gogerddan (also known as Cerrig Llwydion) (Fig. 42)
barrows and   Tirymynach   SN 6265 8351
alleged
standing
stones
218. barrow (d.)
219. barrow (d.)
220. barrow (mutil.)
Murphy, *AW*, 26 (1986), 29–31; Murphy, *Arch. J.* (forthcoming).

Graig Goch
cairns   Trefeurig
221. cairn   SN 7680 8776
222. cairn   SN 7680 8772
223. cairn   SN 7678 8770
224. cairn   SN 7681 8768
225. cairn   SN 7679 8765
Briggs, *AW*, 24 (1984), 33. (1984)

Graig Wen
226. ring   Caron-uwch-   SN 7904 6651
cairn   clawdd
D.K.L. (1981)

Graig Wen
227. cairn   Llanddewi-   SN 6848 5143
                    brefi
OS SN 65 SE 8. (1978)

Graig Wen (recent features)
228. cairns   Ysbyty   SN 813 754
                    Ystwyth
Three or more cairns of white quartz, each about 2–3 m in diameter, used as markers on the packhorse road up Copa Hill. Possibly peat-drying platforms.
(1989)

Groes Fechan (Y Garn)
229. cairn   Caron-is-   SN 7322 6069
                    clawdd
OS SN 76 SW 2. (1978)

Gurnos Mountain (see Trum Llwyd)
barrow and   Llangynllo
cairns
230. barrow   SN 3562 4588
(W)
A ploughed-down bowl barrow 18.5 m in diameter and 0.7 m high with a 0.2 m deep central depression.
231. cairn (E)   SN 3568 4589
A ploughed-down and mutilated turf-covered stony mound 17 m in diameter and up to 0.7 m high.
232. cairn   SN 3562 4586
(middle)
A slightly damaged mound 15.5 m in diameter and 0.6 m high, but a 0.3 m deep ditch visible on the NW may be a later feature.
OS 1835; OS 6-inch 1891; E. Davies, *Hanes Plwyf Llangynllo* (1905), 197–9; *Handlist*; OS SN 34 NE 7. (1975)

Gwarfelin (Fig. 26)
233. barrow   Llanilar   SN 6248 7518
(d.) and pit
cemetery
During building operations in the summer of 1980 an urn fell from the side of a service trench dug on a building site. In November a similar discovery was reported to J. L. Davies at UCW Aberystwyth. It was at a depth of about half a metre from the surface, inverted, and fragmented whilst being removed. The vessel is apparently of Cordoned

Urn or Enlarged Food Vessel type, characterized by massive thumb-impressions along the exterior of the rim. Its rim was partly protected by a stone. Some slight traces of a covering deposit were traced, while the clear outlines of a pit were discerned around the vessel itself. The pot contained a well-compacted deposit of burnt bones and soil, and traces of green copper carbonate indicated the former presence of a small metal artefact deposited in the vessel, possibly an awl or a razor.

Benson *et al.*, *Ceredigion*, 9 (1982), 281–92; report on further excavations in preparation.

Gwarffynnon
234. cairn (d.)   Cellan   SN 6180 4625
NMW Record; OS SN 64 NW 15.

Hafod Ithel (see Llyn Eiddwen)

Hen Hafod (see Lle'r Neuaddau)

Hirnant (N of)
235. kerb   Melindwr   SN 7532 8393
cairn (Fig. 19.2)
This fine example of a kerb cairn lies about 312 m above OD and is situated some 250 m due N of Hirnant farmhouse on Bryn Llwyd. The site was first recorded by W. J. Hemp in 1917 when the orthostats were noted. When Sansbury visited it in 1932 the cairn mass had been practically reduced to ground level.[1] Its condition was little different when examined by Griffiths in 1953.[2] The kerb now comprises 16 stones, encompassing a grass-covered mound of roughly 6 m diameter. The central area has clearly been disturbed in two places leaving a depression about 1 m long and 0.25 m deep to the N alongside a kerbstone; there is also a slight hollow to the W of the mound's centre. Probing failed to determine any new orthostat positions. The site has been listed as a ring cairn by Lynch[3] and as a possible stone circle by Burl.[4]
236. cairn   SN 7527 8382
with cist
Although described by Evans as 'an open cist',[5] 2 m long × 0.6 m wide and 0.6 m deep, aligned NNW—SSE, there is in fact a detectable spread of rocky material, now grass-covered, surrounding this site. Only two of the cist stones survive, along

with the covering stone which is thrown to one side.

[1] Hemp, MSS notes, RCAM (Wales); Sansbury, *Meg. Mons.*, no. 61; Leighton, *PPS*, 50 (1984), no. 23, 342, 344 (fig. 125).
[2] Griffiths, MSS notes, RCAM (Wales).
[3] Lynch, *Scottish Archaeol. Forum*, 4 (1972), 65 (fig. 2).
[4] A. Burl, *The Stone Circles of the British Isles* (London, 1976), 370.
[5] Evans, *Arch. Camb.*, 126 (1977), 36 (site f).
SAM 14; OS SN 98 SE 3. (1990)

Lan Ddu-fawr
237. cairn   Ysbyty   SN 7876 6997
(mutil.)   Ystwyth
OS SN 76 NE 4. (1978)

Llain Villa
238. cairn (d.)   Penbryn   SN 3281 5050
NLW Mapbook 39, fol. 4.

Llain Wen prehistoric and medieval landscape (Fig. 14).
Overlooking the River Cletwr, the south-facing hillside of Llain Wen lies 300–40 m above OD. It is clothed in vestiges of early settlement. Some of this is clearly post-medieval though some may even be medieval, and takes the form of *hafodau* or miners' cottages, the upstanding walls of a handful of which are well preserved on the west of the settlement area. Scattered among these later features, however, are about 40 small cairns, together with several small lynchets or banks, mainly concentrated in an area about 300 m long (NNE–SSW) by about 100 m wide. Although these agricultural clearance features might also be relatively recent in origin, the presence of cairns, clearly of Bronze Age date, suggests a contemporary date for some of them.
239. cairn   Llangynfelyn   SN 6878 9217
A low cairn of stones just over 10 m in diameter and up to 1 m high, roughly circular and of boulders up to 1m in diameter. It displays no structural features but may have been robbed of any orthostats. Noted on the Gogerddan Estate Map of Cae'r Arglwyddes (NLW no. 37.9) as 'Pile of stones'.[1]
240–1. kerb   SN 6903 9220
cairns (2) (Fig. 20.2)
Two small cairns up to 5 m in diameter and less than 0.5 m high, standing close to the fence,

aligned roughly E–W and about 5 m apart. Both are revetted with boulders of white quartz, presenting distinct kerbing. The more easterly has a collapsed cist of local flagstone about 2.5 m long, 0.5 m wide and perhaps 0.3 m deep. The quartz boulders appear to derive from a vein, one of several which traverse the nearby hillslope. Marked on the Gogerddan Estate Map (NLW no. 37.9) as simply 'stones' and lying along the line of the old farm boundary.[2]

242. cairn   SN 6928 9215
with cist
OS SN 69 SE 15. (1988)

243. cairns   SN 6505 9241
(1988)

244. clearance   SN 698 923
cairns
(1988)

[1] Briggs, *Ceredigion*, 9 (1982), 270, pl. 17.
[2] Leighton, *PPS*, 50 (1984), no. 24, 342, 344, fig. 12.

Llandysul (see Ffynnon Tysul)

Llangorwen Church

245. cemetery   Llangorwen   SN 603 838
(?)

'In cutting the foundation for the church, an urn containing bones pronounced by a medical gentleman as definitely those of a human being, was dug up in the south side between the porch and the eastern gable of the nave; and since then, in digging a grave about fifteen yards from the church, and between it and the river, more were found. In both cases the earth was blackened and appeared to have been acted on by fire. The presumption is that this spot was very anciently a place of sepulchre.'

Morgan, *Aberystwyth Guide* (1869), 100.

Llech Cynon (see Carreg y Bwci)

Llech yr Ast (see *Neolithic Burial Monuments*, no. 1)
This may have been a kerb cairn.

Llechwedd Llwyd

246. cairn   Ceulan-a-   SN 7107 9141
              Maesmor
OS SN 79 SW 3. (1978)

Lle'r Neuaddau (S of) (also known as Hen Hafod) (Fig. 19.3)

247. kerb   Melindwr   SN 7554 8465
cairn

Standing on a spur between the Rheidol and Peithnant, at 320 m above OD, this site now comprises 18 uprights (though there were 19 in 1932).[1] A hollow exists on the E side where the missing orthostat was uprooted. Several slabs are a good metre in length; a few lean from their original positions, and one has fallen on the W. In the SW sector there is a large hollow about 1.75 × 1 m and 0.35 m deep, at the E end of which is an orthostat about 0.6 m long, presumably all that remains of a cist. According to Griffiths this pit was lined with stones in 1953, though it now appears to have been excavated.[2]

[1] Sansbury, *Meg. Mons.*, no. 62.
[2] MSS notes in RCAHM (Wales) files; Leighton, *PPS*, 50 (1984), no. 25, 345, fig. 12.
C.S.B.; D.K.L.; D.M.M.; OS SN 78 SE 5. (1990)

Llethr Brith

248. cairn   Gwnnws   SN 7714 6897
              Uchaf
C.S.B.; D.K.L.; D.M.M.; OS SN 76 NE 8. (1978)

Llethr Llwyd

249. cairns   Llanddewi-   SN 736 530
               brefi
D.K.L.; Muckle MS; OS SN 75 NW 15. (1989)

Lletty Lwydin

250. cairn or   Llangynfelin   SN 6683 9297
burial ground
(possibly d.)
(1988)

Lloft Lloyd

251. cairn   Gwnnws   SN 7798 6965
              Uchaf
Stenger, *AW*, 23 (1983), 6; OS SN 76 NE 3.

Llwyn Crwyn (see also Crug Cou)

252. barrow   Llannarth   SN 4127 5311

A barrow about 14 m in diameter and 0.5 m high, from which it is possible the pottery reported from a site about 500 yds NE of Crug Cou may have derived.
OS SN 45 SW 4.

Llyn Eiddwen, Hafod Ithel (Fig. 15)
253. cairnfield   Llangwyryfon   (centred on)
or cemetery   SN 6100 6750
Lying on ground falling to the SSW along a steep-sided ridge at a height of about 350 m above OD is a series of 27 small cairns. A number are disturbed, the cairn mass being scattered around. Most are 3–5 m high. The matrix of the cairns comprises local stones rarely more than about 0.25 m in diameter. Larger slabs promiscuously disposed in some of the larger mounds could formerly have belonged to destroyed cists and to revetments. The site was first noted by E. Whatmore.
E.W.; A.H.A.H.; C.H.H.; *AW*, 14 (1974), 9–10; SAM 132; OS SN 66 NW 7. (1991)

Llyn Moel y Llyn
254. cairn   Ysgubor-y-   SN 7312 9463
                 coed
(1990)

Maen Prenvol (see Carreg y Bwci)

Maen Mynach
255. cairn (d.)   Cilcennin   SN 5387 5967
Handlist; OS SN 55 NW 7. (1976)

Maesnant
256. cairn   Trefeurig   SN 7722 8839
257. cairn x   SN 7690 8769
Briggs, *AW*, 24 (1984), 32.

Maes yr Haf
258. cairn   Llangynllo   SN 3795 4609
A cairn about 10 m in diameter, comprising stones 'none larger than two men could carry',[1] was completely destroyed in turning the open moor to cultivation in 1923, at which time three vessels were noted, possibly from beneath a layer of quartz. No other features appear to have been recorded and the field from which the stones were 'cleared' is now completely devoid of traces of this cairn which had earlier been noted by Evan Davies.[2] The pottery is now in the National Museum of Wales (Acc. No. 39. 563, 1–3) and is described as follows:

(a) Fragmentary Overhanging Rim Cinerary Urn (Fig. 23.4) of tripartite form with smooth buff surface and a deep internal bevel to the rim. The decoration is incised, being of trellis pattern on the inside of the rim and on the concave neck, and a horizontal herring-bone pattern on the outside of the deep collar. Its height (as restored) is 38 cm and diameter (mouth) 18.3 cm. It was found full of ash and cremated bone.

(b) Undecorated Overhanging Rim Cinerary Urn (Fig. 23.2) of poor ware and of devolved, bipartite form, with plain rim and body forming a continuous curve below the collar. Its height is 26 cm and diameter (mouth) 25.5 cm. It was found full of 'black greasy matter'.

(c) Pygmy Cup (Fig. 23.3) of a fine sandy ware with well-smoothed warm buff surface. The form is biconical with a vertical upper portion and is decorated with incised lines, forming a trellis pattern on the internally bevelled surface of the rim; it has alternating panels of horizontal herring-bone and trellis, below which are three grooves on the upper portion, and chevron patterns below the carination. The carination is decorated with three horizontal grooves and two circular perforations 2.3 cm apart. Its height is 5.2 cm and diameter (mouth) 7.2 cm.

Although Evans suggested that vessel (a) was primary, the other two second or even tertiary, no evidence of stratigraphic relationship is available from any of the early accounts.
259. cairn (d.)   SN 3788 4610
A further cairn formerly stood on the other side of the road but this also is no longer traceable. The nearby mound about 5 m in diameter and 0.5 m high, recorded by the OS, is probably modern.
[1] Evans, *Trans. Carms. Antiq. Soc.*, 17 (1923–4), 58–9.
[2] E. Davies, *Hanes Plwyf Llangynllo* (1905), 183.
Further details of the discovery and site appear in the *Western Mail* 29 March 1924; *Welsh Gazette* 3 April 1924; *Welshman* 22 May 1924.
   The finds are described in great detail by Savory, *Arch. Camb.*, 96 (1941), 31–48; *BBCS*, 17 (1957), 196–233; D. Moore (ed.), *Irish Sea Province* (Cardiff, 1970), 38–49; T. G. Jones, *Trans. Carms. Antiq. Soc.*, 1 (1941), 64–5; Grimes, *Prehist. of Wales*, 213 (no. 655).
OS SN 34 NE8. (1975)

Manian Fawr (N of)
260. barrow   Cardigan   SN 1519 4796
(Not located in 1974)

Meineu Hirion near 'Neuodh'
261. cairn   Llangoedmor   SN 258 463
with cists (d.)
Camden, *Britannia* (1722), I, col. 733.

Moelau

262. kerb   Caron-is-   SN 7396 5955
cairn with cist   clawdd

This site is situated to the NE of the 'hafod' site
marked on the 1963 6-inch OS Map and 200 m
NNW of an unmarked settlement complex at the
junction of two streams. It is on the E of a saddle
marked Moelau and about 150 m W of Nant y
Moelau. The site comprises a denuded cairn,
formerly revetted by a kerb about 10 m in
diameter of which about half remains, mostly
leaning outwards, and part of one cist, with the
strong possibility that others formerly existed or
still do so beneath the mound. Ten certain orthostats remain of the original kerb, almost all of
which lie on the W side. A possible further outlier
is to the SE. There is a long, low trough, presumably formed by quarrying, to the NE, about 5 m
long and 2.5 m wide. Within it, at the E end is a
large flagstone 1.75 m by 2 m by at least 0.15 m
thick. This may derive either from the cist or from
the kerb. Two sides of the cist remain, the longer
being a large slab cleaved in two. A further
upright stone some 2 m NW may be part of a
further cist structure.

C.S.B.; D.K.L.; D.M.M.; SAM; Leighton, *PPS*, 50
(1984), no. 28, 345, fig. 13, 346; OS SN 75 NW 19. (1990)

Moelfryn

263. cairn   Llanfair   SN 659 496
                    Clydogau

SAM 115; OS SN 64 NE 3. (1988)

Moel y Garn

264. burial or   Ceulan-a-   SN 6991 9105
clearance   Maesmor
cairn

OS SN 69 SE 17. (1988)

Moel y Llyn (see also *Stone Circles*, no. 6).

265. cairn (N)   Ceulan-a-   SN 7124 9283
                    Maesmor

266. cairn (S)   SN 7126 9168
stone circle   SN 6994 9106

This site, first noted as 'a carnedd' by Meyrick,[1]
was described in 1846 as 'consisting of 26 upright
stones forming a circle of 228 ft (69.5 m) in circumference, situated about Nant y Nod'.[2] The site
was rediscovered by Dr P. Manning in 1980.[3]

[1] Meyrick, *Hist. and Antiq.*, lxxiv.

[2] Aberystwyth Meeting, *Arch. Camb.*, 1 (1846), 357; Anon.,
Arch. Camb., 28 (1873), 292–3 (n.25); T. O. Morgan,
Aberystwyth Guide (1851), 141.

[3] Manning, *Country Quest* (1985), 59–60; Briggs, *J. Landscape History*, 8 (1986), 8.

Moel y Mor

267. barrow   Llandysul   SN 4129 4654
(d.)

268. barrow (d.)

Two circular cropmarks about 10 m in diameter
with a strong resemblance to barrows. These
could not be identified on the ground by the OS.
OS SN 44 NW 9. (1976)

Mynydd Bach (see Garn Wen, Lledrod Isaf)

Nant   Cwmrheidol   SN 737
269. ?cairn
817 OS SN 78 SW 14. (1978)

Nant Bry Isaf (Fig. 19.4)

270. kerb   Gwnnws Isaf   SN 7003 7044
cairn

Sansbury, *Meg. Mons.*, no. 33; Leighton, *PPS*, 50 (1984),
no. 29, 345, fig. 14, 347; OS SN 77 SW 6. (1990)

Nant Geifaes

271. ?ring   Melindwr   SN 7120 8216
cairn

OS SN 78 SW 15. (1979)

Nant Groes Fawr (see also Castell Rhyfel)

272. cairn   Caron-is-   SN 7272 5986
with cist   clawdd

273. cairnfield   SN 727 598

There are six small cairns along the E side of the
track. To the E lie seven smaller, approximately
equidistantly spaced, clearance cairns with others
to the NE and SW. The whole hillside appears to
have been cleared of stone, probably for agricultural purposes.

D.M.M. (1990)

Nant Llechwedd Mawr

274. cairn   Trefeurig   SN 7694 8843

Briggs, *AW*, 24 (1984), 31.

Nant Maesnant Fach (Fig. 37.2)

275. cairn   Melindwr   SN 7632 8687

An earthfast, flat-topped mound measuring

11.5 × 12.5 m and about 2 m high on the plateau above the reservoir. The cairn has been little disturbed, though slightly eroded by sheep. Two slabs, possibly orthostatic, are visible to the E and on the SW a further probable kerbstone is discernible.

A.H.A.H.; Crew, *AW*, 16 (1976), 16, 21; Leighton, *PPS*, 50 (1984), no. 30, 345, 348, fig. 15; SAM 44. (1984)

Nant y   Melindwr   SN 7591 8536
Fedwen
276. cairn
The present form of this site does not inspire great confidence in its antiquity. As surveyed, a rough spread of stones 10 m NE–SW lies across a craggy exposure in which there are two marked hollows, one of which lies adjacent to the outcrop in such a way as to suggest that it might have been suitable as a natural cist. At least half a dozen of the slabs or boulders at this site could have been orthostatic, but it would be best to use the term 'earthfast' when describing them, since they display only the vaguest resemblance to a kerb.
C.S.B.; D.K.L.; D.M.M.; SAM 43. (1990)

Nant-y-moch (E of)
277. cairn   Melindwr   SN 7655 8708
(1984)

Nant y Moelau
278. cist   Caron-is-   SN 7407 5959
                   clawdd
A little over 100 m to the ENE of the cairn on Moelau (see no. 262) is a vestigial cist of which one stone remains on the stream side and a further orthostat, about 0.4 m high and similarly broad, faces downstream. Little remains of the cairn material which attains a maximum height of 0.5 m and a large slab, possibly the capstone or another sidestone, lies 7 m to the S.
C.S.B.; D.K.L.; D.M.M.; *AW*, 17 (1977), 17; OS SN 75 NW 8. (1990)

Neuadd Fawr (possibly nr.)
279. burials   Llanwnnen   Site not
                                    located
In 1931 D. Ernest Davies donated two Pygmy Cups to the National Museum of Wales. These may have been discovered together, or might equally be stray finds, each from a burial (or burials) in the vicinity of Neuadd Fawr.[1]

Grimes describes them as follows:
(No. 666) 'A plain Pygmy cup of coarse, gritty brick-red fabric comparatively thick with internally bevelled rim and vertical upper wall. Quite plain.'[2] Its height is 6.15 cm and diameter 7.15 cm. (National Museum of Wales Acc. No. 31. 470.1). (Fig. 25.8)
(No. 667) 'Pygmy cup, of good thin buff ware with short sub-cylindrical neck and a globular body with a slightly rounded base. Pair of small holes with panels of five or more vertical lines below; on outside of neck, at base: four wide grooves; on body: two zones separated by three grooves and containing triangles with filling of oblique lines; on base (demarcated from body by six grooves): cruciform pattern of incised lines which do not actually meet at centre.'[3] (Fig. 25.12)
[1] Grimes, *Arch. Camb.*, 87 (1932), 410 (fig. 2).
[2] Grimes, *Prehist. of Wales*, 217, no. 666 (fig. 31.2); Savory, *Guide Catalogue*, 154, no. 470 (fig. 71).
[3] Grimes, *Prehist. of Wales*, 217 no. 667 (fig. 31.3); Savory, *Guide Catalogue*, 154–5, no. 471 (fig. 71).

North Fechan
280. cairn (d.)   Penbryn   SN 3234 5105
Handlist; OS SN 35 SW 7. (1973)

Noyadd Trefawr (see also Meini Kyvrivol, *Stone Circles*, no. 5, and *Neolithic Burial Monuments*, no. 8)
281. ?kerb   Llandygwydd   SN 258 463
cairn
This was described in 1722 as follows: '. . . some remaining pillars of such a circular stone monument (though much larger) than as that described in Carmarthenshire by the name of Meini Gwyr'. The site has not been traced.
Camden, *Britannia* (1722), I, col. 733.

Pantglas (Fig. 25.7)
282. burial   Tregaron   SN 695 581
A Pygmy Cup of biconical form with whip-cord decoration in a heavily gritted, light buff material. Two small perforations 0.25 cm in diameter and 2 cm apart occur about halfway down. Horizontal whip-cord lines encircle the rim (one line), the belly (three lines) and the base (two lines) which is omphaloid. Two zones of vertical cording are separated by the belly. The rim decoration may also have been corded but is so water-worn as to

be indistinguishable. Its height is 4.1 cm and its diameter (mouth) 6.8 cm and (belly) 7.7 cm, the base 5 cm. It is now in the British Museum (BM 1846, 3.14.1) simply labelled 'Pantglas' and the Museum Register offers no further clues as to its origins.

J. Abercromby, *Bronze Age Pottery of Great Britain and Ireland* (Oxford, 1912), II, pl. lxxxi, 265; Wheeler, *Prehist. and Roman Wales*, fig. 79.1; Savory, *BBCS*, 17 (1957), 114 (D1).

Pant y Ffin

| 283. cairn with cist | Llanfair Clydogau | SN 6420 4901 |

Probably not a prehistoric feature.

C.S.B.; NAS (1986)

Pen Banc   Cellan

| 284. cairn (mutil.) | | SN 6272 4991 |

A mound of large boulders, reduced through recent field clearance, with a cist measuring 0.8 × 0.4 m exposed at its N end.

| 285. cairn with cist (mutil.) | | SN 6276 4994 |

A further much reduced site now measuring 15 × 18 m, discovered by Mr D. Bark in 1975.

OS SN 64 NW 17. (1975)

Pen Caeau (E of)

| 286. cairn | Llanddewi- brefi | SN 6498 5280 |

D.K.L. (1981)

Pen Craig y Pistyll

| 287. cairn | | SN 7158 8650 |

D. K. L. (1981)

Penlan-poeth

| 288. ?barrow | Llannarth | SN 4726 5241 |

D.M.M. (1977)

Pen Lluest y Carn

| 289. cairn | Cwmrheidol | SN 8012 8657 |

SAM 28. (1988)

Penllwyn Chapel (Fig. 22)

| 290. burial | Melindwr | SN 6531 8035 |

A cist was discovered by a grave-digger in March 1926. It was covered by an unhewn slab measuring 2 ft (0.6 m) × 1 ft (0.3 m), beneath which stood a fine Encrusted Urn, mouth uppermost, filled with burnt bone. There was no trace of a barrow.[1]

The vessel is of well-fired clay, the fabric smooth and buff-coloured with inclusions of large mineral fragments including some slate and quartz. It has been well restored, though it is now impossible to ascertain the true shape, which appears to have been globular. Decoration is by the appliqué method and was effected using both comb and fingernail impressions. The decorative scheme is described as follows by Grimes:

'On the bevels of rim alternating notched triangles (in comb); on the body four zones divided by raised mouldings, the uppermost containing applied "spectacle-ornament" and bosses enriched with notched lines, with a row of triangular impressions at top and bottom; the third a simple plain zigzag, with plain bosses in the lower interspaces; the fourth undecorated'.[2] Its height is 34.6 cm and diameter (mouth) 34.8 cm.

[1] C. Fox, *Ant. J.*, 7 (1927), 115–27; Fox, *TCAS*, 5 (1927), 34–6; *Arch. Camb.*, 88 (1933), 165; Fox, *Life and Death in the Bronze Age* (London, 1959), 36–7; Bowen, *TCAS*, 11 (1936), fig. 111.

[2] Grimes, *Prehist. of Wales*, 212 (no. 647); Savory, 'The later prehistoric migrations across the Irish Sea', *Irish Sea Province*, ed. D. Moore (1970), Pl. Va; *Guide Catalogue*, 81, 82, 144 (fig. p. 208).

NMW Acc. No. 26.252; OS SN 68 SE 13.

Pen Plynlimon Fawr

291. cairn (N)	Cwmrheidol	SN 7904 8701
292. cairn (middle)		SN 7896 8694
293. cairn (S)		SN 7894 8686

Handlist; OS SN 78 NE 8, 9. (1988)

Pen Plynlimon Arwystli

| 294. cairn | Trefeurig | SN 8150 8775 |

On the edge of a 1 m high rock outcrop surrounded by a well-defined bank of small stones. Orthostats may possibly be discerned, and discoloration suggests that it may be a ring cairn.

Crew, *AW*, 16 (1976), 16.

295. cairn		SN 8151 8776
296. cairn		SN 8152 8778
297. cairn		SN 8154 8782

SAM 35. (1988)

Penrhiwlas (S of) (see Gelli (nr.))

Pen Rhiw Llwydog
298. cairn   Llanddewi-   SN 7397 5264
                  brefi
OS SN 75 SW 1.

Penyberth (see also Gloucester Hall and Pyllau
Isaf)
299. multiple   Trefeurig   SN 638 839
burial
The original account is of a 'carnedd' or large
heap of stones, occupying the centre of a level field
on this farm. According to T. O. Morgan, 'the
stony space was of circular form, sixteen yards in
diameter'. Many stones were removed for
building purposes. Beneath the heap was 'pitched
paving leading towards the centre of the heap',
and at the end of these 'a flag-stone was found,
which sounded hollow under the crowbar, on
carefully removing which an earthen urn was
discovered in an inverted position': evidently a
cist. The vessel contained 'human bones and the
pin of a brooch of metal-like pinchbeck'.[1] According to Stanley and Way this pin was 2.75 in.
(7 cm) long.[2] Black ashes and cremated bones
were also found. The urn had a figured design in
diagonal chequering. Some confusion has arisen
over the identification of this vessel with that from
Pyllau Isaf. Further confusion exists in that
Stanley and Way equate Penyberth with
Gloucester Hall (SN 638 840).[3] It is worth noting
that this site had previously produced a similar
urn.[4] Although the finds from these sites have been
confused, it seems likely that those from Penyberth
are now lost.
[1] Morgan, *Arch. Camb.*, 6 (1851), 164–5.
[2] Stanley and Way, *Arch. Camb.*, 23 (1868), 217–19;
Anwyl, *Arch. Camb.* (1906), 83–102; Sansbury, *Meg.
Mons.*, 80.
[3] Stanley and Way, *Arch. Camb.* 23 (1868), 249–51.
4. Morgan, loc.cit., 164, n.1.
OS SN 68 SW 7.

Pen-y-bwlch
300. cairn (E)   Caron-uwch-   SN 7803 6373
                   clawdd
301. cairn (W)   SN 7750 6379
A.H.A.H.; *Handlist.* (1972)

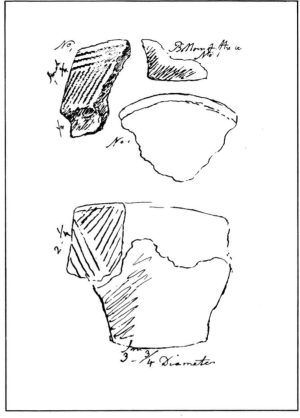

Fig. 40: Early Bronze Age pottery: Gilfach-wen-
isaf (from the MS diary of Richard Fenton).

Pen-y-corn
302. cairn (N)   Llanddewi-   SN 6948 5152
                   brefi
303. cairn (S)   SN 6934 5135

Pen y Daren
304. cairn   Trefeurig   SN 6790 8295
CAS *Melindwr and Trefeirig* (1988), no. 6783/6.

Pen y Garn (see Garn Nant y Llys)

Pen y Garn, Bow Street
305. barrow   Tirymynach   SN 6233 8046
AP, RCAHM 1984.

Pen-y-glogau
306. barrow   Trefilan   SN 5545 5931
with burials
(mutil.)

This substantial circular cairn about 20 m in diameter, apparently almost without structure, was removed for road metalling (some 160 cart-loads). An investigation by informed amateurs revealed a circular cist-grave 1 ft 4 in. (0.4 m) deep, protected by a small slab and lined with stones. A further grave showed cruder signs of walling. After trenching across and around the site, a total of 16 graves were uncovered. Most appear to have been little more than circular holes in the ground, some containing burnt stone and bone. Only two produced grave-goods; in one was a Pygmy Cup, in the other an urn in the Collared and Cordoned tradition, which contained a flint scraper. Three of the graves contained identifiable calcined bones. The presumed primary burial was 3 ft (0.9 m) × 1 ft 6 in. (0.32 m) and contained bones and charcoal.[1] It is possible that some of the holes believed to have been for burial were post holes or pits of a settlement site in the old ground surface.

Vessels in the National Museum are described as:

(a) 'Cast of overhanging rim urn of grey-buff ware. Decoration bands of triangles with fillings of alternating oblique lines; on neck: oblique lines. Crudely modelled and decoration poorly arranged.'[2] Its height is 17.35 cm and it is described by Longworth as a 'Collared Urn, secondary series, form 1A'.[3]

(b) (Fig. 25.11). 'Cast of pigmy cup, of grey-buff ware, with slight internal bevel to rim, and vertical slightly concave upper wall containing pairs of holes just above shoulder. Decoration: incised herring-bone pattern on bevel and upper wall.' Its height is 5.4 cm and diameter at the mouth 7.4 cm.

The cast of the urn could not be located in 1977.

[1] Jones and Davies, *TCAS*, 7 (1930), 118–24; Bowen, *TCAS*, 11 (1936), 15 (fig. IV).
[2] Grimes, *Prehist. of Wales*, 209 (nos. 636–7); Savory, *BBCS*, 18 (1958), 111 (A12) (Pygmy Cup); *Guide Catalogue*, 148, figs. 69 and 71.
[3] I. H. Longworth, *Corpus of Collared Urns* (1984), 322. OS SN 55 NE 4.

Pen y Graig Ddu (see Nant Geifaes)

Pen yr Heol (N of)
307. barrow   Llannarth   SN 4431 5346
(d.)
AP RAF 100G/UK 1470/3267–8; 4272–3.

Plas Gogerddan (see Gogerddan)

Plynlimon Fawr
308. cairn   Trefeurig and   SN 7940 8702
                 Cwmrheidol
Handlist. (1970)

Pontrhydfendigaid (nr.)
309. urn   Gwnnws   SN 73 63
probably from   Uchaf
burial
'Fragment of urn found near Pontrhydfendigaid'. Exhibited by Dr Rowland at the Lampeter meeting of the Cambrian Archaeological Association in 1878.
No further references are known.
Lampeter Meeting (Local Museum), *Arch. Camb.*, 34 (1879), 65–8.

Pont Trecefel (nr. Tregaron)
310. burial   Caron-is-   SN 673 753
                 clawdd
According to Edward Lhuyd, 'an urn [was] found at pont treceval near Tregaron fawr'.
Morris, Lhuyd's *Parochialia* III (1911), 91.

Pyllau Isaf
311. cairn   Llanfihangel-   SN 637 753
                 y-Creuddyn
The early history of this site is mixed up with that of the Penyberth (Gloucester Hall) discovery (see p. 203). The original account states only that a cinerary urn was found here in a cairn. The connection between the urn and Pyllau Isaf is cemented by the inscription upon William Hughes's grave in Llanbadarn churchyard. Dated 1843, and stating clearly that the urn was found in a field called Cae'r-odyn on the farm of Pyllau-isaf, Llanfihangel-y-Creuddyn, in 1840, is the earliest known reference to the discovery though there may be yet undiscovered contemporary accounts. The discrepancies between various early accounts merit fuller discussion. The urn is described as follows: 'Decoration (corded): on internal bevel of rim: three horizontal lines; on collar: alternating triangles with filling of oblique lines, with two enclosing lines above and below; on shoulder: a row of roughly triangular impressions. Lower part missing.'[1] Its diameter is 18.5 cm, and its original height about 20 cm (Fig. 25.5). The accompanying vessel at the museum

(not certainly from the same site) was a 'Pygmy cup of buff ware, with internally-bevelled rim and vertical upper wall. Decoration (incised): on internal bevel, zigzag, all enclosed between horizontal lines'.[2] Its height is 25.3 cm and diameter 7.2 cm. NMW Acc. No. 30.2102 (Fig. 25.4).

[1] Grimes, *Prehist. of Wales*, 210 (No. 640).
[2] Op. cit., 217 (No. 665).
Aberystwyth Meeting, *Arch. Camb.*, 2 (1847), 359; Morgan, *Arch. Camb.*, 6 (1851), 164; Welshpool Meeting, *Arch. Camb.*, 11 (1856), 366; Tenby Meeting, *Arch. Camb.*, 6 (1851), 334; 11 (1856), 366; Stanley and Way, *Arch. Camb.*, 23 (1868), 249–50; Peate, *Arch. Camb.*, 80 (1925), 203–5: *Arch. Camb.*, 87 (1932), 201–2; Savory, *Guide Catalogue*, 149, 427, fig. 62 (Urn); 154, 469, fig. 71 (Pygmy Cup).

Rhos Wylgain
312. burials   Troed-yr-aur   SN 373 495
Lhuyd records that prior to 1700 'There were some urns found lately upon Ros (anciently Moel) Wylgain near to wch Plaen is an old fortification called pen y gar'. The relationship of the discovery to Pen y Gaer (now called Caerau) is unclear and the find may have come from within a wide compass of ground.
Morris, Lhuyd's *Parochialia* III (1911), 90.

Tair Carn (sites of barrows)
313. cairn   Cellan   SN 6233 4950
314. cairn   SN 6375 4950
315. cairn   SN 6313 4931
316. cairn   SN 6262 4950
317. cairn   SN 6278 4940
318. cairn   SN 6309 4937
OS 1820; Lewis, *Topog. Dict.* (1833); OS SN 64 NW 9. (1973)

Tan Bwlchau (S of)
319. kerb   Caron-is-   SN 7243 6040
cairn   clawdd
A cairn 4 m in diameter, 0.3 m high and bordered by a rough kerb of stone slabs. It appears undisturbed.
(1978)
320. cairn   SN 7241 6040
A.H.A.H.; OS SN 76 SW 3. (1978)

Tan yr Esgair
cairns (4)   Blaenpennal   SN 6165 6711
A group of four cairns aligned roughly NNE–SSW on ridge.
321. 8 m in diameter and 0.5 m high.

322. 6 m in diameter and 0.4 m high.
323. 8 m in diameter and 0.7 m high.
324. 4.5 m in diameter and 0.3 m high.
Neil King (for OS in 1974) felt that these were not simply field clearance cairns.
Handlist; OS SN 66 NW 3. (1978)

Trawsallt
325. cairn   Ysbyty   SN 7783 7040
        Ystwyth
OS SN 77 SE 3. (326)

Tremain
326. burial urn   Y Ferwig,   SN 24 49
        Llangoedmor
        or Blaen-porth
The Revd G. Evans exhibited a 'Sepulchral urn (British), with remains of burnt bones' at the Cardigan meeting of the Cambrian Archaeological Association in 1859.
Cardigan Meeting, *Arch. Camb.*, 14 (1859), 349.

Tresaith (see Dyffryn Saith)

Trichrug
A fine group of 4 earthfast cairns:
327. cairn   Cilcennin   SN 5419 5995
3.3 m high with an overall diameter of 19.8 m, with a slight platform on top, 5.6 m across, containing a shallow depression.
328. cairn   SN 5422 5991
2.5 m high with a diameter of 10.6 m with a flat top about 3 m in diameter, surmounted by an OS Trig. Point.
329. cairn   SN 5425 5989
1.4 m high with a diameter of 20 m. The interior is badly damaged, much material apparently having been removed, with a large central hollow about 12 m in diameter filled with rubbish.
330. cairn   SN 5403 5990
A low turf-covered mound, 0.6 m high and 13.2 m in diameter, which may represent the site of a further cairn.
SAM 61; OS SN 55 NW 8. (1990)

These monuments have been much disturbed, the whole area forming a clearing in a forestry plantation. The presence of cemented stone close to the summit of the most northerly cairn gives rise to speculation that this as well as the others may have been altered in recent times.

It is difficult to know how much credence to put upon the account of 1877 stating that: 'fifty years ago the attention of the antiquarians was directed to this spot . . . [and] . . . one of them was examined, and among other relics of war there was found a sword which I believe was for many years at Tymawr, Cilcennin, and is now, I am told, at Glanrydw, Carmarthen.'[1]

[1] *Byegones* (1877), 243.

Trum Llwyd (see Gurnos Mountain)

Twmpath Tylwith Teg
331. barrow   Llangoedmor   SN 212 479
(d.)
Fenton, *Arch. Camb.*, 15 (1860), 58; OS 24 NW 2. (1975)

Tyll Coed, Wervilbrook
332. cairn   Llangrannog   SN 34 52
cemetery (d.)
'A round bottomed cup, holding 1/4 pint, with three holes in the side' was found with eleven urns in a cairn in 1802. All save one crumbled to pieces.
Meyrick, *Hist. and Antiq.*, 228–9, 433; Savory, *BBCS*, 17 (1958), 118 (no. 84); OS SN 35 SW 8. (1972)

Ty'n y Bwlch
333. cairn   Llanddeiniol   SN 544 736

Tyn'reithin
334. barrow   Lledrod Isaf   SN 6302 6855
OS SN 66 NW 10.

Ty'n-yr-helyg
335. cairn   Ceulan-a-   SN 6701 8945
            Maesmor
Meyrick records a cist or stone chest here, and Sansbury noted that there was still the remains of a cairn in 1932. According to C. H. Houlder the hollow could still be seen in 1971, in an area of several large boulders.
Meyrick, *Hist. and Antiq.*, 438; Sansbury, *Meg. Mons.* no. 17; OS SN 68 NE 6.

Ty'n-y-rhos (nr.)
336. cairn   Lledrod Isaf   SN 6302 6855
OS SN 66 NW 10. (1988)

Ty'n-y-rhos (Nancwnlle) (S of) (For burial from site, see Fan, no. 183)

Waun Bant
337. cairn (d.)   Cellan   SN 6208 4633
NMW Rec.; OS SN 64 NW 14. (1975)

Waun Groes
338. cairns   Caron-is-   SN 713 599
(mainly clear-   clawdd
ance)
Muckle MS. (1989)

Waun Maenllwyd
339. barrow   Llanddewi-   SN 6765 5386
            brefi
Morgan, *AW*, 27 (1987), 33.
340. clearance   SN 679 536
cairns
C.S.B. (1986)

Wervilbrook (1 mile from)
341–43. cairns   Llangrannog   SN 34 52
(3, d.)
Meyrick, *Hist. and Antiq.*, 433; OS SN 35 SW 8. (1973)

Whilgarn
344. cairn   Llannarth   SN 4481 5172
Handlist; OS SN 45 SW 2. (1976)

Ynys Tudor
345. barrow   Llangynfelin   SN 6695 9286
SAM 130; *Handlist*; OS SN 69 SE 4. (1978)

Ystumtuen
346. cairn   Cwmrheidol   SN 73 78
Four or five mounds in field.
C.H.H.

Unlocalized, west Wales, probably Cardiganshire
347. A Pygmy Cup was presented by Mr E. Evans to the National Museum of Wales in 1940 (NMW Acc. No. 40.174). No details of its discovery are recorded. Grimes describes it as 'of software with warm-buff, eroded surface and biconical form with internally bevelled rim and flat base; the decoration consists of two pairs of horizontal furrows spanning the carination and just above the base respectively, a frieze of incised, counter-hatched triangles above and below the carination, an incised circle on the base and two perforations 1.7 cm apart on the carination'. It is 5.5 m high and 6.2 cm in maximum diameter.
Savory, *Arch. Camb.*, 96 (1941), 31, 35, 36, fig. 4; Grimes, *Prehist. of Wales*, 218 (no. 672) (Pl. XV3); Savory, *BBCS*, 17 (1958), 109A; Savory, *Guide Catalogue*, 155, Fig. 71.

APPENDIX II: STONE CIRCLES

1. Bryn y   Llanddewi-   SN 7490 5473
Gorlan   brefi
Leighton, *Arch. Camb.*, 129 (1980), 154–7. (1984)

2. Coed   Lampeter   SN 5918 5022
Gwarallt   Rural
(natural
feature)
Meyrick, *Hist. and Antiq.*, 200; Sansbury, *Meg. Mons.* no. 39; Grimes in I. Ll. Foster and L. Alcock (eds.), *Culture and Environment* (London, 1963), 148–9.

3. Hirnant (kerb cairn: see *Cairns*, no. 235).

4. Lle'r Neuaddau (kerb cairn: see *Cairns*, no. 247).

5. Meini Kyvrivol   SN 24
(Cyfrifol) (site of)
Gibson, *Britannia* (1695), col. 647: *Britannia* (1722), col. 773; Sansbury, *Meg. Mons.* no. 54.

6. Moel y Llyn (or Cylch Derwyddol) (Fig. 17.1)
(see *Cairns*,   Ceulan-a-   SN 6994 9106
nos. 265, 266)   Maesmor

T. O. Morgan, *Aberystwyth Guide* (1851); *Arch. Camb.*, 28 (1873), 292; Sansbury, *Meg. Mons.* no. 18.

7. Noyadd   Llandygwydd   SN 258 453
Trefawr (site
of)
Gibson, *Britannia* (1695), col. 647: *Britannia* (1722), col. 773; J. P. A. L. Phillips, *Cardiganshire Pedigrees* (1859); OS SN 24 NE 1.

8. Stepaside,   Cardigan St   SN 17 47
Cardigan   Mary's
(natural
features)
Jones, *Antiq.*, 30 (1955), 34–6; *Cardigan and Tivy-Side Advertiser* 26 Aug. 1955; 2 Sept. 1955. (1989)

9. Ysbyty   Cwmrheidol   SN 752 791
Cynfyn
Grimes in I. Ll. Foster and L. Alcock (eds.), *Culture and Environment* (1963), 127; Briggs, *Arch. Camb.*, 128 (1979), 138–46. (1990)

APPENDIX III: STANDING STONES

1. Allt-ddu   site not
(boundary,   located
site of)
NLW Crosswood Mapbook I, fol. 40.

2. Blaen   Llanddewi-   SN 7694 6310
Glasffrwd (SE   brefi
of)
Leighton, *Arch. Camb.*, 129 (1980), 154–7. (1984)

3. Blaengowen   Llandysilio-   SN 3985 5125
Fawr (site of)   gogo
Sansbury, *Meg. Mons.* no. 47.

4. Bron   Gwnnws Isaf   SN 6943 7031
Caradog
Sansbury, *Meg. Mons.* no. 35; OS SN 67 SE 8. (1978)

5. Bron   Caron-uwch-   SN 7423 6352
Caradog   clawdd
OS SN 76 SW 20. (1978)

6. Bryn y   SN 7494 5473
Gorlan
(fallen)
(see also *Cairns*, nos. 85–6)

7. Bryn y   Gwynfil   SN 633 573
Maen (site of)
OS 1835; anon., *Arch. Camb.*, 16 (1861), 312; Sansbury, *Meg. Mons.* no. 37; OS SN 65 NW 2. (1976)

8. Bryn y   Lledrod Uchaf   SN 6662 6751
Maen (site of)   (site)
Sansbury, *Meg. Mons.* no. 59; OS SN 66 NE 4. (1974)

9. Buwch a'r   Trefeurig   SN 7219 8332
Llo (stone
group)
(see *Cairns*, no. 199)
Sansbury, *Meg. Mons.* no. 64; Bird, *Ceredigion*, 7 (1972),
437; OS SN 78 SW 8. (1978)

10. Byrfaen   Cellan   SN 6328 4733
Gwyddog
Morris, Lhuyd's *Parochialia* III, *Arch. Camb.*, 65 (1911), 86;
Gibson (ed.), *Britannia* (1695), col.62; OS SN 64 NW 7.

11. Cae Brynmaenmawr (see Bryn y Maen,
Gwynfil)

12. Cae   Aberystwyth   SN 591 801
Maen, Pen-
parcau (site
of)
Welsh Gazette 5 Jan. 24; Sansbury, *Meg. Mons.* no. 1.

13. Cair Carn (see Tair Carn)

14. Camddwr   site not
Mawr   located
NLW Mapbook 37, folio 47. (1787)

15. Careg-y-   Ceulan-a-   SN 6785 8620
difor   Maesmor
(gatepost)

16. Carreg y   Cellan   SN 6200 4650
Bwci (site of)
Sansbury, *Meg. Mons.* no. 5; OS SN 64 NW 5. (see below,
II. ch. 4, p. 307).

17. Carreg   Ysbyty   SN 7971 6989
Naw Llyn   Ystwyth
Sansbury, *Meg. Mons.* no. 83; OS SN 76 NE 2. (1978)

18. Carreg   Gwnnws Isaf   SN 7260 7129
Samson
Sansbury, *Meg. Mons.* no. 36; OS SN 77 SW 4. (1978)

19. Carreg   Llanddewi-   SN 6760 5380
Samson   brefi
(Maen
Llwyd)
Sansbury, *Meg. Mons.* no. 29.

20. Carreg   Ysbyty   SN 7414 7038
Samson   Ystwyth
Sansbury, *Meg. Mons.* no. 82; OS SN 77 SW 7. (1978)

21. Carreg   Trefeurig   SN 7190 8355
Slic, Lluest
fach
Sansbury, *Meg. Mons.* no. 76; OS SN 78 SW 18. (1978)

22. Carreg y   site not
Trathen   located
NLW Mapbook 37, fol. 27. (1787)

23. Carreg Tryr/Carreg Tair Croes (see Tair
Carn)

24. Castell   Cwmrheidol   SN 7256 8363
Coch
Sansbury, *Meg. Mons.* no. 63.

25. Castell   Llandysul   SN 4233 4203
Gwynionydd
Sansbury, *Meg. Mons.* no. 49.

26. Cerrig   Faenor Uchaf   SN 6250 8355
Llwydion
(meinihirion)
Marked as 'stones' on NLW Mapbook 37, folio 27;
Sansbury, *Meg. Mons.* no. 73.

27. Cerrig yr   Melindwr   SN 6855 8369
Wyn (stones),
Ty'n y Cefn Brith
Sansbury, *Meg. Mons.* no. 74.

28. Cnwch   Llanddewi-   SN 7504 4966
Eithiniog   brefi

29. Cnwch   Llanddewi-   SN 7575 4965
Eithiniog   brefi
(see *Cairns*, nos. 139–40)
NLW Mapbook 37, folio 27; Sansbury, *Meg. Mons.* no. 27.

30. Cors Pwll- Llanddewi-   SN 7573 4965
y-ci   brefi
OS SN 74 NE 7. (1976)

31. Court   Tirymynach   SN 6613 8568
Grange Mine
(meinhir)
Stone used for Penrhyncoch War Memorial.
Sansbury, *Meg. Mons.* no. 72.

32. Cringae   Llansanffraid   SN 5442 6504
Bird, *Ceredigion*, 11 (1972), 40–5; OS SN 56 NW 6. (1978)

33. Croes-y-   Penbryn   SN 2890 5138
bryn

34. Dinas   Cwmrheidol   SN 729 821
Hillfort (site
of two stones)

35. Disgwylfa   Melindwr   SN 7312 8366
Fach
Bird, *Ceredigion*, 7 (1972), 44. OS SN 78 SW 23. (1978)

36. Esgair Hir   Ceulan-a-   SN 7292 9089
Mine   Maesmor
Sansbury, *Meg. Mons.* no. 19.

37. Ffrwd   Llanrhystud   SN 5475 6840
Farm
D. Evans, *Adgofion Gan Henafwyr* (1904).

38. Gaer Fawr   Llanilar   SN 6508 7198
Sansbury, *Meg. Mons.* no. 69.

39. Garn   Cwmrheidol   SN 7525 8335
Lwyd
Sansbury, *Meg. Mons.* no. 23; OS SN 78 SE 2. (1974)

40. Garn Wen   SN 6898 9274
NLW MS Map R.M. C20. (1820)

41. Garreg   Penbryn   SN 3080 5300
Fawr
Sansbury, *Meg. Mons.* no. 66.

42. Garreg   Penbryn   SN 3070 5290
Llwyd
Sansbury, *Meg. Mons.* no. 66.

43. Garreg   site not
Llwyd (Nant   located
y Brent)
NLW Mapbook 39, fol. 5. (1787)

44. Garreg   Llanfihangel-   not plotted
Llwyd Fawr   y-Creuddyn
and Fach

45. Garreg   Llanfihangel   SN 51 56
Samson, Allt   Ystrad
y Gaer
Sansbury, *Meg. Mons.* no. 51.

46. Garreg   Trefeurig   SN 7037 8351
Hir
OS SN 78 SW 17. (1978)

47. Gilfach-   Llandysul   SN 405 407
wen-isaf
(see *Cairns*, no. 214)

48. Glan-   Ceulan-a-   SN 684 885
yrafon (lost)   Maesmor
Bird, *Ceredigion*, 7 (1972), 40–5; OS SN 68 NE 7. (1978)

49. Hirfaen   Cellan   SN 6245 4645
Gwyddog
Morris, Lhuyd's *Parochialia* III (1911), 86; entered as
'Byrfaen' in Gibson (ed.), *Britannia* (1695), col. 647;
Meyrick, *Hist. and Antiq.*, 218–19; RCAM *Carms. Inventory*
no. 615; Sansbury, *Meg. Mons.* no. 11.

50. Llech   Llanbadarn   SN 5425 6485
Gron   Trefeglwys
Bowen, *The Universal Magazine* (1765); Sansbury, *Meg.
Mons.* no. 42; *Handlist*; OS SN 56 SW 1. (1988)

51. Llech   Llangybi   SN 60 53
Gybi
Morris, Lhuyd's *Parochialia* III (1911), 68, 88. (*c.* 1700)

52. Llech   Lledrod Isaf   SN 6550 6960
Mihangel
(site of, NW of Gilfach-las)
OS 1835; Sansbury, *Meg. Mons.* no. 58; OS SN 66 NE 6.
(1974)

53. Llech yr   Llangoedmor   SN 222 484
Ast (stones)
Gibson, *Britannia* (1695), col. 645; (1723), col. 772; OS SN
24 NW 3. (1975)

54. Llech yr   Penbryn   SN 3070 5240
Ochain (site
of)
Meyrick, *Hist. and Antiq.*, 179; Fenton, *Arch. Camb.*, 15
(1860), 61; Sansbury, *Meg. Mons.* no. 63.

55. Maen Gwyn (site of)   Llanfair-orllwyn   SN 3822 4333
Sansbury, *Meg. Mons.* no. 50; OS SN 34 SE 5. (1975)

56. Maen Gwyn, Ty'n Llidiart   Gwnnws Isaf   SN 6865 6880
Sansbury, *Meg. Mons.* no. 34.

57. Maen Hir   Llanwnnws   site not located
Morris, Lhuyd's *Parochialia* III (1911), 4. (*c.* 1700)

58. Maen y Prenfol (?Carreg y Bwci)   Cellan   SN 6457 4790
Morris, Lhuyd's *Parochialia* III (1911), 86. (*c.* 1700)

59. Maes Mynach   Llanfihangel Ystrad   SN 5195 5061

60. Meini (site of)   Llanychaearn   SN 56 735
Briggs, *Ceredigion* 9 (1982), 266.

Meini Hirion (Noyadd Trefawr: see *Stone Circles*, no. 7)

61. Mynydd March   Melindwr   SN 7217 8332
OS SN 78 SW 20. (1978)

62. Nant Glandwr   Melindwr   SN 7309 8359
OS SN 78 SW 7. (1978)

63. Nant-y-gof   Llangoedmor   SN 2040 4591
OS SN 24 NW 19. (1975)

64. Nant-y-maen   Caron-is-clawdd   SN 7617 5830
Sansbury, *Meg. Mons.* no. 3.

65. Olmarch House (site of Maen Hir)   Llangybi   SN 59 52
Morris, Lhuyd's *Parochialia* III (1911), 87. (*c.* 1700)

66. Old Abbey, Strata Florida (site nr.)   not plotted
NLW Crosswood Mapbook I fol. 40. (*c.* 1800)

67. Pant Garreg Hir   Trefeurig   SN 7037 8351
Sansbury, *Meg. Mons.* no. 75; OS SN 78 SW 17. (1978)

68. Parc Enoch (lost)   Troed-yr-aur   not plotted
Sansbury, *Meg. Mons.* no. 78.

69. Parc Pwdwr   Troed-yr-aur   SN 345 478
Sansbury, *Meg. Mons.* no. 77; OS SN 34 NW 7. (1975)

70. Pen Maen Gwyn   Caron-uwch-clawdd   SN 7521 6506
Bird, *Ceredigion* 11 (1972), 43; OS SN 76 NE 1. (1977)

71. Pen Sarn Gerrig   Troed-yr-aur   SN 3457 4764
OS SN 34 NW 7. (1975)

72. Pen-y-banc   Betws Ifan   SN 311 468
Bird, *Ceredigion*, 11 (1972), 43; OS SN 34 NW 5. (1975)

73. Pen y Castell   Ceulan-a-Maesmor   SN 6913 8447
Wright, *Aberystwyth Studies*, 11 (1912–14), 63; Sansbury, *Meg. Mons.* no. 71; OS SN 68 SE 12. (1978)

74. Pistyll Einion (lost)   Cellan   SN 6256 4864
OS SN 64 NW 23. (1975)

75. Preseb y March   Llanddewi-brefi   SN 60 52
Morris, Lhuyd's *Parochialia* III (1911), 88. (*c.* 1700)

76. Pwll Prydd   Lledrod
NLW Crosswood Mapbook II, 10f. (*c.* 1780)

77. St Michael's   Llangoedmor   SN 2357 4851
Fenton, *Arch. Camb.*, 5 (1850), 59.

78. St Tysilio's Church — Llandysilio-gogo — SN 3633 5749
Evans, *Arch. Camb.*, 73 (1918), 143; H. Allcroft, *The Circle and Cross* (London, 1920), II, 143; Bowen, *Antiq.*, 45 (1971), 213–15.

79. Tair Carn/Carreg Tair Croes/Carreg Tryr Croes (site of) — Cellan — SN 6275 4946
Morris, Lhuyd's *Parochialia* III (1911), 87; Meyrick, *Hist. and Antiq.*, 216–17.

80. Tir Ifan — Cellan — SN 6474 4974
Sansbury, *Meg. Mons.* no. 9.

81. Tre Taliesin — Llangynfelyn — SN 660 917
Sansbury, *Meg. Mons.* no. 45.

82. Troed Rhiw Ruddwen — Llanddewi-brefi — SN 771 478
OS 1831; Sansbury, *Meg. Mons.* no. 26; OS SN 74 SE 8. (1976)

83. Ty-hen (d.) — Cardigan, St Mary's — SN 1938 4909
Sansbury, *Meg. Mons.* no. 70.

84. Ty'r Banc (E of) — Tirymynach — SN 6803 8583

85. Tyr y Swyd — Lledrod
NLW Crosswood Mapbook II, fol. 10 f. (*c.* 1806)

86. Ysbyty Cynfyn (see *Stone Circles*, no. 9) — Cwmrheidol — SN 7528 7907
Briggs, *Arch. Camb.*, 128 (1979), 138–47.

APPENDIX IV: PERFORATED STONE IMPLEMENTS

Full petrographic descriptions, under the given reference numbers of the Council for British Archaeology, are available from the National Monuments Record for Wales, Aberystwyth.

1. Cardiganshire, unlocalized (Fig. 33.4) Miniature pebble macehead of close-grained grit. Dimensions: 101 × 57 mm, and 37 mm thick, with a perforation 17 mm in diameter. Presented to NLW by Mr Robert Kenrick, 20 May 1911, now in the Department of Maps and Prints.
Jerman, *Arch. Camb.*, 91 (1936), 148–9.

2. Cae-y-maes Mawr — Betws Leucu — SN 638 568 (approx.)
A small perforated macehead discovered in 1933 'near the site of a stone monolith ... which had been blown up with gunpowder many years before'. Dimensions: 86 × 63 mm and 28 mm thick, the hole from 38 to 22 mm in diameter.
NMW Acc. No. 33.549.1.
Davies, *TCAS*, 9 (1933), 32–5; Grimes, *Prehist. of Wales*, 268 (field given as Cae bryn maen mawr) (see *Standing Stones*, no. 7).

3. Cwmllech-wedd-isaf — Lledrod Isaf — *c.* SN 667 708
(Fig. 33.3)
Miniature pebble macehead with flattened oval section, oval plan, and cylindrical perforation, found 'in a brook in a dingle leading from Cwmllechwedd-isaf farm to Dolfor Wood'. Dimensions: 69 × 42 mm and 22.5 mm thick. The stone is black and white granodiorite speckled with iron staining (Group XXIIIB; cf. St David's Head).
CA 11. NMW Acc. No. 47.164.146.
Peate, *Arch. Camb.*, 80 (1925), 202–3; Grimes, *Prehist. of Wales*, 171 (no. 364); Shotton in F. M. Lynch and C. B. Burgess (eds.), *Prehistoric Man in Wales and the West* (1972), 90.

4. Cwrt Mawr — Llangeitho — SN 622 619
(Fig. 31.2)
A well-polished axe hammer with flat faces, an oval hour-glass perforation towards the butt which is flattened into an oval facet of grey colour, one face slightly eroded. Found in a peat bog. Dimensions: 242.5 mm tapering to 76 mm and

91.5 mm thick with a perforation 40 × 31 mm inside. The stone is of altered granophyric porphyrite.
CA 9. NMW Acc. No. 33.540.
Davies, *TCAS*, 9 (1933), 32–3; Grimes, *Arch. Camb.*, 90 (1935), 272–4 (fig. 2); Hyde, *PPS*, 5 (1939), 166–72; Savory, *Guide Catalogue*, 92 (fig. 14).

5. Ffosgwy Lledrod Isaf SN 652 687
(Fig. 33.5)
Pebble macehead made from a rounded pebble. Dimensions: 112 × 131 mm, with a perforation narrowing from 45 to 17 mm. The rock appears a blue-green colour where it has been chipped, and is a coarse grit, probably of local origin.
CA 29. TCSM 26.

6. Ffynnon Cwmrheidol SN 722 794
Wen (Fig.
33.8)
A half-made rounded pebble macehead of fine conglomerate with a matrix of quartz, feldspar and fine-grained rock-types.
CA 22. In private possession.

7. Glan Llanfihangel- SN 462 752
Ystwyth (Fig. y-Creuddyn
34.2) Isaf
Perforated axe-hammer with convex sides, flat butt, splayed blade and nearly cylindrical perforation close to butt. It is black in colour and heavily patinated and pitted on one side more so than the other as if it had been exposed to the weather. Dimensions: 250 × 119 mm and ranging from 73 to 60 mm in thickness, the blade 81 mm thick: perforation 49 mm interior (not constant), 56.5 mm exterior. The stone is of picrite (Group XII; cf. Cwrt Mawr).
CA 10. NMW Acc. No. 47.164.142.
Jones, *BBCS*, 3 (1927), 352; Grimes, *Prehist. of Wales*, 170 (no. 357); Savory, *Guide Catalogue*, 93 (fig. 16).

8. Llanddewi- SN 637 541
brefi
(Fig. 33.6)
Pebble macehead, possibly of recent manufacture. Dimensions: 63 × 47 mm and 35 mm thick with a cylindrical perforation 11.5 mm in diameter. The material is either Old Red Sandstone or Carboniferous grit.
CA 18.

9. Llanfeiliog Pen-uwch SN 593 625
(Fig. 31.1)
A diamond-shaped implement, designated by Mrs Roe as a 'double axe-hammer' with an hour-glass perforation. Dimensions: 200 × 70 mm and 34.5 mm thick; of the same stone as no. 12 below.
CA28. TCSM 25
Roe, *PPS*, 32 (1966), 244 (no. 267).

10. Llangybi SN 61 53
(nr.) (approx.)
Pebble macehead(?), 'found within four miles of Lampeter on a hillside overlooking the right bank of the R. Dulas'. A holed stone 3.25 in. (99 mm) in length, the present whereabouts unknown.
Davies, *TCAS*, 9 (1933), 34 (illustrated no. 4, opposite p. 32).

11. Llwyndyrys Llandygwydd SN 238 433
Quarry,
Llechryd
(Fig. 33.10)
Massive oval pebble macehead. Dimensions: 100 × 92 mm and 48 mm thick with an hour-glass perforation. The stone is of rhyolitic ash.
CA 12. NMW Acc. No. 39.563.5.
Grimes, *Prehist. of Wales*, 167 (no. 335).

12. Llwyn- Llanbadarn SN 635 599
rhys (Fig. Odwyn
31.5)
Axe hammer with abrasion at cutting edge. Dimensions: 161 × 68 mm and 39 mm thick. Pecking for perforation effected by the same technique as no. 9. The stone is of arkose grit.
CA 27. TCSM 28.
Roe, *PPS* 32 (1966), 244 (no. 466).

13. Llyn Llangwyryfon SN 61 68
Eiddwen (on
mountainside
N of) (Fig.
31.3)
Axe-hammer heavily patinated and pitted so that the original surface is quite unrecognizable, giving it a grey-brown or black aspect. A ridge of weathering runs along the edge. One face is flat, the other slightly concave longitudinally, so that the edge and butt are wider than the middle. Dimensions: 211 × 101 mm and thickness ranging from 68 mm at the top, to 61 mm in the middle

and to 66.5 mm at the base, the hole having an external diameter of 53 mm and an internal of 38 mm. The stone is of sub-ophitic dolerite.
CA 8. NMW Acc. No. 33.548.
Davies, *TCAS*, 9 (1933), 33–4 (illustrated opposite p. 32 (no. 2)); Grimes, *Arch. Camb.*, 90 (1935), 274–5; Grimes, *Prehist. of Wales*, 169 (no. 347: fig. 56.5); Savory, *Guide Catalogue*, 92 (fig. 14).

14. Pemprys, Ysgubor-y- SN 7136 9414
Ystrad Einion, coed
Furnace (280 yds (*c.* 250 m) from Pemprys)
Large axe-hammer found in the bank of the River Pemprys; composed of Group XII rock.
CA 42. Liverpool Museum 1966—375.

15. Penlan, Lledrod Uchaf SN 679 658
Swyddfynnon
(Fig. 33.1)
Axe-hammer or battle axe, apparently a pebble implement. Dimensions: 75 × 87 mm and 62 mm thick. The stone is grey-green in colour and well-smoothed of ophitic dolerite (cf. Preselite).
CA 25. TCSM 1.
Jones, *BBCS*, 3 (1927), 350 (no. 29).

16. Penlan, Lledrod Uchaf SN 679 658
Swyddfynnon
(Fig. 34.5)
(findspot as no. 15)
Axe-hammer, very badly weathered, red-brown in appearance, the feld spars having broken down leaving large rough hollows throughout. Dimensions: 206 × 88 mm and 58 mm thick. The stone is of picrite (cf. Cwm Mawr, Group XII).
CA 26. TCSM 2.

17. Pisgah, nr. SN 537 527
Lampeter
A large coarse axe-hammer found in a marshy field near the cottage called Pisgah. The butt is rounded and both perforated surfaces slightly dished, the perforation of hour-glass type. Dimensions: 220 × 100 mm and 54 mm thick, the perforation ranging from 63 to 43 mm. The stone is of felspathic dolerite (hand specimen identification only).
In private possession.
Savory, *BBCS*, 15 (1953), 158.

18. Rhiwgoch SN 753 817
Farm,
Ponterwyd
(Fig. 33.2)
Pebble macehead with hour-glass perforation of sub-ophitic gabbro (cf. Preseli area, Group XIII).
CA 21. In private possession.

19. Tafarn Llanbadarn-y- SN 652 785
Crug Isaf Creuddyn
Farm, Capel Uchaf
Seion (Fig.
34.1)
Axe-hammer of well-finished rock with eccentric but almost cylindrical perforation. The two perforated surfaces are slightly dished. Dimensions: 193 × 95 mm, the diameter of the perforation 45 mm. The stone is of picrite (cf., Corndon Hill, Mont.: Group XII).
CA 15. NMW Acc. No. 64. 577.
Savory, *BBCS*, 22 (1967), 202–4: *Guide Catalogue*, 94 (fig. 16).

20. 'Teifiside', unlocalized (Fig. 34.3)
Axe-hammer with convex sides, flat faces, and rounded butt with almost central hour-glass perforation. The implement is slightly grooved, possibly for thonging, but only on one face. Dimensions: 202 × 95 mm and 82 mm thick. The stone is of quartz dolerite (cf. St David's Head, Group XXIIIb).
NMW Acc. No. 47.164.139.
Peate, *Arch. Camb.*, 80 (1925), 202–3; Jones, *BBCS*, 3 (1927), 343–56; Grimes, *Prehist. of Wales*, 170 (no. 354); Shotton in F. M. Lynch and C. B. Burgess (eds.), *Prehistoric Man in Wales and the West*, 90; Savory, *Guide Catalogue*, 93 (fig. 15).

21. 'Teifiside', unlocalized (findspot as no. 20)
Fig. 34.4).
Miniature axe-hammer with convex sides, thin flattened butt, polished blade and hour-glass perforation slightly nearer butt than blade. Dimensions: 81 × 45 mm and 22 mm thick. Made from a pebble of micaceous siltstone.
NMW Acc. No. 47.164.143.
References as no. 20.

22. Ty Neuadd (found in bog nr.), Llangeitho SN 610 634

Pen-uwch (Fig. 33.7)
A small pebble with an hour-glass perforation, chipped at the edge. The stone is of feldspathic volcanic ash or greywacke.
CA 23.

23. Wern Felen Caron-uwch-clawdd SN 723 648
(Fig. 33.9)
A half-perforated, unfinished pebble implement of Aberystwyth Grit. Dimensions: 120 × 67 mm and 37 mm thick with external diameter of perforation 35 mm.
TSCM 39.

APPENDIX V: METALWORK

1. Aberaeron SN 46 63
(Fig. 30.10)
A socketed axe of almost square section with loop and three ribs. In fine condition with a black patina and a small hole through the blade. A tiny deposit of sand or clay is visible at the base of the socket. Dimensions: 110 mm long, the blade 52 mm wide and the socket 56 × 46 mm.
NMW Acc. No. 56.487.
Sansbury, *TCAS*, 7 (1930), 83; Savory, *Arch. Camb.*, 107 (1958), 43 (fig. 2.5): Savory, *Guide Catalogue*, 110 (fig. 26).

2. Aber-mad SN 604 760
Mould for socketed chisel. Found during dredging operations in the bed of the Mad, close to its junction with the Ystwyth, in 1944. 'One valve of a mould, of fine gritstone, without grooves or dowels, for casting a socketed chisel with a simple collar.' Dimensions: 73 mm long and 35 mm wide at the edge.
NMW Acc. No. 44.292.
Jones, *Arch. Camb.*, 98 (1944), 146; Savory, *BBCS*, 12 (1948), 60; Grimes, *Prehist. of Wales*, 192 (no. 553); Hodges, *Ulster J. Arch.*, 17 (1954), 78; Savory, *Guide Catalogue*, 125 (fig. 40).

3. Abermeurig SN 56 56
(nr.) (approx.)
(Fig. 29.7)

Looped-socketed spearhead with kite-shaped blade. Circumstances of discovery not clear, but almost certainly not associated with the Pygmy Cup from Ty'n-y-rhos (see *Cairns*, no. 183). Slightly damaged, the casting seams still visible. Dimensions: 169 mm long, its socket 18.5 mm wide and blade 27 mm wide.
NMW Acc. No. 15.139.2.
Lampeter Meeting, *Arch. Camb.*, 34 (1879), 65; Anwyl, *Arch. Camb.*, 61 (1906), 114; Sansbury, *TCAS*, 7 (1930), 79–81 (fig. 7); Grimes, *Prehist. of Wales*, 198 (no. 585 (2)); Savory, *Guide Catalogue*, (1980), 132, no. 336, fig. 71.

4. Ash Grange Faenor Uchaf SN 612 825
(Fig. 30.5)
A plain, loopless palstave with incipient shield-pattern. Found with a piece of worked quartz, thought to have been an end scraper, along with the remains of a fire, during drainage operations.[1] Much corroded, with the butt damaged and casting flaws and a hollow below the stop-ridge. Dimensions: 149 mm long, the blade 53 mm wide and 28.5 mm thick.[2]
NMW Acc. No. 47.164.179.
[1] Sansbury, *Arch. Camb.*, 82 (1927), 200; *BBCS*, 4 (1927), 93; *TCAS*, 7 (1930), 82–3.
[2] Grimes, *Prehist. of Wales*, 177 (no. 441); Burgess, *J. Flints. Hist. Soc.*, 20 (1962), 94 (fig. 3c); Savory, *Guide Catalogue*, 103 (no. 137).

5. Carn Saith Llanddewi- SN 771 530
Wraig, Nant brefi
Llwyd (Fig. 29.8)
Socketed spearhead, broken off near socket and
displaying no rivet holes: exact dimensions not
ascertained. In private possession. Information
and sketch from Mr E. R. D. Prosser, Tregaron.

6. Cae Maen Ysbyty SN 729 729
Arthur, Ystwyth
Pant-y-gorlan (Fig. 30.11)
Plain bag-shaped socketed axe, the socket badly
damaged but displaying a slight collar. Casting
bubbles visible on both faces and its interior still
retains traces of (?)clay. Dimensions: 9 mm long,
the blade 55 mm long, the socket 32 × 38 mm and
loop 7.5 mm long.
TCSM 45.

7. Cefn Coch SN 745 965
Sheepwalk,
nr. Glandyfi
(Fig. 29.1)
Flat axe, the blade slightly damaged and
somewhat corroded, 131 mm long, and blade
72 mm wide. Formerly in Powysland Museum.
Machynlleth Meeting, *Arch. Camb.*, 21 (1866), 544; *Powys-land Museum Catalogue* (1922), 16; Wheeler, *Prehist. and Roman Wales* (1925), 140; Sansbury, *TCAS*, 7 (1930), 84; Savory, *Trans. Carms. Antiq. Soc.*, 4 (1962), 75.

8. Ffynnoncadno Quarry, SN 741 808
nr. Ponterwyd
A socketed axe with loop and a reasonable depth
of collar. Sansbury suggests that the body is oval
in section and possibly faceted. Burgess (*in litt.*)
notes its length as 105 mm and blade width as
55 mm; in private possession.
Sansbury, *Arch. Camb.*, 82 (1927), 200–1; *BBCS*, 4 (1927), 93; *TCAS*, 5 (1927), 108 ; 7 (1930), 83 (and illustration); 11 (1936), fig. 11 (opp. p. 14).

9. Glanrheidol Cwmrheidol SN 663 794
(Fig. 30.8)
A loopless palstave 'with hollow below stopridge',
169 mm long and the blade 68 mm wide.
NMW Acc. No. 47.164.185 (cast): the original in
private possession.
Sansbury, *Arch. Camb.*, 82 (1927), 200; *BBCS*, 4 (1927), 93; *TCAS*, 5 (1927), 108; 7 (1930), 81 (and illustration);

Grimes, *Prehist. of Wales*, 177 (no. 444); Savory, *Guide Catalogue*, 103, 168, fig. 20, no. 138.

10. Nant Llanfair SN 670 510
Clywedog Clydogau
Ganol (Fig. 29.3)
Dirk of ovoid cross-section with narrow blade with
central thickening with expanded butt with
remains of two rivet holes. There are numerous
scars and small rivet holes near butt. Dimensions:
233 mm long.
NMW Acc. No. 09.130.
Davey, *Arch. Camb.*, 46 (1891), 235–6; Wheeler, *Prehist. and Roman Wales*, 149; Sansbury, *TCAS*, 7 (1930), 84; Bowen, *TCAS*, 11 (1936), 15 (fig. 11); Grimes, *Prehist. of Wales*, 183 (no. 513); Savory, *Guide Catalogue*, 112 (fig. 27).

11. Nant Llanfair SN 640 510
Clywedog Clydogau (approx.)
Ganol (Fig. 29.10)
Socketed looped spearhead almost serrated at
socket, the blade fairly sharp, casting seams
prominent, with ochreous green patina. Dimensions: 92 mm long, 16 mm in diameter at the
socket, the blade 14 mm wide, loops 14.5 mm long,
and hammered flat to 0.4 mm thick.
NMW Acc. No. 09.131.
Davey, *Arch. Camb.*, 46 (1891), 235–6; Wheeler, *Prehist. and Roman Wales*, 149: Sansbury, *TCAS*, 7 (1930), 84; Bowen, *TCAS*, 11 (1936), 15 (fig. 11); Grimes, *Prehist. of Wales*, 182 (no. 501: Fig. 62. 13); Savory, *Guide Catalogue*, 113 (fig. 28).

12. Llandysul SN 42 41
(Fig. 29.11) (approx.)
Gold bar torc of square section, 2.6–2.7 mm thick.
The terminals hammered a little, almost to square
section of 4.6 × 4.3 mm and 4.2 × 4.5 mm.
BM WG.9
Wheeler, *Prehist. and Roman Wales*, 169 (fig. 63.6); Bowen, *TCAS*, 11 (1936), 16.

13. Llan-non SN 52 67
(Fig. 30.6)
Palstave of looped trident-pattern with broken
loop. The surface is a little pitted with light green
patination and some iron-staining. Dimensions:
157 mm long and 28 mm thick, the blade 62 mm
wide.
NMW Acc. No. 35.622.
Grimes, *Prehist. of Wales*, 177 (no. 448: fig. 60.2); Savory, *Guide Catalogue*, 105 (fig. 22).

14. 'Pen Dinas', Aberystwyth   SN 584 803
(Fig. 30.2)
Palstave of unlooped variety with vestigial shield-
pattern. One wing of blade broken. Possibly part
of a hoard, allegedly from 'Castle Hill'.
NMW Acc. No. 47.164.177.

Meyrick, *Hist. and Antiq.*, 421 (illustration facing p. 418
(no. 3)); Meyrick and Skelton, *British Arms*, I (London,
1830), pl. 47.1; Lewis, *Topog. Dict.*, *s.v.* Aberystwyth;
Way, *Arch. Camb.*, 11 (1856), 124; Pritchard, *Arch. Camb.*,
29 (1874), 13; J. Evans, *Ancient Bronze Implements* (London,
1881), 79; Jerman, *Arch. Camb.*, 89 (1934) 125; Savory,
Guide Catalogue, 105.

15. Pen Dinas,   SN 584 903
Aberystwyth
A barbed copper spearhead of dubious antiquity
and unknown whereabouts: if genuine it is almost
unique in Britain.
Sansbury, *BBCS*, 4 (1927), 81; *TCAS*, 7 (1930), 8; Saer,
TCAS, 9 (1934), 81.

16. Plynlimon (not plotted)
A spearhead or dagger described as a 'British
spear or spike . . . of brass and nails of the same
material' dug up 'on the side of Plynlymmon
mountains' before 1755. At one time in Lewis
Morris's collection but its present whereabouts are
unknown.
Owen, *Gent. Mag.*, 61 (1791), 116 (Pl. 1, no. 6).

17. Pontrhyd-   Ysbyty
ygroes, 'near a   Ystwyth
copper mine',
(Fig. 29.4)
A copper halberd 'with heavy asymmetrical blade
with strong central rib and expanded rounded
butt containing three large rivets. A straight cast
ridge obliquely across the base of the blade
probably represents the position of the shaft'.
Dimensions: length 292 mm, width 102 mm,
0.5 mm thick.
NMW Acc. No. 22.178.
Fleure, *Aber. Studs.*, 4 (1922), 117; Wheeler, *BBCS*, 1
(1922), 171; *BBCS*, 2 (1923), 88; Wheeler, *Prehist. and
Roman Wales*, 141; Sansbury, *TCAS*, 7 (1930), 84; Grimes,
BBCS, 6 (1932), 278; Bowen, *TCAS*, 11 (1936), 14, (fig.
2); O'Riordain, *Arch.*, 86 (1937), 275, 313 (fig. 57. 4);
Savory, *Guide Catalogue*, 99 (fig. 29.100).

18. Rhos   SN 54 65
Haminiog   (approx.)
Spearhead '. . . found in a turbary near Rhos
Haminiog . . . nine feet below the surface . . . of
bronze copper'. Its present whereabouts is not
known.
Dolgelley Meeting, *Arch. Camb.*, 5 (1850), 331.

19. Rhos   Llanychaearn   SN 575 745
Rydd (a peat
bog called),
Glan-rhos, Aberllolwyn (Fig. 35)
A circular shield 665 mm diameter of sheet bronze
decorated with twenty concentric rings of
repoussé bosses with raised ribs between. The
metal is bent over at the edges to form a rim 7 mm
wide, of oval section and 4 mm thick. The hand-
grip is a separate piece, 145 mm long and almost
40 mm wide, folded over and riveted on with three
rivets, the heads of which are about 8 mm
diameter (behind) and 5 mm (front). The handle
is protected by a hollow conical boss protruding
about 45 mm at the front of the shield. On the
back there is a small pointed tongue rivet, 28 mm
long, halfway in from the edge, and a second rivet
but no tongue in a corresponding position on the
other side of the shield. The shield is in an excellent state of preservation. There is a considerable
body of literature on it, some of which incorrectly
suggests that it was found in Borth Bog.
BM Cat. 73, 2–10, 2. Copy in NMW Acc. No. 39.
69.1.
Meyrick, *Hist. and Antiq.*, 338–9 (pl. 20, fig. 2); Evans,
Ancient Bronze Implements (1881), 251; Grimes, *Prehist. of
Wales*, 184 (no. 521 copy); Coles, *PPS*, 28 (1962), 188 no.
16; Savory, *Guide Catalogue*, 114 (Pl. IIIa).

20. Rhydlwyd   Lledrod   SN 645 707
A haft-flanged axe, with incipient stop-ridge
'ploughed up 200 yards from the Sarn Helen'.
Now in private possession.
Sansbury, *TCAS*, 7 (1930), 82; Savory, *Trans. Carms.
Antiq. Soc.*, 3 (1960), 58 (no. 1); *BBCS*, 21 (1964), 64.

21. Rhyd-y-   Llan-non   SN 529 660
torth,
(Fig. 29.5(i), 29.6(ii))
Two fragments of flat bronze axes found 'on the
Cardiganshire coast near Llansantffraid':

(i) The butt end of a narrow butted flat axe, in very rough condition, pitted dark-brown or black showing signs of flattening on one side, 98 mm long.

(ii) The blade end of a similar axe, not in very good condition; dull green to brown; recently filed showing gold colour of metal. Dimensions: 75 mm long, the blade 82 mm wide and 22 mm thick. Both now in Carmarthen Museum.

Lloyd, *Trans. Carms. Antiq. Soc.*, 4 (1904) 9; Fleure, *Arch. Camb.*, 78 (1923), 239; Sansbury, *TCAS*, 7 (1930), 83–4; Bowen, *TCAS*, 11 (1936), fig. II.

22. Rhyd-y-pennau bridge, Bow Street (200 yds NE of) (Fig. 29.2)   SN 631 860

A bronze flat axe of the thin-butted variety, slightly hammered along its edges, one face smooth, the other showing traces of tooling. A copper colour beneath the black patina. Dimensions: 144.5 mm long, its blade 77 mm wide, the butt 37 mm long and 12 mm thick.
NMW Acc. No. 37.152.

Grimes, *Prehist. of Wales*, 174 (no. 407, fig. 58.4); Savory, *Guide Catalogue*, 100 (fig. 17.104).

23. Tan-y-bwlch, Tair Carn Mountain (at a height of over 1,000 ft (or 304 m)) (Fig. 30.9)   Cellan   SN 629 490

Socketed axe 'much worn and corroded, looped, socket plain and rectangular externally, double moulding at mouth'. Dimensions: 595 mm long, the socket diameters 45 × 36 mm.
NMW Acc. No. 46.419.1.

Savory, *BBCS*, 12 (1948), 126; Grimes, *Prehist. of Wales*, 181 (no. 492); Savory, *Arch. Camb.*, 100 (1948), 40 (no. 1), 43 (fig. 2.7); *Guide Catalogue*, 109 (fig. 24).

24. Tan-y-bwlch (Fig. 30.3)   Tirymynach   SN 680 859

Two looped practically identical palstaves were found in 1880 and 1930. One (Fig. 39.3) was formerly in UCW Arts and Crafts Gallery, the latter is probably in private possession.
Sansbury, *TCAS*, 7 (1930), 82.

25. Tregaron, found in a bog near, in the north part of the parish (Fig. 29.9)   SN 68 60 (approx.)

A spearhead and two palstaves, described as 'two celts, all bronze, and a *framea* or light javelin, used in the chase . . . found in a peat bog near Tregaron'. They were exhibited at the Dolgellau meeting of the Cambrian Archaeological Association in 1850. The spearhead may be identified with some confidence as that now in Carmarthen Museum. It is looped and socketed, with a sharp midrib and blade, the loop flattened, though not lozenge-shaped. It has a smooth, dark-green patina. Dimensions: 147 mm long, 21 mm wide, and 15 mm in diameter (socket).

Dolgelley Meeting, *Arch. Camb.*, 5 (1850), 331; *Trans. Carms. Antiq. Soc.*, 5 (1909–10), 66; 21 (1927–9), 8; Sansbury, *TCAS*, 7 (1930), 81; Bowen, *TCAS*, 11 (1936), 15; fig. 2, opposite p. 14.

26. Tŷ-gwyn, Cwmere, Elerch (Fig. 30.7)   Ceulan-a-Maesmor   SN 685 877

Loopless palstave with shield pattern. Discovered in 1965 in the abandoned cottage of Tŷ-gwyn, and presumed to have been found locally. The surface is corroded though some brown-coloured patina remains. It has a well-developed septum and an irregular hole through the septum immediately above the stop. Dimensions 172 mm long, the blade 75 mm and 31 mm thick.

Savory, *BBCS*, 22 (1967), 402–5; Savory, *Guide Catalogue*, 104 Fig. 21.

27. Ysbyty Cynfyn (Fig. 30.1)   Cwmrheidol   SN 753 791

Looped palstave with central rib. Cast in NMW; Acc. No. 47.164.187. Whereabouts of original not known. Length 151 mm.

Fleure, *Aberystwyth Studs.*, 4 (1922), 116; Sansbury, *TCAS*, 7 (1930), 1–2; Bowen, *TCAS*, 11 (1936), Fig. 11 opp. p. 14; Burgess, *Arch. J.*, 126 (1969), 150, Fig. 1d; Savory, *Guide Catalogue*, 107, Fig. 22 (stating only 'probably from Wales').

28. Ystrad-   Lledrod Uchaf   SN 702 675
meurig Castle

?Lost. 'Celt': 'in clearing the moat, which surrounded the keep an ancient celt was found'. This need not necessarily have been of bronze.
Meyrick, *Hist. and Antiq.*, 312.

CHAPTER 3

THE IRON AGE

J. L. Davies and A. H. A. Hogg†

AN INTRODUCTION

J. L. Davies

THE archaeological record of the later first millennium in the County differs dramatically from that of its inception. A seemingly sparsely populated landscape with a monument range heavily biased towards those of funerary or ritual purpose—characteristic of the second millennium—gives way to a heavily settled landscape dominated by settlements of overwhelmingly defended character, whose occupants are engaged in the exploitation of a wide range of resources, including the working of iron. Burial and ritual are expressed differently, or at least in a manner which leaves fewer archaeological traces. As is the case with all such episodes the pace and scale of change is difficult to quantify and the causal factors little understood, though it is generally agreed that the period *c.* 800–600 BC is the watershed which ushers in the new era. In Cardiganshire evidence from this critical period is virtually non-existent. No archaeological site with a suite of structures and diagnostic objects can be referred to which, when compared with others elsewhere, would allow us to see more clearly the process whereby the County's social and economic base was transformed. It is, therefore, necessary to extrapolate data from elsewhere in order to throw light on these complex processes, environmental, economic and social.

One of the catalysts of change was undoubtedly environmental; a climatic deterioration with a change to cooler and wetter conditions beginning *c.* 1250 BC, occurring more rapidly after 850 BC and reaching its climax between 850 and 650 BC.[1] Lamb estimates that there was a 2°C fall in temperature which reduced the growing season by about five weeks.[2] It has been suggested that this severely affected marginal landscapes, the western uplands in particular, where anthropogenic factors—deforestation, soil degradation and loss of fertility—sharply compounded the problem. Increasing wetness furthermore led to soil acidification, gleying and large-scale peat formation inhibiting woodland regeneration. Communities which had hitherto won a precarious

---

[1] H. H. Lamb, 'The Late Quaternary history of the climate of the British Isles', *British Quaternary Studies: Recent Advances*, ed. F. W. Shalton (Oxford, 1977), 283–98; idem, 'Climate from 1000 BC to 1000 AD', *The Environment of Man: The Iron Age to the Anglo-Saxon Period*, ed. M. Jones and G. W. Dimbleby (BAR 87: Oxford, 1981), 53–65; J. Turner, 'The Iron Age', *The Environment in British Prehistory*, ed. I. G. Simmons and M. J. Tooley (London, 1981), 250–81; A. F. Harding (ed.), *Climatic Change in Later Prehistory* (Edinburgh, 1982).
[2] H. H. Lamb, 'Climate from 1000 BC to 1000 AD', 53–65.

livelihood through the exploitation of marginal upland zones were eventually forced off the land, some of their fields disappearing beneath blanket bog. In Cardiganshire J. Turner's work on the raised bog at Tregaron showed recurrence surfaces between 1004 and 696 bc, and the rapid growth of the bog from *c.* 700 bc onwards, which is a classic indication of wetness.[3] Certainly the effects are likely to have been felt more keenly in upland areas west of the Cambrian Range.

Opinion is sharply divided as to the overall effects of this climatic and environmental change. Some writers suggest that they were comparable to the effects of the Black Death of the fourteenth century which brought about a population collapse.[4] Others hold that the results were not catastrophic and that the recovery of population and economic activity was rapid. Most, however, are agreed that the combination of climatic and anthropogenic factors was serious.

In the County, and for west Wales as a whole, the virtual disappearance of settlement sites is symptomatic of these changes, though it is difficult to believe that all the lowlands and river valleys were depopulated. It may well be that the land which was occupied and regularly used *c.* 1000–650 bc was considerably reduced in extent compared with the previous period. Certainly there appears to be a notable dearth of settlement sites of Late Bronze Age date in west Wales when compared with the eastern parts of the Principality,[5] though this may be redressed with the recent discovery of occupation at sites such as Dale Fort and Bosherston Camp, Pembs.,[6] and activity of some kind intimated by a charcoal-filled pit with a C14 date of 820 ± 60 bc at Plas Gogerddan.[7] It would be wise to refrain from making any definitive statements pertaining to demographic collapse, curtailment of settlement density, land use and economic activity in general until our regional data base becomes more reliable.

According to Turner there appears to have been an improvement to a warmer and drier episode after 450 bc, though the climate was still considerably cooler and wetter than a millennium before.[8] It seems to have allowed an agricultural and demographic recovery—evidenced throughout the British Isles—with some areas experiencing a substantial rise in population. The recovery was sufficiently strong to force farmers out into marginal zones once again, clearing forest, if such existed, and establishing new settlements. Such appears to be the case in Cardiganshire where there is palynological evidence for deforestation in the neighbourhood of Tregaron Bog *c.* 400 bc and for the extensive burning of woodland on the lower slopes of the Ystwyth Valley in the third century and the Ystwyth Forest plateau in the third to second

[3]J. Turner, 'The anthropogenic factor in vegetational history. 1. Tregaron and Wixall Mosses', *New Phyt.*, 63 (1964), 73–90; idem, 'The vegetation', *The Environment of Man: The Iron Age to the Anglo-Saxon Period*, 67–74.

[4]C. Burgess, 'Population, climate and upland settlement', *Upland Settlement in Britain. The Second Millennium BC and After*, ed. D. Spratt and C. Burgess (BAR 143: Oxford, 1985), 195–230.

[5]G. Williams, 'Recent work on rural settlement in later prehistoric and early historic Dyfed', *Ant. J.*, 68 (1988), 40.

[6]Ibid., 40, 48.

[7]K. Murphy, 'Plas Gogerddan, Dyfed: a multi-period ritual and burial site', *Arch. J.* (forthcoming).

[8]J. Turner, 'The Iron Age', op. cit., 261; idem, 'Post-Neolithic disturbance of British vegetation', *Studies in the Vegetational History of the British Isles*, ed. D. Walker and R. G. West (Cambridge, 1970), 81–96.

century BC.[9] Whether this was designed to facilitate agriculture as opposed to pastoralism is uncertain. Certainly there seems to have been an agricultural intensification at this time, embracing a wide range of habitats in the British Isles,[10] supported in some cases by an emphasis on the cultivation of crops which were better suited to the prevailing climate[11]—though we shall presently see that there is evidence for both agriculture and pastoralism in Iron Age Cardiganshire. Given the possibility that agricultural yields, at least in the earlier Iron Age, are likely to have been low and erratic, animal husbandry may have been pre-eminent. Such practices will have required even more land to support an equivalent number of families.[12] Pressure upon, competition for, and protection of land and its produce appears to be one of the recurrent and indeed over-riding themes of this era; it is graphically recorded in the settlement record and goes some considerable way towards explaining other changes in the archaeological record of the later first millennium BC.

One of these was the introduction of an iron technology.[13] British smiths had certainly begun to experiment with iron from c. 650 BC, possibly because the increased demand for bronze tools and weapons could not be satisfied; in effect an alternative was being forced upon the community at large because of a consumer-led shortage. The production of cheaper, if not technically more efficient, iron artefacts was a gradual process, iron never completely ousting bronze which continued to be utilized for the production of fine metalwork such as the Castell Nadolig collar or the La Tène III brooches from Plas Gogerddan (see Appendix II, p. 272). The new technology which gave its name to one of the three great Ages in the early nineteenth century is significant in the context of its socio-economic rather than its technological impact. By virtue of its widespread ores it allowed communities to bypass the complex social and economic networks which were a prerequisite for the accumulation of the constituents of bronze, thereby permitting much greater freedom of action and allowing hitherto relatively weak or subservient communities to challenge those who had dominated them. It has been suggested that the net result was not only the loosening of social and economic bonds but also the fostering of regionalism and aggression.

The transition from a bronze to an iron technology is not clearly evidenced in the archaeological record of the County, nor is anything known about subsequent organization of the industry. Iron slag is recorded from the hillforts of Caerau (Henllan), Caer Cadwgan, Pen Dinas (Aberystwyth) and from the lower levels of the outer ditch at Odyn-fach,[14] but the quantities are unimpressive

[9]J. Turner, 'Post-Neolithic disturbance of British vegetation', op. cit., 81–96; J. A. Taylor, 'The role of climatic factors in environmental and cultural changes in prehistoric times', *The Effect of Man on the Landscape: The Highland Zone*, ed. J. A. Evans *et al*. (C.B.A. Res.Rep. 11; London, 1975), 6–19; idem, 'Man-environment relationships', *Culture and Environment in Prehistoric Wales*, ed. J. A. Taylor (BAR 76: Oxford, 1980), 311–36. For a recent study of the later prehistoric vegetational sequence just beyond the County boundary, see F. M. Chambers, 'Environmental history of Cefn Gwernffrwd, near Rhandirmwyn, mid-Wales', *New Phyt.*, 92 (1982), 607–15.

[10]H. H. Lamb, 'Climate from 1000 BC to 1000 AD', 53–65; J. Turner, 'The Iron Age', op. cit., 275.

[11]H. H. Lamb, 'Climate from 1000 BC to 1000 AD', 53–65.

[12]R. Mercer, *Farming Practices in British Prehistory* (Edinburgh, 1981).

[13]For the general background, B. Cunliffe, *Iron Age Communities in Britain* (3rd edn., London, 1991). For Wales, H. N. Savory, 'The Early Iron Age in Wales', *Culture and Environment in Prehistoric Wales*, ed. J. A. Taylor (BAR 76: Oxford, 1980), 287–310. For the social impact of iron technology, R. Bradley, *The Social Foundations of Prehistoric Britain* (London, 1984), 128ff.

[14]K. Murphy and M. Johnson, 'Odyn-Fach Enclosure', *AW*, 29 (1989), 43–4.

and all probably relate to forging. So far there is nothing comparable to the large-scale iron production, from ore to billet, evidenced from the small fort of Bryn y Castell, Merioneth, or the unenclosed settlement at Crawcwellt, Merioneth.[15] Finished objects, all seemingly utilitarian, are known from Caerau (Henllan) and Pen Dinas (Aberystwyth),[16] though there must be some doubt as to the pre-Roman date of the nails from the former. Such a small total reflects the low survival of iron objects in the acid soils of the County together with small-scale excavation.

More contentious in terms of its chronology and process is that transition which led to the Celticization of the County, both linguistically and culturally, and embraced it within a pan-Celtic region which by the close of the first century BC stretched from Ireland to Czechoslovakia. Mediterranean sources of the fourth century BC indicate that Celtic names were already prevalent in the British Isles, whilst the earliest references to Celtic river and place-names in Cardiganshire belong to the second century AD.[17] When was a language ancestral to modern Welsh first spoken in Wales? Was it introduced by new settlers who were sufficiently numerous to change the linguistic basis in the first millennium, or was it an antique language even then?

In the past it was fashionable to explain this process by grafting an archaeological 'package' to it and thereby identifying 'A Coming of the Celts'. Supposed linguistic change was seen as being the product of successive waves of Celtic immigrants whose origins lay in a notional central European 'homeland' and whose material culture, labelled Hallstatt and La Tène, could be distinguished from that of the indigenes by a continentally inspired range of artefacts. These settlers were credited with land-taking and the subduing, enslaving or displacing of the indigenes —or at the very least with the imposition on them of a warrior-aristocracy, thereby bringing about changes in language and material culture. The interpretation of changes in material culture (metalwork, pottery and even new settlement types such as hillforts) was subordinated to this thesis, fostered by the implicit belief that cultural change, or the Model thereof, was largely brought about by 'invasion' or 'diffusion'.

Whilst popular movement into and within Britain cannot be entirely discounted, current archaeological opinion tends to play this down as the sole explanation for cultural change. It is generally acknowledged that both linguistic transmission and cultural changes involve complex, interactive processes which need not involve external stimuli; for example, long-term climatic changes which affect the subsistence base, demographic levels and ultimately social organization as reflected in the archaeological record.

Renfrew has recently argued that Indo-European speakers reached those areas where Celtic was, and still is, spoken by c. 4000 BC.[18] The Celtic languages then eventually emerged by a process

[15]For Bryn y Castell, see P. Crew, 'Bryn y Castell Hillfort—a late prehistoric iron working settlement in north-west Wales', *The Crafts of the Blacksmith*, ed. B. G. Scott and H. Cleere (Belfast, 1986), 91–100; for Crawcwellt, see P. Crew, 'Excavations at Crawcwellt West, 1986–89: A late prehistoric upland iron-working settlement', *AW*, 29 (1989), 11–16.

[16]For Caerau (Henllan) see A. Williams, 'A promontory fort at Henllan, Cardiganshire', *Arch. Camb.*, 96 (1945), 236; for Pen Dinas see C. Daryll Forde *et al.*, 'Excavations at Pen Dinas, Aberystwyth', *Arch. Camb.*, 112 (1963), 151.

[17]See A. L. F. Rivet and C. Smith, *The Place-Names of Roman Britain* (London, 1979), 10–11, who suggest that Celtic reached the British Isles in the Late Bronze Age/Early Iron Age. For a contrary view see C. Renfrew, *Archaeology and Language: The Puzzle of Indo-European Origins* (London, 1987), 211–49.

[18]C. Renfrew, *Archaeology and Language*, 249.

of differentiation and crystallization from an undifferentiated Indo-European language. As far as he is concerned, the process of becoming Celtic began at a very early stage, certainly long before the first millennium BC, and was later reinforced through the workings of the process of 'cumulative Celticity'.[19] A cultural overlay was thereby produced, reflected in the changes in the material evidence, particularly that associated with the upper class, and bringing about a continuum of change effected by 'constant trickles' of foreign goods and the workings of environmental and sociological factors. This thesis invokes some degree of external stimulation, archaeologically recognizable by the importation and copying of high-status items such as arms, armour and the decorative arts—the panoply of the high-ranking warrior and his retainers— reinforced by recurrent contact between British- and continentally-based élites. Cumulatively these links may have reinforced ethnic and perhaps linguistic cohesion over time with a continental 'core-zone'. Thus, no specific 'Coming of the Celts' needs to be invoked to explain the similarities which the County shares in terms of language, society and economy with other parts of Britain in the later first millennium BC.

Celtic society

Celtic society was not fossilized. Pluralistic, dynamic and variable in its structure, it was the product of different economic bases and degree of interaction with the west-central European 'core-zone'. As such the social pattern was variable from central Europe to the Atlantic seaboard. In part it represents a continuum, as illustrated by the attention given to high-status metalwork. These prestige goods continue the theme of élite display evident in the archaeological record of the Middle and Later Bronze Age, and thus suggest the continuance of a highly stratified society. Status and wealth may also have continued to be expressed in less tangible fashion; ownership and control of land, livestock, and metal production, together with the amassing of clients. Certainly the sparsity of examples of 'exotic' Iron Age metalwork from the County, in themselves the products of exchange or knowledge of current modes, should not betoken the absence of élites.

The key to comprehending the social pattern of the County lies in the settlement record, the hillforts and enclosures. It is the investigation of these monuments—their internal arrangement, chronology and inter-relationship—which will reveal the socio-economic systems of the first millennium. As elsewhere there are hints that the settlement pattern in Cardiganshire seems to have been variable over time, with the implication that communities may have been organized in different ways. But such evidence as there is is largely analogous, the problem being exacerbated by minimal excavation on all types of presumed first millennium BC settlements.

Settlement evidence

One of the most notable features of the latter half of the first millennium BC is the proliferation of settlements delimited by palisades, earthworks, stone walls or composite defences. Many are

[19]C. F. C. Hawkes, 'Cumulative Celticity in Pre-Roman Britain', *Études Celtiques*, 13, 2 (1979), 607–28.

obviously sited with a view to maximizing a defensive potential and, in consequence, are termed hillforts, though not all hillforts are so sited. Cardiganshire is typical of most of Wales insofar as its Iron Age settlement pattern is composed of defended, or at least enclosed, settlements, many of which have a propensity to survive later denudation or agricultural obliteration. Whether there was ever a substantial unenclosed (or simply fenced or lightly walled) element in the settlement pattern, as in north-west Wales,[20] is uncertain. There are tantalizing hints that such may have existed, as at Stackpole Warren, Pembs.,[21] or on palisaded sites later enclosed by earthworks,[22] but such lightly delimited sites are extremely vulnerable to destruction by ploughing and their frequency is speculative. What we can show through the application of air photography to the problem of settlement archaeology is that hillforts or the more obviously defensive settlements, represent only one element in the Iron Age landscape and must be supplemented by a large number of lightly enclosed, small 'farms'. To date, these are best known on the sands and gravels of the south of the County, the geology of which is particularly susceptible to cropmark formation. Defended or otherwise, and irrespective of morphological similarities, these settlements were not always strictly contemporary. Recent work has shown that they often represent a succession, and a proliferation, of settlement over time.[23]

Hillforts

Detailed discussion of the morphology and distribution of this class of settlement will be found on pp. 234–8. What follows is a discussion of the Cardiganshire forts in the context of those in south-west Wales as a whole, with particular reference to the contribution of evidence from recent excavations, together with an analysis of their socio-economic significance. The dearth of excavation on sites within the County prohibits the reconstruction of an evolutionary sequence and clear-cut relationships between the various forts. This does not, of course, prohibit the reconstruction of hypothetical sequences and relationships (see pp. 234ff.).

It has long been recognized that the story of hillfort development is complicated, with some sites being apparently founded in the Late Bronze Age, though no site in south-west Wales, with

[20]RCAHM *Caernarvonshire* III (1964), lxxxvii ff.; E. G. Bowen and C. A. Gresham, *History of Merioneth* I (Dolgellau, 1967), 176–224. For a recension of the settlement evidence see R. S. Kelly, 'Recent research on the hut group settlements of north-west Wales', *Conquest, Co-Existence and Change: Recent Research in Roman Wales*, eds. B. C. Burnham and J. L. Davies, *Trivium*, 25 (1990), 102–11.

[21]H. N. Savory, 'Welsh hillforts. A reappraisal of recent research', *Hillforts: Later Prehistoric Earthworks in Britain and Ireland*, ed. D. W. Harding (London, 1976), 2–51. For C14 dates from Stackpole, see G. Williams, 'Recent work on rural settlement in later prehistoric and early historic Dyfed', *Ant. Journ.*, 68 (1988), 51–2.

[22]For example, Dale Fort (Pembs.) where eighth century BC radiocarbon dates are associated with a sequence of palisades, succeeded by a rampart, in what is apparently a Late Bronze Age horizon. Information from G. Williams. For the radiocarbon dates, see G. Williams, 'Recent work on rural settlement in later prehistoric and early historic Dyfed', 48.

[23]G. Williams, 'Recent work on rural settlement in later prehistoric and early historic Dyfed', esp. 33–40. ✦

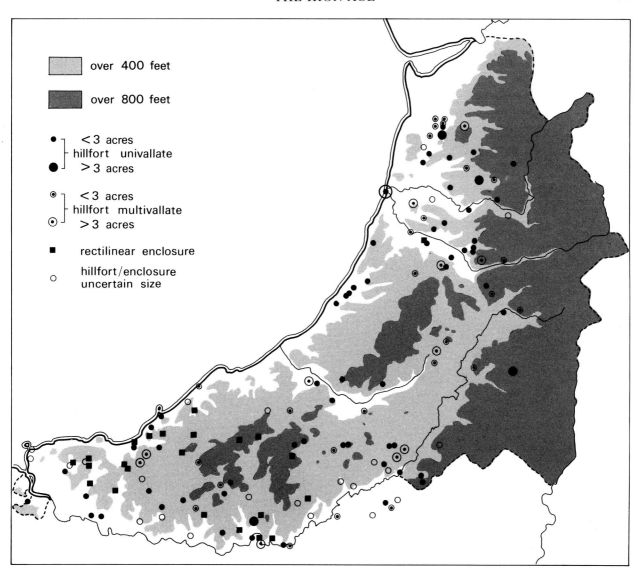

Fig. 41: Distribution of hillforts and enclosures.

the possible exception of Dale Fort, Pembs.,[24] can claim such an early foundation. The earliest radiocarbon dates from hillforts in our County lie within the seventh to fifth centuries BC, thus sharing a trend common to Welsh hillforts as a whole.[25] At Bryn Maen Caerau, Cellan, a general layer associated with pits and postholes, possibly but not certainly associated with pre-rampart occupation and a palisade trench, has a single date of 570 ± 70 bc. At Caer Cadwgan two dates are available for the destruction of the Phase 1 gate; 630 ± 70 bc and 410 ± 70 bc, an

[24]See above, n. 22. For a classic fortification of Late Bronze Age date in Wales, see C. R. Musson *et al., The Breiddin Hillfort* (CBA Res. Rep., no. 76: London, 1991).
[25]See above, n. 23, Appendix pp. 48–52.

inconsistency which presently cannot be resolved. These dates are respectably early and are not incompatible with those from early contexts at other medium-sized Welsh hillforts.

It has long been recognized that there are regional differences in hillfort types, mirroring environmental differences, social trends and the history of each region.[26] South-west Wales is essentially a zone of small hillforts and enclosures, few of which exceed 1.2 ha (3 acres) in size, the great majority of the smaller sites being concentrated in the far south-west. Within this region Cardiganshire contains a high percentage of medium/small true hillforts, together with a few larger examples, intermixed with farmstead-type enclosures (see Fig. 41).

No single explanation will suffice to explain the appearance of this proliferation of defensible settlements. Certainly, the notion of a colonization by newcomers (see p. 236) must be treated with extreme caution, if not immediately rejected.[27] The emphasis on community defence, implicit in the larger and more complex sites, indicates an increasingly convulsed, warlike society, in which competition for resources and status played a key role in social relationships. Such pressures are thought to have demanded an increased level of organization for the management of an increasingly stratified, parochial society, periodically wracked by the raids and clan wars of petty chiefs and their war-bands. These individuals exercised control over the lesser orders, subsistence, exchange and external relationships. The hierarchy of settlement, therefore, reflects an increasingly elaborated social network dependent upon different economic systems and, ultimately, environmental differences between geographical regions. It also reflects population recovery, growth and the colonization of new land in the latter half of the millennium.

If settlement size, then, is a function of socio-political systems and ultimately of subsistence strategies which dictate population density, what the Cardiganshire evidence indicates is that for most of the County the dearth of high-quality soils and a climate more conducive to pastoral regimes was more suited to settlements of relatively small, uniform size and low density than to settlements of large, nucleated character. G. Williams, drawing an analogy with central southern England, has suggested that the sprinkling of larger forts, particularly in the north and east of the County, may possibly reflect a more complex, hierarchical system based upon the production of surpluses—presumably of livestock products rather than cereals[28]—but this is a thesis which requires testing through large-scale excavation.

Attention has already been drawn to the relatively early radiocarbon dates from two medium-sized forts, Bryn Maen Caerau, Cellan, and Caer Cadwgan, though none are available for their abandonment. Consequently it is not known whether they represent a short-lived phase in the story of Iron Age settlement in the County or have an enduring significance. In other parts of Wales and Britain in general we can demonstrate that by the middle phase of the Iron Age some hillforts were abandoned, whilst others seemingly acquired an enhanced significance with their

[26]H. N. Savory, 'The Early Iron Age in Wales', *Culture and Environment in Prehistoric Wales*, ed. J. A. Taylor (BAR 76: Oxford, 1980), 287–310.

[27]H. N. Savory, 'Welsh hillforts: a reappraisal of recent research', *Hillforts: Later Prehistoric Earthworks in Britain and Ireland*, ed. D. W. Harding (London, 1976), 237 ff.

[28]G. Williams, 'Recent work on rural settlement in later prehistoric and early historic Dyfed', 30–54.

own large, dependent 'territories'—the phenomenon of the so-called 'developed hillfort'.[29] It is uncertain whether such a progression is a feature of south-west Wales. At the 3.5 ha hillfort of Merlin's Hill, Abergwili,[30] two radiocarbon dates suggest that this site was either founded or possibly enlarged in the middle phases of the Iron Age, whilst the complexity of the defensive sequence at Pen Dinas, Aberystwyth, which on the basis of ceramic evidence has an occupation sequence to the second or first century BC, makes this site a prime candidate for a 'developed hillfort'.[31] It may be necessary, however, to add a caveat; complexity need not necessarily betoken continuous, long-term occupation. There is good reason to believe that some have a spasmodic occupation—at least as reflected in their defences—though their importance or tradition as territorial foci was probably retained.[32]

Judging by the results of recent excavation in west Wales the fourth to second centuries BC seem to have been the heyday for the construction and occupation of a great variety of defensible sites, ranging from true hillforts to small but strongly defended sites with elaborate outworks termed 'ringforts'.[33] Several examples have now been totally excavated and show occupation sequences in the second or first centuries BC.[34] A late Iron Age origin may thus be suggested for this class, of which there are good examples in Cardiganshire; for example, Coed-parc Gaer (SN 592 514). Also seemingly of late Iron Age date are the numerous small, lightly-embanked oval, or frequently sub-rectangular enclosures, such as Ffynnon Wen, Y Ferwig (SN 2308 4929). The sub-rectangular enclosures appear to form a tightly circumscribed group comprising a minimum of twenty settlements lying west of a line drawn from New Quay to Llanybydder. They also appear prominently in the settlement spectrum of Pembrokeshire and west Carmarthenshire. Though none of these have been excavated in Cardiganshire, judging by the evidence from similar enclosures at Pen-y-coed[35] and Llangynog[36] in Carmarthenshire, and Whitton and Cae Summerhouse in Glamorgan,[37] they appear to be no earlier than the second century BC and seemingly continued to be built into the early first century AD.

[29]For a general discussion of the 'developed hillfort', see B. Cunliffe, 'Iron Age Wessex: continuity and change', *Aspects of the Iron Age in Central Southern Britain*, eds. B. Cunliffe and D. Miles (Oxford, 1984), 12–45.

[30]G. Williams, 'Merlin's Hill', *AW*, 26 (1986), 33.

[31]C. Daryll Forde *et al.*, 'Excavations at Pen Dinas, Aberystwyth', *Arch. Camb.*, 112 (1963), 149–50, for the pottery associated with the Period IV enlargement of the fort.

[32]For example, Moel y Gaer (Flints.), G. Guilbert, 'Moel y Gaer (Rhosesmor) 1972–1973: an area excavation in the interior', *Hillforts: Later Prehistoric Earthworks in Britain and Ireland*, ed. D. W. Harding (London, 1976), 303–17; idem, 'Planned hillfort interiors', *PPS*, 41 (1975), 203–21; J. Collis, 'A theoretical study of hill-forts', *Hill-Fort Studies: Essays for A. H. A. Hogg*, ed. G. Guilbert (Leicester, 1981), 66–76.

[33]G. Williams, 'Recent work on rural settlement in later prehistoric and early historic Dyfed', 31.

[34]Ibid, 34–40.

[35]K. Murphy, 'Excavations at Penycoed, Llangynog, Dyfed, 1983', *Carmarthenshire Ant.*, 21 (1985), 75–112.

[36]R. Avent, 'Excavations at Llangynog II, 1972', *Carmarthenshire Ant.*, 9 (1973), 33–52; 'Excavations at Llangynog II, 1974', *Carmarthenshire Ant.*, 11 (1975), 21–53.

[37]Whitton: M. G. Jarrett and S. Wrathmell, *Whitton: An Iron Age and Roman Farmstead in South Glamorgan* (Cardiff, 1981). Cae Summerhouse: J. L. Davies, 'Cae Summerhouse, Tythegston', *Morgannwg*, 17 (1973), 53–7 and D. M. Robinson (ed.), *Biglis, Caldicot and Llandough: Three Late Iron Age and Romano-British Sites in South-East Wales. Excavations 1977–79* (BAR 188: Oxford, 1988), x–xvii.

Social organization

There is still a great debate about the function and relative status of this settlement spectrum spanning half a millennium or more. Does it represent the continuation of a hierarchy of settlement throughout the Iron Age, or, as the excavation evidence suggests, were some settlements strictly circumscribed chronologically? Did their functions remain constant through time? What were their inter-relationships? What do we know of the social units? Social units are, at least in part, represented by evidence of size and complexity and the survival of internal structures within settlements, though we must bear in mind the likelihood of changes in social organization and, hence, of settlement over time. There is a strong likelihood, therefore, of a series of 'overlays' in the settlement record as investigated by archaeologists. Whilst there are grounds for suggesting that the larger or middle-sized hillforts were built by and served the needs of larger populations, and by implication had their own catchment areas or 'territories' in which other settlement types existed, there are no reliable means of establishing populations, 'territories' or relationships with cognate sites.[38]

In the absence of excavated evidence the presence of emplacements for buildings in the sloping interiors of some sites represents a rough, if by no means reliable, guide to their relative populations.[39] Four are visible within Caer Cadwgan, augmented by another two from partial excavation of the interior: the total could be doubled. Similarly, at Pen Dinas, Aberystwyth, about a dozen 'house-platforms' are visible within the 'South Fort', but the total of structures could have been considerably higher since terracing was unnecessary within the 'North Fort' and a substantial strip of level ground in the lee of the eastern rampart of the 'South Fort' could also have been built upon. These building emplacements with their post-settings, wall-trenches and drainage gulleys for the most part relate to circular or oval timber round-houses of a type common in the British Iron Age.[40] Elements of four such buildings were discovered just within the inner rampart at Caerau, Henllan; the best-preserved being 8.2 m in diameter, its wall set in a continuous trench, an internal ring of posts supporting the rafters and a doorway facing the interior of the site. Such houses, together with four-post structures—conventionally interpreted as storage-structures or granaries,[41] a solitary example of which was discovered just within the north gate at Pen Dinas, Aberystwyth, with others emerging at Caer Cadwgan—represent part of the recurring structural range of this period.

Although these buildings provide crude data for population estimates, they represent minima. Once again we have to interpolate data from elsewhere. On this basis the larger hillforts may have been high-status settlements, but whether they were occupied—permanently or otherwise —by chieftains and their retinues is impossible to say. Also of high status, it is suggested,[42] were

[38]J. Collis, 'A theoretical study of hill-forts', 66–7; B. Cunliffe, 'Iron Age Wessex: continuity and change', 12–45.

[39]G. Guilbert, 'Hill-fort populations: a sceptical viewpoint', *Hill-Fort Studies* (Leicester, 1981), 104–21.

[40]G. Guilbert, 'Double-ring roundhouses, probable and possible, in prehistoric Britain', *PPS*, 47 (1981), 299-317.

[41]H. Gent, 'Centralized storage in later prehistoric Britain', *PPS*, 49 (1983), 243–67.

[42]G. Williams, 'Recent work on rural settlement in later prehistoric and early historic Dyfed', 45–6.

the smaller forts and 'ringforts' which, it is thought, supported extended family units by reason of their densely packed interiors with numerous round-houses and storage-structures, with evidence biased towards 'consumption' rather than production. The lightly embanked, small enclosures with one or two round-houses and relatively few storage structures seemingly represent the lowest observable element (if not the very bottom) of the hierarchical system, family farms. The fruits of their labours will presumably have supported chiefs and their retinues residing in minor hillforts or 'ringforts', or if such existed, in the larger hillforts.

Élites are elusive in the archaeological record of the later first millennium in Cardiganshire. The evidence is confined to a few items of metalwork such as the bronze half-collar found within the hillfort of Pencoed-y-foel or the late La Tène brooches accompanying burials at Plas Gogerddan, and the necrological record itself. Indeed the artefactual range which can illuminate social and territorial distinctions is extremely meagre and limited to the more durable end of the artefactual spectrum—the metalwork, a few items of worked stone and glass beads. Pottery is very rare since the County shares a distinction common to much of Wales in this period; it is essentially aceramic. Potsherds, representing at least one vessel of Malvernian origin (see Appendix II, p. 273), have been found at Pen Dinas, Aberystwyth, but no local production is known. Its absence prohibits the drawing of any distinction between social groups (clans or tribes) inhabiting the County and their neighbours, both on grounds of common ethnicity or cultural links in respect of trade/exchange. However, this apparent concentration of 'foreign' material at Pen Dinas, coupled with the size and 'developed' character of this hillfort suggests that by the second or first century BC it served the needs of long-distance exchange networks, perhaps manipulated by a residential élite.

We may conclude that by the close of the millennium the County's inhabitants were organized on a tribal basis—a commonplace in the Celtic world. No certain political foci can be identified in the settlement record and a fragmented political structure is implied. The absence of a convenient pre-existing, urban-type focus for the region is implicit in the Roman creation of a *civitas* town for the dominant tribe—the Demetae—at Carmarthen.

The economy

It has already been argued that the settlement archaeology reflects socio-political differences which in turn reflect differing economic systems. Data pertaining to the latter is small, imprecise and scarcely quantifiable. Farming represents our starting-point since, as is the case with all primitive societies, the economy depended upon the winning of a livelihood from the land, either on a subsistence basis, or, as is being increasingly recognized, on the basis of a surplus giving way to specialization and interdependence.[43]

It is difficult to estimate the extent of arable or its relative importance against stock-raising. Because of later agricultural activity field-systems do not survive in those parts of the County where soil types suggest that arable could have been significant. Nothing much is known of the

[43]M. Jones, 'Regional patterns in crop production', *Aspects of the Iron Age in Central Southern Britain*, eds. Cunliffe and Miles, 120–5.

pastoral base either because of the overwhelmingly acid soils. At Pen Dinas, Aberystwyth, spindle-whorls and loom-weights indicate that sheep were either reared in the locality or their wool was brought to the fort, perhaps as part of a tithe. Spindle-whorls also occurred at Caerau, Henllan, whilst mutton was consumed here, sheep bones being represented among the small, fragmentary assemblage. Calcined bone was also recovered from Caer Cadwgan and Bryn Maen Caerau, Cellan, though it has not been analysed in respect of species and their relative proportions. The morphological characteristics of some settlements such as the 'south-western type' hillforts (Castell Nadolig being a prime example) or the ringforts with droveways (for example, Derry Ormond) also suggest the importance of stock-rearing. Certainly, animal husbandry will have played an important role in the food-producing economy, as well as producing the normal range of by-products. The evidence of palynology is crucial in this respect, as it is in determining evidence for cereal cultivation as opposed to consumption.

The large-scale deforestation of the environs of Tregaron Bog after c. 400 BC[44] and of the Ystwyth Forest and the lower slopes of the Ystwyth Valley in the third century,[45] indicated by pollen spectra, seems to relate entirely to pastoral activities, though in these marginal areas an arable input is inherently likely to be low or absent. Turner has demonstrated the minimal cereal pollen from Tregaron Bog in Iron Age/Romano-British contexts.[46] Clearance could even be the product of a search for building timber or firewood. More surprising, though, is the complete absence of cereal pollen in a pre-Roman buried soil beneath the *vicus* of the Roman fort at Trawscoed.[47]

Despite the overwhelmingly negative palynological evidence it is inherently likely that there was always an arable component in the economy. At Caer Cadwgan[48] excavations revealed much crop-processing waste to the rear of the rampart, though pollen analysis of the soils within the hillfort apparently indicate a change from a pastoral economy with some arable to a pastoral monoculture.

Querns, or the presence of four-post structures on settlement sites, might be considered good evidence for an arable element in the economy. No certain specimen of Iron Age quern has been recovered, however, through excavation in the County, and that recorded as having been found at Dinas Cerdin, Llandysul,[49] could well be of Roman or even later date. So may others so recorded. It is interesting to note that the excavation of ringforts in the Llawhaden group, where agriculture is attested through environmental evidence, produced only two querns, though prolific four-post structures.[50] By way of contrast the excavation of Pen-y-coed[51] produced evidence

[44]J. Turner, 'Post-Neolithic disturbance of British vegetation', *Studies in the Vegetational History of the British Isles*, eds. D. Walker and R. G. West (Cambridge, 1970), 81–96.

[45]J. A. Taylor, 'Chronometers and chronicles: a study of the Palaeo-environments of west central Wales', *Progress in Geography*, 5 (1973), 248–334.

[46]J. Turner, 'The anthropogenic factor in vegetational history. 1. Tregaron and Wixall Mosses', 78.

[47]F. Dilnot, 'Palaeobotanical investigations at the Roman fort excavations, Trawscoed' (unpublished University of Wales B.Sc. dissertation, Environmental Science, Aberystwyth, 1986).

[48]D. Austin et al., 'Caer Cadwgan', *AW*, 27 (1987), 36.

[49]C. S. Briggs, 'Quernstones', *AW*, 26 (1986), 32.

[50]G. Williams, 'Recent research on rural settlement in later prehistoric and early historic Dyfed', 44.

[51]See above, n. 35.

of a four-poster and two querns on a functioning farm, where, to judge from environmental data from waterlogged deposits, there was an overwhelming dominance of pastoralism over arable. Clearly, the absence or presence of querns and four-post structures may not be a reliable indicator of the relative importance of arable as against pastoralism.

What of external economic relationships? This is entirely dependent upon the evidence of durable objects, and as such amounts to very little. The Malvernian pottery from Pen Dinas, Aberystwyth, has already been mentioned, representing a rare outlier in west Wales.[52] That the vessel implies contact with an area some eighty miles distant is certain. It is the nature of that contact which is shadowy. It can scarcely imply trade in pottery as such, though it could well be that it was its contents which were valued (cf. the distribution of briquetage (VCP) salt-containers in Wales).[53] The reason for and the mechanics of its transportation remain unknown, as must the duration and volume of this 'trade'. It is not impossible that it represents contact of an altogether different kind, perhaps a family or marriage link. Even more difficult to account for is the gold stater of 'proto-Coritanian type' found in Penbryn parish (Appendix II, pp. 271–2). The only other Welsh example of this type of Celtic coin comes from the Great Orme's Head.[54] Like its northern counterpart the 'Penbryn' coin evidently arrived and was presumably held as bullion, since no gold coinage circulated in pre-Roman Wales. The mechanism which transmitted it from its east-Midland place of origin is unknown. The amber bead from Caerau, Henllan (Appendix II, p. 273), arrived as an easily portable trade good, and there is a possibility that the glass beads from Pen Dinas, Aberystwyth, Castle Hill, Aberystwyth and Caer Cadwgan (Appendix II, pp. 272–3) may be 'imports' to the County, though that from Pen Dinas—a Meare 'spiral' bead—is a clear western variant.[55]

Burial

If much needs to be learned about the day-to-day life of the County's Iron Age inhabitants their fate after death remains even more enigmatic. Though there are hints as to where we might seek answers the lack of a consistent, widely recurring burial rite remains. As such the County shares a problem common to much of western Europe in the Celtic Iron Age. Most of the dead were disposed of in a manner which leaves little or no archaeological trace.[56] Cremation is one such rite, now attested in several Welsh contexts.[57] Inhumations also occur, either within or in the vicinity

---

[52]D. P. S. Peacock, 'A petrological study of certain Iron Age pottery from western England', *PPS*, 34 (1968), 414-26.

[53]E. Morris, 'Prehistoric salt distributions: two case studies from western Britain', *BBCS*, 32 (1985), 336–79.

[54]For a list of Celtic coins found in Wales see G. C. Boon, 'British coins from Wales', *Biglis, Caldicot and Llandough*, ed. D. M. Robinson, 92.

[55]For the Pen Dinas bead see M. Guido, *The Glass Beads of the Prehistoric and Roman Periods in Britain and Ireland*, Society of Antiquaries Research Report 35 (London, 1978), 79, 189.

[56]R. Whimster, *Burial Practices in Iron Age Britain: A Discussion and Gazetteer of the Evidence c. 700 BC–AD 43* (BAR 98: Oxford, 1981).

[57]G. Williams, 'An Iron Age cremation deposit from Castle Bucket, Letterston, Pembrokeshire', *AW*, 25 (1985), 13–15.

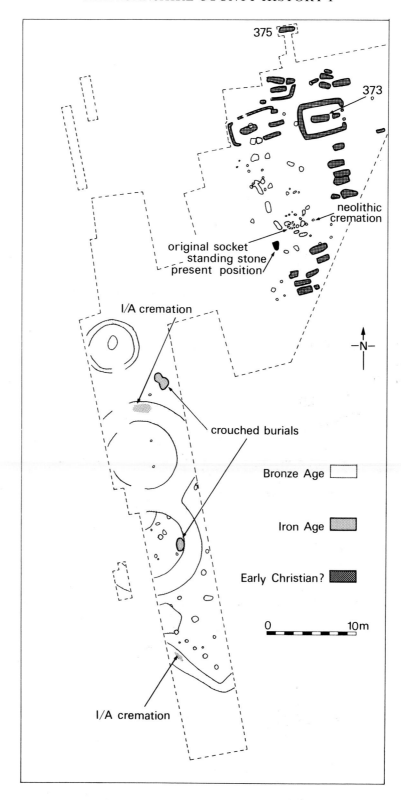

Fig. 42: Multi-period burials, Plas Gogerddan (after Murphy).

of settlements, some accompanied by grave-goods. In this respect the two bronze 'spoons' found within Castell Nadolig may have accompanied a burial, these objects frequently occurring in funerary contexts.[58] Cremations recorded within this hillfort could also have been of Iron Age date.[59] These putative burials apart, genuine Iron Age burials are only attested at Plas Gogerddan (Fig. 42).[60]

The setting for these comprises three axially arranged ring-ditches, one of which had a pit set slightly off-centre. Phosphate analysis suggests that it may have contained a cremation. A mass of burnt bone and charcoal was deposited in one of the ditches, whilst four to five pits set concentric to the ditches also contained burnt human bone. Radiocarbon dates suggest that the ring-ditches and cremations belong to the period c. 1000–200 BC. It has, furthermore, been suggested that inhumations covered by a low mound may have been placed on the ground surface within the ditches, the acid soil being responsible for their non-survival.

Barrows of this period are very rare and hitherto none have been recorded in Wales, though others may be conceivably masquerading as funerary monuments of the Bronze Age. Murphy suggests that the closest parallels for these burials seem to be Irish.[61]

At a time when one of these ring-ditches was already silted, a pit containing a crouched inhumation accompanied by a pair of late La Tène bronze fibulae was dug just within its margin; whilst a further two interlocking pits, dug between two of the ring-ditches, contained a crouched inhumation, possibly accompanied by a bronze brooch, and a further cremation was made in the silted ditch. These burials may well have been broadly contemporary as indicated by a radiocarbon date of 200 ± 60 bc for the cremation and a date range of the first century BC to early first century AD for the fibulae.

These interments cannot be regarded as the norm since it is presently impossible to determine what *is* the norm among the small number of Iron Age burials in Wales. It is likely that they represent the interments of a privileged group (as is so often the case in the prehistoric necrological record) and as such members of a discrete, local kin-group. Their location at the foot of the ridge dominated by the hillfort of Hen Gaer (Broncastellan) recalls a similar close relationship between cemeteries and early settlements dealt with elsewhere in this volume (II.7.c, pp. 402–3), but it is unwise to press this juxtaposition too far.

The Cardiganshire burials such as they are represent a not inconsiderable addition to the small number of Iron Age burials in Wales. These represent different funerary rites, some being situated close to or within settlements, as in England, with others now seemingly focused on the sites of early prehistoric ritual/funerary complexes, in this case a standing-stone and ring-ditch of a large barrow. Whimster has already noted a tendency for Iron Age burials to recur on similar sites in England.[62] Now that the Plas Gogerddan evidence indicates that the practice is prevalent in Wales as well, we have an important pointer towards future research.

[58] A. Way, 'Notices of certain bronze relics of a peculiar type assigned to the Late Celtic Period', *Arch. Camb.*, 26 (1870), 205–7; B. Cunliffe, *Iron Age Communities in Britain* (London, 1978), 318–19.
[59] 'Cardigan Meeting', *Arch. Camb.*, 15 (1859), 328.
[60] K. Murphy, 'Plas Gogerddan, Dyfed. A multi-period ritual and burial site', *Arch. J.* (forthcoming).
[61] See above, n. 60.
[62] See above, n. 56.

THE HILLFORTS AND LATER PREHISTORIC SETTLEMENTS

A. H. A. Hogg†

Some seventy hillforts survive in the County together with a large number of small enclosures, probably of similar date. To these can be added seven field-names or other evidence suggesting the former presence of hillforts.

The distribution pattern (Fig. 41)

Topographically the hillforts fall into two distinct groups.[1] The northern group comprises thirty-one (or perhaps thirty-three) surviving hillforts, and one 'gaer' name. All lie within the historic County. On the south the valley of the Wyre forms a boundary for this group, a boundary probably continued eastward by the Ystwyth, though the correct attribution of the forts at Penffrwdllwyd (SN 709 688) and Pen y Bannau (SN 742 669) is not certain and for convenience they have been arbitrarily assigned to the southern group.

The southern group seems to extend a little beyond the County boundary into Carmarthenshire, where eight forts may belong to it. Including these, the total in this group is forty-eight, and six 'gaer' field names or other evidence.

The appearance of two distinct groups may be illusory but they do display some rather different features and can conveniently be treated separately.

In what follows the lack of firm evidence will be very apparent. Nevertheless, some attempt at interpretation seems preferable to a purely factual description. Strictly, almost every statement needs to be hedged round with qualification and reservations, which would be wearisome and which are, therefore, omitted. So the following statements and deductions should be regarded only as reasonable hypotheses consistent with the very sparse evidence available, not as firmly established facts.

i) *The northern group*

Of the thirty-one identifiable sites, twenty-six are either univallate or seem to have been so originally. Treating these as corresponding to the first phase of Iron Age settlement in this area, the pattern which emerges is of a scatter of small defensible enclosures ranging from single-family

---

[1]Since the late Dr A. H. A. Hogg prepared this section, K. Ray and J. Thorburn, 'Ceredigion hillforts: recent survey evidence' (forthcoming), have cast doubt on the criteria for the division of the County's hillforts into a northern and southern group, a division first proposed by J. G. Williams in 1867 and thereafter further defined by Sayce in his paper on 'Hill top camps' (*Trans. Hon. Soc. Cymmrodorion* (1920–1), 97–134), with distributional, historical and linguistic criteria being adduced for group definition. Ray and Thorburn, however, have demonstrated that the only evidence from the hillforts themselves in support of such a division was the apparent break in their distribution, with a southern boundary for the northern about the line of the Wyre. Recent work by the authors has suggested that this supposed 'break' is a fallacy. No convincing archaeological arguments, such as differences in site morphology, can be made for retaining this division (Eds.).

farms of about 0.1 ha (0.25 acre) up to perhaps 2 ha (5 acres); the largest enclosure, at Nanteos (SN 615 789), is so overgrown that its area is uncertain. Omitting the half-dozen at each end of the range, the remaining fourteen all range between 0.25 and 0.75 ha (0.6 to 1.9 acres), but throughout the sequence there is no sharp break which can be regarded as separating 'farms' from 'villages.'

Bearing in mind the criticisms of the use of numerical calculations and having regard to the very arbitrary assumptions involved, any attempt at an estimate of the population of these sites may be looked upon as of questionable value. Nevertheless, provided these reservations are kept in mind, such calculations are of some use for they give a rough idea of the probable order of magnitude of the true figures and permit valid comparison with calculations for other areas made on the same basis.

Subject to these reservations, the following results apply to the northern group. The total known enclosed area in univallate forts is about 16 ha (0.6 ha per fort on average), which should perhaps be brought up to 18 ha to allow for 'lost' forts. The sites are close enough together to suggest that there were few, if any, unfortified settlements at this stage. Since the rare surviving huts are circular, the population density within the forts may reasonably be taken as similar to that found in Caernarfonshire,[2] roughly 20 per acre or 50 per hectare. This indicates a total population of the order of 900, the largest single settlement containing perhaps 100 people and the smallest 8. Assuming that the 'territory' associated with any fort may extend to a distance of 5 km, the area corresponding to the group would be nearly 500 square kilometres, 19 square kilometres per fort or very roughly an average population density of about 1.8 persons per square kilometre.

Anticipating the discussion of later developments, the final enclosed area, assuming that all forts remained in use, increased by 6 ha, corresponding (on the assumptions given) to an additional 300 persons and increasing the average density to 2.3 per square kilometres, but these figures have little real significance, being well within the range of uncertainty of calculations of this kind.

Assuming subsequent development to correspond to the appearance of multivallation, there seem to have been only five new forts, all bivallate, including one with wide-spaced ramparts, founded after the initial phase. Five or six univallate forts were modified to make them wholly or partly multivallate. One inland univallate fort (New Cross SN 628 772) was enlarged, its area being nearly trebled.

The most interesting changes took place at Pen Dinas, Aberystwyth. The earliest fort, on the northern knoll, enclosed 1.6 ha within an earthen rampart and accompanying ditch; the rampart was faced with a timber revetment. This was replaced by a fort of similar size on the southern knoll, protected by a much stronger, stone-revetted rubble rampart. Finally, a similar rampart was built to bring the whole top of the ridge, including both north and south knolls, within the enclosure, giving a final area of 3.8 ha (9.5 acres), nearly twice the size of any other fort in this group. In its very latest phases it may have been partly bivallate.

[2]A. H. A. Hogg, 'Garn Boduan and Tre'r Ceiri, excavations at two Caernarvonshire hill-forts', *Arch. J.*, 117 (1962), 22.

Unfortunately, there is no way of testing the attractive possibility that the original North Fort was merely a temporary base occupied during the construction of the first defences on the southern knoll. So far as its later history is concerned, the settlement seems to have prospered, at least in contrast to its neighbours, and its position would be appropriate to a trading-centre. Nevertheless, if that is the explanation of its prosperity, the goods imported must have been mainly perishable, for although the pottery recorded from the site indicates distant contacts it is hardly enough to imply a prosperous port-of-trade. In this context it is worthwhile recalling a suggestion made many years ago[3] that the hillforts in this area were deliberately sited to control the exploitation of the local lead ores, for Pen Dinas would be admirably suited as a port associated with such activity. Regrettably, though, there is as yet no evidence either way to support this hypothesis, for veins of lead are so plentiful in northern Cardiganshire that almost any hillfort would be near one. Nevertheless, the possibility deserves investigation. Evidence should be available, if anywhere, at Darren (SN 679 830), for part of the ditch of that fort follows the line of a vein which was later worked as opencast by the seventeenth-century miners.

It remains to attempt to date the stages in this hypothetical evolution of settlement. Excavations at sites in this group have failed to produce radiocarbon-dated sequences. The only reasonably firm evidence derives from sites in the south group, Bryn Maen Caerau, Cellan and Caer Cadwgan, where radiocarbon dates in the sixth century and seventh to fifth centuries BC respectively relate to a pre-rampart occupation at the former and the destruction of the Phase 1 gate at the latter. But, judging from evidence from elsewhere, not all such sites need be early. The interesting sequence at Pen Dinas, Aberystwyth, beginning with what may have been a Poundbury-type defence[4] on the North Fort, is undated, though Cunliffe considers this type of defence to date broadly to the fourth to third centuries BC. By the time that a Malvernian vessel had been deposited in a midden of the second or first century BC the site had been enlarged to encompass the whole ridge.

The development of multivallation has also been considered to be of chronological validity. Omitting the single example in this group of the use of wide-spaced ramparts at Cefn Blewog (SN 697 725), which is apparently unfinished, four new forts seem to have been built in this style and five older, univallate ones appear to have been modified. Multivallation, at least in this region, is probably to be assigned to the latest phase of the Iron Age.[5] The entrances are uninformative. Most, so far as surface evidence goes, are simple gaps. Gaer Fawr, Llanilar (SN 649 719), has inturns, but this style without guardchambers probably had a long life.

Very tentatively, then, the history of the northern group may be summarized as follows. Hillfort building probably began in the sixth/fifth century BC. One interpretation of the distribution pattern suggests that the impetus came from the arrival of new settlers at Pen Dinas (but see p. 222), their spread inland perhaps taking a generation or more and indicated archaeologically by the scatter of univallate enclosures. Towards the end of the second century BC Pen Dinas

[3]J. G. Williams, 'Ancient encampments near Aberystwyth', *Arch. Camb.*, 22 (1867), 284–91.
[4]B. Cunliffe, *Iron Age Communities in Britain* (London, 1978), 246.
[5]H. N. Savory, 'Welsh hillforts: a reappraisal of recent research', in D. E. Harding (ed.), *Hillforts: Later Prehistoric Earthworks in Britain and Ireland* (London, 1976), 279; B. Cunliffe, *Iron Age Communities in Britain*, 249–50.

Plate XI: Inscribed building stones, Llanio. (a) RIB 407. (*Copyright St David's University College, Lampeter*). (b) RIB 409. (*Copyright St David's University College, Lampeter*).

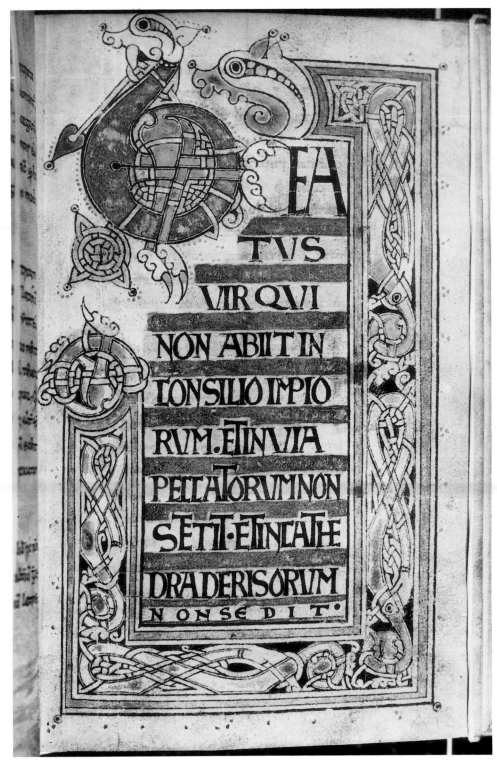

Plate XII: The beginning of Psalm 1 and the first full-page decoration in the Rhygyfarch Psalter from Llanbadarn Fawr. (*Copyright Trinity College, Dublin, MS 50, fol. 35r*).

Plate XIII: Plas Gogerddan: special grave 373, viewed from the east. (*Copyright Dyfed Archaeological Trust*).

Plate XIV: An example of a circular churchyard within a possible larger enclosure: St Silian's Church, Cribyn, SN 5715 5124, viewed from the north-east, showing a possible outer enclosure around the churchyard. (*Copyright Dyfed Archaeological Trust*).

Plate XVI: Llandysul: churchyard. (Crown copyright RCAHM (Wales)).

Plate XVII: Maes-llyn, Llangwyryfon. (Copyright National Museum of Wales).

Plate XV: Llanddewibrefi: churchyard.
(Crown copyright RCAHM (Wales)).

Plate XVIII: Near Dyffryn Bern, Penbryn. (*Crown copyright RCAHM (Wales)*).

Plate XIX: Crug-y-whil, Llanwenog. (*Copyright National Museum of Wales*).

Plate XX: Silian: church. (*Crown copyright RCAHM (Wales)*).

Plate XXI: Tregaron: church. (*Copyright National Museum of Wales*).

was extended as a univallate enclosure to its full extent, though the defences underwent some further modifications, perhaps becoming bivallate in part; and during the first century a few multivallate forts were constructed, either on new locations or by altering earlier defences.

ii) The southern group

This is less homogeneous than the northern group, and its boundary on the south is less sharply defined. Generally, the Teifi seems to form the limit, but Craig Gwrtheyrn and three adjacent forts on the Carmarthenshire side of the river fall naturally into this group, as do half a dozen sites mostly on the high ground south and west of Lampeter, four of which also lie in Carmarthenshire. Including these, the total number of forts in this group is forty-eight, together with six field-names or sites otherwise known. Of these, only thirty-one (including five in Carmarthenshire) seem either to be or to have been originally univallate. Three of these have stone walls. Gaer Wen (SN 396 471), on an inland promontory, and Gelli-gaer (SN 622 480) are without ditches. Craig Gwrtheyrn (SN 433 402) had a ditch and was reinforced with *chevaux-de-frise*; in its latest form multiple defences were added. Perhaps Pen-y-gaer, Llanybydder (SN 523 434), with slab revetments, should be added to this list. Savory's map of walled forts[6] supports the derivation suggested below for the introduction of hillforts into this area.

Nevertheless, although the distribution-pattern of the univallate forts in this group would be consistent with the idea of settlers moving from Pembrokeshire up the Teifi valley and over the hills north of it, it does not offer a strong argument for this hypothesis as against possible alternatives. The main support, such as it is, for the view that the appearance of hillforts implies new arrivals rather than indigenous development comes from the hint offered by the distribution of stone-walled forts and from the probability that conditions in the south of the County would resemble those in the north. Although the recently discovered fort at Craig-y-Gwbert (SN 159 502) offers protected beaches where small boats could be drawn up in safety, there seems to be no need to postulate sea-borne invaders to explain the southern group. The beach at Castell Bach (SN 303 536) is not sheltered and is not now easily accessible.

The enclosed areas are known for thirty of these forts. Two, Craig-y-Gwbert (2.9 ha) and Castell Goetre (SN 603 510, 2.8 ha but probably only 1.1 ha originally), are very much larger than any of the other twenty-eight, which total 17.3 ha, an average of 0.6 ha per fort. For all thirty forts, the total is 24.1 ha, which should perhaps be increased to, say, 28 ha to allow for possible 'lost' forts represented by field-names, corresponding, according to the same assumptions as for the north group, to some 1,400 persons. The warning must be repeated that this figure is primarily for comparative purposes and needs to be treated with reserve. The associated area is about 1,120 square kilometres, about 30 square kilometres per fort, or 1.3 persons per square kilometre.

The thirty forts range in size from 0.05 to 2.9 ha, but, omitting the smallest (which may be medieval) and the largest two, the remaining twenty-seven range from 0.1 to 1.5 ha. If the half-dozen at the end of the range are omitted, the figures for the remaining fifteen are 0.36 to 0.88 ha. The general character of the occupation is thus closely similar to that of the north group, though rather less intense.

[6]H. N. Savory, 'Welsh hillforts: a reappraisal of recent research', 452, Fig. 10.

With one exception, to be discussed below, the later development of the southern group seems to have been similar to that in the north. Seven new multivallate forts were built and four formed by altering earlier univallate sites. It is noteworthy that four of the apparently new forts were on inland promontories; of the altered sites, one was on a promontory and one on a cliff-edge, also inland. There is nothing known in the south group to compare with the development of Pen Dinas, but the largest fort, Castell Goetre, seems to have developed from an earlier enclosure of only 1.1 ha.

The exceptional development referred to earlier was the appearance of multivallate enclosures with wide-spaced ramparts such as Castell Nadolig (SN 298 504; Fig. 43). Characteristically, a small inner ring, presumably enclosing the actual dwellings, is surrounded by one or more ramparts all widely spaced, which can be regarded as providing protection for cattle. The type has a very markedly south-western distribution in Britain. Indeed, the unfinished fort on Cefn Blewog (SN 697 725), within the area of the north group, seems to be the most northerly example known. There is no dating evidence from Cardiganshire. What evidence is available, mostly from Devon and Cornwall, suggests that the type originated in the third/second century BC.

Five of these sites are known within the area of the southern group (Gaer Pwntan, SN 282 494; Castell Nadolig, SN 298 504; Henllan, SN 358 402; Cwmtudu, SN 360 581; Cilcennin, SN 529 590) and imply the introduction of cattle-raising as a specialized activity on a fairly large scale, possibly even trading. Other forts seem to have annexes (Cribyn Gaer, SN 520 509; Caer Argoed SN 616 710; New Cross, SN 628 772; Gaer Fawr, SN 649 719; Darren, SN 679 830). Some may be the result of superimposing two enclosures of different date, but some may correspond to modifications of an earlier fort to fulfil the same purpose as the wide-spaced ramparts; all but Cribyn Gaer are in the north group. At Castell Goetre, also in its final phase, one of the two compartments could have formed a separate area for cattle. For Wales as a whole, the evidence for pastoralism is well displayed by Savory.[7]

It would seem reasonable to assume that the chronological evolution of the southern group was essentially similar to that in the north. The small amount of dating evidence has already been discussed relative to the two groups as a whole. As noted above, the appearance of wide-spaced multivallate forts implies the development of pastoralism, perhaps to be dated very roughly to about the beginning of the second century BC. Continued occupation of some sites in the group, at least to the close of the millennium or even later, is indicated by the decorated bronze half-collar from Pencoed-y-foel (SN 425 428) and the pair of 'spoons' from Castell Nadolig (SN 298 504), both regarded as products of a western school of metalworking.[8] In the south group, as in the north, there is no evidence at present for the continued occupation of any hillfort after the Roman conquest.

[7]Ibid., Fig. 13.
[8]H. N. Savory, *Guide Catalogue of the Early Iron Age Collections* (Cardiff, 1976), 40–1.

APPENDIX I: GAZETTEER OF HILLFORTS AND ENCLOSURES

A. H. A. Hogg† and J. L. Davies

A list of hillforts in Cardiganshire was first published by A. H. A. Hogg over thirty years ago.[1] Since that time there have been additions to the factual evidence with the publication of the report on the excavations at Pen Dinas, the excavations at Bryn Maen Caerau and Caer Cadwgan and the discovery of a considerable number of new sites—hillforts, such as Tre-Coll and Craig-y-Gwbert, and especially enclosures, particularly in the south of the County. Background knowledge, derived from research elsewhere in Britain, has also greatly increased. The main immediate effect of this increased information has been to show that the development of hillforts, both as a class and individually, is very much more complex than previously supposed; satisfactory generalization has not yet become possible again. Nevertheless, some attempt at the explanation of the evolution of the defences seems desirable, at least on the more complex sites. In describing the remains, therefore, the aim has been to give an objective description of what was visible when the site was visited, followed where appropriate by a more subjective interpretation (obviously, complete objectivity in description is usually unattainable in practice). Except for Pen Dinas, the accompanying plans are not generally accurate surveys but are based on the older 1 : 2500 OS maps revised from examination of the actual remains. The form-lines are merely intended to give a general indication of the form of the ground; they are not accurate contours, being interpolated and sketched in using those on the 6-inch and 1 : 2500 OS maps.

The contents, arrangement, and classification (or rather the absence of classification) require a brief explanation.

Although this History is only concerned with Cardiganshire, the hillforts, as explained above, have sometimes been thought to fall into two fairly well-defined groups, one of which includes a few sites which now lie in Carmarthenshire. For completeness and to assist identification these outliers have been included in their appropriate places in the Gazetteer but without detailed description. Other forts in Carmarthenshire and Pembrokeshire are shown on the map but are not listed. 'Gaer' farm or field names are also noted but only when they do not seem to apply to a fort/enclosure otherwise recorded and where their situation supports the implication that a fort/enclosure formerly existed there. A supplementary list of rejected sites includes such names when inappropriately situated, as well as sites which have been or might be regarded as hillforts but which do not now seem to be such.

The lists are arranged in numerical order of the 10 km squares of the National Grid (and thus also of the sheets of the 1 : 2500 map). Within each square, the entries are in numerical order of six-figure grid references. Since a site is generally identified by name, though not always by the same name, an alphabetical index which leads to the appropriate 10 km square is also given.

In each entry the name of the site is followed by the approximate area in hectares (1 ha = 2.47 acres) where known, parish and grid reference. The parish is generally taken from the index to the OS *Map of Southern Britain in the Iron Age*; since the civil and ecclesiastical parishes have different

---

[1] A. H. A. Hogg, 'List of hill-forts in Cardiganshire', *BBCS*, 19 (1962), 354–66.

boundaries, and these are liable to administrative alteration, the site may often appear in other records under a different parish name. The descriptive entries which follow are mostly based on visits made by A. H. A. Hogg between 1955 and 1965, but some of the major sites have been re-examined. All are simple ovals unless otherwise noted. The bibliographical references given are only those which seem to be of some value; no attempt has been made to include every mention. Unfortunately, many of the thirty or so plans published by F. S. Wright and I. T. Hughes are inaccurate in detail and some are seriously misleading even as sketches.

In the 1962 list the entries were classified under various headings but such an arrangement seems presently undesirable since it imposes on the data an interpretation which is partly subjective and may be misleading.

Alphabetical list of hillforts and enclosures by 10 km square

All are in 100 km square
SN

R = Rejected Sites

Aberdeuddwr, Castell	35
Aberystwyth, Pen Dinas	58
Allt-goch, Caer	68
Allt-goch, Castell	55
Allt y Cadno	24
Allt y Ddinas	34
Argoed, Caer	67
Bach: see next word	
Banc y Castell	68
Banc y Gaer, Blaen-plwyf	57
Betws Bledrws, Coed-parc	55
Blaen-Barre, Caerau	34
Blaen-Igau, Castell	35
Blaen Nant	24
Blaen-plwyf, Banc y Gaer	57
Bow Street, Hen Gaer	68
Broncastellan	68
Bronfre Ganol	45
Bryngwyn-mawr	68
Bryn Maen Caerau	54
Bryn Teifi Farm	33
Bwa-drain, Castell	77
Cae Perth Caerau	44
Caer, Caerau: see next word	
Cadwgan, Caer (Gelli-gaer)	64
Capel Bangor	68
Capel Seion, Hen Gaer	67

Carreg-wen, Castell	67
Castell, Castle: see next word	
Castell	77
Castle Hill, Foel Dihewid	45
Cawrence	24
Cefn Blewog	67
Cellan, Gelli-gaer (Caer Cadwgan)	64
Ceulan-a-Maesmor	68
Cerdin, Dinas	34
Cilcennin	55
Clawdd Buarth	44
Clyn yr Ynys	15
Cnwc y Bugail	67
Coed Allt Fedw	67
Coed Lluest	67
Coed-parc Gaer	55
Coed-parc Gaer, E and NE of	55
Craig Gwrtheyrn	44
Craig Pentre	35
Craig-y-Gwbert	15
Cribyn Clottas	55
Cribyn Clottas, Gaer Fach	55
Cribyn Gaer	55
Crugiau, Castell	35
Crug Llwyn Llwyd	24
Crug y Balog	34
Cwm Castell, Llan-narth	45
Cwmtudu, Castell Bach	35
Darren	68
Deri Odwyn, Pen-y-gaer	66
Derry Ormond	55

Dinas: see next word	
Disgwylfa, Castell	67
Dol-llan, Yr Hen Gastell	44
Dyffryn Saith Farm	25
Elerch, Pen Dinas	68
Esgair Graig	34
Esgair Nantyrarian	78
Fach: see next word	
Fach, Gaer	55
Fawr: see next word	
Fawr, Gaer	67
Felin Cwrrws	34
Fflemish, Castell	66
Ffynnon Groes, Castell	35
Ffynnon Wen	24
Fisher's Arms (Bryn-maen Caerau)	54
Flwyn	54
Foel, Y	56
Foel Dihewid, Castle Hill	45
Gaer: see next word	
Gaer	24
Gaergywydd	68
Garreg Lwyd	76
Garth Penrhyn-coch	68
Gelli-gaer, see Caer Cadwgan	64
Gilfach-hafel	57
Glaneirw	24
Glan-ffrwd	68
Glan Rhyd	65
Goetre, Castell	65
Gogerddan	68
Goginan Fach	68
Gors	34
Gors (New Cross)	67
Grogwynion, Castell	77

Key

CUC = Cambridge University Collection of Aerial Photographs
PRN = Dyfed Archaeological Trust Provisional Record Number

SN 14

Gwbert Hotel Enclosure PRN 8899	Y Ferwig	161 499

SN 15

Craig-y-Gwbert (2.9 ha)	Y Ferwig	159 502

This headland is almost isolated by two small coves which cut into the promontory from the north-west and south-west, leaving only a narrow isthmus for access. The position has been strengthened by a rampart following the north-west margin of the coves, with a gap at the end of the isthmus. North of the gap the bank is about 10 m wide and 1.50 m high, apparently of earth and rubble, with no revetment visible, except perhaps at the entrance passage which has been eroded by modern use. South of the gap it is cut into by a limekiln, beyond which it is reduced to a scarp. The interior, much of which is base rock with only a thin soil cover, displays no ancient features.

The coves, which are easily accessible, have sandy beaches on which small boats could be drawn up above high-water mark.
Hogg & Williams, *AW*, 17 (1977), 15.

Clun yr Ynys   Y Ferwig   16 51
Hillfort
PRN 5323

SN 24

Crug Llwyn   Cardigan   202 484
Llwyd
(0.8 ha)
A single rampart, now reduced to a scarp some 4 m high, cuts across the neck of an inland spur. The remains have been heavily eroded by former cultivation and the position of the entrance is uncertain.

Llan-y-cwm   Y Ferwig   208 493
Cropmark of enclosure.
PRN 8384

Tre Cefn Isaf   Y Ferwig   2106 4941
Cropmark of sub-rectangular enclosure.
CUC BZW 66; PRN 12135

Cawrence   Llangoedmor   226 456
(c. 0.8 ha)
Possible cropmark of univallate, kidney-shaped enclosure situated on level ground.
Meridian Airmaps, 1955, 220/240, 12256–7; PRN 11267.

Waunlle   Y Ferwig   2257 4912
(Pl. VIa)
Cropmark of enclosure/hill-fort.
PRN 5838

Treferedd   Y Ferwig   227 499
Uchaf
Cropmark of enclosure/hill-fort.
PRN 8386

Ffynnon Wen   Y Ferwig   2308 4929
Cropmark of rectangular enclosure.
CUC BZW 71; PRN 8388

Rhos y   Y Ferwig   230 499
Gadarn Uchaf
CUC BZL 69; PRN 8387

Portis   Llangoedmor   231 470
An L-shaped cropmark, probably representing about a third of an enclosure of *c.* 30 × 45 m, whose other two sides appear to be coincident with surviving hedge-banks. It is apparently bisected internally.
Meridian Airmaps 1955, 220/240, 12254–5; PRN 11268; Stenger, *AW*, 25 (1985), 47.

Onnen-deg   Llandygwydd   235 434
(0.25 ha)
A promontory between a small stream and the flood-plain of the Teifi has been fortified by a straight length of bank and ditch, *c.* 75 m long, 18 m wide and 3 m in overall height, with an entrance near the centre. Although the choice of site is unusual, it seems likely to be pre- rather than post-Roman.

Caer   Llandygwydd   246 433
Llandygwydd
A circular enclosure of some 23 m in diameter formed by a bank about 1.5 m high. It is on a gentle slope falling to the south-west. The site has been damaged by ploughing.

Allt y Cadno   Llandygwydd   263 463
Three sides of a sub-rectangular enclosure encompassing an area of about 60 × 45 m.
Meridian Airmaps, 1955, 220/240, 12193–4; PRN 11269; Stenger, *AW*, 25 (1985), 47.

Blaen Nant   Aber-porth   274 491
Cropmark of rectilinear enclosure measuring about 50 × 40 m.
Meridian Airmaps, 1955, 220/240, 12243–4; PRN 11270; Stenger, *AW*, 25 (1985), 47.

Glaneirw   Llandygwydd   277 487
Cropmark of rectilinear enclosure measuring about 35 × 30 m.
Meridian Airmaps, 1955, 220/240, 11904–5; Stenger, *AW*, 25 (1985), 47.

Gaer   Llandygwydd   291 428
Hill-fort
PRN 2084

Gaer Pwntan   Penbryn   292 494
(2.6 ha
(1.4 int))
This appears to be the remains of a wide-spaced multivallate hill-fort of the concentric enclosure type, now almost destroyed by ploughing and quarrying. The inner circuit was of oval plan, roughly 150 m east–west by 120 m; the outer about 180 m in diameter. The interspace between the ramparts varies from 15–30 m.
A. Fox, 'South-western hill-forts', in S. S. Frere (ed.), *Problems of the Iron Age in Southern Britain* (London, 1961), 37.

Pontdaniel   Betws Ifan   294 475
Hill-fort/enclosure.
PRN 5848

Ty Hen   Penbryn   286 517
(*c.* 0.25 ha)
Cropmark of a roughly rectangular, univallate enclosure situated on a level shelf on a hillside. A 30 m stretch of the western rampart was visible in 1987.
PRN 2104; CUC BZX 15; *Arch. Camb.*, 14 (1859), 328; *Arch. Camb.*, 17 (1862), 215–16. Additional information from Dr K. Ray for Ceredigion Archaeological Survey.

SN 25

Dyffryn Saith   Penbryn   284 512
Farm
A promontory fort occupying a west-facing spur, with steep scarps on all sides except the east where a broad, outward-curving and much-eroded bank is situated. A slight hollow to its east may possibly represent a ditch.
Information from Dr K. Ray for Ceredigion Archaeological Survey.

Castell   Penbryn   298 504
Nadolig
(3.2 ha
(0.8 int))
(Fig. 43; Pl. Vc)
The site occupies the summit of a gently rounded hill. Its ramparts mostly survive in fair condition, though incorporated in modern field-banks whilst the whole area has been cultivated. It is an example of a concentric enclosure with widely-spaced ramparts.

The inner enclosure is defined by a bank 6 m wide and 1.5 m high with a ditch of similar dimensions, now almost filled. A rough stone outer revetment to the bank is almost certainly modern. On the east there is a gap of almost 40 m in the circuit. A modern field-bank runs close to its approximate line but is slighter than those which elsewhere follow the course of the rampart, and the difference in level between the upper and lower sides is small, far less than where the neighbouring stretch of outer rampart has been ploughed. The rampart here may have been completely levelled before the present field system was laid out but it seems more likely that the above gap was original. The rampart north of the gap is linked to the outer rampart by a scarp representing a ploughed-out bank, and the field-bank in the corresponding position south of the gap is substantial and may indicate the existence of a similar bank.

The outer rampart is slightly smaller than the inner. There is no visible ditch but lusher grass suggests that one may have originally existed. To the east there is a small, crescentic annexe of about 0.5 ha protected by a similar bank.

On the east the outer banks have been partly levelled by ploughing but seem to have been composed mainly of earth, with no revetment. Owing to modern disturbance, the entrance cannot be identified.

Two bronze 'spoons' were found within the enclosure (*Arch. Camb.*, 17 (1862), 214–15).

The folk-tale implied by the site-name seems to be lost.

SN 33

Bryn Teifi   Orllwyn Teifi   3838 3980
Farm (0.2 ha)

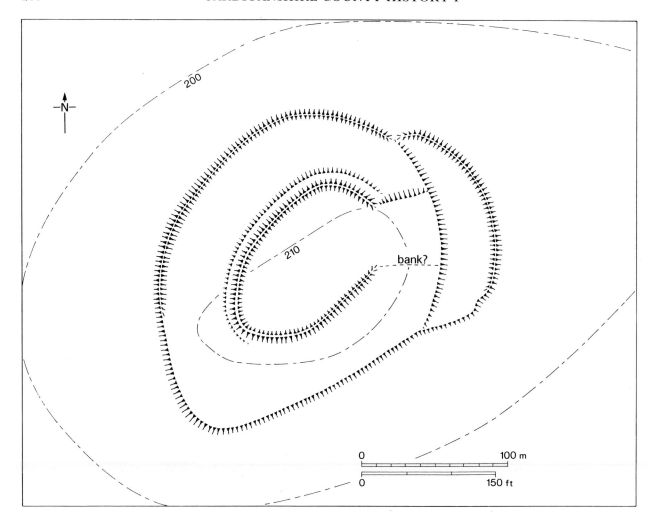

Fig. 43: Castell Nadolig.

Cropmark of a sub-rectangular, univallate enclosure, about 45 m square, with a single entrance.
CUC BVP 036.

SN 34

Esgair Graig   Betws Ifan   3028 4633
A much-reduced circular earthwork, about 40 m in diameter, sited on a spur.
Meridian Airmaps, 1955, 230/240, 18101–2; Stenger, *AW*, 25 (1985), 47; PRN 12118.

Allt y Ddinas   Betws Ifan   317 432
Hillfort/enclosure.
PRN 5764

Pant y Bwla   Betws Ifan   316 444
A spur on the west side of the River Dulas has been fortified by a single bank and ditch, now almost entirely destroyed.

Crug y Balog   Troed-yr-aur   341 452
(*c.* 1.0 ha)
A slight earthwork, with no visible ditch, almost obliterated by a field-bank, delimits an oval enclosure of about 140 × 90 m. The location of the entrance is uncertain. The situation is a commanding one but the slopes of the hill are very gentle.

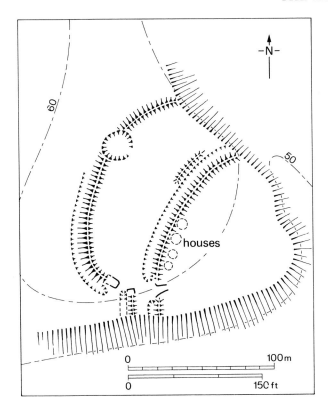

Fig. 44: Caerau, Henllan.

Caerau, Henllan	Orllwyn Teifi	358 402

(1.2 ha)
(Fig. 44)
The fort occupies an inland promontory, the northern side of which falls to the Teifi and the north-east to a tributary. The defences, comprising two widely spaced ramparts, crossed the level ground between these valleys. The site is a good example of a wide-spaced multivallate enclosure of south-western type.

The site was excavated prior to the building of a prisoner-of-war camp, having been previously under plough. Only a few short and barely visible traces of the ramparts remain but much of the interior is still open.

Both ramparts were essentially similar, being composed of upcast from ditches, faced on both sides with a rough stone revetment. They are unlikely to have stood more than 2 m high, and were separated from the ditches by berms 0.6–1.3 m wide. The ditches were 6–8 m wide but only

about 0.8 m deep and flat-bottomed. The inner had a low, unrevetted counterscarp bank about 5 m wide.

The outer entrance was a simple, 6 m wide gap between the rampart ends, but half obstructed by the ditch, with no trace of timberwork. At the inner entrance the rampart ends were thickened, giving a passage 7 m long, tapering from 6 to 3.6 m wide at its inner end where a pair of post-holes indicated the position of a gate.

Clearance of a strip about 9 m wide and 110 m long against the rear of the inner rampart exposed traces of four circular timber buildings. The best preserved was almost circular and 8.2 m in diameter. Its wall was about 0.1 m thick, composed of small posts probably adzed flat and set in a slot cut into the bedrock. The roof was supported by a ring, probably of seven posts located 1–2 m within the wall; four of these had been renewed, one twice. A doorway 2 m wide faced the interior. Six other posts, of uncertain relative date, may have been for partitions or additional roof supports.

The other buildings were probably similar but had lost the wall-slot owing to ploughing. There were also indications of a four-post setting 2 m square, and near the edge of the promontory was a line of post-holes indicating a fence.

Finds were few and gave no evidence for dating. They comprised two beads (one of amber), a spindle-whorl, two iron nails and a piece of iron slag.
Williams, *Arch. Camb.*, 96 (1945), 226–40.

Felin Cwrrws Hillfort	Llandyfrïog	3515 4112

PRN 3243

Penbeili Mawr	Llangynllo	3663 4352

Crop-mark of a rectangular, ?ditched platform about 55 × 40 m.
Meridian Airmaps, 1955, 23/240, 34844–5; PRN 12119

Caerau, Blaen-Barre	Troed-yr-aur	360 495

(0.4 ha)
(Fig. 45)
A blunt spur projecting from ground rising gently towards the south has been fortified by two banks

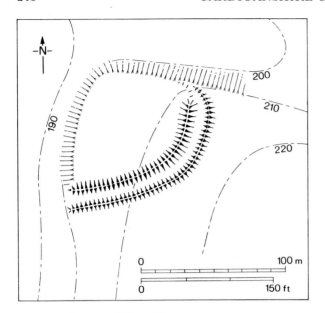

Fig. 45: Caerau, Blaen-Barre.

on that side, the rest of the circuit being merely scarped. The banks are of equal height, nearly 2 m above ground level, with a median ditch. The whole system measures about 30 m wide by 5 m high overall. The entrance was probably a simple gap at the north end of the banks.

Near Gors   Orllwyn Teifi   389 414
Crop-mark of a circular, univallate enclosure, about 45 m in diameter, with a ditch 3.5–4.5 m wide and a single entrance.
CUC BVP 038

Dinas Cerdin   Llandysul   386 470
(0.5 ha)
This fort occupies a raised knoll at the southern end of a steep-sided spur. It is oval, measuring about 100 m north–south by 60 m wide. Around most of the circuit the rampart is single, now a scarp 5–6 m high with a silted ditch forming a shelf at its base. Where it crosses the spur on the north there is an additional outer rampart and the system, which measures some 30 m overall, comprises an outer scarp 3–4 m high, a shelf 3 m wide and then the main rampart; this has been partly robbed, but still stands over 2 m high externally and nearly 10 m thick. The entrance, a simple gap, is a little west of the northern apex of the enclosure. The interior seems undisturbed.
Hughes, *TCAS*, (1930), Fig. 2, 112.

Gaer, Troed-   Llandysul   390 460
y-rhiw
(0.2 ha)
A slight bank and ditch, now about 4 m in overall width and 0.6 m high, forms an oval enclosure at the southern tip of a spur. The entrance is a simple gap on the south-east.

Gaer Wen   Llandysul   396 471
(now Garn Wen, Pen-y-graig)
(0.5 ha)
A blunt, steep-sided spur has been fortified by a slightly curved wall across its base. The wall seems to have been mainly of stone with a small admixture of earth. It is much damaged but still stands about 6 m wide and 2 m high. There seems to have been no ditch, but the presence of a ruined cottage and garden prevents certainty.
    The name Gaer Wen is that given in the Tithe Award survey.

SN 35

Caer Lwyd   Penbryn   301 524
(0.5 ha)
A sub-rectangular, univallate enclosure measuring about 75 × 65 m with its interior sloping gently from west to east. It is bordered by a steep crag on the south. The rampart on the east is overlain by a hedge whilst the northern arc has been much reduced through ploughing. The western arc has been damaged by quarrying.
Additional information from Dr K. Ray for Ceredigion Archaeological Survey.

Castell Bach,   Penbryn   303 536
Penbryn
(*c.* 0.6 ha)
A straight bank and ditch, 100 m long and 18 m wide overall and more than 2 m high cuts across the base of a promontory between the sea-cliff and a small stream-valley to the south. The entrance gap and accompanying causeway across the ditch lies near the mid-point. The interior appears to have been ploughed.

Llangrannog   314 512
A promontory fort situated on a northward-jutting spur. The defences comprise a short length of bank, apparently without an accompanying ditch. Much of the neck of the promontory has

been lost to coastal erosion and the remainder of the bank is similarly threatened.
Information from Dr K. Ray for Ceredigion Archaeological Survey.

Castell Ffynnon Groes   Penbryn   317 529

A sub-rectangular enclosure lying just south of the crest of a low hill. Only one section of the bank survives clearly, along the north side. Part of the southern circuit may survive in a field-bank, but the remainder of the site has been almost wholly ploughed-out.
Information from Dr K. Ray for Ceredigion Archaeological Survey.

Craig Pentre   Llangrannog   311 538

Though recognized as a potential site by the Ordnance Survey in 1973 it was thought to be too severely damaged by quarrying for certain attribution. It has since been verified as a small fort from the air, and surveyed by the CAS. It is situated in a scarp-edge position on the end of a long, seaward-running spine of land. A crag standing high above the Nant Hawen forms the eastern side of the fort, whilst a simple, curving bank encompasses the north, south and west sides. Two or three areas within are occupied by quarries; much of the rest is taken up with seven platforms scarped into the hillside.
PRN 1373; Ray and Thorburn, 'Ceredigion hillforts: recent survey evidence' (forthcoming).

Pen Dinas Lochdyn   Llangrannog   315 549
(*c.* 1.08 ha)

The fort occupies a strong position on a steep-sided coastal hill with exceptional views. The summit is occupied by a Ministry of Defence tracking station whose building has damaged the interior. The defences are poorly preserved but whether this is because some parts were never constructed to any great size or because there has been subsequent erosion or damage is not entirely clear. The best surviving portions lie towards the 'weaker' southern end of the hill, though generally reduced to scarps, nowhere more than 2 m high. On the west the scarp appears to run within the line of a natural drop, producing a slight terrace with a counterscarp as an additional defence at a

point where access is marginally easier. The Ceredigion Archaeological Survey suggests that the terrace represents the line of an almost completely filled ditch, lengths of which survive along the south and south-western part of the circuit.

The original entrance probably lay south of the point where the modern access road breaches the defences but the whole area has been disturbed by earlier tracks. The interior is fairly level and may have been ploughed in the past. The CAS have noted two narrow, elliptical platforms facing north-east immediately to the north of the modern entrance gap.
B. and H. Burnham, *Hillfort Study Group Meeting 1988: Lampeter and the Surrounding Area* (Lampeter, 1988), 10–12; Ray and Thorburn, 'Ceredigion hillforts: recent survey evidence' (forthcoming).

Castell, Blaen-Igau   Penbryn   341 506
(0.3 ha)

The enclosure is sub-rectangular, bounded on the north and west, where the ground falls steeply, by a scarp some 2 m high, and on the south and east by a bank and ditch 15 m across and 3 m high. There are gaps at the north corner and near the middle of the south side. The latter was probably the entrance.

Gaer Wen   Llandysiliogogo   346 563
(*c.* 0.5 ha)

This nearly circular enclosure is sited in a hollow on the south-east facing slope of the coastal ridge. The bank was composed of earth and rubble, the eastern half of which has been extensively damaged by ploughing. The ditch, if such existed, has been obliterated. The site can never have been defensible. Irregular, stony hollows suggest the former presence of buildings within.

Castell Crugiau   Penbryn   354 528
(*c.* 0.2 ha)

This site has been completely over-ploughed, with the exception of its south-east corner. It appears to have been truly rectangular with fairly sharp angles, measuring about 50 × 45 m. The bank seems to have been doubled on the north. The position is not naturally strong but has excellent views.
PRN 1386

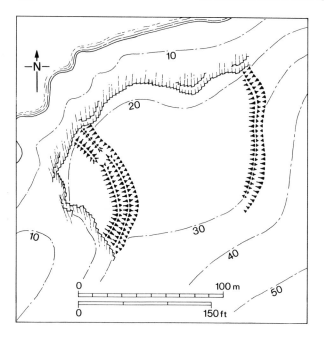

Fig. 46: Castell Bach, Cwmtudu.

| Castell | Llandysiliogogo | 355 555 |
Aberdeuddwr
(0.2 ha)

This univallate enclosure is rectangular with fairly sharp corners, and measures about 60 × 45 m. The bank is about 10 m wide and 2.5 m high fronted by a 3.5 m wide ditch, rock-cut to a depth of more than 1.5 m. The present entrance near the south-east corner appears to be a modern break, and access may have originally been via a bridge. A. H. Williams suggests that it may have been the original Caerwedros.

PRN 1357; A. H. Williams, *Introduction to the History of Wales* I, 122.

| Castell Bach, | Llandysiliogogo | 360 581 |
Cwmtudu
(1.1 ha)
(Fig. 46)

The fort occupies a coastal promontory. Although appearing to be an example of the 'South-Western Type' of multivallate enclosures with wide-spaced ramparts, the defences may well be of different periods. The site comprises a double set of curving banks and ditches enclosing a small area of cliff-edge (about 0.1 ha), and beyond this an almost level area bounded by scarps running to the east

and north-east. The north-east margin of this level area is defined by a curving bank and ditch broadly concentric with the inner defences.

The inner defences comprise two banks: the inner about 7 m wide and 2 m high with a section exposed in the eroding cliff-face. The outer bank is about half the size of the inner. The system measures about 12 m wide overall.

The outer defences are separated from the inner by about 100 m. They consist of a bank and ditch, 7 × 2 m overall. A stone revetment is visible on the inner face.

A recent survey suggests that the site has a complex history. A small bank within the outer area appears from aerial photographic evidence to form a roughly rectangular enclosure, the west side of which runs beneath part of the outer bank. The eroding cliff-face also seems to show that the inner enclosure initially comprised a single bank and ditch, subsequently remodelled apparently at the same time as an outer bank and ditch were first built. This sequence was apparently followed by a rebuild of the outer bank. There is some evidence for a possible entrance at the northern end of the inner enclosure.

Additional information from Dr K. Ray for Ceredigion Archaeological Survey.

SN 44

| Castell | Llandysul | 408 418 |
Gwilym

A slight bank, with no visible ditch, apparently formed the corner of a rectangular enclosure. The site is heavily overgrown and largely obliterated.
PRN 7658

| Gaer, near | Llandysul | 419 456 |
Gyfeile

This is indicated on the first edition of the Ordnance Survey one-inch map, but nothing is now visible.

| Yr Hen | Llanfihangel- | 421 409 |
Gastell, Dol- ar-arth
llan

This small, univallate enclosure is in Carmarthenshire but seems to belong to the south Cardiganshire group of forts.
Carmarthenshire, RCAHM *Inventory* (London, 1917), no. 394; *BBCS*, 16 (1954), 64.

Pencoed-y-foel Llandysul 425 428
(1.5 ha)

The position is strong but the defences measure only 11 by 2.5 m overall, comprising a bank, ditch and slight counterscarp. The crest of the bank has been robbed, as it is likely to have consisted largely of rubble. The entrance lay probably on the north but here the rampart has been destroyed. The interior is covered with small, shallow quarries for stone (D. C. Evans's 'huts'). A bronze half-collar, probably of the first century BC, was found here (*Proc. Clifton Antiq. Club.*, 2 (1896), 210).

Evans identifies the site with Caer Hyfaidd, mentioned in a charter of Talley Abbey. Hyfaidd was the name of a ninth-century *regulus* of Dyfed. Hughes, *TCAS* (1929), Fig. 5; Evans, *TCAS*, 9 (1931), 24; H. N. Savory, *Guide-Catalogue of the Early Iron Age Collections* (Cardiff, 1976), No. 30, Pl. IVb.

Craig Llanfihangel- 433 402
Gwrtheyrn ar-arth
(1.5 ha)

Traditionally associated with the legend of the death of Gwrtheyrn (Vortigern) in the early ninth-century *Historia Brittonum*, this is one of the major hillforts of the region and, though in Carmarthenshire, belongs naturally to the south Cardiganshire group. It is defended by a stone wall and on the south-west (entrance) side by two further banks and a belt of *chevaux de frise*. Gardner, *Arch. Camb.*, 87 (1932), 144–50.

Llanfair Farm Llandysul 4315 4090

A sub-rectangular enclosure noted on low-lying ground. PRN 11818 (AP/84/112.38); James, *AW*, 24 (1984), 23.

Cae Perth Llandysul 433 435
Caerau
(*c.* 0.2 ha)

This seems to have been a truly rectangular enclosure, measuring 55 × 40 m, with slightly rounded corners. It has been badly damaged by ploughing. The bank and ditch are some 15 m in width, the bank standing to a height of 0.6 m. The site has good views in all directions. PRN 7668; Hughes, *TCAS*, (1930), 114.

Gwar Ffynnon Llandysul 4483 4093
Sub-rectangular enclosure.
Meridian Airmaps 1955, 240–220, 34912–3; PRN 12127.

Castell Pant Llanfihangel- 461 401
Wen (0.73 ha) ar-arth
This is a small, univallate enclosure which seems to belong to the south Cardiganshire group. Carmarthenshire, *Inventory* No. 395; Savory, *BBCS*, 16 (1954) 64.

Castell Pyr Llanllwni 469 400
(0.3 ha)
This is a small, multivallate enclosure with fairly strong defences. It seems to belong to the south Cardiganshire group. Carmarthenshire, *Inventory* No.522; Savory, *BBCS*, 16 (1954) 63.

Caerau, Llan- Llanwenog 478 449
wenog
This farm name implies the former existence of some earthwork but nothing is now visible.

Clawdd Llanwenog 489 451
Buarth
Rectilinear enclosure.
PRN 8215; D. C. Evans, *TCAS*, 7 (1930), 65–7.

Pen y Cwrt Llanwenog 493 433
Earthwork
PRN 8214

SN 45

Mynachlog- Llandysiliogogo 408 521
uchaf (0.1 ha)
A nearly ploughed-out, sub-rectangular enclosure situated on ground falling to the north. OS Record.

Gaer Rhyd- Llannarth 430 525
lydan (Pen-y-
gaer)
Examination of aerial photographs have led to the rediscovery of an earthwork recorded by Meyrick in 1810 and Lewis in 1831. Photographs show a much-reduced, univallate, sub-rectangular enclosure of about 190 m north–south × 120 m east–west. There are possible annexes to the west

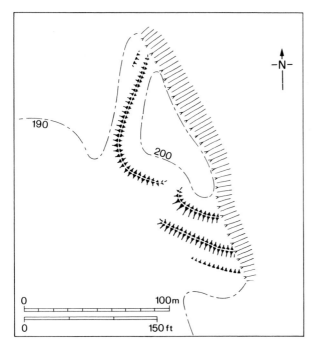

Fig. 47: Cwm Castell.

and north-east, but these are much less clearly defined.
Meridian Airmaps 1955, 240/250, 17990–1. PRN 12280; Stenger, *AW*, 25 (1985), 18.

Gaer, Pen-yr-   Llannarth   442 555
heol, Llan-
narth
This field-name recorded in the Tithe Award survey would be an excellent position for a hill-fort, but nothing is now visible.

Cwm Castell   Llannarth   469 554
(0.44 ha)
(Fig. 47)
This enclosure is identified by Meyrick (in the only early reference) as the castle of Mabwinion, but it is almost certainly pre-Roman. It occupies an oval knoll with the River Feinog on the east, protected on the north and north-west by a small stream which joins this and on the south by a stretch of marshy ground joining the two streams. Around most of the circuit the defence is a single bank but on the south it is doubled. The inner bank is 7 m wide and stands 3 m high, possibly fronted by a wholly silted ditch, now a flat space

of 10 m; then the outer bank measuring 17 m by 2 m overall. There is a trace of a stone revetment at the eastern end of the inner bank but otherwise both seem to be composed of earth and rubble. There is a slightly inturned entrance on the north-west at the terminals of the double rampart. Just north of this there is a slight trace of a levelled platform, possibly for a round house.
Meyrick, *History and Antiq.* (1907 ed.), 234.

Rhos Garn   Llannarth   471 502
Wen
Soilmarks define a concentric enclosure situated on ground sloping gently to the north-east. The inner enclosure appears sub-rectangular; the outer sub-ovoid.
CUC BHJ 9

Castell   Llannarth   474 515
Moeddyn-fach
(0.05 ha)
A bank and ditch, 35 m long, 13 m wide and 2 m high overall, cuts across an inland spur about 30 m from its top. The entrance is a simple gap about 4 m wide near the middle of the bank.

The age of the structure is uncertain. Its very small area suggests that it may be medieval and it is listed by King as a 'possible castle', but the relatively slight defences and the central entrance gap would be consistent with a pre-Roman date.
Evans, *TCAS*, 9 (1931), 24; King, *Ceredigion*, 3.i (1956), 67, No. 30.

Castell   Llannarth   485 520
Moeddyn
(1.0 ha)
(Fig. 48;
Pl. IVb)
The position chosen is a blunt spur which falls steeply to the south but with a very easy approach from the north. The defences consisted of a strong bank, ditch and counterscarp-bank, about 18 m in overall width by 4–5 m high where best preserved (for about 30 m on the north-west), but reduced to a scarp on the south end with the ditch silted up elsewhere. The steepness of the outer face of the main bank suggests the presence of a stone revet-ment, now entirely concealed by turf. The entrance, on the north-east, is a simple gap.
Evans, *TCAS*, 9 (1931), 23.

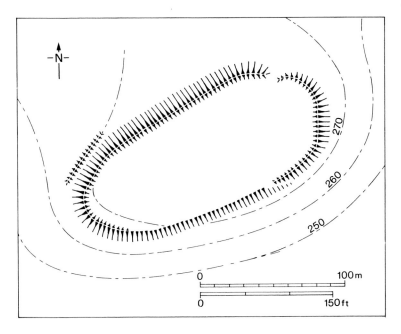

Fig. 48: Castell Moeddyn.

Maes-y-gaer   Ciliau Aeron   499 585
This field name in the Tithe Award survey probably refers to the slight univallate enclosure of about 40 m diameter, situated on a steep slope, recently discovered by Ordnance Survey staff.

Bronfre Ganol   Ciliau Aeron   491 587
Aerial reconnaissance has revealed the remains of a hillfort surviving as a slight earthwork on the north-east, with a modern hedge-bank marking the course of the rampart on the south-east. The course of a ditch can be seen as a faint cropmark to the west, giving the site an overall diameter of about 120 m. Traces of a possible outer ditch are also visible on the west.
PRN 11831; AP 84/111.1.

Foel Dihewid   Llanfihangel   495 552
(Castle Hill)   Ystrad
This site, recorded by Lewis and Meyrick, is no longer visible on the ground.
Meyrick, *History and Antiq.* (1907 edn.), 212; Lewis, *Topog. Dict.*, s.v. 'Llanfihangel Ystrad'; Evans, *TCAS*, 9 (1931), 22.

SN 54

Pen-y-gaer,   Llanybydder   523 434
Llanybydder
(0.6 ha)
This is a substantial hillfort, partly bivallate, overlooking the Teifi from the south. Though in Carmarthenshire, it falls naturally within the south Cardiganshire group of forts.
Carmarthenshire, *Inventory*, No. 600; Savory, *BBCS*, 16 (1954), 61.

Castell Flwyn   Pencarreg   566 437
(0.8 ha)
This is a univallate enclosure situated on a fairly steep hillside. It seems to fall within the south Cardiganshire group.
Savory, *BBCS*, 16 (1954), 66.

Tŷ Newydd   Lampeter Rural   5422 4690
Earthwork.
PRN 9536

Henfeddau   Lampeter Rural   5673 4951
Earthwork.
PRN 9541

Llety-twppa Lampeter Rural , 584 485
Wood
Earthwork.
PRN 8922

Castell Olwyn Llanfair 580 492
  Clydogau
A pear-shaped knoll, probably of glacial origin, is
fortified at its broad northern end, the weakest
side, by a bank and ditch 23 m wide by 4 m high
which die out round the steeper flanks. The
position of the original entrance is unknown. King
suggests this as a 'possible castle', but it seems
much more likely to be pre-Roman.
King, *Ceredigion*, 3.i (1956), 61. No. 29.

Pen-gaer-wen Pencarreg 581 449
(0.1 ha)
A small hill-slope enclosure discovered by the
Ordnance Survey. Though in Carmarthenshire,
its seems to belong with the south Cardiganshire
group.

Mynydd Pen- Pencarreg 589 444
carreg
(0.76 ha)
This multivallate fort occupies a strong position in
the hills south of the Teifi. Though in Carmarthenshire, it seems to belong with the south
Cardiganshire group.
Carmarthenshire, *Inventory* No. 690; Savory, *BBCS*, 16
(1954), 66.

Bryn Maen Cellan 597 483
Caerau
(Fisher's
Arms)
(0.9 ha)
(Fig. 49)
This curiously sited enclosure occupies a low, oval
knoll on the margin of a gravel terrace in the Teifi
valley. It is defined on the south-east by a bank
and ditch with traces of a counterscarp-bank,
rather less than 2 m high, and on the north-west
by the scarping of the margin of the terrace. The
defences are overlain by modern boundaries and
buildings and bisected by the modern road. Its
internal area is about 125 × 90 m. An entrance
lay on the south-west, of which only its eastern
side, defined by an expanded rampart terminal,

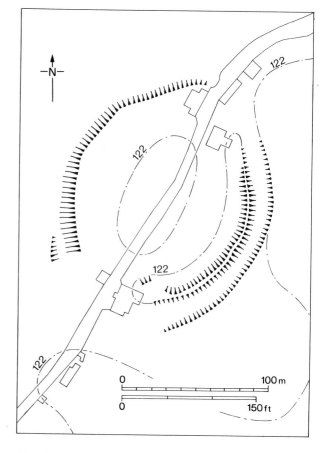

Fig. 49: Bryn Maen Caerau.

survives. An early estate map shows what appears
to be a 'banjo' approach, fossilized in present-day
field boundaries (information from D. Austin).
  Limited rescue excavations have been undertaken within the site by the Dyfed Archaeological
Trust. The earliest features discovered comprised
a number of ill-defined pits and hollows. A C14
date of 2870 ± 70 bc (CAR-1071) from charcoal
in a large pit clearly indicates Neolithic occupation long prior to the construction of the
defences. Later occupation, broadly relateable to
the enclosure, began with a pre-rampart phase
represented by debris comprising burnt stone,
charcoal and a little burnt bone, together with pits
and post-holes. This occupation was very extensive, a number of phases being represented.
Charcoal from this general layer produced a C14
date of 570 ± 70 bc (CAR-1070). There may
have been a period of abandonment between this

pre-rampart occupation and the construction of the defences, although it need not have been of any great duration. The bank appears to have been of one phase and incorporated posts suggestive of an internal, and possibly external, revetment.

Williams, *AW*, 27 (1987), 32–3. Additional information from G. Williams for Dyfed Archaeological Trust.

SN 55

Caer Lifry   Llanfihangel   516 565
(0.3 ha)   Ystrad

A single bank and ditch follow the sides of a ridge and cut across the ends to form a roughly rectangular enclosure about 105 m long and 30 m wide, with the long axis running east-north-east to west-south-west. The bank is much ploughed but at the west end the bank and ditch are over 20 m wide by nearly 3 m in overall height. At the east end the defences are similar in width but only about a metre high, and a further bank, measuring about 10 m wide and 2.5 m high, crosses the ridge 55 m further east. It is not parallel to the east end of the fort. The entrance seems to have been a simple gap about 10 m from the north-west corner.

Evans, *TCAS*, 9 (1931), 22, under 'Pen-y-gaer'. The older name may be inferred from that of a farm about a quarter of a mile to the south-west.

Cribyn Gaer   Llanfihangel   520 509
(Caer   Ystrad
Maesmynach)
(0.8 ha)
(Fig. 50)

The fort occupies the north-west end of a ridge, with ground falling steeply on all sides except the south-eastern. The defences comprise a strong bank and ditch, 15 m by 5 m high overall, partly levelled on the north and north-west and replaced by a steep scarp on the south-west. On the south-east there is an additional bank and ditch, 14 m by 3 m overall, separated from the main ditch by a berm, and with another, rather smaller, bank and ditch curving away from it. The entrance, at the north-east end of these additional defences, is a simple gap.

Evans, *TCAS*, 9 (1931), 23.

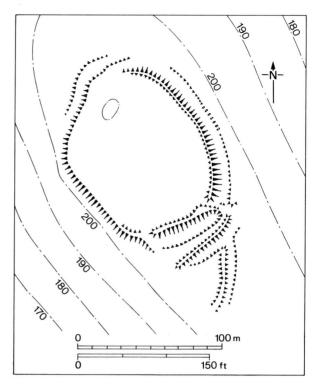

Fig. 50: Cribyn Gaer (Caer Maesmynach).

Castell, Cil-   Cilcennin   528 589
cennin
(Perthi Mawr)
(0.5 ha)
(Fig. 51)

The fort occupies a strong position. It is protected by two widely separated banks, without ditches, now turf-covered but probably masking ruined walls, surviving to a height of nearly 2 m. The entrance is of zigzag type. The interior has escaped cultivation and the footings of a round-house 6 m in diameter, surviving as a low turf-covered wall, can be seen within.

Gaer Fach,   Llanfihangel   531 514
Cribyn   Ystrad
Clottas
(0.2 ha)

Although the surrounding bank is fairly substantial, 4 m wide and 1.5 m high, this small, oval enclosure is hardly defensible. It stands on ground falling to the west, with a good view in all directions except to the east. There are slight traces of an external ditch on the south and modern gaps to

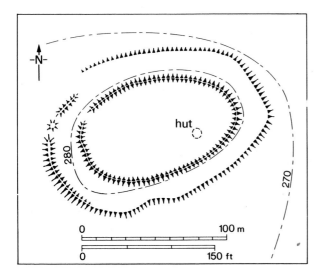

Fig. 51: Castell, Cilcennin (Perthi Mawr).

the north and south, one of which may have destroyed the original entrance. Traces of a cottage remain within the enclosure.

Cribyn   Llanfihangel   536 515
Clottas   Ystrad
(0.88 ha)
A slight bank of earth, about 6 m wide and a metre high with no visible ditch, forms an almost circular enclosure on a gently rounded summit. The slopes are not steep but the view in all directions is excellent. The remains have been greatly damaged by agriculture.
Evans, *TCAS*, 9 (1931), 20.

Derry   Betws Bledrws   589 515
Ormond
Aerial photographs show a bivallate, oval enclosure in close proximity to Coed-parc Gaer.
CUC BUP 046,052; St Joseph, *AW*, 15 (1975), No. 94.

Coed-parc   Betws Bledrws   592 514
Gaer, E of
Cropmark of a roughly circular enclosure which lies close to the Gaer. It has a single, broad ditch with a 'banjo'-type entrance.
CUC BUP 046,052; St Joseph, *AW*, 15 (1975), No. 97.

Pen-clawdd-   Llanfihangel   555 553
mawr (0.7 ha)   Ystrad
This fort occupies the end of an inland pro-

montory, on ground falling to the west. All that now remains is a short length of bank about 15 m wide by nearly 2 m high, but according to Evans there were originally two or three banks and ditches. The same account gives the area as 270 sq yds but the situation suggests that this is far too small. The position is overlooked by higher ground to the east but is otherwise strong.
Evans, *TCAS*, 9 (1931), 21.

Pen-y-gaer,   Nancwnlle   577 583
Nancwnlle
(0.5 ha)
A bank and ditch, now almost obliterated by cultivation, follow the shape of the hill to form an enclosure with parallel sides and semicircular ends, roughly 140 (north-east–south-west) × 45 m. The entrance seems to have been at the north-east end. The position is very commanding and defensible.

Coed-parc   Betws Bledrws   588 514
Gaer
(Betws Bledrws)
(0.5 ha)
This enclosure is formed by a bank and ditch measuring about 18 m by nearly 2 m overall. The rampart ends overlap to form an entrance on the south-east. The site lies on sloping ground, with a steep scarp to the south and overlooked by higher ground immediately to the north-east. When visited the interior had been recently ploughed, exposing some burnt stone but no other relics.

Castell Allt-   Llanfair   594 501
goch (1.4 ha)   Clydogau
This contour fort occupies a gently rounded summit, defensible but not naturally of great strength. For most of the circuit cultivation has destroyed all except the inner rampart and the position of the entrance is lost, but on the north and east the defences survive as two close-set banks and ditches and a counterscarp bank, measuring 45 m wide overall. The inner rampart still stands over 4 m high above the ditch bottom.

SN 56

Troed-y-rhiw   Llansanffraid   523 676
(0.34 ha)
A lightly embanked, univallate enclosure,

measuring about 70 × 50 m, sited on ground falling gently to the west.
Discovered by Ordnance Survey staff.

| Y Foel | Llanrhystud | 543 693 |
| | Anhuniog | |

Cropmark of a single-ditched, circular enclosure of about 75 m diameter, situated on the end of a spur with good all-round views except to the south.
CUC BUP 060,062

Castell Mawr,	Llanrhystud	537 686
Llanrhystud	Anhuniog	
(1.2 ha)		

This was a roughly circular univallate enclosure, almost obliterated in 1923 and no longer recognizable.
Hughes, *TCAS*, 4 (1926), 26, 50, Fig. 25.

Castell Bach,	Llanrhystud	539 688
Llanrhystud	Anhuniog	
(0.2 ha)		

This fort occupies a small knoll forming the end of a promontory projecting westwards and with steep slopes on all sides except the south-east, which has been fortified by a single bank and ditch whose original dimensions are uncertain. When visited in 1952 a short length of stone revetment was visible on the east, but the whole site has long been cultivated and the rampart robbed.
Hughes, *TCAS*, 4 (1926), 26, 41, Fig. 26.

SN 57

Gilfach-hafel	Llanrhystud	559 701
(Tan-yr-allt)	Anhuniog	
(0.7 ha)		

The position chosen is the side of a ridge, the south side of the enclosure being on the margin of a steep fall to the River Wyre. The remainder of the circuit, which faces uphill, is protected by a single bank, now some 2 m high, with traces of a ditch in places. The whole has been much reduced by cultivation.
Hughes, *TCAS*, 4 (1926), 26, 50, Fig. 23.

Banc y Gaer,	Llanychaearn	567 745
Blaen-plwyf		
(0.12 ha)		

This fort, whose presence was implied by the name in the Tithe Award Survey, has been dis-

covered by Ordnance Survey staff. It is an oval, 50 m north–south by 30 m, and is much reduced by cultivation.

SN 58

Pen Dinas,	Llanbadarn-y-	584 805
Aberystwyth	Creuddyn Isaf	
(Fig. 52;		
Pl. IVa)		
1.6 ha (Phase 1);		
3.8 ha (Phase 4)		

This fort occupies the summit of a steep-sided ridge between the Rivers Rheidol and Ystwyth, about a kilometre south-east of the point at which they now enter the sea. Both rivers would have provided accessible and sheltered landing-places for small boats, especially if the shingle bank which now diverts the Ystwyth were absent.

Excavations were carried out here in 1933–7 by Prof. Darryll Forde. The account which follows is based on the results of these excavations but the detailed arguments and reservations given there are not discussed. Inevitably, many problems remain to be investigated.

The ridge on which the fort stands is long and narrow with its major axis, of 500 m, almost due north–south. Its top forms two knolls of about equal size, the northern rising about 115 m above OD, the southern to 125 m; they are connected by a saddle (or 'isthmus') some 10 m lower.

The probable evolution of the defences is as follows:

Initially, the northern summit was defended by an earthen rampart 4–5 m thick at the base, with a sloping timber revetment at the front only, separated by a berm 3 m wide from a ditch 5 m wide and 2 m deep, becoming narrower and deeper as it approached the sides of the ridge. The area enclosed was 1.6 ha. These defences are almost entirely destroyed or concealed by later work.

After an unknown interval a fort of similar size (1.5 ha) but with much stronger defences was built on the south knoll. The rampart was composed of rubble revetted on both sides in stone, 4.3 m thick, separated by a berm 1.5 m wide from a ditch 3.7 m wide and 2.5 m deep; these are the dimensions where it crossed the 'isthmus'. There were gateways at the north and south ends. Details are partly obscured but the ramparts were

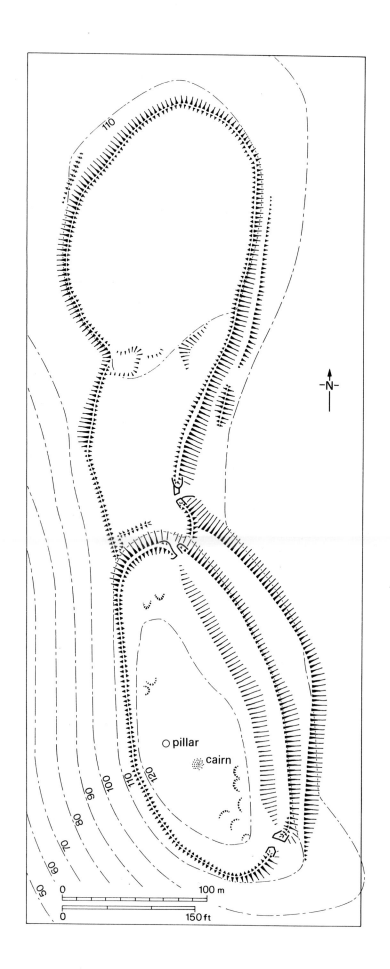

○ pillar

cairn

110

120

90

100

110

120

80

70

60

50

0   100 m

0   150 ft

Fig. 52: Pen Dinas, Aberystwyth.

thereafter thickened in Phase 2. The gate passages, some 5.8 m wide, probably had a rectangular setting of four posts (though only three post-holes of this were identified at each gateway) for a bridged gate.

The third phase saw a reconstruction of this fort to essentially the same plan but there seems to have been an interval of sufficient length for the Phase 2 defences to fall into ruin and to become partly turf-covered.

Finally, in the fourth main phase, which can be subdivided into four or five subsidiary phases, a wall 4 m thick was carried along the sides of the 'isthmus' and around the northern knoll (North Fort), bringing the enclosed area to 3.8 ha. The north gate of the South Fort giving access from the 'isthmus' as well as its rampart barring the approach from that side, seems to have remained in use, and it is possible that Phase 3, the reconstruction of the South Fort, is contemporary with Phase 4a.

The subsidiary divisions of Phase 4 are indicated by the evolution of the gate giving access to the 'isthmus' through the added wall. Initially (Phase 4a) this was a gap some 12 m wide, apparently with no timberwork. It was narrowed by successive additions to the rampart ends (phases b*i*, b*ii*, c) until it was reduced to an opening 3–4 m wide with a rectangular setting of large posts, about 0.6 m in diameter. Finally, in phase d, after the phase c rampart had begun to show signs of incipient collapse, an additional wall, with an accompanying ditch, about 4 m wide and 2.5 m deep, was built against the outer face of the rampart south of the gate. Surface appearance suggests strongly that this new wall was continuous along the whole of the eastern side of the South Fort as far as its south gate, although no attempt was made to demonstrate its veracity through excavation.

Although the interior has been cultivated, about a dozen house-platforms can still be recognized, terraced into the sloping ground within the South Fort: the 'isthmus' and North Fort have been cultivated. One excavated platform shows the house to have been D-shaped in plan, with a flat facade 10 m wide facing downhill, probably with four posts symmetrically placed. The curved back was cut into the hillside to a depth of a metre; it may originally have been vertical. The platform

so constructed is 6 m wide at its broadest point. Such a plan is very unusual indeed but the results of the excavation cannot be reconciled with the assumption that the platform was roughly circular and that the lower half had been eroded.

Another structure, immediately within the 'isthmus' gateway on its south side, was represented by a rectangular setting of post-holes, 2.1 × 1.7 m, with a small hearth (not necessarily associated) in the middle of one side. Too little of the surrounding area was cleared to determine whether this was a free-standing, four-post structure of a type common to Iron Age settlements or whether the posts formed part of a larger building, not necessarily of rectangular plan.

The structural development of the defences shows that the hillfort must have had a history measured in centuries but only two dateable relics were found. One, a bead similar to some found at Meare (Som.), came from an occupation layer within the South Fort. The other, a pot of a type manufactured near Malvern (Worcs.), lay against the outer face of the Phase 4 wall where it crossed the ditch of the North Fort, apparently having been broken *in situ* about the time the wall was built. A date within the second century BC would now be acceptable for this vessel, though the type seems to have had a long life. The bead may be rather later in date.

Forde *et al.*, *Arch. Camb.*, 112 (1963), 125–53.

SN 64

Caer Hwch   Cellan   624 472
A very small enclosure bearing this name appears on early editions of the 1-inch Ordnance Survey Map, but nothing is now visible.

Caer   Cellan   622 480
Cadwgan
(Gelli-gaer)
(Total,
1.27 ha)
(Fig. 53)
The main enclosure of about 0.42 ha occupies the summit of a steeply sloping hill, the circuit being marked by spreads of rubble, except on the south where it has been more extensively robbed. An entrance, approached by a hollow way, lies at the south-west end, its western terminal marked by

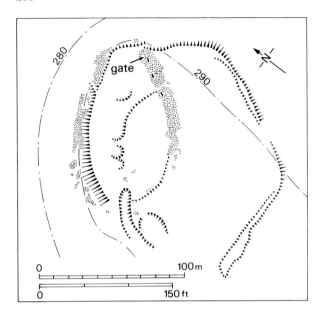

Fig. 53: Caer Cadwgan (Gelli-gaer).

several vertical slabs. A second entrance lies on the north-east and was the focus of excavation between 1984 and 1986. A third gap on the south may also represent an original entrance.

The inner enclosure is partially divided by a prominent stony bank, later revealed to be a wall 1 m wide. Four semicircular building platforms were visible in the interior prior to excavation.

An outer enclosure of about 0.85 ha, marked by insubstantial earthworks on the east and west and by a low, stony bank on the south, is appended to the south and east of the main enclosure. There is a 17 m gap on its south-west side but its interpretation, with other features, is complicated by partial reclamation. Traces of earthworks are visible along the line of the modern boundary wall, including a semicircular building platform.

Excavations have examined the north-east entrance and rampart. The rampart was 3–4 m wide with boulder faces revetting a rubble core, fronted by a ditch/quarry scoop. The rampart terminals sealed concentrations of charcoal either representing pre-rampart clearance or an earlier phase of occupation. What is essentially a two-phase sequence was observed at the gate. In Phase 1 it probably comprised a simple six-post gate, the two central posts being joined by a shallow gully and probably supporting the gate itself. Sometime after, the outer enclosure was constructed. Phase

2 saw modifications to the gate passage, and the possible disuse of some of the earlier posts. The gate was then destroyed by fire, an event for which two C14 dates are available: 2360 ± 70 bp (CAR-968) and 2580 ± 70 bp (CAR-969). The gate passage was then blocked. Extensive occupation deposits accumulated immediately to the rear of the rampart and the blocked gate; two substantial post-holes probably represented part of a contemporary structure.

The internal dividing wall was found to overlie an unsuspected building-platform. Another platform to the north-west was excavated, revealing a complex of post-holes and burnt daub. It had been occupied by at least one timber structure of uncertain plan which had been burnt down. Traces of a further, unsuspected platform entirely filled with natural hillwash were noted on the steep slope down to the rampart on the west.

Finds from the site include calcined animal bone, carbonized cereals, iron slag and glass beads.

D. Austin *et al.*, *The Caer Cadwgan Project: Interim Reports* (St David's University College, Lampeter, 1984, 1985, 1986, 1987); B. and H. Burnham, *The Hillfort Study Group: Lampeter and the Surrounding Area* (Lampeter, 1988), 19–24. Additional information from Dr B. Burnham.

SN 65

Castell Goetre   Llanfair   603 510
((1)1.1 ha,   Clydogau
(2)2.8 ha)
(Fig. 54)

Re-examination suggests that the evolution proposed in 1962 regarding the internal cross-bank as a later addition is probably incorrect. The following interpretation seems more likely, but certainty is impossible without excavation since the ramparts have been much disturbed by incorporation in modern field-banks and have been almost levelled over a large part of the circuit. The three possible entrances mentioned below have all been damaged and it is impossible to be sure which was the original.

The first phase seems to have comprised an oval enclosure measuring roughly 100 m north–south by 90 m. The rampart where it crosses the supposed later enclosure is some 6 m wide and 1.5 m wide on the west and rather less than a metre on the east. A gap, now about 4 m wide,

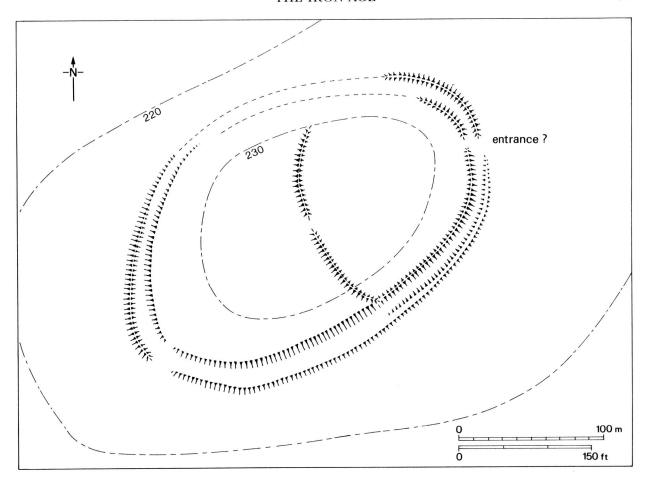

Fig. 54: Castell Goetre.

near the middle of this side probably corresponds in position to an original entrance.

The eastern two-thirds of this rampart seems to have been incorporated in the much stronger defences of an enclosure of more than twice the size, measuring about 240 × 140 m. These defences comprise a substantial inner bank, 8–10 m wide and 2.5 m high above the ditch bottom with a counterscarp bank of about half the dimensions of the main rampart; the whole system being nearly 20 m across. The banks are of earth, with no trace of revetment now visible. There was almost certainly a gateway at the south-west end of the long axis, where a lane now enters the enclosure, and probably another at the north-east end.

On the north side the rampart has been almost certainly destroyed for about 120 m but the general line can just be traced. Apart from this most of the circuit of the supposed original enclosure is fairly well preserved. To the west the inner bank has been reduced to a scarp, and the counterscarp bank only survives in part beneath modern hedges.

Glan Rhyd   Llanfair   6395 5138
                      Clydogau
Earthwork
PRN 9502

SN 66

Pen-y-gaer,   Tirymynach   640 609
Deri Odwyn
(0.36 ha)
The older 6-inch Ordnance Survey map indicates an enclosure measuring about 100 × 50 m, with

traces of an outer enclosure of about twice these dimensions. No evidence for this outer enclosure survives on the ground and the inner has been almost destroyed by cultivation. On the north part the rampart survived (1955) to a height of nearly 2 m, with probable traces of a ditch, but the rest is reduced to a scarp.

Tre-Coll	Llanbadarn	641 622
(1.5 ha)	Odwyn	

A tongue of land naturally protected on three sides by small, steep-sided valleys has been fortified by three banks separated by two ditches across its accessible north side. The inner bank and ditch measure about 30 m wide by 6–7 m high overall. About 12 m outside this ditch are a rather larger bank, ditch and counterscarp bank. The entrance probably lay between the western end of these defences and the adjacent valley.

Hogg, *Ceredigion*, 6.4(1971), 436 (sketch plan).

Castell	Caron-is-	654 632
Fflemish	clawdd	
(0.7 ha)		

This may be an example of the wide-spaced multivallate hillforts of 'South-Western Type', but is more probably two superimposed works of different periods. Both enclosures are nearly circular, the inner protected by a bank and ditch about 3 m high overall, with a small counterscarp bank. The outer defences are slighter, separated from the inner by a wide space on the west but converging to coalesce with the counterscarp bank on the east. When first visited (1951) the interior had been ploughed, revealing burnt stones but no other relics.

PRN 5167

Castell,	Caron-is-	687 602
Tregaron	clawdd	
(Sunnyhill)		
(0.7 ha)		

The site chosen is a blunt promontory which rises to form a small knoll and thus provides a good defensive position although overlooked by higher ground on the north-east. Two strong ramparts cut across its base but the steeply sloping sides are undefended. The outer bank and ditch measure 20 m by 3 m overall and are separated from the inner defences by a 6 m wide berm. The inner defence comprises a bank and ditch 24 m wide and 4 m high overall. The entrance lies on the east and is approached by a narrow, levelled track.

PRN 5168

SN 67

Caer Argoed	Llangwyryfon	616 710
(0.45 +		
0.2 ha)		

The main enclosure occupies the summit of a low ridge. It is protected by a single rampart about 15 m wide by more than 2 m high. To the north-west was an annexe defended by two banks with accompanying ditches; the inner about 16 × 3 m overall, the outer of about half these dimensions. The whole site has been ploughed, obscuring detail.

Hughes, *TCAS*, 4 (1926), 26 and Fig. 27 (inaccurate in detail).

Castell, Pant-	Llanbadarn-y-	611 756
mawr	Creuddyn Isaf	
((1)0.5 ha.		
(2)0.4 ha)		

The site is a steep-sided spur projecting from the north side of the Ystwyth Valley. Surface evidence suggests two periods of fortification but the remains are covered by vegetation even in winter and interpretation is difficult.

In Phase 1 a bank about 15 m wide and over 2 m high forms a rough semicircle across the neck and continues as a slighter bank around the edge of the spur. In Phase 2 an unusually strong bank and ditch, nearly 35 m wide and some 7–8 m in overall height, with the bank still nearly 6 m high on its inner side owing to the slope of the ground, runs for 35 m straight across the spur, about 30–5 m behind the Phase 1 rampart. A small section of rear revetment is visible near its western end. The entrance in each phase seems to have followed the eastern margin of the spur.

Old Warren	Llanbadarn-y-	615 789
Hill, Nanteos	Creuddyn Isaf	
(*c.* 2 ha)		

The plateau between the Rheidol and Ystwyth Valleys is cut by a small stream, Nant Paith, whose valley has left a spur which is easily accessible from the north but otherwise steep-sided. The enclosure is pear-shaped with the narrow end towards the south. Around the steep sides the rampart is reduced to a scarp but where it cuts across the spur it consists of an earthen bank and ditch about 15 m by 3 m overall. No revetment is visible. Ten metres further north another defence, of similar width but only a metre high, runs for 25 m across the spur. The site is heavily wooded and the location of the entrance is uncertain.

Hughes, *TCAS*, 4 (1926), 45 (fig. 13); Wright, *Aberystwyth Studies*, 2 (1914), 56 (Fig. 7). Wright's plan is poor. Neither shows the additional rampart on the north.

New Cross	Llanbadarn-y-	628 772
Camp (Gors)	Creuddyn Isaf	

((1) 0.4 ha;
(2) 1.1 ha)

The remains have been very badly damaged by cultivation and modern field-banks; hence they are difficult to interpret. Initially a single bank and ditch seems to have formed a nearly circular enclosure on the summit of the hill, which was later extended by carrying a rampart round the contour to the west at a rather lower level.

Hughes, *TCAS*, 4 (1926), 25 and Fig. 18.

Penycastell,	Llanilar	630 745
Llanilar		

(0.56 ha?)

Interpretation of this site is difficult. In the writer's opinion (A.H.A.H.), it is a pear-shaped enclosure protected by a fairly substantial bank with no surviving ditch but mutilated by a disused quarry excavated through the middle. Alternatively, the quarry may be an enlargement of an original ditch separating a low motte from a small bailey on the south.

King, *Ceredigion*, 3.1 (1956), 62 (but see Hogg and King, *Arch. Camb.*, 112 (1962), 101); Hughes, *TCAS*, 4 (1926), 25, and Fig. 19.

Penycastell,	Llanilar	6297 7469
near		

(*c.* 0.45 ha)

A trapezoidal, univallate enclosure about 65/70 m square across its banks, lies on the hillslope to the north of Penycastell. Noted from the ground by J. L. Davies in 1974 and subsequently seen from the air.

RCAHM (Wales) photographs 881363/1–6.

Hen Gaer,	Llanbadarn-y-	638 793
Capel Seion	Creuddyn Uchaf	

This field name occurs in the Tithe Award survey but although the position would be suitable for a hillfort nothing is now visible.

Pen y Wern	Llanfihangel-	640 760
	y-Creuddyn Isaf	

Cropmark of a single ditched enclosure of some 45 m diameter, situated on ground sloping gently to the south-west.

CUC ASR 21–2.

Gaer Fawr,	Llanilar	654 719
E of		

A univallate enclosure of about 80 (east–west) × 50 m (north–south) has been noted on a spur some 500 m east of the above-named hillfort.

PRN 11828; AP/84/38.20; James, *AW*, 24 (1984), 24.

Gaer Fawr,	Llanilar	649 719
Llanilar		

(1.7 ha)
(Fig. 55)

The fort is strongly sited on a knoll at the south-western end of a ridge which extends a short distance to the north-east at a generally lower level. The main enclosure is formed by a strong bank of shaly rubble, probably originally accompanied by a ditch though that is now silted except for about 60 m on the north. Here these defences measure about 10 m wide by about 4 m high overall. Around the north-western half of the enclosure and separated from it by a wide space is a smaller, outer bank with traces of an accompanying ditch. There are entrances through the inner rampart at the north-east and south-west ends and in the north-west side, the first two being flanked by short, inturned lengths of rampart. That on the south-west is not accompanied by any corresponding gap in the outer rampart, which suggests that it may have been an addition, perhaps unfinished, to the original enclosure.

The remains have recently been badly damaged by ploughing.

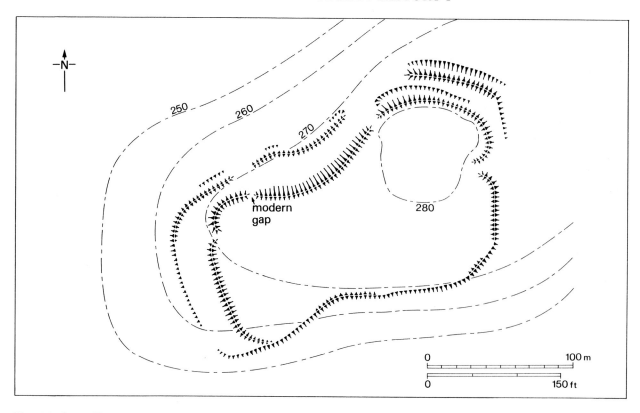

Fig. 55: Gaer Fawr.

Llwyn y Brain   Llanfihangel-   6520 7676
(Plate VIb)   y-Creuddyn
                 Isaf
Cropmark of ovoid enclosure.
CUC ASR 22; PRN 7699

Coed Allt   Llanilar   661 729
Fedw (0.6 ha)
This fort occupies a knoll projecting north-east-wards from higher ground. The whole area has been heavily cultivated and planted as a conifer nursery. The rampart now appears as a bank about 6 m wide and 2–3 m high, any ditch which may have existed having been ploughed-out.

About 150 m to the east a curved line of bank and ditch, with the ditch on the convex, uphill side, runs for 140 m across the end of the spur, just before the ground steepens sharply. The rampart dies out on slopes which, though steep, are not difficult to climb. The system measures about 15 × 3 m overall. Its function is obscure. It is difficult to see how it can be related to the nearby

enclosure and it may be another unfinished example.
Hughes, *TCAS*, 4 (1926), 25 and Fig. 20.

Trawscoed   Llanfihangel-y-   677 736
Park   Creuddyn Isaf
Cropmark of a ditched enclosure, about 50 × 40 m, with a major disturbance (?quarry-pit) to one side.
CUC BUB 038; PRN 8620, AP/84/41.34

Castell Disg-   Llanbadarn-y-   687 737
wylfa   Creuddyn Isaf
(0.15 ha)
(Pl. IVc)
From the hill called Disgwylfa two spurs extend westwards, ending in small knolls with sides falling steeply in all directions except the east. Both are fortified. The more southerly, called 'Castell' on older editions of the OS map, has a bank 6 m wide and 2 m high externally, with no ditch, along the crest and part of the north sides. There is a possible entrance on the north.

Cnwc y   Llanbadarn-y-   687 740
Bugail   Creuddyn Isaf
(0.45 ha)
(Pl. IVc)
This site (named in the earlier 1-inch OS maps) occupies the most northerly of the knolls mentioned in the previous entry. A bank about 7 m wide and just over a metre high externally encloses the whole summit. There is a short detached section of bank about 50 m south of the main enclosure; its relation to it is uncertain.

Castell   Llanfihangel-   688 749
Carreg-wen   y-Creuddyn
(0.1 ha)   Isaf
This fort, marked on the earliest 1-inch OS maps, has been rediscovered by Ordnance Survey staff. A slight bank, some 20 m by 0.7 m overall, isolates the end of a ridge.

Coed Lluest   Llanbadarn-y-   682 783
Camp   Creuddyn
(0.32 ha)   Uchaf
A blunt spur with steep flanks, projecting north-westwards above the Rheidol valley, has been fortified by a bank and ditch, measuring nearly 20 × 3 m overall, running straight across the base of the spur. From each end a slighter bank and ditch follow the flanks of the spur for about 30 m. The entrance seems to have been about 25 m west of the north end of the main bank.

Cefn Blewog   Llanafan   697 725
(0.45 ha
interior)
(1.6 ha total)
(Fig. 56)
Although this fort stands within an afforested area it has been left clear of trees; however, the thick tussocky grass makes interpretation difficult. It appears to be an unfinished example of a 'wide-spaced multivallate' fort of 'South-Western Type'. The intention was apparently to build two roughly concentric, oval enclosures, each with a single, rather slight, enclosing bank accompanied by a small ditch, measuring about 12 m wide and a little over 1 m high overall. Only about 100 m of the inner bank seems to have been built, forming roughly the western third of the intended circuit.

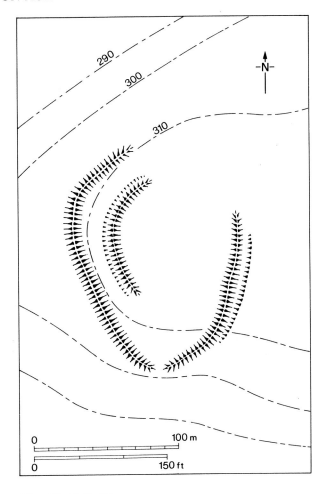

Fig. 56: Cefn Blewog.

The outer bank, separated from the inner by 30 m, is about three-quarters built, but a gap 100 m wide remains to the north.
Hughes, *TCAS*, 4 (1926), 25 and Fig. 21.

SN 68

Gogerddan   Tirymynach   6260 8350
Circular crop-mark, about 80 m in diameter, noted near barrow complex.
PRN AP 84/48.22; 49.23–5. James, *AW*, 24 (1984), 24.

Gaergywydd   Tirymynach   6273 8519
A very large ditch, 6 m wide and at least 2 m deep, running east–west, was noted during the construction of a gas pipeline in 1986. The farm immediately to the east is called Gaergywydd.
PRN 13052; *AW*, 26 (1986), 32.

Hen Gaer, Tirymynach 633 844
Bow Street
(Broncastellan)
(0.8 ha)
This roughly pear-shaped enclosure is strongly sited. It is protected by a single bank and ditch, measuring about 12 m wide overall and still standing in places to a height of 3–4 m. The original entrance seems to be a simple gap near the middle of the west side, with a large mound just outside it resembling a Roman *titulum*. Although certainty is impossible without excavation, this seems likely to be merely spoil from cutting a modern gap.
Hughes, *TCAS*, 4 (1926), 42, Fig. 42 (very misleading); Wright, *Aberystwyth Studies*, 2 (1914), 53, Fig. 4.

Glan-ffrwd Genau'r-glyn 635 878
(0.6 ha)
Aerial photographs show the crop-mark of a pear-shaped enclosure about 100 m east–west by 65 m, on a spur between the River Leri on the north and a small tributary stream on the west. A ditch, which to judge from the crop-mark was defensive, extends round the whole circuit and is doubled on the east. Marks which appear to show pits and perhaps a large round-house appear within.
St Joseph, *AW*, 15 (1975), No.95; CUC BUB 050.

Caer Pwll-glas Genau'r-glyn 634 867
(1.0 ha)
The position chosen is naturally strong and the defences are substantial, except towards the south-east where the hillside is very steep, so that the outer rampart becomes unnecessary and the inner is replaced by a scarp. On the other sides the enclosure is protected by two banks with accompanying ditches, the inner measuring 17 m by 3.5 m overall, the outer 10 m by 2 m. There is a level berm, 6 m wide, between the lip of the inner ditch and the tail of the outer rampart. The entrance, towards the south-west, is a simple gap; near it the inner ditch is rock-cut. The interior is planted with conifers.
Hughes, *TCAS*, 4 (1926), 41, Fig. 7; Wright, *Aberystwyth Studies*, 2 (1914), 58, Fig. 9.

Odyn-fach Ceulan-a- 648 877
Maesmor
Aerial photographs show a double-ditched enclosure encompassing a low hillock. The outer ditch formed an oval enclosure, 100 × 65 m; the inner, apparently dug in straight segments, forming a circle of 50 m diameter. Unlike the outer ditch which followed the contours, the inner lay on sloping ground to the east of the summit and was not concentric with the outer. This may indicate two periods of construction. The entrances through both ditches lay on the least steep, eastern side of the hillock. Within, and centrally placed to the inner enclosure, was a dark, circular crop-mark, about 12 m in diameter, possibly the site of a round-house terraced into the hillside.

A gas pipeline traversed the western side of the site in 1986, but did not affect the inner enclosure. Excavation by the Dyfed Archaeological Trust examined the outer ditch on the south-west, showing it to have been V-shaped, 4.5 m wide and 1.5 deep. The only find was a fragment of iron slag in the lower levels of the ditch.
AW, 26 (1986), 32. Additional details were kindly provided by Mr K. Murphy in advance of publication.

Caer Allt- Genau'r-glyn 641 884
goch (0.8 ha)
A strong, stony bank, 3–4 m high externally and nearly a metre high internally, follows the margins of a rocky knoll, forming a rather pointed, oval enclosure. There are steep slopes to the Leri valley on the south, the gentlest approach being that from the north-east along the ridge. There are some traces of a ditch but generally the bank merges into the hill-slope. The entrance is ill-defined but seems to have been a simple gap at the northern apex of the enclosure. About 30 m further north is a fragment of bank 10 m long, perhaps the remains of an additional defence across the easiest approach.

The Ceredigion Archaeological Survey notes about six house-emplacements in the interior, mostly in the south-western portion.
Hughes, *TCAS*, 4 (1926), 39, Fig. 3 (poor); Wright, *Aberystwyth Studies*, 2 (1914), 52, Fig. 3. Additional information from Dr K. Ray for Ceredigion Archaeological Survey.

Bryngwyn- Ceulan-a- 649 867
mawr Maesmor
Aerial photographs show the crop-mark of a slightly curving ditch cutting across a ridge. If the

remains of a hillfort, the enclosure would be of the order of about 350 m north-south by 90 m wide. The ditch appears to be about 2 m wide.
CUC AYJ 41

Capel Bangor   Parsel Canol   658 808
(0.27 ha)
This badly damaged site is situated on the highest point of a ridge overlooking the Rheidol Valley to the south; there are steep slopes to the north and south. The site was apparently univallate, with an entrance, flanked by its own outer bank, on the north-east. The remainder of the circuit has been destroyed by cultivation. The Ceredigion Archaeological Survey has noted traces of house-platforms within.
Hughes, *TCAS*, 4 (1926), 43, Fig. 11 (the central mound indicated on this plan is a natural outcrop); Wright, *Aberystwyth Studies*, 2 (1914), 57, Fig. 8.

Garth Pen-   Trefeurig   658 840
rhyn-coch
(0.17 ha)
This oval, univallate enclosure has been ploughed over, obscuring all detail. The position chosen is the end of a ridge, with good views except to the east. The entrance seems to have been on the north.
Hughes, *TCAS*, 4 (1926), 42, Fig. 9; Wright, *Aberystwyth Studies*, 2 (1914), 57, Fig. 6.

Caer Llety-   Ceulan-a-   651 882
llwyd (0.5 ha)   Maesmor
This enclosure is roughly circular, protected on most sides only by a single bank, perhaps originally ditched but now almost wholly reduced to a scarp 3–4 m high; it roughly follows the margin of a steep-sided spur which falls to the south-west. On the north-east the highest point of the knoll is crossed by two additional banks, the inner accompanied by a ditch; the whole system of three ramparts measures about 50 m overall. It may originally have extended further around the enclosure. Outside these defences the ground falls to a saddle, partly occupied by a streamlet, and then rises steeply. The position of the entrance to the enclosure is uncertain.
Hughes, *TCAS*, 4 (1926), 39, Fig. 4; Wright, *Aberystwyth Studies*, 2 (1914), 34, Fig. 5 (poor).

Excavation of a gas pipeline in 1986 revealed two parallel ditches 10 m apart running north–south, each being 3.5–4 m wide and at least 2 m deep, and showing evidence of recuts. To the east the presence of a buried soil suggested the former presence of a bank. The ditches may possibly be associated with Caer Llety-llwyd 100 m to the south-west.
AW, 26 (1986) 32; PRN 13045.

Darren   Trefeurig   679 830
(0.44 ha)
(Fig. 57)
The fort occupies a strong position on a hilltop overlooking the deep Nant Silo valley to the north. The easiest approach is from the west. A bank and ditch measuring about 30 m by 4 m overall encloses an oval area of about 100 × 55 m. In 1960 a short length of dry-stone walling was visible in the outer face of the rampart. The entrance is a simple gap.

On the west side of the hill, separated from the main rampart by about 25 and 50 m respectively,

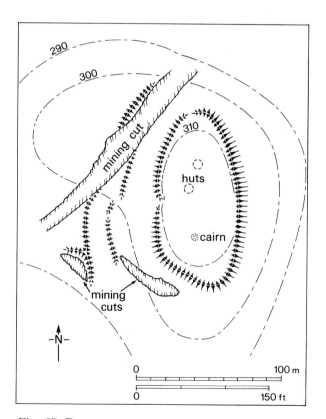

Fig. 57: Darren.

are further banks and ditches which merge to the north but are separated by about 20 m at their southern limits. The inner measures about 14 m by 3 m overall and contains a slightly overlapping entrance as well as a simple gap, also apparently original, nearby. The outermost bank is rather slighter. Both these ramparts have been destroyed near their northern ends by an opencast cut following a vein of lead ore.

The area directly behind the inner rampart has been terraced to provide, on the west side in particular, a level area. Further up-slope, around the summit, are a series of terraces (some artificial, some natural) which provide level areas on the steep north and east sides. There are also traces of 7–8 house-platforms in the interior.

Hughes, *TCAS*, 4 (1926), 43, Fig. 10 (inaccurate); Wright, *Aberystwyth Studies*, 2 (1914), 51, Fig. 2. The fort is shown in an engraving of the mine works published by Sir John Pettus, *Fodinae Regales* (London, 1670). The nearer detail in this picture seems fairly accurate, despite the scepticism aroused by the appearance of the sea, with ships on it, to the east.

Pen Dinas,   Ceulan-a-   677 877
Elerch   Maesmor
(0.35 ha interior, *c.* 3 ha total) (Fig. 58)
The position chosen is a rocky knoll from which the ground falls steeply on the north-east to the River Leri; and which is protected on the other sides by a marshy hollow. Access was from the south, where a rocky ridge projected into the marsh. The crossing was completed by a short length of artificial causeway, which has dammed the natural flow of water from the marsh on the west.

For convenience of description the remains are treated as if of three periods but they may in fact correspond to a single-period site of complicated plan. The slight resemblance to the 'nuclear forts' found in Scotland is probably misleading. According to local information the site was partly ploughed a few years ago and this has obscured some features which were noted on an earlier visit.

The first enclosure occupies the summit of the knoll. It is oval, 90 m (north–south) by 40 m, protected on the west by a slight, stony bank about 2–3 m wide and 0.3 m high following the margin of the steep slopes and on the east by a scarp. Where it crosses the knoll on the north this bank becomes much more substantial, about 6 m

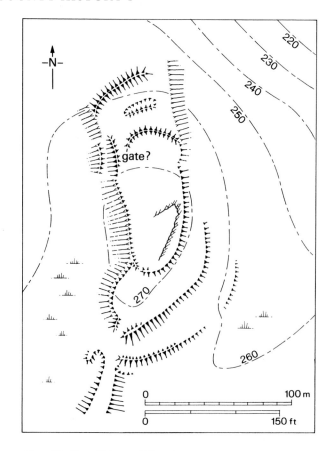

Fig. 58: Pen Dinas, Elerch.

wide and 3 m high on its north side. There is no ditch. There are three entrances, all simple gaps, about 3–4 m wide, but rather ill-defined. At the south apex the bank on each side is rather stronger for some 4–5 m. The gap on the north-west is ancient but may be a break made of the supposed later alterations. The age of that on the north-east is uncertain and there has been a little recent digging for stone here.

In the second(?) phase a rampart loops out from the enclosure to incorporate part of the northern slopes of the knoll. It is substantial, about 1–1.5 m high on the inner side, for a short distance on each side of the entrance. On the west it continues as a very slight bank following the crest of the slope to join the inner enclosure just north of the entrance. On the east it becomes a steep scarp, the toe of which emerges into the natural slope, and curves round towards the inner enclosure. It now dies away into the hillside and the old 1:2500 OS map does not show it as continuing much further, but Hughes's plan shows it joining the inner rampart just north of the north-eastern gap. Wright shows it curving to run parallel to the inner bank.

In the third(?) phase the whole top of the knoll was enclosed. On the south a third rampart begins at the north end of the causeway and curves round to the east and north. Initially it stands about 0.5 m high on the inner side and 3 m externally but soon becomes a scarp which now dies away after about 120 m. Formerly, after a (modern?) gap some 30 m wide, it could be traced along the top of a low, natural crag, curving round as if to join the second rampart. It is accompanied by a ditch, 5–6 m wide and about a metre deep at the causeway but generally very shallow and only about 3 m wide. A fallen stone lies at the west end of the ditch, and level with its outer lip there is a small, upright stone on the west side of the causeway. These suggest the presence of a gateway but not carrying anything more substantial than a field-gate, and not necessarily ancient. Running alongside the causeway, on its west side, is another short length of ditch.

At the northern end of the knoll a bank, rather more substantial than the rampart of the inner enclosure, branches off from it just south of the north-western gap. It is accompanied for about 20 m by a ditch over 10 m wide, which also extends 10 m to the south. This outer bank curves round to cross the knoll and increases to 15 m wide and over 3 m high on the northern face and nearly 1.5 m on its southern. It ends about 60 m before reaching the eastern side of the ridge.

Midway between this rampart and that of the inner enclosure, a low bank with traces of a ditch to the north, about 8 m wide by less than a metre high overall, extends for about 30 m.

Although the remains have been described as if of three periods, two considerations need to be set against that view. The defences of all three 'phases' are strikingly similar in character, especially in the way that they are increased considerably in size for a very short distance on each side of the southern entrance; and since the access-causeway would logically be one of the first structures on the site, the defences at its southern end, here treated as belonging to the 'third phase', might be expected to be early also.

Hughes, *TCAS*, 4 (1926), Fig. 5; Wright, *Aberystwyth Studies*, 2 (1914), 64, Fig. 11. Wright records the discovery of two silver coins, since lost, in the marsh just west of the causeway.

Penycastell,   Tirymynach   689 848
Llety-Evan-
Hen (0.5 ha)

The site is situated on a small spur, with steep slopes on the north, west and south, and is of oval plan, about 110 × 60 m, with defences comprising a rampart and ditch, generally of slight proportions. The circuit is not continuous and cannot be traced for a length of about 40 m on the south. The entrance is a simple gap, some 12 m wide, at the north-east end of the long axis. For about 20 m on each side of the entrance the rampart is much more substantial, the bank and ditch measuring 12 m wide and 3 m high overall, with a slight counterscarp bank. The Ceredigion Archaeological Survey notes that where the rampart has been eroded it is possible to discern how it was revetted with horizontally laid stone slabs. The inner face on the north also seems to have possessed a stone kerb. They also note the existence of six house-platforms in the interior, the best-preserved being sub-circular, measuring 10 × 7 m and constructed as a rock-cut scoop to the rear and a built-up platform at the front.

Hughes, *TCAS*, 4 (1926), 40, Fig. 6; Wright, *Aberystwyth Studies*, 2 (1914), 62, Fig. 10; Ray and Thorburn, 'Ceredigion hillforts: recent survey evidence' (forthcoming).

Goginan Fach   Melindwr   694 818
(Banc y
Castell)
(1.4 ha)

This site is spectacularly situated on a spur high above the Melindwr valley. It is essentially a promontory fort, the rampart running almost straight for 200 m across the more accessible (north) side of a roughly triangular knoll. The other two sides, which have been artificially scarped, measure about 140 and 230 m. The main defence, where best preserved, is a bank some 6 m wide and 2 m high, but is generally reduced to a scarp. The entrance is about 30 m from the east end of the rampart. Its arrangement is difficult to follow. On its east side the rampart turns inwards for a short distance, and at the angle a natural mound which seems to have been scarped, projects northwards;

beyond this is a further natural mound, but that does not seem to have been incorporated in the entrance works. About 30 m west of the gap a smaller bank diverges outwards from the main rampart, and then also turns inwards. Functionally, the final result is a funnel-shaped entrance passage with a bastion (formed by the natural mound) on the east; but how much of this is original and how much the result of later disturbance is uncertain.

Hughes, *TCAS*, 4 (1926), 25, 46, Fig. 16 (lacks detail at entrance).

SN 75

Castell Rhyfel (1.4 ha)	Caron-is-clawdd	732 599

This fort is far more remote and exposed than any other in the County. It is an irregular oval, in a very strong position, but the single rampart is slight, rather less than 5 m wide and only about 0.5 m high. There is no ditch. The bank material has been obtained from a line of small quarry-pits to its rear. No masonry is visible and the bank seems to be almost entirely composed of earth. The entrance, a simple gap, is on the south-east. PRN 2031

Penffrwdllwyd (0.4 ha) (Fig. 59)	Gwnnws Isaf	709 688

The enclosure is roughly semicircular of about 90 m diameter. It is partly protected by a line of crags, lacking any artificial defences, whilst around the remainder of the circuit there are generally two ramparts, separated by about 12 m of undisturbed, steep hillside. The inner rampart is the slighter, only about 5 m wide and a metre high, with no ditch. The outer bank was accompanied by a ditch, now mostly silted up. Where best preserved these measure about 10 m wide by 2 m high overall. At the ends of the enclosure conditions are a little different. On the south the outer rampart in part follows a line of crags, where it is accompanied by a rock-cut ditch with near-vertical sides, and continues to the western cliff; but the inner rampart dies out before reaching these. On the north all the defences are more substantial and between the entrance and the cliff a further bank and ditch protect a small, triangular annexe. This is accessible by way of a

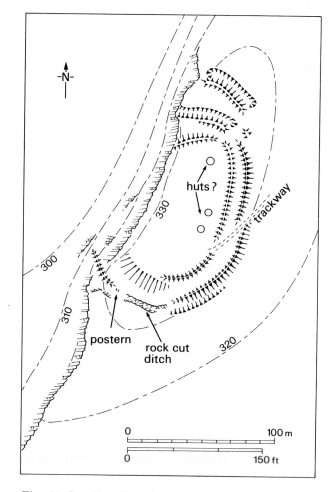

Fig. 59: Penffrwdllwyd.

causeway along the edge of the cliff and from the main entrance to the fort.

The only certain entrance is the straight passage through both ramparts at the northern end. Near the middle of the east side of the enclosure a terraced trackway cuts diagonally through both ramparts. It cannot be dismissed as a modern break, for the line of the outer rampart is distorted here; but there seems to be no reason why a second, original entrance should exist so close to the other. Finally, there is a gap 1.3 m wide through the outer rampart at the south end which may be original, but not certainly so.

The interior is undisturbed. One certain house-platform about 5 m in diameter, can be seen as well as two other probables, but no other structures can be traced.

Hughes, *TCAS*, 4 (1926), 26; 52, Fig. 29 (inaccurate).

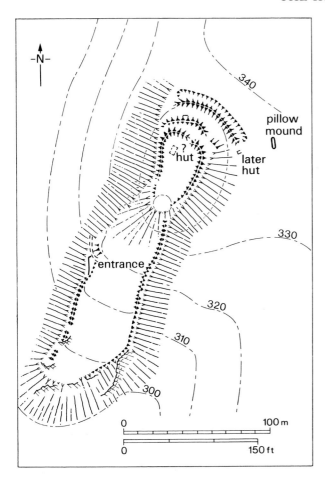

Fig. 60: Pen y Bannau.

Garreg Lwyd   Gwnnws Isaf   701 697
(0.12 ha)
This oval enclosure stands in a weak position on ground falling gently to the west. The defences comprise a dry-stone wall about 3 m thick but heavily robbed and now only about 0.5 m high. The interior has been ploughed.

Y Gaer,   Caron-uwch-   722 666
Pencefn   clawdd
(0.4 ha?)
This field, so named in the Tithe Award survey, lies on a ridge which would be a good position for a fort. The 6-inch Ordnance Survey map (County Sheet series, 21 NE) shows a small 'Gaer' about 30 × 25 m, at 716 661. It seems likely that both refer to the same site. A. H. A. Hogg, visiting the site in 1955, could see nothing at either point, but the

Ordnance Survey staff have now identified faint traces of an enclosure, perhaps 80 × 50 m, at 722 666.
PRN 2047

Pen y Bannau   Gwnnws   742 669
(1.1 ha)   Uchaf
(Fig. 60;
Pl. Va)
The fort occupies a very strong position with a wide outlook. It forms an irregular oblong measuring roughly 180 m (north–south) by 60 m. The defences comprise either a wall (as on the east and south), now reduced to rubble, or (as on the west) by scarping. About 50 m from the north end the ground falls steeply to a lower level. This scarp is shown, incorrectly, as the southern end of the fort in Hughes's plan. At the northern end the wall increases in size to a substantial bank and two similar banks curve round from the western side of the ridge to overlap the gap in the inner wall, forming an oblique entrance.
Hughes, *TCAS*, 4 (1926), 27; 53, Fig. 30 (misleading except for entrance detail).

SN 77

Castell Bwa-   Cwmrheidol   713 795
drain
(0.48 ha)
The position is strong, with an almost precipitous fall to the Rheidol valley on the north-west. With the exception of that side the site is enclosed by a single strong bank of shaly rubble about 3 m high: no revetment is visible. There is an indication of a rock-cut ditch on the east. The bank is set out in straight sections with sharp angles. There is a modern gap near the middle of the north-east side but the original entrance, about 5 m wide, is at the north-east corner. Near the middle of the site, just north-east of a natural rocky hummock, there seems to be a house-platform about 6 m in diameter.
Hughes, *TCAS*, 4 (1926), 45, Fig. 14 (inaccurate).

Castell   Llanafan   721 725
Grogwynion
(0.8 ha)
This fort is roughly rectangular owing to the shape of the ground. It occupies a hillock which falls almost precipitously to the Ystwyth on the south, requiring no defence on that side. The west

side is also very steep and only one bank was required. Around the remainder of the circuit are two strong ramparts running nearly parallel, about 20 m apart along the north side and 40 m on the east. The outer rampart is accompanied by a ditch for part of the northern circuit. The entrance at the north-east corner is rather elaborate. The outer eastern rampart curves west for a short distance and ends in a mound a little north of the terminal of the outer northern rampart, forming an oblique entrance. To gain the interior it is necessary to go south for a short distance between the inner and outer ramparts and then turn west past the line of the inner rampart. The 'banks' and mounds within the fort are of natural origin.
Hughes, *TCAS*, 4 (1926), 26; 49. Fig. 22.

| Castell | Llanfihangel-y-Creuddyn Uchaf | 7270 7761 |

Earthwork.
PRN 2057

SN 78

| Esgair Nant-yrarian (0.4 ha) | Melindwr | 710 817 |

The end of a west-facing spur rises to form a knoll, and has been fortified by the construction of two banks and ditches across the base of the spur. The inner measures about 10 m by 2 m overall; the outer about 12 m by 4 m, with a rock-cut ditch. They are separated by about 20 m. The whole area is thickly planted with conifers, obscuring all detail.
Hughes, *TCAS*, 4 (1926), 25; 47, Fig. 47. The delineation of the earthworks seems correct so far as can be judged, but the contours to the west are completely wrong, showing a steep slope where there is, in fact, a considerable hillock.

| Dinas, Melindwr (0.44 ha) | Melindwr | 743 834 |

The position is strong, the steep-sided hill being almost encircled by the Rheidol and tributary streams. The rampart is a stony bank, about 5.5 m wide and just over a metre high externally. It has been composed of material from a large, internal quarry-ditch, and there is no external ditch. The entrance, on the north, is a simple gap. There is one certain house-platform, 5 m in diameter, just north of the centre of the enclosure, and perhaps three others, one (recently destroyed) near the northern end and two near the entrance.

A similar platform exists on the open hillside about 450 m north of the fort. It is probably a house-site, since charcoal-burning platforms are not common in the area.
Hughes, *TCAS*, 4 (1926), 46, Fig. 15.

Rejected sites

Structures which have at some time or another been accepted as pre-Roman, or which might be mistaken for such. Earthwork castles listed in *Arch. Camb.*, 112 (1963), 91–3 are not included; all, unless otherwise noted, are probably medieval. 'K' refers to D. J. C. King's descriptive list of castles in *Ceredigion*, 3 (1956), 50–68.

SN 14

| Castell, Manian Fawr K No. 33 | St Dogmaels | 151 479 |

| Castell, Nantperch-ellan K No. 34 | St Dogmaels | 173 433 |

SN 56

| Castell (or Caer) Penrhos (1.8ha) | Llanrhystud Mefenydd | 552 696 |

At first glance this earthwork seems to comprise a univallate hillfort with a medieval ringwork superimposed upon it, but the detailed relation between the 'hillfort' rampart and the ringwork strongly supports King's view that they are contemporary. Subject to the possibility that excavation might show surface appearances to be misleading, it therefore seems possible that the whole site was built by Cadwaladr ap Gruffydd in 1148.
King, *Ceredigion*, 3.i (1956), 63, No.22; Hughes, *TCAS*, 4 (1926), 26, 51, Fig. 24.

SN 57

Pen-y-gaer,   Llanrhystud   583 705
near Tycam   Mefenydd

This field, so named in the Tithe Award survey, is on a steep north-facing slope and in a very unlikely position for a hillfort. Aerial photographs show nothing.

SN 67

Cae Castell   Llanilar   650 735

The field of this name in the Tithe Award survey lies in steeply sloping ground, a very unlikely position for a hillfort. Nothing is visible on aerial photographs.

SN 69

Moel-y-garn   Ceulan-a-   692 911
                Maesmor

This appears as Moel y Gaer on the older editions of the 1-inch Ordnance Survey map, but probably by mistake, for no trace of fortification can be seen although the ground has never been cultivated.

APPENDIX II: IRON AGE FINDS

J. L. Davies

a) Burials

Plas Gogerddan   SN 6264 8351
(Fig. 42)

Excavations by the Dyfed Archaeological Trust in 1986 in advance of the laying of a gas pipeline examined part of a complex, multi-period site spanning the fourth millennium BC to the fourth/fifth century AD.

Part of the complex included an axial arrangement of three ring-ditches; the northernmost (237) 6 m in diameter, the others (266 and 365) coeval and 11.6 and 12 m in diameter respectively. A shallow pit set off-centre within 237 had (on the basis of phosphate analysis) contained a cremation, whilst it is also possible that burials had lain beneath (now vanished) mounds within ring-ditches 266 and 365. A *terminus post quem* of 820 ± 60 bc (CAR-1073) was obtained for the digging of 365, whilst a mass of burnt bone and charcoal incorporated in the fill of 266 gave a *terminus ad quem* of 200 ± 60 bc (CAR-1072) for this ring-ditch.

A number of pits were concentric to 266 and 365; all contained evidence for human burials. Pit 340, just within the margin of 365, contained the stain of a crouched or contracted inhumation with the head to the north, accompanied by a pair of bronze fibulae (brooches) of first century BC to first century AD type.

Two interlocking pits between ring-ditches 237 and 266 each probably contained a crouched/contracted inhumation. A fragment of bronze in the southern pit probably represents the remains of a fibula, and the burial may be of similar date to that in Pit 340.

The inhumations and cremation may all be broadly contemporary and belong to the first century BC.

K. Murphy, 'Plas Gogerddan, Dyfed: a multi-period ritual and burial site', *Arch. J.* (forthcoming).

b) Metalwork

1. Gold

Stater (Mack 50) of Corieltauvian A type, said to have been found in the parish of Penbryn before 1722. It is a rare example of a Celtic coin from Wales. Date: *c.* 70–55 BC.

Camden, *Britannia*, ed. Gibson (London, 1722), 42, 75 No. 1; J. Evans, *The Coins of the Ancient Britons, Supplement* (London, 1890), 433; D. F. Allen, 'The origins of coinage in Britain. A reappraisal', *Problems of the Iron Age in Southern Britain*, ed. S. S. Frere (London, 1960), 180; R. P. Mack, *The Coinage of Ancient Britain* (London, 1964); R. D. Van

Arsdell, *Celtic Coinage of Britain* (London, 1989), 216–19 and Map 39.

2. Bronze

(a) A half-collar found *c.* 1875 during ploughing within the hillfort of Pencoed-y-foel (SN 425 427). H. N. Savory describes it thus: '. . . a thick, semi-circular plate with the remains of the attachment for a hinge at one end, and a groove for a fastening pin at the other. The inside is plain, the upper decorated in low relief with a series of pointed leaf-forms with hemispherical raised bosses riveted to the plate, forming trumpet units linked by S-scrolls. It was probably completed with a detachable beaded segment. Damaged and corroded towards the hinged end.' Overall diameter 150 mm, width 22 mm, thickness 7 mm. First century BC–first century AD. Megaw (under 'Birdcombe Camp') considers the form to be 'provincial Roman rather than Celtic', and later 'that a mid- or late first-century date would not be unreasonable'.
Barker, *Proc. Clifton Antiquarian Club*, 3 (1896), 210; J. V. S. Megaw, *Art of the European Iron Age* (New York, 1970), 171; J. V. S. Megaw, 'A group of Later Iron Age collars or neck-rings from western Britain', *Prehistoric and Roman Studies*, ed. G. de G. Sieveking (London, 1971), 145–55; H. N. Savory, *Guide Catalogue of the Early Iron Age Collections* (Cardiff, 1976), 40–1, 61–2, Pl. IVb.

(b) A pair of spoon-like objects said to have been found about 1829 under a heap of stones within the hillfort of Castell Nadolig (SN 298 503). They have shallow, pointed oval bowls, wide flat handles (one damaged) 'decorated in low relief with assymetrical La Tène scrolls (the designs differ slightly). One bowl (present length 120 mm; width 74 mm) has an incised cross, the other (length 123.5 mm; width 73 mm) a hole near the right edge.' Such objects are not infrequently associated with Iron Age burials. This may be the case here, the heap of stones representing a burial cairn. The absence of any reference to human remains may possibly be accounted for by their total disappearance in an acid soil.

G. Williams has drawn attention to the possibility that records of cremations within Castell Nadolig may refer not to Bronze Age burials, but to those of Iron Age date.
'Cardigan Meeting—Report', *Arch. Camb.*, 14 (1859), 328; E.L.B., *Arch. Camb.*, 17 (1862), 214–15; H. N. Savory, *Guide Catalogue*, 41, 61, 106 (Fig. 36, 4); R. Whimster, *Burial Practices in Iron Age Britain* (BAR 90: Oxford, 1981), 172; Williams, *AW*, 25 (1985), 14.

(c) Two fragmentary late La Tène fibulae accompanying an inhumation from Pit 340 at Plas Gogerddan.
(i) A low bow made of wire approximately 2 mm thick, with a bilateral spring 8 mm in diameter at one end. Overall length 33 mm, but foot and pin missing.
(ii) A very fragmentary brooch composed of wire 1 mm thick with a bilateral spring 6 mm in diameter, two coils on either side of the bow. The catch-plate was of the solid variety. The brooch may be an example of the 'Nauheim derivative' type.

(d) Fragments of a brooch from grave 335 at Plas Gogerddan. Possibly part of the open catch-plate of La Tène II or III type.
K. Murphy, 'Plas Gogerddan, Dyfed: A multi-period ritual and burial site', (forthcoming).

(e) Two tubular fragments found in excavations at Pen Dinas, Aberystwyth in 1933.
Forde, *BBCS*, 7 (1933), 80.

(f) Fragment of semi-cylindrical bronze binding found in excavations at Pen Dinas, Aberystwyth, in 1934.
Forde, *BBCS*, 7 (1934), 327.

3. Iron

(a) Numerous fragmentary objects, including some of large size, were found in excavations at Pen Dinas, Aberystwyth, though only a nail could be identified.
Forde *et al.*, *Arch. Camb.*, 112 (1963), 151.

(b) Fragmentary nails were found during the course of excavations at Caerau, Henllan.
Williams, *Arch.Camb.*, 98 (1945), 236 Fig. 5.

c) Glass

(a) Globular bead 11.5 mm in diameter, of pale yellow translucent glass decorated with three spirals of yellow opaque glass threads. Found

during excavations at Pen Dinas, Aberystwyth. It belongs to Guido's Class 10, a Meare 'spiral'. These have a western British distribution.
Forde, *BBCS*, 7 (1934), 326; *BBCS*, 8 (1936), 380; M. Guido, *Prehistoric and Roman Glass Beads in Britain and Ireland*, Soc. Antiquaries Research Report 35 (London, 1978), 189.

(b) Bead, of unknown type, said to have been found on Castle Hill, Aberystwyth (SN 579 815).
Calendar of the University of Wales, Aberystwyth (1879), 66; Sansbury, *TCAS*, 7 (1930), 78–9.

(c) Three glass beads of unstated types found in excavations at Caer Cadwgan (SN 623 480).
AW, 25 (1985), 18.

d) Amber

(a) Bead 14 mm in diameter with 2.5 mm central perforation, found in excavations at Caerau, Henllan.
Williams, *Arch. Camb.*, 98 (1945), 236, Fig. 5. 1.

(b) An amber bead found in excavations at Caer Cadwgan. *AW*, 25 (1985), 18.

e) Pottery

A number of potsherds were found during excavations at Pen Dinas, Aberystwyth, and represent a minimum of two vessels. One was decorated with a deeply impressed horizontal groove with oblique incised ornament above. It probably belongs to the same variety of 'Malvernian' pottery described below.

Several sherds have allowed the reconstruction of a vessel of ovoid profile with a plain, slightly flattened rim. It is 183 mm high and 145 mm in diameter at the mouth. The ware is smooth, varying from buff to reddish brown in colour and the fabric is of Peacock's 'Group A' ('Malvernian'). It is decorated externally just outside the rim with a frieze of irregular comma-shaped impressions in close order.
Forde *et al.*, *Arch. Camb.*, 112 (1963), 151; D. P. S. Peacock, *PPS*, 34 (1968), 416, 427 no. 2; Savory, *Guide Catalogue*, 71, 111, Fig. 41. 10.

f) Clay

Baked clay spindlewhorl 20 mm in diameter with 4 mm central perforation found in excavations at Caerau, Henllan.
Williams, *Arch. Camb.*, 98 (1945), 236, Fig. 5.2.

g) Stone

(a) Mudstone spindlewhorl of convex form, 48 mm in diameter with an irregular central perforation of 7.7 mm. Upper surface decorated with two parallel grooves and diagonal grooves in two planes.
Williams, *Arch. Camb.*, 98 (1945), 236, Fig. 5. 3.

(b) Spindlewhorl from excavations at Pen Dinas, Aberystwyth.
Forde, *BBCS*, 7 (1933), 80.

(c) Spindlewhorl from excavations at Pen Dinas, Aberystwyth.
Forde, *BBCS*, 7 (1934), 326.

(d) Stone bead from excavations at Pen Dinas, Aberystwyth.
Forde, *BBCS*, 7 (1933), 80.

(e) Loom weight.
Forde, *BBCS*, 7 (1934), 327.

(f) Loom weight.
Forde, *BBCS*, 8 (1936), 379.

(g) A stone head found in the bank of the River Ystwyth between Llanfarian and Llanilar. It measures 50 × 30 mm and is fashioned from a water-worn pebble. While the use of a natural pebble and the association with a river or stream has parallels in pagan Celtic traditions, the object does not have any particularly 'Celtic' features.
Delaney and Williams, *AW*, 22 (1982), 42; PRN 10500 (drawing in Dyfed Archaeological Trust files).

(h) Pierced stone (?loomweight) showing traces of cord wear. Found at Ffosgwy Farm, Lledrod Isaf (SN 65 68).
Sansbury, *TCAS*, 7 (1930), 72.

(i) Disc-shaped spindlewhorl 38 mm in diameter, decorated on one face with ten pits standing in circles close to the perforation, and on the other side with thirteen pits and a zigzag line. Found in a garden in Bryn Road, Aberystwyth. (SN 58 81).
Savory, *Guide Catalogue*, 65, Fig. 34, A12.

(j) Disc-shaped spindlewhorl 41 mm in diameter, decorated on each face with eight radiating incised lines and with a single incised line around the edge. 'From the Teifiside district'.
Savory, *Guide Catalogue*, 65, Fig. 34, A5.

(k) Spindlewhorl, found in the parish of Caron-is-clawdd (SN 668 625). In private possession.
PRN 8988

(l) Two spindlewhorls found in Tirymynach parish (SN 63 84).
RCAHM Field observation in 1961; *Handlist*, 1976; PRN 5166.

(m) 'Half of the upper stone of a rotary quern decorated with concentric grooves, the outer one carrying transverse radials'. Present whereabouts unknown. Said to have been found at Dinas Cerdin, Llandysul (SN 386 469).
Briggs, *AW*, 26 (1986), 32.

Items (g)–(m) can only be provisionally ascribed to the Iron Age. Their date-range probably lies between the early first millennium BC and the mid-first millennium AD.

CHAPTER 4

THE ROMAN PERIOD

J. L. Davies

'... the promontory of the Ganganoi; the mouth of the river Stuccia; the mouth of the
river Tuerobis; the Octapitarum promontory ...'

It is with these few geographical details from Ptolemy's coastal survey of Britain that the
County briefly transcends the divide between prehistory and history before once again lapsing
into obscurity until the early medieval period. Albeit a compilation of the mid-second century
AD the *Geographia* utilized much earlier source-material for its British section and there is little
doubt that the bulk of the information pertaining to Wales will have been gleaned directly after
its conquest between AD 74 and 77.[1] Ptolemy's *Stuccia* (properly *Stuctia*) is manifestly the modern
Ystwyth, mentioned again in a late seventh-century AD document known as the Ravenna
Cosmography where it erroneously appears as the *Iuctius* (= *Stuctius*). The Latinized Celtic name
admirably suits the topography of 'the winding river'.[2] Despite some philological reservations the
Tuerobis can be none other than the Teifi, the only river with a *ta*-root south of the Ystwyth and
north of St David's Head—the promontory of the Octapitai.[3] The reason why specific rivers were
singled out in this manner is unknown although a connection between the river name and an
important native centre—or more likely a Roman fort—has been postulated, with the transfer
of the river name to settlements along their banks.[4] Only one place-name—*Bremia*—is probably
to be located within the County. This figures in a somewhat tangled list in the Ravenna
Cosmography and is customarily equated with the well-known Roman fort at Llanio.[5] The name
is thought to derive from a river of that ilk (= 'the roaring stream') and the Brefi, a tributary
of the Teifi, does indeed come to a confluence a mile to the south of the fort. Early antiquaries
equated Llanio with the *Luentinum* cited by Ptolemy as one of the two *poleis* of the Demetae (here
utilizing the term *polis* to mean 'a place' rather than a town), but there is no evidence to support
such an identification. Indeed Pumsaint Roman fort and the probable gold-mining complex at
Dolau Cothi is a far more likely candidate.[6] The other *polis*, *Moridunum* (Carmarthen), may have

[1]Ptolemy, *Geographia* II, 3, ed. C. F. A. Nobbe (Leipzig, 1898–1913). For further discussion see
below, n. 2.
[2]A. L. F. Rivet and C. Smith, *The Place Names of Roman Britain* (London, 1979), 462.
[3]Ibid., 480; also A. L. F. Rivet, 'Some aspects of Ptolemy's Geography of Britain', *Caesarodunum*,
9 (1974), 64.
[4]I. A. Richmond and O. G. S. Crawford, 'The British section of the Ravenna Cosmography',
Arch., 93 (1949), 1–50; W. H. Davies, 'The Romans in Cardiganshire', *Ceredigion*, 4 (1961), 85–93.
[5]Rivet and Smith, *Place Names*, 277.
[6]A. L. F. Rivet, 'Some aspects of Ptolemy's Geography of Britain', 71.

similarly originated as a fort but had probably attained the status of the tribal *caput* by the later second century AD[7].

The identity of the socio-political group(s) who inhabited Cardiganshire in the pre- and early Roman period is unknown since the sparse sources pertaining to the Romano-British *civitates* (tribes) make it impossible to allot specific localities to these political entities with any degree of precision. None of the Welsh tribes produced an indigenous pre-Roman coinage, which would have signified the concentration of power in the hands of chieftains, evolving into the 'tribal-states' of the early first century AD whose boundaries may be broadly determined with reference to the distribution and exclusivity of these coinages.[8] This process of political centralization, well advanced over much of southern England by the Roman conquest and even recognizable in north-eastern England in the middle of the first century, is nowhere evidenced in Wales. Even within those politically advanced communities in England the prevalent Celtic patron-client system generated a shifting pattern of political alliances which could lead to fragmentation on the death of a paramount chieftain, before a further period of coalescence and the rise to power of another individual. The power of the pre-eminent chieftain rested upon his ability to coerce an aggregate of kin-groups, dominated by his own clan, through success in war or the giving of gifts. It would have been perhaps the temporarily pre-eminent clan which would attract the attention of Roman writers, to be utilized as a socio-political focus for a tribally-based administrative framework.

The situation in Wales with its relatively low population density, inferior agricultural potential and often inhospitable terrain leading to dispersed settlement, may have been a positive disincentive to political cohesion at a regional level, except in exceptional circumstances. Although Roman sources remark upon the hostility of tribes such as the Silures and the Ordovices, many groups may have been divided in their attitude to Rome, this divided loyalty perhaps reflected in the later selective placement of Roman garrisons. There is a further complication: following conquest there are instances of territories dominated by anti-Roman clans being handed over to a pro-Roman section in whose hands local administration was invested. In this case the *civitates* thus formed were probably given the name of the favoured clan, whose name was applied to the rest or assumed through common usage. Other *civitates* were wholly artificial groupings, created through the amalgamation of a number of smaller units to suit Roman administrative convenience. In conclusion then we might bear in mind the woeful inadequacy of the sources pertaining to the identity of the immediate pre-Roman inhabitants of our region. Whilst Jarrett and Mann[9] in their discussion of the Welsh evidence suggest that the territory of Ptolemy's Demetae may have extended into southern Cardiganshire on the grounds that Roman forts are absent from this region—a characteristic which it shares with Pembrokeshire and western

[7]H. James, 'Excavations at Church Street, Carmarthen, 1976', *Monographs and Collections I, Roman Sites*, ed. G. C. Boon (Cambrian Archaeological Association, Cardiff, 1978), 63–4. For a summary of recent work see *Archaeology in Dyfed. A Review of Ten Years' Work by the Dyfed Archaeological Trust, 1976–86* (Dyfed Archaeological Trust, Carmarthen, 1986), 20–2.

[8]L. Sellwood, 'Tribal boundaries viewed from the perspective of numismatic evidence', *Aspects of the Iron Age in Central Southern Britain*, ed. B. Cunliffe and D. Miles (University of Oxford: Committee for Archaeology Monograph No.2, Oxford, 1984), 191–204.

[9]M. G. Jarrett and J. C. Mann, 'The tribes of Wales', *WHR*, 4, 2 (1968), 161–74.

Carmarthenshire—fort distribution, on its own, is too coarse an indicator to make such a fine distinction.

We have already noted a tendency on the part of Roman sources to oversimplify the contemporary indigenous socio-political situation. Consequently the identity of smaller tribes or important clans could be submerged in that of larger, more powerful or philo-Roman neighbours, the Octapitai of western Pembrokeshire being a case in point.[10] An eminent writer such as the elder Pliny had never heard of the Demetae, and, consequently, boldly states that the shortest crossing to Ireland could be made from the district of the Silures; in this instance utilizing the well-known tribal name for the inhabitants of south Wales as a whole, since they were to Roman eyes the most notable *gens* in the region.[11] Roman documentary sources apart there is one interesting piece of evidence which may relate to the identity of the inhabitants of Roman Cardiganshire, namely the post-Roman inscribed stone from Penbryn bearing the epitaph of Corbalengus.[12] He is described as an Ordous, an Ordovician, a tribe with an extensive territory in mid Wales.[13] Despite arguments to the contrary it seems best to regard Corbalengus as a 'foreigner' in southern Cardiganshire, otherwise the tribal *origo* would have been superfluous. It would, therefore, appear that when the epitaph was set up (for a discussion of its date see p.314), southern Cardiganshire, at least, was excluded from Ordovician territory.

Archaeology cannot be of much assistance in isolating the immediate pre-Roman inhabitants of Cardiganshire. They appear to have shared the same cultural traits of many of the contemporary inhabitants of mid-Wales, the lacking of an indigenous 'tribal' coinage, or a distinctive ceramic or artefactual range. Nor is settlement morphology of much assistance except insofar as it links our area in the most general terms with south-west Wales as a whole, and in drawing a thin veil between those dwelling on opposite banks of the Dyfi. To the east the spine of the Cambrian range, apparently bereft of any overt settlement in the later prehistoric period, may well have isolated our area from communities dwelling in the upper Wye and Severn valleys. For what it may be worth—clan/tribal complexities and Roman administrative interference apart —it would not be unreasonable to suggest that by the mid-second century (the date of the compilation of Ptolemy's Geography) south Cardiganshire at least formed a *pagus* (a rural district of local government) of the Demetae. Their eastern neighbours, and perhaps their northern too, will have been the Ordovices.[14] However, we may note the propensity of Cardiganshire to have an identity all of its own, certainly as a kingdom by the eighth century AD, and if not already a political entity by the early Roman period then very likely assuming a role as a border territory.

Broad historical events related by first century AD writers such as Cornelius Tacitus, involving dominant tribes such as the Silures and Ordovices, certainly embraced our region, but the

---

[10]Ptolemy, *Geographia* II, 3, 3; J. L. Davies, 'Roman and native in Wales, I–IV AD', *Roman Frontier Studies 1969*, ed. E. Birley (*et al.*) (Eighth International Congress of Limesforschung, Cardiff, 1974), 35–6.
[11]Pliny, *Natural History*, 4, 103.
[12]V. E. Nash-Williams, *The Early Christian Monuments of Wales* (Cardiff, 1950), 102.
[13]Jarrett and Mann, 'The tribes of Wales', 167–70.
[14]Ibid., 169. For the Ordovices in Merioneth see J. E. Lloyd, *A History of Wales* I (London, 1911), 250. For a discussion of whether north-west Wales lay within their territory see R. B. White, 'Excavations at Brithdir, near Dolgellau, 1974', *Monographs and Collections I: Roman Sites*, ed. G. C. Boon (Cambrian Archaeological Association, Cardiff, 1978), 46.

paucity both of literary evidence and a substantial corpus of epigraphic data militates against the writing of a meaningful history of Roman Cardiganshire. Indeed the techniques available for its study in this period are essentially those of the prehistorian, with all their imprecision and inherent defects. We should also bear in mind that the history of what is after all a minute portion of a remote province of a far-flung empire lacks any real meaning unless viewed against the background of the political, social and economic developments of the Roman West. The immense value of this imperial connection cannot be overstated. First it provides a relatively firm chronological framework for some three centuries. Second, a vast body of comparative material —literary, epigraphic and archaeological—is available for study. Together they allow the student to interpret a variety of archaeological phenomena with a fair degree of confidence, thereby presenting a much more human face to the emergent picture of Cardiganshire in the Roman period.

The conquest and military occupation

In the half-century following the Claudian invasion of AD 43 the conquest of southern Britain never conformed to what we might consider a master plan. Three major factors dictated its speed and course: imperial interest in the province; the attitude of British communities towards Rome; and external factors, largely of a military/political nature, which on occasion might be so overriding as to have a substantial effect upon insular operations. On occasion Roman campaigning against the Welsh tribes was constrained by all three. It would be reasonable to conclude that the Emperor Claudius envisaged the eventual conquest of the whole of Britain. An advance into the west midlands, and thence into the central and southern Marches in AD 48, although provoked by an attack on tribes allied to Rome, appears to have been a preparatory phase to an offensive against certain of the Welsh tribes by the second governor of the province, Ostorius Scapula (AD 47–52). Roman forces were already engaged against the Decangi (Deceangli) of north-east Wales in that year, and were then drawn into a protracted war against the Silures of south-east and the Ordovices of north-central Wales in the following year. That war was still in full swing, at least against the Silures, in AD 52 and had resulted in the first major defeat for Roman arms on British soil.[15] Scapula's successor Didius Gallus (AD 52–7), despite Tacitus' critical comments, may not have been unsuccessful.[16] There may well have been subsequent gains in the Welsh borderland—including the conquest of Gwent and Glamorgan as far west as Cardiff, where a large fort of this period has come to light beneath the medieval castle [17]— redressing the reverses of 52. The archaeological evidence, spanning some twelve years of campaigning, is complex, and the primary chronological indicators—coinage in particular—are incapable of differentiating between the work of successive late Claudian and earlier Neronian

[15]Tacitus, *Annals*, 12, 40.
[16]M. G. Jarrett, 'Early Roman campaigns in Wales', *Arch.J.*, 121 (1965), 31–3; W. H. Manning, *Report on the Excavations at Usk. The Fortress Excavations 1968–1971* (Cardiff, 1981), 29–31.
[17]J. L. Davies, 'Roman military deployment in Wales and the Marches from Claudius to the Antonines', *Roman Frontier Studies 1979*, ed. W. S. Hanson and L. J. F. Keppie (BAR 71: Oxford, 1980), 258–60.

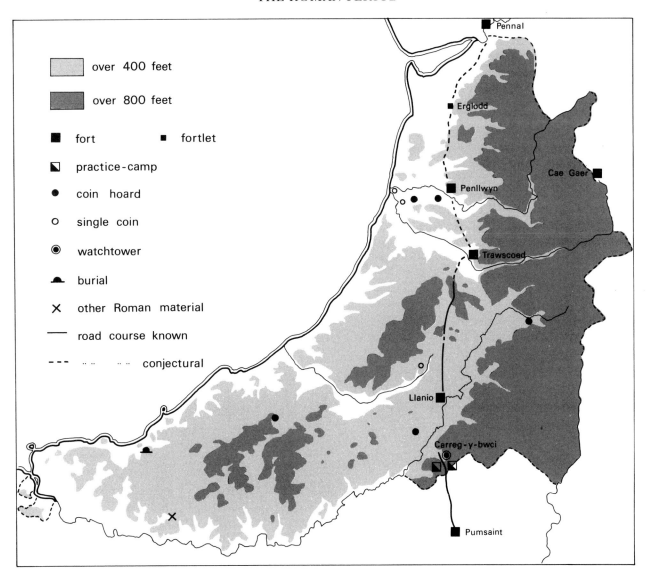

Fig. 61: Map of Roman Cardiganshire.

governors. However, the meagre documentary evidence hints that the governorships of Didius Gallus, Quintus Veranius and the first two years of Suetonius Paulinus (AD 52–60) saw a substantial reduction in the fighting potential of the Silures and Ordovices. By AD 60 Paulinus was able to launch a successful assault on Anglesey—a campaign which must surely have been regarded as the culmination of the Neronian offensive, but the outbreak of the Boudiccan rebellion brought all to nought. Consolidation of Paulinus' fresh Welsh conquests had to be forsaken to facilitate the concentration of the army to meet this emergency, whilst the quelling of the insurrection necessitated the re-garrisoning of disaffected areas in eastern England and led to a reappraisal of the situation in Wales. Seemingly, all thought of resuming operations in Wales was abandoned. Indeed, for more than a decade it appears that the army was largely concerned with maintaining the status quo from its bases in the Welsh March. A quiet state of affairs is indicated by the temporary withdrawal of Legio XIV Gemina from its Wroxeter base in AD 66 and its dispatch to Italy, with a concomitant redeployment of the legionary garrison of Britannia. Legio XX Valeria Victrix seems to have been moved north from its base at Usk to fill the lacuna at Wroxeter whilst elements of Legio II Augusta may have been redeployed at Gloucester. The status of the Usk fortress in this period is uncertain.[18]

Archaeological traces of Rome's attempt to grapple with the problem of Wales in the period AD 48–74 are substantial, though tantalizing. They include short-lived field-entrenchments such as marching-camps, and permanent or semi-permanent works such as legionary fortresses, 'vexillation fortresses' and auxiliary forts. Many more temporary works, and doubtless a number of forts, remain to be detected. Of those known, relatively few have been the subject of intensive archaeological investigation and their relative chronologies and spatial relationship remain problematical.[19] Chronology and inter-relationship is undoubtedly complex with sites being founded, abandoned, reoccupied or succeeding one another with bewildering rapidity in the ebb and flow of frontier warfare. No certain pre-Flavian (i.e. pre-AD 69) military sites are known in south-west Wales, but permanent sites situated further east could have been used for offensive operations striking far to the west. In this context we may note that the Severn valley in particular offered a prime invasion route into the heart of Wales. With a legionary base at Wroxeter from circa AD 55, itself apparently succeeding a campaign base, or bases, it is not surprising to find what may be equally early auxiliary forts upstream at Brompton (Salop.) and Llwyn y Brain, near Caersŵs (Mont.). Although unexcavated the latter occupies a nodal position at the confluence of the Severn with a number of minor rivers forming an upland bowl, and its size suggests that it functioned as the base for a substantial force (1,000–1,500 men) whose operational range could have included the headwaters of the Severn/Wye, if not Cardigan Bay. Further south the valleys of the upper Wye and Usk served as further avenues into the heart of Wales, with a large pre-Flavian base at Clyro (Rads.) and a legionary fortress established in the mid-50s at Usk (Mon.). Two marching-camps flanking the upper Wye at St Harmon and Esgairperfedd form part of an incomplete series indicating a line of march towards Plynlimon and the headwaters of the Ystwyth. Neither have been dated, but they may be pre-Flavian.[20] Even more enigmatic is the site of the Flavian fort at Llandovery, which on the strength of a small amount of what is presumed to be pre-Flavian pottery and a recently observed ditch-system and destruction deposit sealed by the defences of the Flavian fort, may be considered as a candidate for a pre-Flavian installation and an early Roman presence approaching Cardiganshire from the south-east.[21] In default of unimpeachable evidence we cannot be certain that south-west Wales, and the tract between the Dyfi and the Teifi in particular, had been penetrated by the Roman army prior to the 70s. The region was remote and probably did not figure large in the plans of the Roman high command for the reduction of Wales. Even trade-goods, contained within durable ceramic containers, and fancy metalwork of early Romano-British provincial origin, are

[18]W. H. Manning, op. cit; see above, n. 16.
[19]See above, n. 17.
[20]V. E. Nash-Williams, *The Roman Frontier in Wales*, ed. M. G. Jarrett (Cardiff, 1969), 124–6.
[21]Ibid., 96; *Brit.*, 14 (1983), 281.

absent from the excavated settlement sites of early to mid-first-century AD date in south-west Wales, further emphasizing its peripheral nature and the unreceptive, if not overtly hostile attitude of the region's native aristocracy.[22] The placement of Roman garrisons in the County certainly indicates that its populace was initially hostile.

The accession of Flavius Vespasian to the throne in AD 69 marks a turning-point in the history of Roman Britain. The new administration, facing a crisis with the collapse of the Brigantian client-state in northern England, concentrated military resources to finish the task and bring the whole island under Roman control. This resolute policy was initiated with the subjugation of the Brigantes by Vettius Bolanus (AD 69–71) and Petilius Cerealis (AD 71–4): then Julius Frontinus (AD 74–7) was given a brief in which the conquest of the Welsh tribes figured large. Tacitus refers solely to his subjugation of the Silures but subsequent events—in particular the Ordovician rebellion of the late autumn or early winter of AD 77—indicate that his achievement was considerably greater.[23] He was certainly responsible for the reduction of south Wales—the Demetae included—and much of mid and north Wales too, although we have no means of determining whether it was he or Cerealis who initiated this advance. It is probably in Frontinus' governorship that we might reasonably expect to find the first permanent military installations in Cardiganshire. Of the course of the campaigns which preceded the more evident phase of consolidation, we know nothing, although a woefully incomplete series of marching-camps of presumed Flavian date survives in south and mid Wales. Attention has already been drawn to the camp at Esgair Perfedd which points to a large expeditionary force moving west from the upper Wye probably towards the headwaters of the Ystwyth. The upper Severn also provided ready access to north Cardiganshire, Roman concern for the security of this route being indicated by the siting of the small fort at Cae Gaer (Mont.), well placed to supervise this mountainous route linking the valleys of the Rheidol, Wye and Severn. The southern portion of the County, doubtless, will have been penetrated via the upper Usk and Tywi, whilst the sea could have offered an alternative approach if the *Classis Britannica* was thus employed.[24] Certainly the siting of some Flavian forts—Pennal (Mer.) being the only instance along Cardigan Bay—suggests that the advantages of seaborne supply, if not the transport of troops, was much appreciated.

The conquest phase is not reflected at the three extensively investigated Cardiganshire hillforts; Caerau (Henllan), Caer Cadwgan and Pen Dinas (Aberystwyth). None have yielded evidence of assault or of the slighting of their defences at Roman hands, but such proven instances are rare and their discovery fortuitous.[25] There is nothing to indicate that they were occupied in the first century AD in any case. Once local war-bands had been eliminated, or the military had reached an accommodation with friendly communities, then forts housing regiments of auxiliary (i.e. non-citizen) soldiers, together with other, smaller types of military installations were established according to strategic requirements. In Cardiganshire the primary arrangement

[22]Cf. pre-Flavian pottery from Mynydd Bychan (Glam.) and pre-Flavian glass from Whitton (Glam.).

[23]Tacitus, *Agricola*, 17.

[24]C. G. Starr, *The Roman Imperial Navy 31 BC–AD 324* (Cambridge, 1960), 154.

[25]For a discussion of the Welsh evidence see J. L. Davies, 'Roman and native ...', *Roman Frontier Studies 1969*, ed. E. Birley, B. Dobson and M. Jarrett (Cardiff, 1974), 36–7; J. L. Davies, 'Roman arrowheads from Dinorben and the Sagittarii of the Roman army', *Brit.*, 8 (1977), 257–70.

seems to have comprised three such forts—Penllwyn, Trawscoed and Llanio, each sited at the point where the axial north–south military road (an essential element in the system of control) crossed the major rivers, the Rheidol, Ystwyth and Teifi respectively. They were also in all probability placed with a view to supervising concentrations of population. In addition, a fortlet at Erglodd accommodated an outposted detachment stationed in a position intermediate between Penllwyn and the fort at Pennal (Mer.) on the north bank of the Dyfi; whilst the small fort at Cae Gaer, again just beyond the County boundary, probably housed an incomplete unit or *vexillatio*. In no case is the initial garrison of these garrison posts known, although on grounds of size alone (itself a most uncertain criterion) we might tentatively suggest a cavalry regiment (*ala quingenaria*) or two brigaded part-mounted regiments each 500 strong (*cohortes quingenariae equitatae*) at Penllwyn, an infantry regiment 1,000 strong (*cohors milliaria peditata*) or two part-mounted regiments each 500 strong) at Trawscoed, and a regiment 500 strong (possibly part-mounted) at Llanio. Only at the last-named do we have an epigraphically attested unit, *Cohors II Asturum equitata*, but at an uncertain date and, therefore, not necessarily the primary garrison.

These installations represent only a very small portion of a much more extensive, selectively placed network of forts, fortlets and possibly watch-towers employed for the policing of those communities who had offered resistance, with the legions ensconced in their bases at Caerleon, Wroxeter and Chester acting as a strategic reserve. The forts, probably built by legionary work-parties (Legio II Augusta, XX Valeria Victrix and II Adiutrix are known to have been active on the Welsh front), conformed to the standard near-square or playing-card shape, with earthwork defences, timber gateways and interval-towers and buildings of timber-framed construction. They could be rapidly constructed of locally available materials and swiftly refurbished or rebuilt as circumstances dictated. Only the stone bath-houses which lay outside their defences required a sophisticated building technology. These garrisoned posts, eventually linked by an all-weather road-system which penetrated valley and upland tract, were normally placed a day's march (12–15 miles) apart; they were mutually supportive and capable of rapid reinforcement or concentration should rebellion be in the offing. The whole system was probably complete by the close of the 70s AD.

The military dispositions of Julius Frontinus and Cn. Iulius Agricola's governorship did not remain unaltered for very long. A reduction in the Welsh garrison had to be expedited as quickly as possible to facilitate the release of troops for service in northern Britain in the wake of the territorial gains of Agricola's governorship (AD 77–83). Agricola's campaigns placed what transpired to be an intolerable strain on manpower, whilst Continental exigencies compounded the situation. Legionary detachments drawn from Britain were already serving in Domitian's German war in AD 83; and in AD 86, or soon thereafter, Legio II Adiutrix stationed at Chester was permanently withdrawn from Britain,[26] a move which it is thought was probably accompanied by the transfer of a complement of auxiliary regiments. There is no certain evidence that these troop movements affected Cardiganshire although a hiatus has been detected in the Flavian occupation within and without the fort at Trawscoed (see p.301) and possibly at Erglodd too.[27]

---

[26]One of its centurions was decorated in a Dacian War, possibly in AD 88 (*ILS* 9193).

[27]J. L. Davies, 'Excavations at Trawscoed Roman Fort, Dyfed', *BBCS*, 28 (1980), 723, 727.

For the remainder of the century the military situation in Wales is unclear although there may well have been some selective thinning through a reduction in the size of individual garrisons rather than by outright abandonment. This process quickened in Trajan's reign (AD 98–117) with forts either being abandoned, reduced in size to accommodate smaller garrisons as at Caerau, Beulah (Brec.), Tomen y Mur (Mer.) and Gelli-gaer (Glam.), or simply accommodating sub-divided units.[28] By the beginning of Hadrian's reign (AD 117–38) the process had been accelerated and embraced forts in many parts of the Principality; for example, at Pen Llystyn (Caerns.), where a fortlet replaced the cohort fort (with the possibility of a similar sequence at Llanio), and *Segontium* (Caernarfon), where the barracks in the *praetentura* of the fort were replaced by buildings of manifestly different function. In the period AD 100–140 the establishment of fortlets housing elements of subdivided units may have been an efficient way of reducing the military commitment to Wales as a whole, whilst still maintaining an effective presence.

This phase, highly subjective in terms of chronology and almost unknowable in terms of strict overall site-relationship, ended sometime early in the reign of Hadrian insofar as Cardiganshire is concerned. Wherever excavations have been conducted on Roman military sites in the County they have consistently failed to reveal concrete evidence of occupation beyond *c.* AD 130 at the latest. This is certainly the case at Trawscoed and Llanio. Although the chronological indices from Penllwyn and Erglodd leave much to be desired, if the emergent pattern is regarded as meaningful then these two sites are likely to have followed suit. This process of military disengagement which left the greater portion of the Principality bereft of garrisons by the 140s was partly a response to the prevailing situation in northern Britain which led to the stationing of the bulk of the army on, and south of, the Tyne–Solway isthmus from *c.* AD 90, and partly to the quiescence of the Welsh tribes as a whole (north-west and east-central Wales seemingly excepted). By the middle of the century, with the exception of the great fortress of II Augusta at Caerleon, retained by reason of military inertia or investment in its facilities as a Roman equivalent of an Aldershot or Catterick, the territory of the Silures had been stripped of its garrisons, whilst romanized building projects had certainly been initiated at incipient villa sites and at their tribal town of *Venta*. Further west no military installations can be shown to have been occupied within or bordering the putative territory of the Demetae after the 140s, and, although romanization may have been less thorough here, their right to administer tribal affairs as a full-blown *civitas* was probably delayed no later than the Antonine period (AD 139–92) on the basis of perceived developments at their tribal town of *Moridunum* (Carmarthen).[29] It is manifest that the population of Cardiganshire was now regarded as wholly pacific and reconciled to its lot. There is no hint that this area gave Rome any further trouble.

With the quiescence of south Wales it was only necessary to maintain troops at select forts in north-west and east-central Wales—broadly the territory of the Ordovices—from the Antonine period: even then there is no reason to believe that the occupation of forts such as Brecon Gaer, Castell Collen or Caersŵs was full-scale or continuous.[30] The political and military tribulations

[28]J. L. Davies, 'Roman military deployment . . .', *Roman Frontier Studies 1979*, 264, 269.

[29]H. James, 'Carmarthen—Moridunum', *Conquest, Co-existence and Change : Recent Work in Roman Wales*, ed. B. C. Burnham and J. L. Davies, *Trivium*, 25 (1990), 86–93.

[30]V. E. Nash-Williams, *The Roman Frontier in Wales*, 22–8; J. L. Davies, 'Soldiers, peasants and markets in Wales and the Marches', *Military and Civilian in Roman Britain, Cultural Relationships in a Frontier Province*, ed. T. C. F. Blagg and A. C. King (BAR S136: Oxford, 1984), 93.

which beset the Empire in the mid–late third century AD are reflected in a Welsh context by the retention of some key sites, but the archaeological evidence suggests the run-down of an already small garrison whose prime concern had been the provision of the equivalent of police-posts in areas where there may have been some recurrent localized problems—more likely inter-clan feuding on the Afghan model rather than insurrection against Rome. Whatever the precise status of these late forts, no example is known in west Wales.

The third century AD is characterized by an increasing concern for the littoral defence of Britain from raiders whose homelands lay across the North and Irish Seas. It is exemplified by the appointment of officers such as M. Aurelius Mausaeus Carausius (pre-AD 286) with a brief to rid the English Channel of pirates, and by the extension of a defensive system based upon powerfully defended shore bases for elements of the Roman fleet and regular army units. In Wales the construction of a new-style fort at Cardiff in the last quarter of the third century will have blocked passage of the Bristol Channel to enterprising sea-borne raiders threatening the towns and rich villa estates bordering the Severn estuary, whilst in the north the retention of the fort at Caernarfon and the subsequent building of a small naval fort at Caergybi (Holyhead) and an associated watch-tower on Holyhead Mountain in the late fourth century perhaps form an integrated system designed to protect north-west Wales, uncomfortably exposed to the depreda-tions of the *Hiberni*.[31] Despite the high degree of exposure there is no evidence that the west and south-west coast of Wales was similarly protected.[32] The consequences of this threat, imaginary or real, have in the past been evidenced by the high incidence of later third-century AD coin hoards from this region. Three such hoards have been found in Cardiganshire: Rhiwarthen-isaf, Bwlch-bach and Strata Florida (see p.313). But hoarding need not specifically relate to a localized threat, least of all from Irish raiders, since the numerous political and monetary crises across the years AD 259–96 led to catastrophic debasement, demonetization and revaluation which will have encouraged the practice of hoarding in anticipation of re-tariffing and the restoration of stability, or quite simply the doubtless reluctant disposal of now worthless coinage.[33]

Raiding and the subsequent settlement of large tracts of south-west Wales by Irish colonists has always figured large in the late and post-Roman history of the region, a link which is strongly marked in the documentary and epigraphic record spanning the Irish Sea. Irish sources relate how the Uí Liatháin and the Déisi of Munster were jointly associated in their raids on western Britain, whilst the genealogy of the early medieval kingdom of Dyfed shows how the dynasty

---

[31] *Hiberni* and *Picti* figure as the enemies of the Britons in the Panegyric of AD 297. For Caernarfon see P. J. Casey, 'Magnus Maximus in Britain: a reappraisal', *The End of Roman Britain*, ed. P. J. Casey (BAR 71: Oxford, 1979), 76–7. For Holyhead fort and watch-tower, P. C. Crew, *Holyhead Mountain Roman Watch Tower: Interim Report on the 1980–1 Excavations* (privately circulated).

[32] Later third-century activity at the site of the early forts at Loughor and Neath could be significant in this respect. See J. L. Davies, 'Roman military deployment in Wales and the Marches from Pius to Theodosius I', *Roman Frontier Studies 1989. Proceedings of the 15th International Congress of Roman Frontier Studies*, ed. V. A. Maxfield and M. J. Dobson (Exeter, 1991), 52–7. *Moridunum* (Car-marthen) could have intermittently served as a base for troops since these were often billeted in towns in the fourth century.

[33] G. C. Boon, 'The Penard Roman imperial hoard: an interim report and a list of Roman hoards in Wales', *BBCS*, 22 (1967), 291–310; idem, 'Counterfeit coins in Roman Britain', *Coins and the Archaeologist*, ed. J. Casey and R. Reece (London, 1988), 102–88 (*passim*).

traced its origins to one Eochaid mac Artchorp, leader of the Déisi.[34] Place-name studies also indicate a strong Irish-speaking element in the population by the early medieval period, whilst the corresponding distribution of memorial stones of fifth–sixth century AD date, with epitaphs written in the ogam alphabet (itself of Irish origin), often accompanied by parallel versions in Latin, reinforces the place-name evidence.[35] Other inscriptions, if not in ogam, commemorate persons with Irish names, such as Dumelus, buried at Llanddewibrefi.[36] It has long been customary to think of this Irish presence in south-west Wales, and also that in Gwynedd traditionally obliterated by the movement of Cunedda and his followers from the eastern lowlands of Scotland, as the product of land-winning by raiders-turned-settlers at a date which it was thought—on a comparison of the Welsh and Irish king-lists—should lie at the turn of the fourth and fifth centuries. More recently it has been suggested that Rome herself played a positive role in this context with the usurper Magnus Maximus settling the Déisi as *foederati*, entrusted with the defence of a threatened south-western littoral prior to his bid to oust the Emperor Gratian in AD 383.[37] The validity of this claim will be dealt with presently. Let us first consider the evidence for the preparatory phase; third- and fourth-century raiding.

There are no obvious tempting targets for raiders along the relatively inhospitable coasts of west Wales: Carmarthen was a walled town, and the few examples of villas known in south Carmarthenshire and south Pembrokeshire are relatively unsophisticated in comparison with those of, for example, the West Country. However, the relative military weakness of the late Empire coupled with a dramatic decline in its population and a concomitant abandonment of land may have acted as a magnet for Irish communities themselves affected by insular demographic or military pressures.[38] But Bateson has demonstrated the sparsity of later third-century Romano-British finds in Ireland, precisely that period when other evidence suggests that raiding should have been rife.[39] Whilst it is not uncommon for loot to leave no trace, fourth-century AD material is more common and, significantly, concentrated in the southern, inland region of Munster, the heartland of the Déisi—finds which it is suggested may be related to Irish raiding in Dyfed, perhaps a preliminary to settlement.[40] But contact between Wales (or rather the British

---

[34]K. Meyer, 'The expulsion of the Dessi', *Y Cymmrodor*, 14 (1901), 101–35, and *Eriu*, 3 (1907), 135–42.

[35]M. Richards 'The Irish settlements in south-west Wales', *JRSAI*, 90 (1960), 133–62.

[36]V. E. Nash-Williams, *The Early Christian Monuments of Wales*, 98.

[37]L. Alcock, *Arthur's Britain* (London, 1971), 96–8; W. Davies, *Wales in the Early Middle Ages* (Leicester, 1982), 87–8.

[38]For population decline see M. E. Jones, 'Climate, nutrition and disease: an hypothesis of Romano-British population', *The End of Roman Britain*, ed. P. J. Casey, 231–51.

[39]J. D. Bateson, 'Roman material from Ireland: a re-consideration', *PRIA*, 73 (C) (1973), 21–97; idem, 'Further finds of Roman material from Ireland', *ibid.*, 76 (C) (1976), 171–80.

[40]R. B. Warner, 'Some observations on the context and importation of exotic material in Ireland, from the first century BC to the second century AD', *PRIA*, 76 (C) (1976), 267–92. Contrast with the third–fourth-century gold ornaments from Conyngham and the similarly dated gold and silver coins from a cult site at Newgrange; also the hack-silver from the hoards of Ballinrees (Co. Derry) and Balline (Co. Limerick), which might be loot, though the latter with its late Roman silver ingots might even represent part of a concealed accession donative acquired by an Irishman serving in the Roman army. On Newgrange see R. A. G. Carson and C. O'Kelly, 'A catalogue of the Roman coins from Newgrange, Co. Meath', and 'Notes on the coins and related finds', *PRIA*, 77 (C) (1977), 35–55.

mainland) and Ireland need not necessarily always have been violent.[41] Trading and broad cultural contacts are apparent long before the pre-Roman Iron Age, whilst a kinship link antedating the Roman period is provided by Ptolemy who records Gangani in Llŷn and Galloway: the Irish tribe of the Lagin are also considered to have given their name to Llŷn and Leinster.[42] Attested contacts between Ulster and Gwynedd certainly enhance the possibility of similar links between Munster and Dyfed, contacts which may well have smoothed the path for later migration and the assimilation of the newcomers. That such settlement may be attributed to deliberate Roman policy seems doubtful in the light of fresh evidence.[43] This hypothesis was heavily dependent upon the idea of a traditional abandonment of Welsh military installations by the usurper Magnus Maximus, who in turn invited Irish and British dynasts to take over the task of defence— if not administration—in his absence. An abandonment of Wales under Maximus must now be dismissed, excavations at *Segontium* (Caernarfon) having conclusively demonstrated that the fort continued to be garrisoned beyond its traditional abandonment date of AD 383.[44] The presence of regular troops in north-west Wales will surely have precluded Irish settlement, official or otherwise. If such was the case then an Irish settlement of the south-west within the Roman period becomes less credible. Certainly, Carmarthen, the tribal centre of the Demetae, continued to flourish into the second half of the fourth century AD with no apparent diminution in its 'Roman' characteristics. Whilst an Irish settlement could have been effected in a rural hinterland (for which there are good Continental parallels) which never seems to have been particularly romanized anyway, there is no evidence for it, notwithstanding the uncertainties of archaeological criteria which could withstand rigorous examination of their so-called 'Irish' attributes. A dearth of Roman coinage in south-west Wales after the middle of the fourth century might be considered significant, but, again, this might reflect nothing more than the operation of socio-economic factors rather than a settlement of the region by a community unfamiliar with the use of coinage.[45]

It is the dynastic link between southern Ireland and south-west Wales which apparently provides the strongest case for an Irish settlement in the late Roman period. The earliest native genealogical tradition about the post-Roman kings of Dyfed was that they were of Irish descent; only later like their counterparts elsewhere in Europe were they anxious to gain a measure of respectability, wishing to emphasize their 'legitimacy' and the continuity of their rule with late-Roman forms of administration. This ambition could best be served by anchoring their claims—even to the extent of inventing family ties—to the great Roman figures of the fourth century AD, Constantine the Great, and especially that 'British' hero, Magnus Maximus.[46] The

[41]Warner, *PRIA*, 76 (C) (1976), 276–83.

[42]H. N. Savory, 'Later Prehistoric migrations across the Irish Sea', *The Irish Sea Province in Archaeology and History*, ed. D. Moore (Cardiff, 1970), 38–49; L. Alcock, 'The Irish Sea Zone in the pre-Roman Iron Age', *The Iron Age in the Irish Sea Province*, ed. C. Thomas (CBA Research Report 9, London, 1972), 99–108.

[43]D. N. Dumville, 'Sub-Roman Britain: history and legend', *History*, 62 (1977), 173–92.

[44]P. J. Casey, 'Magnus Maximus in Britain: a reappraisal', *The End of Roman Britain*, ed.P. J. Casey, 76–7; P. J. Casey and J. L. Davies, *Excavations at Segontium (Caernarfon) Roman Fort 1975-79* (CBA Research Report 90, London, 1993).

[45]J. L. Davies, 'Coinage and settlement in Roman Wales and the Marches: some observations', *Arch.Camb.*, 132 (1983), 90–4.

[46]See above, n. 42.

dynastic link with Rome, therefore, may have been a fictive one, developed in that synthetic milieu which resulted from an Irish colonization of parts of south-west Wales—an extensive tract of Cardiganshire included—in a sub-Roman context.

Civilian life

Nothing is known of the fate of the inhabitants of Cardiganshire after their conquest in the 70s of the first century AD. Literary and epigraphic sources spanning the subsequent three centuries are wholly lacking, whilst the Romano-British settlement sites which should produce illuminatory evidence are presently unknown. Whilst the County presents a major lacuna in the distribution of civil settlements of this period their absence, however, may be more apparent than real. Although a drastic depopulation of the region is not beyond the bounds of possibility (note the violent Roman reaction to revolt in AD 77 when Agricola is said to have virtually wiped out the Ordovices), a more cogent explanation is that Roman-British settlements will be difficult to distinguish from those of the pre-Roman era, a consequence of Cardiganshire's relative cultural poverty throughout the period.[47]

The distribution of Roman forts in the northern portion of the County indicated that administratively a substantial proportion of the population will have fallen under direct military control, the inhabitants ranking as *dediticii*, possessing no rights in the field of government or taxation. Doubtless chiefs or clan leaders, especially those who were prepared to reach an accommodation with the new Power, will have continued to exercise certain of their customary rights—food and service-renders and the like—because it was the tribal aristocracies which became the focus of socio-economic manipulations; but even the most favourably regarded will have done so under the supervision of military *tribuni* and *praefecti*. Military administration will certainly have been a feature of the County down to the reign of Hadrian, if not beyond. Some tribal lands may even have been forcibly appropriated since each auxiliary fort will have required its own *territorium*—land in military ownership—necessary for the partial provisioning of the garrison. Within that *territorium* a measure of self-government may have been permitted the immigrant inhabitants of the *vici* or villages which developed outside the forts, but the authority of their elected councillors—if such existed—will have been exceedingly limited, encompassing community affairs only.[48]

For much of southern Britain military government was of relatively brief duration: for those areas under the control of client rulers it will have been virtually absent. Thereafter it became customary to utilize the existing tribal structure (or not infrequently an artificial grouping)—suitably modified to run on Roman lines—as the basis for local administration. The *pax Romana* also facilitated the enhancement of pre-existing native centres to the status of *civitates*, or the creation of urban centres for those tribally based administrative units or *civitates peregrinae* which

[47]For native communities in Roman Wales see J. L. Davies, 'Aspects of native settlement in Roman Wales and the Marches' (unpublished University of Wales Ph.D. thesis, Cardiff, 1980).

[48]C. S. Sommer, *The Military Vici in Roman Britain. Aspects of their Origins, their Location and Layout, Administration Function and End* (BAR 129: Oxford, 1984).

lacked them, administration in Roman eyes being indivisible from urbanization. Town foundations were not an imperial 'gift', rather they were the product of the necessity of maintaining control over subject peoples through the manipulation of the aristocracy.[49] Quite simply, the aristocracies were 'targeted'. Prior to the conquest they had retained and enhanced their status through war and gift-exchange designed primarily to win and maintain a large body of clients. Dependants would have rendered service or tribute to their superiors. With the Roman conquest much of that tribute (in the form of money taxes) was now forwarded to the office of the *procurator Britanniae*, the aristocracies being made responsible for its collection. Now that social and political advancement through war was impossible the energies of the Celtic aristocracies had to be harnessed to non-destructive pursuits, namely competition for status in accordance with time-honoured Roman precepts—i.e. through holding public office as an elected magistrate on an urban-based council. Status-building activities, and the centralization of the activities of a tribal council, would probably have been sufficient inducement for the aristocracies to acquire urban property. Urban foundation, itself the product of emulations as well as of native energies and financial resources, then satisfied the socio-political aspirations of the aristocracies, ultimately preparing the ground for a piece of social engineering which led to the emergence of a new, romanized class of wealthy, landowning tribal councillors or *decuriones*. Their responsibilities, though locally important, were limited to the fields of organizing the collection of taxes, public works and judicial matters of a non-capital nature, but office-holding was a matter of great significance, conferring prestige on the holder and ultimately preparing the way for the coveted Roman citizenship and the possibility of a career in imperial service.

Two *civitates peregrinae* are known in Wales; that of the Silures, with its *caput* at *Venta* (Caerwent), and the Demetae based upon *Moridunum* (Carmarthen). When *civitates* were created (and the chronology of the above remains uncertain) existing tribal boundaries were doubtless taken into consideration, but they had to suit Roman administrative convenience. Boundary changes could take place, enlarging some at the expense of others, whilst there is a high degree of artificiality in other cases.[50] The situation in west Wales is as nebulous as elsewhere. We simply do not know whether the whole, or even part, of Cardiganshire lay within the *civitas Demetarum*. The southern portion may have done so but the post-Roman history of the County suggests a high degree of independence which may reflect the situation in earlier times.[51] If Cardiganshire was excluded wholly or in part then the administrative arrangements which followed the departure of the army are unknown, a problem embracing the greater portion of Wales where a *civitas*-based administrative framework does not appear to have evolved. Whatever the precise arrangement it will surely have functioned only through the aristocracy, further emphasizing the essential continuity in administrative frameworks which Rome was anxious not to disturb.

Further south Carmarthen had evolved as the tribal town of the Demetae by the later second century at least, when in common with many contemporary British urban centres it was provided with earthwork defences. The reason for its singular development depended upon a combination of 'central-place' function combined with political overtones, production beyond subsistence in

[49]S. S. Frere, *Britannia. A History of Roman Britain* (London, 1987), 190–2.
[50]Ibid., 192.
[51]See p. 277 and Chapter 5, p.320.

the locale and the investment of capital in urban building projects by a receptive aristocracy.[52] It was the only Roman town in west Wales, its importance manifest not only by its role as a major market centre but also by the partial adoption of Roman life-styles by the southern Demetic aristocracy.[53] Elsewhere, in mid and north Wales the conspicuous absence of urbanization betokens a continuance of native tradition.

Prior to the creation of differential forms of local administration the Roman army not only exercised a tight reign on tribal affairs but in some respects indirectly influenced the lives of the inhabitants long after the abandonment of military installations. The army will have been instrumental in opening up the region through the construction of the first all-weather road network to supplement existing trackways, a communications system which not only facilitated military transport but all types of traffic and the movement of merchandise. Moreover, permanently stationed, regularly paid regiments of auxiliary soldiers had the potential to affect profoundly the economic basis of their locale and even region. Much has been written concerning the likely stimulation of food-producing economies resulting from the supposed difficulties of provisioning forts with supplies garnered from the more fecund parts of Britain.[54] It is clear that these supposed difficulties have been exaggerated: the imperial propensity to 'administrative distribution' (i.e. ignoring cost/distance factors) in terms of army supply is manifest, particularly in the first century AD. Whilst it would have been sensible to supply as much food as possible from local resources, the impact on local economies may have been small, minor stimulation and little else, and then only for as long as the garrisons remained.[55] This is an issue whose parameters continue to be highly speculative, and will remain so until palaeoenvironmental data pertaining to the nature of pre-Roman and Roman-British food-production has been obtained from settlement sites in the vicinity of military establishments. Only then will the issues of 'stimulation' as against 'fossilization' of native economies become somewhat less clouded.

We can only hypothesize, or extrapolate data from elsewhere, as to the socio-economic impact of the military presence. Much would have depended upon the attitudes of the local population, but liaisons and 'unofficial' marriages with local women spring to mind (soldiers being forbidden to marry before the early third century AD), with the further possibility of local recruitment into the *auxilia*. The forts themselves acted as magnets for persons who had anything marketable, whether professional camp-followers (*lixae*), merchants (*mercatores*) or local people. The result was normally the establishment of a *vicus*[56] (village) immediately outside the defences, traces of which are known at Trawscoed and Llanio (see pp.300, 302). At the former the most extensive development lies to the north-west of the fort where a rudimentary street-grid aligned on that of the fort could point to an officially constituted Flavian settlement. At the latter the *vicus* lies astride a road junction west of the fort, and it is again seemingly a Flavian foundation. In some instances (Trawscoed may be a case in point) it may well be that the origin of the *vicus* has as

[52]See above, n. 7.

[53]H. James and G. Williams, 'Rural settlement in Roman Dyfed', *The Romano-British Countryside. Studies in Rural Settlement and Economy*, ed. D. Miles (BAR 103: Oxford, 1982), 289–312.

[54]W. H. Manning, 'Economic influences on land use in the military area of the Highland Zone in the Roman period', *The Effect of Man on the Landscape: The Highland Zone*, ed. J. G. Evans (*et. al.*) (CBA Research Report 11, London, 1975), 112–16.

[55]J. L. Davies, 'Soldiers, peasants and markets in Wales and the Marches' (see above, n.30), 112.

[56]C. S. Sommer, *The Military Vici of Roman Britain* (Oxford, 1984).

much to do with military requirements as with civilian entrepreneurship. Relatively little can be said of the morphology or size of these *vici* since their investigation has been small-scale. The only known stone building is the military bath-house south of the fort at Llanio, though a comparable structure undoubtedly existed at Trawscoed. A *mansio* or inn for accredited persons travelling by the *cursus publicus* (the imperial posting-service) is also likely. Although considerable building variety is evidenced in *vici*,[57] most buildings seem to have been of the relatively simple, single-storey strip-type which can be readily paralleled elsewhere. Rectangular timber-framed buildings up to 15 m or more in length and 6–8 m wide, clustering in the most advantageous positions along the roads leading to the fort gates (or occupying a block 36 m deep as at Trawscoed), will have provided domestic accommodation, stores and workshops as well as shops and *tabernae* (bars). Lead weights found within buildings at Trawscoed testify to commercial activity, whilst the presence of ovens, and numerous amphora, jug and wine-cup fragments conjure up a picture of off-duty soldiers purchasing *ofellae* ('pizzas') and quaffing *acetum* (cheap wine) or *cervesa* (Celtic beer).[58] Small-scale industrial activity, featuring tanning and metalwork (the latter evidenced by the contents of rubbish-pits at Trawscoed) is another feature of *vici* and is normally either of military origin, constrained to areas outside the fort by reason of smell or fire-risk, or is the product of craftsmen satisfying the military craving for 'personalia'—brooches, rings, armlets and other items of adornment.

In the frontier zone of north Britain the social and economic impact of the long-occupied *vici* was considerable. Their relatively short-term impact in west Wales is problematic, but most likely significant within a limited context. They might have been in receipt of the produce of upland economic zones—animal products and metals—thereby acting as intermediaries between the urban markets of southern England and ultimately the Continent. If such was the case they could have provided a considerable boost to native economies, functioning in turn as market centres for the distribution of a variety of goods—the principal survivals being ceramics and metalwork—in return for cash or barter. One concomitant, at least, will have been the introduction of a money economy, but other features of a markedly alien culture—language, customs and religious observances, to name the obvious—could have been imparted via the army and its dependants. Indeed the military *vici*, for all their humble, if not rudimentary, characteristics, will have been the nearest thing to a romanized township that most natives are likely to have encountered. But however tempting it may be to emphasize this role as catalysts for socio-economic change, it is evident that the symbiosis between *vicus* and fort was infinitely more significant than that between *vicus* and native hinterland. The beneficiaries were soldiers, *lixae* and *mercatores*. The stimulus to native economies is likely to have been minimal, with no growth of true market centres.[59] Commerce probably remained dependent upon the activities of enterprising traders or the exchange which appears to have been an essential feature of the religious assemblies (the *oenach* in Ireland) of the Celtic year.

[57]See pp.301–2 for somewhat more complicated buildings at Trawscoed. For *comperanda* see J. Britnell, *Caersws Vicus, Powys. Excavations at the Old Priory School 1985–86* (BAR 205: Oxford, 1989).
[58]For alcoholic drinks see A. K. Bowman and J. D. Thomas, *Vindolanda. The Latin Writing-Tablets* (Britannia Monograph Series 4, London, 1983), 85–6.
[59]G. D. B. Jones, '"Becoming different without knowing it". The role and development of the Vici', *Military and Civilian in Roman Britain*, ed. T. F. C. Blagg and A. C. King, 75–91.

The symbiosis between fort and *vicus* is graphically illustrated at Trawscoed where the numismatic and ceramic assemblage suggests a concurrent abandonment. No post-Hadrianic material is known from the Llanio *vicus* either, although the small-scale nature of the excavations precludes certainty. There is little doubt that the *vici* were an unnatural growth existing by virtue of the army and its regular pay, and testify to the commercial exploitation of its personnel by professional camp-followers. Once that *raison d'etre* had gone by the decade AD 120–30, many *vici* will have been immediately abandoned, or at best withered and died. Southern and central England, and possibly south-east Wales, on the other hand, seem to have examples of military *vici* which apparently continued in occupation after the abandonment of the parent fort. This was a matter of deliberate choice, coupled with favourable economic factors, in particular a high population density, and the proximity of an extant native settlement. In Cardiganshire, as is so often the case in upland contexts, forts did not experience a 'drift' of enterprising natives to their vicinity and economic conditions seem to have been unfavourable for the retention of *vicus* communities once the troops had gone. The lack of such quasi-urban centres undoubtedly had an adverse effect upon the course of romanization in the County.

Since overt traces of Roman cultural influence in respect of spontaneous moves towards urban development or growth of villas, with their sophisticated architectural tradition, are conspicuously absent in Cardiganshire and rare in Wales as a whole, romanization (in its widest sense) will manifest itself only indirectly at an economic level through minor changes or innovations in building technology and the appearance of coins and consumer goods on settlements of 'native' character—sites which may be desperately poor in material remains, and whose buildings and economic practices may be little different from those of the pre-Roman Iron Age.

Among the most manifestly 'Roman' items to appear in a rural context are coins, representing a store of wealth and a medium of exchange. No pre-Roman coins were minted or circulated in west Wales[60] and a money economy, introduced by the Flavian army, will have been initially confined to forts and *vici*. Even though coinage gained a wider currency in a post-military context it was a transient phase, coins disappearing from circulation in the fourth century AD[61] before their reintroduction under Anglo-Norman rule. A perusal of the short list of hoards and single losses from the County (see pp.312–14) indicates that coins may not have been universally or continuously used from the first to the fourth century AD, although the scarcity or even absence of coins in periods other than the later third and earlier fourth centuries AD is not statistically meaningful.[62] None has been found on an undoubted 'native' settlement in the County, thereby pointing to a dearth of communities fully or partially integrated into the Roman currency system. Indeed, it is possible that coins may have rarely circulated as money in the conventional sense, not only in our County but over much of Wales. Whilst tax payments will have been normally discharged in the form of silver coin, it is most likely that flocks, herds and the produce of the

[60]For pre-Roman coinage in Wales see G. C. Boon's list in *Biglis, Caldicot and Landough. Three Late Iron Age and Romano-British Sites in South-East Wales. Excavations 1977–79*, ed. D. M. Robinson (BAR 188: Oxford, 1988), 92.
[61]J. L. Davies, 'Coinage and settlement in Roman Wales and the Marches: some observations' (see above, n. 45), 90–4.
[62]Ibid., 78.

land, rather than bullion, remained the basis of personal wealth, at least in the countryside, for the whole of the Roman period.

The supply of ceramic containers (and their contents) and other consumer products emanating from within the Province, and from more distant parts of the Empire in respect of amphora-borne commodities such as wine and olive oil or high-quality table ware such as samian, will have been initially geared to military requirements, although a surplus for local consumption is assumed. Insofar as pottery is concerned, none of the military posts in the County has produced any which need be much later than c. AD 130, and it may well be that the cessation of military contracts with insular manufactories, as well as merchants who arranged imports, will have seen the termination of large-scale ceramic importation into the region. South-west Wales apparently lacks kiln-sites of Romano-British date and was far removed from the major production centres of the second–fourth centuries AD. Although Carmarthen as a Roman town was in receipt of the standard southern British ceramic range, and most certainly will have served as a distribution centre for these products, settlement sites in its catchment area appear to have used pottery sparingly.[63] Remoteness, a small market and high transportation costs may have rendered such a trade uneconomic in rural west Wales, although we may note the incidence of Dorset black-burnished wares at remote Castell Henllys (Pembs.) and Corsygedol (Mer.).[64] Whilst it is unwise to be dogmatic, negative evidence may be significant, and it may be that the failure of putative Romano-British settlements in Cardiganshire to produce a few diagnostic sherds indicates that their inhabitants largely relied upon time-honoured metal, wooden or leathern containers for storage and cooking.[65]

It is evident that the native mode, drawn from the traditions of the first millennium BC, was the more conspicuous in the material culture of much of Wales in the Roman period. Broad continuity of settlement type and location appears to be the rule with economies developing along traditional lines. The County appears to be no exception. Nevertheless any assessment of the effects of absorption within the imperial framework depends upon the recognition of contemporary settlements and comparison with those of neighbouring regions. In this respect we begin with a major handicap: not one certain Romano-British settlement of native origin has been identified in the County. The solitary coin from Pen Dinas (Aberystwyth) (see p.314) is most likely a casual loss since excavations demonstrated no late Roman phase at this large hillfort. In contrast the discovery of nails in the post-holes of Huts II and III at Caerau (Henllan) might well indicate the rebuilding of round-houses within the promontory fort in the Roman period, albeit without an accompanying ceramic assemblage.[66]

Doubtless some of the enclosures which represent such a prominent feature of the Iron Age settlement pattern in the County must be prime candidates for Romano-British occupation,

[63]For the poverty of farmsteads see K. Murphy, 'Excavations at Penycoed, Llangynog, Dyfed, 1983', *Carms.Antiq.*, 21 (1985), 75–112.
[64]Castell Henllys, *AW*, 23 (1983), 24; 24 (1984), 45. On Corsygedol see W. E. Griffiths, 'The excavations of a Romano-British hut-group at Cors-y-Gedol in Merionethshire', *BBCS*, 18 (1958), 189–229.
[65]W. E. Griffiths, 'The excavations of a Romano-British hut-group', 126.
[66]There are no authenticated instances of the use of nails for domestic purposes in Wales in the pre-Roman period. Professor W. H. Manning has kindly discussed this matter with the writer. For Henllan see A. Williams, 'A promontory fort at Henllan, Cardiganshire', *Arch.Camb.*, 98 (1945), 226–40.

thereby repeating a pattern well evidenced elsewhere in Wales. Even if the larger hillforts were abandoned, the great diversity of settlements, ranging from small forts of less than 1 ha enclosed, to much smaller, weakly defended, enclosures of oval or rectilinear form are likely to have been occupied. It is precisely these less impressive types of settlement which produce the bulk of the evidence pertaining to Romano-British rural settlement in Dyfed.[67] Until such time as a representative sample has been investigated in the County it is in neighbouring Carmarthenshire and Pembrokeshire that we must seek information pertaining to the putative socio-economic systems of Roman Cardiganshire. Even then we could be dealing only with one element within the settlement hierarchy; that conferring high status, by virtue of the possession of defences.[68]

At one end of this group of larger enclosures, such as Dan-y-coed (Pembs.),[69] Walesland Rath (Pembs.)[70] and Coygan Camp (Carms.),[71] vernacular architecture can range from traditional timber round-houses to some relatively crude, composite rectangular buildings and four or six-post structures, or a mixture of all these forms. The smaller farmsteads such as Pen-y-coed (Carms.)[72] or Knock Rath (Pembs.)[73]—presumably of lesser status—are just as conservative in their building forms. Environmental data suggests that the occupants of both categories practised a mixed farming economy, although in some instances, such as Pen-y-coed, pastoralism may have been the mainstay. Certainly in north Cardiganshire, where geomorphology favours livestock production, there may well have been a bias in this direction. For example, the pollen record from Trawscoed[74] shows no evidence for cereal production in the immediate vicinity of the fort and *vicus*, nor subsequent to their abandonment. Cereal grains from *vicus* deposits are themselves, therefore, most likely imports. Presently the negative evidence speaks loudest but the situation may well change.

In south-west Wales as a whole the Roman impact on native society and economy does not appear to have been great. Had the inhabitants been more receptive or wealthy a larger crop of *villae*, the homes of a romanized native aristocracy, might be expected, but these are rare and, with the exception of Llys Brychan (Carms.),[75] restricted to the relatively simple cottage-block variety as at Trelissey (Trelisi) (Pembs.) and Cwmbrwyn (Carms.).[76] The reasons for this sparsity

[67]H. James and G. Williams, 'Rural settlement in Roman Dyfed', *The Romano-British Countryside. Studies in Rural Settlement and Economy*, ed. D. Miles (BAR Reports 103: Oxford, 1982), 289–312; G. Williams, 'Recent work on rural settlement in later prehistoric and early historic Dyfed', *Ant.J.*, 68 (1988), 30–54, especially 41–3.

[68]'Open' or palisaded forms may be difficult or impossible to locate in well-farmed landscapes.

[69]See above, n. 3; G. Williams, 'Recent work on rural settlement in later prehistoric and early historic Dyfed', *Ant.J.*, 68 (1988), 30–54.

[70]G. J. Wainwright, 'The excavation of a fortified settlement at Walesland Rath, Pembrokeshire', *Brit.*, 2 (1971), 48–108.

[71]G. J. Wainwright, *Coygan Camp. A Prehistoric, Romano-British and Dark Age Settlement in Carmarthenshire* (Cambrian Archaeological Association, Cardiff, 1967).

[72]K. Murphy, 'Excavations at Penycoed, Llangynog, Dyfed', *Carm.Ant.*, 21 (1985), 75–112.

[73]D. W. Crossley, 'Excavations at Knock Rath, Clarbeston, 1962', *BBCS*, 21 (1965), 264–75.

[74]F. Dilnot, 'Palaeobotanical Investigations at the Roman Fort Excavations, Trawscoed' (unpublished University of Wales B. Sc. dissertation, Aberystwyth, 1986).

[75]M. G. Jarrett, 'Excavations at Llys Brychan, Llangadog, 1961', *Carm.Ant.*, 4 (1962), 1–8.

[76]W. G. Thomas and R. W. Walker, 'Excavations at Trelissey, Pembrokeshire, 1950–51', *BBCS*, 18 (1959), 295–303; J. Ward, 'Roman remains at Cwmbrwyn, Carmarthenshire', *Arch.Camb.*, 62 (1907), 175–209.

are simple: the source of the aristocracy's wealth lay in the countryside, their estates and the rents and tithes rendered by their clients. Where wealth could not be readily accumulated through increased agricultural production destined for market, or exactions from tenants, moves towards romanized life-styles were slow or minimal. The presence or absence of romanized rural settlement could also be a function of the degree of social stratification within a region, perhaps pointing to the relative weakness of a coercive aristocracy as well as an expression of absolute distinctions in landed wealth over time and space, rather than reflecting cultural predispositions. In Cardiganshire, then, the apparent poverty of the landscape seemingly disallowed the accumulation of aristocratic wealth which could otherwise have been invested in land and capital projects such as a new-style *domus* (house).

The 'barbarian' parts of Europe incorporated into the Roman Empire were subjected to social and economic influences which could sometimes lead to radical changes. Insofar as Cardiganshire is concerned our minimal knowledge allows us only to theorize as to whether any changes may have occurred. Large-scale immigration, whether from abroad or elsewhere within the British province, is inherently unlikely. The only attested newcomers are auxiliary soldiers and *vicani*, and their presence was transient. We have seen that only the Celtic aristocracy, managing a socio-economic system which may have survived more or less intact through the Roman period, was likely to profit from the imperial connection. But, as we have surmised, its status was more likely to be reflected through clientage rather than in garnering cash and its translation into gracious living. Some aristocrats became romanized to the extent that they—or rather their descendants (following early Christian practice)—either latinized their names, or took Latin ones: witness Domnicus and Potentina.[77] Here 'civilized' nomenclature could be adopted without any other signs of romanization. There may have been other linguistic borrowings too but British undoubtedly remained the vulgar speech, even if Latin was universally used for writing.

Elsewhere in Britain one well-evidenced product of the conquest was the importation of foreign religious cults, the not infrequent dramatic rendering of an architectural expression for native cults, and a Romano-Celtic synthesis. Whilst no certain evidence for a cult site exists in the County, the small, female bust of yew-wood found in peat close to the fort at Llanio (see pp.316–17), if indeed a votive object, suggests the presence of a sacred pool or spring and an essential continuity of Celtic cult-practice into the Roman period.[78] Also possibly significant is an otherwise inexplicable circular shaft, containing a sharpened post, dug through the silted Period 1 fort ditch at Llanio, for whose cultic origins, if not context, there are good parallels.[79]

Burial is another aspect of religious practice for which there is some evidence in Roman Cardiganshire. The considerable diversity of necrological practices in late prehistoric Britain and our woeful ignorance of the Welsh scene as a whole has already been noted (see above, II.3). Both inhumations and cremations of probable Roman date are known in the County, inhumation becoming the dominant rite in the Empire after the third century. Of four cremations at Plas Gogerddan, the site of a much earlier prehistoric ritual complex and cemetery, one at least could possibly belong to the first century AD.[80] By the time that the site was being used for burial once

---

[77]V. E. Nash-Williams, *The Early Christian Monuments of Wales*, Nos.122, 132.

[78]M. Green, *The Gods of the Celts* (Gloucester, 1986), 150–66.

[79]*Brit.*, 5 (1974), 400.

[80]K. Murphy, 'Plas Gogerddan, Dyfed: a multi-period ritual and burial site', *Arch. J.*(forthcoming).

again the rite represented was inhumation in a cemetery of oriented graves, some coffined and three with surrounding rectangular structures. A solitary radiocarbon date of 370 ± 60 ad from a coffin provides the only firm dating for the cemetery, a date which when calibrated (AD 285–525) spans the late Roman and early Christian period. A late Roman origin for this, thereafter increasingly common, burial practice seems likely.[81] What we appear to have at Plas Gogerddan is the sporadic use of a long-standing ritual focus by what is probably a discrete kin-group, further emphasizing the element of continuity in terms of social grouping and land use. The location of the complex at the foot of the ridge crowned by the hillfort of Hen Gaer is intriguing, recalling a similar juxtaposition of early settlement site and cemetery at Cribyn Gaer. We may simply beg the question as to whether those buried at Plas Gogerddan had their Iron Age and Romano-British domicile at Hen Gaer.

Of earlier date than the above inhumations is the cremation contained within a pot dated c. AD 120–60, possibly accompanied by coins (including an *aureus* of Titus) said to have been found 'within a small heap of stones' at Penbryn (Appendix V, no. 1; cf., II.7.c (p.399)). This discovery is not without considerable interpretative problems, given the relationship of the 'cairn' to the early Christian monument bearing the epitaph of 'Corbalengus, the Ordovician'. Does the cremation signify the continued use of an earlier sepulchral site (the cairn?)? Do the coins represent a hoard, or is the surviving *aureus* a splendid Charon's obol? Is the inscribed stone of Roman date and the cremation that of Corbalengus, or have we another example of the reuse of a sepulchral site in early Christian times? Given the date of the vessel containing the cremation we cannot rule out the possibility of a Roman military origin although the context would best fit a member of the native élite.

Industry

Economic activity in Roman Cardiganshire appears largely to have been geared to the needs of a subsistence economy focusing on pastoral and agrarian pursuits. Of what may be termed industrial activity there is little sign. Although iron-smelting and bronze-working is attested at Trawscoed and Llanio, it probably served military and *vicus* requirements only. Hitherto the extensive rural iron and bronze-working evidenced on defended and unenclosed settlements in north-west Wales is unattested.[82] But what of the rich lead/silver and copper lodes of north Cardiganshire? British mineral wealth was, after all, according to Tacitus, one of the eagerly sought fruits of conquest.

Anxious to prove the antiquity of non-ferrous mineral exploitation in Cardiganshire, O. Davies in his pioneering study drew attention to primitive stone implements—hammer-stones, mauls and grinders—from several mines and waste-tips; for example, the mines at Nant yr Eira and Goginan (where Roman coins had been reputedly found in the mine, together with bronze vessels of purportedly Roman date).[83] However, positive proof of Roman working is obstinately lacking.

---

[81]H. James, 'Excavations at Caer, Bayvil, 1979', *Arch.Camb.*, 136 (1987), 51–76, especially 70–6.
[82]P. Crew, 'Crawcwellt West', *AW*, 26 (1986), 36; 27 (1987), 41.
[83]O. Davies, *Roman Mines in Europe* (Oxford, 1935), 155–6; idem, 'Cwm Ystwyth Mines', *Arch.Camb.*, 99 (1946), 57–63.

Indeed, recent research suggests that 'hammerstone technology' is pre-Roman and increasingly linked to a mid-second millennium BC phase of exploitation specifically directed at the mining of copper in north Cardiganshire.[84] Was there, then, a phase of Roman exploitation? To quote one view: 'It is difficult not to envisage at least some continuity of mining activity between prehistoric and historic periods, and it seems unlikely that all the evidence for this could have been destroyed by later mining.'[85] Certainly, traces of early workings are all too prone to extensive disturbance or obliteration by later enterprises, yet, in the Mendips and Flintshire lead/silver fields, extraction sites and processing areas are known, together with extensive dependent settlements such as Charterhouse and Pentre Ffwrndan, Flint.[86] Had Roman working of the Cardiganshire field been extensive, comparable settlement traces (or at least finds therefrom) might be expected, unless their working was vested entirely in the military, some of whose bases (e.g. Erglodd, Trawscoed) are conveniently sited as foci for ore-processing and the administration of mines.[87] We must conclude that at present the evidence for the Roman exploitation of the north Cardiganshire mineral deposits is tentative and inferential for the most part. Unless there are concrete examples of objects of Roman date in association with mine-waste, or at least Roman-British radiocarbon dates from the same, then it seems best to regard the case as unproven.[88]

The inhabitants of Roman Cardiganshire undoubtedly experienced some degree of socio-economic change between the late first and early fifth century AD. What archaeology cannot reveal, however, is the changes in thought processes and attitudes. Were some, at least, imbued

[84]J. Pickin, 'Stone tools and early mining in Wales', *AW*, 28 (1988), 18–19; S. Timberlake, 'An archaeological investigation of early mineworkings on Copa Hill, Cwmystwyth', *AW*, 27 (1987), 18–20.

[85]S. Timberlake, 'Excavations at Parys Mountain and Nantyreira', *AW*, 28 (1988), 17.

[86]T. J. O'Leary (*et al.*), *Pentre Farm, Flint 1976–81: An Official Building in the Roman Lead Mining District* (BAR 207: Oxford, 1989).

[87]Tacitus informs us that in AD 48 Curtius Rufus, governor of Germania Superior, used troops to sink a silver mine in the territory of the Mattiaci. Note the fort which lies close to the lead/silver workings at Charterhouse on Mendip: B. Jones and P. Lewis, 'Ancient mining and the environment', *Rescue Archaeology*, ed. P. A. Rahtz (Harmondsworth, 1974), Map p.139.

[88]Mr Simon Hughes's dissertation, entitled *Ancient Mining in Mid-Wales* for the degree of MA of the University of Manchester, argues persuasively for a very early origin for some mining operations in Cardiganshire. One of the most exciting aspects of his work has been the analysis by gamma-ray spectrometry of lead samples from a variety of sources in mid Wales (Cardiganshire and western Montgomery) with a view to determining their probable origin. Five lead samples from objects discovered during the course of the writer's own excavations at Trawscoed and Llanio Roman forts were submitted for analysis. The results proved to be exceptionally interesting. Two of the samples from Trawscoed taken from a lead lampholder (Hughes No.101/A) and a weight (No.009/A) respectively proved to be of mid-Wales origin. Indeed the former contains trace elements which can be compared with lead samples obtained from Strata Florida Abbey. Of the three samples from Llanio, one (No.007/A) shows trace elements which are alien to mid Wales, and containing as it does an insignificant proportion of silver may prove to be of Derbyshire origin. The second (No.008/A), a fragment from a large lead pipe, may represent recycled material: there are trace elements which represent metal of external provenance, but the presence of nickel in the sample suggests a Cwmystwyth provenance for part of the metal content. The third sample (No.006/A) is statistically grouped with samples obtained from mines in the Tal-y-bont area of Cardiganshire.

with a sense of *romanitas*—a feeling of belonging to an imperial whole—or was Roman rule simply regarded as an irritant, represented by the grasping hand of the tax-collector or officialdom requisitioning supplies irrespective of local shortfall? We will never know. It is instructive to note, however, that the epitaphs of the late fifth- to seventh-century élite reveal that they too, like their Christian counterparts elsewhere in western Europe, felt themselves to be the inheritors and defenders of a Roman tradition (exemplified by the Christian faith of later emperors) in an increasingly convulsed world, however diluted and misrepresented that tradition may have been.

APPENDIX I: ROMAN MILITARY SITES

Six certain and one probable military installations are known in the County: three auxiliary forts; one fortlet; two practice-camps, and one possible watch-tower emplacement. All lie on, or close to, the line of the military road running north–south through the County and thereby form integral parts of the late first-century AD scheme for the maintenance of security in the newly conquered region. No large permanent sites are thought to remain undetected. Marching-camps, however, are conspicuous by their absence. Aerial reconnaissance may be instrumental in their future discovery, possibly in proximity to the known permanent sites.

Because of its proximity the small fort of Cae Gaer, sited only just beyond the County boundary, has also been included in the list of auxiliary forts. The sites are described as follows:

(a) Auxiliary forts
(b) Fortlet
(c) Practice-camps
(d) Possible site

a) Auxiliary forts

1. Cae Gaer   SN 824 818
(Mont.)
This small fort lies 100m east of the County boundary and occupies the north-facing slopes of a plateau set in a bowl surrounded by the Cambrian massif. The spot is one of the few locations where a fort could have been built. It overlooks the Tarennig, a tributary of the upper Wye, and the pass through which the A44 now runs.

The plateau slopes quite sharply on all sides except the south where there is a further level expanse in what is now a forestry plantation. The fort is a rhomboid measuring 125 × 91 m (410 × 300 ft) over the ramparts with an area of 1.05 ha (2.82 acres). The ground within is exceedingly broken. A marshy hollow transverses the site from the south to the north-west and a peat-flow has destroyed a substantial portion of the south defences, together with the south gate if such had existed.[1] The north gate is visible as a centrally placed gap. There are no eastern or western gates.

In 1913 F. N. Pryce[2] examined parts of the defences, including the north gate and the western rampart terminal next to the site of the then presumed south gate, as well as parts of the interior. The rampart, 3.5 m wide, was composed of turf and surmounted by a timber breastwork. A low counterscarp bank, apparently running the full circuit of the defences, accentuated a shallow external ditch 2.5 m wide and 0.75 m deep. A classic, seven-post, fan-shaped timber tower was found at the south-east corner; presumably with others at the remaining angles. The north gate, now a 3.5 m wide gap, was also examined but no coherent gate-plan could be reconstructed from a palimpsest of post-holes.

Limited trenching in the interior revealed no structures of Roman date other than a possible hearth/oven within the rampart roughly midway between the north gate and the north-east corner.

The site has been variously termed a fortlet[3] and temporary fort.[4] Although about 0.2 ha smaller than the normal small infantry *castellum* and thereby with a commensurately smaller garrison, forts of substandard size are not infrequent in

Flavian and later contexts. Despite the narrowness of its rampart its defences are in other respects characteristic of a fort designed for long-term occupation. The lack of evidence for timber buildings in the interior may be attributed to the small-scale nature of the exploration and the failure to recognize construction trenches for timber buildings. The lack of Romano-British pottery and other diagnostic finds is probably the result of the extreme acidity of the subsoil. The fort may, however, have had a short life.

Its siting, in particular the way in which it is thrust to the northern margin of the plateau with the best views north, indicates a clear concern with maintaining the security of a communication route, if not a road, between the valleys of the Rheidol and Ystwyth to the west and the upper Wye and thence the Severn to the east. The ultimate eastern link will have been with the fort(s) at Caersŵs.

[1] V. E. Nash-Williams, *The Roman Frontier in Wales*, ed. M. G. Jarrett (Cardiff, 1969), 132–5 (with plan).
[2] F. N. Pryce, 'Excavations at Cae Gaer, Llangurig', *Arch. Camb.* (1914), 205–20.
[3] See above, n. 1.
[4] I. A. Richmond, 'Trajan's army on Trajan's Column', *Papers of the British School at Rome*, 13 (1935), 22–4.

2. Penllwyn   Parsel Canol   SN 650 806
Pl. IX; Fig. 62

This large fort was discovered during aerial reconnaissance in the drought of 1976.[1] It occupies a strong position on an uneven west-sloping ridge on the north bank of the Rheidol, presumably guarding the point where the Roman road crossed the river. Its course is probably represented by the minor road that ascends the ridge immediately east of the fort.

Crop-marks define a playing-card-shaped enclosure of approximately 185 × 142 m within triple ditches: the area enclosed is about 2.65 ha (6.5 acres). The fort faces south-west with its angles aligned on the cardinal points. Its defences lay on the margin of sharp scarps, only the western approach being easy. The interior is unusually irregular with a sharp internal fall from the north-west defences. The defences have been completely levelled except at the south-east corner. The sites of the north, east and west gates are visible on aerial photographs, but no internal features, whether streets or buildings, are visible.

The fort lies within a large, incompletely known single-ditched enclosure which has an entrance-gap opposite the west gate of the fort. Excavation showed the ditch to be V-shaped, 3 m wide and 1.2 m deep. It apparently combines the functions of an outwork with a large annexe to the south.[2]

Small-scale excavations in 1976–7 and 1983 examined the defences on the south-west and close to the north gate (*porta decumana*), together with parts of the interior. Within a triple and apparently contemporary system of three V-shaped, rock-cut ditches were the remains of a turf and gravel rampart about 5 m wide. A large, contemporary post-pit probably belonged to the south-east corner tower. A hearth/oven lay within, together with the foundation trench for a rectangular timber building. The defences had been deliberately demolished upon the abandonment of the fort.

Apart from two post-holes there was no evidence for buildings in the north-western portion of the interior, but the limited excavations preclude certainty as to whether the area was occupied by post-built structures or left vacant.

Only a small amount of datable pottery was recovered, which might indicate a short occupation were it not for a few sherds conventionally dated post-AD 120.[3] Only larger-scale work in the less plough-damaged southern portion of the fort will clarify the occupation sequence, whose parameters are unlikely to be very different from those of Trawscoed or Llanio (AD 70–130).

Although one of the largest forts in west Wales, its size may have been a function of the topography rather than space for the building requirements of the original garrison. It is certainly sufficiently large to have held a cavalry regiment 500 strong (*ala quingenaria*), an infantry regiment 1,000 strong (*cohors milliaria*) or two brigaded part-mounted quingenary cohorts (*cohortes quingenariae equitatae*).

[1] J. K. St.Joseph, 'Air reconnaissance in Roman Britain, 1973–76', *JRS*, 67 (1977), 152–4. For complementary aerial views of the site see the following photographs in the Cambridge University Collection: BZX 61, 63, 67; CCU 30, 37, 40; CJZ 2, 4; CKS 11.
[2] D. R. Wilson, 'Defensive outworks of Roman forts in Britain', *Brit.*, 15 (1984), 51–61.
[3] J. L. Davies, 'Excavations at Pen Llwyn Roman fort, Capel Bangor, Dyfed', *BBCS*, 33 (1986), 414–28.

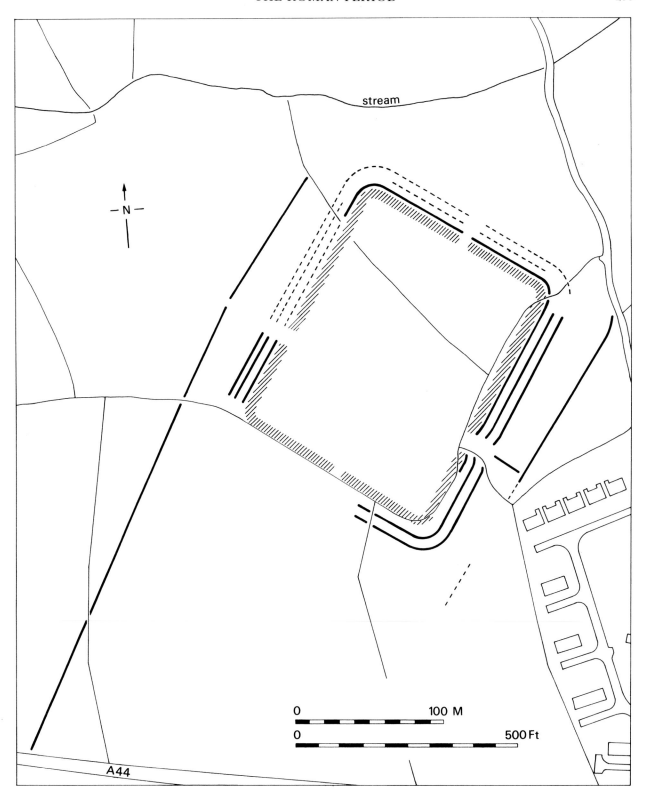

Fig. 62: Penllwyn Roman fort.

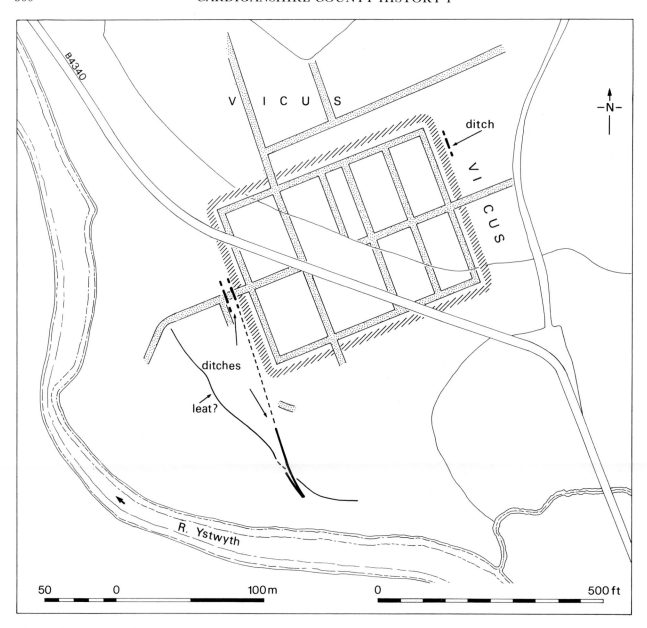

Fig. 63: Trawscoed Roman fort.

3. Traws-coed   Llanafan   SN 671 727
Pl. VII;
Fig. 63
This fort, discovered in 1959,[1] is situated on a level gravel terrace on the north bank of the Ystwyth within the grounds of the ADAS Experimental Husbandry Farm. The B4340 traverses the site leaving about two-thirds of the fort in parkland next to Trawscoed House, where the north corner,

the north-western and part of the north-eastern defences are visible as low mounds 12–14 m across. A plantation north of the road obscures much of the central portion of the fort, whilst the southern third has been extensively ploughed.

It commands the point at which the Roman road crossed the river. A short section of the road can be seen on aerial photographs zigzagging up the steep river-bank towards the south-west gate (*porta praetoria*), whilst south of the river another length is visible as a parch-mark aligned on Hendre Villa.[2]

Aerial photographs and a ground survey have revealed a comprehensive plan of the site.[3] It faced towards the river, its overall dimensions within the ditch-system being approximately 170 × 128 m with an area of 2.1 ha (5.4 acres). Parch-marks of exceptional clarity define the *viae praetoriae* and *decumanae*, but only the northernmost part of the *via principalis*. Three streets running parallel to the *via principalis* delimit a narrow block within the *latera praetorii* before the *via quintana* is reached, with another street dividing the *retentura* into equal-sized segments. A small parch-mark south of the B4340 could represent the south corner of a stone-built *principia* facing the junction of the *via principalis* and *via praetoria*. If such is the case then it appears to have occupied a frontage of about 25 m and a maximum depth of 30 m. Another indistinct parch-mark north of the modern road may represent a stone building set back from the *via principalis*; possibly a *horreum* or store-building.

Small-scale excavations in the eastern portion of the fort in 1962[4] and 1974[5] revealed defences of two periods and apparent differences in the ditch system to either side of the east gate (*porta decumana*). The primary defences comprised a turf and clay rampart 5.9 m wide fronted by two V-shaped ditches, 3.25 m wide × 1.95 m deep and 2.60 m × 1.75 m respectively to the west of the gate. The defences were rebuilt early in the second century AD, the rampart being widened to 8.5 m over the inner ditch.

A complex sequence of perimeter roads, ovens and drains lay inside the rampart together with timber buildings of at least two periods. These were set *per scamna* (across the fort axis), their timber frames set in foundation trenches and the walls of wattle and daub. The Period 1 building north of the *via decumana* was 8 m wide and probably a barrack. It faced another building, only the east wall of which was found, across an' unmetalled space. Both were burnt down before the close of the first century AD. Their Period 2 replacements were similarly aligned but of different plan. That nearest the rampart was narrower than its precursor and of uncertain use. Its partner to the west was an L-shaped barrack, *c*. 7.50 m wide excluding the officers' quarters

which occupied some 16 m of a barrack which could not have exceeded 52 m in length. A barrack which allows only 34 m for the *contubernia* (mess-units) is most likely to represent accommodation for two *turmae* (cavalry squadrons), 64 men in all, of an *ala* or a *cohors equitata*.[6] Excavations across the *via decumana* in 1962 revealed another timber building aligned *per scamna*, 7.30 m wide and at least 12.8 m long, with a west-facing verandah and rooms of equal size. It is doubtless a barrack, but of uncertain period.

No inscriptions exist to record the building unit or any garrison. It could have accommodated an *ala quingenaria*, a *cohors milliaria peditata* or two *cohortes quingenariae peditatae*. The closely spaced Period 2 buildings suggest a different unit, including cavalry, in garrison, but further speculation is fruitless.

Pottery and coins point to a foundation in the 70s of the first century AD, with an apparently short abandonment indicated by the burning of the fort before the close of the century (a phenomenon which seemingly extends to the *vicus* as well) and a final abandonment *c*. AD 125–30.

The vicus: The extra-mural settlement (*vicus*) to the north and east of the fort is one of the most significant features of the site. Its focus appears to have lain to the north where a rudimentary street-grid, based upon the prolongation of the *via principalis*, a parallel street 45 m to its east and a perimeter road bordering the fort ditches, is visible on aerial photographs.

Excavations in 1985–6 demonstrated a complex building sequence in this area.[7] One of the earliest structures outside the north-west gate was a brick/tile kiln. Thereafter at least four phases of timber buildings, with associated rubbish-pits, flanked both sides of the *via principalis* extension for at least 36 m and also occupied frontages on the parallel street. Two of these buildings were at least 7 and 11 m-long strip-buildings probably functioning as shops/taverns. These early buildings were burnt down and replaced by others of uncertain plan, one lying close to the fort gate being multi-roomed. Metal-working in bronze, and to a lesser extent in iron, is evidenced in the later phase, this part of the *vicus* being seemingly abandoned concurrently with the fort.

Excavations outside the north-east gate in 1984

and 1987–8[8] showed that *vicus* structures were also plentiful in this area. Buildings cluster outside the gate, but are also known to occupy areas immediately on the margin of the defences 35 m to the north and 25 m to the south. Buildings in such positions presuppose a need to get close to the fort, not because of any consideration of security but because of the needs of trade, the prime locations along the road leading from the gate having been already occupied. Two major phases of timber buildings were noted here. The earliest buildings were of Flavian date, one being gable-end on to the road, 8 m wide and at least 15.5 m long, with a bench-oven within. It was burnt down. Its successor was of a more complex, multi-roomed plan. Occupation here seemingly ended *c.* AD 100–10, at least a decade or more prior to that outside the north-west gate.

The symbiosis between fort and *vicus* is particularly striking at Trawscoed.[9] What may be an officially constituted settlement sprang up soon after the establishment of the fort in the early Flavian period, its history thereafter seemingly mirroring that of the fort. No Romano-British activity is indicated following its abandonment.

[1] V. E. Nash-Williams, *The Roman Frontier in Wales*, ed. M. G. Jarrett (Cardiff, 1969), 113–16.

[2] Cambridge University Collection RC 8; BC 32.

[3] Photographs taken in the summer of 1975–6 and ground survey in 1984 and 1987. One of the most informative photographs is in the Cambridge University Collection K17 A1 178. See also S. S. Frere and J. K. St.Joseph, *Roman Britain From the Air* (Cambridge, 1983), 101–3.

[4] V. E. Nash-Williams, *The Roman Frontier in Wales*, 115–16.

[5] J. L. Davies, 'Excavations at Trawscoed Roman Fort, Dyfed', *BBCS*, 31 (1984), 259–92.

[6] Ibid., 274–5. For a discussion of fort garrisons see D. Breeze and B. Dobson, 'Fort types as a guide to garrisons: a reconsideration', *Roman Frontier Studies 1969*, ed. E. Birley *et al.* (Cardiff, 1974), 13–19; M. Hassall, 'The internal planning of Roman auxiliary forts', *Rome and her Northern Provinces*, ed. B. Hartley and J. Wacher (Gloucester, 1983), 96–131.

[7] J. L. Davies, 'Trawscoed Roman Fort', *AW*, 25 (1985), 27–8; 26 (1986), 43–4.

[8] J. L. Davies, 'Trawscoed Roman Fort', *AW*, 24 (1984), 50; 18 (1978), 44; 28 (1988), 58–9.

[9] J. L. Davies, 'Excavations at Trawscoed Roman Fort, Dyfed', 262; idem, 'Three Welsh vici: analysis and implications', *Akten Des 14 Internationalen Limeskongresses 1986 in Carnuntum*, ed. H. Vetters and M. Kandler (Österreichischen Akademie der Wissenschaften, Wien, 1990), 341–51.

4. Llanio   Llanddewi-   SN 644 564
Pl. VIII,   brefi
Fig. 64

The probable existence of a fort at Llanio-isaf Farm has been known since the late seventeenth century, with the evidence consistently pointing to Cae'r Castell, immediately east of the farm, as its site. Edward Lhuyd recorded two building inscriptions found here and also noted the discovery of Roman coins, bricks and pottery.[1] His observations were echoed by Meyrick who refers to the discovery of Roman antiquities in Cae'r Castell after ploughing, together with foundations of a building '150 ft long and 72 ft in breadth'.[2] He also noted two inscriptions built into nearby cottages. The excavation of a cutting for the Manchester and Milford Railway in 1865 unearthed further Roman material,[3] and three years later W. D. Jones began the investigation of the fort bath-house.[4] Thereafter Lloyd-Williams's excavations of this building, commencing in 1888, were extensive,[5] and followed by further small-scale work in 1910.[6]

J. Willis-Bund, reporting the excavations of 1888, was especially perceptive and describes the first instance of an archaeological crop-mark in the County. He saw the parch-mark of the Roman road bypassing the fort to the west, and noted how 'the corn withered up in two broad lines across the fields (*sic* in Cae'r Castell), the lines crossing each other at right angles'.[7] This phenomenon recurred in 1975–6 and was seen to represent the main streets within the fort.

No further work is recorded at Llanio until 1961 when Professor M. G. Jarrett excavated in the field west of the lane leading to the farm in the erroneous belief that 'earthworks' in this area were the defences of the fort.[8] The earthworks can now be shown to be the *agger* of the Roman road and a branch to the west gate of the fort.

The question of the precise location of the fort rested there until 1969 when the writer excavated a trench across the probable course of the southern defences in Cae'r Castell and duly confirmed the traditional siting.[9] Later work was directed at the bath-house in 1970–1,[10] and parts of the interior in 1972–3.[11] This small-scale work, coupled with probing, enabled the street-grid of the central and southern portion of the fort to be established, a plan whose accuracy was confirmed and refined

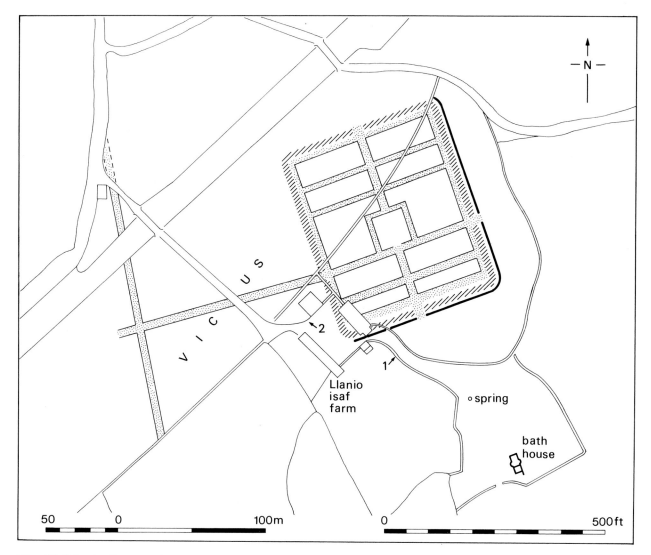

Fig. 64: Llanio Roman fort.
1. Roman ironworking debris.
2. Timber building.

by excellent aerial photographs of the site in 1975.[12]

The fort, tentatively equated with the *Bremia* of the Ravenna Cosmography,[13] occupies a gravel terrace on the north bank of the Teifi and was sited to command the river crossing. It consequently faced the river, with its long axis lying north-west to south-east. Its overall dimensions are *c.*134 × 115 m enclosing an area of 1.55 ha (3.84 acres). To the east the defences are sited on a scarp above the flood-plain, whilst they also lie on a slight break of slope to the south. Otherwise there are no natural

obstacles. Ploughing has virtually obliterated all traces of the fort other than a short length of scarp on the line of the western defences east of the farmhouse, whilst a slightly dished area in Cae'r Castell marks the site of the *principia*. A hedgebank bisects the fort from its north-east corner to a point approximately midway along its west side, whilst Llanio-isaf Farm overlies its south-west corner.

The fort was established early in the Flavian period and had defences comprising a turf and gravel rampart 5.5 m thick and a V-shaped ditch, 3.30 m wide and 1.20 m deep. The defences appear to have been refurbished at the north-east corner, possibly in the period AD 100–120, a phenomenon whose significance will be discussed later. Judging by aerial photographs the *principia* measured 23–4 m square and may have been of stone. The *praetorium* to its west was apparently of half-timbered construction but of uncertain plan. At least one *horreum* probably lay west of the principia. The arrangement of buildings in the *retentura* of the fort is unknown although the street-system allows sufficient space for a minimum of two pairs of barracks set *per scamna*. Aerial photographs also hint that the *principia* did not extend as far as the *via quintana*, thereby allowing space for a further range of buildings to its rear as at Traws-coed.

Limited excavations show that buildings in the eastern division of the *praetentura* were of timber throughout, and arranged *per scamna*. Three main periods were represented here. The primary arrangement seems to have comprised two barracks (?), *c.* 8 m wide, facing onto a common street with another building of uncertain function fronting the *via principalis*. The latest period (early Hadrianic) again comprised two barracks(?), 8.5 m and 9.75 m wide respectively. In the western division only the building sequence next to the *via sagularis* has been examined, two periods being represented, in both instances comprising barracks(?) *c.* 8 m wide. The *praetentura*, then, has sufficient space to accommodate at least four barracks or two sets of barracks and stables.

Pottery evidence shows that the fort was established in the 70s and occupied up to *c.* AD 130. At the north-east corner the defences were recast early in the second century after a circular shaft containing an upright post was dug through the primary ditch—strongly hinting at an abandonment. It is tempting to associate this activity with what appears to be a 3 m-wide ditch dug across the site of the *praetorium*. If this was of Roman date it may have been either intended to reduce the area of the fort by a third—cutting off the *praetentura*—or possibly relates to the construction of a fortlet in the north-east corner. A reduced early second-century garrison appears probable.[14]

The garrison: Llanio has produced five inscribed stones,[15] two of which apparently record legionary work[16] with another two attesting the presence of the quingenary unit *Cohors II Asturum* in garrison. It has been assumed that this unit, part of the army of Germania Inferior, was transferred to Britain sometime after AD 89,[17] but Dr M. Roxan has mooted the possibility of two such units in existence. She suggests that the cohort in Germany was equitate and later transferred to Egypt whilst the British homonym could either have formed part of the Claudian expeditionary force or arrived in Britain sometime thereafter. *Cohors II Asturum* could, then, have represented the primary garrison, or even the last to occupy the full-sized fort. Certainly excavation suggests that there was plenty of space for such a regiment, whether equitate or not.

Despite the fact that the regiment was raised among the Astures of north-western Spain—a region famed for its auriferous deposits—there is no need to suggest, as formerly, that its stationing at Llanio was occasioned by the requirements of mining expertise at the not too distant gold-bearing deposits of Dolau Cothi.[18] Such views were formulated before the recognition of the fort at Pumsaint. Secondly, the 'national' characteristics of auxiliary regiments were, with a few exceptions, short-lived. Its posting to Llanio is coincidental. Since the defences of the fort were never rebuilt in stone the building inscriptions recording the regiment either relate to work on one of the major internal buildings or on the bath-house.

The bath-house: Fig. 65: This sadly dilapidated building, with that at Tomen y Mur (Mer.), constitute the only visible examples of full-sized auxiliary bath-houses in Wales. It lies *c.* 100 m south of the fort in water-meadows, its water supply being probably provided by a copious spring which rises to the north-west.

Although robbed, its substructural walling still survives one metre high, and the remains, though incompletely exposed, indicate a simple, row-type bath-house some 30 m long.[19] The *frigidarium/apodyterium* lay to the south, its site covered by a nineteenth-century spoil-heap. The *tepidarium*, 6 m square internally, lay to its north with a booster-flue in its south-west corner. Its masonry is of excellent quality and includes some decorated stones. Nothing remains of the brick *pilae* and suspended floor recorded by Willis-Bund.[20] Three arched flues connected the heating arrangements

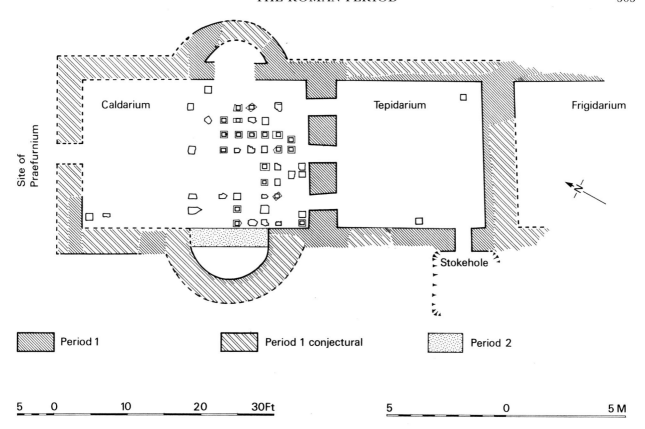

Site of Praefurnium

Caldarium   Tepidarium   Frigidarium

Stokehole

Period 1   Period 1 conjectural   Period 2

5 0   10   20   30Ft

5   0   5 M

Fig. 65: Bath-house, Llanio.

of the *tepidarium* to the hottest room, the *caldarium*, 9.30 m long and 6 m wide internally. A shallow apse lay on the east with a corresponding, but deeper, apse on the west; the former presumably functioned as an alcove, possibly with a water-basin, the latter possibly as a hot bath. The main hot bath (*alveus*), however, seems to have been sited directly over the furnace on the north. Fragments of painted wall-plaster and window glass testify to its refinement.

The overall arrangements are strikingly similar to those of the auxiliary bath-house at Castell Collen (Rad.)[21] and the legionary baths at Inchtuthil (Perth.),[22] the latter certainly of Flavian date. The bath-house at Llanio must be broadly contemporary. The writer has already suggested that it was built by a legionary work-party.[23]

A secondary phase in its history is represented by the reflooring of the *tepidarium* and the blocking of the western apse in the *caldarium*. Its abandonment is presumably coeval with the fort.

The vicus: The extra-mural settlement (*vicus*) appears to have been centred upon the road by-passing the fort on the west and a branch to the west gate. Excavations by Professor M. G. Jarrett[24] examined a few of its buildings whilst aerial photography has revealed traces of pits, a possible rectangular enclosure and at least two four-post structures lying south of the branch road. Four-posters are common on Iron Age sites but also continue into the Roman period.[25] In this context they may relate to the agricultural role of the *vicus* complex.

Excavations revealed the clay and gravel *agger* of the bypass road, 6.4 m wide, flanked on the west by a timber building and rubbish-pits. At least two phases of building were noted east of the road, the second represented by two or more timber strip-buildings, internally partitioned and perhaps *c.* 10 m long. The branch road, again 6.4 m wide, overlays a timber building and was later flanked by pits and other structures.[26]

Other features probably relating to the *vicus* include traces of a timber building 15 m west of the fort and 18 m south of the branch road,[27] whilst pottery found north of the bath-house may indicate buildings in this area as well. In 1969 ditching revealed dumps of iron slag and burnt clay associated with Flavian pottery immediately south of the farmyard.[28]

Pottery evidence indicates a Flavian origin for the *vicus* with occupation continuing to *c.* AD 130. Presumably it did not long outlive the abandonment of the fort.

[1] J. Camden, *Britannia*, ed. Gibson (1695), 645.

[2] S. R. Meyrick, *The History and Antiquities of the County of Cardigan* (1808), x.

[3] W. D. Jones, 'The Loventinum of Ptolemy', *Arch. Camb.*, 23 (1868), 450–2.

[4] See above, n. 3.

[5] J. Willis-Bund, 'Reports on Llanio and on church restoration', *Arch. Camb.*, 43 (1888), 297–317.

[6] *TCAS*, 1 (1910), 1ff.

[7] J. Willis-Bund, *Arch. Camb.*, 43 (1888), 300.

[8] *JRS*, 52 (1962), 161.

[9] *Brit.*, 1 (1970), 269.

[10] *Brit.*, 2 (1971), 243; 3 (1972), 300.

[11] *Brit.*, 4 (1973), 271; 5 (1974), 400.

[12] Cambridge University Collection BUB 22, 22A and 16.

[13] A. L. F. Rivet and C. Smith, *The Place Names of Roman Britain* (London, 1979), 277.

[14] See my comments, J. L. Davies, 'Roman military deployment in Wales and the Marches from Claudius to the Antonines', *Roman Frontier Studies*, 1979, ed. W. S. Hanson and L. J. F. Keppie (BAR 71: Oxford, 1980).

[15] R. G. Collingwood and R. P. Wright, *The Roman Inscriptions of Britain*, I, Nos. 407–10.

[16] Ibid., Nos. 409, 410.

[17] M. Roxan, 'Pre-Severan auxilia named in the Notitia Dignitatum', *Aspects of the Notitia Dignitatum*, ed. R. Goodburn and P. Bartholomew (BAR S15: Oxford, 1976), 63–4.

[18] V. E. Nash-Williams, *The Roman Frontier in Wales* (Cardiff, 1954), 40.

[19] *Brit.*, 2 (1971), 243; 3 (1972), 300.

[20] J. Willis-Bund, *Arch. Camb.*, 43 (1888), 297–317.

[21] L. Alcock, 'Castell Collen excavations, 1957', *Trans. Rads. Soc.*, 27 (1957), 5–11.

[22] L. F. Pitts and J. K. St Joseph, *Inchtuthil. The Roman Legionary Fortress Excavations 1952–65* (Britannia Monograph Series 6, London, 1985), 214–18.

[23] J. L. Davies, 'A legionary inscription from Llanio, Dyfed', *BBCS*, 28 (1978), 157–8.

[24] *JRS*, 52 (1962), 161.

[25] For example, at Cae Summerhouse (Glam.). See A. Ellison and P. Drewett, 'Pits and post-holes in the British Early Iron Age: some alternative explanations', *PPS*, 37 (1971), 185–9.

[26] Reinterpretation of the structural sequence by the writer. Professor Jarrett kindly made his field-notes available.

[27] Revealed during the course of building activity in April 1970.

[28] *AW*, 9 (1969), 17.

b) Fortlet

Erglodd	Llangynfelyn	SN 653 903

Pl. X

This site was discovered by aerial reconnaissance in the drought of 1976.[1] The differential parching of a rounded hillock forming a low spur of the Coed Erglodd ridge revealed a rectangular enclosure *c.* 50 m square with rounded corners and angles aligned on the cardinal points. It encloses 0.25 ha (0.625 acres). Ploughing has removed all surface traces but the ditch and external palisade-trench, a pit and gulley and a U-shaped feature in the interior are visible on aerial photographs. There is no trace of a causeway across the ditch, but the entrance probably lay on the north-east where a saddle joins the ridge and hillock. The site has good views to the west and north, the Leri valley to the south being invisible.

Excavations examined the north-western defences in 1976–7.[2] These proved to be of two periods, apparently separated by a phase of abandonment. Initially the defences comprised a 3 m-wide turf rampart and V-shaped ditch fronted by a palisade set 3 m beyond it. This phase ended wih the slighting of the rampart and the possible demolition of internal structures. The defences were then recast on a slightly different alignment, the Period 2 rampart overlying the Period 1 ditch. The Period 2 ditch was itself deliberately filled upon the abandonment of the site.

Datable finds were meagre but suggest a Flavian origin. The date of abandonment is unknown, but unlikely to be later than *c.* AD 130.

The fortlet lies in an intermediate position 7.5 miles from the fort at Pennal (Mer.) and 6 miles from Pen Llwyn and was presumably sited to supervise traffic between these sites and to patrol the surrounding countryside. It is not inconceivable that it may have had a role in the early exploitation of the lead/silver deposits in the neighbourhood (see p.296). Indeed, it is possible that in Roman times a tidal creek from the base of the hillock may have facilitated the shipment of bulk cargo. Little is known of its internal arrangements but comparative data suggests that its garrison would either have been drawn from Pennal, or more likely the larger fort at Pen Llwyn. It is unlikely to have numbered fewer than a century.[3]

The easement for a gas pipeline which transected the saddle immediately east of the fortlet in 1988 showed no trace of Roman features.

[1] J. K. St Joseph, 'Air reconnaissance in Roman Britain, 1975–76', *JRS*, 67 (1977), 152–3.
[2] J. L. Davies, 'A Roman fortlet at Erglodd, near Talybont, Dyfed', *BBCS*, 28 (1980), 719–29.
[3] Ibid., 724–6.

c) Practice-camps

Two small earthworks at Pant-teg Uchaf are the sole representatives in west Wales of field-entrenchments built by detachments of the Roman army on manœuvres.[1] Their constructional techniques imitate those of marching-camps insofar as they are rectangular or square with rounded corners, the rampart and ditch being insubstantial. The entrances—where they survive —are normally protected by a *titulum* or *clavicula*. These camps, furthermore, are not only much smaller than the smallest marching-camp, but are frequently found in clusters, commonly close to a Roman road and rarely more than a few hours march from an auxiliary fort.[2] The camps at Pant-teg Uchaf lie almost equidistant from the forts at Llanio and Pumsaint (4.5 and 5 miles respectively) and could, therefore, represent exercises by detachments from either fort.

Camp 1   Cellan   SN 641 493
When first detected by Professor J. K. St Joseph it was considered a fortlet;[3] the subsequent discovery of Camp 2 showed this not to be the case. It is sited on the level crest of what was formerly high moorland, now a clearing in a plantation. The course of the Roman road lies just to the south. The camp appears secondary since its axis lies parallel to it. The interior has been ploughed and only the north-east side and north angle survive.

The defences comprise a rampart about a metre high, a shallow ditch and 0.6 m high counterscarp. Traces of an entrance survive midway

along the north-east side with possible traces of another facing the road to the south-west. Its dimensions over the ramparts appear to have been 32 × 26 m (105 × 85 ft).

Camp 2   Cellan   SN 647 485
This lies some 0.75 miles south-east of Camp 1. It is of interest in that it appears to be the only unfinished example known in Britain. The north-east rampart survives 0.75 m high, whilst 18 m and 9 m lengths of the north-east and south-west sides survive respectively, these two remaining incomplete.

[1] For fieldcraft see Vegetius, *Epitoma rei militaris I*, 21–5.
[2] V. E. Nash-Williams, *The Roman Frontier in Wales*, ed. M. G. Jarrett (Cardiff, 1969), 126–30; R. W. Davies, 'Roman Wales and Roman military practice-camps', *Arch. Camb.*, 117 (1968), 103–20.
[3] J. K. St Joseph, 'Air reconnaissance in Britain 1958–60', *JRS*, 51 (1961), 127–8. See RAF cover 106G/UK/1471, 1063–4.

d) Possible site

Careg y Bwci   Cellan   SN 6457 4790
This circular earthwork, variously described as a prehistoric 'burial chamber' or 'barrow'[1] occupies a moorland knoll beween two ridges. It is 22 m in overall diameter and defined by a rock-cut ditch 2.4 m wide and 0.30–0.45 m deep with a partial counterscarp, and a bank 3.60 m wide and 0.60 m high. An entrance causeway 3.60 m wide is sited on the south-west. A massive recumbent boulder lies within, the interior having been damaged by digging around its base.

The writer has suggested that in view of its morphology and position only 20 m west of the putative course of the Roman road the site may be that of a Roman watch-tower.[2] It has panoramic views along the road, particularly to the south. It is almost equidistant between Llanio and Pumsaint and commands a strategic col traversed by the road. If this identification is accepted then it is not impossible that it formed part of the chain of some three, intervisible towers between these forts.

Excavations within in the late nineteenth century produced no Romano-British or prehistoric artefacts.[3]

[1] G. E. Daniel, *The Prehistoric Chamber Tombs of England and Wales* (1950), 216; OS SN64 NW1.

[2]J. L. Davies, 'Careg y Bwci: A Roman watch-tower?', *Arch. Camb.*, 135 (1986), 147–53.

[3]D. R. Thomas, 'Prehistoric and other remains in Cynwil Gaeo', *Arch. Camb.*, 34 (1879), 55–62.

APPENDIX II: THE ROMAN ROAD SYSTEM
(Fig. 61)

Judging by the distribution of forts and marching-camps early Roman military operations in Wales utilized natural lines of communication and such trackways as existed. However, as soon as conditions permitted, an essential requirement for the maintenance of security would have been the provision of all-weather roads linking garrison posts. The acquisition of a road system, therefore, will have been piecemeal and dependent upon the retention of conquered territory. Without doubt the construction of a lateral communication route between the principal operational bases at Wroxeter and Usk belongs to the late 50s or early 60s, but it was only with the Flavian conquest that a comprehensive network came into being. The recognition and tracing of certain elements of that system remain difficult; nevertheless its basic outline is clear.[1]

The Flavian and later road network in Wales forms a grid. Three main north–south routes form its warp: a road from Caerleon to Chester; a 'Cambrian' route from Cardiff to Caersŵs and beyond; and, finally, a western route running probably from Carmarthen to Caernarfon. The weft consisted of at least four east–west routes; one each along the north and south coasts, and two others along the valleys of the Severn and the Usk. The final element comprised a number of diagonal routes linking the corners of this grid. Cardiganshire, as we shall see, possesses a portion of the western north–south road ('Sarn Helen') and elements of perhaps two diagonal routes.

For most of Wales the construction and repair of the road system to the mid-second century will have been a military responsibility. Their needs were paramount, the roads enabling the rapid movement and deployment of troops, guaranteeing an adequate food supply to the garrison posts, and the provision of building materials. This was a period which may also have seen the transportation of mineral resources—principally lead and silver—from the mining areas to where they were required, or for export. With the relinquishing of military administration over much of southern and eastern Wales from the mid-second century, civilian authorities may have been charged with the upkeep of the road system. Milestones of the third and fourth centuries point to repair and perhaps even the rebuilding of certain stretches.[2] Unfortunately, no such epigraphic evidence exists for the continued maintenance of the road system in Cardiganshire, although there is little doubt that 'Sarn Helen'—the prime north–south route in west Wales—will have remained important. As elsewhere in Wales the road system will have been instrumental in opening up the country, facilitating the exploitation of natural resources and enhancing the opportunities for trade. Of no less importance was the unifying role of the road system, easing the movement of people and ideas. For the first time formerly isolated, introspective and economically backward communities were made aware of the new *modus vivendi*, emulated with varying degrees of enthusiasm and success by communities elsewhere in Britain. Indeed, the psychological effects of this communications network cannot be overestimated, linking communities along the length and breadth of Roman Britain and giving them an identity which they were anxious to preserve in post-Roman times.

The road system in Cardiganshire is incompletely known. Only the north–south route has been surveyed on the ground and from the air; even so some stretches are problematical.[3] Though there is a tendency for Roman roads to be laid out in straight lengths from elevated sighting points, the straight line which passes as an almost proverbial description of a Roman road should not be taken too much to heart. This applies just as much to the well-researched 'Sarn Helen' as to the more uncertain routes.[4] Only four roads merit consideration: (1) a north–south route ('Sarn Helen') linking Pennal and Llanio; (2) a diagonal route linking Llanio and Pumsaint; (3) a probable extension of this route to Carmarthen; (4) a possible route linking Penllwyn with Cae Gaer, and thence on to the Severn valley. It is immediately noticeable that this leaves southern Cardiganshire and northern Pembrokeshire without a road system, but it must be remembered that it was not the Roman intention to create an overall road network but merely to facilitate communication beween military posts situated in, and on the flanks of, the mountainous spine of Wales. It has already been suggested that the far south-west may have been inhabited by a community who were well-disposed towards the Romans; therefore military establishments and a concomitant road system was rendered unnecessary. It must also be borne in mind that any discussion of the Roman road system invariably ignores earlier tracks which linked native settlements and which will have played no small part in the Roman communications network. These are for the most part undetectable.

(1) *'Sarn Helen': Pennal to Llanio:*[5]   This route begins at Pennal (Mer.) where the first certain traces of the road are discernible. Aerial reconnaissance of the fort in 1975 showed the parchmark of the road issuing from the south-west gate, traversing a marshy area at the base of the slope and making for the crossing of the Dyfi half a mile distant.[6] Two opposing tongues of land make fording possible at this point.[7] South of the Dyfi no certain traces of the road are known until Trawscoed is reached. However, there is general agreement as to its probable course and the discovery of Erglodd and Penllwyn has clarified the problem to some extent.

The course of the road for some seven miles south of the Dyfi is dictated by high ground to the east and low-lying, marshy ground extending along its south bank to Borth Bog. North of Furnace (SN 684 952) the course of the road is undetermined, but thereafter it was formerly believed to correspond with a minor road running about a mile inland of the A487 as far south as Tal-y-bont. This is a good, direct alignment which has much to recommend it. However, the discovery of the fortlet at Erglodd makes such a supposition uncertain since that fortlet was clearly sited to command the north end of the pass through which a road presumably ran to the Leri

crossing (see p.306). It is a reasonable assumption, therefore, that the course of the A487 from Furnace to Tal-y-bont approximates to that of the Roman road. This route takes the easiest line through country which exhibits a marked ridge and valley physiognomy as far south as the Ystwyth.

Beyond the Leri the course of the Roman road may be marked by the minor road that forks left at SN 652 889 and runs as far south as Penrhyn-coch. Thereafter its course is uncertain. Some years ago D. P. Jones suggested that after crossing the Silo the road ascended the steeply sloping ridge to Llwyngronw Farm, crossed the intervening ridge via a low saddle and made for the crossing of the Peithyll at Rhyd-lwyd.[8] Indeed, the northward deviation of the parish boundary at SN 644 833 could well mark such an ancient feature. Jones suggests that the road ascended the ridge by way of Ty'n-y-cwm Farm and descended to the Rheidol close to Cwm Mwythig. As supporting evidence he cites the discovery of 'an ancient road' in a field significantly called Cae Pen Sarn, just east of Cwm Mwythig in 1885. An alternative route, and one which continues the alignment of the modern road north of Penrhyn-coch, is that which runs south through the village, ascending the ridge via a carefully engineered gradient to Pen-y-berth, its course to the Peithyll being conterminous with the modern road. Beyond the stream the road picks up a southerly alignment once more before it descends to the Rheidol crossing via a saddle immediately east of the fort at Penllwyn. In view of the general alignment, and the close relationship between roads and forts the writer prefers the latter route, but the matter awaits conclusive proof.

Beyond the Rheidol the road would have assumed a south/south-east alignment making for the river crossing at Trawscoed, but its course is uncertain. Meyrick speaks of the road being visible both at a farm called Brennan and at another called Llwynrhyngyll.[9] D. P. Jones, following Meyrick and asserting local tradition, states that the road ascended the steep slopes on the south bank of the Rheidol through Pwllcenawon Wood, where it appeared as a terraceway 11.5 ft in width. Its course was then indicated by a track through Rhiwarthen-isaf, the road surface 12 ft in width being visible following ploughing near SN

639 790 in 1885. The road then continued through Nantybenglog-isaf Farm, crossing the Paith at Cae Sarn, where Jones states that it was clearly visible following ploughing in *c.* 1840.[10] The Revd D. J. Evans records the same phenomenon after ploughing near Cae Sarn in about 1930 where the course of the 'Roman' road was visible as a crop-mark four yards across.[11] An alternative route to that described above takes a more easterly alignment and commences near Tan-yr-allt (SN 657 789) where a carefully engineered terraceway ascends the wooded slope from the floor of the Rheidol valley and thence around the shoulder of the ridge at Llety-bach. Thereafter the old road through Llanfihangel-y-Creuddyn could represent its course, passing the significantly named farm and house at Sarnau-fawr and Nant-y-sarnau. Beyond Llanfihangel the road ascends the ridge and then descends via a zigzag near Llannerch-yr-oen. Beyond Pen-y-pont-bren, where the road fords the Nant Magwr, there are no further possible traces towards Trawscoed, a mile to the south-east but aerial photography has revealed extensive traces of the road system in the vicinity of this fort (see p.300).

South of the Ystwyth the road has been intensively researched, and because of the divergence of modern roads and tracks from its line more survives above ground. Field boundaries west of Trawscoed station and a sharp modern road alignment making for Lisburne House and Hendre Rhys may mark the first indications of the road south of the river. Beyond this point the westerly alignment changes to the south/south-west and is continued by a trackway which brings the road around the spur on which Gaer Fawr is situated and the re-entrant between this and the afforested Banc-cwm-llechwedd. This track continues as far as the significantly named farmstead Sarn Ellen, where a long field boundary undoubtedly marks its course to SN 6550 6940. Thereafter, a short length of the road is visible as a grassmark at approximately SN 6548 6940,[12] the alignment being almost due south. It is then lost until the minor road picks it up at Llwyn-merch-Gwilym (SN 654 685). At SN 653 676 the modern road makes a detour to the east before recommencing the same alignment a quarter of a mile further south, but aerial photographs[13] demonstrate that at the northern end of this detour the Roman road

continued its southerly course and is now visible as a low *agger* some 6m wide for a distance of about 160 m. The Roman and modern road are thereafter conterminous until the crossing of the Camddwr at SN 6505 6686. Beyond this stream the alignment is continued, first as a fieldbank, then as a footpath as far as SN 646 646 where aerial photographs again clearly reveal the road as a grass-mark traversing pasture and moorland for 750 m.[14] It appears to join the modern A485 close to Taihirion-rhos (SN 644 651) a spot where the road was formerly visible.[15] Road metalling was also apparently encountered during the course of pipe-laying just west of Penbryn (SN 646 656) in 1964.[16] In 1959 the structure of the Roman road in this area was investigated by members of the Cardiganshire Antiquarian Society, three sections being excavated: (1) At SN 6480 6618 showed the road to have a foundation of cobbles and clay 4 ins thick resting on peat, overlain by 6 ins of soil representing the last vestiges of its *agger*. (2) At SN 6488 6635 showed the road to have a substantial foundation of boulders or cobbles 4.25 m wide capped with layers of clay and soil 0.40 m thick. (3) At SN 6485 6630 showed the road to be 4.5–4.8 m wide, and composed of a mix of clay and stones 0.25 m thick resting on peat.

For the next 1.5 miles the modern road continues the Roman alignment as far as the Tyncelyn crossroads where the A485 turns sharply to the east. Immediately to the north-east of the crossroads the pebble metalling of the Roman road was observed by the writer following spring ploughing in 1971. Beyond the crossroads the B4578 and the Roman road are conterminous as far as SN 642 572 where the Roman alignment diverges for some 150 m to the west until once again taken up by the modern road for a further half mile. Thereafter, aerial photographs indicate that the southerly alignment was continued passing close to the cottages which lie west of the trackway leading to Llanio-isaf Farm and then bisecting the angles formed by the railway and the road bridge.[17] The road is then seen to continue for some 130 m, either as a slightly raised *agger* 9 m wide or as a cropmark heading for a crossing of the Teifi close to SN 643 559. Aerial photographs also show a branch road running from this road to the west gate of the fort at Llanio (see p.302).

(2) *'Sarn Helen': Llanio to Pumsaint:* The existence of this route is not in doubt but its course is problematical. Tradition has it that south of Llanio the Roman road crossed Llanfair Mountain on a south-easterly alignment to the church of Llan-y-crwys (SN 645 453), and, thence, through Caio to Pumsaint.[18] Margary suggests that after crossing the river opposite Llanio the road skirted Garth, crossed the Brefi and took a south-westerly alignment along the east bank of the river as far as Llanfair Clydogau (SN 624 513), the B4343 marking its course.[19] Thereafter he suggests that the road took a south-easterly alignment, marked by the minor road over Llanfair Mountain, until it left the County at SN 646 479. The presence of the two practice-camps at Pant-teg Uchaf (see p.307) supports the Roman origin of the latter part of this route, camps of this type being frequently sited close to Roman roads.[20]

The north-western portion of Margary's putative route has an uncharacteristically steep descent to the valley floor, and a valley bottom route to the crossing of the Brefi seems unlikely. Alternatively the road may have changed alignment on Llanfair Mountain, a north-easterly course taking it across a series of spurs and minor stream valleys before the descent to the Teifi. Whilst this gives a more direct northerly route it presents topographical difficulties. Defining the course of this road requires further fieldwork.

(3) *Llanio to Carmarthen:* The existence of this route is once again vouched for by early antiquaries although few traces have been observed. In the summer of 1989 T. James of the Dyfed Archaeological Trust noted part of its course just to the north of Carmarthen as a parch-mark from SN 4305 2312 to 4370 2420.[21] Meyrick states that after passing through Llanybydder the road entered Cardiganshire by way of a ford across the Teifi at Lampeter, and then keeping to the north bank made for Llanio.[22] Margary favours the same course but maintains a route along the south bank with a branch from Pumsaint making a junction at Llanfair Clydogau.[23] This route requires further investigation.

(4) *Penllwyn to Cae Gaer:* The siting of the small fort of Cae Gaer undoubtedly denotes the existence of a link with Caersŵs in the upper Severn and either the fort at Penllwyn or that at Trawscoed (or perhaps both). Both routes (the former being the most likely) would present considerable, but not insuperable, difficulties for Roman engineers, the situation being roughly comparable to that of linking Caersŵs and Pennal by road. The only tentative piece of evidence for a road was noted prior to afforestation by Dr A. H. A. Hogg and comprised a short length of ancient-looking trackway on a south-westerly alignment close to Cae Gaer.[24] This may possibly relate to an unfinished road-building project in this inhospitable region.

[1] For the road system in general see I. D. Margary, *Roman Roads in Britain* (London, 1969).

[2] R. P. Wright, 'Roman milestones found in Wales', *The Roman Frontier in Wales*, ed.M. G. Jarrett (Cardiff, 1969), 182–8.

[3] Margary, *Roman Roads*, 356–7.

[4] O'Dwyer, *Roman Roads in Cardiganshire* (1936).

[5] The writer acknowledges the valuable assistance given by Messrs C. Houlder and E. Whatmore in tracing this route, and for placing their maps and field notes at his disposal.

[6] Airviews (Manchester) Ltd. No.47655; 47669.

[7] E. G. Bowen and C. A. Gresham, *History of Merioneth*, I (Dolgellau, 1967), 238.

[8] D. P. Jones, 'The Roman road from Carmarthenshire to Pennal', ed. G. E. Evans, *Trans.Carms.Nat.Soc.*, 19 (1925–6), 43–8.

[9] S. R. Meyrick, *The History and Antiquities of the County of Cardigan* (1808), xi.

[10] D. P. Jones, *Trans Carms.Nat.Soc.*, 19 (1925–6), 45.

[11] D. J. Evans, *Hanes Capel Seion* (Aberystwyth, 1935), 116–17.

[12] RAF cover No.541–464–4058.

[13] RAF cover No.541–464–3021/2.

[14] RAF cover No.541–464–4020/2; Cambridge University Collection AUB 97.

[15] Meyrick, *History and Antiquities*, xi.

[16] Information from Ordnance Survey.

[17] Cambridge University Collection AYJ 26; BUB 22, 26.

[18] Meyrick, *History and Antiquities*, xi. Also the correspondence between Robert Greville and Thomas Leman, *W. R. O.* 383–907. I am indebted to Dr C. S. Briggs for this reference.

[19] Margary, *Roman Roads*, 335, 357.

[20] V. E. Nash-Williams, *The Roman Frontier in Wales*, ed. M. G. Jarrett (Cardiff, 1969), 127.

[21] Information from Mr Terry James, Dyfed Archaeological Trust.

[22] Meyrick, *History and Antiquities*, xi.

[23] Margary, *Roman Roads*, 357.

[24] Information from Dr A. H. A. Hogg.

APPENDIX III: INSCRIBED STONES FROM LLANIO-ISAF

1. Pl. XI (a)
A building slab measuring 104 x 33 cm, seen in, or before, 1806 when it was built into the wall of a cottage. Now in the National Museum of Wales. The Dept. of Geology at the Museum has identified it as of Lower Silurian greywacke, readily available in the locality. The inscription lies within an ansate border, a feature that Meyrick's illustration and the recent photograph both bear out. In this respect Collingwood's drawing does not do it justice.

The text reads: COH (ORS) II ASTVR (VM)/ ... 'The Second Cohort of Asturians ...' The second line is illegible but probably comprised a centurion's mark and name.
R. G. Collingwood and R. P. Wright, *The Roman Inscriptions of Britain* I, No.407.

2. A fragment measuring 23 x 20 cm of what may have been a dedication slab. Now built, at ground level, into the east jamb of the south arch of the doorway into the church tower at Llanddewibrefi. An incised line shows that it represents part of the last two lines of the text. It reads: ...] MIBVS [.../...I] I. AST [VR (UM)
']mibus [.../... the Second Cohort of Asturians'
Collingwood and Wright, No. 408.

3. Pl. XI (b)
A building-stone measuring 30 x 18 cm first recorded by Edward Lhuyd who drew it at Llanio-isaf Farm a little before 1695. Both he and Meyrick illustrate the stone which was then undamaged. It is now deposited at the library of St David's University College, Lampeter. The Dept. of Geography at St David's has identified the stone as of Ordovician or Silurian greywacke of local origin. The text lies within an ansate panel and reads: > . ARTI. M./ ENNIVS/PRIMVS 'The century of Artius. Marcus Ennius Primus (built this).'

Despite his unusual *nomen* the centurion Artius seems to have been a Roman citizen, since the names of his subordinate indicate that he was a citizen of long standing. This inscription, and No.4 below, comprise the only evidence for building activity by a legionary work-party at Llanio.
Collingwood and Wright, No.409; J. L. Davies, 'A legionary inscription from Llanio, Dyfed', *BBCS*, 28 (1978), 157–8.

4. A centurial stone measuring 38 x 18 cm found built into a wall bounding Cae'r Castell in 1888. It was drawn by Collingwood in 1929 but its present whereabouts is unknown. The left-hand side of the stone was damaged but part of an ansate border survived on the right. It read: > ARTI 'The century of Artius (built this).'
Collingwood and Wright, No.410.

APPENDIX IV: ROMAN COINS FROM CARDIGANSHIRE

a) Hoards

1. Mydroilyn   circa SN 442 544
R. E. M. Wheeler refers to the discovery of 'two Roman brass found some years ago in a peat bog about a mile south-west of the village of Mydroilyn, Felinfach'. They were presumably shown to him at the National Museum of Wales. Their present whereabouts are unknown. G. C. Boon suggests that they may have been *sestertii* of the period AD 67–8.

R. E. M. Wheeler, 'Roman coins from Cardiganshire', *BBCS*, 2 (1923), 88; G. C. Boon, 'The Penard Roman Imperial Hoard: An interim report and a list of Roman hoards in Wales', *BBCS*, 22 (1967), 302.

**2. Tan-y-   Llangybi   SN 608 523
Fforest**
Ellis Davies records the discovery of a hoard sometime between 1830 and 1840, 37 coins being found whilst stacking turf in a farmyard.
E. Davies, 'Coin finds', *Arch.Camb.*, 73 (1918), 362.

3. Bwlch-bach SN 608 793
Farm,
Nanteos

Under the title 'Treasure Trove' *The Welshman* states that on 25 November 1841 a ploughman at Bwlch-bach turned up a large copper pot full of ancient coins. The edition for 31 December carried a further report wherein some of the coins were said to be silver-plated. Ten coins out of 'many hundreds' corroded together were identified by Revd I. Bonsall as issues of Gallienus, Salonina, Postumus, Laelianus, Victorinus, Aurelian, Tetricus I and II, Tacitus and Carausius. The hoard, or a large portion of it, passed into the hands of T. O. Morgan of Aberystwyth who exhibited the coins and their fragmentary container at the Tenby meeting of the Cambrian Archaeological Association in 1851. There is no subsequent record of their whereabouts.

One of those identified by Bonsall was an ORIENS AVG (not Oriens Vic as stated) issue of Carausius, of a type intermediate between RIC 293 and 297, with the C mint-mark (AD 286–9). The hoard was probably of Carausian date.

The Welshman 3/12/1841 and 31/12/1841; G. E. Evans, 'Two Forgotten Hoards, 1841 and 1881', *Trans.Carm. Nat.Soc.*, 19 (1925–6), 41.

4. Rhiwarthen- SN 639 795
isaf ('Goginan')

This hoard, within a cooking-pot, was ploughed up in 'the third field south-east of Rhiwarthen-isaf Farm' in 1881. The total is uncertain. *Archaeologia Cambrensis* 1880 states 'some thousands', whilst G. E. Evans says that a Mrs Morgan who bought the vessel and the coins is said to have purchased 7,000: these she made into bracelets, chains, earrings etc. The remainder eventually passed to D. T. Harris who presented the pot and coins to the National Library of Wales. These were sought in vain by the writer.

A few coins were identified by Professor Angus at the University College of Wales, some 70 per cent of which were issues of Victorinus and the Tetrici. Forty coins ranging from Valerian to Probus (AD 253–82) are said to have been presented to the College, but most appear to have been lost in the fire of 1885, although an *antoninianus* of Victorinus and three of Victorinus and Tetricus I, fashioned into a tie-clip, are still preserved in the

College collection. W. H. Davies illustrated some of those said to have been part of the hoard in the possession of R. E. Bonsall. Seven of these made into a chain are *antoniniani* of Victorinus and Tetricus I; with two others of Tetricus I and Claudius II. A further 47 coins said to have formed part of the hoard are preserved in the National Museum of Wales and range from Valerian to Probus. The closing date for the hoard appears to lie within the reign of Probus (AD 276–82).

G. C. Boon has shown that the coins said to have been found at Aberystwyth Castle (the so-called Aberystwyth hoard) formed part of the Rhiwarthen-isaf hoard.

Anon., 'Miscellaneous notices. Roman coins', *Arch.Camb.*, 35 (1880), 238; *University of Wales Calendar* 1882–3, 81; G. E. Evans, 'Two forgotten hoards, 1841 and 1881', *Trans. Carm. Nat. Soc.*, 19 (1925–6), 41; W. H. Davies, 'The Romans in Cardiganshire', *Ceredigion*, 4 (1961), 72, Pl.IV, 10–12; G. C. Boon, 'The Penard Roman Imperial Hoard: An interim report and a list of Roman hoards in Wales', *BBCS*, 22 (1967), 305; idem, 'A list of Roman hoards in Wales—first supplement 1973', *BBCS*, 26 (1975), 238.

5. Strata SN 746 658
Florida

R. E. M. Wheeler's list includes a hoard of 'upwards of 16 Roman coins' found within a bronze bowl ploughed up 'some years ago' (i.e. *c*. 1850) at Strata Florida. Those seen by Wheeler included *antoniniani* of Gallienus, Victorinus (4), Claudius II (2), Tetricus I and II (7) and a rare *denarius* of Carausius. There is no further record of this hoard for which G. C. Boon suggests a deposition date of *c*. AD 290.

R. E. M. Wheeler, 'Archaeological lists. Roman coin hoards in Wales', *BBCS*, 1 (1923), 346–7; Boon, 'The Penard Imperial Hoard...', *BBCS*, 22 (1967), 306.

b) Single finds

1. Nero, *dupondius*. Very much worn with very little patination. Found in a garden at Tal-y-bont: possibly a modern loss. Information from G. C. Boon.

2. Domitian, *denarius* (RIC 174), AD 92–3. Found 'on a rock in the R. Ystwyth'. Shown to G. C. Boon in 1965.

3. Faustina I, *as*. Slightly worn with no patination. Said to have been found 'in a street at Llandysul'. Probably a modern loss. Now in the National Museum of Wales.

4. Tetricus I, *antoninianus*, AD 270–3. Found during the course of building work in 1977 at Lluest, Aberystwyth. Seen by the writer. It remains in the possession of the finder, D. Williams, Pendaro, Church St., Llanrhystud.

5. Diocletian, *antoninianus*. Found 'with' a north Wales farthing in 1968 in a garden at Rhydyfelin, Aberystwyth. Probably a modern loss. Information from G. C. Boon.

6. *Follis* of Constantine I struck for Maximian (RIC 90), London mint, AD 307. Found in April 1930 in a mole hill a few yards from the monument within Pen Dinas, Aberystwyth. Now in the National Museum of Wales.
V. E. Nash-Williams, 'Roman coin from Aberystwyth, Cardiganshire', *BBCS*, 6 (1931–3), 94.

7. A coin of Constantine I is said to have been found within Aberystwyth Castle. It may possibly be the *Urbs Romana* illustrated by W. H. Davies and said to have (impossibly) formed part of the Rhiwarthen-isaf hoard.
Anon. 'Miscellaneous', *Arch.Camb.*, 12 (1857), 402; W. H. Davies, 'The Romans in Cardiganshire', *Ceredigion*, 4 (1961), Pl.IV.

8. W. H. Davies reports that he saw a coin (of third-century date?) said to have formed part of a hoard found at Trawscoed.
W. H. Davies, 'The Romans in Cardiganshire', *Ceredigion*, 4 (1961), 95.

APPENDIX V: ROMANO-BRITISH BURIALS

1. Penbryn   SN 289 513

The Romano-British inurned cremation, associated coin and memorial of Corbalengus were first recorded by Meyrick,[1] though the memorial stone and a small heap of stones (cairn?) had been noted by Camden. The latter states that, 'It (*sic* the stone) stood not long since (as I was informed) in a small heap of stones, close by the place where it lies now on the ground.'[2] By Meyrick's time, '... the heap of stones he mentions were removed about two years ago, when some silver coins were found, and an urn containing ashes'. No trace of the cairn(?) survived by 1861.[3] The coin was first exhibited at the Cardigan meeting of the Cambrian Archaeological Association in 1859, and subsequently at the Carmarthen meeting when it was displayed with a cinerary urn and a Roman bronze key said to have been found at Penbryn.[4]

Some uncertainty exists in respect of the record of silver coins (a hoard?) from the site and the gold coin exhibited, although an association is not improbable. The coin is an *aureus* of Titus (RIC Vespasian 177a), *c.* AD 74; the pot containing the cremation is a small black-burnished cooking-pot of the type current *circa* AD 120–50. They are both preserved in the National Museum of Wales (Acc.No.29.433/2).

Despite its association with an Early Christian memorial stone of Class I (see p.414)[5] there is no doubt that the cremation is a genuine burial of the Hadrianic–early Antonine period. Its closest parallels appear to be the barrow burials of first/second-century AD date in south-eastern England, a cairn being substituted for a barrow.[6] That the cremation is that of Corbalengus himself is an attractive proposition, but the epigraphic links would seem to be more in keeping with memorial stones of the Early Christian period than those of Roman date. Corbalengus's grave may, possibly, have been a secondary interment (almost certainly an inhumation) either in the body of an earlier cairn, or close to it. Instances of the reuse of much earlier cemetery sites are not uncommon,[7] and burials in or beneath cairns or barrows in early Christian times are not infrequent.[8]

[1] S. R. Meyrick, *The History and Antiquities of the County of Cardigan* (1810), 178–9.
[2] J. Camden, *Britannia*, ed. Gibson (1695), 648.
[3] H. L. J..., 'Early inscribed stones in Wales' *Arch.Camb.*, 16 (1861), 305–8.

[4] *Arch.Camb.*, 14 (1859), 350.
[5] V. E. Nash-Williams, *Early Christian Monuments of Wales* (1950), 102.
[6] G. C. Dunning and R. F. Jessup, 'Roman barrows', *Antiq.*, 9 (1936), 37–53.
[7] Plas Gogerddan (Cards.); Tandderwen (Denbs.).
[8] V. E. Nash-Williams, *The Early Christian Monuments of* *Wales*, No.41, 294, 409. No.101 from Penmachno bears the formula, 'In congeries lapidum'.

2. Plas Gogerddan   SN 675 483

For the possibility that some of the inhumations (and possibly some of the earlier cremations) belong to the Romano-British period, see p.294.

APPENDIX VI: OTHER ROMANO-BRITISH FINDS

a) Metalwork

1. Trawscoed   SN 6725 7315
(Fig. 66)

A bronze cart/waggon fitting found on the surface of an experimental grass-seeding plot, to the north-east of the fort.[1] It represents the fore-part of a griffin whose body terminates in a socket designed for attachment in the horizontal plane. It measures 48 mm from the stumps of the legs to the remains of the ear-tufts; 57 mm from the beak to the end of the socket, which is of oval section, 11.5 × 9 mm, decreasing rapidly in diameter from a depth of 7 mm. A cast perforation in the vertical plane, 7 mm in diameter, is situated immediately in front of a collar encircling the socket. A roughly square-sectioned, anteriorly inclined bronze pin, 5.5 mm square and 10 mm long, with an expanded but broken end, fully pierces the socket. It may have been designed for affixing this decorative fitting to a projection on the vehicle. Now in the Ceredigion Museum.

A close parallel comes from the Roman fort at Strageath (Scotland).[2]

[1] J. L. Davies, 'A Bronze vehicle mount from Trawscoed, Dyfed', *Brit.*, 18 (1987), 277–8.
[2] S. S. Frere and J. J. Wilkes, *Strageath: Excavation within the Roman Fort 1973–86* (Britannia Monographs Series 9, London, 1989), 146, 149, Fig. 50.

2. Aber-porth   SN 26 51

A bronze roundel found on the beach 'near Aber-porth' by Mrs A. Watkiss of Coventry, in whose possession it remains. It comprises a damaged roundel of bronze foil, 8.5 cm in diameter. An irregular central perforation is encircled by a diagonally slashed moulding, which is in turn surrounded by a symmetrical arrangement of five petals. Springing from between these are groups of S-coils with fleshy terminals curved around berried rosettes.

It was presumably originally mounted on a wooden or leather base. Decoratively it combines elements of both Celtic and Roman art. Its function is uncertain although M. Simpson draws parallels with Roman military *phalerae*. He suggests a late first/early second-century AD date. M. Simpson, 'A bronze mount from Aberporth', *Arch.Camb.*, 117 (1968), 72–6.

b) Pottery

1. Aberaeron

A sherd of samian is said to have been found by staff of the Ordnance Survey.
Dyfed Archaeological Trust PRN 1868.

2. Peraidd   SN 815 822
Fynydd

A pottery lamp said to have been found in digging in a fox earth between 1962 and 1967. It is an Egyptian product of the second–fourth century AD. It is difficult to believe that such an exotic object was lost in the Roman period, particularly in such an isolated spot. It may, therefore, be a modern loss. Now in Ceredigion Museum, Access No.1845.
D. Browne, 'Peraidd Fynydd', *AW* 26 (1986), 43.

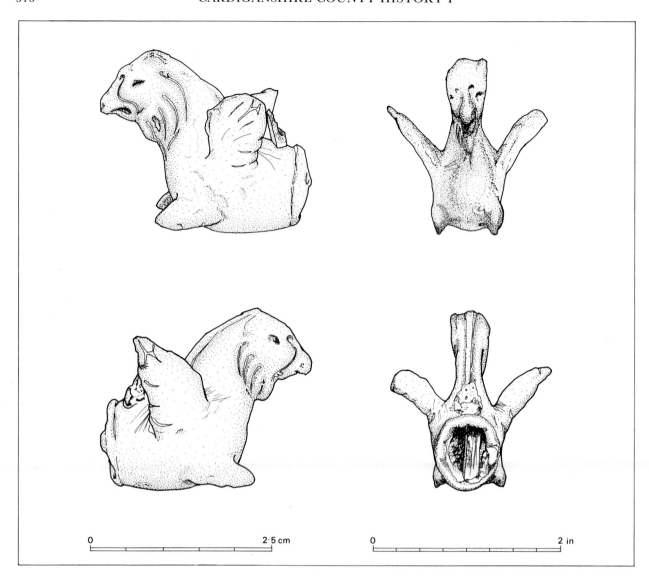

0   2·5 cm

0   2 in

Fig. 66: Bronze cart fitting, Trawscoed.

c) Wood

Llanio   *circa* SN 643 567
A carved female head first exhibited when the
Cambrian Archaeological Association visited the
site of the Roman fort in 1878.[1] On that occasion
the farmer stated that it had been found some fifty
years previously during the course of peat-digging
in Cae Gwerful. 'Hands with part of an arm,
belonging to the head' had also been found but
subsequently lost. According to the Tithe

Schedule the field in question is Parcel 297
situated beyond the abandoned railway, just
north of the fort.

The head is composed of yew, is 17.6 cm high
and depicts a female with a melon-style coiffure.[2]
The features are plain but well carved (considerable effort having gone into the treatment of the
hair) with a flattened profile and deeply-sunk eye
sockets. A plain collar encircles the base which has
a socket some 2 cm across and up to 5 cm deep,
indicating that the head was intended for attach-

ment to some sort of dowel. Stylistically it is unquestionably Romano-British and G. C. Boon dates it to *c.* AD 200 on the basis of the coiffure. The object has no ready parallels though Boon suggests that it had a prosaic function as a key or knife-handle. However, the writer prefers an alternative explanation as a small cult statue or *ex voto* from a shrine situated in or close to a spring or pool in the previously marshy Cae Gwerful. The 'hands with part of an arm' said to have been found with it could have formed part of a composite statue, or alternatively were individual *ex votos* akin to those known from both Romano-British and Gallo-Roman contexts.[3]

It remains in private possession.

[1] R. Willis-Bund, 'On a wooden female head found at Llanio', *Arch.Camb.*, 34 (1879), 81–5.

[2] G. C. Boon, 'A Romano-British wooden carving from Llanio', *BBCS*, 27 (1978), 619–24.

[3] For similar carved wooden heads see *Antiq.*, 46 (1972), 39–42.

d) Stone

Dinas Ceri   SN 316 434
Farm

The upper stone of a rotary quern was found on the farm by Mr E. Wynn. It is fashioned from a water-worn boulder and decorated with two concentric circles around the pivot-hole, and with five radial lines extending from the outer circle. Decorated querns of this type are common in Romano-British contexts in north-west Wales. Now in Ceredigion Museum.

A. H. A. Hogg, 'Dinas Ceri Farm', *AW*, 12 (1972), 22; see *Ulster J. Arch.*, 14 (1951), 49–61 for a discussion of the type.

CHAPTER 5

THE POLITICAL DEVELOPMENT OF CEREDIGION, *c*.400–1081

D. P. Kirby

IN the early Middle Ages Wales was a collection of kingdoms ranging across into the west midlands of what is now England, part of a complex of British kingdoms extending from the valley of the Clyde to Cornwall, subject not only to continual curtailment by the expanding authority of neighbouring Anglo-Saxon rulers but also to a wide range of different regional factors and external influences.[1] Distant from the main theatres of border warfare with the Anglo-Saxons, Ceredigion was a compact kingdom on the shores of the Irish Sea, partitioned administratively in the course of time into four *cantrefi*, the name of only one of which, Penweddig in the north, has survived. The *cantrefi* were in turn subdivided into ten commotes, four in Is Aeron (below the River Aeron) and six in Uwch Aeron (above the River Aeron).[2] Ieuan ap Sulien, writing at Llanbadarn Fawr *c*.1090, the first Cardiganshire man to write about his *patria* or 'homeland', as he calls it, describes the 'fertile region' of Ceredigion as bounded by Plynlimon to the east and the sea to the west, and to the north and south by the Rivers Dyfi and Teifi.[3] When Gruffudd ap Rhys attacked Ceredigion across the Teifi from the south in 1116 'he came first',

---

[1] The most recent study of Wales as a whole in this period is Wendy Davies, *Wales in the Early Middle Ages* (Leicester, 1982), but there is still a great deal of value in J. E. Lloyd, *A History of Wales from the Earliest Times to the Edwardian Conquest*, 2 vols. (3rd ed., London, 1939). See also M. Lloyd Jones, *Society and Settlement in Wales and the Marches, 500 BC–AD 1100*, 2 vols. (BAR British Series 21, 1984). I am grateful to Professor J. Beverley Smith and to Professor R. Geraint Gruffydd for their helpful comments on this chapter.

[2] Melville Richards, 'Local government in Cardiganshire: medieval and modern', *Ceredigion*, 4 (1962), 1–11, and 'The significance of *Is* and *Uwch* in Welsh commote and cantref names', *WHR*, 2 (1964), 9–18. For maps, see W. Rees, *An Historical Atlas of Wales* (London, 1951), plates 28 and 33, and Melville Richards, *Welsh Administrative and Territorial Suffixes* (Cardiff, 1969), 1, 27, 28. For further comment on the administrative organization of early Ceredigion, see below, II, ch. 6.

[3] M. Lapidge, 'The Welsh-Latin poetry of Sulien's family', *Studia Celtica*, 8 (1973), 68–106 (pp. 82–3).

say the Welsh annals,[4] 'to the place called Is coed' (one of the commotes of Is Aeron), while, certainly in the twelfth century, the line at which princes crossed from north Wales into Ceredigion was the Dyfi. To the north of the Dyfi lay Meirionydd, to the south of the Teifi, Ystrad Tywi, and to the east of Plynlimon, Arwystli. When men and women in Ceredigion fled before the avenging royal forces of Henry I, king of England, as his forces searched for Owain ap Cadwgan in 1109, some sought refuge in Arwystli, others in Ystrad Tywi. Ceredigion's maritime character exposed it to seaborne influences, particularly Irish in the fifth and sixth centuries and Scandinavian in the age of the Vikings. The former were by far the more significant. In time a cultural and linguistic divide between Irish or Goedelic influences and British or Brythonic emerged in the area between the River Ystwyth and the River Arth.[5] As a consequence Ceredigion, extending north of the Ystwyth and south of the Arth, was a divided, non-homogeneous region, a meeting-ground of Irish and Welsh, a corridor of territory linking a Goedelic south to a Brythonic north. Primarily, however, it was Ceredigion's position between the two more powerful British kingdoms or over-kingdoms of Gwynedd in the north and Dyfed (subsequently Deheubarth) in the south which dictated its political development in the early Middle Ages. Though Ceredigion appears to have enjoyed an independent existence until the late ninth century as a separate kingdom, from the end of the ninth century onwards the region was subject to the control of the royal family either of Gwynedd or of Deheubarth and experienced two centuries of instability consequent upon the dynastic rivalries of these 'super-powers', both of which appear to have regarded possession of Ceredigion as a right and as essential to the furtherance of their particular interests. This is what makes Ceredigion an integral part of the whole sequence of events in the history of west Wales in the period before the attacks of the Normans transformed the nature of Welsh political and cultural life.[6]

[4] The Welsh annals are found in the texts of the *Annales Cambriae* and the *Brut y Tywysogyon* which represent annalistic compilations possibly from the late eighth century, otherwise from the mid-tenth, onwards: K. Hughes, 'The Welsh Latin Chronicles: *Annales Cambriae* and related texts' and 'The A-text of *Annales Cambriae*', *Celtic Britain in the Early Middle Ages*, ed. D. Dumville (Studies in Celtic History II; Woodbridge, 1980), 67–85, 86–100. For the text of the *Annales Cambriae*, E. Phillimore (ed.), 'The *Annales Cambriae* and the Old Welsh Genealogies from *Harleian MS 3859*', *Y Cymmrodor*, 9 (1888), 141–83 (cf. *Nennius: British History and the Welsh Annals*, ed. and trans. J. Morris (London and Chichester, 1980)) and *Annales Cambriae*, ed. J. W. ab Ithel (Rolls series: London, 1860); cf. J. E. Lloyd, 'Wales and the coming of the Normans (1039–1093)', *THSC* (1899/1900), 122–79, with its appendix (pp. 166–79), 'The text of MSS B and C of the "Annales Cambriae" for the period 1035–1093'. For the texts of the *Brut y Tywysogyon* see T. Jones (ed.), *Brut y Tywysogyon or The Chronicle of the Princes* (Cardiff, Board of Celtic Studies, University of Wales History and Law Series), no.VI (1941) (Peniarth MS 20), no.XI (1952) (Peniarth MS 20 (trans.)), no.XVI (1955) (Red Book of Hergest), and no.XXV (1971) (Brenhinedd y Saesson).
[5] Melville Richards, 'The Irish settlements in south-west Wales', *JRSAI*, 90 (1960), 133–62 (pp. 151–2); cf. M. Dillon, 'The Irish settlements in Wales', *Celtica*, 12 (1977), 1–11; B. Coppleston-Crow, 'The dual nature of the Irish colonization of Dyfed in the Dark Ages', *Studia Celtica*, 16/17 (1981/2), 1–24; D. Simon Evans, 'The Welsh and Irish before the Normans—contact or impact', *Proc. British Academy*, 75 (1989), 143–61 (pp. 145 ff.).
[6] On early Ceredigion see J. E. Lloyd, *The Story of Ceredigion, 400–1277* (Cardiff, 1937); cf. D. P. Kirby, 'The place of Ceredigion in the early history of Wales, *c.*400–1170', *Ceredigion*, 6 (1970), 265–84.

The Romano-British legacy

The political geography of post-Roman Wales was shaped by its prehistoric and Roman past. The tribal pattern of the pre-Roman Iron Age was one formative influence.[7] The Demetae, for example, gave their name to Dyfed. Another was undoubtedly the Roman *civitas* organization. Just as Roman terminology persisted on memorial stones,[8] so the kingdom of Gwent in south-east Wales emerged out of the *civitas Silurum*, centred upon Caerwent. Powys represented the *pagus* (territory) of the *civitas Cornoviorum*, centred on Wroxeter.[9] In addition, however, the presence of Celtic personal names in the toponymic appellations of a number of early medieval kingdoms in Wales suggests that a further important development was the ascendancy of native dynasties in the power-vacuum created by the withdrawal of the Roman government.[10] Part of the Silurian territory from the Usk to the Tawe, for example, emerged as Glywysing, taking its name from an eponymous founder-figure with a British name, Glywys. The name of the tribe which dominated Cardiganshire in the pre-Roman Iron Age is unknown. Part of the region at least seems to have lain outside Ordovician territory,[11] and part could have been absorbed into the *civitas Demetarum*, centred on *Moridunum* (Carmarthen),[12] before eventually splintering apart in the upheavals of the immediate post-Roman period. The most distinctive feature of Ceredigion is that its name derives from the eponym, Ceredig, so that the kingdom appears most clearly as one of the Celtic successor-states of post-Roman Britain. Geographically, the clearly delineated natural frontiers of Plynlimon and the Dyfi helped to forge an independent realm which could force an Irish population south of the Ystwyth into submission as far as the Teifi. There is no reason to assume that this was done swiftly, however, and the kingdom of Ceredigion, like all the kingdoms of Dark Age Wales, will have taken decades, even centuries, to evolve, only slowly attaining its maximum territorial extent. Professor R. R. Davies has stressed the fluidity of 'the political geography of power' as late as the eleventh century as kingdoms 'expanded, contracted, fragmented, and even disappeared, as military fortunes ebbed and flowed'.[13] This was probably even more true in the highly disturbed conditions of the fifth, sixth and seventh centuries.

Irish immigration and the Britons

About the year 900 Cormac mac Cuilennáin, king of Cashel, in his *Sanas Cormaic*, a glossary of

---

[7]J. M. Reynolds, 'Legal and constitutional problems', *The Civitas Capitals of Roman Britain*, ed. J. S. Wacher (Leicester, 1966), 70–5 (p. 72); cf. C. E. Stevens, 'Gildas and the civitates of Britain', *EHR*, 52 (1937), 193–203 (p. 193).

[8]*ECMW* no.103.

[9]Cf. I. A. Richmond, 'The Cornovii', *Culture and Environment*, ed. I. Ll. Foster and L. Alcock (London, 1963), 251–62.

[10]Cf. M. Richards, 'Places and persons of the early Welsh Church', *WHR*, 5 (1971), 333–49 (p. 334).

[11]M. G. Jarrett and J. C. Mann, 'The tribes of Wales', *WHR*, 4 (1968–9), 169–71 (p. 170); see now J. L. Davies, above, II, ch. 4, 277.

[12]But see now J. L. Davies, above, 288ff.

[13]R. R. Davies, *Conquest, Coexistence and Change: Wales 1063-1415* (History of Wales II: Oxford, 1987), 59.

Old Irish, refers to the time when 'great was the power of the Irish over the British', so that 'they divided Alba (Britain) among them in districts ... and the Irish dwelt on the east of the sea no less than in Scotia (Ireland), and their mansions and their royal forts were built there'.[14] There is no doubt that at some point in time there was an eastward expansion from Ireland which resulted in Irish-speaking colonies along the coasts of western Britain from Argyll to Cornwall. The Irish were raiding Britain by the end of the third century, intensifying their assault in the course of the fourth and developing also new commercial contacts,[15] and there is reason to believe that an Irish presence became critical in the years after the abandonment of Britain by the Imperial government. According to Gildas in his *De Excidio Britanniae (The Ruin of Britain)*, written in the early sixth century, the attacks of Picts and Scots constituted the earliest phase of invasion of Britain at the end of the Roman period and on the eve of the *adventus Saxonum*.[16] It was in the course of the endeavours of the Britons in Wales in the fifth and sixth centuries to contain this Irish invasion and settlement that a number of British kingdoms emerged. Ceredigion was one of these kingdoms, a Brythonic or Brittonic spearhead against Goedelic intrusion.

Little is known of the details of this Irish settlement for, as N. K. Chadwick observed, no Gildas recorded the *adventus Scottorum*.[17] The rath ('a small univallate enclosure of circular shape'), the most common homestead type in early Christian Ireland, is morphologically paralleled in Britain, but reservations have been expressed about the 'Irish' origin of raths in south-west Wales. These may well represent rather an indigenous development, perhaps strengthened by Irish settlement but not wholly due to it.[18] Place-names of Irish origin, however, are found in concentrated groups in certain areas along the west coast and in south-west Wales, for example, leaving no doubt as to the reality of Irish or Scottish settlement. Further confirmation of such settlement is provided by the evidence of Ogam-inscribed stones and memorials to persons with Irish names, found particularly in south-west Wales but scattered elsewhere in the Principality. Ogam script was a feature of southern Ireland and the Ogam alphabet was developed there during the Roman period.[19] The not infrequent presence of Christian *formulae* on these stones would seem to locate them in the fifth century or early sixth.[20]

Irish literature contains a number of accounts of expeditions by Irish heroic figures to Britain, not least Níall of the Nine Hostages (fifth-century ancestor of the Uí Néill dynasty which provided the successive kings of Tara in the early medieval period) and Crimthann mac Fidaig, king of Munster, uncle and foster-father of Conall Corc of Cashel (fifth-century ancestor of most of the Eóganachta dynasty which provided the successive kings of Munster in the early medieval

[14]'Sanas Cormaic: an Old Irish Glossary', ed.K. Meyer, *Anecdota from Irish MSS* IV (1912), 75.

[15]See now J. L. Davies, above, 284ff. Cf. also L. and J. Lang, *Celtic Britain and Ireland, AD 200–800: The Myth of the Dark Ages* (Dublin, 1990), 165–8.

[16]*De Excidio*, ed. and trans. H. Williams, *Gildas* (Cymmrodorion Record Series 3: 2 vols., London, 1899, 1901), ch. 19. On Gildas, see *Gildas: New Approaches*, ed. M. Lapidge and D. Dumville (Studies in Celtic History V; Woodbridge, 1984).

[17]N. K. Chadwick, *Early Brittany* (Cardiff, 1969), 190.

[18]L. Alcock, 'Was there an Irish Sea culture-province in the Dark Ages?', *The Irish Sea Province in Archaeology and History*, ed. D. Moore (Cambrian Archaeological Association: Cardiff, 1970), 55–65 (p. 63); cf. L. Alcock, *Arthur's Britain* (London, 1971), 268.

[19]See A. Harvey, 'Early literacy in Ireland: the evidence from Ogam', *Cambridge Medieval Celtic Studies*, 14 (1987), 1–16.

[20]See below, II, ch. 7c.

period).[21] It is quite possible that the rising fortunes of the Uí Néill and the Eóganachta were in part at least the consequence of the prestige and booty gained from successful raiding expeditions to Britain, though the extant material is late and legendary. More secure is the evidence bearing on attacks on late Roman and post-Roman Britain by the Déisi and the Uí Liatháin, from southern Ireland, and by the Laigin, men of the region of Leinster in south-east Ireland.[22] In north-west Wales the name of the Llŷn peninsula is derived from the Laigin.[23] According to British tradition, the Déisi and the Uí Liatháin were associated together in an attack on south Wales.[24] The most substantial piece of evidence relating to the Irish presence in south Wales is the eighth-century saga known as *The Expulsion of the Déisi*[25] and a later mid-tenth-century genealogy of the kings of Dyfed.[26] After recounting the legendary history of the wandering of the Déisi in Ireland, the *Expulsion of the Déisi* claims that they went overseas to Dyfed, in the time of Eochaid, son of Artchorp; and the descent from Eochaid of Tewdwr (Tualodor), uncle or father of King Maredudd, whose death is recorded in the Welsh annals in 796, is given as follows:

> Tewdwr ap Rhain ap Cadwgan ap Clothen ap Nowy ab Arthur ap Pedr ap Cyngar ap Gwrthefyr ab Erbin ab Aircol Lawhir ap Tryffin ab Aed Brosc ap Corath ab Eochaid.

Gwrthefyr is the British king Vortepor denounced by Gildas in the early sixth century, and this, it has been suggested, could date Eochaid to *c*.400–25.[27] It certainly seems unlikely that he is to be placed earlier and it could be that he belongs more properly in the second half of the fifth century.[28] From this it follows that there is little or no case for arguing that the Déisi were settled in south Wales by the Roman government of Britain. On the other hand, Vortepor's memorial stone, inscribed 'memoria Voteporigis Protictoris', which originally stood at Castelldwyran, near Narberth,[29] the principal court of the princes of Dyfed according to the Mabinogion, and the inclusion of the term 'protector' as a remote forebear of the kings of Dyfed,[30] could suggest that he thought of himself as occupying a responsible military position in south-west Wales in the early sixth century. The movements of the Déisi into the territory of the Demetae appear, however, to have only been one element in the Irish colonization of Wales at this time. The *Historia Brittonum* (*History of the Britons*), compiled in Gwynedd in 829/30 traditionally by Nennius, declares that 'the sons of Liathan prevailed in the region of the Demetae and in other regions,

---

[21]See T. F. O'Rahilly, *Early Irish History and Mythology* (Dublin, 1946), 209ff., and F. J. Byrne, *Irish Kings and High Kings* (London, 1973), 70ff.

[22]F. J. Byrne, *Irish Kings*, 72, 135.

[23]J. E. Caerwyn Williams, 'Mallaen, Dinllaen, Lleyn', *BBCS*, 22 (1966), 37–45. Cf., on a group of place-names in Anglesey containing the Irish element *cnwc*, Melville Richards, 'The Irish settlements in south-west Wales', 149.

[24]This evidence is reviewed by Melville Richards, 'The Irish settlements in south-west Wales', 135–41.

[25]K. Meyer (ed.), 'The expulsion of the Dessi', *Y Cymmrodor*, 14 (1900), 101–35 and *Eriu*, 3 (1907), 135–42; cf. V. Hull, 'The Book of Uí Maine version of the expulsion of the Dessi', *Zeitschrift für celtische Philologie*, 24 (1954), 266–71 and 'The later version of the expulsion of the Dessi', *Zeitschrift für celtische Philologie*, 27 (1958/9), 14–63.

[26]*Early Welsh Genealogical Tracts* (hereafter cited as *EWGT*), ed. P. C. Bartrum (Cardiff, 1966), 9 ff. (cf. p.4).

[27]M. Miller, 'Date-guessing and Dyfed', *Studia Celtica*, 12/13 (1977–8), 33–61 (p. 36).

[28]T. O Cathasaigh, 'The Déisi and Dyfed', *Eigse*, 20 (1984), 1–33.

[29]*ECMW*, no.138 (p. 107), plate III, and cf. L. Alcock, *Arthur's Britain*, 243–4 and plate 27a.

[30]*EWGT*, 10.

that is Gower and Cydweli'.[31] Furthermore, there is the evidence of later Welsh traditions and the distribution of Ogam memorial stones and place-name elements of Irish derivation to suggest that Brycheiniog constituted an overspill area for Irish settlement in south Wales—'an extension of Irish influence eastward from Dyfed along the line of the Roman roads'.[32]

Irish tradition suggests that the tide of Irish attack on Britain turned in the reign of Loeguire, reputedly a son of Níall of the Nine Hostages, approximately in the mid-fifth century.[33] An account of the British response to the Irish presence is preserved in the *Historia Brittonum*, which claims that Cunedda, a North British chieftain from Manaw (in the) Gododdin, the northern-most territory (around Stirling at the head of the Firth of Forth) of the Votadini, moved to north Wales with his sons and expelled the Scots from those regions, and this event is dated by the *Historia Brittonum* to 146 years before the reign of his descendant, Maelgwn.[34] Maelgwn died, according to the Welsh annals, in 547 (*recte* 549).[35] The period of 146 years may represent a calculation based on an assumption that Cunedda belonged to the time of Magnus Maximus, who died in 388 (to which an addition of 146 gives 534 for Maelgwn's accession which is in fact a date recorded for the death of his father, Cadwallon Llawhir ('Long Hand')).[36] This does not, though, necessarily give us the true date of Cunedda, only what antiquarian learning proposed as Cunedda's date.[37] In the Welsh genealogies, Cunedda appears as Maelgwn's great-grand-father,[38] on the basis of which Cunedda could perhaps be assigned to the period *c.*450, assuming the pedigree to be sound.[39] In the *Historia Brittonum*, however, Cunedda is described as the *atavus* of Maelgwn, which signifies not great-grandfather but grandfather's great-grandfather.[40] This would mean that names representing two generations have dropped out of the list of Maelgwn's

[31]*Historia Brittonum*, ch.14, ed. T. Mommsen, *MGH Auctores Antiq.*, 13 (Berlin, 1894), 111 ff., currently being re-edited in successive volumes by D. N. Dumville, beginning with *The Historia Brittonum*, vol.3: *The Vatican Recension* (Cambridge, 1985). For a translation see J. Morris, *Nennius* (London and Chichester, 1980).

[32]Melville Richards, 'The Irish settlements in south-west Wales', 144.

[33]F. J. Byrne, *Irish Kings*, 83.

[34]*Historia Brittonum*, ch.62. On the geographical situation of Manaw in the Gododdin, see K. H. Jackson, *The Gododdin: The Oldest Scottish Poem* (Edinburgh, 1969), 69–75.

[35]Maelgwn is said to have died in a plague, for the date of which (549) see A. P. Smyth, 'The earliest Irish annals', *PRIA*, 72, Section C (1972), 1–48 (pp. 14–16). P. Sims-Williams, 'Gildas and the Anglo-Saxons', *Cambridge Medieval Celtic Studies*, 6 (1983), 1–30, suspects that this date (for Maelgwn's death) may represent a late and unsupported guess by the annalist (p. 4); cf. D. N. Dumville, 'Gildas and Maelgwn: problems of dating', *Gildas: New Approaches*, ed. M. Lapidge and D. Dumville, 51–60.

[36]M. Miller, 'Date-guessing and pedigrees', *Studia Celtica* 10/11 (1975–6), 96–109 (p. 103).

[37]The date of Cunedda has been the subject of continuing speculation and for earlier views ranging from *c.*380 to *c.*450, see A. H. A. Hogg, 'The date of Cunedda', *Antiq.*, 22 (1948), 201–5, and P. Hunter Blair, 'The origins of Northumbria', *Archaeologia Aeliana*, 25 (1947), 1–51 (pp. 35–6), reprinted in P. Hunter Blair, *Anglo-Saxon Northumbria* (1984). For a review of a wider selection of interpretations, see M. Miller, 'The foundation-legend of Gwynedd in the Latin texts', *BBCS*, 27 (1976–8), 515–32 (p. 517, n.3). I am most grateful to Dr R. Geraint Gruffydd for allowing me to consult his paper, 'A new look at Cunedda Wledig', read at the VIIth International Celtic Congress at Oxford in July 1983, in which he first suggested that Cunedda may have made Dinorben, near Abergele, his stronghold; see now R. G. Gruffydd, 'From Gododdin to Gwynedd: reflections on the story of Cunedda', *Studia Celtica*, 24/5 (1989–90), 1–14.

[38]*EWGT*, 9ff.

[39]M. Miller, 'Date-guessing and pedigrees', 107; cf., based on a different approach, D. P. Kirby, 'British dynastic history in the pre-Viking period', *BBCS*, 27 (1976), 81–113 (p. 99).

[40]L. Alcock, *Arthur's Britain*, 127; cf. M. Miller, 'The foundation-legend of Gwynedd', 531.

ancestors, which could suggest a date for Cunedda *c*.400. Most recently the suggestion has been made that it was not Cunedda who moved from north Britain to north-west Wales but his grandfather, Padarn (Paternus) *Peisrud* (of the Red Robe), who will indeed (if the genealogy is correct) have been Maelgwn's *atavus*; the original settlement of Padarn and the subsequent organization of a kingdom in north Wales by Cunedda then becoming confused as a result of a telescoping of tradition.[41] In this case, again if the genealogy is correct, Padarn would date to *c*.400. This would perhaps be just early enough for the movement of some of the Votadini to north Wales to have been a deliberate act by the Roman government in Britain. But the genealogy is not necessarily historical. Historians are now aware that a genealogy should be seen more as 'a legal title, a political weapon and an expression of learning' than as a statement of 'biologico-historical' fact. [42] The genealogical material alone cannot demonstrate the arrival of Padarn or Cunedda to have been so early or their activities anything other than the uncontrolled movements of people in the aftermath of the Roman abandonment of Britain. There seems no reason to suppose that a migration of some Votadini from Manaw to north Wales could not have taken place and therefore did not.[43] At a time of far-reaching movements of people round Britain —Irish or Scots, Picts, Anglo-Saxons—some degree of internal displacement is perfectly intelligible. Certainly, an original homeland among the Gododdin for the traditional ancestor of the later kings of Gwynedd could help to explain their subsequent involvement against the Northumbrians, at a time when the survival of the Votadini was threatened by the Northumbrian advance to the Forth.[44]

The formation of Ceredigion

The expulsion of the Irish from north Wales appears to have been a slow process, not completed until the time of Cadwallon 'Long Hand', the father of Maelgwn, in the early sixth century,[45] and even then the persistence of Irish memorial stones into the sixth century indicates that the 'expulsion' of the Irish should probably be understood to mean only 'dispossessed' or 'relegated to dependent status'.[46] As a result of persistent British opposition, however, Irish settlement was minimized over a wide area of north Wales. British tradition preserved in the early ninth-century

[41]M. Miller, 'The foundation-legend of Gwynedd', 531.

[42]D. N. Dumville, 'Kingship, genealogies and regnal lists', *Early Medieval Kingship*, ed. P. H. Sawyer and I. N. Wood (Leeds, 1977), 72–104 (pp. 74, 84); cf. D. Ó Corráin, 'Irish origin legends and genealogy', *History and Heroic Tale*, ed. T. Nyberg (Odense, 1985), 51–96 (pp. 83–4).

[43]N. K. Chadwick, 'Early culture and learning in north Wales', *Studies in the Early British Church*, ed. N. K. Chadwick (Cambridge, 1958), 29–120 (pp. 32 ff.) was inclined to be dismissive, and was followed by J. Mann, 'The Northern Frontier after AD 369', *Glasgow Arch. J.*, 3 (1974), 34-42 (p. 42, n.73), who asked, 'What more striking way could there be for the kings of Gwynedd to bolster up their prestige than to claim descent from the Gwyr y Gogledd?' D. N. Dumville, 'Sub-Roman Britain: history and legend', *History*, 62 (1977), 173–92 (pp. 181–2), is also sceptical. See also below, n.57.

[44]D. P. Kirby, 'Northumbria and the destruction of the Votadini', *Trans.East Lothian Antiq.and Field Nat.Soc.*, 14 (1974), 1–13. Cf. also idem, *The Earliest English Kings* (London, 1991), 86.

[45]J. E. Lloyd, *History of Wales* I, 120; cf. R. Bromwich, *Trioedd Ynys Prydein* (Cardiff, 1961), no.62 and pp.126–7.

[46]M. Richards, 'The Irish settlements in south-west Wales', 145, 147.

Historia Brittonum records that Cunedda and his eight sons expelled the Irish with immense slaughter 'from all the regions of Britain', and even attributes the expulsion of the Uí Liatháin from Gower and Cydweli to them.[47] The mid-tenth-century Harleian Genealogies give further details, namely that the number of Cunedda's sons was nine (not eight) but that the eldest, Tybion, died in Manaw so that it was his son, Meirion, who came in his place,[48] the other sons being Osfael, Rhufon, Dunod, Ceredig, Afloeg, Einion Yrth, Dogfael and Edern, and the boundary of their territories is defined more narrowly as the Rivers Dee and Teifi. These sons of Cunedda, with the exception of Einion Yrth, ancestor of the kings of Gwynedd, were thought of as having given their names to the kingdoms bordering Gwynedd—Osfeilion, Rhufoniog, Dunoding, Ceredigion, Meirionydd, Afloegion in Llŷn, and Dogfeiling and Edeirnion in Powys, for the genealogies of their respective ruling houses (where they survive) are traced back to them.[49] In this 'origin-legend', for that is what it is, Cunedda's sons are represented as eponymous founding-figures of kingdoms in north Wales clustered around Gwynedd. Ceredigion appears as the kingdom of Ceredig, son of Cunedda, its creation part of that same process which established Cunedda in north Wales.

Was Ceredig really the son of Cunedda? There can be no certain answer to this question but, though historians have often accepted the relationship in the past, it seems unlikely that he was. Of the surviving genealogies of the ruling families of Ceredigion, Dunoding and Meirionydd, the patrilineages of which go back to Ceredig, Dunod and Meirion respectively, the princes of Dunoding cannot be dated and the pedigree could be corrupt.[50] Of the princes of Meirionydd, Cynan, whose lineage it represents, may be dated to the late eighth century if Brochwel, his great-great-grandfather, is to be identified with the Brochwel whose death is recorded in the Welsh annals in 662, but no further precision is possible; Cynan may not have been the last of his line and nothing is known of what became of the princes of Meirionydd. That Meirion shows every sign of having been attached at a later stage to the eight sons of Cunedda, however, could suggest that Meirionydd passed into Gwynedd's political control later than the territories represented by other eponyms.[51] Ceredigion is better documented and provides crucial evidence. The Welsh annals record the death in 807 of Arthen, king of Ceredigion, and in 871 or 872 the drowning of Gwgon, king of Ceredigion. The Harleian Genealogies give the following patrilineage for Gwgon:

Gwgon ap Meurig ap Dyfnwallon ab Arthen ap Seisyll ap Clydog ab Arthlwys ab Arthfoddw ap Boddw ap Serwyl ab Usai ap Ceredig ap Cunedda.[52]

---

[47] *Historia Brittonum*, chs. 14, 62.

[48] Unless, that is, there has been a misunderstanding at this point by a later genealogist and originally Cunedda was thought to have nine sons apart from Tybion: M. Miller, 'The foundation-legend of Gwynedd in the Latin texts', 524, n.7. For a general comment on this type of origin-story, cf. P. Sims-Williams, 'Some functions of origin stories in early medieval Wales', *History and Heroic Tale*, ed. T. Nyberg, 97–132 (pp. 102–3).

[49] *EWGT*, pp. 9 ff.

[50] M. Miller, 'The foundation-legend of Gwynedd', 526 (with a suggestion that one of the princes of Dunoding, Pobddelw, may be identical with the Pobddelw of stanza A74 of the *Gododdin*: cf. K. H. Jackson, *The Gododdin*, 21).

[51] Cf. M. Miller, 'Date-guessing and pedigrees', 102, note 1; idem, 'The foundation-legend of Gwynedd', 524–6; idem, *The Saints of Gwynedd* (Woodbridge, 1979), 105–10.

[52] *EWGT*, 12.

The number of generations involved here, anchored to a *floruit* in the third quarter of the ninth century for Gwgon ap Meurig supported by a date for the death of Arthen, his great-grandfather, locates Ceredig as a younger (perhaps a much younger)[53] contemporary of Maelgwn, reputedly a great-grandson of Cunedda. Unless a number of generations have been omitted, therefore, it seems unlikely that Ceredig was originally seen by the ruling family of Ceredigion as a son of Cunedda.[54]

It has to be emphasized that the names of the sons of Cunedda appear for the first time only in genealogical material of the mid-tenth century. This is over a century after the eclipse of the descendants of Cunedda as kings of Gwynedd and their replacement in 816–25 by a new dynasty, that of Merfyn Frych ('the Freckled') who was not a prince of Gwynedd at all; if his place of origin can be determined it was the Isle of Man, with a further crucial Powys connection.[55] This has been termed the Second Dynasty of Gwynedd to distinguish it from a Cuneddan or First Dynasty.[56] The story of Cunedda from Manaw Gododdin with his unnamed sons and their wars with the Irish in the *Historia Brittonum* almost certainly originated in the time of the First Dynasty whose origin-story it is.[57] Some of the sons may even have been identified with the eponyms of adjacent territory—for example, the petty commote of Afloegion—at an early stage. Nevertheless, the details of the story were evidently subject to increasing elaboration. The reference in the *Historia Brittonum* to eight sons reveals that in the early ninth century Cunedda was already thought of as the father of a numerous progeny, but we do not know how his sons were currently being identified. The fact that only eight sons are referred to in the *Historia Brittonum* indicates that this figure was then still evolving towards the nine of the Harleian Genealogies in the mid-tenth century. Secondly, the details were being more precisely localized. Having earlier been thought of as having expelled the Irish from all the regions of Britain, Cunedda and his sons and their activities are more narrowly located in the Harleian Genealogies between the Teifi and the Dee.

The concept of Cunedda as the father of Ceredig, for example, could have arisen, therefore, in the time of the Second Dynasty when an older body of tradition was being redefined in a new political situation. Angharad, the sister of Gwgon ap Meurig, is said to have married Rhodri

---

[53]Cf. the parallel genealogies in M. Miller, 'Date-guessing and Dyfed', 58. Dr Miller would place Ceredig (on the evidence of the genealogy) in 'the last quarter of the sixth century' (art.cit., 59).

[54]D. P. Kirby, 'British dynastic history in the pre-Viking period', 92. The alternative explanation, that a number of names have dropped out of this Ceredigion genealogy, simply justifies a tradition that we do not know to be historical.

[55]On a possible Manx connection, see N. K. Chadwick, 'Early culture and learning in north Wales', 79–80, and on the Powys association, D. P. Kirby, 'Vortigern', *BBCS*, 23 (1968), 37–59 (p. 51).

[56]The terms are used by M. Miller, 'The foundation-legend of Gwynedd', 515 ff., and *The Saints of Gwynedd*, 1 ff., and in other papers.

[57]Note that the Isle of Man is Manaw (cf. Manaw in the Gododdin) but M. Miller, 'The foundation-legend of Gwynedd', 517, considers it 'unlikely that Cunedda's migration from Manaw to Gododdin was a simple invention to provide a precedent for Merfyn'. Dumville, however, thought that at least 'it presented a welcome parallel, no doubt much cultivated by the Second Dynasty of Gwynedd, of an outside dynasty coming to power in Gwynedd': D. N. Dumville, 'Sub-Roman Britain: history and legend', 182. Subsequently, he has suggested that the Gwynedd origin-legend 'may have been the creation of the genealogists for the newly-established Second Dynasty': D. N. Dumville, 'The historical value of the *Historia Brittonum*', *Arthurian Literature*, 6 (1986), 1-26 (p. 23).

Mawr, son of Merfyn Frych and king of Gwynedd, and to have become the mother of most of Rhodri's sons,[58] and at some point after the death of Gwgon in 871 or 872 Ceredigion passed under the control of Rhodri or his sons. It is possible that this was a forceful annexation of Ceredigion by Rhodri. It was certainly part of a long process of dynastic expansion. Gwriad, father of Merfyn Frych, had married into the ruling family of the First Dynasty of Gwynedd and Gwynedd was subsequently annexed by Merfyn, who married into the ruling family of Powys which was subsequently annexed by Rhodri or his sons.[59] The marriage of Hywel, grandson of Rhodri, into the ruling family of Dyfed was followed by the apparently forceful seizure of Dyfed —the Welsh annals record the beheading of Rhodri, son of Hyfaidd, king of Dyfed, in 904 or 905 in Arwystli.[60] The ascendancy of Merfyn and his descendants, therefore, represented the rise of an intrusive dynastic force which transformed the political face of north and west Wales in the ninth century, terminating the independent existence of Ceredigion and of other neighbouring kingdoms and bringing them into closer relationship with Gwynedd. It may not be without significance that the background to the ascendancy of Merfyn and Rhodri was a Scandinavian presence in the Irish Sea and the new dangers of Viking attack, coupled with deeply penetrative Saxon offensives from the 790s to the 870s. Rhodri was driven out of his kingdom by the Vikings in 877 and slain by the Saxons in 878. Such pressures may have encouraged memories of an earlier resistance to Irish attack in the north and west and provided a context for the cultivation of older legends about the eponymous founders of the kingdoms of the region—with Ceredig, for example, now identified as a son of Cunedda—as the Second Dynasty of Gwynedd extended its lordship over them and probably sought to strengthen ties of loyalty.

J. E. Lloyd hinted that the so-called sons of Cunedda were rather his followers and lieutenants.[61] Some would argue that even this relationship may be too close. Melville Richards was prepared only to regard the establishment of these chieftainships, as he called them, in west and north-west Wales 'as the expression of a Brythonic surge'.[62] The circumstances of the struggle with the Irish may have helped to shape a British identity in north and west Wales in which a sense of kinship was heightened, subsequently to find expression in a crystallization of genealogical relationships perhaps as late as the ninth and early tenth centuries when a series of dynastic revolutions at a time of external danger really did produce a greater coalescence of older groups. It seems, therefore, most likely that Meirion, Osfael, Rhufon, Dunod, Afloeg, Dogfael, Edern and Ceredig were military leaders thrown by the convulsions of society into the same conflict as Cunedda with

[58]*EWGT*, 46–7, 49.

[59]See on the chronology of the rise of Merfyn's descendants D. N. Dumville, 'The "six" sons of Rhodri Mawr: a problem in Asser's *Life of King Alfred*', *Cambridge Medieval Celtic Studies*, 4 (1982), 5–18 (pp. 14 ff.).

[60]D. P. Kirby, 'British dynastic history in the pre-Viking period', 97. J. E. Lloyd, *History of Wales* I, 324 ff., whose reconstruction of events historians have generally followed (but see now, D. N. Dumville, 'The "six" sons of Rhodri Mawr', 14 ff.), understood the rise of Merfyn's family to have been essentially legitimate, successive territories passing under its control by the right of inheritance as a consequence of marriages (followed to some extent by D. P. Kirby, art.cit., 97): but it must be regarded as more likely (not just because of the beheading of Rhodri ap Hyfaidd) that these were all forceful annexations to which the dynastic marriages afforded only the thinnest veneer of legitimacy, if that.

[61]J. E. Lloyd, *History of Wales* I, 119.

[62]M. Richards, 'The Irish settlements in south-west Wales', 138.

the Irish but all probably essentially independent of one another and not necessarily even contemporaneous.

The historical kingdom of Ceredigion probably only began to take shape in the time of Ceredig, who, if he can be dated on the evidence of the Ceredigion genealogy, belonged not to the mid-fifth but to the mid-sixth century (or later).[63] Nor would it be unnatural for Ceredigion, running south towards Dyfed and the area of most substantial Irish settlement, to have been brought under British domination at a later stage than the heartland and more immediate border-territories of Gwynedd. Ceredig was certainly pictured in later hagiographical tradition as having been part of the military forces which repulsed the Irish. The twelfth-century *Vita* II of the *Life of St Carantoc*, a Cardiganshire saint, portrays an aged Ceredig being asked to appoint one of his sons, Carantoc, or Carannog, as king to wage war on the Irish.[64] In the genealogies Carantoc was regarded as the grandson of Ceredig.[65] Though the details are unhistorical, Mrs Chadwick suggested that the *Life* preserves 'a tradition that a strong military king was essential to the kingdom of Cardigan'.[66]

The patrilineage of Gwgon ap Meurig, last recorded king of Ceredigion in the ninth century, represents only one segment of descent from Ceredig. Not all of Gwgon's lineal ancestors necessarily reigned as kings of Ceredigion and his patrilineage should not be regarded as a king list. There must have been collateral royal lines from whom kings of Ceredigion in this period would also be drawn.[67] Medieval genealogical compilations (*Progenies Keredic*, *Plant Ceredig* and *Bonedd y Saint*) catalogue some of Ceredig's alleged descendants but their historical nucleus, if it exists, is so overlaid with hagiographical legend and historiographical convention that (pending further study) it is not easy now to perceive it.[68] Ceredig appears in the genealogical material as the grandfather of two saints, Dewi ap Sant and Carannog ap Corun, and the great-grandfather of another, Teilo ab Ensic ap Hydwn Dwn. The commote of Anhuniog, however, probably derived its name from the Anhun who appears in the genealogies as a son of Ceredig,[69] and it is probable that other names in these genealogies—for example, Gwgan Gleddyfrudd ('Red Sword') ap Llawch ap Llucho (ap Ceredig), Cynidr Gell ('the Brown') ap Cynon (ap Ceredig) and Cyndeyn ap Cyngar ap Garthog (ap Ceredig)—represent individuals who, whatever their actual blood relationship, played a part in the early history of Ceredigion. Other such men who gave their names to commotes in Ceredigion do not appear in the genealogies—Gwynion, whose name is enshrined in Gwynionydd in Is Aeron, Mebwyn in Mebwynion, also in Is Aeron, and

[63]There seem to be no grounds, however, for thinking that Ceredig represents an intrusive British element from Severnside, displaced by the advance of the West Saxons and the British defeat at Dyrham, as M. Miller suggested, 'Date-guessing and Dyfed', 59.

[64]*Vitae Sanctorum Britanniae et Genealogiae*, ed. A. W. Wade-Evans (Cardiff, 1944), 149–50.

[65]*EWGT*, 55.

[66]N. K. Chadwick, *Early Brittany*, 177.

[67]On the kindred group and royal succession in the Celtic world, see, for example: D. A. Binchy, 'Secular institutions', *Early Irish Society*, ed. M. Dillon (Dublin, 1954: repr.1959), 52–65 (p. 58); idem, *Celtic and Anglo-Saxon Kinship* (Oxford, 1970), 25; two papers by T. M. Charles-Edwards, 'Some Celtic kinship terms', *BBCS*, 24 (1971), 105–22 and 'Kinship, status and the origin of the hide', *Past and Present*, 56 (1972), 3–33, and F. J. Byrne, *Irish Kings*, 35 ff., 122 ff. See also, however, for a different view, D. Ó Corráin, 'Irish regnal succession', *Studia Hibernica*, 11 (1971), 1–39.

[68]*EWGT*, 20, 49, 54–5.

[69]J. E. Lloyd, *History of Wales* I, 258.

Mafan in Mefennydd in Uwch Aeron.[70] The location of the commotes of Mebwynion and Gwynionydd along the border with Ystrad Tywi could suggest that they originated as military units disposed against the kings of Dyfed. The role of Ceredig's descendant, Seisyll ap Clydog, in the second half (not the first half)[71] of the eighth century was certainly significant in this context. 'Seisyll', wrote J. E. Lloyd, 'embarked on a career of conquest and added to Ceredigion the three cantrefs of Ystrad Tywi, the whole dominion being henceforth known from the name of its founder as Seisyllwg.'[72] The evidence for this is the story of Pwyll, prince of Dyfed, the first 'branch' of the Mabinogion, which concludes with a reference to 'the three cantrefs of Ystrad Tywi and the four of Ceredigion, and those are called the seven cantrefs of Seisyllwg'.[73] Seisyll appears to have been king of Ceredigion and his annexation of Ystrad Tywi—which included Cantref Mawr as it was later known—represented a substantial inroad by the rulers of Ceredigion into the territory of the kings of Dyfed. It was possibly a continuation of that push southwards against the Irish in south Wales which played such a part in the evolution of Ceredigion. Dyfed contracted to form Rheinwg, a territory probably named not after Rhain ap Cadwgan of Dyfed,[74] who belongs to the first half of the eighth century, but rather Rhain ap Maredudd, king of Dyfed, who died, according to the Welsh annals, in 808. If it was Maredudd, who died in 796 or 797, who lost the land to Seisyll, his son, Rhain, will have been the first king of Dyfed to face the reconstruction of a dismembered territory. Whether the kings of Ceredigion still controlled Ystrad Tywi at the time of King Gwgon's death has been questioned[75] but a reference in the Welsh annals to Anarawd ap Rhodri, king of Gwynedd, deploying Saxon troops in a 'harrying' of Ceredigion and Ystrad Tywi in 895 would suggest that the two territories were by then traditionally associated.

The dynasty of Merfyn Frych

The First Dynasty of Gwynedd, therefore, was eclipsed by the family of Merfyn Frych in the late ninth century. The way in which Merfyn and his descendants appear to have married into ruling families must have been a commonplace of aristocratic and royal society but the consequences were unusual. Merfyn's father, Gwriad, married Essyllt, daughter of Cynan,[76] within nine years of whose death in 816 Merfyn had succeeded as king of Gwynedd. This was not, however, without parallel at the time. Maredudd, king of Dyfed, died in 796 or 797, his sons Rhain and Owain in 808 and 811, and his grandson Tryffin, son of Rhain, in 814. After this date there is a long period when we know very little of the royal succession in Dyfed until the time of Hyfaidd

[70]M. Richards, 'Early Welsh territorial suffixes', *JRSAI*, 95 (1965), 205–12.

[71]As J. E. Lloyd, *History of Wales* I, 257.

[72]Ibid., I, 257.

[73]*The White Book of the Mabinogion*, ed. J. Gwenogvryn Evans (Pwllheli, 1907), cols.37–8 (p. 19); translated Gwyn Jones and Thomas Jones, *The Mabinogion* (Everyman Library, 1949; repr. 1966), 24.

[74]As J. E. Lloyd, *History of Wales* I, 262, 281–2, thought, dating Seisyll also to the early eighth century: similarly M. Richards, 'Early Welsh territorial suffixes', 207.

[75]D. N. Dumville, 'The "six" sons of Rhodri Mawr', 15–16.

[76]*EWGT*, 9, 36, 38, 47, 95; J. E. Lloyd, *History of Wales* I, 323.

ap Bleddri (*c*.870–892/3). Hyfaidd was the son of Tangwystl, daughter of Owain ap Maredudd,[77] and is referred to in Asser's *Life of King Alfred*, written in 893–4.[78] Described in a Welsh triad as one of the 'kings sprung from villeins',[79] he also represents a family which married into the old ruling dynasty of Dyfed and then supplanted it, as Merfyn ap Gwriad did in Gwynedd. By the ninth century the older patrilineages of the ruling dynasties were evidently losing their dominant positions, and what we see by the end of the ninth century in west Wales is a confrontation between two new ruling families, one in Gwynedd and the other in Dyfed.[80] The acquisition of Ceredigion by Rhodri ap Merfyn or his sons is another example of the apparent collapse of the royal patrilineage of an older dynasty.

When Rhodri was killed by the Saxons in 878 he left several sons. Asser refers specifically to Anarawd ap Rhodri, who, with his brothers, made an alliance with the Vikings of Northumbria and then abandoned it.[81] In England by this time the Danes had conquered or partitioned all the major kingdoms of the Anglo-Saxon heptarchy except Wessex, which under Alfred (871–99) survived the attack of the Danish king Guthrum in 878–80. In the 880s the kings of Gwent and Glywysing placed themselves under Alfred's lordship for protection (which must have taken the form of military aid) against the ravages of Æthelred, ealdorman of west Mercia (east Mercia being by now in the hands of the Danes), and Hyfaidd ap Bleddri, king of Dyfed, and Elise ap Tewdwr, king of Brycheiniog, did the same for protection against the sons of Rhodri. In 886 Alfred captured London from the Danes and Æthelred submitted to Alfred in return for possession of London and the king's daughter, Æthelflaed, in marriage, but on terms that in every respect he would be obedient to Alfred. The *Anglo-Saxon Chronicle* A records that at this point all the Anglo-Saxons not under subjection to the Danes submitted to Alfred. In this way a formidable alliance was created against the sons of Rhodri, Anarawd and his brothers. Anarawd's reaction was evidently to ally with the Danes of York. In 892 Viking reinforcements landed in England and the Danes attacked Æthelred's Mercia. In the following year they were defeated at Buttington on the Severn whence they may have proceeded with the intention of joining forces with Anarawd. In the following year they plundered in Wales before withdrawing to Northumbria and East Anglia. According to Asser, Anarawd's alliance with the Danes brought him nothing but harm, to which must have been added the fear of political isolation, and he in turn now submitted to Alfred in person. Alfred was vengeful enough to impose quite humiliating terms on Anarawd who, though a Christian ruler, had to undergo confirmation with Alfred as sponsor (an expression of his political superiority) and accept the same terms as Æthelred of Mercia, undertaking to obey Alfred in all things.[82]

[77]*EWGT*, 9, 106.

[78]W. H. Stevenson (ed.) *Asser's Life of King Alfred* (Oxford, 1904: 1959 impression), chs.79–90. Cf. also now *Alfred the Great: Asser's Life of King Alfred and other Contemporary Sources*, trans. S. Keynes and M. Lapidge (Harmondsworth, 1983).

[79]R. Bromwich (ed.), *Trioedd Ynys Prydein*, no. 68. See also on Hyfaidd ap Bleddri, R. Geraint Gruffydd, 'The early court poetry of south-west Wales', *Studia Celtica*, 14/15 (1979–80), 95–105 (pp. 96–7).

[80]The poem *Etmic Deinbych* contains an allusion, possibly of the ninth century, to warfare between Dyfed and Gwynedd: I. Williams, *The Beginnings of Welsh Poetry: Studies by Sir Ifor Williams*, ed. R. Bromwich (Cardiff, 1972), 155 ff.

[81]*Asser's Life of King Alfred*, ch.80.

[82]*Asser's Life of King Alfred*, ch.80; cf. D. P. Kirby, 'Asser and his *Life of King Alfred*', *Studia Celtica*, 6 (1971), 12–35.

Having brought about an 'Alfredian settlement', as it were, of Wales, the West Saxons could not keep the situation under control. The kings of south Wales had submitted and received military aid. Anarawd must also have desired some reciprocal token on Alfred's part of his new relationship with the West Saxon king, and the Welsh annals record that in 894 or 895 Anarawd, with Anglo-Saxon assistance, devastated Ceredigion and Ystrad Tywi. It may be that the rulers of Gwynedd failed to extend their authority into Ystrad Tywi when they succeeded in Ceredigion and that Rhodri's sons were endeavouring to possess themselves of the whole of Seisyllwg, but it is certainly probable that it was West Saxon aid which enabled Hyfaidd to resist them in Ystrad Tywi and even to extend his authority into Ceredigion. This would explain the tension between the sons of Rhodri and Hyfaidd. Hyfaidd died in 892 or 893 and his son Llywarch would seem to have maintained his position at least until Anarawd's campaign of 894/5, but Anarawd's brother Cadell was probably established in the territories of Ceredigion and Ystrad Tywi in the years after 894/5.[83] This, therefore, was the background to the marriage of Hywel ap Cadell to Elen, daughter of Llywarch ap Hyfaidd,[84] the sequel to which was the collapse of the fortunes of Hyfaidd's family in 904 or 905 with the beheading of Rhodri ap Hyfaidd in Arwystli. Cadell lived until 909 or 910 and was traditionally remembered as having been lord of Dinefwr, the capital of the kings of Deheubarth, that is, ancient Dyfed with the addition of Seisyllwg and all land west of the Tawe, but the creation of Deheubarth should perhaps more properly be seen as the work of his son Hywel Dda, 'head and glory of all the Britons' as the annals style him when recording his death in 950.

Hywel's ascendancy in west Wales occurred at a time when the Alfredian settlement in Wales was collapsing in the aftermath of Saxon support for the sons of Rhodri. By 916 Æthelflaed of Mercia was at war with Brycheiniog, formerly allied to her father. A new settlement was soon to be imposed on the family of Anarawd by Æthelflaed's brother, Edward, king of Wessex (899–924), to whom Hywel and his cousin, Idwal Foel ab Anarawd, king of Gwynedd, submitted in 918. This new settlement was extended to embrace Gwent and consolidated by Alfred's grandson, Athelstan, king of Wessex (924–39), who received the submission of Welsh rulers, including Hywel, at Hereford in 927 and imposed upon them a huge tribute. Hywel and Idwal regularly attended the formal gatherings of Athelstan's court and may have been compelled to accompany him on campaign against his northern adversary, Constantine son of Aed, king of the Scots, in 934. There is no need to see, as Sir John Lloyd did, any admiration on Hywel's part for the West Saxons to account for his presence at the West Saxon court, but merely the prevailing might of the contemporary kings of Wessex. Athelstan was a prodigious legislator, concerned with the suppression of lawlessness and disorder in Wessex and with speeding the development of efficient royal government, and if the legislation with which Hywel is credited in Welsh medieval legal tradition owed its inspiration to West Saxon legislative activity, again it is not so much a reflection of Hywel's admiration for Athelstan as of concern with similar disorders and a corresponding desire to increase his royal power and authority.[85] Moreover, as Sir John Lloyd remarked, 'the union of Dyfed and Seisyllwg ... would bring him early in life face

---

[83]D. N. Dumville, 'The "six" sons of Rhodri Mawr', 17.
[84]*EWGT*, 9, 106.
[85]D. P. Kirby, 'Hywel Dda: anglophil?', *WHR*, 8 (1976), 1–13.

to face with the inconvenience of conflicting tribal custom',[86] a problem intensified by an expansion of his authority within Wales.

The Welsh kings appear to have had no part in the great Viking–Scottish–North British coalition, organized by the Vikings of Dublin and Constantine, king of the Scots, against the West Saxons in 937 which was defeated at *Brunanburh*,[87] but that the Britons, under the banner of St David, should ally with the Dublin Vikings against the West Saxons, was the belief of the author of *Armes Prydein Vawr*,[88] inspired either by the build-up of anti-English forces before *Brunanburh* or (as now seems to be thought more likely) by the reversal of West Saxon military fortunes in the early years (939–42) of Athelstan's brother and successor, Edmund, king of Wessex (939–46), at the time when Idwal, king of Gwynedd, was killed by the Saxons in 942 or 943, or just conceivably even later still.[89] Hywel, however, was not drawn into war against the West Saxons, again not because he stood for 'peace and friendship with the English', as Sir John Lloyd also thought, but because his personal dynastic ambitions attracted him more to intervention in Gwynedd; on Idwal's death in battle, Hywel invaded and expelled his sons, Iago and Ieuaf. In addition, it may have been Hywel who brought to an end the independence of Brycheiniog, so that from 942/3 to his death in 950 Hywel could have ruled all Wales with the exception of the south-east. Possession of Ceredigion was probably fundamental to the security of Hywel's position in west Wales as a whole.

The union of Gwynedd and Deheubarth which Hywel brought about collapsed upon his death. In 950 or 951 Iago and Ieuaf ab Idwal recovered Gwynedd and its northern dependencies, fought the sons of Hywel at Nant Carno and in 952 twice laid Dyfed waste. In the fighting of 954 Ceredigion, now a war-zone, was ravaged by the sons of Idwal. The attacks of the Vikings and internal struggle in Gwynedd precluded a further offensive until 983 when Hywel ab Ieuaf, having established himself in Gwynedd, attacked Brycheiniog and the lands of Einion ab Owain ap Hywel in alliance with the Saxons. The year after Hywel ab Ieuaf's death in 985, Maredudd ab Owain, king of Deheubarth, slew Cadwallon ab Ieuaf in battle and gained possession of Gwynedd and Anglesey. These northern territories he may then have held with Deheubarth and its dependencies for eleven years—far longer than Hywel Dda—until his death in 999,[90] at which point Cynan ap Hywel ab Ieuaf established himself in Gwynedd until his death in 1003.

From the end of the tenth century onwards new princes of unknown or uncertain ancestry emerge, in particular Llywelyn ap Seisyll in Gwynedd and, perhaps but not certainly in

---

[86]J. E. Lloyd, *History of Wales* I, 338.

[87]For a detailed review of material relevant to the battle, see A. Campbell, *The Battle of Brunanburh* (London, 1938), and now also the discussion by A. P. Smyth, *Scandinavian York and Dublin: The History and Archaeology of Two Related Viking Kingdoms*, II (Dublin, 1979), 31 ff.

[88]*Armes Prydein: The Prophecy of Britain*, ed. Sir Ifor Williams; English version by Rachel Bromwich (Medieval and Modern Welsh Series VI, Dublin Institute for Advanced Studies, 1972).

[89]A. P. Smyth, op.cit., II, 71–2; D. N. Dumville, 'Brittany and "Armes Prydein Vawr"', *Études Celtiques*, 20 (1983), 145–59 (pp. 150–1).

[90]W. Davies, *Patterns of Power in Early Wales* (Oxford, 1990), 57–8, however, argues for an independent Viking presence in Gwynedd in the late 980s and 990s. See also now on Wales in the late tenth and eleventh centuries, K. L. Maund, *Ireland, Wales and England in the Eleventh Century* (Woodbridge, 1991) (commenting on Maredudd's possibly continuing overlordship of Gwynedd, 58).

Gwynedd, Aeddan ap Blegywryd, killed by Llywelyn in 1018.[91] The appearance of these princes gives the impression of dynastic instability and indeed what we see here is a rise of new royal families in the eleventh century analogous to the rise of Merfyn's family in the ninth. In exactly the same way as Merfyn's family married into the older ruling dynasties, Llywelyn ap Seisyll married Angharad, daughter of Maredudd ab Owain,[92] a marriage which was to form an important strand in the web of dynastic relations in this period. In 1022 Llywelyn marched against a claimant to the kingship in Dyfed, Rhain, who claimed—falsely, so the annals maintain —to be a son of Maredudd ab Owain, and overthrew him at Abergwili.[93] But Llywelyn died the next year and Deheubarth emerged as an independent realm again under Rhydderch ab Iestyn (1023–33), generally seen as another of the intrusive kings of this period but who came to be regarded as a grandson of Owain ap Hywel Dda.[94] The descendants of Idwal ab Anarawd temporarily recovered power in Gwynedd in the person of Iago, grandson of Meurig ab Idwal, but it was Llywelyn's son Gruffudd who came to power in Gwynedd in 1039 on the slaying of Iago and who next united Deheubarth to Gwynedd. In Dyfed, on the death of Rhydderch ab Iestyn, Hywel and Maredudd ab Edwin, great-grandson of Hywel Dda, restored the fortunes of their family but Maredudd was killed in 1035[95] and Hywel suffered repeated attacks from Gruffudd ap Llywelyn. In 1039 Gruffudd is said to have pillaged Llanbadarn Fawr and held all Deheubarth, driving Hywel ab Edwin from his kingdom. Two years later he defeated Hywel at Pencader on the confines of Ceredigion and captured his wife, whom he took for his own. Hywel allied with Irish mercenaries in 1044 but was slain by Gruffudd ap Llywelyn at the mouth of the Tywi. The sons of Rhydderch ab Iestyn continued to resist Gruffudd until the slaying of Gruffudd ap Rhydderch in 1055, in the course of which phase of the war Dyfed and all Deheubarth were ravaged by Gruffudd ap Llywelyn. Mastering also Morgannwg, from *c.*1060 Gruffudd was 'in some sense ruler of all Wales',[96] a unique position. With the killing, however, of Gruffudd by a certain Cynan, possibly but not certainly Cynan ab Iago,[97] in 1063 in the course of a great English offensive against him led by Harold Godwinesson, 'the chaos of contention . . .

[91] J. E. Lloyd, *History of Wales* I, 346–7. For poetic material possibly relevant to Aeddan, see *The Beginnings of Welsh Poetry : Studies by Sir Ifor Williams*, ed. R. Bromwich, 172 ff. Wendy Davies, *Wales in the Early Middle Ages*, 106–7, sees Aeddan and Llywelyn as men of Dyfed. K. L. Maund comments in *Ireland, Wales and England*, 59–62, 90–2.

[92] *EWGT*, 101.

[93] For a discussion of the record of this event in the Welsh chronicles, see Thomas Jones, 'Historical writing in Medieval Welsh', *Scottish Studies*, 12 (1968), 15–27 (pp. 25 ff).

[94] P. C. Bartrum, 'Pedigrees of the Welsh tribal patriarchs', *National Library of Wales J.*, 13 (1963), 93–146 (no. 37 and p.125). It would be more convincing, genealogically, if Rhydderch were a great-grandson of Owain. He appears, however, to have been associated with Gwent Uchaf and Erging: J. E. Lloyd, *History of Wales*, II, 361; Wendy Davies, *An Early Welsh Microcosm: Studies in the Llandaff Charters* (London, 1978), 74, 89, 186. Both his son Gruffudd and grandson Caradog seem to have ruled in Morgannwg: J. Beverley Smith, 'The kingdom of Morgannwg and the Norman Conquest of Glamorgan', *Glamorgan County History*, ed. T. B. Pugh, III (Cardiff, 1971), 1–43 (pp. 4–7). See now, K. L. Maund, *Ireland, Wales and England*, 20–2.

[95] His name is inscribed on a memorial stone near Carew, *ECMW* no.303 (p. 182), plate XLI.

[96] Wendy Davies, *Wales in the Early Middle Ages*, 106. See also, however, her reservations in *Patterns of Power in Early Wales*, 81. K. L. Maund, *Ireland, Wales and England*, 64–8, 123–39, 163–6 reviews the different aspects of Gruffudd's reign.

[97] K. L. Maund, 'Cynan ap Iago and the killing of Gruffudd ap Llywelyn', *Cambridge Medieval Celtic Studies*, 10 (1985), 57–66 (cf. idem, *Ireland, Wales and England*, 163).

TABLE 4: Genealogical chart indicating the principal descendants of Rhodri by 1080

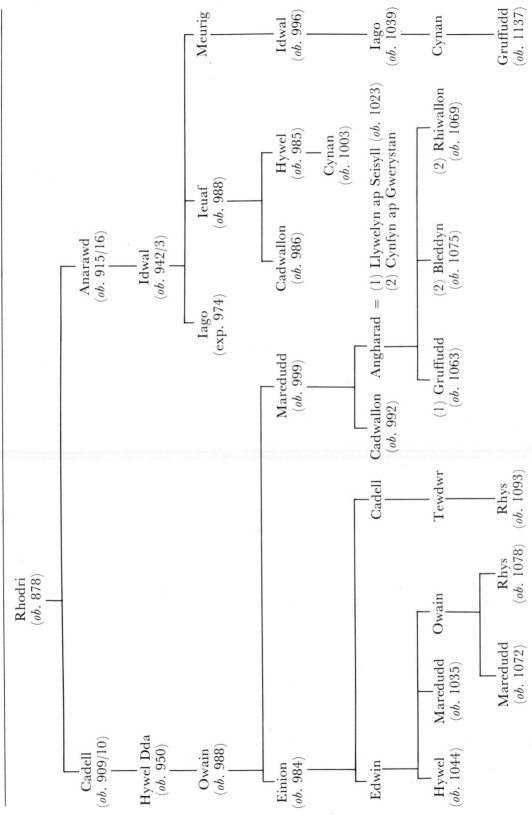

returned'.[98] Bleddyn and Rhiwallon, sons of Cynfyn ap Gwerystan, Gruffudd's half-brothers (Cynfyn ap Gwerystan having married Angharad, widow of Llywelyn ap Seisyll)[99] and representing a further intrusive element, were established as subject kings in Gwynedd and Powys by Edward the Confessor, presumably with English military support; while in Deheubarth Maredudd ab Owain ab Edwin re-established his family, although his position was threatened by the continuing hostility and aspirations of the descendants of Rhydderch ab Iestyn. Rhiwallon was killed in battle with the sons of Gruffudd ap Llywelyn in 1069 and Bleddyn in 1075 by Maredudd ab Owain's brother Rhys. Trahaearn ap Caradog succeeded him in Gwynedd and Powys. He was Bleddyn's cousin according to the annals, so that Trahaearn's mother 'must have been a sister of Cynfyn or of Angharad ferch Maredudd'.[100] Trahaearn ruled jointly with Cynwrig ap Rhiwallon at first, and they were opposed by Gruffudd ap Cynan ab Iago, returning from exile in Ireland with Irish mercenaries. Cynwrig was slain and the *Historia Gruffud vab Cynan* tells how Gruffudd defeated Trahaearn at the battle of *Gwaet Erw* in Meirionydd but was in turn defeated by Trahaearn in Gwynedd at *Bron yr Erw* after Gruffudd's Welsh supporters turned against his Irish followers.[101] Trahaearn was then able to avenge Bleddyn's death in 1078 at the battle of *Pwllgwdig* but he could not prevent Rhys ap Tewdwr, a cousin of Rhys ab Owain, establishing himself in Deheubarth.

It is apparent in these wars that, in the struggle between the two branches of the descendants of Rhodri Mawr, in the tenth century the princes of Dyfed prevailed over those of Gwynedd with a contrary tendency in the early eleventh, at a time when intrusive kings were seizing power and endeavouring to found new dynasties. It is likely that strong feelings were generated both in Gwynedd and Dyfed in the course of these wars. The relationship between Gruffudd ap Llywelyn and Deheubarth was extremely uneasy. In 1047 approximately 140 of Gruffudd's warband were slain through the treachery, according to the Welsh annals, of the leading men of Ystrad Tywi. In 1075 Rhys ab Owain was able to slay Bleddyn ap Cynfyn through what the annals describe as 'the evil-spirited treachery' of the princes and leading men of Ystrad Tywi. The activities of these kings south of Ceredigion certainly appear to have been bitterly resented. What these struggles meant for Ceredigion is revealed only occasionally in the annals but it is sufficient to give an impression of the situation. In 952 and 954 Ceredigion was ravaged by the sons of Idwal the Bald. In 992 in the course of a struggle in Deheubarth between Maredudd ab Owain ap Hywel Dda and his nephew Edwin ab Einion, Edwin, with Saxon aid, ravaged all Maredudd's territory including Ceredigion. In 1039, the year of his accession, Gruffudd ap Llywelyn pillaged Llanbadarn Fawr in Ceredigion while advancing to drive Hywel ab Edwin out of Deheubarth. When Hywel returned from Ireland with Viking mercenaries, Gruffudd defeated him at the mouth of the Tywi. Ceredigion provided the northern princes with a direct approach to Ystrad

---

[98]Wendy Davies, *Wales in the Early Middle Ages*, 112. Cf. now on the period after 1073 R. R. Davies, *Conquest, Coexistence and Change*, 24 ff., and K. L. Maund, *Ireland, Wales and England* (for example, 141 ff.).

[99]*EWGT*, 39, 47, 95, 104, 151.

[100]*EWGT*, 141. See on Trahaearn now, K. L. Maund, 'Trahaearn ap Caradog: legitimate usurper?', *WHR*, 13 (1987), 468–76 (cf. idem, *Ireland, Wales and England*, 76–82).

[101]D. Simon Evans, *Historia Gruffud vab Kenan* (Caerdydd, 1977), 10–11. There is an English edition with English translation by A. Jones, *The History of Gruffydd ap Cynan* (Manchester, 1910). See also now D. Simon Evans, *Medieval Prince of Wales: The Life of Gruffudd ap Cynan* (Llannerch, 1990).

Tywi. Similarly it provided the rulers of Deheubarth with direct access to the north and Gwynedd. It would have been through Ceredigion that the army of Maredudd ab Owain advanced against Cadwallon ap Ieuaf to subdue Gwynedd and Môn 'with great treasure' in 986. It was in Ceredigion as well as Dyfed that Maredudd regrouped displaced persons after a Viking attack on Môn. But the main pressure was undoubtedly exerted by Gwynedd upon Deheubarth. Ceredigion provided the route for Llywelyn ap Seisyll to advance to Abergwili in 1022 and for Gruffudd ap Llywelyn to ravage Dyfed and Ystrad Tywi in 1047. In short, Ceredigion was a military route from north to south Wales and whoever controlled this coastal strip was well placed to attack his opponent across its borders. It is difficult to see how, under such circumstances, Ceredigion can have had much of a political life of its own except as a satellite of Gwynedd or Deheubarth, and difficult to imagine to what allegiances the men of Ceredigion in these centuries felt themselves primarily bound. There can have been no sense of identity or self-consciousness other than to the transient overlord of the moment, and it is probable that the most fundamental allegiances were to local lords within Ceredigion itself about whom the records in this period are entirely silent.

Saxons, Vikings and Normans

Ceredigion does not appear to have been exposed to further Irish attack after the force of fifth-century Irish immigration had spent itself or had been checked, though there are some indications that Irish kings in the eleventh century, for example the Leinster king Diarmait mac Máel-na-mBó, styled 'king of Wales' as well as of the Hebrides, Dublin and southern Ireland,[102] exercised some overlordship in Wales, presumably specifically in Gwynedd and Dyfed, the rulers of which territories used Irish mercenaries against each other. There is no evidence, however, that Diarmait ever personally campaigned in Wales. Nor did the activities of Anglo-Saxon rulers normally intrude across Ceredigion borders. The military expeditions of Anglo-Saxon kings into Wales in the course of the eighth and ninth centuries—into Powys and Gwynedd—must have left Ceredigion largely untouched. The impetus of a Mercian attack on Gwynedd in 865 took them up into Môn, not down into Ceredigion. It is possible, however, that when Cœnwulf, king of Mercia, ravaged the land of Dyfed in 818, he attacked through Ceredigion, though an invasion through south Wales is not inconceivable. Certainly Ceredigion must have been vulnerable in the ninth and tenth centuries to Scandinavian attack from the sea. The great sweep of Cardigan Bay naturally lured to its shores the ships of the Vikings from Ireland and the Irish Sea, ships which, in R. R. Davies's words, 'terrorized the coastal lowlands'.[103] The records are imperfect, but north and south Wales experienced serious assaults and Ceredigion is unlikely to have been entirely bypassed. In 988 Llanbadarn Fawr and Llandudoch (St Dogmaels) are known to have been ravaged. It may even be that Hywel Dda and his contemporary Welsh rulers did not join forces in the great Scandinavian, Scottish and North British coalition against Athelstan, king of

---

[102] *Annals of Tigernach*, ed. W. Stokes, *Revue Celtique*, xvii (1896), 410.
[103] R. R. Davies, *Conquest, Coexistence and Change*, 25. Cf., in general for Wales and the Irish Sea province in the age of the Vikings, A. P. Smyth, *Scandinavian York and Dublin* (2 vols.: Dublin, 1975, 1979) (see also above n. 87) and idem, *Scandinavian Kings in the British Isles 850–880* (Oxford, 1977), and H. R. Loyn, *The Vikings in Wales* (Dorothea Coke Memorial Lecture: London, 1976).

Wessex, which was crushed at *Brunanburh* in 937, for fear of encirclement by the Scandinavians.[104] Not, however, that the Vikings proved a permanent danger to the Welsh. Dyfed was a primary area of Scandinavian influence but this influence was eventually confined purely to coastal regions and off-shore islands and evidence for Scandinavian settlement on the mainland is very slight indeed.[105] Wales was not on the main Viking sea-ways across north-west Europe and Scandinavian activity in the British Isles was concentrated elsewhere. Nearly ninety years later, however, raiders appeared in Ceredigion who, though not at first distinguishable from other marauders, were forerunners of what was to be eventual total conquest. These raiders did not come by sea; they came through the defiles of Plynlimon. In 1066 the Normans under their duke, William the Bastard, defeated Harold Godwinesson at the battle of Hastings. In 1073 'the French', as the Welsh chroniclers called them, 'ravaged Ceredigion and Dyfed', and in 1074 'the French ravaged Ceredigion by itself'. Twenty years after that first raid on Ceredigion the Norman invasion of west Wales began in earnest and with it the inexorable erosion of the native culture and traditional society.

The Anglo-Saxons, scourge of lowland Britain in the time of Gildas, had come to dominate most of what is now England by *c.*650, but beyond the border area running roughly from the Dee to the Wye they had been unable to make further inroads into what is now Wales. The great dyke, constructed by Offa, king of Mercia, in the eighth century from Treuddyn to Chepstow, marked roughly the frontier zone between Saxons and Welsh and was complemented by Wat's Dyke across Shropshire to Basingwerk on the Dee.[106] It was subject, as all frontiers, to fluctuating fortunes. In the 820s the Mercians annexed the whole of Powys for a while. In the mid-eleventh century Gruffudd ap Llywelyn, king of Gwynedd, carried his frontier several miles to the east along the whole line of Offa's Dyke. Subject also to vicissitudes was the hegemony exercised by successive Anglo-Saxon kings in Wales. Offa may have enjoyed some acknowledgement of overlordship by the Welsh. When papal legates visited England in 786 to enquire into the state of the Anglo-Saxon Church, Theophylact, bishop of Todi, one of the legates, visited 'the king of the Mercians and parts of Britain', by which Wales could be implied. According to a rather grandiose claim by the Alfredian chronicler in the *Anglo-Saxon Chronicle* A, Ecgberht, king of Wessex, and grandfather of Alfred, led an army among the Welsh in 830 and reduced them all to 'humble submission'. The *Chronicle*, on the other hand, says nothing of Alfred's diplomatic

[104] D. P. Kirby, 'Hywel Dda: anglophil?', 8.

[105] B. G. Charles, *Non-Celtic Place-Names in Wales* (London, 1938), xxxiii–iv. Cf., on place-names, B. G. Charles, *Old Norse Relations with Wales* (Cardiff, 1934), and M. Richards, 'Norse place-names in Wales', *The Impact of the Scandinavian Invasions on the Celtic-speaking Peoples c.800–1100 AD*, ed. B. Ó. Cuív (International Congress of Celtic Studies, 1959; Dublin, 1975). See also now, however, on a possible Viking presence, particularly in Gwynedd, at the end of the tenth century, W. Davies, *Patterns of Power in Early Wales*, 51 ff.

[106] The standard work is C. Fox, *Offa's Dyke* (London, 1955) but see also now D. Hill, 'Offa's and Wat's Dykes: some exploratory work on the frontier between Celt and Saxon', *Anglo-Saxon Settlement and Landscape*, ed. T. Rowley (BAR 6, 1974), 102–7; idem, 'The inter-relation of Offa's and Wat's Dykes', *Antiq.*, 48 (1974), 309–12; and idem, 'Offa's and Wat's Dykes: some aspects of recent work', *Trans.Lancs.and Cheshire Antiq.Soc.*, 79 (1977), 21–33. M. Worthington comments on the Offa's Dyke project in *AW*, 25 (1985), 9–10. See also P. Wormald, 'Offa's Dyke', *The Anglo-Saxons*, ed. J. Campbell (Oxford, 1982), 120–1. For two guides (with maps) to Offa's Dyke see F. Noble, *The Shell Book of Offa's Dyke Path* (London, 1969), and C. J. Wright, *A Guide to Offa's Dyke Path* (London, 1975). More recently has appeared F. Noble, *Offa's Dyke Reviewed*, ed. M. Gelling (BAR British Series 114, 1985).

ascendancy over the rulers of Wales, attested by Asser, in the 880s and 890s. This Alfredian position, as has been seen, was shattered in the years immediately following Alfred's death. By 918 Alfred's son, Edward (899–924) (with his sister, Æthelflaed) had so restored West Saxon military fortunes that Hywel ap Cadell, king of Deheubarth, and Idwal the Bald, king of Gwynedd, 'sought to have him as lord'. Athelstan (924–39), Edward's son and successor, kept the leading Welsh princes, including Hywel, attendant upon him at regular intervals from 928 to 934. Hywel's last appearance at the court of a West Saxon king was in 949, the year before his death. The West Saxon kings presumably held their neighbouring rulers in subjection to prevent, by intimidation, an alliance of Welsh leaders with Vikings. Athelstan was too powerful for Hywel to challenge, but Hywel's death coincided with an abatement of Viking pressure on Wessex. When pressure on Wessex built up again under Æthelred II the Unready (978–1016), the West Saxons were then themselves too hard-pressed and disorganized to counter the renewed assault, and incapable of attempting any further subjugation of the Welsh. Though Harold Godwinesson in the reign of Edward the Confessor (1042–66), son of Æthelred II, campaigned effectively against Gruffudd ap Llywelyn, and Bleddyn and his brother Rhiwallon, as the *Anglo-Saxon Chronicle* D records, swore an oath in 1063 to serve Edward by land and sea and paid great tribute, the Confessor's authority over the Welsh was only partial. After the battle of Hastings Bleddyn and Rhiwallon supported the Saxon rebels in the midlands in 1067 against the new king of England, William of Normandy.

Many of these events belong to the history of Wales rather than specifically to the history of Ceredigion, but Hywel's subjection to the West Saxons, for example, is in a sense part of the history of Ceredigion because Ceredigion was in his possession. Moreover, in the fighting between Deheubarth and Gwynedd, Ceredigion was the territory through which plunder as well as armies moved and some of this probably found its way into Saxon hands during periods of subjugation as tribute or peace-offering. The Lichfield Gospels, otherwise known as the Book of St Chad, may well have been conveyed into England by this route. Its marginal memoranda of early land grants reveal quite clearly that this was at one time the Gospel Book of the church of St Teilo at Llandeilo Fawr in Ystrad Tywi.[107] The mystery is how St Teilo's Gospel and deed book came to rest in Lichfield. It has been suggested that Hywel Dda and Tewdwr ap Gruffudd, king of Brycheiniog (one of the Welsh kings who witnessed Athelstan's charters), brought the book voluntarily to King Athelstan to give to Ælfwine, bishop of Lichfield, in 934. This is because the name 'Teudur' appears in it and such a transfer, it has been argued, could not have been accomplished on the authority of 'anyone but Hywel Dda' who is known to have attended a gathering at the court of Athelstan on 28 May 934 with Tewdwr, king of Brycheiniog, present.[108] The name 'Teudur', however, is not certainly that of the king of Brycheiniog who was Hywel's contemporary, and the crucial piece of evidence for dating the book's arrival at Lichfield is the appearance on the very first page of the name 'Wynsi', Wynsige, bishop of Lichfield (964–75).[109] The probability, therefore, is that it was acquired by the church of Lichfield in the time of Wynsige. In 973 at Chester, Edgar, king of Wessex (959–75), strong in the temporary absence

---

[107] Melville Richards, 'The "Lichfield" Gospels (Book of "Saint Chad")', *Nat. Library of Wales J.*, 18 (1973), 135–45 (pp. 137–8), and D. Jenkins and M. E. Owen, 'The Welsh marginalia in the Lichfield Gospels, Part I', *Cambridge Medieval Celtic Studies*, 5 (1983), 36–66 (pp. 48–9).

[108] Melville Richards, 'The "Lichfield" Gospels (Book of "Saint Chad")', 138–9.

[109] Cf. D. Jenkins and M. E. Owen, art. cit., 48–9.

of Viking incursions, received the 'submission' of several British rulers including Iago ab Idwal, king of Gwynedd.[110] It does seem highly unlikely that any king of Deheubarth would have freely given away the Gospel and muniments book of one of the principal churches in the kingdom, but Iago might well have given it away had it come into his possession. Iago had attacked Owain ap Hywel, king of Deheubarth, in 951 and in 952 twice laid Dyfed waste. On any of these expeditions, Llandeilo Fawr could well have been plundered, and the booty including the Gospel book of Llandeilo Fawr carried back through Ceredigion into Gwynedd. If in 973 Iago felt it appropriate to make gifts to King Edgar, the Gospel book could have been easily parted with. Chester was in the diocese of Lichfield, and for Edgar to have handed it on to the bishop of Lichfield would have been a natural enough gesture. It may be, therefore, that the Lichfield Gospels represent one item of plunder taken from south Wales by a king of north Wales and subsequently given into Saxon keeping, reaching Lichfield from Llandeilo indirectly via Ceredigion and Gwynedd.

When William the Bastard defeated Harold, king of England, at Hastings in 1066, there was no immediate awareness on the part of the Saxons that their new conqueror had come to stay. Still less can the Welsh leaders have regarded the arrival of the Normans in England as presaging disaster for themselves; at first Normans as well as Irish were used as mercenaries. In 1072 Caradog ap Gruffudd ap Rhydderch, now king of Morgannwg, used Norman mercenaries to overthrow and slay Maredudd ab Owain, king of Deheubarth, on the banks of the Rhymni. Nevertheless, it did presage great adversity. The history of the Norman advance into Wales during the reign of William the Conqueror (1066–87) is essentially the history of the three border earldoms which William established on the Anglo-Welsh frontier, those of William fitz Osbern at Hereford, Roger de Montgomery at Shrewsbury and Hugh d'Avranches at Chester.[111] The death of fitz Osbern was followed by the rebellion of his son Roger in 1075 against the Conqueror, after which the earldom escheated to the Crown, so that the Norman advance in south Wales at this stage proceeded no further than the annexation of Gwent. Roger de Montgomery, however, built and garrisoned a proliferation of castles in the Vale of Montgomery, with his principal holding at Hen Domen (Old Montgomery), from whence a military advance could be pressed deep into Powys and even into Ceredigion.[112] In north Wales, Robert, nephew of Hugh d'Avranches, established himself at the forward base of Rhuddlan probably by the mid-1070s: from there he advanced west to Degannwy by 1086 and possibly by 1081.[113] This was the situation

---

[110] *Florentii Wigorniensis Monachi Chronicon ex Chronicis*, ed. B. Thorpe, 2 vols. (London, 1848), I, 142; J. E. Lloyd, *History of Wales* I, 349. See on the meeting at Chester as a royal conference, A. P. Smyth, *Warlords and Holy Men: Scotland AD 80–1000* (London, 1984), 228.

[111] J. E. Lloyd, *History of Wales* II, 371 ff.: an earlier important paper by Lloyd was 'Wales and the coming of the Normans (1039–93)' (see above, n.4). Cf. L. H. Nelson, *The Normans in South Wales 1070–1171* (Austin and London, 1966); D. Walker, *The Norman Conquerors* (Swansea, 1977) and I. W. Rowlands, 'The making of the March: aspects of the Norman settlement in Dyfed', *Proc. of the Battle Conference on Anglo-Norman Studies* III (1980), 142–57.

[112] D. J. Cathcart King and C. J. Spurgeon, 'The mottes in the Vale of Montgomery', *Arch. Camb.*, 94 (1965), 67–78.

[113] *The Ecclesiastical History of Orderic Vitalis*, ed. M. Chibnall, IV (Oxford, 1973), 138–9. Robert was apparently established at Rhuddlan before 1081 and Hugh d'Avranches and Robert of Rhuddlan were also apparently campaigning in Llŷn by 1081. But for a note of caution on the precise chronology of these years, see *The Ecclesiastical History of Orderic Vitalis*, VI (Oxford, 1978), xxxiv–viii, and K. L. Maund, *Ireland, Wales and England*, 148.

regarding the Norman advance into north Wales as a harassed Trahaearn ap Caradog turned to meet a new threat from his dynastic adversaries.

Gruffudd ap Cynan, exiled in Ireland, made two attempts to take the kingship of Gwynedd from Trahaearn by force, the first in 1075, the second in 1081. With more Irish-Norse mercenaries, Gruffudd crossed in 1081 to Porth Glais, near St David's, where he met with Rhys ap Tewdwr, king of Deheubarth, against whom Trahaearn had been campaigning in alliance with Caradog ap Gruffudd ap Rhydderch. The *Historia Gruffud vab Kenan* is undoubtedly concerned to present Rhys in the most desperate straits and dependent for his very survival on the help of Gruffudd, [114] but it is probable that Gruffudd was even more dependent on the aid of Rhys. The two princes went to St David's 'and received the bishop's blessing', [115] the bishop at the time being Sulien of Llanbadarn. A great battle was fought at *Mynydd Carn*, which has been located near Newport (Pembs.) in the commote of Uch Nyfer at Y Garn Fawr, about twenty miles from St David's.[116] Caradog was slain and the *Historia* provides a grim picture of Trahaearn, sorely wounded, biting the grass in agony and groping vainly for his weapons until one of Gruffudd's mercenaries 'made bacon of him as of a pig'. Trahaearn's army fled, pursued by Gruffudd. Rhys, fearing treachery from Gruffudd according to the *Historia*, withdrew into the night, for which Gruffudd ravaged his land. Gruffudd then set off through Ceredigion and in Arwystli, Trahaearn's centre, he 'destroyed and slew the common folk there: and he burnt its houses, and bore into captivity its women and maidens ... From there he approached Powys where he displayed cruelty to his opponents according to the custom of a conqueror, and he spared not even the churches.'[117]

It must strike the modern observer as peculiar that with the threat of Norman conquest so close in time and space these kings could remain so preoccupied with the pursuit of what seem by comparison petty dynastic feuds; and, indeed, an element of 'political chaos' has been discerned as segmentary conflict between royal lineages became acute and the links between rulers and their subjects were weakened in the pursuit of further territorial aggrandisement.[118] But in the first place, these dynastic feuds were not petty. They were the essence of political life and men were fighting for power and wealth. Both Gruffudd and Rhys were in danger of losing everything to Trahaearn. Such tensions and conflict undoubtedly also attended the rise of Merfyn Frych and his family. Secondly, as Marc Bloch put it with regard to the political and military leaders of Europe as a whole in the early Middle Ages, 'The truth is that the leaders were far more capable of fighting (if their own lives or property were in jeopardy) than of methodically organizing a defence. Moreover with very few exceptions they were unable to understand the connection between their particular interests and the general interest.'[119] These Welsh princes were typical, therefore, of the age in which they lived and of the common mentality of the ruling element of that age. Thirdly, the socio-economic development of Wales at this time was such that they were presiding only over what archaeologists and anthropologists would now describe as 'chiefdoms'

[114]*Historia Gruffud vab Kenan*, 13–14.
[115]Ibid., 14.
[116]E. D. Jones, 'The locality of the battle of Mynydd Carn, AD 1081', *Arch.Camb.*, 77 (1922), 181–97.
[117]*Historia Gruffud vab Kenan*, 16. The circumstances surrounding the battle of *Mynydd Carn* and the careers of Gruffudd and Rhys are examined in detail by K. L. Maund, *Ireland, Wales and England*, 33–8, 82–90, 142–4, 148–55, 168–82.
[118]W. Davies, *Patterns of Power in Early Wales*, 80 ff.
[119]M. Bloch, *Feudal Society*, trans. L. A. Manyon (London, 1961), 55.

as opposed to 'states'; that is to say, by contrast with an early state in which a centralized monopoly of coercive force, the economic base of which is a thriving market economy, maintains internal stability and territorial integrity, a chiefdom is characterized by its non-coercive government, its relatively weak market economy and its fissiparous tendencies.[120] Whereas tenth- and eleventh-century England, therefore, may be seen as a state with a highly developed administrative organization, the hegemonies of these Welsh rulers still belong to what have been defined as 'cyclical' chiefdoms; that is, though for a time they may have established a firm control over their own and adjacent territory, this control was temporary because the absence of an adequately advanced administrative framework and of a sound enough economic base ensured its relative transience.[121] 'Power', writes Professor R. R. Davies, 'lay more in the control of peoples and moveable wealth and in the collection of renders and tributes than in the control and exploitation of land.'[122]

Before the end of 1081 Gruffudd ap Cynan had been captured by the Normans at Rhug near Corwen by Hugh d'Avranches and Hugh, son of Roger de Montgomery, and had been imprisoned at Chester. There he was to remain for twelve years.[123] In the same year Rhys ap Tewdwr in Deheubarth, certainly with Gruffudd's capture the dominant leader of the western Welsh, came face to face with the Conqueror. The Welsh annals state that William went to St David's to pray. The *Anglo-Saxon Chronicle* E records, 'This year the king led an army into Wales and there liberated many hundreds of men.' Once in Deheubarth William may have made a pilgrimage to St David's but he was there with the army first and foremost to assert his authority and protect the Norman troops already far flung across Wales.

Sulien of Llanbadarn, bishop of St David's from 1073 to 1078 when he resigned, and then again from 1081, had been present at the meeting of Gruffudd ap Cynan and Rhys ap Tewdwr at St David's. There is no reason to suppose that Rhys dealt with William before the battle of *Mynydd Carn*, and the capture of Gruffudd may have been a significant factor in bringing William into Wales. Nevertheless Sulien's family, though based at Llanbadarn Fawr in Ceredigion, had important connections with St David's, and it is not impossible that Bishop Sulien acted in some way as mediator between Rhys and William.[124] But he was essentially at St David's in 1080, as the Welsh annals record, 'against his will'. It would appear that Sulien was uneasy as bishop and in 1085 he resigned his see a second time. With such a disposition it seems unlikely that he

[120]Cf. E. R. Service, *Origins of the State and Civilization* (New York, 1975); H. J. M. Claessen and P. Skalnik (eds.), *The Early State* (The Hague, 1978); W. T. Sanders and D. Webster, 'Unilinealism and multilinealism and the evolution of complex societies', *Social Archaeology*, ed. C. L. Redman *et al.* (New York and London, 1978), 249–302; and J. Bintliff (ed.), *European Social Evolution: Archaeological Perspectives* (Bradford, 1984).

[121]R. Hodges, *Dark Age Economics: The Origin of Towns and Trade AD 600–1000* (London, 1982), 26–8, 185 ff.

[122]R. R. Davies, 'In praise of British History', *The British Isles 1100–1500: Comparisons, Contrasts and Connections*, ed. R. R. Davies (Edinburgh, 1988), 9–26 (p. 20). He writes (p. 21) that the 'economic backwardness' of Celtic regions—'or perhaps more accurately their very different ways of organizing economic relationships and transferring wealth'—meant that their rulers 'could not command the regular resources in liquid assets and patronage which might have begun to transform their political power and extend the effective range of their political demands'.

[123]*The Ecclesiastical History of Orderic Vitalis* IV, xxxvi–viii.

[124]Cf. I. Williams, 'An Old Welsh verse', *Nat.Library of Wales J.*, 2 (1941–2), 69–75, from which 'it appears that Padarn's episcopal staff was famed as a peacemaker' (p. 71).

welcomed any diplomatic activity into which his position as bishop may have forced him. What does seem certain is that the 'Riset de Wales' who held south Wales (including Ceredigion) in fee of the Crown of England at an annual *ferm* of forty pounds was Rhys ap Tewdwr;[125] 'and if a formal agreement may be presumed, no time is so likely to have produced it as the year of his expedition undertaken by the Conqueror to the uttermost parts of Dyfed'.[126] The scene was set, however, for a second Norman offensive on west Wales in the 1090s in which Ceredigion—'once' in the words of Ieuan ap Sulien 'extremely rich, spiteful to enemies, kind to travellers, excelling all Britain in hospitality'[127]—would again play a vital strategic role, as indeed it always had done across these distant centuries.

[125]J. H. Round, 'Introduction to the Herefordshire Domesday', *VCH Hereford*, ed. W. Page (London, 1908), I, 281 (n.209).
[126]J. E. Lloyd, *History of Wales* II, 394.
[127]M. Lapidge, 'The Welsh-Latin poetry of Sulien's family', *Studia Celtica*, 8/9 (1973/4), 68–106 (pp. 84–5).

CHAPTER 6

EARLY SOCIETY AND ECONOMY

R. A. Dodgshon

THE six or seven centuries following the Roman withdrawal have rightly been called a 'hazy period of little truth and much fiction' in Welsh history.[1] Indeed, few other periods admit of more dispute between historians. Even discussion of a central theme like the character of the native society and economy is marked by sharply divided opinions. Thus, some would have us believe that the period from the fifth century to the eleventh saw the continuation of an archaic, tribally organized society which practised a pastoral and semi-nomadic economy. Others would argue that early Welsh society and economy displayed more capacity for change and propose that, even by the fifth century, native society was organized around the extended family or clan-group rather than the tribe, that it already had a significant arable sector to its economy, and that the landscape was already, in part, made up of permanent fields and farms. Trying to resolve this fundamental conflict of views in the context of Cardiganshire brings with it additional problems. If the evidence for Wales as a whole casts only a shadowy, flickering light on the matter, it could be argued that no light at all is thrown on the scene in Cardiganshire. Relevant studies of the period tend to ignore the County or refer to it only in passing. Yet without wishing to deny this very real deficiency of material, we can—by culling evidence from a range of material and by looking back from the better documented conditions of the thirteenth and fourteenth centuries—sketch the possible outlines of its character.

The problem can be viewed through a number of sources. Firstly, there is the evidence of early manuscripts, of which the most informative are the early Welsh Law Codes. The extant thirteenth-century texts of the Laws of Hywel Dda are of inestimable value because they represent a documentary link, albeit several stages removed in manuscript transmission, with the period under review. Extents and accounts compiled during the thirteenth and fourteenth centuries or even later can be used to set the evidence of the Codes in a more specific context. Secondly and potentially the most fruitful, we have field-work and archaeological evidence. This potential is still largely latent, but an attempt has been made here to determine what kind of sites may typify Dark Age settlement in Cardiganshire. The third source is place-name evidence. Again, its full potential has still to be realized. Much more work is needed on early Welsh place-names before we can use them to distinguish between different phases or types of settlement.

Our view of Cardiganshire society and economy in the early Middle Ages and the questions which can be posed and discussed are wholly dependent on the nature and limitations of these

---

[1] W. H. Davies, 'The Romans in Cardiganshire', *Ceredigion*, 14 (1962), 85–92 (p. 93).

three sources. For this reason the discussion has been structured around the evidence and ideas that can be gleaned from each in turn.

The documentary evidence

The tradition behind the compilation of the Law Codes is well-known. In the tenth century Hywel Dda gathered together lawyers from the different parts of Wales beside the Tywi and from their combined knowledge of long-standing custom and legal practice assembled the nucleus of what we now know as the Codes,[2] thereby affording a valuable insight into the structures of Dark Age society. It must be stressed that we do not possess an original copy of the Codes. The earliest text dates from the thirteenth century. It is believed that three separate versions of the Codes were drawn up initially, embodying the custom and practice of three different parts of Wales, and hence their description as the Venodotian appertaining to Gwynedd, the Gwentian to Gwent and the Demetian to Dyfed. Although the Demetian is still thought to have a loose relationship with Dyfed, doubt over the strict regional applicability of the three Codes has led to their retitling on the basis of supposed authorship. Thus, the Venedotian has been redesignated the Book of Iorwerth, the Gwentian the Book of Cyfnerth and the Demetian the Book of Blegywryd, but even this new categorization has been criticized on the grounds that no one lawyer was responsible for any single redaction.[3]

    The Laws shed considerable light, first, on the complex territorial system of administration and social order into which *gwledydd* or the larger districts like Cardiganshire were divided; secondly, on the different social groups or grades of society and the rules which governed their inter-relationships; and thirdly, on the ways in which the different groups or grades were related to the possession of land in terms of tenure and inheritance.

i) The territorial organization of early Cardiganshire

At some stage during the immediate post-Roman period Wales came to consist of large tribal districts or *gwledydd*, each with its own royal dynasty. Ancient Cardiganshire was one such district. In time each *gwlad* came to be composed of a cluster of territorial units. The Laws depict an ideal pattern in which each *gwlad* was subdivided into *cantrefi*, *cymydau* and *maenorau*. The exact derivation and precise meaning of the term *cantrefi* is uncertain. Its most likely meaning is of a territory comprising a hundred *trefi* or settlements. We must not assume that there must have been exactly a hundred settlements in each *cantref*. Essentially, the term expressed the amount

[2]See, for example, G. R. J. Jones, 'Post-Roman Wales', *The Agrarian History of England and Wales*, I,ii, ed.H. P. R. Finberg (Cambridge, 1972), 281–382 (pp. 284, 324); T. Jones Pierce, 'The social and historical aspects of the Welsh laws', *Medieval Welsh Society: Selected Essays by T. Jones Pierce*, ed. J. Beverley Smith (Cardiff, 1972), 353–68 (pp. 367–8).

[3]G. Edwards, 'Studies in the Welsh Laws since 1928', *WHR* (Special Number, 1963: *The Welsh Laws*), 1–17 (pp. 8–9); D. Jenkins,'Introduction', *Celtic Law Papers: Introductory to Welsh Medieval Law and Government*, Studies Presented to the International Commission for the History of Representative and Parliamentary Institutions, no. XLII, ed. D. Jenkins (Brussels, 1973), 3–22 (pp. 9–10).

of responsibility which the *cantref* bore in respect of renders and obligations, that is, it answered for a hundred houses or settlements. Initially, the *cantrefi* may have been the only subdivision of *gwledydd*, but they appear later subdivided into *cymydau* or commotes. The Laws fix the number of *cymydau* per *cantref* at two. The Demetian Code makes it clear that each *cwmwd* was further subdivided into four *maenorau*. The *maenor* was not an elemental unit but covered a fairly spacious area and usually contained a group of settlements. Its description by some historians as a 'multiple estate' embodies something of its character. Of the four in each *cwmwd*, three were said to be in the hands of freemen and the fourth in those of bondmen. Each *maenor* was itself further subdivided into townships. If a free *maenor*, it contained thirteen and, if a bond *maenor*, seven townships. This meant that there were forty-six townships in a *cwmwd*. To this total need to be added two townships held by the king in demesne plus one by his reeve and another by his chancellor, to produce a total of fifty settlements, or precisely what one would expect of a unit rated as half a *cantref*.[4] Each township was further subdivided into *rhandiroedd* or sharelands, their precise number varying between free and bond settlements. If the former there were deemed to be four sharelands but if the latter only three. As well as declaring that a shareland comprised 312 acres, the Laws assign one shareland for pasture and the remainder for arable. Although there were exceptions, these sharelands did not occupy the entire territory of a township; instead, we should see them as forming, initially, disjoined blocks around which were positioned the farmsteads of the township, with common waste lying in between.

By contrast with this legal scheme, the on-the-ground arrangements in Cardiganshire display a number of differences. The area encompassed by the modern County comprised four *cantrefi*. Early lists name only one, Cantref Penweddig (also called *Cantref Gwarthaf*), the most northerly or 'upper' *cantref*,[5] though references occur in the sixteenth century to 'Hischohit et Hufchit Penwedhic et Stradmauric'[6] and to *Cantref Canawl*, *Cantref Sirwen* and *Cantref Castell*.[7] Although these names are repeated by the antiquary Samuel Meyrick,[8] some doubt exists over their authenticity. Alone among writers, he also envisaged an earlier stage when Cardiganshire was divided into only three *cantrefi*, namely *Cantref Gwarthaev*, the 'upper' cantref, *Cantref Mabwyniawn*, the 'Cantref of the sons of Wyneon', and *Cantref Caer Wedros*, 'Gwedros's Fortress'. Judging by the composition of these three, the later grouping into four was produced by the subdivision of *Cantref Caer Wedros* into two. Meyrick also repeats the old folk tradition regarding an offshore territory known as *Cantref Gwaelod*, the 'lowland *cantref*', which had become submerged. He peopled it and filled its landscape with roads and towns. The shingle banks which run seaward were transformed by him into routeways with names like Sarn Dewi (St David's Causeway) and Sarn Cynfelyn (St Cynfelyn's Causeway). Its principal town, Caer Wyddno, was named after its

[4]Cf. G. R. J. Jones, 'Post-Roman Wales', 299–300; W. Davies, *Wales in the Early Middle Ages* (Leicester, 1982), 43–4.

[5]M. Richards, 'Local government in Cardiganshire, medieval and modern', *Ceredigion*, 4 (1962), 272–82 (p. 273); J. E. Lloyd, *The Story of Ceredigion* (Cardiff, 1937), 13.

[6]The reference occurs in sixteenth-century marginalia in the *Red Book of the Exchequer* inserted on an extent drawn up in 8 Edward I. For a facsimile of this see E. M. Pritchard (ed.), *The Taylors Cussion by George Owen of Henllys* (London, 1906).

[7]H. Owen (ed.), *The Description of Pembrokeshire by George Owen of Henllys* (Honourable Society of Cymmrodorion, part IV: London, 1936), 480.

[8]S. Meyrick, *The History and Antiquities of the County of Cardigan* (London, 1808), 48.

last ruling prince, Gwyddno.[9] Whereas Meyrick assiduously dated the inundation which caused the loss of this hypothetical *cantref* to AD 520, work on changes in sea-levels would date it to the Mesolithic era. [10]

The obscurity which surrounds the exact toponymy of Cardiganshire's early *cantrefi* is probably a consequence of the fact that they were supplanted as major units of administration by commotes. The County was composed of ten commotes, Genau'r-glyn, Perfedd, and Creuddyn which formed *Cantref Gwarthaf*, Mefenydd, Anhuniog and Pennardd which formed another (Meyrick's *Cantref Canol*) and Mabwynion and Caerwedros which formed another (Meyrick's *Cantref y Castell*) and Gwynionydd and Is Coed which formed another (Meyrick's *Cantref Caer Wedros*).[11]

The names of these commotes yield clues as to how they may have originated. A few appear to have derived from personal names—Anhuniog from Anhun, for example, Mefenydd perhaps from Mafan. Others appear based on topographical names, like Genau'r-glyn meaning 'the mouth of the defile'. Of particular interest is the widespread use of the prefixes *Is/Uwch* in commote names. Melville Richards has questioned the conventional, purely topographic interpretation of these prefixes as meaning below and above. Instead, he has suggested that they had a geographical-political meaning: the former signifying an area close to a local political centre and the latter an area that was more peripheral or further away.[12] However, a more likely explanation is that such prefixes represent the residual use of dual classificatory schemes. Under such schemes, tribes and other large kin groupings would have ordered themselves into two symbolic or classificatory halves: these opposed or interdependent halves served to regulate marriage, ritual and succession. So long as the socio-political organization of landscape revolved around such kin groups, then we can also expect such schemes to have played a part in the way landscape was ordered and symbolized, with districts and settlements being imprinted with the same symbolic or classificatory order as the kin groups that occupied them. Arguably, it is for this reason that we find farmsteads and districts within the Cardiganshire landscape distinguished through prefixes like *Is/Uwch*. Restored to their original context of use, such prefixes need to be seen as directly equivalent to, even interchangeable with, a range of other classificatory oppositions (eg. east/west, great/little, fore/back). Though they could be used to create a geographical order—both in a relative and absolute sense—their primary intent was symbolic and classificatory. With the feudalization of the area and the need to territorialize jurisdictions

[9]Ibid., 50–78.

[10]J. A. Taylor, 'Chronometers and chronicles: a study of palaeo-environments in west central Wales', *Progress in Geography*, ed. C. Board, R. J. Chorley, P. Haggett and D. R. Stoddart, 5 (London, 1974), 250–334 (pp. 312–14); P. Evans, 'The intimate relationship: a hypothesis concerning pre-Neolithic land use', *The Effect of Man on the Landscape: The Highland Zone*, ed. J. G. Evans, S. Limbrey and H. Cleere (CBA Research Report No. II, 1975), 43–8 (p. 46).

[11]A number of early commote lists are available, some complete, others incomplete. See National Library of Wales (hereafter NLW), E. A. Lewis Facsimiles, No. 84, S. C. II/770/1–19; NLW, E. A. Lewis Facsimiles, No. 84, S. C. 1160/1; E. M. Pritchard, op. cit.; M. Rhys (ed.), *Ministers' Accounts for West Wales 1277 to 1306* I, Honourable Society of Cymmrodorion Record Series, No. XIII (London, 1936), 269–87; E. A. Lewis 'The Account Roll of the Chamberlain of West Wales from Michaelmas 1301 to Michaelmas 1302', *BBCS*, II (1925), 49–86; H. Owen (ed.), *Description of Pembrokeshire*, 480–6.

[12]J. E. Lloyd, *The Story of Ceredigion*, 15–17; M. Richards, 'The significance of Is and Uwch in Welsh commote and cantref names', *WHR*, 2 (1964), 9–18.

—a process certainly in progress by the twelfth century—elements of this earlier symbolic system appear to have been carried over into the new system simply because it was the way communities thought about space and how they ordered themselves within it. In short, the use of prefixes like *Is/Uwch* carry us back to a much older layer of landscape history, one in which they had a quite different context of use.[13]

According to the Laws commotes were subdivided into multiple estates (multiple = covering more than one settlement) called *maenorau* but the documentary evidence for twelfth-century Cardiganshire suggests its *maenorau* had already disappeared, though their former existence is revealed by place-names incorporating the element *maenor*. Rather than the *maenor*, the administrative unit which appears to dominate the local landscape is one called the *gwestfa*. Except where *gwestfau* provided the basis for later parishes such as Gwestfa Cilcennin and Gwestfa Lledrod, the meaningful use of these units did not outlast the medieval period. However, we can reconstruct the former *gwestfau* within each commote by using early extents. A thirteenth-century extent gives the number of *gwestfau* within north Cardiganshire commotes; an extent of 1303 provides an incomplete listing for the County as a whole; whilst another of fifteenth-century date provides a check on those in the south of the County.[14]

The most northerly commote in the County, Genau'r-glyn, was rather curiously divided into $5\frac{1}{2}$ *gwestfau*, four of which, *Gwestfa Oeron Oweyn*, *Gwestfa Oeron Ynoi Moryddyg.*, *Gwestfa Oeron Gruff. ab Wyron* and *Gwestfa Oeron ab ph.*, were clearly named after kindred groups. The remaining *gwestfa* was called *Gwestfa Goythenes*. The commote of Perfedd comprised only four *gwestfau*, in all probability equivalent to the four *parsels* into which Perfedd was divided during more recent times,[15] and the names of two of which—*Gwestfa Trefmeyric* and *Gwestfa Dyffryn Reydaul*—are preserved in the names of two *parsels*, Trefeurig and Cwmrheidol. The third commote in Cantref Penweddig, Creuddyn, was subdivided into six *gwestfau*, again probably corresponding to the six *parsels* into which Creuddyn appears divided in more recent times—Llanfihangel Upper, Llanfihangel Lower, Llanbadarn Upper, Llanbadarn Lower, Llanafan and Gwestfa.[16] Matching particular *gwestfa* units with *parsels*, though, is complicated by the fact that the relationships have been obscured by changing nomenclature. The commotes of Anhuniog and Mefenydd boasted more complex patterns of *gwestfau*. The former was arranged into nine: *Llandewi-Aberarth*, *Llan-non*, *Morfa Mawr*, *Trefethwal*, *Gwascarawg*, *Llansanffraid*, *Llyswen*, *Ciliau* and *Cilcennin*; the latter was arranged into eight: *Blaenaf*, *Rhosdie*, *Redogoed*, *Garth Meyt*, *Morfa Bychyn*, *Goyllwyd*, *Maes Meyderuf* and *Lledrod*. The commote of Pennardd had only four, incompletely recorded but including *Gwestfa Llandewi* and *Gwestfa Betws Leucu*. In the south of the county, the commotes of Caerwedros, Gwynionydd and Is Coed had four *gwestfau* apiece. Those of Caerwedros were *Gwestfa Mawr*, *Gwestfa Gruff.*, *Gwestfa Hyscoed Bwedr* and *Gwestfa Mochros*; those of Gwynionydd were *Gwestfa Aber Drammell*, *Gwestfa Vawr*, *Gwestfa Bedwyt* and *Gwestfa Abernython*, and those of Is Coed were *Gwestfa Cauros*, *Gwestfa Verwig*, *Gwestfa Blaynannerch* and *Gwestfa Lancoydmawr*. Finally,

[13]R. A. Dodgshon, 'Symbolic classification and the making of early Celtic landscape', *Cosmos. The Yearbook of the Traditional Cosmology Society*, 1 (1985), 61–83.

[14]F. Seebohm, *The Tribal System in Wales* (London, 1904), 116–22; NLW, E. A. Lewis Facsimiles, No. 84, S. C. 1160/1 and S. C. II/770/1–19.

[15]L. Morris, *A Short History of the Manor of Perverth* (1751), reprinted in Meyrick, op. cit., 568–75.

[16]L. Morris, *A Short History of the Crown Manor of Creuthyn* (1751), reprinted in Meyrick, op. cit., 555–67. Significantly, Morris says that locals referred to the manor as 'Cwmmwd y Creuythyn'.

the commote of Mabwynion comprised eight *gwestfau*, including *Gwestfa Lanerch Ayron*, *Gwestfa Dyhewyd* and *Gwestfa Llanwyr*, but the identity of others is hidden behind the names of kindred, such as *Gwestfa Gruff.*, or place names which cannot now be located, such as *Gwestfa Kestyll Bygeyd*.

Early extents indicate that each *gwestfa* comprised five sharelands, the only exceptions being the *gwestfau* of Llys-wen and Cilcennin in Anhuniog which comprised only four.[17] Assuming that five sharelands existed in most *gwestfau*, this gives a total of 260 for the county. Of these, the names of barely one-sixth have been recovered. Thanks to a Ministers' Account for the years 1277/80, those of Creuddyn are especially well documented. They include *Randir de Kevene*, *Meuric*, *Randir Kevene Grug*, *Randir apud Yweloc*, *Randir apud Glascrug*, *Randir apud Castelou*, *Randir apud Mayskan-herein*, *Randir apud Mananam*, *Randir apud Vandu*, *Randir apud Oisrestendk*, *Randir David ap Howel*, *Randir Kiwarchin* and *Randir quondam ad Velin*.[18] An extent of 1303 also contains a useful list of some of the sharelands in Genau'r-glyn. Those of *Kefyn*, *Elgar*, *Rylbach* and *Wilheyraug* can be linked to present-day farms in the vicinity of Llandre. Edward Lhuyd provides names of other sharelands, such as *Rhandyr pen y Coed*, *Rhandyr y dre* and *Ollmarch Randyr* in Betws Bledrws (now Llangybi) parish, or those of *Rhandir Tir y Wlad*, *Rhandir y Gairron*, *Rhandir Ceven Meirig*, *Rhandir pen y Panne* and *Rhandir Lhwyn y maen* in Llanwnnws (now Gwynnws Uchaf and Isaf) parish.[19] Isolated references to others occur in early sources whilst Rhandir occurs as a place-name element, as in Rhandir-hen (SN 588 720), Bwlch-y-Randir (SN 591 730), Randir Uchaf (SN 604 715) and Randir Isaf (SN 605 709), all farms around Llangwyryfon.

T. Jones Pierce drew attention to what he saw as an apparent regularity in both the size and composition of *gwestfa* units. Contrasting this regularity with the more complex and varied appearance of *maenorau* and *trefi* in areas like north Wales, he suggested that those of Cardiganshire must form part of a later, more artificial system, one that could not have existed before the late twelfth century.[20] Such a view, though, needs qualification. There are two points at issue here. First, it places too much emphasis on the regularity of *gwestfau*. Admittedly, there is an impressive regularity in the number of sharelands per *gwestfa*, but there is no convincing regularity in the physical size of *gwestfau* or in the number of *gwestfau* per commote. A comparison between the nine *gwestfau* which made up the relatively compact commote of Anhuniog with the four that made up the larger, more expansive commote of Pennardd demonstrates this. Second, and providing a more serious qualification to his argument, is the way Jones Pierce handles the question of what the creation of *gwestfau* actually involved. His argument is bound up with his wider view that west and north-west Wales enjoyed a pastoral, nomadic economy down to at least 1100 AD. He assumes no permanent settlement, no layout of arable sharelands, prior to this

---

[17]Seebohm, op. cit., 116–22; NLW, E. A. Lewis Facsimiles, E/142/51/1–10.

[18]R. A. Roberts, 'Cymru Fu: some contemporary statements, appendix inc. Ministers' Account 1277–80', *THSC*, 4 (1895–6), 104–37.

[19]*Archaeologia Cambrensis Parochialia. Being a Summary of Answers to 'Parochial Queries'*, By Edward Lhuyd, part III (Cardiff, 1911), 4 and 87–8; *Calendar of Various Chancery Rolls AD 1277–1326, Supplementary Close Rolls, Welsh Rolls, Scutage Rolls* (London, 1912), 325; D. C. Rees, *Tregaron: Historical and Antiquarian* (Llandysul, 1936), 1.

[20]Meyrick, op. cit., 332. T. Jones Pierce, 'Medieval Cardiganshire—a study in social origins', *Ceredigion*, 3 (1959), 1–19; 'Pastoral and agricultural settlements in early Wales', *Geografiska Annaler*, XLIII (1961), 182–9; and 'Agrarian aspects of the tribal system in medieval Wales', *Geographie et Histoire Agraires: Annales de L'Est*, Memoire No.21 (1959), 329–37 (all three being reprinted in T. Jones Pierce, *Medieval Welsh Society* (309–27, 339–51 and 329–37 respectively).

date.[21] In quick succession over the twelfth century, though, he sees kin-groups being allocated fixed blocks of arable land and—as a separate but roughly contemporaneous process—the boundaries of sharelands and *gwestfau* being superimposed on the landscape. Thus, the creation of *gwestfau* was seen as part of the complex process whereby the landscape was carved up into fixed arable settlements and brought within a framework of administrative order. Unfortunately, his case for such a late development of fixed arable settlements is unconvincing. The early medieval evidence for fixed settlements is indisputable.[22] Furthermore, it would be difficult to make sense of Welsh legal processes relating to land if permanent settlement only emerged during the twelfth century. A process like *dadannudd*, for instance, enabled the descendant of a landholder to bring a claim for the repossession of abandoned land within nine generations of its being abandoned. Such a process would defy explanation if there was not already a tradition of permanent settlements or sharelands at the point when the Welsh Laws were first redacted in the tenth century. Clearly, once we accept that fixed settlements long predated the twelfth century, the problem of *gwestfau* changes.

In origin, the term *gwestfa* derives from a food render long paid by freemen to their king or lord. By the time we find references to it in sources like the Law Codes it had been converted into a cash payment, a *tunc* pound of 240*d.* payable by each *maenor* or, as in the case of Cardiganshire, by each *gwestfa*. Documents like the Minister's Accounts for 1277/80 and the 1303 extent for Cardiganshire show that local payments had certainly been converted into cash by then.[23] Noting the conversion of *gwestfa* into cash, though, provides only partial understanding of the problem. We still need to explain why—in Cardiganshire and adjacent parts of the Teifi valley but nowhere else in Wales—this conversion involved the creation of a system of territorial order based on units called *gwestfau*. In one sense this is a simple problem. If *gwestfa* was also converted from being levied on the person or kin group to being levied directly on land, then there would be good reasons for creating a system of territorial order based on the payment of *gwestfa*. Those *gwestfau* which incorporate the names of kin groups (e.g. *Gwestfa Wyrion Llawden, Gwestfa Wyrion Owain, Gwestfa Wyrion Ieuan Foel* and *Randir David ap Howel*) clearly symbolize this shift in meaning. However, to see how such a system could be meaningfully reused as a system of territorial order does not explain why such a solution was adopted in Cardiganshire but not, apparently, elsewhere. We can only presume that socio-political conditions in the County during the twelfth century favoured this solution.

ii) The social structure of early Cardiganshire

In the words of the Law Codes, there were 'three kinds of persons, a king, a breyr, and a villein, with their near relations'.[24] The king or chief *(pencenedl)*, together with those of princely or lordly status, formed the apex of the social system, beneath whom were the *breyr* or freemen, a social group distinguished above all else by the fact that they were members of a kindred, and below

---

[21]T. Jones Pierce, *Medieval Welsh Society*, 323, 339–42.

[22]G. R. J. Jones, 'Post-Roman Wales', 281–382; D. Jenkins, 'A lawyer looks at Welsh land law', *THSC* (1967), 220–47 (pp. 241–7.)

[23]Most *gwestfau* were recorded as paying 13*s.*4*d.*: see, for example, NLW, E. A. Lewis Facsimiles, No. 84, S. C. II/770/1–19.

[24]A. Owen, *Ancient Laws and Institutes of Wales* (London, 1841), 169.

whom was arguably the most numerous element in early Welsh society—the villeins of servile status.

Each of the districts into which sub-Roman Wales appears divided was ruled over by its own royal dynasty. As a separate *gwlad*, Ceredigion was no exception. During the eighth century the domain of its ruling dynasty was extended across the Teifi as far as the Tywi, to create the larger kingdom of Seisyllwg which had a relatively fleeting life in the political geography of early Wales, being soon after absorbed into the kingdom of Deheubarth. Against this backcloth, the ruling hierarchy in Ceredigion probably became more numerous and the position of the king more defined and powerful.

The main focus of royal or lordly power was the *llys*, the principal administrative centre within each commote. Thus, the commote of Anhuniog had its own court at Llys-wen on the Aeron, and Genau'r-glyn at Henllys on the Leri near Dôl-y-bont. These courts could either be royal or lordly, but they enforced the renders and obligations due to the king or lord from the communities within their territories. The most important render discharged by freemen was that of *gwestfa*. Freemen were also obliged to provide accommodation for the king's officers when they toured each *tref*, collecting *gwestfa*. Bondmen were liable to a more varied range of renders, from payments for the upkeep of the lord's war-horse to payments for the maintenance of his officials. In later documents, such payments were referred to collectively as 'rents of extent'. Originally, the dues rendered by freemen were collected by a royal officer known as the *rhingyll*, whilst those paid by bondmen were collected by one of their own called a *maer* or reeve.

Beneath those of royal or lordly status were the *breyr* or *bonheddig*, the freemen who knew their *heddig* or lineage. All their rights in law and property derived from this.[25] Within known degrees of affinity which T. P. Ellis called 'responsible kinship', each man owed to another 'certain duties which varied according to the proximity of relationship'.[26] The kinship group, within which the freeman was most immediately placed, comprised all males within four degrees, that is, all those who were descended from a common great-grandfather on the male side. Kinsmen related within four degrees constituted the social units or lineages around which rights of property and inheritance developed. Important rights and obligations were also attached to kinsmen within seven degrees. Those comprising this group were eligible for the payment of *galanas* or honour price, the damages which one kinship group paid to another in the event of injury, the amount varying according to the nature of the injury inflicted and the status of the injured party. The existence of a wider network of kinship up to nine degrees of relationship is hinted at by the legal process of *dadannudd*. These different kindred groupings are important, for Irish Law reveals that the degrees of kinship which mattered for different kinds of assessment—land-rights, blood-fine —underwent modification as population grew, land became scarce, and rights, in consequence, had to be more and more restricted.[27] It might be possible to read into the scaling of kinship responsibilities in Wales a similar narrowing of kinship definition.

[25]See Meyrick, op. cit., lxvi: 'Geneologies were preserved as a principle of necessity ... A man's pedigree was in reality his title deed, by which he claimed his birthright in the country.'
[26]T. P. Ellis, *Welsh Tribal Law and Custom in the Middle Ages* (Oxford, 1926), I, 82, 88–9.
[27]T. M. Charles-Edwards, 'Kinship, status and the origins of the hide', *Past and Present*, 56 (1970), 3–33.

Beneath freemen in the social scale were bondmen, men whose rights derived not from their membership of a lineage but from the fact that they were legally tied to a lord. They carried more onerous personal burdens and—where appropriate—performed labour services for their lord. Whereas freemen held land allodially, by descent from their ancestors, bondmen held land from their lord. Given the stereotypes of early Celtic society as a society of freemen, the existence of bondmen has always posed a tantalizing problem. Resolving this problem has not been made any easier by the wide disagreements that exist between scholars over their relative importance within early Welsh society. For Jones Pierce, they were a minority element, whose settlement was mainly to be found in coastal areas.[28] In Cardiganshire, Llan-non provides what he saw as a typical bond settlement. For others, like Glanville Jones, they were a majority element, to be found in upland no less than lowland areas.[29] Indeed, Glanville Jones has argued for the presence and importance of bondmen by the late Iron Age. Their numbers may have been added to by the impoverishment of freemen lineages. This could have occurred during phases of population growth, reducing the ability of freemen lineages to provide for their members.[30] In such circumstances, we can expect some to have rented land from their king or lord, a relationship whose ultimate price may have been a loss of free status.

iii) Land tenure, landholding and settlement in the early Middle Ages

The distinction between freemen and bondmen expressed itself through both landholding and settlement. As regards landholding, freemen held their land by *tir gwelyawg*, literally 'resting place tenure'. The precise nature of *tir gwelyawg* has been the subject of much debate, particularly the question of whether it dates in origin from before or after *c.* 1100. It has already been noted that Jones Pierce saw early Welsh society as consisting largely of freemen who practised a pastoral, nomadic economy. Freemen, he argued, did not convert to a settled, arable economy until after AD 1100. Over the century or so which followed, he had the tribes which previously 'roamed at will with their flocks and herds' dividing up their territories between the various kinsmen of the tribe through a process of primary appropriation. When the first occupant, the *gwr dfod*, of such a share died, his land was divided equally between his sons or grandsons. It was this partition of the holdings created by the 'primary appropriation' of tribal land which, in Jones Pierce's view saw the creation of *gwelyau*, each named after the son or grandson who occupied it.[31] Once created, the number of *gwelyau* remained fixed, with descendants of its first occupier holding it as 'joint proprietary units'. His case for such a late formation of the *gwely* was based on three sorts of evidence. First, as an institution, it scarcely rates a mention in the Law Codes. Second, *gwelyau* invariably carry the name of an individual who lived there during the twelfth century. And third, in areas like Cardiganshire, *gwelyau* have a youthful appearance in terms of the number who shared them as joint proprietary units. For Jones Pierce, the *gwely* was 'a relatively fleeting

[28]T. Jones Pierce, *Medieval Welsh Society*, 342–3 and 350.

[29]G. R. J. Jones, 'The distribution of bond settlements in north-west Wales', *WHR*, 11 (1964), 19–36. For a detailed discussion of Llan-non, see G. R. J. Jones, 'Forms and patterns of medieval settlement in Welsh Wales', *Medieval Villages*, ed. D. Hooke (Oxford University Committee for Archaeology, Monograph no. 5, 1985), 165–7.

[30]T. M. Charles-Edwards, art. cit., 20–1.

[31]T. Jones Pierce, op. cit., 334–9.

phenomenon in the Welsh landscape'.[32] By *c.* AD 1300 it had already begun to decay rapidly as a joint proprietary unit, dissolving into individual freeholds. Needless to say, such an interpretation of the *gwely* would make it irrelevant to any history of the County prior to 1081 AD.

There is, however, a strong counter view for seeing the *gwely* as a much older institution. Glanville Jones, for instance has argued for its association with a settled, arable economy long before 1100.[33] By extension, he sees the institution of the *gwely* as equally deep-rooted and as always having the character of a joint proprietary unit. Indeed, in origin, the term probably applied to the grouping of kinsmen who possessed the land rather than the land itself. This shift in meaning probably took place as pressure on land mounted and the interests of the group became focused more and more on controlling access to property. Those who favour an early development of the *gwely* make a further assumption about how its character changed. Initially, it represented a continually developing institution. The source of this dynamism was the customary definition imposed on the *gwely* as a grouping of kinsmen. The Law Codes suggest a restriction to all males linked together across four generations or a founder plus his sons, grandsons and great-grandsons. So long as these limits on the social extent of *gwelyau* operated, then we can expect new *gwelyau* to have formed with each passing generation through fissioning of an existing *gwely* into two or more *gwelyau* or by a new one budding off from it. For those who believe in the antiquity of the *gwely*, the significance of the twelfth century lies not in the creation of the *gwely* but in the fact that this process of fissioning ceased. The number of *gwelyau* then existing remained fixed or even declined, the latter occurring where lineages died out. A number of reasons have been put forward to explain why this fissioning process should have ceased. First, in a society in which status and the possession of land went together, a point may have been reached at which the fragmentation of estates could have threatened the status of *gwelyau*. Certainly, we know from a variety of work that such fragmentation did occur over the early medieval period. Secondly, the change may have sprung from the inability of Anglo-Norman lawyers to cope with an institution which could duplicate itself each generation.

Evidence for the existence of *gwelyau* in Cardiganshire can be derived from *The Black Book of St David's*, a survey of the bishop's lands compiled in 1326. In it are detailed a number of '*gwely*' or '*lecti*' in the south of the County that were held '*comporciones de consanuinitate*'. At Llanddewibrefi, for instance, it brings the two forms of reference together in the phrase that there were 'viii lecti qui vocantr *Gwely*'. Each is shown to have been held by a number of possessors plus '*descendentes*'. One *gwely*, for instance, was held by 'David ap Trahan, Philip ap Cadogan, Eynon Vaughan and their descendants'.[34] Further examples can be inferred from an extent drawn up in 1303. Detailed discussion of these *gwelyau* must be left until Volume II of the *Cardiganshire County History*. However, one aspect does deserve comment. For Jones Pierce, the *gwelyau* evident in the County had a distinctly youthful appearance, a genealogical shallowness, as if they had not long been formed. Their apparent shallowness, though, need only tell us about when,

---

[32] Ibid., 342.

[33] G. R. J. Jones, 'The tribal system in Wales: a re-assessment in the light of settlement studies', *WHR*, 1 (1961), 111–32 and 'Post-Roman Wales', 281–382. Amongst other work supporting the deep roots and settled history of freeholding, see W. Davies, 'Land and power in medieval Wales', *Past and Present*, 81 (1978), 3–23; idem, *Wales in the Early Middle Ages*, 41–7.

[34] J. W. Willis-Bund (ed.), *The Black Book of St David's* (The Honourable Society of Cymmrodorion Record Series, No. 5, London, 1902), 197–234.

roughly, the regular fissioning of *gwelyau* ceased, not when the institution of the *gwely* was first created. In fact, when we survey the Cardiganshire evidence, there are ample signs that the pattern of landholding had more depth and maturity than Jones Pierce was prepared to concede it. Some *gwelyau* were quite large in terms of membership, with some being shared between ten to fifteen shareholders. Others were scattered between settlements. Most revealing of all, we find examples of *gwestfau* named after kin-groups which, by the early fourteenth century, were further subdivided into *gwelyau*. Thus, payments of *gwestfa* in *Gwestfa Aeron Oweyn* in north Cardiganshire, for instance, were subdivided between seventeen units, fourteen of which involved joint-proprietary units that were presumably *gwelyau*.[35] Clearly, the kin-based possession of land has been imprinted on the landscape at different scales, a sign that landholding has evolved through successive stages of fissioning. In fact, in those parts of Wales where we can probe the history of landholding over the early medieval period, it appears to be one of estates becoming progressively smaller, with large multi-settlement units giving way gradually to single settlement estates and, ultimately, to settlements that contained more than one estate.

Bond communities inhabited small nucleated hamlets sometimes referred to as *trefgordd* or bondvills. By *tir cyfrif*, 'register' or 'reckoned-land' tenure, every adult male member of a bondvill was entitled to an equal share of arable along with other bondmen in the community when he came of age. Lineage was irrelevant and there was no question of land being possessed on a hereditary basis as of right. On the basis of references in the Laws to their land as divided *per stirpes*, bond communities are thought to have been farmed on an open-field basis, with each individual's holding fragmented and scattered in the form of intermixed strips.[36] A particularly important feature is that within each bond *maenor* there existed a bondvill known as the *maerdref* where the lord's power and authority were centred. This was where the lord's local representative lived, where he usually had his *llys*, and where the demesne land, worked by the labour services of bondmen, was located.

It has been argued that bond communities may have originated in the Iron Age and that, initially, the *maerdrefi* of multiple estates may have been represented by hillforts. Setting hillforts in such a context, of course, would help explain the large amounts of labour invested in them. With the arrival of the Romans, however, the occupation of such patently defensive sites was abandoned and *maerdrefi* may have been re-established on lower, less defensive sites nearby. Vestiges of these low-ground *maerdrefi* have survived in the form of place-names (for example, Maerdy in Llangrannog parish), long after bondmen and their tenures disappeared.

Some Cardiganshire *maerdrefi* appear to bear out this point, being located in close proximity to hillforts.[37] One clear example is the hillfort of Pencoed-y-foel, Llandysul, overlooking Castell

---

[35]NLW, E. A. Lewis Facsimiles, No. 84, S. C. II/770/1–19.

[36]As a cautionary note, it is worth mentioning that the Codes specifically state that in a register *tref* or a bond settlement 'every one is to have as much as another, yet not of equal value'. A. Owen, *Ancient Laws and Institutes of Wales* (London, 1841), 5. Why this may *not* lead to open fields is explained in R. A. Dodgshon, 'The landholding foundations of the open field system', *Past and Present*, 67 (1975), 3–29.

[37]G. R. J. Jones, 'The distribution of bond settlements in north-west Wales', *WHR*, II (1962), 19–36, and 'Post-Roman Wales', 380.

Gwynionydd, a defensive site of possibly Dark Age origin,[38] beside which is the divided *maerdref* of Faerdrefawr and Faerdrefach. It may be that the six townships of Llandysul parish—Borthin, Capel Dewi, Llanfraid, Faerdre, Llandysulfed and Llanfair—were *ab origine* bond settlements, appendaged to this *maerdref*.[39] The hillfort at Llety-twppa Wood may bear a similar relationship to the sites around its base. In the Middle Ages it is likely that most ecclesiastical property in Cardiganshire, especially in the lowlands of the east and along the major river valleys, was originally bond land.[40] Though some of it appears in later medieval records as *tir gwelyawg*, at the time of its acquisition by the Church the probability is that it was servile or bond *tir cyfrif* which was being given away by kings and nobles. Significantly, when we look at the distribution of Church land within the County, it embraces upland no less than lowland. The church at Llanbadarn, for instance, held the entire commote of Perfedd, a commote which stretched inland to the slopes of Plynlimon.[41] Likewise, Strata Florida Abbey was granted extensive areas of upland to the east and north of Tregaron as well as large blocks of lowland to the west.[42] Another possible indicator of where bond settlements were to be found is provided by those early churches which now stand in isolation, such as Llanbadarn Odwyn, Llangynllo, Bangor Teifi, Llanfairorllwyn and Rhostïe. Though tradition has associated these early Celtic churches with eremetical figures, there is a case for seeing them as having once been surrounded by bond settlements. During periods of political and military disturbance, like the twelfth century, their bond inhabitants may have absconded—or even have been slaughtered—leaving the church as the only reminder of a once thriving settlement.[43]

The archaeological evidence

The archaeological evidence for early Welsh society offers few clues to those who see it as providing a context for concepts derived from the Laws. In terms of reliably dated field evidence the County only possesses commemorative standing stones and early church sites. This lack of verified settlement sites is a problem which Cardiganshire shares with the whole of Wales. In a discussion of the field evidence for Wales as a whole, Professor Alcock stressed that only a handful of settlement sites can be confidently dated to the Dark Ages, none of which are to be located

[38]For comment on Pencoed-y-foel and Castell Gwynionydd, see I. T. Hughes, 'Some south Cardiganshire earthworks', *TCAS*, VII (1930), 112–17; 'The background of Llandysul', *Ceredigion*, 3 (1957), 101–15.
[39]G. R. J. Jones, 'Post-Roman Wales', 305, argues that Llandysul itself was a settlement of importance as early as the sixth century, and that it later emerged with a local *maerdref* as a centre for a group of seven hamlets.
[40]T. Jones Pierce, *Medieval Welsh Society*, 316–17.
[41]J. E. Lloyd, *The Story of Ceredigion*, 15.
[42]A discussion of the abbey's granges can be found in T. Jones Pierce, 'Strata Florida Abbey', *Ceredigion*, I (1950), 18–33. On p. 29 he suggests that when first conveyed (mid-twelfth century), the abbey's granges were 'developed hamlets, many of them with servile tenants, transferred by charter from secular to monastic lordship'.
[43]G. R. J. Jones, 'The tribal system in Wales', 127.

in Cardiganshire.[44] In large measure, though, the problem is one of identification and recognition of contemporary secular occupation.

Clearly, if we accept Jones Pierce's thesis, we would not expect much evidence to have survived for settlement in upland areas where freemen, in his view, practised a nomadic, pastoral economy. Only in low-lying, coastal areas would stable, arable-based settlements have occurred. In fact, such an interpretation would be difficult to sustain in the light of recent thinking about the extent to which both upland and lowland areas of Britain were settled by the end of the Iron Age. In keeping with those who argue for bond communities being more numerous and widespread and with those who argue for a deeper and settled history for free *gwelyau*, we are on a more secure footing if we assume that low-ground and valley sites in Cardiganshire were already widely settled during the early medieval period. The problem then becomes one of use/disuse. We can only expect early medieval settlement and field patterns to be detectable if subsequent changes in type and location left them as relict systems. However, even if such archaeological or fossil systems are not apparent, it does not necessarily follow that few fixed settlements could have existed prior to AD 1081. We must consider the possibility that many farm sites and even fields dating from this period may have continued in use down to modern times. In other words, the problem facing us may be the more difficult one of isolating pre-1081 sites from within the present-day landscape.

Reviewing the question of archaeological evidence for early medieval settlement, one type of site that merits consideration is that identified by the place-name *Gaer*. Although, literally translated, *gaer* means a fort, a large number of *gaer*-sites have a surrounding rampart less obviously defensive than hillforts and lack their naturally defensive position. Indeed, many are sited on low ground, within the fields of present-day farms. Illustrative of this is the *Gaer* at Ffos-y-ffin, a site on the Teifi floodplain. It consists of a slight, perfectly circular enclosure, now dissected by a road. Other *gaerau* which occupy lowland settings include Gaer Wen, Caer Argoed and Caer Llety-llwyd. It is impossible to date them accurately, but it is possible that they were occupied during the Roman period and immediately after.

In a valuable paper, K. H. Jackson has argued that an equivalent term, *Car-* was used in place-name formation by the Britons of Cumbria and southern Scotland and that during the later phases of its use it became attached to farms or hamlets 'protected by some kind of stockade'.[45] Gaer Ffos-y-ffin fits into this latter category. Overall, Jackson suggests a possible sequence from well-defended hillforts in the later Iron Age, through the less defensive character of early *gaerau* and the enclosed but more open character of the late *gaerau* being replaced, during the fourth and fifth centuries AD, by non-defensive sites identified by the place-name element *Tref-*, meaning a farm or, later still, a township. Such a sequence may have relevance to an area like Cardiganshire. If so, it would suggest that *gaerau* were part of its settlement pattern during the second and third centuries AD, with the more open, less defensive examples being the last established. By the fourth and fifth centuries AD, we can expect them to have been replaced or

[44]L. Alcock, 'Some reflections on early Welsh society', *WHR*, 3 (1964), 1–7 and 'Wales in the fifth to seventh centuries AD: archaeological evidence', *Prehistoric and Early Wales*, ed. I. Ll. Foster and G. Daniel (London, 1965), 177–211.

[45]K. Jackson, 'Angles and Britons in Northumbria and Cumbria', *Angles and Britons* (O'Donnell Lectures) (Cardiff, 1963), 60–84 (pp. 80–3).

supplemented by sites with the place-name prefix *Tref-*. Indeed, work in south-west England suggests that, there, the element *Car-* or *Ker-* was actually replaced by *Tref-*.[46]

There is, however, another point to be drawn from Jackson's discussion. Though early medieval settlements may have involved timber-framed buildings, perhaps with wattle and daub walls,[47] and, for this reason, be more difficult to detect in an archaeological sense, there is also the possibility that they were surrounded by an earthwork, a feature that we can expect to be a more durable element in the landscape. In fact, the Laws and other sources provide some suggestive clues on the continuing use of settlement enclosures. The *tir cordllan* or nucleal land of the Laws[48] was probably land which was not divided among co-heirs but enclosed land around which the dwellings of a family-group were disposed and in which the members of the family had a common interest. Considering the derivation and meaning of the terms *trefgordd* and *cordref*, H. Lewis reasoned that the *tref* element signified in origin the family and the *cor* or *gordd* element indicated a circle or enclosure.[49] The term *gwelygordd* which means 'a circle of ancestors' could indicate that *cordllan* was enclosed land which symbolically bound family groups or *gwelyau* together.[50] Similarly, early Celtic churches are associated with circular, or oval-shaped cemetery enclosures. Indeed, it is now thought likely that these cemetery enclosures actually preceded the establishment of the church itself.[51] In fact, the place-name element which signifies the presence of such churches, *llan*, was originally the term for the cemetery enclosure[52] and may, at a still earlier date, have been used of any form of enclosure, secular or religious. As churches came to be built within the cemetery enclosures, the meaning of the term was redefined and used of the church itself. But the presence of an enclosure need not necessarily signify an early ecclesiastical foundation. In Britain and Ireland generally such enclosures were also constructed around purely secular settlements.

Significantly, a search through nineteenth-century tithe maps and modern aerial photographs of the County has revealed a fair number of farmsteads surrounded by or linked to small enclosures; *ab origine*, some may represent medieval *trefgordd*. Most comprise circular or oval enclosures, 0.75–2 acres in extent, and either encircle or lie adjacent to present-day farmsteads. In a few cases they have been mutilated by subsequent building activity or the construction of new banks. In one or two cases, the enclosure around the farmstead is only one of two concentric enclosures, as at Blaenhoffnant Isaf and Uchaf and at Tyn y Coed, Garn Fach and Pantanamlwg. Also interesting are those which form the centre of a radial field pattern, as at Ciliau Uchaf beside the Aeron and Tyn y Gwndwn, now Bryneithin.

Although examples occur widely throughout the County, local concentrations can be detected. Relatively few are to be found in the extreme north of the County, in what was Cantref Penweddig. The most northerly cluster is scattered through Llanfihangel-y-Creuddyn parish. Further east, around the upper reaches of the Teifi, quite a number of farms have well-preserved examples but few are to be found in Llanddewibrefi parish. The latter, though, has many farms

[46]C. Thomas, 'The character and origins of Roman Dumnonia', *Rural Settlement in Roman Britain*, CBA Research Report 7 (1966), 74–98 (p. 97).

[47]*Giraldi Cambrensis Opera*, ed. J. F. Dimock, VI (Rolls Series: London, 1868), 200–1.

[48]G. R. J. Jones, 'Post-Roman Wales', 340–9.

[49]H. Lewis, *The Ancient Laws of Wales*, ed. J. E. Lloyd (London, 1892), 92–4, 101–2.

[50]H. Lewis, *The Ancient Laws of Wales*, 101.

[51]C. Thomas, *Britain and Ireland in Early Christian Times AD 400–800* (London, 1971), 109.

[52]E. G. Bowen, *The Settlements of the Celtic Saints in Wales* (Cardiff, 1956), 1–2.

on its lower ground associated with small, irregular fields whose origin may be late prehistoric or early medieval.[53] Lower down the Teifi around Lampeter and beyond, examples of farmstead enclosures are more abundant. A further grouping occurs in the south-west of the County in the parishes of Llangoedmor, Llanfairorllwyn, Llandysiliogogo, Y Ferwig, Aber-porth and Penbryn. Although some are to be found along the Vale of Aeron, they are not numerous, though a small concentration is to be found in the parish of Nancwnlle, that at Llys-wen being especially fine. At Tal-sarn early plans show the houses, disposed around a large oval-shaped enclosure, facing a central green. When Leland saw it in the sixteenth century, prior to the alterations which have changed its character, it was 'caullid Talessarne Greene'.[54] Only excavation can establish the true antiquity of such settlement enclosures. However, morphologically, they embody a late prehistoric tradition that certainly survived into the early medieval period.

An alternative approach to the investigation of early settlement lies in the investigation of local boundaries and watercourses. As well as providing procedures for dividing land between individuals of different rank or status, the Law Codes also legislated for the drawing of boundaries; the more important the boundary, the wider and more substantial its marker. Thus, the boundary between *cantrefi* is nine feet, between *cwmwdau* seven, between *trefi* five and between *randiroedd* three, while 'the meer of erws, two furrows, is called a balk'.[55] Where possible, the more important boundaries were fixed on rivers or streams. In a society deficient in the skills of land surveying, it was important to have a 'stay' of boundary, a boundary which could not be moved or ploughed out and which could be recognized by all. Watercourses satisfied these conditions. Indeed, where natural watercourses failed to extend far enough or were not conveniently placed, artificial ditches or fosses were dug. Because of their permanence, quite a number of these boundary ditches survive in the modern landscape. Equipped with the knowledge that the more important the boundary the wider it should be, it may be possible to disentangle the boundaries of some early territorial units in the County.

There are a number of well-known earthworks which may also qualify as major early boundaries, the most notable being that of Cwys yr Ychen Bannog in Caron parish. This is a ditch between twelve and fifteen feet in width which now divides the parish into Caron-is-clawdd and Caron-uwch-clawdd. It runs from Maes-llyn Lake past Blaengorffen to Garn Gron, and from there to the megalithic monument at Nant-y-maen. Local tradition has cast this fosse in the role of a road that continued beyond Maes-llyn Lake to the coast near Llanrhystud,[56] though its character is consistent with that of an early boundary of some importance. A good example of the way in which ditches were used by local communities to supplement natural watercourses is provided by the boundary of Trefilan parish where both the Wallen and Wion brooks (today known as Nant Rhiwafallen and Nant Bwlch y Werne) appear to have been artificially extended by the digging of ditches, thus establishing a water-based 'stay' of boundary for virtually all of

[53] The early field pattern of the area is best examined through the magnificent survey by T. Lewis in 1791 of the Llanfair Clydogau and Llanddewibrefi property of Thos. Johnes: NLW, Map Collection, vol. 26.

[54] J. Leland, *The Itinerary of John Leland in or about the years 1535–1543*, ed. L. T. Smith, III (London, 1964), 51.

[55] A. Owen, *Ancient Laws and Institutes of Wales*, 525.

[56] D. C. Rees, *Tregaron: Historical and Antiquarian*, 73–4.

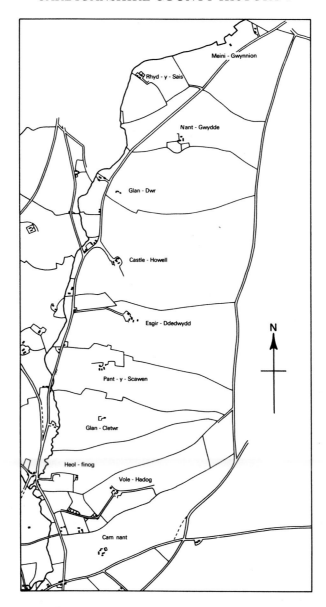

Fig. 67: Landholding along the Cletwr Fach: based on NLW Tithe Map, parish of Llandyssil, 1841.

Trefilan's bounds. In view of the antiquity of Trefilan as a territorial unit,[57] these extensions may well date back to pre-Conquest times.

One way of establishing early patterns of landholding and settlement is to reconstruct the layout of early charter grants in the landscape. This approach can be demonstrated by reference to the farms which lie along the Cletwr Fach. As Figure 67 shows, the farms along the east bank —Healfeinog, Pantscawen, Esgair-ddedwydd, Castell Howell, Glandŵr and Nantygwyddau

[57]It is referred to in medieval documents: see M. Rhys (ed.), *Ministers' Accounts for West Wales, 1277–1306*, Part I (Cymmrodorion Record Series, vol. XIII; London, 1936).

—have the appearance of having been laid out at the same time. Each has the Cletwr Fach at its foot and each runs to the boundary of Llandysul parish, the latter being formed by a fairly straight and well-entrenched lane that conceivably began life as a boundary ditch. This seemingly planned appearance is crucial because at least two of these farms—Moel Ehedog and Rhyd Owen—were held by Talley Grange.[58] Given their location, it seems unlikely that the monks of Talley pioneered them when they first received possession in the twelfth century. It is more likely that these farms existed before the twelfth century. What makes this an appealing interpretation is that, opposite Glandŵr, the farm of Gwaralltferdre may have been the *maerdref* for a cluster of settlements that stretched along the Cletwr Fach.

A form of field evidence that can be more reliably dated are the various standing stones inscribed in Latin or Ogam or bearing early Christian motifs. Some are clearly memorial stones, though whether they were originally erected as gravestones is unclear for many have been removed from their original location. Others may mark places of worship and prayer. One stone of particular interest is that from Llanllŷr, dated to the fifth or sixth century, the inscription of which records how Occon, the son of Asaitgen, gave Madomnuac the waste plot of Ditoc.[59] In Ireland inscribed stones of this same period served not only as memorials but as estate boundary markers, burial on the boundary of an estate being thought to invest it, and hence the owner, with inalienable rights.[60] An interesting subgroup in the County are those which betray more direct Irish influence, recognizable either by the use of Irish personal names or Ogam. Two examples of the former exist at Llanllŷr and Llanddewibrefi, and two of the latter at Llannarth and Rhuddlan.

The place-name evidence

Place-names have considerable potential for the study of early society and its settlements. Three types of information may be derived from them; firstly, the influence of the major cultural groups, secondly, the character or status of a particular settlement, and thirdly, the chronology of settlement.

The current view is that Goidelic place-name elements in Wales are to be ascribed to the settlement of Irish-speaking groups during the fifth and sixth centuries AD. Though northern Cardiganshire was less affected by this settlement,[61] the evidence of standing stones testifies that Irish was spoken in Dyfed up to the close of the sixth century, and the probability is that the Irish in Wales remained in contact with their Irish kinsmen as late as the mid-eighth century.[62] It follows, therefore, that Irish place-name elements may be expected to have survived from this contact phase. The distribution of the element *cnwc* or *cnwch*, derived from the Irish word for hill,

[58]H. Owen (ed.), *The Description of Pembrokeshire*, part IV, 458.

[59]R. A. S. Macalister, 'The sculptured stones of Cardiganshire', *TCAS*, 5 (1927), 7–20 (pp. 10–11), and M. Richards, 'The Irish settlements in south-west Wales', 142.

[60]T. M. Charles-Edwards, 'Boundaries in Irish Law', *Medieval Settlement*, ed. P. H. Sawyer (London, 1976), 83–90 (pp. 84–5). Similarly, the Welsh Laws refer to stones and water-courses as preserving boundaries.

[61]M. Richards, 'The Irish settlements in south-west Wales', 133–62.

[62]I. Ll. Foster, 'The emergence of Wales', *Prehistoric and Early Wales*, ed. I. Ll. Foster and G. Daniel, 213–35 (p. 219).

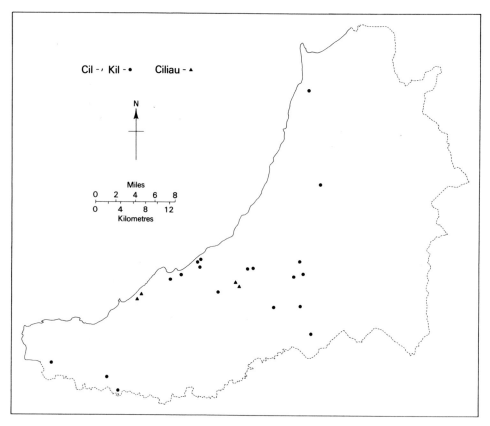

Fig. 68: Distribution of place-name element *cil-*, *kil-*, *ciliau-*.

has been discussed by Richards.[63] Apart from a scattering along the Teifi, Wyre and Ystwyth, they occur in a broad belt along the coast from Cardigan to the mouth of the Wyre, in some of the best farming land in the County. Only the Vale of Aeron seems deficient in examples, though there is quite a concentration towards its mouth. Although the writer has found other examples as far north as Genau'r-glyn, these do not materially alter the basic pattern.

The distribution of other Irish place-name elements is not so revealing. The element *loch*, for instance, is thought to be of Irish origin, but it occurs only once in the County in Lochdyn, near Llangrannog.[64] Another element, the Irish connections of which still have to be affirmed, is of *cil-* or *kil-*,[65] signifying in Irish a church or cell though in Wales commonly understood to denote a nook or narrow way. When mapped (Fig. 68), the distribution of *cil-* or *kil-* elements certainly overlaps with *cnwc*, *cnwch*, but *cil-*, *kil-* elements are better represented in the Vale of Aeron and have a slightly greater presence north of the Rheidol. Another relevant place-name element is that of *gwyddel*, a Welsh word signifying Irishman, which occurs at a number of locations—for example Waun y Gwyddel, a mile north of Elerch, and Coed y Gwyddel at Llandre. A small

---

[63]M. Richards, art. cit., 148; cf. M. H. Jones, 'Some of the historical associations of Penllyn', *TCAS*, 5 (1927), 37–47 (p. 41).
[64]M. Richards, art. cit., 149.
[65]For a comparative view of how *Cil-* or *Kil-* were introduced by the Irish into Brythonic-speaking south-west Scotland during the fourth to sixth centuries, see W. H. L. Nicolaisen, 'Gaelic place-names in southern Scotland', *Studia Celtica*, 5 (1970), 15–35.

cluster of examples is also to be found in the upper reaches of the Teifi, with several farms called Llwyn y Gwyddel. On the coast Wig y Gwyddel occurs near Aberystwyth, and a Cefn Gwyddel near New Quay. How we interpret these *gwyddel* place-names, though, is a matter for debate. Some may genuinely reflect early Irish settlements[66] but others may indicate the presence much later of itinerant Irish farm-workers.[67]

Some place-name elements can be linked to the socio-legal context of early settlement. Township names which doubled as *gwestfa* names (Llan-non or Cilcennin), those prefixed by the element *randir* (*Rhandir Ceven Meirig* or *Rhandir Lhwyn y maen*), and those which incorporated the elements *maerdref* or *llys*, are obvious examples. To these, we might add the element *hendref*. This has been interpreted as meaning not just an 'old settlement', but the original focus of settlement for a particular *gwely* or lineage, the point from which their proprietary rights sprang. As these proprietary rights became extended through a number of townships or *rhandiroedd*, it was only natural that a name like *Hendref* should have been conferred upon the original focus of the *gwelyau*. Thus in Cardiganshire there is a Hendre Rhys (Llanilar), Hendre Philip (Llanfair Clydogau) and a Hendre Lewis (Llangrannog). Another element of interest is that of *pentref*, literally 'township end', the meaning of which has been interpreted as the part of a township occupied by bondmen.[68] Concerning freemen, the element *rhyd* is commonly interpreted as 'ford', but when combined with a personal name—as in the case of Rhyd Lewis, Rhyd Owen or Rhyd Merionydd—there is a strong case for arguing that it signifies a freeholding. Even where a personal name is not involved, *rhyd* often occurs in situations where there is no adjacent ford. Because of these interpretative problems no attempt has been made to exclude those examples which may, therefore, mean ford when mapping the element *rhyd* (Fig. 69). Their pattern shows few examples in the south-west but a sizeable number occur in the parishes of Llandysul, Llanwenog, Llannarth and Llandysiliogogo, in the upper Teifi, along the Vale of Aeron, and north to the Dyfi.

Other place-name elements which may also be linked to early settlement are *llan* and *tre* or *tref*. Although primarily associated with early ecclesiastical sites, *llan* is also incorporated in the names of scattered farmsteads, its original meaning being an enclosure, whether secular or religious. There is no doubt that many *llan* settlements date back at least to the immediate post-Roman era. Some secular examples may be even earlier. When mapped, *llan* names show a fairly wide scatter (Fig. 69), but with relatively few along the coast from Cardigan to the mouth of the Wyre or north of the Ystwyth. Those along the lower reaches of the Teifi include some which put the defining element first and *llan* second, an inversion which may conceivably indicate Irish influence. Further north, a number of examples can be seen strung out along either side of the Vale of Aeron (rather than within it) linking up eventually with those around the upper Teifi. Equally diagnostic is the element *tref*, *tre* or *dre*. Originally meaning 'family', it eventually came to signify 'township'. A possible measure of its antiquity is the fact that it was used as a

---

[66]The *Tref y Gwyddel*, described as one of the 'more eminent places' in the confirmation charter of 1184 for the lands of Strata Florida, is clearly a genuine early name.

[67]See on this, with reference not only to Irish agricultural labourers but also to Irish influence on the numeration system of these south Welsh areas, D. Greene, 'The Irish numerals in Cardiganshire', *Studia Celtica*, X/XI (1975/6), 305–11.

[68]E. Jones, 'Settlement patterns in the middle Teifi Valley', *Geography*, 30 (1945), 109–10.

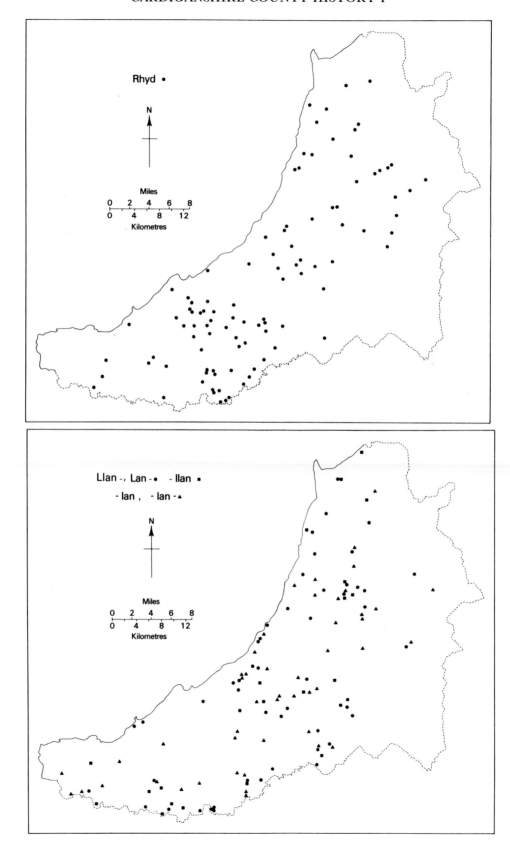

Fig. 69: i. Distribution of place-name element *rhyd*, ii. Distribution of place-name element *llan-, lan-, -llan*.

place-name prefix in south-west Britain, Cumbria and southern Scotland, a distribution which suggests that it was used prior to the political fragmentation of the British West in the centuries following the Anglo-Saxon invasions. Like other early elements, a fair number in Cardiganshire are combined with personal names, such as Tre Taliesin or Treddafydd. The most notable feature of its distribution in the County is the concentration in the south-west, around Cardigan, but lesser groupings occur along the Teifi and Aeron and north of the Rheidol. (Fig. 70).

This discussion of early society and economy has necessarily been suggestive rather than conclusive. The inadequacy of data prevents it from being otherwise. The overall impression gained is of a settled, sedentary society, not a nomadic one. As with other parts of Wales, early sources suggest that the County was organized into a hierarchy of territorial units—*cantrefi, cymydau* and *maenorau*—though there is no way of knowing exactly when each scale of unit took shape. As regards landholding and settlement, the dominant themes of the post-Roman period appear to have been those of fission in respect of landholding and expansion in respect of settlement. Initially, landholding probably involved large estates, embracing a number of settlements. As time went by, partible inheritance produced smaller and smaller estates. This was not a uniform process. Kings and nobles managed to expand their estates, at the same time as they enhanced

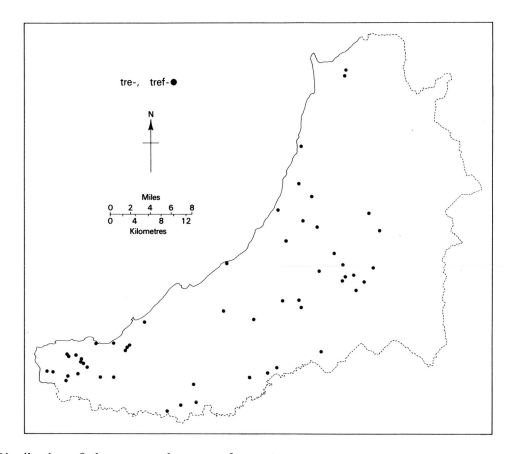

Fig. 70: Distribution of place-name element *tref-, tre-*.

their status. But no matter how slowly, the bulk of estates must have become smaller through partition, such that by the end of our period we can expect individual townships to have been divided between more than one estate or *gwely*. By this point, though, the fissioning of *gwelyau* into new *gwelyau* had virtually come to an end. Our insight into bondmen is less satisfactory. It is doubtful whether questions about their numerical importance or the amount of land which they occupied can be answered definitively using Cardiganshire material. Yet there can be no doubting their importance during the early Middle Ages. Because of their differences in tenure and landholding, the distinction between freemen and bondmen greatly affected their impact on landscape. But whether they were bond or free, we can expect the settlement associated with them to have expanded over the early Middle Ages. Even allowing for a substantial continuity of farm-sites and fields from late prehistory down into the historic period, and admitting the possibility that the County may have shared the sharp reduction in population that seems to have affected other parts of Britain during the sixth and seventh centuries AD, we can expect that, overall, the early Middle Ages saw large amounts of woodland and waste cleared, new fields pioneered and new farmsteads created. In terms of how much was achieved in these terms alone, the period can lay strong claim to being a formative one in Cardiganshire's history.

Plate XXIV: Tregaron: churchyard. (*Crown copyright RCAHM*
(*Wales*)).

Plate XXIII: Tregaron: churchyard.
(*Crown copyright RCAHM* (*Wales*)).

Plate XXII: Llanwnnws: churchyard.
(*Crown copyright RCAHM* (*Wales*)).

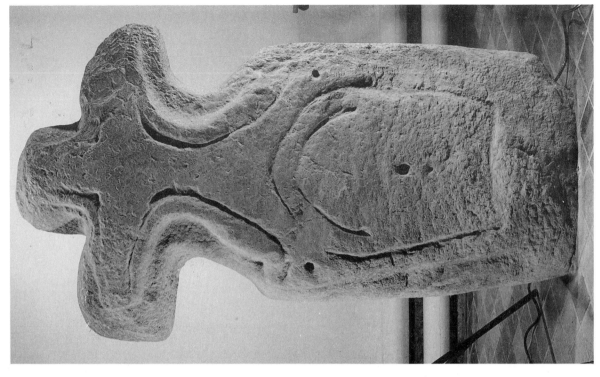

Plate XXVI: Llanbadarn Fawr: churchyard. (*Crown copyright RCAHM (Wales)*).

Plate XXV: Llannarth: churchyard. (*Crown copyright RCAHM (Wales)*).

Plate XXIX: Cribyn, Llanfihangel Ystrad. (*Crown copyright RCAHM (Wales)*).

Plate XXVIII: Llanddewi Aber-arth: church. (*Crown copyright RCAHM (Wales)*).

Plate XXVII: Llanddewi Aber-arth: church. (*Crown copyright RCAHM (Wales)*).

Plate XXXI: Silian: churchyard (rear). (*Crown copyright RCAHM (Wales)*).

Plate XXX: Silian: churchyard (front). (*Crown copyright RCAHM (Wales)*).

CHAPTER 7

THE CHURCH IN CEREDIGION IN THE EARLY MIDDLE AGES

a. THE COMING OF CHRISTIANITY

D. P. Kirby

WHEN Augustine and his companions arrived in Kent from Rome in 597 a pagan Germanic hinterland stretched far to the north and west. Augustine had been daunted by the immensity of the task facing him and had nearly abandoned his mission. Papal encouragement drove him on but another factor may have been the knowledge that beyond the Germanic pagans to the west the clergy of the Christian Britons could be brought under his authority as archbishop and the ecclesiastical unity of the province of Britain re-established.[1] The Church in Rome believed the Britons to be living in accordance with the customs of the Catholic Church[2] and there is no doubt that Pope Gregory the Great intended that Augustine should exercise authority as archbishop over the Britons. 'We commit to you, my brother', he told him, 'all the bishops of Britain.'[3]

Such was the context for the meeting or meetings between Augustine and the British bishops at 'Augustine's Oak' in Anglo-Saxon territory bordering the Bristol Channel about the year 600. The only source for these conferences is the well-known account by Bede in which Augustine, by his seemingly intolerant and arrogant conduct (not least in his remaining seated in the presence of British bishops), so alienated the British clergy that they refused to accept him as archbishop or to join with him in preaching to the Anglo-Saxons.[4] This story quite vividly illustrates some of the issues in dispute in Bede's time between the British clergy and the church of Canterbury —differences over the dating of Easter and in the performance of the rite of baptism, and a refusal to submit to the authority of the archbishop of Canterbury—which must have been present at 'Augustine's Oak' at least in embryonic form and which were cumulatively deeply disturbing to both sides.

It must not be thought that all the Britons felt equally strongly about these differences. Some

---

[1] P. Wormald, 'Bede, *Bretwaldas* and the origins of *Gens Anglorum*', *Ideal and Reality in Frankish and Anglo-Saxon Society: Studies presented to J. M. Wallace-Hadrill*, ed. P. Wormald (Oxford, 1983), 99–129 (p. 124).
[2] *Bede's Ecclesiastical History of the English People*, ed. B. Colgrave and R. A. B. Mynors (Oxford, 1969), 146–7 (II, 4).
[3] Ibid., 88–9 (I, 27).
[4] Ibid., 134–43 (II,2). See on this episode, N. K. Chadwick, 'The battle of Chester: a study of sources', *Celt and Saxon: Studies in the Early British Border*, ed. N. K. Chadwick (Cambridge, 1963), 167–85. H. Mayr-Harting, *The Coming of Christianity to Anglo-Saxon England* (London, 1972), 72, thinks that elements in the story 'may originally have come from the British themselves'.

British bishops did consort with Anglo-Saxon clergy. Two of them assisted one Saxon bishop at the consecration of the Northumbrian Chad among the western Saxons in the mid-660s. In the 760s, as the Welsh annals record, Bishop Elfoddw championed acceptance by the Britons of the Roman Easter, imposed on the churches in Wales in 768. On the other hand, there can be no doubt about the strength of feeling in some circles. Aldhelm, abbot of Malmesbury, writing to Geraint, king of Dumnonia, in the late seventh or early eighth century, alleges that the clergy of *Demetia* on the other side of the Severn (apparently referring to south Wales as a whole rather than specifically to Dyfed) refused to have communion with Anglo-Saxon clergy and obliged anyone visiting them from English regions to undergo penance for forty days; he reveals that, because the Britons did not observe Roman rites—he mentions specifically the British rejection of the Petrine tonsure—nor keep (at that time) the Roman Easter, they were seen as placing themselves outside the Catholic Church.[5] Such men were not in harmony with the Catholic faith and could be seen as schismatics, so that Aldhelm could say, 'he who does not follow the teaching and rule of St Peter boasts vainly and idly about his Catholic Faith'.[6]

There were probably Christians in Wales long before Christianity became the official religion of the Roman Empire in the course of the fourth century. Julius and Aaron were two Christians who were martyred at Caerleon, probably in the mid-third century.[7] In the mid-fifth century the Romano-British Church was also in close contact with the Church in Gaul and leaders of the Gallic Church had intervened in Britain to suppress the Pelagian heresy which found support among some of the Britons.[8] 'Not only a British Church in contact with Gaul but an orthodox one triumphing over heresy' is how Dr Charles Thomas describes the Church in Britain in the mid-fifth century.[9] Though some areas in western Britain may well have remained pagan into the fifth century, with others only semi-Christianized, the earliest memorials of the Church in Wales, the inscribed stones from the late fifth century and the sixth on which occur the terms *sacerdos* (normally in this period signifying 'bishop') and *presbiter* ('priest'), suggest that Christianity was 'the accepted official religion of a stable kind of society' in fifth-century Wales.[10] Stones with Irish inscriptions and Christian symbols, having close connections with Christian sites in west Wales, indicate that many of the Irish immigrants, if not Christian when they reached Wales, were converted soon after.[11] The memorial stone of Vortepor, for example, stood in the

[5]*Aldhelmi Opera*, ed. R Ehwald (MGH Auct.Antiq., 15 : Berlin, 1909), 480 ff. (cf. *Councils and Ecclesiastical Documents of Great Britain and Ireland*, ed. A. W. Haddan and W. Stubbs, III (Oxford, 1871), 268 ff.); trans. M. Lapidge and M. Herren, *Aldhelm: The Prose Works* (Ipswich, 1979), 155ff.

[6]M. Lapidge and M. Herren, op.cit., 160; cf. *The Life of Bishop Wilfrid by Eddius Stephanus*, ed. B. Colgrave (Cambridge, 1927), chapter 5.

[7]C. Thomas, *Christianity in Roman Britain to AD 500* (London, 1981), 48.

[8]E. A. Thompson, *Saint Germanus of Auxerre and the End of Roman Britain* (Studies in Celtic History VI: Woodbridge, 1984).

[9]C. Thomas, *Christianity in Roman Britain*, 59. But see also now for the possible absence of a coherent doctrinal tradition in Britain in the early fifth century, R. A. Markus, 'Pelagianism: Britain and the Continent', *J. Eccles.Hist.*, 37 (1986), 191–204.

[10]W. H. Davies, 'The Church in Wales', *Christianity in Britain 300–700*, ed. M. W. Barley and R. P. C. Hanson (Leicester, 1968), 131–50 (p. 137).

[11]Melville Richards, 'The Irish settlements in south-west Wales', *JRSAI*, 90 (1960), 133–62 (p. 144); cf. C. Thomas, 'The Irish settlements in post-Roman Western Britain: a survey of the evidence', *J. Royal Institute of Cornwall* (1972), 251–74 (pp. 258–60).

churchyard of Castelldwyran. There were Christian communities in Ireland by 431[12] and the mission of Patrick, who came from western Britain, to the Irish in the course of the fifth century is generally considered to have been directed from Britain.[13]

With the Anglo-Saxon invasions ecclesiastical organization in lowland Britain disintegrated but the derivation of the not uncommon place-name in England, Eccles, from Latin *ecclesia* through a Primitive Welsh *egles*, indicates a spread of churches in the late Roman period in the areas which passed under the control of the Anglo-Saxons.[14] There is no reason to suppose that a comparable disruption of ecclesiastical communities occurred in western Britain in this period as a consequence of Irish attack. Here, early church foundations were not obliterated. It used to be thought that a Gallic connection revitalized the Christian communities of western Britain, if not actually re-establishing Christianity in many areas,[15] but such a hypothesis is probably unnecessary. There certainly did exist in these centuries what had been described as 'a long-lived straggling sea trade' in the Irish Sea between the Continent and the British Isles, demonstrated by the imported pottery from Gaul and the Mediterranean which is so characteristic a feature of the western seaboard in this period.[16] This trade, however, is now seen as having brought ideas rather than Gallic missionaries,[17] leading not to a process of reconversion but to the development first in Gaul and then in Britain of a monasticism, commonly thought to have been of south-Gallic type, perhaps derived ultimately from the Egyptian practices of the Desert Fathers and characterized by a combination of communal and eremetical activity.[18]

[12]D. N. Dumville, 'Some British aspects of the earliest Irish Christianity', *Irland und Europa: Ireland and Europe: Die Kirche im frühmittelalter: The Early Church*, ed. Ní Chatháin and M. Richter (Stuttgart, 1984), 16–25.

[13]R. P. C. Hanson, *St Patrick: His Origins and Career* (Oxford, 1968) and C. Thomas, *Christianity in Roman Britain*, 295 ff. See also now, however, E. A. Thompson, *Who was Saint Patrick?* (Woodbridge, 1985).

[14]K. Cameron, 'Eccles in English place-names', *Christianity in Britain, 300–700*, ed. Barley and Hanson, 87–92.

[15]V. E. Nash-Williams, *The Early Christian Monuments of Wales* (Cardiff, 1950); E. G. Bowen, *Saints, Seaways and Settlements* (Cardiff, 1969).

[16]L. Alcock, *Arthur's Britain* (London, 1971), 197 ff.; L. Laing, *The Archaeology of Late Celtic Britain and Ireland c. 400–1200 AD* (London, 1975), 268 ff.; and C. Thomas, 'East and West: Tintagel, Mediterranean imports and the early insular Church', *The Early Medieval Church in Western Britain and Ireland*, ed. S. M. Pearce (BAR British Series 102, 1982), 17–34. See also now C. Thomas, '"Gallici Nautae de Galliarum Provinciis"—a sixth/seventh-century trade with Gaul, reconsidered', *Medieval Archaeology*, 34 (1990), 1–26.

[17]C. Thomas, *Christianity in Roman Britain*, 268 ff., and cf. 'East and West: Tintagel', 30–1.

[18]Cf. G. MacGinty, 'The influence of the desert fathers on Irish monasticism', *Monastic Studies*, 14 (1983), 85–91. For reviews of monastic developments in the Mediterranean and west Europe, with specific concern for the origins of Celtic monasticism, see J. Ryan, *Irish Monasticism* (Dublin, 1931), 52 ff., and, more briefly, N. K. Chadwick, *The Age of the Saints in the Early Celtic Church* (London, 1961), 35 ff. Much of what has been written about the earliest monasticism of the Celtic areas, however, will need qualifying in the light of further study. The surest guide is the corpus of Irish monastic Rules (cf. Ryan, *Irish Monasticism*, 194–5 and J. F. Kenney, *Sources for the Early History of Ireland* I, *Ecclesiastical* (Columbia, 1929: reprinted New York, 1966), 315, 472–5), but most of these are probably no earlier than the ninth century. One exception is the Rule of Columbanus (G. M. Walker (ed.), *Sancti Columbani Opera* (Dublin, 1957), 122 ff.). Cf., on early Irish rules, V. O. Maidin, 'The Monastic Rules of Ireland', *Cistercian Studies*, 15 (1980), 24–38, and E. de Bhaldraithe, 'Obedience: the doctrine of the Irish Monastic Rules', *Monastic Studies*, 14 (1983), 63–84 (pp. 71–2). For some general comments see C. Evans, 'The Celtic Church in Anglo-Saxon times', *The Anglo-Saxons: Synthesis and Achievement*, ed. J. D. Woods and D. A. E. Pelteret (Waterloo, 1985), 77–92 (pp. 80–1).

Monastic centres had been established by the time Gildas wrote the *De Excidio Britanniae*. Maelgwn, king of Gwynedd in the early sixth century, spent some time in a monastery and Gildas was consulted by a certain Vinnian on the subject of monks who left their monastery to seek a stricter discipline elsewhere.[19] But Maelgwn had been taught originally by a distinguished 'magister elegans', signifying probably a rhetorician, and the evidence of Gildas's Latin suggests that Gildas was also first and foremost the product of professional rhetorical training.[20] The possible survival of traditional Roman schools in Britain into the later fifth century indicates that the new monasticism was introduced into a society still far from divorced from its Romano-British antecedents. The whole tone of Gildas's *De Excidio* and his use of Old Latin versions of the Scriptures 'presupposes a continuous history of Christianity reaching well back into Roman Britain'.[21] This is confirmed by the evidence of pre-Norman Welsh manuscripts which give some indications of an extremely archaic and conservative tradition stretching back probably into the fifth century[22] (a pre-Gregorian liturgy, for example, was still in use in Wales in the ninth century).[23] That the British Church in western Britain derived essentially from the Church of Roman Britain, therefore, has been the conclusion of a number of scholars who would accept J. C. Toynbee's description of the 'Celtic Church' as 'thoroughly Roman in creed and origin; Roman too, initially, in its organization and practice'.[24] Despite evidence for a 'British background to Irish Christianity',[25] however, how far or for how long the organization and practice of the Irish Church reflected that of the Church in Wales in the early Middle Ages remains a major unresolved problem of the ecclesiastical history of these regions.[26] Even within Wales there are likely to have been 'considerable differences in the nature of ecclesiastical organization from one part of the country to another',[27] (between, for example, the possibly more precocious

---

[19]R. Sharpe, 'Gildas as a Father of the Church', *Gildas: New Approaches*, ed. M. Lapidge and D. Dumville (Woodbridge, 1984), 193–205 (pp. 196 ff.); on Vinnian, see D. N. Dumville, 'Gildas and Uinniau', ibid., 201–14. See also now M. W. Herren, 'Gildas and early British monasticism', *Britain 400–600: Language and History*, ed. A. Bammesberger and A. Wollmann (Heidelberg, 1990), 65–78.

[20]M. Lapidge, 'Gildas's education and the Latin culture of sub-Roman Britain', *Gildas: New Approaches*, 27–50.

[21]W. H. Davies, 'The Church in Wales', 140.

[22]D. N. Dumville, 'Some British aspects of the earliest Irish Christianity', p. 23.

[23]M. Lapidge, 'Latin learning in Dark Age Wales: some prolegomena', *Proc.of the Seventh International Congress of Celtic Studies*, ed. D. Ellis Evans *et al.* (Oxford, 1986), 91–107.

[24]J. C. Toynbee, 'Christianity in Roman Britain', *JBAA*, 16 (1953), 1–24. Cf. also P. A. Wilson, 'Romano-British and Welsh Christianity: continuity or discontinuity?', *WHR*, 3 (1966), 5–21, 103–20, and C. Thomas, *Christianity in Roman Britain*, 274, 347 ff. W. F. Frend, 'Ecclesia Britannica: prelude or dead end?', *J. Eccles. Hist.*, 30 (1979), 129–44, however, and more recently 'Roman-British Christianity in the West: comparison and contrast', *The Early Church in Western Britain and Ireland*, ed. S. M. Pearce, 5–13, continued to doubt whether 'The Celtic Church of the late fifth and sixth centuries' was 'a direct heir to that of Roman Britain' (p. 11).

[25]Ibid., 93.

[26]Cf. H. Pryce, 'Church and society in Wales, 1150–1250: an Irish perspective', *The British Isles 1100–1500: Comparisons, Contrasts and Connections*, ed. R. R. Davies (Edinburgh, 1988), 27–47 (p. 29).

[27]R. R. Davies, *Conquest, Coexistence and Change: Wales 1063-1415* (Oxford, 1987), 173. See also now W. Davies, 'The myth of the Celtic Church', *The Early Church in Wales and the West*, ed. N. Edwards and A. Jane (Oxbow Monograph 16, Oxford, 1992), 12–21.

south-east and the more remote north-west, or the south-west where Irish settlement had occurred).

The hope that saints' *Lives* would yield information about monastic founders in the sixth century in the 'age of the saints' has largely faded. Welsh saints' *Lives* were mostly compiled at the time of Norman reconstruction of the Church in Wales, six hundred years after the traditional 'age of the saints'. The *Life* of St David by Rhygyfarch is the oldest of these late *Lives* and it belongs to the 1080s or 1090s.[28] Consequently, there is generally very little of historical value concerning the sixth century in these compositions. The twelfth-century *Life* of St Carannog, reputed founder of the Ceredigion church of Llangrannog, for example, has been described as 'based on dedications linked together by legendary motifs',[29] and in the *Life* of Cadog of Llancarfan, written by Lifris, probably in the 1090s, 'the emphasis is on the status and importance of Llancarfan rather than on the "historical" Cadog'.[30] A saint's *Life* took the oral tradition of the saint's cult and the property rights of the monastery and set them in the framework of a devotional image of the saint as founder figure,[31] not least for purposes of liturgical celebration. Unfortunately, even the oral tradition which was preserved in this form was invariably 'abbreviated, enfeebled and but half-understood'.[32] Similarly, the belief that a map of churches dedicated to a particular saint 'is likely to represent those churches and chapels whose sites were originally associated with a settlement made by the particular itinerant saint whose name they bear'[33] has been abandoned. Dedications cannot be shown to be contemporaneous with specific saints and are most likely to be a later and secondary feature.[34] It is not possible, therefore, to view the dedication of certain churches to Padarn, for example, as reflecting the movements of an original historic Padarn.[35]

[28]For the most recent discussion of the date of the *Life* of David, see *The Welsh Life of St David*, ed. D. Simon Evans (Cardiff, 1988), xxv–xxxi (Professor Evans favouring 1081–5). See also, below, n. 59.

[29]L. Olson, 'Crantock, Cornwall, as an early monastic site', *The Early Church in Western Britain and Ireland*, ed. S. M. Pearce, 177–85 (p. 177). On Carannog, see also P. Ó Riain, 'The saints of Cardiganshire', II, ch. 7.c.

[30]J. K. Knight, 'Sources for the early history of Morgannwg', *Glamorgan County History* II, ed. H. N. Savory (Cardiff, 1984), 387.

[31]See the writings of P. Ó Riain, 'Towards a methodology in early Irish hagiography', *Peritia*, 1 (1982), 146–59, 'St Finbarr: a study in a cult', *J. Cork Hist. and Arch. Soc.*, 82 (1977), 63–82, and 'Cainnech *alias* Colum Cille, patron of Ossory', *Folia Gadelica*, ed. P.de Brun *et al.* (Cork, 1983), 30–5. Of particular relevance to Wales is idem, 'The Irish element in Welsh hagiographic tradition', *Irish Antiquity*, ed. D. Ó Corráin (Cork, 1981), 291–303, and also below, idem, 'The saints of Cardiganshire', II.ch.7.c. See also now J. M. H. Smith, 'Oral and written: saints, miracles and relics in Brittany, *c*. 850–1250', *Speculum*, 65 (1990), 309–43 (which includes valuable observations on Welsh saints' cults and hagiography, especially pp.388 ff.). See also on property rights, W. Davies, 'Property rights and property claims in Welsh "Vitae" of the eleventh century', *Hagiographie cultures et sociétés IVe–XIIe siècles* (Actes du Colloque organisé à Nanterre et à Paris, 1979) (Études Augustiniennes, Paris, 1981), 515–33.

[32]K. Hughes, *Celtic Britain in the Early Middle Ages* (Studies in Celtic History II: Woodbridge, 1980), 60.

[33]E. G. Bowen, *Settlement of Celtic Saints in Britain* (Cardiff, 1954), 3.

[34]See O. Chadwick, 'The evidence of dedications in the early history of the Welsh Church', *Studies in Early British History*, ed. N. K. Chadwick (Cambridge, 1955), 173–84, and more recently N. Yates, 'The "Age of the Saints" in Carmarthenshire: a study of Church dedications', *Carms. Antiq.*, 9 (1973), 53–81. Cf. W. Davies, *Wales in the Early Middle Ages* (Leicester, 1982), 146, and note that the dedication patterns do not even exclusively represent properties of the main house, ibid., 162–3. Cf. also, M. Lloyd Jones, *Society and Settlement in Wales and the Marches*, 2 vols. (BAR 121, 1984), ii, 273–5.

[35]On Padarn, see also P. Ó Riain, 'The saints of Cardiganshire', II.ch.7.c.

The British Church was no longer regarded as Catholic in the seventh century. Why not? It had clearly emerged in isolation from developments at Rome across the intervening period. The use of old-fashioned Easter tables demonstrates this. So does papal ignorance of the character of the British Church before Augustine's encounter with its leaders at 'Augustine's Oak'.[36] The Church on the Continent had retained the urban-based organization of the late Roman world. The Church in British territories, on the other hand, appears to have lost any association it may once have had with the few urban centres of western Britain. There is no evidence for bishops of Caerwent, for example, in the early Middle Ages. Bishops, however, continued to dominate the Church in British territories. Indeed, bishops were absolutely essential to the maintenance of pastoral activity and the ordering of religious life among the laity. They ordained priests and consecrated churches and generally supervised the ecclesiastical life of the communities over which they possessed jurisdiction. 'Gildas's church is definitely run by bishops and priests', wrote Dr Kathleen Hughes.[37] With the advent of the Normans, the diocesan boundaries of the twelfth century were drawn roughly to conform with the boundaries of the eleventh-century Welsh kingdoms—Bangor (Gwynedd), St Asaph (Powys), St David's (Deheubarth) and Llandaff (Morgannwg)[38]—but not all of these bishoprics necessarily had a continuous history from the post-Roman period to the Norman invasion (Llandaff, for example, may have been of very recent origin). Nor was there only one bishop for each Welsh kingdom before the arrival of the Normans. A legal tract on the bishop-houses of Dyfed, probably dating to the early tenth century, numbers them as seven, one for each of the seven cantrefs of Dyfed.[39] Interestingly, Bede says that seven British bishops were involved in the discussions at 'Augustine's Oak'. The *Anglo-Saxon Chronicle* A records in 914 the capture by the Vikings of Cyfeiliog, bishop of Archenfield or Erging. Archenfield was a region, probably of late or sub-Roman origin (its name derives from the Roman settlement of *Ariconium*), subsequently absorbed into Gwent,[40] in which enlarged kingdom the bishop of Erging will have been only one among several episcopal leaders.[41] It is evident, therefore, that there was a multiplicity of bishops in early Wales. Among them was the bishop of Llanbadarn. Ieuan ap Sulien, writing at Llanbadarn Fawr in the late eleventh century, refers to Llanbadarn as 'a high city where the holy bishop Padarn led an outstanding life'.[42] As

---

[36]See also J. Stephenson, 'The liturgy and ritual of the Celtic Churches', introduction to F. E. Warren, *The Liturgy and Ritual of the Celtic Church* (2nd edn., by J. Stephenson: Woodbridge, 1987), xi–cxxviii.

[37]K. Hughes, 'The Celtic Church: is this a valid concept?', *Cambridge Medieval Studies* I (1981), 1–20 (p. 3) (reprinted K. Hughes, *Church and Society in Ireland AD 400–1200*, ed. D. Dumville (Variorum Reprints: London, 1987)).

[38]Cf. A. Hamilton Thompson, 'The Welsh medieval dioceses', *J. Hist. Soc. of the Church in Wales*, I (1947), 91–111; *Episcopal Acts and Cognate Documents Relating to Welsh Dioceses 1066–1271*, ed. J. Conway Davies, 2 vols. (Historical Society of the Church in Wales, 1946, 1948), I, 38 ff., and G. Williams, *The Welsh Church from the Conquest to the Reformation* (Cardiff, 1976), 2 ff.

[39]T. M. Charles-Edwards, 'The seven bishop houses of Dyfed', *BBCS*, 24 (1971), 247–72.

[40]W. Davies, *An Early Welsh Microcosm: Studies in the Llandaff Charters* (London, 1978), 93–4.

[41]On the bishops of south-east Wales, see W. Davies, *An Early Welsh Microcosm*, 139 ff.

[42]M. Lapidge, 'The Welsh-Latin poetry of Sulien's family', *Studia Celtica*, 8/9 (1973–4), 68–106 (pp. 84–5). On the monastic city, see L. A. S. Butler, '"The monastic city" in Wales: myth or reality', *BBCS*, 28 (1978–80), 458–67 (but note Wyn Evans's words of caution in *BBCS*, 31 (1984), 323), and on the classification of early Christian sites, L. Laing, *The Archaeology of Late Celtic Britain and Ireland*, 377 ff.

late as 1188 the people of Llanbadarn remembered that bishops had resided there, and even that one of them had been murdered by the men of Llanbadarn.[43]

There is some evidence to suggest that, perhaps as early as the first years of the fourth century, metropolitan bishops, each based on a metropolis or centre of a province, with authority over the other bishops in that province, directed the affairs of the Church.[44] Such a development would be in keeping with the practice of the Church on the Continent. The metropolitan bishop for the province of *Britannia Prima*, which embraced Wales, was probably that of Cirencester,[45] a town captured by the Saxons in the late sixth century but which had probably ceased to be the administrative centre of an ecclesiastical province some time before. No other metropolitan was immediately established for the bishops of the British west, and the emergence of the kingdoms of early Wales further fractured any concept of a single ecclesiastical province. It must be stressed that what we describe as the British Church in the early Middle Ages was in reality several Churches, each circumscribed to a degree by the political configuration of the kingdom of which it was a part. In the resulting decentralized world of the Church in sixth-century Wales, it is highly probable that there were irregularities in the ordering of ecclesiastical life. The same situation prevailed in Ireland where, again, no metropolitan had oversight of ecclesiastical affairs and a multitude of bishops existed independently of one another.[46] Certainly, at a time of concern with Catholic orthodoxy, the missionaries of the Roman Church in England suspected the Irish and the Britons of irregularities. Though Irish clergy are known to have been sporadically present in England in the pre-Viking period and again in the tenth century,[47] the Church in England from the archiepiscopate of Theodore (668–90) onwards officially refused to accept the ministrations of Irish or Scottish clergy. This was because, in the absence of metropolitans to exercise proper control, 'we are not certain', as the council of Chelsea put it in 816, 'how or by whom they were ordained'.[48] The fundamental issue, that is, was the validity of the orders of Irish clergy and therefore of the sacraments administered by them. Exactly the same considerations seem to have applied in the case of British clergy. Archbishop Theodore reordained Chad 'after the Catholic manner' through every ecclesiastical gradation,[49] because Chad's earlier consecration by one

[43]*Giraldus Cambrensis Opera*, ed. J. C. Dimock, vi (Rolls series: London, 1868), 121. Cf. *Gerald of Wales: The Journey through Wales and the Description of Wales*, trans. L. Thorpe (Harmondsworth, 1978), 181.

[44]C. Thomas, *Christianity in Roman Britain*, 198.

[45]Ibid., 197.

[46]K. Hughes, *The Church in Early Irish Society* (London, 1966), 39 ff. For an abortive attempt at Armagh in the seventh century 'to project a notion of metropolitan and hierarchical organization' in Ireland, see R. Sharpe, 'Armagh and Rome in the seventh century', *Ireland and Europe*, ed. P. Ní Chatháin and M. Richter, 58–72.

[47]K. Hughes, 'Evidence for contacts between the churches of the Irish and the English from the Synod of Whitby to the Viking Age', *England Before the Conquest*, ed. P. Clemoes and K. Hughes (Cambridge, 1971), 49–67. Cf. J. F. Kelly, 'Irish influence in England after the Synod of Whitby: some new literary evidence', *Eire-Ireland*, 10 (1975), 35–47.

[48]*Councils and Ecclesiastical Documents*, III, 581. Cf. the observations of K. Hughes, 'Evidence for contacts between the churches of the Irish and the English', 64–5.

[49]*Bede's Ecclesiastical History*, ed. B. Colgrave and R. A. B. Mynors, 334–5 (IV, 2); *The Life of Bishop Wilfrid by Eddius Stephanus*, ed. B. Colgrave, chapter 15.

Saxon and two British bishops was quite unacceptable to him. Even Chad's original ordination was unacceptable. It is likely that the issue of the validity of orders emerged as fundamental in the aftermath of the conference at 'Augustine's Oak', if not actually during it, though brought into sharper focus by the authoritarian Theodore who was committed to a wholesale reorganiz-ation of the Anglo-Saxon diocesan structure under the direction of Canterbury.[50] Basically, therefore, it is to this that the gulf between the two Churches, the Anglo-Saxon and the British, should be attributed and exactly the same applies to the Anglo-Saxon and Irish Churches. The appearance of individuals styled 'archbishop' in Gwynedd and Dyfed in the ninth century may reflect changing political circumstances in Wales at that time and the emergence of a more clearly defined political order. The author of the tract on the seven bishop-houses of Dyfed regarded St David's as the principal church in Wales[51] and in the twelfth century first Bernard, bishop of St David's, and then Giraldus Cambrensis, claimed that St David's had been an archbishopric.[52] But no metropolitan structure was ever securely established in Wales, and in the tenth and eleventh centuries some of the bishops of St David's and certain of the bishops of St Teilo (at Llandeilo Fawr) (subsequently regarded as of Llandaff), seeking authentic validation of their orders, went to England for consecration, either to the archbishop of York or of Canterbury.[53]

It is extremely difficult to assess the degree to which the Welsh Church was particularly 'archaic and backward looking' as opposed to merely seeming so by 'the idealised and theoretical standards of reforming churchmen' when the Normans intervened in the late eleventh century.[54] A similar dilemma has beset consideration of the Anglo-Saxon Church on the eve of the Norman Conquest. But the Church in Wales appears to have lacked even the Anglo-Saxon experience of Benedictine monasticism, nor did it have any familiarity with communities of regular canons, or experience of archdeacons, parochial development or tithes. It must necessarily, therefore, have appeared to the Norman clergy to lag behind contemporary European developments.

Nevertheless, the Norman reorganization of the Church in Wales probably recognized the traditional importance in the life of the Welsh Church of certain particular centres associated with which were 'chief bishops', who, even if they did not rule an ecclesiastical province, nevertheless enjoyed personal prestige. It is quite possible that Elfoddw, who died in 809, styled 'archbishop ("chief bishop") of Gwynedd' in the Welsh annals, was associated with Bangor.[55] Towards the end of the ninth century, Asser similarly describes his kinsman, Nobis, bishop of St David's, who died in 874, as 'archbishop', and refers to Hyfaidd, king of Dyfed, as having

[50]For discussion of Theodore, H. Mayr-Harting, *The Coming of Christianity to Anglo-Saxon England*, 121 ff., and N. Brooks, *The Early History of the Church of Canterbury* (Leicester, 1984), 71 ff., and for material on the issue of reordination, L. Saltet, *Les Réordinations: Étude sur le sacrament de l'ordre* (Paris, 1907).

[51]T. M. Charles-Edwards, 'The seven bishop houses of Dyfed', 250.

[52]M. Richter, 'Canterbury's primacy in Wales and the first stage of Bishop Bernard's opposition', *J. Eccles. Hist.*, 2 (1971), 177–89, and idem, *Giraldus Cambrensis: The Growth of the Welsh Nation* (Aberystwyth, 1976), 38 ff., 83 ff.

[53]J. Conway Davies, *Welsh Episcopal Acts* I, 54 ff. was too dismissive of the evidence for this, in the opinion of F. Barlow, *The English Church 1000–1066* (2nd edn., London, 1979), 232.

[54]An issue raised by R. R. Davies, *Conquest, Coexistence and Change: Wales 1063–1415*, 178, 179: cf. the response of H. Pryce, 'Church and society in Wales, 1150–1250', 29–30.

[55]N. K. Chadwick, 'Early culture and learning in north Wales', *Studies in the Early British Church*, ed. N. K. Chadwick (Cambridge, 1959), 29–120 (p. 44).

plundered the monastery and *parochia* of St David, signifying by the *parochia* of St David probably the kingdom of Dyfed.[56] There can be no doubt that the most important church in Ceredigion on the eve of the Norman invasion was that of St Padarn at Llanbadarn Fawr, the 'maritime church', as the twelfth-century *Vita Sancti Paterni* calls it.[57] The association of Padarn with David (and Teilo) in the story of their visit to Jerusalem implies that originally Padarn was regarded as of comparable status. According to the *Life of Padarn*, the patriarch of Jerusalem consecrated Padarn, Teilo and David bishops and they divided 'Britain' into the three episcopies of Seisyllwg, Rheinwg and Morgannwg.[58] The *Life of David* represents the patriarch as consecrating Padarn and Teilo bishops and David archbishop, but this, of course, is a reflection of a St David's view of its own importance.[59] The indications are that the principal church of St Padarn at Llanbadarn Fawr possessed the same standing in Ceredigion as St David's in Dyfed. The *Life of Padarn* refers to it as 'the metropolis' of St Padarn[60] and the division of Ceredigion into four cantrefs may suggest, by analogy with Dyfed, four bishop-houses in Ceredigion, with Llanbadarn in Penweddig claiming an 'archiepiscopal' pre-eminence in Ceredigion and subsequently in Seisyllwg similar to that claimed by St David's in Dyfed and subsequently in Deheubarth. Llanbadarn Fawr, however, unlike St David's was not situated advantageously enough in relation to the secular royal power bases of Hywel Dda and his successors in Deheubarth to rival St David's, and by the tenth century was merely the principal church of a dependent territory. Llanbadarn, therefore, failed to survive as a cathedral community in the pre-Norman period and emerged only (as did most of the *llanau* of early Wales) as a parish church, an important rich church certainly,[61] but still only a parish church in the immense diocese of St David's. It may be that the great emphasis in the *Life of Padarn* on Llanbadarn Fawr as a former bishopric reflects the concern of the churches of west Wales as Bishop Bernard claimed metropolitan status for St David's in the 1120s and after.

Part of the problem with the establishment of British archiepiscopal churches was that the authority of an 'archbishop' in Wales could not easily transcend the political boundaries of the kingdom in which his church was situated. The Church of St David's could extend its authority and influence into Seisyllwg only because that region was under the political control of the kings of Deheubarth for much of the tenth century and early eleventh. This may have been when the

[56]T. M. Charles-Edwards, 'The seven bishop houses of Dyfed', 258.

[57]A. Wade-Evans (ed.), *Vitae Sanctorum Britanniae et Genealogiae* (Cardiff, 1944), 252–69 (pp. 254–5).

[58]Ibid., 258–61, 266–7.

[59]References to David as 'archbishop' in Rhygyfarch ap Sulien's *Life* (J. W. James (ed.), *Rhigyfarch's Life of St David* (Cardiff, 1967)) should be treated with care. The *Life* was written between 1081 and 1099. Rhygyfarch died in 1099. James argued that the *Life* dates to 1093–5 (p. xi). N. K. Chadwick's suggestion that the *Life* was written in the year of the Conqueror's visit to St David's in 1081 ('Intellectual life in west Wales in the last days of the Celtic Church', *Studies in the Early British Church*, ed. N. K. Chadwick, 174–6) has not won general acceptance but must be borne in mind (cf., above, n.28). The *Life* was substantially interpolated and rewritten in the time of Bishop Bernard's campaign for the establishment of St David's as an archiepiscopal see (James, op.cit., xxix ff.). Cf. D. P. Kirby, 'A note on Rhigyfarch's *Life of St David*', *WHR*, 4 (1969), 292–7, though M. Richter's consideration of 'The *Life of St David* by Giraldus Cambrensis', *WHR*, 4 (1968–9), 381–6 would suggest that Rhygyfarch did refer to David as 'archbishop' at the synod of Llanddewibrefi. For evidence of an originally modest view of David, H. D. Emanuel, 'An analysis of the composition of the "Vita Cadoci"', *NLWJ*, 7 (1951–2), 216–27 (p. 221).

[60]*Vitae Sanctorum Britanniae*, 260–1.

[61]N. K. Chadwick, 'Intellectual life in west Wales', 179.

churches of *Vetus Rubus*—a translation of Henfynyw (Old Mynyw or Old Menevia)—where David is said, in his *Life* by Rhygyfarch, to have been educated, and Llanddewibrefi, the alleged site of a synod at which David is said to have presided to suppress Pelagianism,[62] became part of the *parochia* of St David's. Nor did the Church in Wales evolve on purely diocesan lines. The monastic character of the Church in Wales may not have been as marked as that of the Church in Ireland, where a monastery under the rule of an abbot could serve as an episcopal centre for a network of dependent houses no matter how geographically separated from one another, but it undoubtedly shared some of these features. The monastic element in the Church was significant. 'When the Normans arrived in Wales in the late eleventh century they found groups of *claswyr* (men of the Church) established at the major churches, headed by abbots whose title points to their monastic origin. The *clasau*, or mother churches, were responsible for subordinate or daughter churches, a pattern which is similar to the monastic groupings found in Ireland.'[63] The *Life of Samson*, the earliest saint's *Life* to shed light on developments in Wales, presents a picture of monasteries as in some cases family foundations and hereditary possessions, and in particular reveals the monastery of Illtud, perhaps that at Llanilltud Fawr, where Samson was educated, as under the episcopal jurisdiction of the local bishop.[64] A succession of bishops is recorded for the monastery of Menevia, the church of St David, and the bishop of St David's appears also to have ruled the monastery in the same way as 'Teilo's bishop' ruled the *familia* of the church of Llandeilo Fawr.[65] This is how David is represented in Rhygyfarch's *Life of David*, and Kathleen Hughes believed that 'the Welsh bishops appear to have become monastic bishops, probably quite early on.'[66] The important role of monasticism in the history of the early Church in Wales is certainly reflected in Bede's account of the British background to the conference at 'Augustine's Oak', which so closely associates the monks of the monastery of Bangor Is-coed with the British bishops in consultation with a holy hermit before the final confrontation with Augustine as to suggest that by Bede's time of writing, and probably earlier when the the story took shape, the British bishops were more intimately associated with their monastic communities than was normal in many parts of west Europe at this time. They would still, however, retain responsibility for the supervision of pastoral work among the laity and for the ordination and direction of priests, and within the monastic community the bishop's authority even eventually eclipsed that of the abbot.[67]

---

[62]*Life of David*, chs. 8 and 49–52.

[63]S. Victory, *The Celtic Church in Wales* (London, 1977), 54. The term 'abbot' was being used less by the eleventh century: W. Davies, *Wales in the Early Middle Ages*, 149.

[64]F. Fawtier (ed.), *La Vie de saint Samson* (Paris, 1912), chs. 13, 15, and trans. T. Taylor, *The Life of St Samson of Dol* (London, 1925). For a study of the Samson material, Joseph-Claude Poulin, 'Hagiographie et politique: la première vie de Saint Samson de Dol', *Francia*, 5 (1977), 1–26, and see also now I. Wood, 'Forgery in Merovingian hagiography', *Fälschungen im Mittelalter* (Internationaler Kongress der Monumenta Germaniae Historica), V (Hanover, 1988), 369–84 (pp. 380–4).

[65]Cf. W. Davies, *An Early Welsh Microcosm*, 146 ff.

[66]'The Celtic Church: is this a valid concept?', 12.

[67]For a valuable review of the evidence concerning the distinction between the *paruchia* of a church and the *familia* of a monastery but the obscuring of the distinction between secular and regular in religious life 'in Ireland as in Britain', see R. Sharpe, 'Some problems concerning the organization of the church in early medieval Ireland', *Peritia*, 3 (1984), 230–70 (pp. 243–7, 260 ff.).

Not a great deal is known of the character of Welsh monastic life. It is easy to allow Rhygyfarch's account of the austere rule of St David's, with its emphasis on dietary abstemiousness and manual labour, a rule clearly influenced by the ascetic Irish monastic reform movement of the Céli Dé (Culdees) ('Servants of God') of the eighth century,[68] to colour our view of Welsh monasticism as a whole from the sixth century onwards. The implication of the *Life* of Carannog, written in the early twelfth century, is that the church of Llangrannog in Ceredigion was believed to have had a strong eremetical background,[69] but the rule of life at Illtud's monastery appears to have been conducive rather to learning and Samson is represented as having abandoned its relatively comfortable practices for a more demanding way of life elsewhere.[70] There was probably a wide variety of rules of life in early Wales.

Nor should it be thought that the same intensity of monastic experience characterized the Church in Wales throughout the whole of the early Middle Ages. 'The tendency of an early monastic or quasi-monastic establishment to develop into a corporation of secular clergy is apparent',[71] and the normal *clas* church became in the course of time 'hardly monastic any more since the *claswyr* no longer had to take monastic vows such as the vow of celibacy but formed a corporation, usually consisting of one or more kindreds in possession of the church and its lands'.[72] Hereditary succession to ecclesiastical property and office was probably accentuated as time passed, and examples of hereditary families are those of Herewald of Llancarfan in the eleventh century[73] and Sulien at Llanbadarn Fawr, whose son Ieuan died as 'arch- priest of Llanbadarn' in 1137.[74] Another well-known feature of the Church in Celtic areas was for laymen to hold high monastic office, that is, for lay abbots to emerge, perhaps because, in unsettled conditions, 'the monastic families wanted as abbot some lord in the vicinity with forces of his own to protect them'.[75] This must have been particularly so in the face of Viking attacks. Such an impression, however, may be misleading. Giraldus Cambrensis attributed the prevalence of lay abbots in Ireland and Wales to the custom of the clergy of appointing powerful men of the district first as steward and then as protectors of their churches, with such men eventually usurping all rights to themselves, appropriating the lands and styling themselves abbots.[76] The key to what he is describing lies in the application of the title of abbot or *coarb* to the individual who controlled the estates and temporalities of the church. Such an individual by the tenth century might well be a layman, but a layman who had no responsibility for the religious life of the community whose interests he was there to protect. This religious life would continue under separate direction though the members of the religious community might well become impoverished as

[68] K. Hughes, *The Church in Early Irish Society*, 173 ff., and N. K. Chadwick, 'Intellectual life in west Wales', 143.

[69] *Vitae Sanctorum Britanniae*, 142–9 (pp. 144–5).

[70] *La Vie de saint Samson*, ch. 20.

[71] A. Hamilton Thompson, 'The Welsh medieval dioceses', 102.

[72] T. M. Charles-Edwards, 'The seven bishop houses of Dyfed', 256.

[73] J. Conway Davies, *Welsh Episcopal Acts* II, 493 ff.

[74] On the family of Sulien, see J. E. Lloyd, *The Story of Ceredigion*, 30–9; J. Conway Davies, *Welsh Episcopal Acts* II, 493 ff.; N. K. Chadwick, 'Intellectual life in west Wales', 121 ff. and M. Lapidge, 'The Welsh-Latin poetry of Sulien's family', *passim*.

[75] K. Hughes, *The Church in Early Irish Society*, 213.

[76] *Giraldus Cambrensis Opera*, vi, 120; *Gerald of Wales*, trans. L. Thorpe, 180.

its interests and those of the lay abbot continued to diverge.[77] Giraldus was familiar with this phenomenon in a twelfth-century context, not least at Llanbadarn Fawr.[78] We should not view such developments as abuses, therefore, but as 'continuous practices of early usages or direct developments from the social environment', [79] even if, to the reforming Normans, they afforded still further evidence that the Church in Wales needed drastic reorganization at diocesan and monastic level.

The coastal churches of west Wales were clearly vulnerable to seaborne attack. St David's, Llandudoch (St Dogmaels) and Llanbadarn Fawr were ravaged by Vikings in 988. St David's suffered also in other years and Llanbadarn was attacked by Llywelyn, king of Gwynedd, in 1039. But they were also in close contact with the ecclesiastical communities of Ireland. However minimal may be the archaeological evidence for an 'Irish Sea Culture Province' in the early Middle Ages,[80] the transmission of Hiberno-Latin texts from Ireland to Wales is certain, [81] and the literary evidence indicates 'a close and long-standing unity of culture among the Celtic peoples around the shores of the Irish Sea'.[82] An important reflection of this can be seen in the literary and artistic productions of the family of Sulien at Llanbadarn Fawr.[83] There is no doubt that Irish influence on the Church in west Wales was strong. Llanbadarn Fawr enjoyed a cultural flowering in the late eleventh century which belongs essentially to the period after 1081 and demonstrates an area of Irish vitality in the Church in Wales on the eve of the Norman attack. One of the decorated manuscripts from Llanbadarn, the psalter and martyrology of Rhygyfarch ap Sulien (MS Trinity College 50 [A.4.20]) (Plate XII) was transcribed in 1079 at Rhygyfarch's request by a certain Ithael and illuminated by Rhygyfarch's brother Ieuan.[84] Copied out in Irish minuscule,[85] it contains, in addition to Jerome's translation of the psalms, a martyrology which, judging by its inclusion of Irish saints, may derive from an Irish exemplar, whilst Ieuan's decorative work resembles Irish manuscript art in its zoomorphic capitals and foliage ornaments.[86] Ieuan's poem on the life and family of his father Sulien, written in 1085–91, sheds

---

[77]K. Hughes, *The Church in Early Irish Society*, 223, and in particular, R. Sharpe, 'Some problems concerning the organization of the church in early medieval Ireland', 264–5: 'The status of the temporalities of a church is the most unusual feature of Irish ecclesiastical organization' (p. 266). The same may be true of the Church in Wales.

[78]*Giraldus Cambrensis Opera*, vi, 121; *Gerald of Wales*, trans. L. Thorpe, 180–1. Cf. J. Wyn Evans, 'The survival of the *clas* as an institution in medieval Wales: some observations on Llanbadarn Fawr', *The Early Church in Wales and the West*, ed. Edwards and Jane, 33–40 (p. 34).

[79]K. Hughes, *The Church in Early Irish Society*, 166.

[80]L. Alcock, 'Was there an Irish Sea Culture Province in the Dark Ages?', *The Irish Sea Province in Archaeology and History*, ed. D. Moore (Cardiff, 1970), 55–65.

[81]M. Lapidge, 'Latin learning in Dark Age Wales', 97.

[82]N. K. Chadwick, 'Early literary contacts between Wales and Ireland', *The Irish Sea Province*, 66–76 (p. 76).

[83]C. H. Slover, 'Early literary channels between Ireland and Britain', *Texas Studies in English*, 7 (1927), 5–111 (e.g. pp.89 ff.); N. K. Chadwick, 'Intellectual life in west Wales', 137 ff.; M. Lapidge, 'The Welsh-Latin poetry of Sulien's family', *passim.*, and P. Ó Riain, 'The Irish element in Welsh hagiographic tradition', *passim*. See also D. Simon Evans, 'The Welsh and the Irish before the Normans—contact or impact', *Proc. British Academy*, 75 (1989), 143–61 (p. 159).

[84]*The Psalter and Martyrology of Ricemarch*, ed.H. J. Lawlor (Henry Bradshaw Society: 2 vols., London, 1914), xix, xxi–ii.

[85]W. M. Lindsay, *Early Welsh Script* (Oxford, 1912), 32 ff.

[86]M. Lapidge, 'The Welsh-Latin poetry of Sulien's family', 77.

further light on the antecedents of this activity.[87] He declares that the land of Ceredigion is his homeland and that his father Sulien was born at Llanbadarn Fawr where he subsequently educated the people, including his four sons, Rhygyfarch, Ieuan, Arthgen and Daniel. Sulien, born c.1012, studied first in British schools, according to Ieuan, but then resolved to go to Ireland, perhaps when he was in his early twenties. It was evidently customary to do this for the Welsh regarded the Irish as distinguished for their remarkable learning and famous for their writers and teachers. An adverse wind, however, drove Sulien to the shores of Alba (Scotland), which destination appears to have proved equally attractive. Sulien remained there for five years, and then proceeded to Ireland where he studied for another ten, after which he returned home to teach the people and clergy of his native land. An approximate chronology for these events would be c. 1035–40 for his sojourn in Alba, and c. 1040–50 for that in Ireland, with the establishment of his own school at Llanbadarn c. 1050–5. Sulien's own education, 'whether in Scotland or Ireland, must have been wholly Irish in character'.[88] An analysis of the poems of his sons reveals familiarity with a wide range of classical and early medieval texts (including the works of Vergil, Ovid, Lucan, Juvencus, Prudentius, Martianus Capella, Sedulius, Boethius and Aldhelm), possibly culled from a library established by Sulien at Llanbadarn.[89] The education which Sulien made available at Llanbadarn seems to have been of a conservative kind, reminiscent of ninth-century Carolingian learning rather than of contemporary European scholarship, but it established Llanbadarn as a centre of intellectual and artistic excellence in west Wales in the late eleventh century.

In 1073 Sulien became bishop of St David's. Five years later he resigned his bishopric but when Bishop Abraham, his successor, was slain by Vikings in 1080 Sulien was 'led away', in the words of Ieuan, and induced 'against his will', as the annals say, to assume the office of bishop for a second time. He remained at St David's until 1085 when he once more resigned, dying in 1091, 'the most learned and most pious of the bishops of the Britons, and the most praiseworthy for the instruction of his disciples and his parishes'. Sulien's second episcopate was far from uneventful. In 1081 Gruffudd ap Cynan and Rhys ap Tewdwr both visited St David's for the bishop's blessing before marching against Trahaearn ap Caradog; also in 1081, in the words of the annalist, 'William the Bastard came on the Menevian pilgrimage'. He came with an army but it is probably unlikely that the full extent of Norman ambition was yet perceived by those present on that occasion.

The Church in Cardiganshire was an integral part of the Church in Wales, particularly west Wales, and developments in Cardiganshire can be illuminated directly in three ways which deepen our knowledge of the life of Christian communities between the Dyfi and the Teifi in the early Middle Ages—through the more detailed study of the cults of the saints of Ceredigion (see below II. ch.7.b), of the Early Christian monuments of the area (see below II. ch.7.c) and of the archaeology of the Early Christian cemeteries (see below II. ch.7.d).

[87] Ibid., 70–1, 80–1 ff.
[88] N. K. Chadwick, 'Intellectual life in west Wales', 166.
[89] M. Lapidge, 'The Welsh-Latin poetry of Sulien's family', 69–70. On the possibility that this library contained at least one Welsh manuscript, ibid., 72.

b. THE SAINTS OF CARDIGANSHIRE

Pádraig Ó Riain

Introduction

Various lines of enquiry may be brought together to show that the story of early Christianity in south-west Wales must have had a predominantly Irish character. K. H. Jackson has observed that the distribution of ogam stones 'agrees closely with what is known about [Irish] colonies'.[1] Moreover, according to the same authority, 'the colonists continued to speak Irish into the second half of the sixth century, and very likely as late as the seventh'.[2] Linguistic traces of the Irish colonies survived, as Melville Richards has shown, in the topography and dialects of south-west Wales.[3] The saints also succumbed to Goidelic influences; Elltud, the correct Welsh form of the saint's name, is attested only in north Wales. Elsewhere, the Irish form Illtud prevailed.[4] The southern part of Cardiganshire came within this early Christian sphere of Irish influence. The bilingual stone at Llanfechan, which is dated to *c.* 600, has been taken by J. E. Lloyd as 'proof positive' that south Cardiganshire was—'at least, in part'—a Goidelic country.[5] Similarly, *meid(i)r/moydir*, the Welsh reflex of Irish *bóthar* 'road', while mainly attested in north Pembrokeshire, also occurs in the Cardiganshire parishes of Cardigan, Y Ferwig and Llangoedmor.[6] But Irish influence on the saints of Cardiganshire has been largely obscured by the effects of localization. The purpose of this essay is to show that the distribution of saints' cults in south Cardiganshire in particular is largely a legacy of its early Christian Irish population.

The sources

By the time documentary coverage of the Cardiganshire saints begins in the eleventh century, Irish connections with the area had become a dim and distant memory. Furthermore, whenever saintly origins are mentioned, they reveal the unmistakable effects of rampant localization. Thus, in the earliest surviving list of local saints, the eleventh-century *Progenies Keredic*, individual descent is from the local eponymous ancestor, Ceredig, regardless of historical accuracy.[7] The same is true, needless to say, of the somewhat later but similar lists preserved in *Plant Ceredig* and *Bonedd y Saint*.[8] The fate of the biblical figure, Pedr (St Peter), patron of Lampeter, who is added

---

[1]K. H. Jackson, *Language and History in Early Britain* (Edinburgh, 1953), 154.
[2]Ibid., 171.
[3]M. Richards, 'The Irish settlements in south-west Wales. A topographical approach', *J. Royal Soc. Antiq. Ireland*, 90 (1960), 133–62.
[4]For comments on the forms by Sir J. Rhŷs and H. Lewis see G. H. Doble, *Saint Iltut* (Cardiff, 1944), 33n. Cf. E. G. Bowen, *The Settlements of the Celtic Saints in Wales* (Cardiff, 1954), 43–4.
[5]J. E. Lloyd, *The Story of Ceredigion* (Cardiff, 1937), 3.
[6]M. Richards, 'Welsh *meid(i)r, moydir*, Irish *bóthar* "lane, road"', *Lochlann*, 2 (1962), 128–33.
[7]*EWGT*, 20. The text is not confined to saints.
[8]Ibid., 49, 54–5. The precedence given to the saints of Cardiganshire in the *Bonedd* text indicates a local provenance.

to the descendants of Ceredig, must seem the perfect *reductio ad absurdum* of this approach.[9] Almost all the local saints of any importance were accounted for—through the male line—in this way. In the case of Padarn, however, whose father is invariably set down as an Armorican from Letavia—whatever that may mean[10]—a change had to be made. Accordingly, in at least one source it is Padarn's mother who is said to have been descended from Ceredig.[11]

Concern with descent, however inaccurate, formed part of the inherited stock-in-trade of the medieval Welsh hagiographer. It was, however, a peculiarly Celtic legacy. Nowhere else in western Christendom—excepting Ireland—were collections made of saints' pedigrees.[12] Indeed, the Celtic saint's pedigree has been put on the same plane as the two basic *bona fides* of the western European saint—the date of his feast and his place of burial.[13] In reality, however, the pedigree does no more than provide the saint with a place on the genealogical map. For the medieval hagiographer this was obviously the map that counted.

A far more important map may be drawn up by reference to the distribution of church dedications. The evidence of dedications is potentially one of the earliest surviving sources of information on the saints. It is only in this century, however, that the potential of this map as a source of information on the Celtic saints has been fully appreciated. The credit for having pioneered distribution-related studies goes to R. Largillière who applied the method very successfully to the Breton saints,[14] whilst in Britain it was first used in connection with the Cornish saints by G. H. Doble.[15] Some of its possible implications for the Celtic saints in general, however, have been worked out in the writings of the late E. G. Bowen.[16] Bowen, who took the distribution pattern to be generally much 'older than the lives of the saints', sometimes even drew from this kind of evidence 'a dim reminiscence of historical fact'.[17] That dedications to saints Carannog, Pedrog, Briog and Meugan, for instance, are grouped together in different parts of the Celtic world, including 'the lands bordering the Teifi estuary', led him to suggest that these saints were 'companions in some great missionary enterprise'.[18] But it is necessary to be cautious; the fact is that the Celtic saints were not really the great travellers tradition later made them out to be. What travelled were their cults and these, depending on their local reception, often left traces in the pattern of dedications.

[9]It is nowhere stated that Pedr of Lampeter was the apostle of that name but this must seem very likely. Cf. S. Baring-Gould and J. Fisher, *The Lives of the British Saints*, 4 vols. (London, 1907–13), 4, 88–9.

[10]Doble's view, based on a suggestion by A. W. Wade-Evans, that Armorica, otherwise Letavia or Llydaw, in fact referred to a place in south-east Wales has been endorsed by E. G. Bowen, *A History of Llanbadarn Fawr* (Llandysul, 1979), 32–3.

[11]*EWGT*, 58 (§21).

[12]D. Dumville, 'Kingship, genealogies and regnal lists', *Early Medieval Kingship*, ed. P. H. Sawyer and I. N. Woods (Leeds, 1981), 72–104; P. Ó Riain, 'Irish saints' genealogies', *Nomina*, 7 (1983), 23–9.

[13]By P. Grosjean in *Analecta Bollandiana*, 76 (1958), 389n.

[14]R. Largillière, *Les saints et l'organisation chrétienne primitive dans l'Armorique Bretonne* (Rennes,1925).

[15]G. H. Doble, The Cornish Saints series, vols. 1–48 (1923–44) (reprinted *The Saints of Cornwall*, 5 parts, (Truro, 1960–70).

[16]E. G. Bowen, *The Settlements of the Celtic Saints in Wales* (Cardiff, 1954), and idem, *Britain and the Western Seaways* (London, 1972), 70–91.

[17]E. G. Bowen, *The Settlements of the Celtic Saints*, 88, 91.

[18]Ibid., 91.

Other early sources, notably the calendars of saints or martyrologies, enable us to probe the evidence of dedications. An illuminating case in point is provided by the absence of traces in Wales of the cult of St Gildas. Despite his connections with Wales, Gildas never became the subject of a flourishing local cult; Llanildas survives as a dedication only in the pages of the Iolo manuscripts.[19] In fact, the saint's only 'church' as such in Wales was on the tiny island of Flatholm —formerly Echni—off the Glamorgan coast.[20] The location of this island is of particular interest because it adjoins the much larger Barry Island whose patron, St Barrug, is a realization of the Irish cult of St Finnian.[21] In this case, the proximity of dedications may lend support to historical fact. Gildas and Finnian are known to have corresponded from a letter written by the Irishman Columbanus to Pope Gregory the Great c. AD 600.[22] Moreover, the two saints are again brought together in a breviate version of the Hieronymian Martyrology compiled in about 830 at the Irish monastery of Tallaght.[23] Significantly, the day chosen to bring them together, 28 September, directly follows the date of the *gwyl mab sant* observed on Barry Island according to the earliest Welsh calendar.[24]

The value of the calendar for the study of dedications—and as a source of information in its own right—has not received the recognition it very richly deserves. The feasts recorded in the calendar often date in origin to the period immediately following the so-called Age of Saints.[25] The comparatively late date of extant Welsh calendars of the twelfth century and later obscures to some extent the early character of their materials.[26] Together with its Irish counterpart, however, which was already set down in writing by the early ninth century,[27] the Welsh calendar can shed a great deal of light on the origins of local saints. Moreover, when applied to the saints of Cardiganshire, it enables us to give due recognition to the important role played by the Irish colonists in the formation of the local pattern of dedications.

The saints

E. G. Bowen's discussion of the composition of the surviving dedications showed that, of the seventy or so early Cardiganshire church sites, forty are dedicated to Celtic saints.[28] The remainder commemorate foreign or biblical saints including Mary, the Archangel Michael, Peter and the two Johns. Michael with seven and Mary with five lead in the number of dedications, and

[19]T. Williams (ed.), *Iolo Manuscripts: A Selection of Ancient Welsh Manuscripts* (Welsh MSS Society, 1848), 220.

[20]J. G. Evans and J. Rhŷs (eds.), *The Text of the Book of Llan Dav* (Oxford, 1893), 138–9.

[21]P. Ó Riain, 'The Irish element in Welsh hagiographical tradition', *Irish Antiquity*, ed. D. Ó Corráin (Cork, 1981), 291–303.

[22]G. S. M. Walker, *Sancti Columbani Opera* (Dublin, 1957), 8.

[23]R. I. Best and H. J. Lawlor, *The Martyrology of Tallaght* (London, 1931), 75.

[24]S. Baring-Gould and J. Fisher, *The Lives of the British Saints* 1, 194–6.

[25]H. Delehaye, *Cinq leçons sur la méthode hagiographique* (Bruxelles, 1934), 12, 42–74.

[26]For a discussion of the earliest Welsh calendar, see K. Hughes, 'British Museum MS Cotton Vespasian A. XIV (*Vitae sanctorum Wallensium*'): its purpose and provenance,' in *Studies in the Early British Church*, ed. N. K. Chadwick *et al.* (Cambridge, 1958), 183–200.

[27]P. Ó Riain, 'The composition of the Irish section of the Calendar of Saints', *Dinnseanchas*, 6 (1975), 77–92.

[28]E. G. Bowen, 'The Celtic saints in Cardiganshire', *Ceredigion*, 1 (1950), 3–17.

this corresponds to the preference shown for these biblical saints in all the Celtic countries. In Ireland, for instance, the townland names, Kilmurry (*cill* or church of Mary) and Kilmichael (*cill* or church of Michael), with forty-nine and fourteen attestations respectively, far outnumber all other such names based on dedications to biblical saints. A non-biblical but foreign saint with a very widely diffused medieval cult, Martin of Tours, was also possibly culted in Cardiganshire, at Capelborthin (Martin's church?) near Llandysul.[29]

Since this correlates well with the situation that prevailed throughout western Europe, and more particularly in other Celtic countries, the distribution of Cardiganshire dedications to biblical and foreign saints must date from the earliest period of church building. Exceptions to this general rule are few.[30] Moreover, when the Normans, for example, introduced new dedications, these seldom fully displaced the earlier cults.[31]

We may assume that the forty Cardiganshire dedications to Celtic saints also date from the earliest period of church building. It has been suggested that the Irish saint Brigit (Welsh 'Sanffraid') may be an exception to this general rule,[32] but the supporting evidence is negligible. Furthermore, the form of the saint's name in Welsh, *Sanffraid*, is the correct modern realization of Middle Welsh *Sanffreit* from Old Welsh *San Bregit*.[33] The dedication to Brigit at Llansanffraid, of course, is in the southern part of Cardiganshire where Irish influence was strongest. The extent of this influence on the composition of the local pattern of dedications was, as we shall now see, very considerable.

St Finnian in Cardiganshire

While E. G. Bowen and Siân Victory have stressed the Goidelic character of early Christianity in Wales, they have taken little or no account of the effect this must have had on the pattern of dedications. 'The hagiological literature', wrote Bowen, 'is suggestive of much closer contact than is indicated by surviving dedications.'[34] This contradiction between the literary evidence and the dedication pattern is apparent only. Many originally Irish cults later masqueraded as Welsh, and foremost among them was the celebrated cult of St Finnian.

By far the most important early Irish cult was that of Colum Cille (Columba) of Iona. This importance did not extend, however, to Wales where the pre-eminent Irish saint was undoubtedly Colum Cille's tutor, Bishop Findbarr, better known under the Brittonic form of his name as

[29]P. Grosjean's 'Gloria Postuma S. Martini Turonensis apud Scottos et Britannos', *Analecta Bollandiana*, 55 (1937), 300–48, omits mention of this possible dedication.

[30]For some early non-Celtic dedications in the Llandaff area, see W. Davies, *An Early Welsh Microcosm* (London, 1978), 132.

[31]This is seen by reference to the introduction of the cult of St Nicholas in place of Barruc of Barry Island and Fymbrianus of Fowey in southern Cornwall. In both cases the Celtic saint held his ground locally; Ó Riain, 'The Irish element in Welsh hagiographical tradition', 300.

[32]E. G. Bowen, 'The cult of St Brigit', *Studia Celtica*, 8–9 (1973–4), 33–47 (pp. 42–4).

[33]K. H. Jackson, *Language and History in Early Britain*, 498. E. G. Bowen, 'The cult of St Brigit', 42–3, makes the point that the title *sant* is rare in Wales. So it is in Ireland, but there also *sanct* is found with Brigit: P. Ó Riain, *Corpus Genealogiarum Sanctorum Hiberniae* (Dublin, 1985), 29 (§178).

[34]E. G. Bowen, *The Settlements of the Celtic Saints*, 96, and cf. 'The cult of St Brigit', 43, 44.

Finnianus (Vinnianus) whence Finnio (Finnian).[35] The reversal of roles in Wales may be explained on chronological grounds. Colum Cille was still a youth (*juvenis*)—or so Adamnán tells us[36]—when Finnian was an old man (*senis*). So, assuming that Finnian's cult spread among the Irish, including those in Wales, shortly after his death, it enjoyed a great advantage over that of Colum Cille. Moreover, by the time Colum Cille died in 597, the Irish community in south-west Wales may no longer have exercised the same influence as before. Certainly, Cardiganshire traces of Finnian's cult are particularly numerous. As might be expected, the local realizations of the saint, which number at least five, invariably include in their names the element *gwyn* (*gwen*) 'fair' corresponding to Irish *find*.[37]

Gwnnws (Gwynws) of Llanwnnws, whose earliest attestation as Guinnius occurs in the twelfth-century Latin *Life of Padarn*, is a possible case in point. Nothing much beyond his name is known. If the evidence of the sixteenth-century Demetian calendar, which may have been compiled at Llangeitho,[38] is reliable, then his Irish origins can hardly be doubted. Firstly, he is described there as one of the children of Brychan, an ancestral figure with strong Irish associations.[39] Secondly and more importantly, he is included in the list for 13 December, a day so close to one of Finnian's principal Irish feasts, 12 December, that it must surely reflect it.[40] The date of Gwnnws's feast is not confirmed in any other source, but accompanying him in the Demetian calendar is St Gwynen who, despite the change of sex, a not uncommon occurrence in Celtic hagiography, must represent the eponym of Llanwnnen,[41] whose *gŵyl mab sant* (at Llanwnnen) was held on 13 December. This was also the feast of Lucy of Syracuse who later displaced the Celtic saint.[42]

The eponym of Llanwnnen is one of two local female realizations of the cult of St Finnian. The other is Gwenog of the neighbouring church of Llanwenog whose day—3 January—coincides with the Irish feast of Fintan (from Find) and Findlug (from Find-Lug).[43] The latter name, also attested locally, is the word-perfect equivalent of Welsh Gwynlleu, the name of the patron of Nancwnlle, a site located about seven miles north of Llanwenog,[44] near to which is a farm named Penlan Wnws.[45] This may indicate that the saint was known by the same pet name, Gwn(n)ws,

[35]For recent articles on the saint and on his name, see P. Ó Riain, 'St Finbarr: a study in a cult', *J. Cork Hist. and Arch. Soc.*, 82 (1977), 63–82; L. Fleuriot, 'Le saint Breton Winniau et le pénitentiel dit de Finnian', *Études Celtiques*, 15 (1976–8), 607–14; P. Ó Riain, 'Finnian or Winniau', *Irland und Europa: Ireland and Europe*, ed. P. Ní Chatháin and M. Richter (Stuttgart, 1984), 52–7; D. N. Dumville, 'Gildas and Uinniau', *Gildas: New Approaches*, ed. M. Lapidge and D. Dumville (Woodbridge, 1984), 207–14.

[36]*Adomnan's Life of Columba*, ed. A. O. Anderson and M. O. Anderson (Edinburgh, 1961), 470 (ch.106b).

[37]It should be noted that all local forms of the saint's name in Wales are hypocoristic.

[38]S. Baring-Gould and J. Fisher, *The Lives of the British Saints*, I, 67–8.

[39]E. G. Bowen, 'Tair Gwelygordd Santaidd Ynys Prydain', *Studia Celtica*, 5 (1970), 1–14 (pp. 11–14).

[40]Finnian's feast was celebrated on this day at Clonard, one of the two most important Irish churches associated with the saint.

[41]S. Baring-Gould and J. Fisher, *The Lives of the British Saints*, III, 230.

[42]Ibid., 230.

[43]Ibid., 198.

[44]E. G. Bowen, 'The Celtic saints in Cardiganshire', 9, gives Cynllo as the patron of Nancwnlle but I do not know on what authority.

[45]S. Baring-Gould and J. Fisher, *The Lives of the British Saints*, III, 247.

as the eponym of Llanwnnws. Moreover, his feast fell on 1 November, a day surrounded in the Irish calendar by associations with St Finnian.[46] One such association is echoed in a very striking fashion in the hagiography of south Cardiganshire. Many years ago A. W. Wade-Evans identified an Irish saint named Crubthir Fintam, who is mentioned in the Latin *Life of Cybi*,[47] with his 'rule-right Welsh equivalent' Gwyndaf,[48] patron, among other places, of Capel Wnda near Troed-yr-aur.[49] This identification is again confirmed by the calendar. Gwyndaf's day, 6 November, was elsewhere observed as the feast of St Winnoc, one of the most celebrated of the Brittonic realizations of the cult of St Finnian.[50] Moreover, not only was the following day, 7 November, observed in Ireland as the feast of St Fintan, but its sequel, 8 November, was Cybi's day in Wales.[51]

The local presence of Finnian's cult, which can now be confirmed only by reference to the calendar of saints, none the less documents—arguably just as unambiguously as the Ogam stones and the evidence of toponymy and dialect—the influence of Irish settlement during the formative period of Christianity in south-west Wales and, more specifically, in south Cardiganshire. His cult may not be the only saintly witness to this influence, but it is surely the most important because, having masqueraded as Welsh for so long, it completely escaped the attentions of later clerics who were often only too eager to affirm the Irish connections of local saints.

Late medieval Irish influence

Among other names in a sixteenth-century Llanbadarn Fawr calendar, Kirianus occurs at 5 March, otherwise the day of the Irish saint, Ciarán. This is no coincidence, as S. M. Harris has shown.[52] In Wales, Ciarán was equated with Caron, the patron and eponym of Tregaron.[53] The question is, however, how far back this equation goes or whether—as Harris has suggested—it is based on a 'mistaken identification'. In fact, in this case the names of the saints reveal no more than a token resemblance. Furthermore, their equation may date to a period when Irish models or parallels seem to have been at a premium.[54] Among those then also affected was a Cornish saint, Piranus, who was not only equated with the Irish Ciarán but fitted out with a *Vita* (*Life*) borrowed in its entirety from the dossier of his Irish 'counterpart'.[55] It must seem likely, therefore, that Caron's equation with Ciarán, if mistaken, was deliberate. Furthermore, unless we assume

[46] 1 November (Fintinna), 6 (Winnoc), 7 (Fintan), 8 (Bairrfhind).

[47] A. W. Wade-Evans, *Vitae Sanctorum Britanniae et Genealogiae* (Cardiff, 1944), 238–42 (chs. 10–15).

[48] Quoted in G. H. Doble, *Saint Cuby*, Cornish Saint Series, no. 22 (1929). Interestingly, the Irish form of the name usually ends in *-n*. It may be, therefore, that the writer was influenced by the local Welsh form of the name, i.e. Gwyndaf.

[49] He is also the eponym of Llanwnda, a parochial name found in Caernarfonshire and Pembrokeshire.

[50] G. H. Doble, *Saint Winnoc*, Cornish Saints Series no.44 (1940). See also P. Ó Riain, 'The Irish element in Welsh hagiographical tradition', 299–301.

[51] In Ireland Cybi's cognate Mochop was culted on 12 November.

[52] S. M. Harris, 'A Llanbadarn Fawr calendar', *Ceredigion*, 2 (1952), 18–26 (p. 21).

[53] The earliest Welsh calendar, the twelfth-century Vespasian A xiv, already records the celebration locally (i.e. at Tregaron?) of Ciarán's feast on 5 March.

[54] P. Ó Riain, 'The Irish element in Welsh hagiographical tradition', *passim*.

[55] G. H. Doble, *Saint Perran or Piran*, Cornish Saints Series, no.29 (1931).

that Caron's feast was also borrowed, which may well be the case, it would perhaps always have fallen on or around 5 March, thus facilitating further the possibility of an identification with Ciarán.

Two Welsh *Vitae* composed *c*.1100, possibly in Ceredigion, of Carannog of Llangrannog and Cybi of Llangybi pose a similar problem.[56] Both *Lives* contain extensive Irish episodes[57] and both saints are equated with Irish counterparts—Cairnech and Mochop—who not only figure in the *Vitae* but also have feasts on or near the same dates as Carannog and Cybi.[58] Extensive use was made of Irish materials—particularly in the Ceredigion *Vitae*—at about this time. The author of Carannog's first *Vita* knew enough of the Irish saint called 'in their language . . . Cernach' and of 'the acts of the blessed Cernach . . . read in Ireland throughout the whole country',[59] to realize that a plausible case could be made for the identity of the saints. Cybi's biographer similarly reveals a remarkable familiarity with the intricacies of Irish personal and place-names. Moreover, in establishing a connection between Cybi and the church 'to the south side of the region of Mide . . . which to this day is called the great church of Mochop', he uses authentic monastic evidence.[60] Clearly, the Irish element in these Welsh *Vitae* was from the first an integral part. The cults of Carannog/Cairnech and Cybi/Mochop—whatever their ultimate origins[61]—were shared by Welsh and Irish in a way that led to their mistaken identification. In fact, as reference to the Appendix shows, Carannog may have originated as quite another Irish saint. Since no local *Vita* was ever composed, the equation of Caron with Ciarán was not explored in the same way. Whether this equation renewed a genuine but much earlier identity, remains very doubtful. The names Caron and Ciarán do not appear to be reconcilable.[62]

David and Padarn

David's *Vita*, which was composed by the Llanbadarn cleric, Rhygyfarch, a little before 1100, gives just as much space to Irish materials as the later Welsh *Vitae*. Indeed, Rhygyfarch's work may have served as a model in this regard. Examination of the Irish personal names in the *Vita*, and of some episodes of the narrative itself, indicates, however, that Rhygyfarch was drawing to some extent on written materials of Irish provenance.[63] Thus, when describing an encounter somewhere on the Irish Sea between St Bairre and St Brendan, Rhygyfarch appears to be drawing on notes added to the Martyrology of Óengus for 2 January. Similarly, in providing

---

[56] A. W. Wade-Evans, *Vitae Sanctorum Britanniae et Genealogiae*, 142–9 (Carannog), 234–51 (Cybi). The same authority discusses the provenance of the *Vitae* at pp.xi–xii. See also K. Hughes, 'British Museum MS Cotton Vespasian A xiv', 188–9.

[57] Carannog (ch. 2), Cybi (chs. 9–15).

[58] Carannog was culted on 16 May. For Cybi see above, n. 51.

[59] A. W. Wade-Evans, *Vitae Sanctorum Britanniae et Genealogiae*, 143.

[60] Ibid., 241.

[61] Both Carannog and Cybi are taken to have been Cornish in Welsh sources. In Irish sources this also applies to Cairnech.

[62] Welsh Caron, earlier Carawn, seems incompatible with Irish Ciarán, from *Ciar* 'dark brown'.

[63] P. Ó Riain, 'The Irish element in Welsh hagiographical tradition', 292–5.

Bairre with a horse as a means of traversing the Irish Sea, Rhygyfarch appears to have been influenced by the Latin *Life* of Máedoc of Ferns. Arguably, therefore, David's Irish record was largely 'invented' towards the end of the eleventh century. Despite Rhygyfarch's claim that 'a third or quarter of Ireland served David', the saint's cult as such is virtually unattested there.[64] This is not to say that David was unknown in Ireland. On the contrary, the earliest documentary reference to the saint is in an Irish martyrology composed *c.* 830 at Tallaght, near Dublin. [65] David's inclusion in this source—which also preserves the earliest recorded references to Deiniol of Bangor and Beuno [66]—is unrelated to the question of his Irish cult. David was then well known in Ireland on account of the importance of his church, Cell Muine (St David's), to which the text actually refers.[67]

Rhygyfarch's demonstrably spurious account of David's influence in Ireland hardly inspires confidence in his other materials, including those which relate to Cardiganshire. Regardless of the vexed question of David's mention in the seventh-century Llanddewibrefi inscription,[68] the name of this church and other local dedications bear clear witness to the early presence of the saint's cult in the County. Despite the views to the contrary expressed by such scholars as E. G. Bowen and D. S. Evans, all other associations with the area are necessarily suspect.[69] When composing saints' *Lives* medieval hagiographers —who often had as little to go by as we have —took some account of dedications, treating them as signposts to the progress of the saint's life. In these circumstances it would naturally fall to the churches furthest removed from the centre —in this case St David's—to fill in the highlights of the saint's early life. This may explain why Cardiganshire with its ready-made cluster of dedications to the saint was chosen as the location of the saint's birth and early education. The names of his parents, Sanctus ('saint')—as unlikely a king of Ceredigion as ever existed—and Nonnita (from *nonna* 'nun'), are clearly fabricated.[70] Similarly, the circumstances of his birth, as was usual in saints' *Lives*, draws heavily on the pattern of the heroic life. As for the saint's pedigree, this is no more reliable than the genre to which it belongs. In other words, unless supported by early evidence, which is completely lacking in David's case, it is an invention. In sum, therefore, while scholars such as E. G. Bowen have insisted on taking the associations of David with Cardiganshire to represent echoes, at least, 'of real historical events',[71] the tradition can only be traced back as far as Rhygyfarch. Whatever

[64] A. W. Wade-Evans, *Vitae Sanctorum Britanniae et Genealogiae*, 162. David's dedications in Ireland (see S. M. Harris, *Saint David in the Liturgy* (Cardiff, 1940), 73) are post-Norman.

[65] S. M. Harris, *Saint David in the Liturgy*, 4. The Martyrology of Tallaght, which Harris mentions, is in fact older than the *Catalogus Sanctorum Hiberniae* which also refers to David: P. Grosjean, 'Édition et commentaire du Catalogus Sanctorum Hiberniae', *Analecta Bollandiana*, 73 (1955), 197–213, 289–322.

[66] R. I. Best and H. J. Lawlor, *The Martyrology of Tallaght* (Henry Bradshaw Society, vol. 68, 1931), 35 (Búgno), 70 (Daniel).

[67] Ibid., 20 (Dauid Cille Mune).

[68] S. Gruffydd and H. P. Owen, 'The earliest mention of St David', *BBCS*, 17 (1956–8), 185–93: cf. ibid. 19 (1960–2), 231–4.

[69] E. G. Bowen, *The St David of History, Dewi Sant: Our Founder Saint* (Aberystwyth, 1982); D. S. Evans, 'Ychwaneg am Ddewi sant—ei fuchedd a'i fywyd', *THSC* (1984), 9–29.

[70] The 'invention' of Nonnita (Nonn) may also have been influenced by the presence locally of a church named Llan-non.

[71] E. G. Bowen, *The St David of History*, 11.

earlier evidence there may be relates to dedications and to the *paruchia*-type organization which may underlie them.[72]

Padarn, the second most important Cardiganshire saint, shares with David a non-Celtic name, from Latin Paternus. There, however, the similarity ends. Padarn's record can be carried farther back than the mention given him in Rhygyfarch's *Life* of David[73] only by reference to the dossier of his Breton namesake and possible double, Patern, bishop of Vannes.[74] Early Irish sources, which give due recognition to the stature of David, Cadog, Gildas and Beuno, ignore Padarn completely. Moreover, the Irish episode in the saint's *Vita*, which may have been composed *c.* 1120, is utterly devoid of local colour.[75] Only Padarn's father, Petran, who is said to have led a religious life in Ireland,[76] has a possible Irish cognate in the Leinster saint, Petrán of Cell Lainne.[77] The saint's Breton connections, on the other hand, loom very large. The consensus view about his *Life* is that it combines separate Breton and Welsh *Vitae*.[78] Padarn's supposedly Armorican origin, which is attributed to confusion between the use of the form Letavia (later Llydaw) as a name not only for Brittany but also—according to Wade-Evans, Doble and Bowen[79]—for a part of south-east Wales, is more likely to be an echo of the cognate Breton cult. In Wales Padarn's dedications, which probably imply a monastic federation centred later on Llanbadarn Fawr, are sometimes adjoined, according to E. G. Bowen,[80] by dedications to 'companion' saints mentioned in the saint's *Vita*. Moreover, as the same authority notes,[81] the dedications to the saint correspond to the course of Roman roads in Wales which may point to an early dissemination of the cult.

Conclusion

The main aim of this brief and necessarily selective survey of Cardiganshire saints has been to investigate the part played by the early Irish colony in the introduction of the cults now represented by the seventy or so surviving dedications. The concentration of Irish dedications south of the River Ystwyth, corresponding to the sphere of influence associated on other grounds with the Irish, has led—mostly by reference to the calendar of saints—to the identification of several saints whose originally Irish character had been obscured by the effects of localization.

[72]For the importance of dedications in relation to *paruchiae*, see W. Davies, *An Early Welsh Microcosm*, 139–46.
[73]A. W. Wade-Evans, *Vitae Sanctorum Britanniae et Genealogiae*, 163–4.
[74]G. H. Doble, *Saint Patern*, Cornish Saints Series no.43 (1940): E. G. Bowen, *A History of Llanbadarn Fawr*, 26–34.
[75]A. W. Wade-Evans, *Vitae Sanctorum Britanniae et Genealogiae*, 254–6.
[76]Ibid, 252.
[77]Petran is attached to the north-east Leinster family of the Dál Meisin Corb, to which Kevin of Glendalough also belonged. His church was at Barrowmount townland, parish of Grangesilvia, Co. Kilkenny; Ó Riain, *Corpus Genealogiarum*, 30.
[78]G. H. Doble, *Saint Patern*, and E. G. Bowen, *A History of Llanbadarn Fawr*, 31.
[79]See above, n. 10.
[80]E. G. Bowen, 'The Celtic saints in Cardiganshire', 9. Cf. idem, *The Settlements of the Celtic Saints in Wales*, 92.
[81]E. G. Bowen, *The Settlements of the Celtic Saints in Wales*, 53–6.

Chief among these saints was Finnian who, whatever may be said of his ultimate origins, was the subject of a cult as typically Irish as that of Patrick. There are two very important implications to this argument. Firstly, along with the Ogam inscriptions, place-name and linguistic traces, the composition of the local pattern of dedications may also now be cited as evidence of early Christian Irish influence in the area. Secondly, these dedications and doubtless others must date from the earliest period of church-building in south-west Wales. If the northern part of the County has scarcely been mentioned, the omission is more apparent than real. Padarn, whose Irish associations—unlike those of David—are not only late but also very vague, belongs to this district. Indeed, he accounts for two of the ten surviving dedications in this part of Cardiganshire. Four of the remaining dedications are to 'foreign' saints, three to Michael, one to Hilary (Ilar). In fact, only one of the saints in the area, Afan of Llanafan Trawscoed, is claimed as a descendant of Ceredig in *Bonedd y Saint*. For all practical purposes, the saints of Cardiganshire were concentrated in the areas south of and immediately north of the River Ystwyth.

APPENDIX: AN ALPHABETICAL LIST OF CARDIGANSHIRE SAINTS

While designed to be as comprehensive as possible, this list does not pretend to be exhaustive. The term 'saint' is used throughout without prejuduce to the often very doubtful origins of the personages under discussion. Place-names are spelt as far as possible according to M. Richards, *Welsh Administrative and Territorial Units* (Cardiff, 1969). Listed below are references additional to those in the footnotes above:

Arnold-Forster: F. Arnold-Forster, *Studies in Church Dedications*, 3 vols. (London, 1899).

Bromwich: R. Bromwich, *Trioedd Ynys Prydein* (Cardiff, 1961).

Evans, *Gaulish Personal Names*: D. E. Evans, *Gaulish Personal Names* (Oxford, 1967).

Evans, *Buched Dewi*: D. S. Evans, *Buched Dewi* (Cardiff, 1959).

Farmer: D. H. Farmer, *The Oxford Dictionary of Saints* (Oxford, 1978).

Fisher: J. Fisher, 'Welsh church dedications', *THSC* (1906–7), 76–108.

Harris, 'Kalendar': S. M. Harris, 'The Kalendar of the *Vitae Sanctorum Wallensium*', *J. Hist.Soc. Church in Wales*, 3 (1953), 3–53.

Jones: E. J. Jones, *Buchedd Sant Martin* (Cardiff, 1945).

Loth: J. Loth, *Les Noms des saints Bretons* (Paris, 1910).

Miller: M. Miller, *The Saints of Gwynedd* (Woodbridge, 1979).

Rees: R. Rees, *An Essay on the Welsh Saints* (London, 1836).

Victory: S. Victory, *The Celtic Church in Wales* (London, 1977).

Wade-Evans, 'Parochiale Wallicanum': A. W. Wade-Evans, 'Parochiale Wallicanum', *Y Cymmrodor*, 22 (1910), 22–124.

AFAN, Llanafan

This saint, who is often called Afan Buellt after the most prominent of his churches, is among those named as descendants of Ceredig (whence Ceredigion). His mother's name is given as Tegfedd which, despite Bromwich, hardly represents *Degfedd* 'tenth'. Tegfedd (from *teg* 'fair'?) is described as the daughter of Tegid Foel of Penllyn, near Bala. Outside Wales Afan's cult is attested at Lanavan (Finistère) in Brittany. The saint's feast fell on 16 or 17 November.

Baring-Gould and Fisher, I, 114; *EWGT* 20; Bowen, *Settlements*, 59, 134–5; Bromwich, 268, 464, 514; Loth, 12.

ALL SAINTS, Cellan

Prior to the ninth century the feast of All Saints was commemorated in Ireland, and presumably also in Wales, on 20 April. By the twelfth century the feast had shifted to 1 November, traditionally one of the four principal days of the pagan Celtic calendar. This day was commonly assigned to saints whose real feasts had been forgotten (see CYNDDILIG, CYNFELIN). A variant tradition asserts that the church of Cellan was dedicated to St Callwen.

Baring-Gould and Fisher II, 67; Farmer, 12; Fisher, 105; Rees, 327; Wade-Evans, 'Parochiale Wallicanum', 59.

BORTHIN (*see* MORTHIN)

BRIGIT (see FFRAID)

BRIOG (see TYFRIOG)

CALLWEN, Cellan

The Demetian Calendar, which may have been compiled at Llangeitho in the sixteenth century, lists Callwen and Gwenfyl under 1 November, describing them as (otherwise unknown) daughters of Brychan. Since Gwenfyl was considered to be patron of Gwynfil, we may take it that Callwen was then also regarded as patron of Cellan. Certainly this is the view advanced later both by Edward Lhuyd and by Browne Willis. Both saints are likely to have been extrapolated from the church names to which they are attached. A variant tradition states that All Saints were commemorated at Cellan.

Baring-Gould and Fisher II, 67; Wade-Evans, 'Parochiale Wallicanum', 59.

CARANNOG (CRANNOG), Llangrannog

Under the Brythonic form of his name, i.e. *carantacos from *caro 'love, friend', this saint is also commemorated in Cornwall (Carantoc of Crantock) and Brittany (Carantec of Tregaran-tec), and his name may lurk behind Carhampton in Somerset. Since at least as early as the twelfth century, when the first of two Lives was composed for the saint, Cairnech (Cernach) of Dulane, Co. Meath, has been regarded as Carannog's Irish equivalent. This would appear, however, to be a misidentification because, linguistically, the names are incompatible. Irish carnthach (carthach) would be the expected realization of *carantacos. Indeed, Carannog's real Irish equivalent may well be the celebrated Carthach (from *caratacos a variant of *carantacos) of Lismore, Co. Waterford. Some of the original Irish settlers in south Wales may have come from the area around Lismore. Moreover, Carthach's feast fell on 14 May which is just two days ahead of that of Carannog. Finally, the Welsh realization of *caratacos is caradog, the name of the remote ancestor of Ceredigion! Possibly, therefore, Carannog originally represented the ancestral deity/saint of the (Irish) people of Ceredigion.

Baring-Gould and Fisher II, 78–90; Bowen, Settlements, 89–91; Doble IV, 31–52; Evans, Gaulish Personal Names, 162–6; Harris, 'Kalendar', 27; Wade-Evans, Vitae, 142–9.

CARON, Tregaron

Derived in all probability from *caranto- (from *caro 'love, friend') the name Caron is ultimately from the same source as Carannog. In other words, the saints Caron and Carannog probably represent the same original cult. Like Carannog, however, Caron fell victim to the late medieval Welsh practice of attaching local saints to unrelated but superficially similar Irish cults. The Irish 'equivalent' chosen in this case, Ciarán of Ossory, seems to have been especially popular among the British Celts. Cornish clerics, for instance, pirated almost verbatim his Irish Vita to serve Perran (from Pezran from Pezr 'Peter') of Perranzabuloe. Obviously, there was a general awareness of the correspondence between Irish c- and Welsh/Cornish p- (cf. CYBI below). The effect of the misidentification on Caron's cult can be seen in the sixteenth-century Llanbadarn calendar where the name is spelt Kirianus, doubtless in imitation of the Irish Ciarán. Similarly, Caron's feast, 5 March, was probably borrowed from the Irish saint. An earlier more local tradition is preserved in the twelfth-century Bonedd y Saint where Caron (written Carawn) is described as a son of Ithael Hael of Brittany.

Baring-Gould and Fisher II, 119–38; EWGT, 58 (§ 25); Doble IV, 3–30; Harris, 'Kalendar', 35.

CEITHO, Llangeitho

Ending in -o (from *auos; cf., -io from *-iauos), Ceitho's name is hypocoristic in form. In other words, it is the pet or familiar form of a name which probably contained the root *catu- 'battle', one of the most prolific of all Celtic name elements. Variant forms like Ceido (Ceidio) are also attested. It could be, therefore, that Ceitho represents a local version of a well-known cult such as that of Cadoc, also from *catu-. Ceitho's feast, 5 August, is recorded in the Demetian calendar which may have been compiled at Llangeitho.

Baring-Gould and Fisher II, 101–2; Evans, Gaulish Personal Names, 171–5.

CHRIST, Capel Crist (Llannarth)

Early dedications in the name of Jesus or Christ are almost non-existent. Almost all Irish examples of Cell Christ, for example, refer to the Norman foundation of Christchurch in Dublin. We may take it, therefore, that the Welsh dedication, which has also been understood to refer to the Holy Cross, is of late origin. As with that to God, the dedication to Christ is interchangeable with the Holy Trinity.

Arnold-Foster I, 18–24; Fisher, 101; Rees, 52.

CRANNOG *see* CARANNOG

CYBI, Llangybi

The earliest recorded references to Cybi—his twelfth-century *Vita* composed, possibly, at Llangybi, and his pedigree as preserved both in his *Vita* and in *Bonedd y Saint* —provide him with a Cornish origin. Through his mother, however, a local relationship is established for him with St David. As fashion demanded (cf. Carannog) Cybi also acquired an Irish 'equivalent'. In fact, his *Vita* names two cognate saints—Pupu of Aran in the west and Mochop of Co. Meath in the east. The choice of Pupu again reveals an awareness of the *c-/p-* correspondence between Irish and Welsh, even if put to work here wrongly. On Aran, Cybi is also met by a saint called 'Crubthir Fintam' who has been identified as Gwyndaf of Capel Wnda (see GWYNDAF). While Cybi's name reveals a superficial similarity to the Irish Mochop (from Copp from Colum/Cormac?), it may be noted that the saints' feasts fell close together at the beginning of November. Mochop's day was 12 November; Cybi's feast fell variously on 5, 7 or 8 November. Possibly, as with Caron, we are dealing here also with a borrowed feast.

Baring-Gould and Fisher II, 202–15; Doble III, 105–32; Harris, 'Kalendar', 31; Miller, 14, 67–8; Victory, 34; Wade-Evans, *Vitae*, 234–51.

CYNDDILIG, Capel Cynddilig (Llanrhystud)

The saint's name is likely to be a diminutive of Cynddelw (from *cuno-deluos*) with which it actually interchanges. In the Iolo MSS he is included among the descendants of Gildas but this record is of little value. Nothing else is recorded of the saint other than the date of his feast which fell on 1 November. The fact that this was All Saints suggests that the date of Cynddilig's original feast may have been forgotten.

Baring-Gould and Fisher II, 230; Rees, 281.

CYNFELIN, Llangynfelyn

In *Bonedd y Saint* Cynfelyn (from *cuno-belinos*)

leads off the list of the descendants of Meiriawn (whence Meirionydd). Mostly, however, the surviving traces of his cult are connected with Ceredigion. A late source names 1 November as his feast but, as with Cynddilig, this may mean that his original day had been forgotten.

Baring-Gould and Fisher II, 243–4; Rees, 260.

CYNLLO, Llangynllo, Llangoedmor

Two pedigrees are on record for Cynllo. One underlines his connection with Cardiganshire by making him a descendant of Ceredig. The other relates to his church at Rhaeadr in Radnorshire. The name of the saint, from *cuno-loig-*, means something like 'wolf-calf'. Its Irish cognate, Conláed, is also used of a saint. Cynllo's feast fell on 17 July.

Baring-Gould and Fisher II, 263–4; *EWGT*, 55, 67.

CYNON, Capel Cynon (Llandysiliogogo)

Of the various saints named Cynon (from *cunonos* 'great hound') the most likely candidate for identification here is Cynon son of Brychan. The saint's feast fell on 9 November, a day shared, perhaps significantly, by the similarly named Irish St Mochonna (from Conna, a familiar form of Colum). More significantly, however, this day follows immediately on that of Tysilio (8 November), patron of the parish containing Cynon's chapel.

Baring-Gould and Fisher II, 272–3; *EWGT*, 17, 18.

CYNWYL, Aber-porth

A genealogy and skeletal history of this saint survive—but only in the suspect Iolo MSS. Elsewhere, in the story of Kulhwch and Olwen, a 'Cynwyl sant' is included among those who escaped after the battle of Camlann. Cynwal (Irish Conall) may be the more correct form of the name. The saint's feast is assigned to 21 November.

Baring-Gould and Fisher II, 275–7; Bowen, 'Celtic saints', 11; Bromwich, 161.

DAVID (*see* DEWI)

DEINIOL, Llanddeiniol

Like David, Deiniol (from Daniel), patron of the very important northern church of Bangor, bears a biblical name. Like David also, one of the earliest mentions of Deiniol is in an Irish source.

The early ninth-century Martyrology of Tallaght includes a reference to *Daniel episcopus Bennchair*. Writing in the late eleventh century Rhygyfarch attests to Deiniol's continuing importance by introducing him into his *Life* of David. He may also have been influenced, however, by the dedication to Deiniol at Llanddeiniol, one of very few southern witnesses to the cult. Deiniol's feast fell on 11 September.

Baring-Gould and Fisher II, 325–31; Miller, 82–5; Wade-Evans, *Vitae*, 165.

DEWI (DAVID), Llanddewibrefi etc.

The saint's churches and chapels in Cardiganshire are Blaenpennal, Capel Dewi (Llandysul), Henfynyw, Llannarth, Llanddewi Aber-arth and Llanddewibrefi. The last-mentioned church is also the most important. The close connection between David's cult and the area is also attested in other ways. The saint's genealogy, for instance, traces his descent from Ceredig. Similarly, Rhygyfarch of Llanbadarn, who composed David's Latin *Life c.* 1090, focuses on local churches and personages in his accounts of the saint's birth and upbringing. Thus the saint's father, Sant, whose clearly spurious name may derive from a misreading of Dewi Sant 'Saint David' as Dewi ap Sant 'David son of Sant', is made king of Ceredigion. The name of his mother, Non, for its part may have been extracted from the church name *Llannon* (more properly *Llan-on(n)* 'church of the ashtree'?). Irish influence probably accounts for part of David's increase in popularity. The spread of his cult, for instance, corresponds closely to the range of Irish settlement in south Wales. He is also the only Welsh saint named in the metrical martyrology composed about 830 by Óengus of Tallaght. David's name, like that of Deiniol, is of biblical origin. His feast falls on 1 March.

Baring-Gould and Fisher II, 285–322; Bowen, *Settlements*, 50–65; Bowen, *St David of History*; Harris, *St David and the Liturgy*; Evans, *Buched Dewi*; Rees, 45–56.

DWY (DUW), Llanddwy (Llanfihangel-y-Creuddyn)

The name of this church preserves, in reduced form, the middle Welsh *dwyw* 'god' (modern Welsh *duw*.) This is one of a small number of Welsh churches dedicated to the Christian deity, and, as with Christ, this dedication sometimes alternates with the Trinity. Thus another name

for Llandrindod was Llandduw. Similarly, a Ffynnon Drindod adjoined Llandduw.

FFRAID (BRIGIT), Llansanffraid etc.

Ffraid, otherwise Brigit, who ranked second only to Patrick among the Irish saints, is remembered in at least seventeen churches, not to mention chapels, in Wales. Two Cardiganshire churches (Llansanffraid and Llanffraid) and one chapel (Capel Ffraid in Llandysul parish) are dedicated to the saint. The uncommon use of *san(t)* 'saint' before the name has led to the claim by Bowen that the person concerned was 'thought of as intrusive'. This may be so in other cases, but *sanct* 'saint' is sometimes prefixed to Brigit in Irish usage. Ffraid's Irish origins appear to have been well remembered. The genealogists named her father Dwthach (Irish Dubthach) Wyddel ('Irishman'). A fifteenth-century Welsh metrical *Life* of the saint also proclaims her Irish ancestry. There is a fairly general view, shared, for instance, by Fisher and Bowen, that the Welsh dedications to Ffraid are comparatively late. Linguistically, however, the name Ffraid corresponds to the Old Irish form Brigit which suggests an early borrowing. The cult may well have been introduced into Wales by early Irish settlers in Dyfed. These came partly from the Déisi of Munster where Brigit's cult was particularly strong. The remote origins of the saint are mythological. Her feast, 1 February, was one of the four principal days of the pagan Celtic calendar.

Baring-Gould and Fisher I, 264–88; Bowen, 'The cult of St Brigit'; Fisher, 101; Jackson, 497–8.

GWBERT, Y Ferwig

This saint was first 'discovered' by Canon Doble who, having observed 'that there is a Gwbert-on-Sea … on the coast of Cardigan near Llangrannog', took the name to represent 'the true patron' of Cubert near New Quay in Cornwall. This claim was subsequently enthusiastically endorsed by Bowen. Lacking any visible sign of sanctity, however, such as a feastday, Gwbert should probably be restored to its previous status as a place-name.

Doble IV, 50; Bowen, *Settlements*, 87, 91.

GWENFYL (GWYNFIL)

While 'discovered' at a much earlier date than Gwbert, this saint may also have originated in the

place-name to which she is attached. Thus her companion, under 1 November, in the local sixteenth-century Demetian calendar, is Callwen who seems to have been foisted on the similarly named church of Cellan, which latter church is otherwise said to be dedicated to All Saints. Gwenfyl and Callwen are described in the calendar as (otherwise unknown) daughters of Brychan.
Baring-Gould and Fisher III, 197; Rees, 153; Wade-Evans, 'Parochiale Wallicanum', 59.

GWENOG, Llanwenog
The several invocations to this saint in the fifteenth-century Llanstephan MS 116 show her to have been the subject of a strong local cult. Her name, from *gwyn* (*gwen*), Irish *finn* 'fair', and the date of her feast, 3 January, which she shares with the Irish saint Fintan (also from *finn* 'fair'), shows her to have originally formed part of the widespread local devotion to a saint best known as (Irish) Finnian. The change of sex involved in this identification was a common enough aspect of Celtic devotion to the saints. See also GWNNEN.
Baring-Gould and Fisher III, 198.

GWNDA *see* GWYNDAF

GWNLLE *see* GWYNLLEU

GWNNEN (GWYNEN), Llanwnnen
Now taken to have been female, Gwnnen is entered in the sixteenth-century Demetian calendar with Gwnnws of Llanwnnws as an (otherwise unknown) son of Brychan. The saint's feast, which fell on 13 December, similarly points to an original identity with the homonymous Irish saint Finnian, whose main feast was on 12 December. If a change of sex did take place at Llanwnnen, then the rededication of the parish church to Lucy of Syracuse, whose feast also fell on 13 December, may have been a contributing factor.
Baring-Gould and Fisher III, 230.

GWNNWS (GWYNWS), Llanwnnws
Gwnnws shares with Gwnnen, his brother according to the Demetian calendar, a feast on 13 December and a name containing the element *gwyn* (Irish *finn*) 'fair'. Like Gwnnen, therefore, Gwnnws no doubt also reflects the cult of the Irish saint Finnian which seems to have been par-

ticularly strong in Cardiganshire. Finnian's main Irish feast was on 12 December. Gwnnws has the distinction of being mentioned in the twelfth-century Latin *Life* of Padarn of Llanbadarn where his name is spelt Guinnius and where he is described as the leader (*dux*) of a local church.
Baring-Gould and Fisher III, 247; Wade-Evans, *Vitae*, 256.

GWYDDALUS, Llanwyddalus
Since at least the sixteenth century, this saint has been (falsely?) identified with Vitalis of Ravenna, a third-century martyr whose feast, well known in Britain, is recorded by Bede and the Old English martyrology. As has often been pointed out, however, Welsh Gwyddalus does not correspond to Latin Vitalis. If false, therefore, the identification may date to the period when it had become fashionable to establish foreign (mostly Irish) equivalents for local cults which also seems to have entailed the borrowing of feasts (see CARANNOG, CARON etc.). Gwyddalus's feast fell on 26 April; that of Vitalis on 28 April. The name Gwyddalus may contain the element *gwyddel* 'Irish (person)'.
Baring-Gould and Fisher III, 217–18; Wade-Evans, 'Parochiale Wallicanum', 59.

GWYNDAF (GWNDA), Capel Gwnda, Troed-yr-aur (Trefdreyr)
As pointed out by Wade-Evans, Welsh Gwyndaf is the 'rule-right' equivalent of Irish Fintam. In all likelihood, therefore, the ostensibly Irish 'crubthir Fintam' (Fintam the priest) of the twelfth-century *Life* of Cybi of Llangybi evokes the local Welsh saint Gwyndaf. In origin, however, Gwyndaf, like Gwnnen and Gwnnws, probably represents the cult of Saint Finnian. Gwyndaf's feast (6 November) is very close to that of an Irish saint Fintan (7 November). A Breton origin is proposed for Gwyndaf in the Iolo MSS.
Baring-Gould and Fisher III, 228–9.

GWYNEN *see* GWNNEN

GWYNLLEU (GWNLLE), Nancwnlle
Gwynlleu figures among the local saints whose descents are traced from Ceredig. Almost nothing else is known of him. The assignment of his feast to 1 November, or All Saints, may mean that his original day had been forgotten. On the other

hand, the Irish saint Finnian, with whom Gwynlleu may be ultimately identical, also had associations with days in early November. His name is the direct equivalent of the Irish Finnlug which is also borne by a saint.
Baring-Gould and Fisher III, 234; *EWGT* 55 (§ 7).

GWYNWS *see* GWNNWS

HILARY *see* ILAR

HOLY CROSS, Mwnt (Y Ferwig)
The dedication to the Holy Cross or Rood at Mount (Mwnt) is preserved in the former name of the place, Y Grog o'r Mwnt. Only a few Welsh churches bear this dedication. Devotion to the Cross is, however, attested in Britain and Ireland at an early date. Oengus's metrical martyrology (*c.* 830 AD) mentions, for instance, the feast of the finding of the Cross on 3 May. Furthermore, there are at least a hundred early dedications to the Holy Cross in England. The dedication at Capel Crist (Llannarth) has also been taken to represent the Holy Cross (see CHRIST).
Farmer, 93–4; Fisher, 101–2.

HOLY TRINITY, Cilcennin (Aberaeron)
The dedication to the Holy Trinity interchanged with that to Christ or God. Another name for Llandrindod, for instance, was Llandduw. Such dedications are, however, rare in Wales, as in Ireland, and probably mostly post-date the arrival of the Normans.
Fisher, 101; Wade-Evans, 'Parochiale Wallicanum', 61.

IFAN (JOHN), Betws Ifan etc.
Of the four dedications to John in Cardiganshire, three—at Ysbyty Ystradmeurig, Ysbyty Cynfyn and Ysbyty Ystwyth—are certainly to John the Baptist, patron of the Knights Hospitallers. Devotion to John the Apostle is attested also, however, from a very early date. His cult is possibly represented by the dedication at Betws Ifan.
Wade-Evans, 'Parochiale Wallicanum', 60–1.

ILAN, Trefilan
Trefilan, which lay formerly within the hundred of Ilan (cf. Llanilar), is taken to derive from *tref* and *Ilan*, a variant of Ilar, the Welsh form of Hilary. This is unproven. Names with *tref* do not normally denote saints. Moreover, there is a variant tradition which maintains that the saint culted in the parish of Trefilan was Cyngar. See also ILAR.
Baring-Gould and Fisher III, 298; Rees, 328; Wade-Evans, 'Parochiale Wallicanum', 63.

ILAR (HILARY?), Llanilar
Celtic devotion to Saint Hilary of Poitiers is already attested in the Martyrology of Tallaght, which was compiled *c.* 830. The cult is also found in a number of Breton churches. Not surprisingly, therefore, the dedication at Llanilar has long been taken to represent Hilary. There is, however, a problem about this identification. Welsh *ilar* does not correspond exactly to Latin *hilarius* (Irish *eláir*). It may be, therefore, that the cult of Hilary at Llanilar dates to the period when foreign saints were being actively promoted as patrons of Welsh churches. The saint's feast at Llanilar, which varied between 13, 14 and 15 January, would have been borrowed at the same time. Hilary's feast fell on 13 January. See also ILAN.
Baring-Gould and Fisher III, 299–300; Loth, 64.

INA, Llanina
According to the eleventh-century tract on the descendants of Ceredig (*Progenies Keredic*), Ina was his daughter, which means that Ina of Llanina was then believed to be the name of a local saint. Otherwise, the saint's origins are obscure. A similarity of name and identity of feast (1 February) indicates that there may be a connection between Ina and Euny (or Uny) of Lalant and Redruth in Cornwall. Euny was regarded by the Cornish clerics as an Irish saint but there is no other support for this. The suggestion that Ina was identical with a West Saxon king of the same name has been rightly rejected.
Baring-Gould and Fisher III, 318; *EWGT* 20; Doble I, 79–88; Fisher, 107.

ITHEL, Bron-gwyn (Teifiside)
Betws Ithel is attested as the former name of Bron-gwyn. When not combined with topographical elements, such as Betws Abergele, *Betws* names are normally accompanied by names of saints, as with Betws Aeddan etc. There is, however, no other record of a St Ithel. On the other hand, a son of Ceredig is said to have borne the name. It may be,

therefore, that we are dealing here with traces of an ancestral cult.
EWGT, 20, 55.

JOHN *see* IFAN

LLEUCU (LUCIA?), Llanwnnen, Betws Leucu
Lleucu is taken to be the Welsh equivalent of Latin *Lucia*. As with *Ilar/Hilarius*, however, the names do not correspond linguistically. The feast of Lucy of Syracuse fell on 13 December and this no doubt led to her substitution for Gwnnen at Llanwnnen. The identity of Lleucu of Betws Leucu cannot now be established, but the name is probably related to the Celtic deity, *Lleu*.
Baring-Gould and Fisher III, 367–8.

LLWCHAEARN, Llanllwchaearn, Llan-ychaearn
This saint reflects the cult of the most widely venerated of all Celtic deities, Lugos (Irish Lug). Thus his name derives from *Lleu* + *teyrn* (the lord Lug), Irish Lugtigern, which was also the name of a saint. Llwchaearn's feast, 11 or 12 January, matches that of two saints in the Irish calendar whose names derive from Lug, Lóichin and Laigne. A Welsh pedigree was provided for Llwchaearn but this reflects the traces of the cult in Montgomeryshire.
Baring-Gould and Fisher III, 381–3; *EWGT*, 60.

LLŶR FORWYN, Llanllŷr
Though it is possible to infer from the saint's name that Llŷr was a (female) virgin, the name is in fact male. The *forwyn* (from *morwyn*) component probably originally derives from *marinus* 'seafarer' which in the form of *marini* often follows (and seeks to explain) Llŷr in the Welsh secular genealogies. *Llyr marini* is named by the genealogists as the father of Caradog, one of the most prominent of the ancestral heroes of Ceredigion. As with Ithel son of Ceredig, we are probably dealing here with traces of an ancestral cult. Llŷr's feast fell on 21 October.
Baring-Gould and Fisher III, 386–7; *EWGT*, 59, 62; Bromwich, 430; Wade-Evans, *Vitae*, 261.

LUCIA *see* LLEUCU

MAIR, Llanfair etc.
With over fifty churches named Llanfair there can be no doubt—despite Fisher and Rees—of the early popularity of the cult of the Virgin in Wales. This is strongly supported by the literary evidence from Ireland. With five or six dedications to Mary, three of them—at Clydogau, Orllwyn and Trelygen—named Llanfair, Cardiganshire was no exception. The dedications at Bron-gwyn, Cardigan and Ystrad-fflur are of later origin. The most important of the Virgin's many feasts was that of the Assumption (15 August).
Fisher, 94–8; Rees, 27–35.

MEILIG, Llannarth
This saint, whose name appears to be a variant of Maelog, was previously honoured at Llannarth. At present the church is dedicated to David. It may be noted that a St Maelog figures in the twelfth-century Latin *Life* of Cybi where he is described as Cybi's disciple. Topographically, this is reflected in the proximity of Llanfaelog to Caergybi in Anglesey. Maelog's cult in Cardiganshire, which is attested in the church name, Llanfeilog near Llangeitho, may also be connected with that of Cybi. The Demetian calendar compiled in the sixteenth century, probably at Llangeitho, lists the saint's feast under 12 November.
Baring-Gould and Fisher III, 405; Wade-Evans, 'Parochiale Wallicanum', 59.

MIHANGEL (MICHAEL), Llanfihangel etc.
The cult of the archangel Michael was by far the single most important Welsh devotion, as nearly one hundred dedications demonstrate. Of these many, if not most, are of early origin. The Welsh annals record the dedication of an unnamed church to Michael under 718. Four of the eight Cardiganshire dedications are named Llanfihangel which also points to an early origin. These are located at Genau'r-glyn, Penbryn, Ystrad and Y Creuddyn. The other four dedications, at Aberystwyth, Ciliau Aeron, Lledrod Isaf and Troed-yr-aur, may be of later origin. A characteristic of Michael's cult is its association with heights. His main feast fell on 29 September.
Fisher, 92–4; Rees, 36–43.

MORTHIN, Capel Borthin (Llandysul)
St Martin was one of the most popular (non-biblical) saints of the early Middle Ages in Britain and Ireland as well as on the Continent. In the time of

Augustine, for instance, a church at Canterbury was dedicated to him. His Latin *Life* by Sulpicius Severus also exercised great influence. One of its most celebrated imitators was Adamnán, abbot of Iona and biographer of Columba. A later Welsh adaptation of Martin's *Life* is also preserved. Despite the saint's popularity, there is no medieval dedication to him in Wales, unless Capel Borthin be regarded as genuine. The problem is, however, that Marthin and not Borthin or even Morthin is the usual Welsh form of the name. Moreover, dedications containing the element *capel* tend to be late. It may be assumed, therefore, that devotion to Martin at Capel Borthin is of more recent date, originating, perhaps, in learned guess-work.
Grosjean; Jones; Rees, 328.

NON, Llan-non

As pointed out above under DEWI, the name Non could have resulted from a (deliberate) mis-interpretation of the church name Llan-on(n) which may in fact mean 'church of the ash(tree)'. Alternatively, Non could represent Latin *nonna* 'nun'. In any event, as with many mothers of saints, Non shows signs of having been invented with a view to fleshing out the story of Dewi's birth and youth in Ceredigion. Even the day of her feast, 3 March, obviously depended on the day of her celebrated son which fell on 1 March. In Rhygyfarch's *Life* of David, the saint's name is spelt Nonnita.
Baring-Gould and Fisher IV, 22–5; *EWGT*, 54–5; Harris, 'Kalendar', 35; Wade-Evans, *Vitae*, 151.

PADARN, Llanbadarn Fawr

After David, Padarn is the most important local saint in Ceredigion. He is commemorated in no less than four local dedications, at Llanbadarn Fawr, Odwyn, Trefeglwys and Y Creuddyn. Yet it is only through his mother, Gwen, daughter of Ceredig, that a local genealogical connection is established for the saint. For the rest Padarn's genealogical associations are with Brittany, where the saint's cult is very strongly represented (indeed, Padarn's early twelfth-century Latin *Life* is thought to be partly based on a continental original). The counter argument to a Breton association, that the Letavia of Padarn tradition represented a place in south Wales, may be discounted. Padarn's *Life* acquired its seemingly indispensable Irish dimension through his father,

Petran, who is supposed to have gone to Ireland where he was visited by his son. In fact, the Irish name Petran represents a diminutive of Petar, 'Peter (the Apostle)'. Since Bowen wrote, attention is often drawn to the conformity between the spread of Padarn's cult in Wales and the course of Roman roads in the area, but cults normally followed available routes. The saint's name derives from the Latin Paternus, a common Roman name. His feast, 15/17 April, was shared by the Welsh and Breton versions of the cult.
Baring-Gould and Fisher IV, 39–51; Bowen 'Celtic saints', 2–9; Bowen, *History*, 26–34; Harris 'Kalendar', 29–30; Loth, 101; Wade-Evans, *Vitae*, 252–69.

PEDR, Lampeter

Almost twenty *llan* churches are named after St Peter. This dedication is almost certainly in all cases, including Lampeter (Llanbedr), to the chief of the apostles. The fact that a Pedr is included among the descendants of Ceredig—in other words among the saints of Ceredigion—merely underlines the strong tendency towards localization of saints which prevailed in Wales, as in Ireland, in early medieval times. This contrasts with the later tendency to externalize the origins of local saints. Peter's principal day, which he shared with Paul, was 29 June.
Baring-Gould and Fisher IV, 88–9; *EWGT*, 55 (§4); Fisher, 100–1.

PEDROG, Y Ferwig

The twelfth-century Martyrology of Gorman, which used as a source a version of Usuard's martyrology prepared in an English church, lists under 4 June 'Petrocus, a chaste, princely chief'. This shows how popular Petroc of Padstow and Bodmin, one of the most celebrated of all Cornish saints, had become. His Welsh cognate, who, according to one genealogical tradition, was Cadog's uncle, no doubt shared in this popularity. A variant genealogy attributes a Cornish origin to the saint. The saint's name derives from **Petracus*, a local variant of *Petrus* (from *Petr/Pedr*) 'Peter' with diminutive suffix. It corresponds to Breton *Perec* (*Perreuc*) which likewise occurs in many church names. This means in effect that we are dealing once more with an original cult of St Peter. In Cornwall, for instance, a 'S. Pedyr's Well' and a 'chapel dedicated to St Pedyr' were located on lands belonging to St Petroc's monastery. Similarly, in the Martyrology of Tallaght under 4 June, Pedrog's day, mention is made among the list of native saints of a certain *Petar* 'Peter'. On the onomastic evidence, therefore, Pedrog's cult could have originated as that of Peter the Apostle who, as we have seen, was very popular in Wales. The placing of his feast on 4 June could possibly be explained by reference to his association with St Kevin of Glendalough, whose 'fellow-pupil' he is reputed to have been. Kevin's feast fell on 3 June. Be this as it may, Doble and, especially, Bowen have drawn attention to the proximity of Pedrog's churches in Cornwall and Wales to the churches of other 'related' saints.

Baring-Gould and Fisher IV, 94–103; *EWGT*, 24–5, 29–30, 60 (§ 39); Bowen, *Settlements*, 87–8, 90–1, 101; Bromwich, 492–3; Doble IV, 132–66; Loth, 103.

RHYSTUD, Llanrhystud

The Welsh genealogists attributed a Breton origin to Rhystud 'of Ceredigion in Deheubarth'. They also found an unlikely brother for him in Cristiolus, the patron of Llangristiolus in Anglesey. Though the subject of various pseudo-etymologies indicating a Welsh origin, Rhystud's name shares with Cristiolus a decidedly non-Welsh appearance. In fact, Rhystud derives from Latin Restitutus which, curiously enough, was also borrowed in Ireland as the name of a Lombardian father of a number of saints. Rhystud's feast was held locally just before Christmas.

Baring-Gould and Fisher IV, 117; *EWGT*, 58 (§ 24a).

SILIN, Capel San Silin (Llanfihangel Ystrad)

The use of *san* with the name may mean that the saint was a (late?) foreign borrowing; (but see FFRAID). The occurrence of the name in association with *capel* is another sign of lateness. The two days attributed to the saint, 27 January and 1 September, show that he was also perceived as a foreigner. The first of the two dates points to Julian, bishop of Le Mans, whose cult had spread to Britain at an early date. The second points to Giles of Saint-Gilles in Provence who was an immensely popular saint throughout Christendom. The patron of Capel San Silin is likely to have been this Giles.

Baring-Gould and Fisher IV, 205; Doble V, 115–16; Farmer, 173; Rees, 220.

SULFED (see TYSULFED)

TYFRÏOG, Llandyfrïog

This saint is to be identified with the patrons of Saint-Brieuc in Brittany and St Breoc in Cornwall. The Welsh form of the name is composed of *Briog* preceded by *ty-* (from **to-* the prefix of endearment). The full Brittonic name was **Brigo-maglos*. In an eleventh-century Latin *Life* of Breton origin, the saint is named 'Brioc-maglus, a native of the Coritician region'. This means that there was a general awareness of the importance of his association with Cardiganshire. The Welsh genealogies, which speak of 'Tyuriawc son of Dyngat of Keredigyawn Is Coet' support this. Llandyfrïog was formerly located in the commote adjoining Is Coed. An English survival of the cult occurs at St Briavels in Gloucestershire, a place formerly known as Little Lidney. Significantly, perhaps, there was a Romano-British dedication near here to Nodens who again figures as Nudd Hael in Tyfrïog's Welsh pedigree. This may mean that the saint's origins were ultimately mythological, which would be in line with the occurrence of his feast on 1 May, one of the main festivals of the pagan Celtic Calendar. Both Doble and Bowen have drawn attention to the proximity in Cornwall and Wales of Tyfrïog's churches to those of other 'related' saints. What this means is that the saint's legend was told along much the same lines in both places.

Baring-Gould and Fisher IV, 292; *EWGT*, 57 (§ 18); Bowen, *Settlements*, 89–91; Bromwich, 476; Doble IV, 67–104; Jackson, 448 (§ 76); Loth, 16.

TYGWY(DD), Llandygwy(dd)

This saint's church is located in fairly close proximity to Llandyfrïog on the southern boundary of Cardiganshire. Not surprisingly, therefore, the genealogists describe Tygwy(dd) and Tyfrïog (whose name is sometimes confused with Tyfrydog) as brothers. Nothing else seems to be known of Tygwy(dd) other than his feast which is variously placed on 13 or 18 January. His name is clearly hypocoristic in form, the first element being *ty-* (from **to-* the prefix of endearment). The second component element consists of a name beginning with *C-*. It may be pointed out that an Irish saint Mochua *al.* Dochua (from **to-* + *cua-*, a hypocoristic form) was also culted on 18 January, Tygwy(dd)'s day at Llandygwy(dd).

Baring-Gould and Fisher IV, 224; *EWGT*, 57 (§18); Wade-Evans, 'Parochiale Wallicanum', 59.

TYSILIO, Llandysiliogogo

This saint is the subject of an extensive dossier. Almost all of it relates, however, to churches in north Wales and Brittany. Thus, what materials survive about Tysilio were transmitted, with some exceptions, by Breton clerics using Welsh sources no longer extant and writing mostly in the interests of Suliac (Suliau, Sulian) of Saint-Suliac, a famous Breton priory. The Breton saint was taken to be identical with Tysilio but this has been disputed. Tysilio's pedigree survives independently in Welsh sources in two conflicting forms. One of these relates to the cult of the saint in north Wales, which centred on Meifod in Powys. The now lost Welsh sources used by Breton clerics also derived from this branch of the cult. The other attributes to Tysilio a descent from Ceredig. In other words, it takes cognizance of the more southern manifestation of the cult. The saint's name is hypocoristic in form and, by way of conjecture, may derive from Irish *sil(l)*-, as in *Sillen*, *Moshiloc* etc. from an original *Sinell*, which contains the element *sen* 'old'. Thus the Irish saint Sinell was commemorated on 1 October, the day of Tysilio's 'equivalent', Suliau. Similarly, a number of Irish saints with names deriving from the root *sen* 'old' were commemorated in early November. Tysilio's Welsh day was 8 November. Alternatively, Loth's suggestion of an origin in **to-suliaw*, from a root **sul* also presumably represented in TYSUL below, may be followed.

Baring-Gould and Fisher IV, 296–305; *EWGT*, 59 (§33) (cf. Baring-Gould and Fisher 4, 296–7); Bowen, *Settlements*, 79–80; Doble V, 104–26; Loth, 115.

TYSUL, Llandysul

Tysul's particular association with Cardiganshire is reflected in the fact that a genealogy was provided for him tracing his descent back to Ceredig and establishing a close relationship with other local saints, including Carannog and Tyfriog. His only other Welsh church was at Llandysul in Montgomeryshire. There his wake was on 11 November which may indicate an association between him and Tysilio whose day fell on 8 November. Tysul's day in Cardiganshire fell on 31 January. This is interesting because it represents the vigil of the feast of St Brigit who, as Ffraid, was culted in the parish. As explained above there may also be a connection between the names Tysul and Tysilio.

Baring-Gould and Fisher IV, 305–6; *EWGT*, 55 (§3); Loth, 138.

TYSULFED, Llandysul

Within the parish of Llandysul there is a church named Llandysulfed. This name is taken to commemorate St Sylvester. It seems very unlikely, however, that such a foreign name underwent hypocoristic treatment in Welsh, as shown by the prefixing of the element *ty*-.

URSULA AND THE ELEVEN THOUSAND VIRGINS, Llangwyryfon, Capel Santesau (Llanwenog)

The supposed British origin of Ursula, patron of the church of St Ursula of Cologne, who is alleged to have been martyred in the company of 11,000 virgins in the fourth century, would be expected to have contributed to the popularity of her legend in Wales. The evidence for the cult is, however, late and mostly confined to Cardiganshire. There it appears to have centred on Llangwyryfon, 'church of the virgins'. The day associated with the cult, 21 October, was also observed locally. All this may derive, however, from a late, deliberate misidentification of a kind so common in Wales. An early sixteenth-century Welsh life of the saint also survives.

Baring-Gould and Fisher IV, 312–47; Farmer, 386–7.

VITALIS (?) (see GWYDDALUS)

c. THE ARCHAEOLOGY OF EARLY CHRISTIANITY IN CARDIGANSHIRE

Heather James

The archaeological evidence for the origins and development of Christianity in western Britain falls into two interrelated parts. Firstly, there is the evidence for burial practices in the form of cemeteries and burial monuments; secondly, there is the evidence, both in the field and through excavation, of early churches, chapels and cult sites such as holy wells. Aerial survey has also produced much new information. A great deal of work has been done on the subject over the last two decades, but coverage is uneven both geographically and chronologically. So the evidence for Cardiganshire will be supplemented by that from west Wales in particular and western Britain in general.

Some of the archaeological evidence, such as the burial formulae or inscribed crosses on the Early Christian monuments, may directly indicate Christian beliefs. There is less certainty now that burial practices of the early medieval period such as orientation, or extended inhumation in stone cists or wooden coffins, unaccompanied by grave goods, are in themselves diagnostic of Christian beliefs.[1] Undoubtedly for west Wales as elsewhere, we must look for the origins of specifically Christian burial practices and sites in native Iron Age/Romano-British traditions as well as in rites imported from the Continent.

It is now well established both by recent excavation and older antiquarian discoveries that many Bronze Age ritual and funerary monuments, such as cairns, standing stones and above all barrows, were reused for burials in the early medieval period. The most numerous examples come from south-west and north-west Wales.[2] There can be no doubt that these structures were recognizable as funerary, if not ritual, monuments in the early medieval landscape. Some may have served as territorial boundary markers. T. M. Charles-Edwards has highlighted from legal sources interesting Irish parallels for the use of a grave mound or mounds as boundary markers.[3] Any claimant to the land had to drive his horses over them in a series of fairly elaborate entry rituals. The phrase 'heir of a gravestone' is used with the implication that men might be buried on the boundaries of their estates. In some instances, their graves may have been marked by stones bearing ogam inscriptions. The likelihood that some of the isolated Class I Early Christian monuments were of this character has long been recognized and some possible Cardiganshire examples are given in the following section. Charles-Edwards further suggests that it was the adoption of overtly Christian burial practices in cemeteries which erased such archaic procedures from Welsh law.

[1] P. A. Rahtz, 'Grave orientation', *Arch.J.*, 135 (1978) 1–14; G. Kendall, A study of grave orientation in several Roman and post-Roman cemeteries from southern Britain', *Arch.J.*, 139 (1982), 101–23.

[2] N. Edwards, 'Anglesey in the early Middle Ages: the archaeological evidence', *Trans.Anglesey Antiq. Soc. and Field Club* (1986), 19–41; H. James, 'A gazetteer of cist cemetery sites in Dyfed' in 'Excavations at Caer, Bayvil, 1978', *Arch. Camb.*, 136 (1987), 51–76.

[3] T. M. Charles-Edwards, 'Boundaries in Irish Law', *Medieval Settlement: Continuity and Change*, ed. P. Sawyer (London, 1976), 83–7.

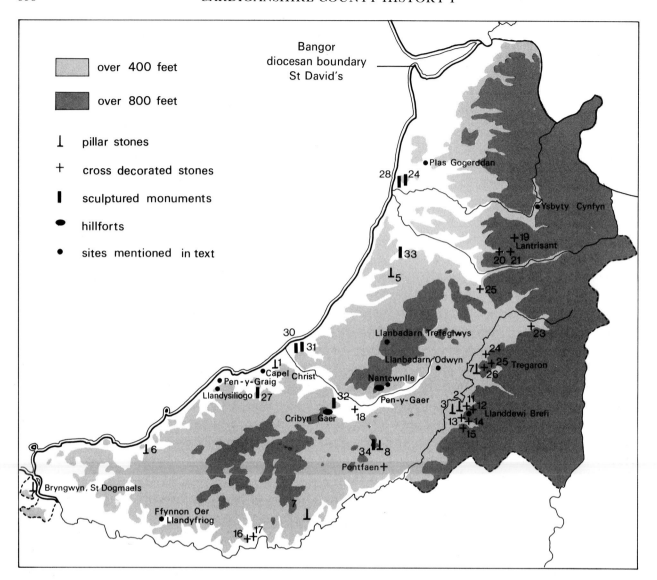

Fig. 71: Distribution of Early Christian monuments and ecclesiastical sites.

We know from place-name evidence and from early poetry, such as the collections of *englynion* known as the *Stanzas of the Graves*, that prehistoric ritual and burial monuments were often considered to be the graves of heroes.[4] Thomas Jones has pointed out how some of the names of these heroes are eponyms derived from natural features like rivers, and cites:

> The grave of Taflogau is in his homestead yonder, as he is in his durance, whoso would dig it would find treasure.

> (Bet Tawlogev man Llut in y trewrud trav, mal y mae in y kystut, ae clathei, [ef] caffei but.)

[4]Thomas Jones, 'The Black Book of Carmarthen "Stanzas of the Graves"', *Proc. British Academy*, 53 (1967), 97–136 (no.61).

Here *Taflogau* is an earlier form of Dologau, which joins the Ystwyth near Hafod Uchdryd. The significance of burial in the homestead is further discussed below.

Examples of the reuse of barrows have not yet been identified in Cardiganshire but a typical example of antiquarian records of such reuse is the account by Edward Laws in 1880 at Brownslade Burrows, Pembs.[5] He opened a barrow where he recognized that the numerous inhumations, 'some protected by an enclosure of long, water-worn stones about the size of ninepins', were secondary to the central square cist. Recent excavations at the barrow cemeteries of Trelystan and Four Crosses, Powys, similarly have located small groups of oriented, simple dug graves of presumably Early Christian date close to the barrows.[6] Elsewhere we also have the well-known phenomenon of the 'christianizing' of pagan sites. Britain can show no examples to equal the Breton practice of carving a cross on top of a large menhir, but, as the following section on Early Christian monuments details, some Bronze Age standing stones may have been reused. E. G. Bowen suggested, admittedly on the basis of inadequate nineteenth-century records, that the large stone found beneath the pulpit during extensive renovation of Llandysiliogogo church may have been deliberately brought into the church from a nearby megalithic site.[7] However, C. S. Briggs has suggested that the supposed prehistoric stone circle incorporated into the churchyard wall of Ysbyty Cynfyn may be an early nineteenth-century creation.[8]

Reuse of earlier ritual and funerary sites, monuments and objects in early medieval contexts is thus quite well attested. It is now beginning to be recognized that in some instances there may have been a continuity of burial on some Bronze Age ritual and funerary complexes during the Iron Age and Romano-British periods. Even the practice of burial in stone cists originated in and developed from Iron Age mortuary traditions; long cists, though rare, are not unknown in Iron Age contexts. What are we to make of three stone-sided and paved graves, with possible headstones, discovered in 1865 near Fynnonoer Farm in the parish of Llandyfriog?[9] They were aligned north–south and contained ash, charcoal and burnt human bone, so cremation seems to have been the burial rite. We can only guess at their date. Other 'long-cist' burials from west Wales have contained traces of ash.[10] The scattering of white quartzite pebbles around graves is also known in Iron Age contexts and has persisted into modern times. The most important change in burial practice in the later Roman period, widely observable across Europe and the Mediterranean, was from cremation to inhumation. It is therefore likely that the cremation burial within a cairn at Penbryn (discussed in detail on p.314 and below II.ch.7.d, No. 6) was of early Roman date. It was reused when a class I Early Christian monument, the Corbalengus stone, was placed over the cairn. But the imperfect nature of our records of this extremely interesting site leaves room for alternative explanations. It cannot be doubted, however, that the use of a cairn of stones to cover a burial or burials, whether in square or long cist, whether cremation or inhumation, flexed or extended, is a continuous tradition in Wales from the Bronze

[5]Edward Laws, *Little England Beyond Wales* (London, 1888), 56–9.
[6]W. Britnell, 'The excavation of two round barrows at Trelystan, Powys', *PPS*, 48 (1982), 161–3; W. Warrilow, G. Owen and W. Britnell, 'Eight ring-ditches at Four Crosses, Llandysilio, Powys, 1981–85', *PPS*, 52 (1988), 53–88.
[7]E. G. Bowen, 'Menhir in Llandysiliogogo Church, Cardiganshire', *Antiq.*, 54 (1971), 213–15.
[8]C. S. Briggs, 'Ysbyty Cynfyn churchyard wall', *Arch.Camb.*, 128 (1979), 138–46.
[9]E. C. L. Fitzwilliams, 'Early interments, Cardiganshire', *Arch.Camb.*, (1865), 395–7.
[10]E.g. at Llanwnwr Farm, Llanwnda, Pembrokeshire, RCAHM, *Pembrokeshire*, 191 (No.559).

Age into the early medieval period. Recent excavations at Tintagel churchyard have explored mounded graves covering encisted inhumations. Such graves, it is argued, should be termed 'special graves', analogous to the western European *inhumations privilégiés*.[11]

The few Welsh examples of Iron Age burials known to date have been listed and discussed by Murphy and Williams.[12] In Cardiganshire the excavations at Plas Gogerddan (see Fig. 42) have provided evidence suggesting the continuity of use of a burial complex from the Bronze Age, through the Iron Age/Romano-British period into the early Middle Ages, combined with change in burial practice. The work at Plas Gogerddan was of a 'rescue' nature, and therefore limited in extent. Before excavation the above-ground remains consisted of a very large barrow (see pp. 187, 271 and Fig. 42), and a standing stone, one of a pair on the gravel ridge between the River Clarach and River Peithyll. Excavation demonstrated that the stone had been re-erected in its present position in modern times. However, it had probably not been moved far since excavation revealed a likely primary socket hole close by. Aerial survey in 1984 had already shown crop-marks around the large barrow and those of smaller ring ditches (ploughed-down barrows) to the west and north.[13] What was wholly unexpected was the discovery of an inhumation cemetery of early medieval date north of the large barrow. Excavation showed that the crop-marks west of the standing stone were of a conjoined double and a single ring ditch of late Bronze Age date. Of great interest was the presence of secondary burials of late Iron Age/Romano-British date. Their date range is suggested by two bronze brooches accompanying a crouched inhumation on the edge of the double ring ditch.[14] There were traces of at least one more such burial close by. All the barrow mounds and the standing stone would have been visible monuments in the early medieval period and the inhumation cemetery seems to have been located with reference to the standing stone.

No bone survived in the acid soils of the site, but several of the grave fills preserved minute traces of wooden coffins. It was from such exiguous remains that the single radiocarbon determination for the cemetery of 370 ± 60 ad (1570 bp) was obtained.[15] At least twenty-two graves were identified in the excavated area with only a slight degree of superimposition. All were oriented, of varying lengths and depths and seemingly arranged in rows. Only on the western side was there any indication of a boundary zone to the cemetery, perhaps precluding encroachment onto the smaller barrows. Its full extent and plan could not be recovered within the confines of the rescue work. Three of the graves may be termed 'special graves' in that they were enclosed within small rectangular wooden structures. In the best preserved of the three (structure 373) (Plate XIII) the evidence took the form of a single foundation trench, straight-sided, but with rounded corners, with an entrance at the eastern end marked by two small post-holes, measuring 5.5 × 3.8 m overall. Within this apparent wooden building was a centrally placed oriented grave with both coffin and bone stains, the bone-staining suggesting that the head was at the west end facing the entrance. Between the grave and the entrance was a small stone-lined pit, which also

[11]J. A. Nowakowski and C. Thomas, *Excavations at Tintagel Parish Churchyard, Cornwall, Spring, 1990*, Cornwall Archaeological Unit and Institute of Cornish Studies (Truro, 1990).

[12]K. Murphy and G. Williams, 'A gazetteer of Iron Age burials in Wales', in K. Murphy, 'Plas Gogerddan, Dyfed: a multi-period ritual and burial site', *Arch.J.* (forthcoming).

[13]T. A. James, 'Aerial reconnaissance in Dyfed, 1984', *AW*, 24 (1984), 12–24.

[14]H. N. Savory, 'Bronze objects', in K. Murphy, *art.cit.*

[15]CAR—1045, context 231.

had timber staining in its fill, possibly the remains of a wooden box. Similar features and arrangements seem to have been present in the other two 'special graves'.

How should we describe these small timber structures at Gogerddan, not all of which may have been standing at the same time? Although Early Christian parallels of special grave surrounds, *martyria*, timber oratories or even chapels all spring to mind, it is perhaps worth noting that small rectangular timber buildings are not unknown in Iron Age cemeteries.[16] The Gogerddan special grave surrounds are very reminiscent in size of the small, rectangular timber structure (4.2 × 3.6 m) built over the site of a levelled Neolithic cursus at Llandegai, Gwynedd.[17] This also contained a single, central, oriented grave. An inhumation cemetery of oriented rows of graves was discovered on the north side of this building, and the grave showed signs of later disturbance. Some 640 m to the east of the site stands the fourteenth-century chapel of St Tegai. The structure associated with the inhumation cemetery was thus, very plausibly, considered by the excavators to be a 'primitive' chapel, and the disturbed grave perhaps evidence for the disinterment of a saint's bones (St Tegai's?) and their translation to the new stone chapel. Another parallel to the Gogerddan structures can be cited at Capel Eithin, Anglesey.[18] The only recognizable above-ground feature of this complex, multi-period prehistoric site to survive into the landscape of the early medieval period, was a small, square, stone building, perhaps of Roman date. An inhumation cemetery of ninety-seven graves was sited north of it. The burials, largely, though not entirely, oriented, fall into three main groups. Those nearest to the building contained three full-size dug graves, and thirteen smaller ones, interpreted as child and infant burials, some incomplete, others in partial stone cists. A second group, on a different alignment to the first, again had a preponderance of probable child/infant burials. On the northern edge of the site was a small robbed-out stone building, 4.9 m square, which contained a deep central grave, partially encisted, with the carbonized remains of a plank beneath the body. Two small child graves were set alongside and finally a full lintel cist grave had been inserted across the threshold of the building. Excavation showed that it had a timber precursor of similar size and dimensions. This structure had evidently served as a focal point for a large group of full-sized graves, with more outside the boundary of the excavation. This building was described as a *cella memoria*, that is, a structure around a martyrial tomb, well known in late and post-Roman continental Christian contexts. Although superficially similar to the special graves at Gogerddan, it is clear that the 'square-ditched' graves at Tandderwen, Clwyd, represent a different tradition. One of these produced a radiocarbon date of 510 ± 60 ad (1440 bp). An inhumation cemetery, where several of the graves were enclosed within square ditches lay to the north of a large Bronze Age barrow, but the ditches did not contain any timber walling or surround, and were seemingly dug to mark off and create a mound over the grave. So far unique in Wales, such graves may be paralleled

---

[16]E. W. Black, 'Romano-British burial customs and religious beliefs in south-east England', *Arch.J.*, 143 (1986), 201–39; R. Whimster, *Burial Practices in Iron Age Britain: A Discussion and Gazetteer of the Evidence 700 bc–ad 43* (BAR 90, 1981).

[17]C. Houlder, 'The Henge Monuments at Llandegai', *Antiq.*, 42 (1968), 216–21.

[18]S. White, 'Excavations at Capel Eithin, Gaerwen, Anglesey; first Interim Report', *Trans. Anglesey Antiq. Soc. and Field Club* (1980), 1527; cf. 'Capel Eithin' in *Med. Arch.*, 25 (1981), 226–7 and 26 (1982), 186.

by those of the East Yorkshire Arras culture of Iron Age date, or Scottish square-ditched graves, which have a longer date range.[19]

To return to Gogerddan, there are no traditions of a lost chapel, no place-name indications of a cemetery, no Early Christian monument, no Roman activity to serve as an interpretative peg for the timber structures around the graves. Perhaps we have a mixture of traditional and innovative burial rites. The location suggests continuity and the possible presence of grave-goods the survival of older pagan practices whereas orientation and special graves may indicate innovative practices from outside. For, as Black wisely reminds us, when discussing Romano-British burial customs and religious beliefs in south-east England: 'Funerary practices are usually based on custom, the continuation of traditional practices by a community. It is usually impossible to tell whether the survivors at a funeral ceremony in Roman Britain would have regarded the form of burial they witnessed as an expression of religious belief.'[20] So far as we can tell the inhumation cemetery at Gogerddan was unenclosed. In his seminal characterization of rural cemeteries as 'the primary field monuments of insular Christianity',[21] Charles Thomas laid particular stress on the significance of circular enclosures. Embanked circular churchyards, usually with a *llan* prefix, have been taken to indicate early church and cemetery sites in Wales, but the enclosures themselves may be of earlier origin and the practice of burial within them another aspect of the continuum of burial practice from the Iron Age/Romano-British period into the early Middle Ages. The gazetteer of Iron Age burials in Wales[22] notes two preferred locations: Bronze Age monuments, already discussed, and within or close by hillforts and defended enclosures (see p.233).

Excavation, aerial survey and a reconsideration of the original location of some Early Christian monuments are all providing a growing number of instances of small defended enclosures of Iron Age date reused as early medieval cemeteries, some developing into fully fledged parish churches and churchyards.

A trial excavation was carried out in 1979 on a small univallate defended enclosure known as Caer, or Y Gaer, Bayvil, Pembs., which as an earthwork site differed not at all from many others of assumed Iron Age date in west Wales.[23] A section across the defensive bank showed that the site may have originated as a palisaded enclosure, and some internal features suggested the gullies of round-houses, but its main interest was its final use as a cemetery. A long-cist burial, cut into the defensive bank was found in 1920 and archaeological excavation found two more, suggesting a possible radial arrangement of burials. The interior was filled with dug graves, some full-size, others small. Some were partially encisted, in others the amount of stone seemed only token. Some small, presumably child, burials were in full cists. Bone survival was very poor but a radiocarbon date of 660 + 65 ad (1290 bp) was obtained from bone in one of the lintel cists cut into the bank. In the interior there was quite a high degree of superimposition, suggesting a fairly intensive use of the enclosure and some patterning in the form of rows was detectable. What the

[19]K. Brassil and P. J. Meredith, 'Square-plan ditches: Dark Age graves at Tandderwen, Denbigh, Clwyd', *AW*, 26 (1986), 21–2; K. Brassil and W. G. Owen, 'Tandderwen, Denbigh', *AW*, 27 (1987), 58; K. Brassil, 'Tandderwen', *AW*, 28 (1988), 51.
[20]Black, 'Roman-British burial customs', 201.
[21]Charles Thomas, *The Early Christian Archaeology of North Britain* (Oxford, 1971), 50.
[22]See above, n. 12.
[23]H. James, 'A gazetteer of cist cemetery sites', see above, n. 2.

limited excavation could not show, however, was whether there was any focal structure or structures. Total excavation would be necessary to discover whether the use of the enclosure as a cemetery came after a period of abandonment or as a change of use in a continuously occupied site.

Only one other defended enclosure in west Wales is known to have cist burials in or at least between its ramparts and that is the multivallate Caerau, Pembs., quite close in fact to Caer, Bayvil. Confusing and circumstantial as the nineteenth-century reports of this site are, they do suggest, with their 'hammers and cutlasses' in graves, the possibility of Iron Age, as well as early medieval, long-cist burials.[24] The number of defended enclosures whose final use was as early medieval cemeteries may be extended if we include those associated with Early Christian monuments, assuming these to be grave markers and thus indicative of cemeteries. A number of these were noted and listed by Lewis, including Cas Wilia, where two inscribed stones, now in Brawdy church, came from the farm which bears the name of the earthwork within which it is partially set.[25]

There are early medieval literary references from Welsh and Irish sources to burial in the ramparts of defended settlements. The dying Irish king, Loeguire, wished to be buried in his armour, facing his enemies, in the ramparts of his fort.[26]

Little new information on the reoccupation of hillforts in the post-Roman period has been produced in the last twenty years. Indeed, rigorous re-examination has actually reduced the number of such instances.[27] Nevertheless the excavation of what must originally have been a large cemetery of sub- and post-Roman date at Cannington, Somerset, remains a potent model for the possibly significant associations of Early Christian cemeteries and hillforts.[28] The Cannington cemetery seems to have originated in the late Romano-British period, its use extending into the eighth century AD. There were two focal elements to the cemetery: the grave of a young girl under a mound in a slab-marked grave, and a circular stone structure on the summit. Rahtz has suggested that the nearby hillfort of Cannington Camp might be the settlement associated with this cemetery.

The association of some Early Christian monuments and other cemetery evidence with hillforts has been pointed out by Lewis.[29] In addition to Pembrokeshire examples, he draws attention to the small hillfort of Cribyn Gaer (SN 520 508). The decorated slab (see below, II.ch.7.d, p.420, No. 32 (Plate XXIX)), which was recorded by Meyrick as coming from the farm of Maes Mynach below the hillfort,[30] may possibly have originally been sited in the fort itself. Another interesting juxtaposition is that of the hillfort at Pen-y-gaer (SN 578 583) with the isolated St Gwynlleu's church at Nancwnlle, with its large oval churchyard, bisected by a stream with a nearby well, in the valley directly below.

[24]H. J. Vincent, 'Caerau', *Arch.Camb.*, 10 (1865), 299–30.

[25]J. Lewis, 'A survey of Early Christian Monuments of Dyfed, west of the Taf', in *Welsh Antiquity*, ed. G. C. Boon and J. M. Lewis (Cardiff, 1976), 177–84.

[26]L. Bieler (ed.), *The Patrician Texts in the Book of Armagh* (Dublin, 1979), 132–3.

[27]N. Edwards and A. Lane (eds.), *Early Medieval Settlements in Wales* AD *400–1100* (Cardiff, 1988).

[28]P. A. Rahtz, 'Late Roman cemeteries and beyond', *Burial in the Roman World* (CBA Res.Rpt.22), ed. R. Reece (London, 1977).

[29]See above, n. 25.

[30]S. R. Meyrick, *The History and Antiquities of the County of Cardigan*, 304.

Aerial survey in west Wales, as in other areas, has discovered more defended enclosures surviving only as crop-marks to add to the already dense distribution of assumed Iron Age/ Romano-British earthworks. Equally significant has been the recognition of larger sites, some of a newly recognized form termed concentric antenna enclosures.[31] Sites surviving as earthworks have been shown from aerial survey to have had larger enclosures of slighter construction around them, and hence perhaps their survival only as faint crop-marks. In the present context, however, it is the recognition of such outer enclosures around small embanked churchyards which strongly suggests that some may have developed from earlier defended enclosures (for a possible example, see Plate XIV).[32] It has long been thought that the substantial embanked circular churchyard enclosure of Eglwys Gymyn (Carms.) was in origin the inner defence of a larger multivallate enclosure. At Llangan (Carms.) the churchyard is sited within or astride a complex crop-mark interpreted as a multivallate enclosure. A second small circular crop-mark in a field north of the church hints at paired enclosures. The rather unusual Class I Early Christian monument, Canna's Chair, is sited in a field called Parc Maen just outside the churchyard. There are also suggestions of a much larger enclosure partly surviving as hedgebanks. We may also cite the crop-mark of a 'concentric-circle' type of prehistoric enclosure discovered near Lan farm, Llanboidy (Carms.) in the dry summer of 1984. Here a 50 m-diameter enclosure lies within a much larger one of 120 m probably enclosed only by a palisade. Is such a feature to be equated with the early Welsh *bangor* (wattle fence), the inner being the *llan*? It is interesting to note that the farm name was *llan* on the first edition of the OS one-inch map and that the field north of the site is called Parc y Fynwent (cemetery field) where there is a local tradition that a church once stood.

The identification of such crop-marks in the grassland conditions prevailing in much of west Wales demands optimum drought conditions and intensive aerial photography over a number of years. Such a programme has not yet been carried out in Cardiganshire, although a preliminary search of a 1989 sortie over the northern half of the County has demonstrated the potential of such a programme.[33] One possible site noted in north Cardiganshire, however, is the isolated St Gwnnws church (SN 6852 6953), beside the Nant Cwm Nel. Faint crop-marks indicate a possible outer enclosure to the south of the oval-shaped churchyard. Strong corroborative evidence that the church lies within an early cemetery site is provided by the explicitly Christian inscription of the 'Hiroidil' stone (see below, II.ch.7.d, p.416, No. 22) from the churchyard. There are several other possibilities. Further aerial survey should certainly be carried out around St Padarn's church, Llanbadarn Odwyn, south-west of Pen-y-gaer hillfort, itself bypassed by the Roman road. A side road deflects around the oval churchyard. Some 200 m to the south west is a curved and substantial hedgebank which might be part of an earlier enclosure. It has been designated as an SSSI by the Nature Conservancy Council because of the very high number

---

[31]T. A. James, 'Air photography by the Dyfed Archaeological Trust 1989', *AW*, 29 (1989), 31–4; T. A. James, 'Concentric antenna enclosures—a new defended enclosure type in west Wales', *PPS*, 56 (1990), 295–8.

[32]T. A. James, 'Air photography of ecclesiastical sites in south Wales', *The Early Church in Wales and the West*, ed. N. Edwards and A. Lane (Oxford, 1992), 62–76.

[33]1989 1:10,000 True Colour Sortie, N. Ceredigion, commissioned by the Welsh Office and the Nature Conservancy, Air Photographs Library, the Central Register of Air Photographs for Wales, Welsh Office, Cardiff.

(seventeen) of hedgerow species it contains, although the possible significance of this in terms of its antiquity has not been recognized. Cardiganshire church sites would undoubtedly benefit from intensive morphological and topographical analysis which has had such striking results, for example, in Cornwall.[34]

Another phenomenon apparent in the distribution of small, defended, Iron Age enclosures in west Wales is the existence of similar-sized sites in close proximity. One such 'pair', Dan-y-coed and Woodside, near Llawhaden (Pembs.), has been totally excavated in recent years.[35] They were occupied in the late Iron Age/Romano-British period, and one continued in occupation as a lower-status farm into the late Roman, possibly sub-Roman, period after the other had been abandoned. Celtic systems of partible inheritance have been suggested to explain such paired sites. At Llangynog (Carms.) the church seems to have been sited within one such embanked enclosure, while aerial survey has shown another similar site surviving in an adjacent field only as a crop-mark.[36] A possible Cardiganshire example may be St Padarn's church at Llanbadarn Trefeglwys, a small, embanked, circular churchyard adjacent to a farm. Across the road to the north-east are faint crop-marks of a second, larger, circular enclosure. Might such sites have been abandoned as a consequence of being given over entirely for burial purposes, perhaps through the presence there of a founder's grave, perhaps by gift, and might they have then become kin burial grounds? Caer Bayvil may plausibly be explained in this way.[37]

It would be incorrect, however, to suggest that all churches and chapels originated as early cemeteries which developed, through the attraction of focal graves, timber oratories and chapels and then stone-built churches. Only total excavation of redundant church sites could demonstrate this sequence. Archaeology has been able to show that not all cemeteries 'developed' in these ways. The isolated grouping of some Early Christian monuments might indicate the existence of 'undeveloped' cemeteries. It may be that the recently discovered stones at Llantrisant churchyard (see below, II.ch.7.d, p.416, Nos. 19–21), might indicate one such cemetery, the possibly reused stone from Maes-llyn, Llangwyryfon (see below, II.ch.7.d, p.414, No. 5) another. Chapel sites, which perhaps pre-date, or were never incorporated into, parochial structures, may indicate other such 'kin burial grounds'. An interesting site of high archaeological potential may be the now deserted Pen-y-graig farm in Llanina parish. When R. E. Bevan perceptively identified some of Llannarth parish's chapels as belonging to the component *Trefi* of the parish, the chapel was identified as Capel Christ and grave mounds could still be seen.[38]

It is generally accepted that the earliest chapels or churches within such cemeteries will have been of wood, not stone. As yet there is very little archaeological evidence for the dating of churches, whether of wood or stone, in Wales. D. B. Hague was able to show that a small wooden structure had served as the direct precursor of the twelfth-century church on Burry Holms, off

---

[34]A. Preston-Jones, 'Decoding Cornish churchyards', *The Early Church in Wales and the West*, ed. Edwards and Lane, 104–24.

[35]G. Williams, 'Recent work on rural settlement in later prehistoric and early historic Dyfed', *Ant. J.*, 68 (1988), 30–54.

[36]See above, n. 33.

[37]H. J. James, 'Early medieval cemeteries in Wales', *The Early Church in Wales and the West*, ed. Edwards and Lane, 90–103.

[38]R. E. Bevan, 'Notes on Llanarth and neighbourhood', *TCAS*, 4 (1926), 60–70.

the north-west coast of Gower.[39] But this was not inevitably the case. The large-scale excavations at Capel Maelog, Llandrindod Wells, have amply demonstrated the development of an early medieval cemetery which perhaps originated in a small post-Roman defended enclosure. Though not primary to the cemetery a special grave served at Capel Maelog as a focus for subsequent development and was seemingly incorporated into the chancel of a small stone church of late twelfth-century date, this church, however, having no timber precursor.[40]

In Anglo-Saxon England the more plentiful survival of documentary evidence and a number of large-scale modern excavations have indicated an intensive period of rural church building —and indeed urban, though such parallels do not apply to Wales—in the ninth, but most especially the tenth and eleventh centuries.[41] These were the churches which in many instances became the parish churches of the twelfth and thirteenth centuries. Some were founded by bishops, or were offshoots from minsters or mother churches, but the majority were proprietal in character, having been founded by local lords. Was Wales so very different?

The failure of some cemetery sites to develop may be due to the lack of sufficiently attractive saints' cults connected with them. It is likely that most cults required an element of organization to develop and Professor Ó Riain's study of the individual saints of Cardiganshire (see above, II.ch.7.b) demonstrates the importance of Irish settlers in the fifth and sixth centuries in the dissemination of saints' cults, both major and minor. The need for active promotion is implicit in parts of the eighth century *Collectio Canonum Hibernensis*, which warn that angels would not visit the souls of Christians who were buried among evil men. Elizabeth O'Brien suggests that such moral blackmail by the Church to ensure burial took place only in Christian cemeteries must mean that mixed pagan and Christian kin burial grounds were still in active use.[42]

Belief in the powers of saints to mediate between God and men mitigated against such traditional practices. Because it was believed that their powers did not die with the saints, burial in close proximity to their graves was thought to confer great spiritual benefit and their ability in life to heal and work miracles to continue through their bodily relics. These powers could even be transferred to objects they had used and owned, such as St Padarn's staff, the *Cyrwen*.[43] The territorial possessions, privileges and protection offered by the greater churches, whatever the nature of their ecclesiastical organization, were derived from the strength of the cult of their founders.

Unfortunately archaeological evidence bearing on the great cult centres of early medieval Cardiganshire, Llanbadarn Fawr and Llanddewibrefi, is virtually non-existent. No such site in Wales has been excavated, even the precise location of many of the monasteries named in historical sources is not known. There is, moreover, an increasing reluctance to assume that Welsh sites would follow the better-known plans, extent and character of Irish monasteries. Reassessment of some British sites, notably Tintagel, has shown how difficult it is to distinguish

[39]RCAHM *Glamorgan* I, 14. See also D. B. Hague, 'Some Welsh evidence', *Scottish Arch. Forum*, 5 (1973), 17–35.
[40]W. H. Britnell, 'Excavations at the early medieval church of Capel Maelog, Llandrindod Wells, Powys. 1984–7', *Med. Arch.*, 34 (1990), 27–96.
[41]R. Morris, *Churches in the Landscape* (London, 1989).
[42]E. O'Brien, 'Late prehistoric–early historic Ireland : the burial evidence reviewed' (unpublished M. Phil. thesis, National University of Ireland, 1984).
[43]E. Henken, *Traditions of the Welsh Saints* (Woodbridge, 1987), 122.

high-status ecclesiastical from high-status secular buildings or occupation simply on the basis of archaeological evidence.[44]

The larger 'mother' or later the *clas* churches may, however, have left their mark on the landscape in one particular way. Among their many rights and privileges, which we find enshrined in the various recensions of the Welsh Laws was that of giving sanctuary—*nawdd*. The fines imposed in the Laws on those disturbing the peace in the cemetery and the much larger *noddfa* imply that both were demarcated by boundaries.[45] Wyn Evans is at present attempting to reconstruct these larger enclosures for the known major pre-Norman churches in Wales.[46] A possible outer boundary delimiting and encircling fields centring on the church seems to be indicated by aerial photography at Llanddewibrefi, although not all the boundaries are of the same, or even early, date.

Excavation and field evidence alone cannot, even under ideal circumstances, tell us all we wish to know about the spread of Christianity and the nature of the early Church in Cardiganshire. We are fortunate, therefore, to have the inscriptions and cross-decorated Early Christian monuments, whose epigraphy, formulae and styles of decoration can tell us more of the diverse influences from other parts of Britain and the Continent.

[44]C. Thomas, 'Tintagel Castle', *Antiq.*, 62 (1988), 421–34.
[45]D. Jenkins, *The Laws of Hywel Dda* (Llandysul, 1986), 81–3, 253.
[46]See also J. Wyn Evans, 'The early Church in Denbighshire', *Denbighshire Hist. Soc.*, 35 (1986), 61–82; J. Wyn Evans, 'The early Church in Carmarthenshire', *Sir Gâr: Studies in Carmarthenshire History*, ed. H. James (Carmarthenshire Antiquarian Society, Monograph series 4: Carmarthen, 1991), 239–54.

d. THE EARLY CHRISTIAN MONUMENTS

W. Gwyn Thomas

Although the thirty and more Early Christian monuments of Cardiganshire form less than 10 per cent of the Welsh total, they cover most of the known types, ranging from natural or roughly shaped boulders inscribed with names to better-shaped stones with incised crosses and brief inscriptions and ultimately to the ornamented sculptured stones of the latest pre-Norman period.[1] The stones carrying merely an inscription and/or an incised cross would seem in most cases to mark burials, as indicated by personal names and the Latin phrase *hic iacet* or *iacit*, 'here lies' (Nos.3, 6–7). Such a phrase shows a specifically Christian usage, as does the use of the cross symbol in a later development, and most of these monuments were first recorded in association with late medieval churches which were also possibly the sites of much earlier Christian centres (see below). One inscription (No.18) records a grant of land, presumably to an ecclesiastical

[1]The basic catalogue is V. E. Nash-Williams, *The Early Christian Monuments of Wales* (Cardiff, 1950), hereafter cited as *ECMW*. The County's monuments had earlier been surveyed by R. A. S. Macalister, 'The sculptured stones of Cardiganshire', *TCAS*, 5 (1927), 7–20. The inscriptions were also catalogued in more detail in his *Corpus Inscriptionum Insularum Celticarum*, I (Dublin, 1945), 333–41 (hereafter cited as *CIIC*).

institution while another (No.22), invoking a blessing for Hiroidil's soul, could have marked either a grave or ecclesiastical property. The tall, decorated cross at Llanbadarn Fawr (No.28) proclaims that this was a major ecclesiastical centre and it could also function as a preaching point, as seems to be true of similar tall crosses at other notable centres like Nevern, Penally, Penmon and Llantwit Major.

The stones employed for these purposes are largely of local origin, the one identified exception being No.28 (at Llanbadarn Fawr), a granitic rock possibly from north Caernarfonshire.[2] The local material does not lend itself to refined carving, but there is a trend from simply dressing one face for an inscription or a cross, to rough shaping of the stone and then with carved decoration to careful shaping of the stone itself. No.29 at Llanbadarn Fawr may show an uncompleted stage or an attempt to sculpt a cruciform monument.

Only one stone (No.6, at Penbryn) can be said to be in its original location, in the middle of a field west of the church. It is a tall, unshaped boulder, larger than other monuments and, were it not for the inscription, might be taken for a Bronze Age standing stone, which it could have been originally in view of the fact that a 'heap of stones' or cairn was formerly recorded there as well as a Roman burial.[3] The slab from Maes-llyn (No.5) was found in what would seem to have been a grave, but was almost certainly reused in this particular case. All the others (except for No.16) were first recorded at existing or former churches or chapels and have been reused as building material. Though one can never be sure that some were not collected from elsewhere, the tradition of burial at such places gives a presumption that they were first set up there, but the practice may have been a development from an earlier pagan custom of wayside burial. The presence of six of these monuments at Llanddewibrefi reinforces the historical indications that this was a site of some importance, possibly a 'mother church' for the area, that was subsequently eclipsed by Llanbadarn Fawr. On the other hand, the recent discovery of the three cross-decorated slabs at Llantrisant (Nos.19–21) indicates not so much its relative importance as the fact that this has been a little-used burial ground in a remote upland location.[4] In more frequently disturbed churchyards such stones are more likely to disappear unless they happen to have been incorporated into the fabric of the church or a surrounding wall.

The inscriptions of the first group of stones (Nos.1–9) are cut in Roman capitals for the most part, with a few half-uncial (or lower-case) letter forms occurring. Over the period from the late fifth century, when such inscriptions were introduced into western Britain, up to the seventh the fact that an increasing proportion of half-uncial letters was derived from manuscript usage indicates a relatively late date. Thus the Penbryn stone (No.6) and that from Llanwenog (No.7), with no half-uncial letters and the inscription set down the face of the stone, are early in the sequence. Datable analogies from continental Christian sites at Lyon, Vienne, Bordeaux and the Rhine Valley provide the basic chronological framework as well as suggesting that Christianity may have been introduced into western Britain from such Gaulish centres, a hypothesis supported by the distribution of finds of post-Roman pottery. The inscriptions in the second and third

---

[2]*ECMW* No.111, citing J. L. Platt.

[3]A definite reuse of a Bronze Age standing stone (identified by a 'cup-mark') is the roadside stone in Llanfaelog parish, Anglesey, inscribed with the name *Cunogus*(*us*) and *hic iacit* (*ECMW* No.9).

[4]J. K. Knight *et al.*, 'New finds of Early Christian monuments', *Arch.Camb.*, 126 (1977), 67–8.

groups (Nos. 14, 18, 22, 24, 27 and 30) are entirely cut in half-uncials and, while later than the seventh century, depend on other features for their dating. The stone from Llanwenog (No.7) with the Latinized name TRENACATVS also has the name in ogam, reading TRENACCATLO. This is the Irish form of the name and is a pointer to a widespread Irish element found not only in other inscriptions in south-west Wales but in place-names too. Ogam lettering is the usual form of inscriptions in south-east Ireland where it is likely to have been introduced by persons who were familiar with the Latin alphabet from Wales or other parts of western Britain; it was subsequently used in west Wales by Irish-speaking settlers.[5]

While some inscriptions consist solely of a name or names (No.2 and possibly but not certainly No.1), the more usual form gives a name in the form 'X son of Y' (Nos. 3, 5 and 7) or (as with No.4) 'X daughter of Y', or (as with No. 9) 'X wife of Y'. These phrases are characteristic of widespread Celtic practice, as is the tendency to place the lettering down instead of across the length of the stone. The formula *hic iacit* (seen on Nos.3, 5–8) derives from ecclesiastical practice at continental Christian centres, as do such biblical and classical names as David, Iacobus and Poten(t)ina. But names such as DUMELUS (No.2), BROHO(MAGLUS) (No.4), COR-BALENGI (No.6), MAGLAGNI (No.7) and others are Celtic, with Latinized endings. The combination of these forms indicates the fusion of different traditions in the early period of Church history in the area. It is to be presumed that the persons named on these monuments were of some consequence in contemporary society, though none of the associated words give any indication of status or rank.

Of particular interest for Welsh history is the record by Edward Lhuyd of the Latin inscription at Llanddewibrefi represented now by fragments only (No.3) which included the words SANCTI DAVID. The letter-forms suggest a mid-seventh-century date, which would indicate a site dedicated to and recording the name of Wales's patron saint within a century of the traditional year of his death and thus significantly earlier than surviving historical references to him. The phrase in which the saint's name occurs, with its reference to spoliation, suggests that here was an establishment of sufficient consequence and wealth to be a target for banditry. It is unfortunate that the other name recorded by Lhuyd as *Idnerth* has suffered damage in the breaking up of the stone, for its recorded form is not altogether consistent linguistically with the proposed date of the inscription.[6]

The effect of manuscript usage on inscriptions of the second and third groups can be seen not only in letter-forms and abbreviations such as $\overline{BT}$ $\overline{DS}$ for *benedicat Deus* on No. 14, and $\dot{H}$ $\overline{NO}$ for *hoc nomen* on No. 22, but is also evident in the small cross with which the original 'IDNERT' inscription (No.3 at Llanddewibrefi) began; a similar instance can be seen on the famous Catamanus stone at Llangadwaladr, Anglesey (*ECMW* No. 13). This could well have led to or at least reinforced the trend towards an incised cross as the primary feature of a monument. Certainly in the case of the inscribed stone at Silian (No. 8) a simple cross has been superimposed on part of an earlier inscription. Cross-bearing stones, often recumbent rather than upright as headstones, become much more numerous than stones with inscriptions alone, and the form of the cross develops a great variety of elaboration from the simple linear Latin cross seen on Nos.

[5]K. H. Jackson, *Language and History in Early Britain* (Edinburgh, 1953), 156–7.
[6]R. G. Gruffydd and H. P. Owen, 'The earliest mention of St David?: an addendum', *BBCS*, 19 (1960–2), 232–4.

11, 20 and 23, or from the ring-cross with a stem of Nos. 18 and 25. The linear and outline forms (Nos. 10, 21) can be matched with those on slabs at Irish monastic cemeteries like St Berrihert's Kyle which existed only during the period from the eighth to the tenth or eleventh centuries.[7] The pointed or spiked foot to the stem of the cross on No. 21 (occurring also on stones in Anglesey and Flintshire) (*ECMW* Nos.11a, 17–30 and p.23) hints at the probability that these cross forms are based on wooden prototypes which could be driven into the ground. The development towards sculptured forms could have been initiated by such features as the cross on the Llanwnnws stone (No.22) where the paired cords which interlace at the junctions are lightly carved in low relief. The similarity of its Latin inscriptions to that on a slab at Tullylease, Co. Cork (the latter reading *Quicumque legerit hunc titulum orat pro Berechtuire*, 'whoever shall read this inscription let him pray for Berechtuire'), has suggested that they are of comparable date; but there were two persons of that name associated with that site, and preference has now been given to Berechtuire the founder *c*.700 rather than to a namesake in the Irish annals in 839.[8] The earlier date suits this roughly shaped slab rather better as does the similar phraseology on the stone at Caldey Island (*ECMW* No.301), which on reconsideration has been attributed to the eighth century rather than to the ninth.[9] A later instance, however, was recorded on Eliseg's Pillar, Valle Crucis (*ECMW* No.182).

The Latin inscription on the stone at Llanllŷr (No.18) deserves notice, recording as it does a gift of land, presumably to the local church. The first name *Ditoc* could be a place-name rather than a personal name, but the letters following suggest not so much the name 'Madomnuac' (the apparent 'M' being a very late form) as Q͡UA(*m*) followed by a personal name, the irregularity of endings in the pronoun being a common feature. The proposed reading DOMNUACOLLON as a personal name may be related to the Old Welsh names *Dumnagual* and *Dumnguallaun*.[10] The earlier reading of the names *Madomnuac* and *Occon* seems to have been affected by the form *Modomnoc(h)* in Rhygyfarch's late eleventh-century *Life* of St David (in other versions it is *Midumnauc*).

A greater concern for shaping the slab and giving more prominence to its carved cross is to be seen on the stone at Llannarth (No. 27) and probably on that recorded by Meyrick at Llangwyryfon (No. 33). The fully sculpted monuments of the ninth and tenth centuries, represented in Cardiganshire by the tall cross at Llanbadarn Fawr (No. 28) and the sadly shattered cross at Llanddewi Aber-arth (No.30), belong to an older widespread practice in Britain and Ireland of erecting standing crosses. Though the arms of the cross-head at Llanbadarn Fawr are so reduced as to be flush with the shaft (a Viking-Age type termed the 'hammer-head cross'), the concept of a distinct three-dimensional cross is still there. This stone (and Nos. 32 and 34) also indicates the introduction of a wider range of carved decoration, in particular plaitwork with derived knotwork, key or fret patterns and human figures in low relief. The rendering of a seated figure (St Padarn ?) on one face and especially the spiral arrangement of the folds of the garment

[7]P. Ó hEailidhe, 'The crosses and slabs at St Berrihert's Kyle in the Glen of Aherlow', *North Munster Studies*, ed. E. Rynne (Limerick, 1967), 102–26.
[8]P. Lionard, 'Early Irish grave-slabs', *PRIA*, 61C (1961), 155.
[9]K. H. Jackson, *Language and History in Early Britain*, 291.
[10]Ibid., 421–2, 668; Cyril Fox *et al.*, 'The Domnic inscribed slab, Llangwyryfon, Cardiganshire', *Arch.Camb.*, 97 (1942–3), 205–12.

clearly owe much to such figures in Irish manuscript illustration as, for example, the portrait of St John in the Stowe Missal, and surviving material from the Llanbadarn Fawr *scriptorium* is similarly characterized by Irish influences.[11] The predecessors of Sulien, Rhygyfarch's father, could, like him, have spent considerable time in Irish monastic houses. But a blend of cultural influences is evident in the simultaneous adoption of the Cumbrian hammer-head and other Anglian features like the paired beasts.

The particular pattern of knotwork that is the only feature on the stone now at Llanilar (No.32) is virtually identical with that on a slab at Silian (No.34), suggesting that both may have been produced by one mason using perhaps the same template for both stones. The Silian stone also shows a good example of diagonal fret-pattern, and the same combination of patterns occurs on a stone at Abercorn, West Lothian.

As well as the links with the north indicated by the Silian stone and some features of the Llanbadarn cross, a more specific link with the Viking Age in the north is the hogback stone at Llanddewi Aber-arth (No.31), in the form of a recumbent, house-shaped stone with a curving roof ridge, often placed against an upright stone. This is the sole example of this type of monument in Wales, a type originating in north Yorkshire by the middle of the tenth century and dubbed by one writer 'a Viking colonial monument', so extensively is it to be found there and in Cumbria and Scotland.[12] But to explain the isolated occurrence of this hogback stone in west Wales remains problematical, so distant is it from sites with either Scandinavian place-names or the few Scandinavian finds of the period.

In the material surveyed here two inferences for the general history of the County can be stressed. One is the ecclesiastical context of many of the stones, whether pointing to primary evangelization or to later major centres, Llanddewibrefi and Llanbadarn Fawr. There are no hints, however, of church organization or of other aspects of life, lay or clerical, as provided by some inscribed stones in other areas of Wales. Another consideration is that despite their relatively small numbers the monuments show evidence of artistic links with more active areas of Christian monumental sculpture, both in the north of England and in Ireland, so that it would be inappropriate to regard life in Cardiganshire over this period as being in a cultural backwater.

In the catalogue which follows, the monuments have been arranged into three groups, reflecting their basic differences in form, purpose and, to some extent, chronology. Within each group the entries are in the alphabetical order of parish names of their original location in so far as this can be established.

[11]Françoise Henry, *Irish Art during the Viking Invasions (800—1020 AD)* (London, 1965), colour pl. J (facing p.187).
[12]J. T. Lang, 'The hogback: a Viking colonial monument', *Anglo-Saxon Studies in Archaeology and History* III, ed. S. C. Hawkes, J. Campbell and D. Brown (Oxford, 1984), 85–176; R. N. Bailey, *Viking-Age Sculpture in Northern England* (London, 1980), 85–100.

APPENDIX: A CATALOGUE OF EARLY CHRISTIAN MONUMENTS

I. Early Inscribed Stones

1. Henfynyw; church   SN 4475 6119

Fragment of a pillar-stone or slab (15 in. by 6 in.), with inscription reading TIGERN[..., for *Tigernus* or *Tigernacus*, a personal name which occurs on a stone at Jordanston, Pembs. The mixture of Roman capitals and half-uncials (T, G) suggests a sixth- to seventh-century date. A dubious letter I after the E is apparently an insertion. The stone was recorded before 1880, set over the north doorway, but it has since been reset inverted in the east gable of the chancel, north of the window.

Arch. Camb., 35 (1880), 299; *Arch. Camb.*, 51 (1896), 110–13; *CIIC* No.990; *ECMW* No.108.

2. Llanddewibrefi;   SN 6635 5529
churchyard (Plate XV)

Rough pillar-stone (44.5 in. by 14 in. and 5–8 in. thick) with inscription in two lines reading down the face DALLVS / DUMELVS, presumably personal names. The inscription is in deeply cut Roman capitals with half-uncial S and ligatured AL; the first letter was recorded before the top of the stone was damaged. The name *Dumeli* (from *Dumelas*) occurs in an ogam inscription in Ireland. A sixth-century date is likely. The stone was noted in 1746 by Lewis Morris as part of the stile on the east of the churchyard, and again by Meyrick about 1808. It is now inside the church.

Meyrick, *Hist. and Antiq.*, 271; *Arch. Camb.*, 51 (1896), 135 (citing Lewis Morris); *Arch.Camb.*, 86 (1931), 390; *CIIC* No. 351; *ECMW* No. 115.

3. Llanddewibrefi; church   SN 663 553

Two fragments of a squared pillar-stone originally at least 40 in. by 5–7 in. and 6 in. thick, with a fragmentary inscription. As recorded by Edward Lhuyd in 1693 and more completely in 1699, the original inscription was in three lines, along the length of the stone preceded by a small cross: HIC IACET IDNERT FILIVS IACOBI / QUI OCCISVS FVIT PROPTER PREDAM / SANC-TI DAVID, 'Here lies Idnerth, son of Jacob, who was slain because of the spoiling of Saint David'

—that is, presumably, in defending the church against despoliation. One fragment (10.5 in. by 5 in.) has only the lower parts of the first two words of line 1 with ....]I OCCISVS [... of line 2; the other fragment (17 in. by 7 in. and 6 in. thick) reads: .]DNERT FILIVS IA[.. of line 1 with .]VIT PROPTER PR[.. of line 2. The lettering is a mixture of debased Roman capitals and half-uncials (reliably shown in Lhuyd's drawing), pointing to a mid-seventh-century date. The initial cross copies the usage in ecclesiastical manuscripts of the period. The inscription provides the earliest known mention of St David (to whom the church is dedicated), probably within a century of his death. Lhuyd saw the complete stone over a doorway in the chancel, and it was seen over a north window there in 1802 and again by Meyrick. It was unfortunately broken when part of the church was rebuilt in 1848, and the two surviving fragments have been built into the external west wall of the nave, near the NW angle.

E. Lhuyd in Gibson (ed.), Camden's *Britannia* (1695 edn.), 644; Meyrick, *Hist. and Antiq.*, 269–70; *BBCS*, 17 (1956–8), 110, 185–93; *BBCS*, 19 (1960–2), 231–2; *CIIC* No. 350; *ECMW* No. 116.

4. Llandysul; churchyard   SN 4187 4072
(Plate XVI)

Fragment of a probable pillar-stone (17.5 in. by 13.5 in. and about 8 in. thick), with part of an inscription in three lines reading: VELVOR[../ FILIA / BROHO[.., 'Velvor(ia), daughter of Broho(...), (lies here)'. The lettering is in lightly cut Roman capitals, the H alone being half-uncial, indicating a sixth-century date. The name *Brohomagli* occurs on a stone at Pentrefoelas, Denbs., and may have been the name commemorated here. The fragment as it is now was noted in the churchyard in 1703 (by Lhuyd—NLW MS 21,001B) and Meyrick saw it in 1810 built into the west gateway. Since about 1905 it has been set into the internal north face of the vestry at the base of the west tower.

Meyrick, *Hist.and Antiq.*, 149 and Pl.IV, 1; *Arch.Camb.*, 11 (1856), 143; *Arch.Camb.*, 77 (1922), 213; *CIIC* No. 349; *ECMW* No. 121.

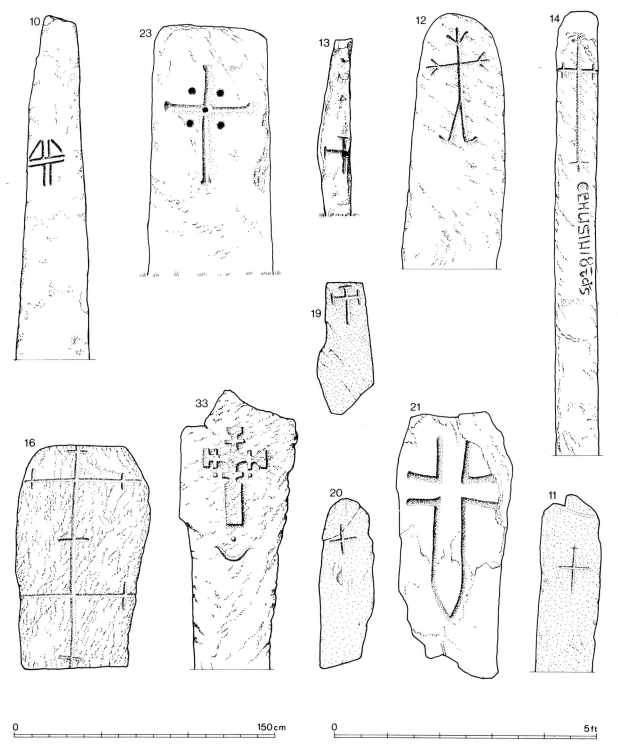

Fig. 72: Cross-decorated stones I. No. 16 is incomplete.

5. Llangwyryfon; at Maes-llyn　　SN 5880 7138
(Plate XVII)
A rough slab (38 in. by 15 in. and 3 in. thick), its edges damaged, with a Latin inscription in three lines: DOMNICI / IACIT FILIVS / BRAVECCI, '(The body) of Domnicus lies here, son of Braveccus'. The lightly picked Roman capitals and open form of the R indicate a late fifth- to early sixth-century date. The stone was discovered in 1942 in ploughing a field, set upright in what may have been a grave, and in the following year was placed in the National Museum of Wales.
Arch. Camb., 97 (1943), 205–12; *CIIC* No. 352A; *ECMW* No. 122.

6. Penbryn: near Dyffryn Bern,　　SN 2890 5137
SW of the church
(Plate XVIII)
A tall standing stone, possibly a prehistoric monument (72 in. above ground, the face 28 in. tapering to 17 in. and 20–6 in. thick), with a Latin inscription in two lines down the east face, reading: CORBALENGI IACIT / ORDOVS, '(The body) of Corbalengus lies here, an Ordovician'. The lettering in deeply cut regular Roman capitals indicates a date in the late fifth century. The Ordovices were named by Classical authors as a tribe probably occupying north Wales. Such tribal areas formed the basis for some post-Roman kingdoms. When first recorded in Lhuyd's additions to Camden (1695) it was described as having recently fallen from a position in a small heap of stones. In levelling this cairn about 1806 a burial urn of Roman date was discovered as well as (apparently) Roman coins of the late first century AD (see p.314). The stone was then re-erected on the site of the cairn.
Lhuyd in Gibson (ed.), Camden's *Britannia* (1695 edn.), 648; Meyrick, *Hist. and Antiq.*, 178; *Arch.Camb.*, 16 (1861), 305; *Arch.Camb.*, 17 (1862), 216; *CIIC* No.354; *ECMW* No. 126.

7. Llanwenog, Crug-y-whîl　　SN 4860 4240
(Plate XIV)
A squared pillar-stone of fine greenstone (72 in. tall by 15 in. and 7.5–8 in. thick) with ogam and Latin inscriptions. The ogam inscription (read upwards on the left edge and the top) gives a personal name TRENACCATLO. The Latin inscription in three lines down the face reads TRENACATVS / IC IACIT FILIVS / MAGLAGNI, 'Trenacatus lies here, the son of

Maglagn(i)'. The lettering is in Roman capitals, with E-shaped F and sickle-shaped G, and dates to the late fifth / early sixth century.

The stone is now in the National Museum of Wales, having been at Highmead until 1950; but it was recorded by Meyrick as being at Llanvaughan (a house since demolished) and was said to have been found built into the footings of a chapel that was demolished in 1796; this chapel stood on Crug-y-whîl near the farmhouse of that name.
Meyrick, *Hist. and Antiq.*, 187, 191; *Arch.Camb.*, 16 (1861), 42; *CIIC* No. 353; *ECMW* No. 127.

8. Silian; church (Plate XX)　　SN 5713 5123
A squared pillar-stone (35 in. by 8 in.) with a Latin inscription and a superimposed cross. The inscription in one line down the face apparently reads: SILBANDVS IACIT, 'Silbandus lies (here)', but the cutting of the cross and the flaking at the upper edge have made the first few letters uncertain, and it is probable that part of the inscription has been lost by fracture, suggesting: ..]FILI BANDVS IACIT, '(The body of X), son of Bandus lies (here)'. The incised linear Latin cross (8 in. by 6 in.), with slightly expanded upper arm-ends, shows a secondary use of the stone. The stone is now incorporated into the external south face of the church near the SW angle; this part of the fabric is older than the restoration in 1873.
Arch.Camb., 33 (1878), 352; *ECMW* No. 128.

9. Tregaron; church (Plate XXI)　　SN 688 596
Part of a roughly squared pillar-stone (29 in. by 6–7 in. and 7–9 in. thick), with two surviving lines of a longer Latin inscription down the face, reading: POTENINA / MΛLIIER (for *Potentina mulier*), 'Potentina, wife of (...)'. The deeply cut lettering is partly in Roman capitals (with reversed Ns and inverted V) and partly half-uncials (T and Es), suggesting a sixth-century date. The misspellings are probably blunders by a cutter copying a written pattern. The stone was noted by Fenton in 1804, built into the south wall of the church, and when seen by Meyrick in the following year while the church was being repaired it was lying loose with three other carved stones. In 1828 it was taken to Meyrick's home at Goodrich Court, Herefordshire, and in 1935 was placed in the National Museum of Wales.
Fenton, *Tours in Wales*, 6–7; Meyrick, *Hist. and Antiq.*, 252; *Arch.Camb.*, 91 (1936), 15–16; *ECMW* No. 132.

II. Cross-decorated Stones

10. Lampeter; Pont-faen   SN 5705 4818
A rough slab 77 in. tall by up to 30 in. wide and 10 in. thick, decorated with an incised outline cross (10 in. long by 8 in.). The stone was recorded in 1878 built into a cottage on the western outskirts of Lampeter but had disappeared by 1971.
Arch.Camb., 46 (1891), 234, 318; *ECMW* No. 109.

11. Llanddewibrefi; churchyard   SN 6635 5531
A roughly shaped slab, 38 in. high (but with the top broken off) by 13 in. and 4 in. thick, with a shallow incised linear cross 10 in. by 7 in. wide, on the dressed face, bearing a small crosslet at the top of the upper arm. This stone and the following four items stand inside the church by the chancel arch.
Arch.Camb., 33 (1878), 354–5; *ECMW* No. 117.

12. Llanddewibrefi; churchyard   SN 6635 5531
A roughly shaped slab, 59+ in. high by 24 in. tapering upwards to 16 in. and 3–4.5 in. thick. On the dressed face, with a rounded top, is an incised linear cross, 24.5 in. long by 14.5 in., in which the lower stem divides and has rounded ends, while the upper arm-ends are of trifid form.
Meyrick, *Hist. and Antiq.*, 271; *Arch.Camb.*, 86 (1931), 390; *ECMW* No. 118.

13. Llanddewibrefi; churchyard   SN 6635 5531
Part of a rough pillar-stone, 76+ in. tall, 11.5 in. (originally *c.* 14 in.) wide and 8 in. thick, the right-hand half of which is lost. On one face is an equal-armed cross with bars on the two surviving arm-ends and a central hole.
Arch.Camb., 46 (1891), 235, 328; *ECMW* No. 119.

14. Llanddewibrefi; churchyard   SN 6635 5531
A very tall squared pillar-stone, 98+ in. high by 9.5 in. and 10 in. thick, bearing an incised cross and an inscription above a flaked-off surface at the base. The linear Latin cross towards the head is 29 in. long, the arm-ends and foot as crosslets. The single-line inscription down the face reads CENLISINI B̄T D̄S, '(The stone or grave?) of Cenlisin(i); may God bless him', formed in regular half-uncials. The contracted forms 'BT' for *benedicat* and 'DS' for *Deus* are common in early manu-scripts, as are the differing forms of 'N'. The probable date is eighth to ninth century.
Meyrick, *Hist. and Antiq.*, 271 and Pl.V, Fig. 3; *Arch.Camb.*, 83 (1928), 307; *ECMW* No. 120.

**15. Llanddewibrefi; south of   SN 6632 5518
church**
A roughly squared slab, 25 in. by 16 in. and 6.5 in. thick (the base broken off), on which is lightly incised a linear Latin cross, edge to edge. Also lightly cut on the face are two cruciform patterns of dots joined by thin incised lines.
Arch.Camb., 126 (1977), 68.

16. Llandysul, Pencoed-y-foel (?)   SN 42 42
A roughly squared slab, 49 in. by 27 in. (tapering to 16 in.) and 5 in. thick, decorated with an incised linear cross. A central stem running edge to edge is intersected by three equidistant arms with crossleted ends and by two shorter bars each set midway between the main arms.

The slab was reputedly found 'below Coedfoel' and brought to the churchyard before 1914. In recent years it has been incorporated into a side altar in the parish church (SN 4187 4072) with other medieval stones which include fragments of two cross-decorated headstones not earlier than the twelfth century. The slab, however, is likely to be of ninth- to tenth-century date.
Arch.Camb., 86 (1931), 413; *ECMW* No.414; *Ceredigion*, 5 (1967), 428.

17. Llandysul; church   SN 4187 4072
Fragment of a shaped headstone, 15 in. long by 10 in. and 8 in. thick, showing a deeply incised outline cross with open arm-ends and framed by a double incised ring. The slab, of eleventh- or twelfth-century date, is built into the SW external angle of the west tower, visible on the south face about 15 ft above the ground.
Meyrick, *Hist. and Antiq.*, 149.

18. Llanllŷr; near the house   SN 542 560
Part of a squared pillar-stone, 50+ in. tall and 9.5 in. by 8.5 in., with incised crosses and an inscription. On the dressed face (the right-hand half of the original stone) is part of a ring-cross about 12 in. diameter when complete, with traces of a stem extending below the ring on the fractured edge and terminating in a divided curved foot. The Latin inscription down the face in four surviving lines may be read as: TESQUITUS

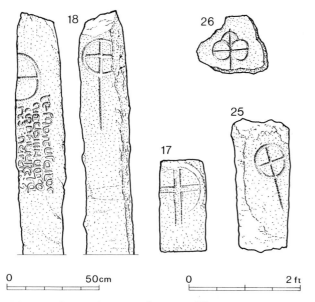

Fig. 73: Cross-decorated stones II.

DITOC / Q̄ŪA DOMNUACO/LLO FILIUS ASA/ITGEN DEDI(T)[.., 'The sacred place (of) Ditoc which Domnuacollon, son of Asaitgen, gave ...', or 'which Ollon, son of Asaitgen, gave to Domnuac...' It probably records the donation of land to the church. Another incised ring-cross on the adjoining right-hand face was originally 8 in. in diameter, with a stem extending 11 in. below. The lettering in regular half-uncials, and the formula, suggest an eighth- to ninth-century date.

The stone was discovered in 1859 in the demolition of the former Llanllŷr House (NW of the present house) which was the site of a chapel presumably older than the medieval nunnery of Llanllŷr. It now stands in the garden SW of the house.
Arch. Camb., 14 (1859), 338; *Arch. Camb.*, 51 (1896), 119–25; *ECMW* No.124.

19. Llantrisant; churchyard   SN 7268 7498
A dressed square-headed slab, 28.5 in. long by 8.25 in. and 1.5 in. thick, a headstone, with at the head an incised linear Latin cross 9 in. high by 6.5 in., with barred upper arm-ends. The stone was exposed in 1970 by grave-digging near the south wall of the nave of the church, and is now kept inside the church.
Arch.Camb., 126 (1977), 65.

20. Llantrisant; churchyard   SN 7268 7498
A slate slab, 38 in. long by 14.5 in. and 2.5 in. thick, one edge squared but the other damaged. At the head is an incised linear cross, 7 in. by 6 in. and below it a half-moon-shaped hollow which is probably natural. It was found with No. 19 (reference as given).

21. Llantrisant; churchyard,   SN 7268 7498
at south side
A roughly shaped slab, 57.5 in. long by 26 in. and 5 in. thick, partly damaged by flaking, of local mudstone. On the main face is an outline Latin cross with open arm-ends and spiked foot (40.5 in. long by 21 in.), chiselled rather than pecked. The stone was probably meant to be recumbent over a grave, and is likely to be late in the period eighth to eleventh century (reference as given).

22. Llanwnnws (Gwnnws Isaf);   SN 6852 6953
churchyard (Plate XXII)
A rough slab of local grit, 56+ in. tall by 15 in. (tapering at the base) and 6 in. thick, with a decorated and inscribed face damaged by fracture of the upper left-hand angle. At the head a ringed Latin cross in low relief is formed of paired cords with interlacing at the centre and where the arms meet the double-corded ring. The only surviving arm-end on the right forms a small Stafford knot beyond the ring, and the stem terminates in a larger similar knot. Each inter-arm space is occupied by a ringed boss. Above the ring on the right are the letters XPS (for *Christus*), probably matched on the left originally with IHS (for *Iesus*), both derived from Greek letters. An inscription in twelve horizontal lines begins on the right of the cross stem and continues below it reading: Q̄ICUNQ̄ / EXPLI/CAŪIT / Ḣ N̄O / DÉT B/ENE/DIXIONE/M PRO ANI/MA HIROID/IL FILIUS / CARO/TINN. The first four lines are contractions of *Quicunque explicaverit hoc Nomen*, thus giving 'Whoever shall have explained this Name (that is *Iesus Christus*), let him give a blessing for the soul of Hiroidil, son of Carotinn'. The lettering in round half-uncials and the abbreviations are found in Insular manuscripts written during the eighth to tenth centuries. Phraseology like this occurs in some of those manuscripts and on inscribed stones too (cf. the Pillar of Eliseg, Llangollen, at Valle Crucis). Two close Irish parallels are the slab of Berichtuire at Tullylease (c.700) and the Gospels of MacRegol (c.800). The

stone, noted by Lewis Morris and Meyrick, is now set up in the west porch of the church.

Meyrick, *Hist. and Antiq.*, 304; *Arch. Camb.*, 29 (1874), 245–6; *Arch. Camb.*, 93 (1938), 44; *ECMW* No. 125.

23. Strata Florida; cemetery of   SN 746 657
Cistercian abbey

A large squared slab, 54 + in. by 27 in. and 6.5 in. thick, with an incised cross on one face. It was found, most probably having been reused, on a grave during excavations at the abbey site in 1848. The deeply cut linear Latin cross, 26 in. long by 19.5 in., has slightly expanded arm-ends and at the intersection are five deep holes, 2 in. deep, set symmetrically. The shaping of the stone suggests a late date, perhaps tenth to eleventh century, but there is unlikely to be any association with the abbey. It has been placed against the east external wall of the parish church.

Arch. Camb., 3 (1848), 131; *ECMW* No. 131.

24. Tregaron; churchyard   SN 688 596
(Plates XXIII, XXIV)

A shaped slab of local gritstone, 25 in. long by 8 in. (tapering to 6 in.) and 4.5 in. thick. One main face bears a form of ring-cross, and one side face is inscribed and decorated. The broad, equal-armed cross with a small central boss is set in false relief by sunken inter-arm spaces within a moulded ring, rounded at the top but with flattened sides and base, with a short incised spike below for a stem. A moulded triangular panel fills a space above the cross. On the decorated left side between an incised saltire cross in a frame at the top and an incised grid pattern at the base is the single-word inscription ENEVIRI, '(The grave) of Enevir', cut in rounded half-uncials to fill a panel. The lettering (which includes the manu-script form of an 'inverted' letter N) and the name form have been accepted as of seventh- to eighth-century date, but some elements of the decoration appear unlikely to be as early as this. Like No. 9, also from Tregaron, the stone was moved by Meyrick to Goodrich Court in 1828, and was transferred in 1935 to the National Museum of Wales.

Meyrick, *Hist. and Antiq.*, 252; *Arch. Camb.*, 91 (1936), 16; *ECMW* No. 133.

25. Tregaron; (as No.24)

Part of a shaped(?) slab recorded by Meyrick

as being 28 in. long by 12 in., with an incised linear Latin ring-cross on a smoothed face. The stone, first seen in 1805, was taken to Goodrich Court where it was noted in 1936 but has since disappeared.

Meyrick, *Hist. and Antiq.*, 252 and Pl. VII, Fig. 4; Rees, *History of Tregaron*, 42; *ECMW* No. 134.

26. Tregaron (as No.24)

Fragment of a slab recorded by Meyrick as 14 in. by 12 in., with an incised, elaborated cross-head in the form of two linked circles surmounted by a semicircle, each divided by an arm of a linear cross, with part of a stem below. The design could well be post-Norman, but like No. 25 the stone cannot now be traced (references as above).

III. Sculptured Monuments

27. Llannarth; churchyard   SN 4230 5773
(Plate XXV)

A shaped slab, 67 + in. high by 24 in. (29 in. at the base) and 6 in. thick (10 in. at base), with a carved cross and inscription, together with reputed traces of ogam letters. The dressed main face (the other faces are left rough) is almost filled by a Latin cross in low relief, with broad squared arms and hollowed angles, a form occurring frequently in Northumbria and on Irish slabs. On the stem, 7.5 in. wide and flanked by narrow sunken panels, is an incised inscription GURHIRT, '(The stone or grave) of Gurhirt', in rounded half-uncials down the face, but most letters are damaged by flaking. The cross is closely paralleled by an un-published slab at Penmon Priory (Ang.) and is of ninth/tenth-century date. On the edge of the left arm-end what appear to be ogam strokes cannot be earlier than the cross and are likely to be strokes made by sharpening tools or weapons. Originally standing south of the church, it is now set within the west tower against the north wall.

Meyrick, *Hist. and Antiq.*, 235, Pl. IV, Fig. 4; *Arch. Camb.*, 29 (1874), 20; *Arch. Camb.*, 51 (1896), 119; *ECMW* No. 110.

28. Llanbadarn Fawr; churchyard   5988 8098

A tall, slender pillar-cross of granitic stone, 120 in. high, rounded at the base but squared to 12 in. by 8 in. in the upper half, decorated on all faces by carved ornament in low relief, somewhat

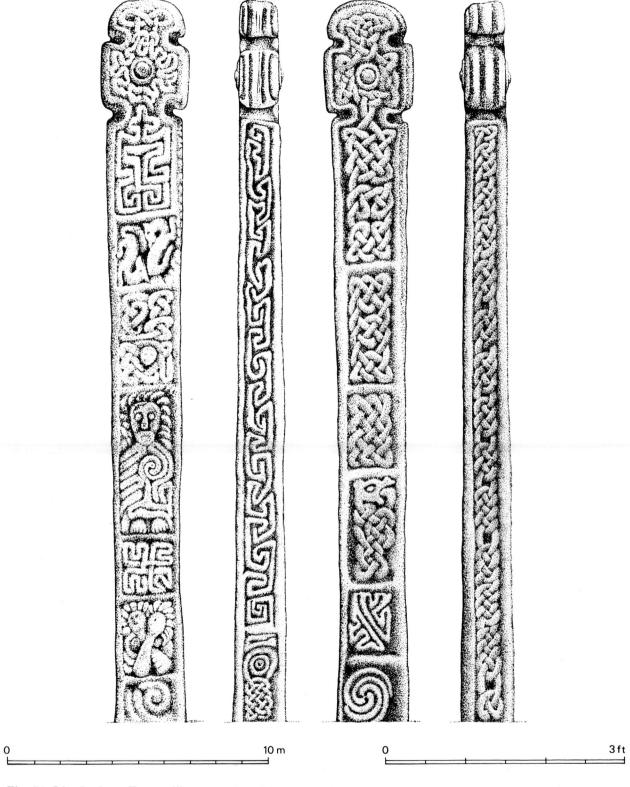

0   10 m   0   3 ft

Fig. 74: Llanbadarn Fawr pillar-cross (no. 28).

weathered. The cross-head is formed by hollows on the narrower faces and rounded at the top, thus resembling 'hammer-head' crosses in Cumbria. The decoration on the main face (originally the east side) is in a series of vertical panels: (1) the head has irregular key-pattern around a central moulded ring-and-boss, continuing on the shaft, and with a small cross at the neck; (2) two animals with heads turned back, resembling paired beasts in Anglian art; (3) knots merging into irregular key-pattern that surrounds a badly weathered human face; (4) a seated figure facing front (hair and feet shown) with drapery folds formed into a spiral, resembling figures of the Evangelists in Insular manuscripts; (5) an unsymmetrical square key-pattern; (6) at the foot, two stylized figures across each other in full-length garments, possibly representing Jacob wrestling with the 'angel' (Genesis 32 : 24), a scene frequently appearing on Irish high crosses. The right side of the cross has a narrow panel of irregular key-pattern and, below it, a panel of plaitwork. The back of the head resembles the front and the shaft is similarly decorated in a series of panels of plaitwork, one with a possible animal head biting its tail, and of diaper key-pattern, terminating in a whorl-pattern. A narrow panel on the left-hand side is filled with figure-of-eight knot-work (Fig. 74).

The pole-like form of the cross and its 'hammer-head' probably imitates a type originating in Breconshire but the other decorative features, particularly the figure representations, show Irish influences which can also be seen in manuscripts produced at this place. The cross, dating from the tenth century, has been reset inside the church, in the south transept.
Meyrick, *Hist. and Antiq.*, 393 and Pl. XVI, 1; *Arch. Camb.*, 72 (1917), 165; *ECMW* No. 111.

29. Llanbadarn Fawr;   SN 5988 8098
churchyard (Plate XXVI)
The roughly shaped cruciform head and wide shouldered shaft of this cross stand 57+ in. high, the arms 31 in. across and the shaft 25 in. wide by 10 in. thick. On the front (originally facing east) the abraded surface has traces of carving in the cruciform head within a bold edge-moulding, possibly a Crucifixion like that on a stone at Llanveynoe (*ECMW* No. 411). A panel on the shaft is framed by incised lines again with edge-moulding but no decoration survives; a deep hole in the

centre and two others outside the head of the panel are probably secondary. The other sides are undressed but a sunken panel on the lower back is incised with something like a Greek *omega*. The date is tenth/eleventh-century. The stone has been reset in the south transept of the church.
Meyrick, *Hist. and Antiq.*, 394; *Arch. Camb.*, 72 (1917), 165–6; *ECMW* No.112.

30. Llanddewi Aber-arth;   SN 4764 6329
church (Plate XXVII)
Two fragments with carved decoration, one with traces of two inscriptions, of local sandstone, discovered during a rebuilding of the church in 1860. One stone, 24 in. long and at 9 in. wide representing about half the original width of what was probably the shaft of a pillar-cross, shows part of a pattern of diagonally set square fret. Both adjacent faces carried inscriptions in round half-uncials set in horizontal lines, but only the first few letters of each line survive, ANI[.. in line 4 on the right suggesting ANIMA ('soul') and ..]RU in line 2 of the other side suggesting CRUX or CRUCEM ('cross'). Below the inscription on the right face is part of a pattern of knot-work. The second stone, 26 in. long by 9.25 in. and probably part of the same shaft, has on the one decorated face traces of two panels, plain knot-work and diagonal key-pattern, of ninth/tenth-century date. Both stones have been clamped against the internal south wall of the west porch.
Arch. Camb., 51 (1896), 113–17; *Arch.Camb.*, 52 (1897), 127; *ECMW* No. 113.

31. Llanddewi Aber-arth;   SN 4764 6329
church (Plate XXVIII)
A hogback stone of local sandstone, 25 in. long by 9 in. high and 12 in. wide at its middle, possibly incomplete. One hipped 'gable-end' is moulded on the edge, but the flat opposite end may have been intended to abut a headstone. The curved ridge moulding is damaged, and on each bombé side below it are ten plain ribs from end to end. This type of monument originated in northern England but the stone is unlike recognized types there or in Scotland. It is of the period tenth to eleventh century, having been found in 1860 with the preceding fragments and like them set in the porch of the church.
Arch. Camb., 51 (1896), 117; *ECMW* No. 114.

32. Llanfihangel Ystrad;   SN 5196 5061
Cribyn
(Plate XXIX)

A shaped quadrangular slab, 69 in. high and 17 in. thick, decorated on one face which is 25.5 in. wide. Above the roughly pointed base-butt, originally set into the ground, the decorated face has a rectangular panel filled with knot-work in shallow relief, formed of three linked pairs of knots (as on No. 34), of ninth/tenth-century date.

Meyrick recorded the stone at Maesmynach, but a later account says it had formerly stood in the hillfort, the Gaer, at Cribyn. It was subsequently taken to Castle Hill mansion, Llanilar, but is now set up in the porch of Llanilar church (SN 6237 7509).
Meyrick, *Hist. and Antiq.*, 238 and Pl. V,1; *Arch. Camb.*, 33 (1878), 351; *ECMW* No. 107.

33. Llangwyryfon; old   SN 5970 7048
churchyard

A rough slab recorded by Meyrick as being about 5 ft. high and 2 ft. wide with a cross in low relief in the upper half. The Latin form of the cross, with squared arm-ends and hollowed angles, is much like that at Llannarth (No. 27), but the bars intersecting the thin arms form a central equal-armed cross with a pellet at each angle of this square. Below the stem is an up-curving bow, not unlike the bow-shaped 'boat' symbol incised on some early cross-decorated stones (for example Newport, Pembs., *ECMW* No. 362). The stone would seem to be of ninth/tenth-century date.

It was seen by Meyrick in 1810 serving as a gatepost to the original churchyard SE of the modern church, but no later record was made. It is said locally that it was used as a foundation for the war memorial erected *c.*1920 at the NW corner of the old churchyard.
Meyrick, *Hist. and Antiq.*, 331, Pl. VII, Fig. 5; *ECMW* No. 123.

34. Silian; churchyard   SN 571 512
(Plates XXX, XXXI)

A roughly squared slab, 37 in. tall, 13 in. wide and 6 in. thick, with a panel of carved decoration in low relief in the upper part of each broad face. One of these (19 in. high) consists of three linked pairs of knots as on No. 32, the other panel (21 in. high) being filled with a diagonally set pattern of square frets. Both patterns occur on another stone at Abercorn (West Lothian). It is of ninth/tenth-century date. The stone was noted by Meyrick in 1810 standing in the churchyard (east of the church in 1878), and it now lies on the floor of the vestry.
Meyrick, *Hist. and Antiq.*, 224; *Arch. Camb.*, 33 (1878), 352; *ECMW* No. 129.

Part of a cross-decorated stone was discovered in 1921 by R. H. S. Macalister at Bryngwyn Farm, St Dogmaels, in what was then part of the borough of Cardigan south of the River Teifi but which until 1832 had been in Pembrokeshire. The roughly shaped slab, 65 in. high and up to 7 in. thick, has a wide head (25 in. maximum but part lost by fracture) and tapering shaft, with incised decoration on the face. The head was formerly filled by a ring-cross with expanded arms and ring in false relief, together with a ring-and-dot device at the centre. Below this is incised a standing figure facing front with arms outstretched in an attitude of prayer, wearing a garment that leaves the feet visible turned in profile to the right. The pear-shaped head with crude facial features (possibly bearded) and the 'orans' posture are similar to human figures in Insular manuscripts and on Irish monuments of the eighth and ninth centuries, its likely date. The stone is now in the National Museum of Wales.
Arch. Camb., 85 (1930), 424; *Arch. Camb.*, 92 (1937), 5; *BBCS*, 8 (1935–6), 279–80; *ECMW* No. 130.

INDEX

LIST OF SUBSCRIBERS

The following have associated themselves with the publication of this volume through subscription:

Professor R. P. Ambler, Edinburgh
David Austin, Lampeter
M. E. Baines, Cilgerran
David Russell Barnes, Caerdydd
Margaret Bateman, Aberystwyth
Dr Martin Bell, Lampeter
S. Benham a Dr S. Byrne, Llangynfelyn
John R. E. Borran, Warrington
Keith Bush, Caerdydd
T. Duncan Cameron, Aberaeron
J. E. R. Carson, Aberystwyth
Harold Carter, Bow Street
A. O. Chater, Aberystwyth
Dr Gilbert W. Clark, Porthcawl
J. A. Corfield, Penrhyn-coch
Heather and John Cowan, Llandysul
Very Revd Canon James Cunnane, Cardigan
Mr and Mrs Alun Eirug Davies, Aberystwyth
David Gwilym Evans Davies, Llandysul
Dr D. H. Davies, Blandford Forum
Dr David R. Davies, Lethbridge, Canada
J. C. Davies, Aberystwyth
Philip Wyn Davies, Aberystwyth
R. R. Davies, Aberystwyth
Dr Susan J. Davies, Aberystwyth
Peter Edward Davis, Aberaeron
Professor Emeritus John Ll. J. Edwards, Toronto, Canada
Drs Richard a Dana Edwards, Aberystwyth
E. D. Ellis, Llan-non
Cyril Evans, Tregaron
David John Evans, Tregaron
Professor D. Ellis Evans, Oxford
Dorothy Ann Evans, Llanfarian
J. M. and B. Evans, Llanrhystud
Y Parch. Ganon J. Wyn Evans, Caerfyrddin
Muriel Bowen Evans, Trelech
Tom a Marilyn Evans, Aberhonddu

T. R. Evans, Llanbedr Pont Steffan
W. Brian L. Evans, Penrhyn-coch
Mrs L. E. Lewes Gee, Lampeter
E. L. Gibson, Llangefni
D. R. Gorman, Aberystwyth
Rhidian Griffiths, Penrhyn-coch
W. I. Griffiths, Comins-coch
Mary Gwendoline Jane Griffiths-Davies, Taliesin
Ceris Gruffudd, Penrhyn-coch
R. Geraint Gruffudd, Aberystwyth
J. Kendal Harris, Bow Street
Colin David Hancock, Waunfawr
John R. Haynes, Aberystwyth
Ann ac Andrew Hawke, Aberystwyth
Marged Haycock, Aberystwyth
Dr Hugh Herbert, Aberaeron
Sonia Hill, Ystradmeurig
William H. Howells, Penrhyn-coch
J. Denys Gwynne Hughes, Aberaeron
Maldwyn Hughes, Lampeter
Kathleen Anne Humphreys, Llanfarian
David James, London
David B. James, Bow Street
E. L. and M. A. James, Penrhyn-coch
John Gwyn Howell James, Swansea
Margaret T. James, Aberystwyth
Dafydd Jenkins, Aberystwyth
David Jenkins, Penrhyn-coch
Yr Athro Geraint H. Jenkins, Aberystwyth
Gwyn Jenkins, Tal-y-bont
Mr and Mrs J. T. Jenkins, Llandysul
Marjorie Jenkins, Stourbridge
D. L. Jones, London
Dafydd Morris Jones, Aber-arth
Huw Bevan Jones, Llandysul
Iwan Meical Jones, Bow Street
Dr J. H. Jones, Rugby
John Meurig Jones, Ystradmeurig
Marian Henry Jones, Aberystwyth
Mr Philip Henry Jones and Mrs M. T. Burdett-Jones, Aberystwyth
Rhys P. Jones, Llanilar
Richard A. Jones, Aberaeron
W. M. Jones, Waunfawr

Dylan Euros Lewis, Llanbedr Pont Steffan
Glyn M. Lewis, London
P. G. T. Lewis, Godalming
P. A. B. and F. M. Llewellyn, Tal-y-bont
Dewi M. Lloyd, Aberteifi
T. G. Lloyd, Aberystwyth
Dr Ceridwen Lloyd-Morgan, Llanafan
Mrs A. A. Lloyd-Williams, Llan-non
H. C. Lloyd-Williams, Llanbedr Pont Steffan
Rheinallt Llwyd, Llanrhystud
Dr W. G. G. Loyn, Aberystwyth
Dr and Mrs Loxdale, Llanilar
M. B. McDermott, Taunton
Mr and Mrs B. A. Malaws, Ystradmeurig
Mrs Shirley A. Martin, Tregaron
Bethan Elin Miles, Waunfawr
Dr R. J. Moore-Colyer, Llanrhystud
Derec Llwyd Morgan, Capel Dewi
Lord Elystan Morgan, Bow Street
Gerald and Enid Morgan, Llanafan
Hywel ap Sion Morris, Caerdydd
A. Moyes, Penrhyn-coch
C. R. Musson, Aberystwyth
D. Huw Owen, Aberystwyth
John Desmond Owen, Aberystwyth
P. Owen-Lloyd, Swansea
B. G. Owens, Aberystwyth
Susan Campbell Passmore, Dolgellau
Martha Phillips, Aberystwyth
Menna Heledd Phillips, Aberystwyth
W. J. Phillips, Chief Executive Dyfed C. C., Lampeter
Marie Powell, Tre'r-ddôl
Revd Canon D. T. W. Price, Lampeter
Emrys R. D. Prosser, Tregaron
Professor and Mrs Graham L. Rees, Aberystwyth
Tudor W. Rees, Caerfyrddin
Capt. and Mrs John Rhydderch, Llanelli
E. L. Richards, Aberystwyth
Enid M. Roberts, Llanrhystud
Hywel Wyn Roderick, Aberystwyth
D. J. Rowlands, Aber-porth
J. G. T. Sheringham, Aberystwyth
Lt. Col. R. J. M. Sinnett, Llanfrynach

J. Beverley Smith a Llinos Beverley Smith, Aberystwyth
Peter Smith, Llanbadarn Fawr
Jack Spurgeon, Waunfawr
Llinos E. A. Taylor, Cwmerfyn
Dr Dulyn Thomas, Cei Newydd
Dr J. Hywel Thomas, Twickenham
Dr Peter Wynn Thomas, Caerdydd
W. Troughton, Aberystwyth
Gwilym Tudur, Aberystwyth
Canon Geraint J. Vaughan-Jones, Mallwyd
Dr R. F. Walker, Waunfawr
Owen Watkin, Llanfihangel Genau'r-glyn
Ei Anrhydedd y Barnwr Watkin Powell, Caerdydd
Department of Extra-Mural Studies, University College of Wales, Aberystwyth
Friends of the Ceredigion Museum
Y Llyfrgell, Coleg y Drindod, Caerfyrddin
Llyfrgell Genedlaethol Cymru/National Library of Wales, Aberystwyth
Llyfrgell Hugh Owen Library, University College of Wales, Aberystwyth
Llyfrgellydd Rhanbarthol, Llyfrgell Cyhoeddus Aberystwyth
University of Wales College of Cardiff Library